DANGER AND SURVIVAL

Choices About the Bomb
in the First Fifty Years

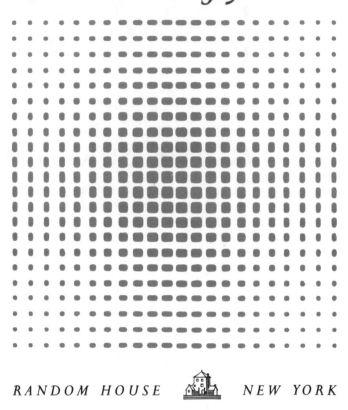

RANDOM HOUSE   NEW YORK

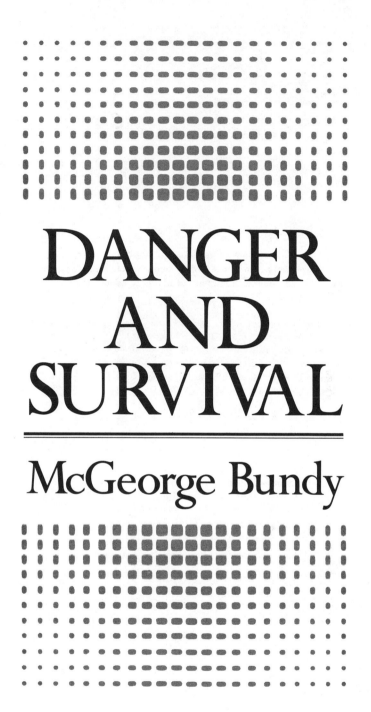

DANGER
AND
SURVIVAL

McGeorge Bundy

All rights reserved under International and Pan-American Copyright
Conventions. Published in the United States by Random House, Inc.,
New York, and simultaneously in Canada by Random House
of Canada Limited, Toronto.

Grateful acknowledgment is made to Farrar, Straus & Giroux, Inc.
and Faber and Faber Limited for permission to reprint
an excerpt from "Fall 1961" from *For the Union Dead* by
Robert Lowell. Copyright © 1962, 1964 by Robert Lowell.
Reprinted by permission of Farrar, Straus and
Giroux, Inc., and Faber and Faber Limited.

Library of Congress Cataloging-in-Publication Data

Bundy, McGeorge.
    Danger and survival.

Includes index.
    1. United States—Military policy. 2. Nuclear
warfare. 3. United States—Politics and government—
1933–1945. 4. United States—Politics and government—
1945– . 5. United States—Foreign relations—1933–
1945. 6. United States—Foreign relations—1945–
7. Arms race—History—20th century. I. Title.
UA23.B786   1988   327.1′1   88-42824
ISBN 0-394-52278-8

Manufactured in the United States of America

24689753

Book design by Carole Lowenstein

For Mary

Foreword

This book is about political choices in the fifty years of man-made nuclear fission. It is not about all such choices, because there have been too many and because there is too much I do not know. It is about choices that meet two standards: first, that they are themselves significant, and second, that I have been able to learn enough about them to believe that I have something useful to say.

There are great matters that I have omitted or sharply compressed: much of the long slow struggle for arms control, most of the complex interconnection between nuclear power plants and nuclear danger, and many subtle problems of technology, service interest, doctrine, and targeting. Sometimes I have found that I had little to add to excellent work by others, and where that is so I have indicated in the notes which books I think outstanding. What I want to emphasize here is that omission and compression are not assertions of unimportance.

By choosing to focus mainly on governments whose choices have led to weapons, I have left out the interesting and almost opposite problem of the reasons for the choices that many countries have made *not* to seek nuclear weapons of their own. That examination of such cases can be highly illuminating has been demonstrated this year by Mitchell Reiss in *Without the Bomb.* Yet I do not think I have been wrong to focus on the choices of states that have crossed the nuclear Rubicon, and especially on the choices of the two superpowers. It is the states with weapons that can decide to use them, and only the governments in Moscow and Washington, so far, have warheads enough to destroy whole civilizations. It is these two governments, above all others, that must stay clear of nuclear war, so the encounters between them have cardinal importance.

Often in recent years, as I have talked about nuclear danger in public meetings, I have been asked if the more immediate threat is not that terrorists or madmen in power might get and use the bomb. That possibility is real; the fact that it has not happened yet does not allow us to assert that it will never happen. But quite aside from the difficulty of addressing this problem primarily through study of the past, there is a different and stronger reason for emphasizing the decisions that relate to large arsenals and the possibility of their use. The terrorist's bomb, and probably also the madman's, would be a matter of a single weapon or a very few. Use of such weapons could be enormously more destructive than the power-plant disaster at Chernobyl, but it would still be much more like that isolated event than like a nuclear war engaging the superpowers. This book, by contrast, is about danger and survival on a planetary scale. Other kinds of nuclear danger may be more probable, but they are not more important.

I should make it clear at the outset that there are three considerably different kinds of inquiry in this book; it may help to consider it as having three sections. In the first section (chapters I–VI), the primary method is that of history. The public record on Franklin Roosevelt and Harry Truman is now about as good as it is going to get (except where official secrecy still hides particular papers), and one can hope to come close to writing history as accurately as another student will in another few years. That is less true of all later administrations and all other countries. I have attempted to write historically about Dwight Eisenhower's first term too.

I begin the second section (chapters VII–X) with events that belong to both the Eisenhower and Kennedy administrations. Here my way of writing changes, and for two reasons. First, in this period the historical record remains seriously incomplete; there are important revelations every year, and on many large questions one cannot yet come close to durable history. Second, and perhaps more important, it is obvious, even to me, that I am not a detached observer of President Kennedy. But while engagement interferes with objectivity, it has some advantages. Being inside a crisis is not the same as observing it or studying it. Memory can easily mislead, but it can also provide clues to understanding. Most of this second section is about matters in which the historical record is less complete and my engagement more direct.

The third section deals with a period that is much too close for history, and I have been much more an observer in that time than a direct participant. Much of this part is concerned with public debates on questions of nuclear choice, and I have had a part in some of those debates. If in the first section I can write mainly as a historian and in the second more as a participant, in the third I am primarily a commentator. These are not black-and-white differences; there is commentary in the first and second sections and history in the second and third, and in a measure all of us are participants all the time in the interaction between nuclear danger and survival. Nonetheless the changes of tone from one section to another have been noted by friends who have read the book in draft, and I share their view that it may help the reader to be forewarned.

For the rest, I let what follows speak for itself, pausing only to invite correction and comment from any reader who can help me understand these matters better, and to express my gratitude to all those who have helped me in nine years of talking, reading, teaching, and writing. In the Acknowledgments I offer more specific thanks.

Acknowledgments

I have been extraordinarily fortunate in finding help for writing this
book. I begin with those who gave me a place to work and the support
that allowed me to make this my central task. It was John Sawhill who
invited me to New York University, and its Department of History,
then led by Carl Prince, that made me welcome as a colleague. Both
were unusual actions that have been generously supported by deans
and librarians. The principal financial partner in this NYU undertaking
has been the Sloan Foundation. I am grateful to its officers and trustees
for their vote of confidence; I do not think the book would have been
possible, in anything like its present form, without the bold and early
backing of Arthur Singer.

It is one thing to get a book written and another to get it published.
George Gallantz gave me excellent advice in the process that led me
to Random House. There my work has been encouraged, improved,
indeed *edited* by Jason Epstein. If there are any unnecessary words left,
or if I seem to accept too readily some unpleasant realities, it is not
Jason's fault. If other people were as clear-eyed as he, discussions could
be more brisk, and realities would be much less unpleasant. I am also
grateful to everyone else at Random House, from my old friend Robert Bernstein to my cheerfully careful copy editor Mitchell Ivers.

In this field all of us are dependent on government documents and
on the scholarly work of those who write with untrammeled access to
them. Librarians and archivists in the presidential libraries, in other
parts of the National Archives, and in the Public Record Office in
London have been unfailingly helpful. I have also relied with confi-

dence on the splendid documentary record in the *Foreign Relations of the United States;* no one can write this kind of history without the prospect of serious correction when he comes closer to the present than the volumes in that series. Those volumes are now published, in general, some thirty years after the events they record. To cut that gap to twenty would be a great improvement and would still leave ample time for the proper temporary protection of the privacy of official and diplomatic discourse. The primary cause of delay as I write is understaffing in the part of the National Security Council staff that handles declassification; the president who wants to change that can do so in ten minutes.

There are too many fellow students to whom I am in debt for me to list them all. Specific obligations are acknowledged in footnotes, but in this field we all learn from one another in all sorts of ways, and most of the good ideas have many sources. I must let a few exemplars stand for a large company: among early students, Bernard Brodie and Raymond Aron; among scientific participants and observers, I. I. Rabi and Herbert York; and among younger writers, David Rosenberg and Strobe Talbott.

I owe a debt for general comradeship and specific critical comment to scholars at many centers of independent study. In citing individual friends I mean to acknowledge their particularly faithful wounds, and not to count out others. In that spirit I am grateful to friends at Harvard, especially Francis Bator and Richard Neustadt; at MIT, especially Carl Kaysen; at Columbia, especially Robert Jervis and Marshall Shulman; at Princeton, especially Richard Ullman; at Cornell, especially Ned Lebow; at Maryland, especially Catherine Kelleher; at Brookings, especially Raymond Garthoff; and at Stanford, especially Sidney Drell. I have a parallel debt to present and past professionals at the Ford Foundation, especially Enid Schoettle. Like all students of the Cuban missile crisis I have had a hard time keeping up with what James Blight and his colleagues are helping us all to find out, but it has been a strenuous delight to try. Among friends abroad I owe most to Solly Zuckerman and Bertrand Goldschmidt. Finally I should acknowledge a debt to those with whom I have had serious differences, and here it is both easy and agreeable to give pride of place to Albert Wohlstetter and Paul Nitze.

In a different way, and even more intensely, I have exchanged thoughts with three old friends, especially while we were writing essays together on current questions: George Kennan, Robert McNamara, and Gerard Smith. Each of them has made his own major individual contribution to both decision and understanding in this field, and each is a teacher by example of the great imperative: Fight the good fight. Still more intimately I am grateful to my brother Bill, who has been improving my prose with editorial zest and fraternal kindness for a very long time.

As truly indispensable partners in the day-to-day work, I have had as successive general assistants Alice Boyce and Patricia O'Sullivan, two of the best colleagues I have ever had. Ms. Boyce lived with these matters day by day before I ever did, as a trusted member of the Eisenhower White House staff, and she played her own critical role in the crises of the Kennedy years. Ms. O'Sullivan has the complementary advantage that she comes fresh to a hard topic and dares to ask enlightening questions. As a beginner in the practice of modern historical research I have also been greatly helped by Donald White, who was research associate in our office for eight years. White's own work in progress, on a still broader canvas of recent American history, has given us much to share beyond the ways and means of using archives and libraries.

Finally, I owe a debt that I could never repay directly to the three people who had most to do with my own education in these matters: Colonel Stimson, Robert Oppenheimer, and President Kennedy. I worked for all three, and these connections are noted in the appropriate places. Different as they were from one another, they shared an approach to nuclear danger that seems right to me: They did their best to understand it; they recognized it as centrally a political problem; and they were not afraid to accept, and even to seek, the responsibility for choice. If this book should be helpful to any of those who have such responsibility in the future, that is as much as any of the three would want of me, and none of them would be surprised if it should be mistakes, including their own (or mine), that are most instructive.

Contents

DANGER AND SURVIVAL

I

How the Americans Went First

THE DECISION that the United States would see if it could make an atomic bomb was made in the deepest secrecy by Franklin D. Roosevelt on October 9, 1941. The president did not commit himself that day to the approval of plant construction and still less to the fabrication of bombs. At that stage no one had more than the sketchiest impression of the size and shape of the construction that would be needed, and the materials from which a bomb might be made did not yet exist. The immediate requirement was for greatly intensified research.

Here as so often Roosevelt decided only what had to be decided—but it was enough. He heard a recommendation for action from his chief of defense research, Vannevar Bush, and he told Bush to move ahead as fast as he could. Roosevelt knew that he was giving broad authority to a man who would make full use of it. If the intense effort of research and development he thus authorized were to succeed, he could expect further recommendations for larger actions and he would expect to approve them. Thus, two months before Pearl Harbor, the president of the United States became the first political leader to set his country firmly on a course that could lead to a bomb. This decision did not determine the outcome of the effort, but it did determine that the effort would be made. Two months later this determination was hardened beyond further argument by the outbreak of open war with Japan and Germany.

What caused this decision? Why did it come when it did, not sooner or later? Why did no other leader of that time make a parallel decision? What can the circumstances of this fateful choice tell us about the ways in which men began to think about politics and physics, war and peace, in the nuclear age?

The Discovery of Fission

Twentieth-century physics, quite aside from nuclear energy and nuclear weapons, is a great adventure of human imagination and intelligence, and until 1939 it was carried on quite outside the world of politics. It was "pure" science—a matter of the contest of the human mind with nature; the object was not to change the world, but to understand it. Scientists could and did argue about the meaning of what they were doing, but like artists they were wary of their own explanations. They did physics because it was there to be done and because it was wonderfully interesting. The transcendent individual achievement is that of Einstein, who transformed man's understanding of physical reality by his special and general theories of relativity; but it is only by invidious comparison that the work of others is less grand.

No field of inquiry was more wonderful than that of subatomic or nuclear physics. The idea of the nucleus, a central core of the atom, ten thousand times smaller than the atom itself, was developed by Ernest Rutherford only in 1911, and while his model allowed extraordinary advances in the understanding of the outer parts of the atom, and of the small particles that it could admit and reject, the nucleus itself remained largely inviolate for another twenty years, acquiring a reputation for solidity and impenetrability that affected later investigators.

It was this apparent impenetrability that made the best of physicists believe there was no early hope or danger of getting large amounts of energy from the atom. The most famous declaration on this point was made by Rutherford in 1933: "Anyone who says that, with the means at present at our disposal and with our present knowledge we can utilize atomic energy, is talking moonshine."[1] The judgment was not universally shared; out in California, Ernest Lawrence had invented the cyclotron, a large and powerful device for bombarding the nucleus by particles of high energy and intensity. Lawrence believed that someday somehow this process might lead to the production of energy—but neither he nor anyone else could say how.

But the energy was known to be there; that indeed was one of the earliest and most powerful results of Einstein's work; energy and mass are interchangeable—$e = mc^2$, where c is the speed of light. In the world of earthly objects visible to the naked eye, Einstein's equivalence was of only theoretical interest, but inside the atom, as inside stars, it was a different matter. Rutherford himself had argued from the beginning, even before Einstein's formula of 1905, that the energy released in radioactivity came from inside the atom, and in 1903 his collaborator Frederick Soddy had speculated boldly on the implication of that insight:

> But it is probable that all heavy matter possesses—latent, and bound up with the structure of its atom—a similar quantity of energy to that possessed by radium. If it could be tapped and controlled, what an agent it would become in shaping the world's destiny! The man who first put his hand upon the lever, by which a parsimonious nature regulates so jealously the output of this store of energy, would possess a weapon by which he could destroy the earth if he chose.[2]

Soddy's speculations caught the imagination of H. G. Wells, who published in 1914 one of the first novels of atomic war and peace, *The World Set Free*.[3] The book was overtaken at the time by a war that was "only" conventional, but years later it stirred another imagination, that of the young physicist Leo Szilard. Meanwhile the world of nuclear physicists gradually accepted the notion that there were vast amounts of energy bound up in the atom.

Finally, in 1932, Einstein's equation was experimentally verified, by John Douglas Cockcroft and E.T.S. Walton, in a famous experiment which demonstrated that protons bombarding the light element lithium gave off energy and reduced the mass of the resulting fragments in amounts that matched the Einstein formula. And by that formula a single gram of hydrogen and seven grams of lithium might produce half a million kilowatt hours of energy. Their paper later won Cockcroft and Walton the Nobel Prize.[4]

But all this energy was still tightly locked up. Lawrence's cyclotrons used billions of times more energy than they released, and Cockcroft's bombardments, while much less profligate, were still vastly more powerful than the energy they set free. Indeed the nucleus seemed in some ways to become more solid the more one learned about it; the binding energy that held it together also seemed to present an electrical defense against any invader. To some degree that defense could be overcome; chips could be knocked off; helium could even be split—but in the language of a later day, the balance of advantage appeared to favor the defense. You could learn by your bombardments, but no one could describe a way of getting any net release of energy. Lawrence and others might cherish their hopes, but on the evidence Rutherford seemed right. Yet already one of his own students had found the particle that would transform Soddy and Wells from visionaries to prophets.

Early in 1932 James Chadwick of Cambridge discovered the neutron, and at once the nuclear physicists found themselves with a new instrument for exploration and explanation of the nucleus. Rutherford, Chadwick's teacher, had believed such a particle was needed to explain the nucleus, but he had not found it experimentally. Chadwick's work won him a prompt Nobel Prize.

The neutron not only helped to explain the composition of the nucleus, but because it had no electrical charge to arouse a repellent, it could be used to get close to the nucleus—to enter it, indeed—and so tell more about it. As it turned out the neutron did much more; in the words of Henry D. Smyth, the first recorder of the development of the atomic bomb, the neutron was "practically the theme song of this whole project." At the beginning, before bombs were thought of, it was a research tool.[5]

If 1932 is the year of the neutron, 1933 is the year of artificial radioactivity, a discovery of Frédéric Joliot-Curie and his wife, Irène. Their demonstration that properly aimed particles could change ordinary atoms of one element into another was a signal to the world of physics that the elements were no longer to be considered immutable, and radioactivity no longer a property confined by nature to radium and a few other less active elements. The notion of alchemy was no longer merely magical. They promptly shared the Nobel Prize.[6]

It was Enrico Fermi in Rome who entered most eagerly upon the exploration of artificial radioactivity. The neutron was his principal instrument of experimentation, and he rapidly demonstrated that nearly every element in the periodic table might undergo a nuclear transformation when bombarded by neutrons. His most important target element was uranium, the heaviest then known; its bombardment produced results that the physics of the day did not explain. Fermi concluded that he had probably found new radioactive elements still heavier than uranium—"transuranic." He rested this tentative conclusion on a demonstration that the radioactive substances he had produced were *not* elements lighter than uranium but near it in atomic number. For his basic demonstration of transformation all through the periodic table he won the Nobel Prize, but the real nature of his transuranics remained uncertain.[7]

The most sustained and careful attack on this transuranic problem was mounted by Otto Hahn and his colleagues in Berlin: Hahn was a radiochemist of great experience; he and Lise Meitner, a physicist, had worked together since 1907. Hahn and Meitner were drawn to Fermi's transuranic problem by their own intense interest in all sorts of radioactive substances, and over a course of years they found "a great number of radioactive transmutation products, all of which we had to regard as elements beyond uranium."[8] Their findings were not wholly persuasive to themselves or to other scientists, and the unresolved puzzle led Irène Curie back to the attack. In the summer of

1938 she and Pavel Savitch announced the discovery of what seemed to be yet another transuranic element—but one which matched badly with those already tabulated by Hahn. Hahn and his colleague Fritz Strassmann undertook to test her results with renewed experiments of their own.

What followed is a story about science that no scientist or nonscientist should forget. When Hahn and Strassmann made their own experiments along the lines of the work in Paris and then removed all the recognized transuranic elements, they found that the remaining solution still contained some unidentified radioactive products. Twenty years later Hahn described what happened in words whose power and tension overtake his own modesty: "Experiments in chemical separation of these substances now gave a remarkable result. When we used barium as the carrier, three radioactive isotopes, with different half-lives, came down with the barium. We were certain that these could not be accidental impurities, because our barium precipitates were extraordinarily pure. . . . Now the precipitates had to be either barium or radium, which is chemically similar to barium."[9]

But it made a truly enormous difference which one it was. Radium is element 88; to get radium from a bombardment of uranium, element 92, required only that the uranium nucleus lose four protons—a small chip off the block; it would be startling, but not revolutionary. But barium is element 56, near the middle of the table of elements. If they had produced barium from uranium, they had done something that physicists still considered impossible—they had truly split the atomic nucleus. Chemists were accustomed to respect the rules of physics as laid down by physicists.

Hahn and Strassmann persevered. There were good reasons to doubt that what they had was radium; to get radium from uranium under the conditions of their experiment would in itself be "a strange affair." But if it *was* radium they should be able to separate it from the barium carrier, one way or another. They were excellent and experienced chemists; the separation of elements is one of the things chemists do best. They tried two tested techniques; both failed. Then they tried two more experiments, adding small amounts of radium that they *knew* was radium. The known radium separated from the barium, but in the very same circumstances the puzzling radioactive isotopes did not. The conclusion literally forced itself upon them: "Our artificial 'radium' could not be separated from barium for the simple reason that it was barium!"[10] It was either A or B; it did not do what A did; it always did what B did; it was not A; it was B.

This was no ordinary conclusion. In their first report, Hahn and Strassmann acknowledged the problem—their experiments were at variance with "all previous experience of nuclear physics." They had originally written "all previous laws," but a law of nature is no law if it is not obeyed.[11] They knew they had a remarkable result, and they also knew they had set large new problems for their friends in nuclear physics. Their own interest was in the clarity and accuracy of their chemical experiments. Within the scientific world of the day they were not the most fashionable or famous—they were challenging an orthodoxy supported by men who knew much more than they did about the atom and the nucleus (and indeed their decisive article contained a physically nonsensical speculation about what might be happening). But they knew their chemistry. So they decided; they published; and for this work Hahn much later received the Nobel Prize. Within weeks it was clear to all the world of physics that their report marked the beginning of a wholly new adventure in nuclear physics, full of intellectual challenges of all sorts and also reversing the judgment of Rutherford. Nuclear energy and nuclear explosions might or might not be practicable, but they would never again be merely "moonshine."

BEFORE we join in that new adventure let us pause to notice just three striking characteristics of the story so far. First, it is all in the open; no one is hiding results; indeed there is no true success without publication—no merely private discovery is part of science. Second, it is quite unaffected by national boundaries. The decisive steps have been taken in Cambridge, Paris, Rome, and Berlin. Third, these are very small groups, and each of them is governed, in its choice of topic, target, instruments, and colleagues, by its own sense of what is most worth doing next. This was not merely the custom of some scientists; it was the ethos of the science of the day.

This ethos of independence did not imply that government should be kept at a distance. On the European continent, indeed, the financial support of science and scientists was assumed to be at least partly the task of government. Einstein, the preeminent theorist, and Marie Curie, the wonder-worker of radium, were both sustained by governmental appointment in the early decades of the century. The governments were repaid by the reflected honor of scientific distinction. The partnership might be easy or uneasy in particular cases, but the condition of its success was that control over their own work remained with the scientists. There was therefore no fundamental difference between the publicly supported national institutes in Paris, Berlin, or Copenhagen, and the university laboratories, largely private, of the English-speaking world.

Twentieth-century physics was already growing in cost, however, and in the years after World War I there did develop, especially in France and the United States, a new and important kind of scientific entrepreneur: the man or woman who could attract enlarged financial support because of a persuasive claim for what science might produce.

These enterprising scientists sought support where they could hope to find it—from government in France, from foundations and private philanthropy in the United States, from a liberal complex that was essentially the universities in Britain. Measured against the standards of later years, these efforts were small, but they encouraged the development of a considerable practical connection with sources of money and power, at least on the part of those at the head of large laboratories. In some countries this sense of connection was increased by the experience of World War I, in which a number of scientists were exposed to the needs and the peculiarities of governments at war. When we say that the scientists of 1939 were men and women shaping their own agenda, driven by the ethos of science itself, we are not discussing people to whom the other currents of society were always irrelevant.

The barium in Otto Hahn's solution did not in fact strike the world of physics as unlawful. His result was confirmed almost immediately by two excellent physicists who learned it from him privately before the end of 1938. Lise Meitner, now in Sweden, had been his partner too long to mistake him for a blunderer—she and her visiting nephew Otto Frisch talked it over. Frisch was a young Austrian physicist based at Copenhagen in the Institute of Theoretical Physics led by Niels Bohr. In two days of thought they not only recognized that the Hahn-Strassmann result was probably correct but found a theoretical explanation for it: It might be a process in which a uranium nucleus hit by a neutron was agitated into a division much as a liquid "drop could divide itself into two smaller drops." If so, they pointed out, the two new nuclei would repel each other with a total kinetic energy of two hundred million electron volts—a lot for a single split. And they presently named all this "nuclear fission."

Frisch returned from Sweden to Copenhagen where he reported the Hahn-Strassmann results and his and Meitner's reflections to Niels Bohr, who was just leaving for the United States. In the world of nuclear physics Bohr was then the greatest authority of all, and his judgment was immediate. As Frisch recalled it, "I had hardly begun to tell him when he smote his forehead with his hand and exclaimed: 'Oh what idiots we all have been! Oh but this is wonderful! This is just as it must be!' "[12] This judgment was promptly confirmed experimentally, first by Frisch and then by others on both sides of the Atlantic.

Two laboratories were especially well equipped to understand and move on. In Paris Joliot and Curie were distressed that they had not found fission first and determined to take the lead in going further. What Joliot wanted to know was the answer to the next question: Did the neutron-caused fission itself produce more neutrons? If it did, there might be a "chain reaction." And the same question, with just a bit less urgency, was posed at Columbia University in New York. The French team got there first, but the difference was one of days. Both groups determined that the process did indeed produce more neutrons. The French overestimated the number at about 3.5, and Fermi at Columbia was characteristically cautious—perhaps 2. The right number is about 2.5. These results completed the first stage of the revolution Hahn and Strassmann had set off. Fission by uranium reactions existed; it liberated energy; it also released more neutrons that might or might not cause more fission. And Bohr had himself already reached one sharply pertinent theoretical judgment: Very probably the nuclear fission under analysis was taking place in one isotope of uranium, a rare one, U-235, present as only one part in 140 of natural uranium.

We shall be considering how governments did and did not make decisions to try to make a bomb, and it will help us to review briefly the questions of physics and technology that remained open after the Paris and Columbia teams had confirmed the production of extra neutrons. Those extra neutrons opened an extraordinary possibility: that somehow a self-sustaining chain reaction could be achieved.

The most obvious possibility was simply that this process might take place in some arrangement that would produce usable heat—a uranium engine, or reactor. This was what was most interesting to both Joliot and Fermi at the time. The chain reaction that both of them set as their objective would probably take place in natural uranium, and the main problem they faced was to determine what arrangement of uranium and neutrons might do the job. What had to be learned was that the process would require the presence of a moderating element. Two substances were to prove practicable for this purpose: carbon, in the form of graphite, and heavy water.

But a reactor was not and never would be a bomb. A reactor could also be called an engine or a boiler; both terms were used. A bomb would be something else, as different from a reactor as TNT from a bonfire. The difference was not at first understood.

There were—and are—two possible ways to get a bomb from uranium. One is to separate the light isotope U-235. To choose that path one must acquire confidence that the properties of U-235 would be so significant that the recognized difficulty of separating it out would be acceptable. One must have confidence that one or another method of separation could be made to work. One must understand that when the stuff was separated it would produce a chain reaction if it reached a certain "critical" size, and one must believe that "subcritical" amounts of separated material could be brought together in some almost instantaneous way, so as to produce a true explosion and not a fizzle.

The other way to get a bomb from uranium was to produce what we now call plutonium. Unlike U-235, plutonium is not present in natural uranium, and in 1939 it still remained to be imagined, produced, and identified. It is the product of transformation induced by neutrons in U-238, one product, indeed, of any successful uranium reactor. To recognize this possibility was the first and most important step along this second path. Next would come the achievement of a laboratory reactor; then the design, construction, and operation of large production reactors, the chemical separation of the resulting plutonium, and the design of a means of detonation that would respect the extraordinary properties of the man-made element.

With this thin sketch of the roads not yet understood or traveled as the Second World War began, let us now consider what different governments did, and why.

The French

To begin in France is to recognize that the most zealous and deeply committed group of investigators at work on these problems in the spring of 1939 was in Paris.[13] At the Collège de France, Frédéric Joliot had with him two talented younger men, Hans Halban and Lew Kowarski, one born Austrian and the other Polish, both in their early thirties, and both naturalized as French citizens only in 1939. The three were united in the double conviction that nuclear reactions would be turned into usable power and that they, the French team, should show the way, as they had led in the discovery that fission produced additional neutrons. As Halban later recalled their mood, "We were absolutely bent on creating a nuclear chain reaction which could be used for industrial power."[14] In this highly practical objective there is something characteristic of the culture of French science in those years. Joliot belonged to a group whose commitment to the international freemasonry of science for its own sake was matched by a conviction that science also offered great prospects for the improvement of the social condition of man, and that the scientists themselves should have a role in ensuring this result. There were strong ties of sympathy and common purpose between scientists of this persuasion and reformist political circles, and the enormous prestige of Joliot's mother-in-law, Madame Curie, rested precisely on the combination of her scientific distinction with the value of radium as a healer. Thus when it began to appear that the new world of fission offered not just a chance of better understanding of the nucleus but a prospect of power that would give benefit to all mankind, and leadership to France, the choice of target made by the French team was almost foreordained.

Through the spring and summer of 1939 the French pursued their experiments with neutrons and uranium and learned that the conditions for a chain reaction were not likely to be fulfilled by uranium and neutrons alone. They were not the strongest in theoretical calculation, and with the outbreak of war their team was weakened further in this respect by the decision of the theoretical physicist Francis Perrin to join the army without requesting a scientific assignment. Yet the war at first produced no other interruption. The French military did not have good connections to French science, and military requests for help from Joliot were modest and routine. Believing the war would be long and new energy sources valuable, Joliot and his colleagues continued. They worked their way, by the end of the year, to the correct understanding that for a chain reaction they would probably need either graphite or heavy water; they preferred heavy water; it was scarce, but they could and did persuade their government to help them get what there was. Nearly all the world's stock was in Norway—186 liters—and in March, less than a month before the Germans took Norway, it was secretly brought to France.[15]

By the spring of 1940 the French team was preparing for an expansion of its work—a larger budget, more workers, more uranium, graphite, and one two-ton truck. At the time this was the most purposive and best focused program of uranium research in the world, and the total amount of additional money that Joliot asked for was a purchase outlay of 500,000 francs (then $20,000) and an increase of 170,000 francs a year in his salary budget. Compared to what lay around the corner elsewhere, the effort was extraordinarily small. It was also about to be overwhelmed by Hitler.[16]

But it would be a mistake to suppose that because it was so sharply interrupted in June 1940 the French effort of 1939–40 was unimportant. Joliot's team was dispersed, but Halban and Koworski pursued their scientific and political purposes with extraordinary determination and energy in England and North America. Joliot himself remained in France, presently joined the Resistance, and then resumed his leadership with renewed political strength when France was free again in 1945. What is still more striking is that already in 1939–40 the French scientists had worked out a comprehensive plan for a cooperative effort of development engaging the scientists themselves as full partners with government and industry, and designating French science as a major beneficiary of the fruits that were confidently expected. The matter was complicated by the fact that the industrial partner was to be the Belgian firm Union Minière. No final agreement was reached before Paris fell to the Germans, but the record of ready three-way cooperation established in the preceding year was highly promising. The objective was clear, and Spencer Weart's description is compelling:

> For a generation the liberal scientists had believed that science would produce measureless practical benefits, and would do so best under

centralized control exercised by themselves; they had insisted on entering the thick of politics. So it is not surprising that Joliot and his team, unlike most scientists in other countries, determined to take over the development of the practical applications of fission themselves. . . .

In their agreements with [industry and government], the Collège de France team said in almost so many words: give us money, supplies, personnel, and authority for our research; guarantee that a share of the profits from our discoveries will be used for pure science, partly under our control; and we will find out how you may build devices that will greatly profit the company and strengthen and protect the nation.[17]

This grand design could not have been executed in wartime, even if the French had successfully resisted the Germans in 1940. The task of developing profitable nuclear power was to prove vastly larger and more complex than Joliot and his colleagues could guess when they began, and in World War II no such efforts ever moved beyond the laboratory level. It is more interesting to speculate on the direction and pace of the French effort if it had *not* coincided with World War II. That would have been to Joliot's advantage, as against competitors elsewhere, precisely because the French had a head start in thinking about the role of science and government and industry in cooperation for peaceful progress. Many have guessed, with P.M.S. Blackett of England and Bertrand Goldschmidt of France, that in a peacetime competition the French would have achieved the first self-sustaining chain reaction.[18] And beyond that is the shining possibility that France might have shown leadership also in a great and fruitful partnership of science, industry, and government for peaceful nuclear energy. That vision, in 1939, was unique to France.

Even in the presence of war, the French under Joliot were at no time on the track of a bomb. The only avenue to an explosion of which they were aware, the road through uranium 235, was one which they thought both uncertain and difficult; it would require chemical and industrial skills and resources that were not in sight for France. But in any case nuclear weapons did not interest them. In making the case for support from the Ministry of Government, after the war began, Joliot would regularly explain that a uranium weapon might be obtainable in the long run, but he would just as firmly insist that the immediate prospect was for new sources of energy. If he had been pressed to explain how any weapon at all would emerge from his attempt to achieve a chain reaction, he would have given less than satisfactory answers; at the time no one in France knew the right answer to that question, even in principle. This difficulty would not have distressed Joliot. Although ministers were sometimes stirred by the possibility of weapons, especially in the aftermath of an adventure like the timely rescue of the heavy water, Joliot and his team had no such objective.

The Germans

Germany played a decisive role in the development of the first atomic bomb. German scientists made the crucial discovery in 1938, and fear that Hitler might be the first to have a bomb was the nightmare that gave compelling force to the inquiries and actions that led to Roosevelt's decision of 1941. But the Germans themselves never came close, and this result was not merely accidental; it was the consequence of deep-seated realities in German physics, German politics, and the German military situation.

The physicists of Germany in 1939 were numerous and able. They were as much interested as their colleagues abroad in the scientific revolution set off by Hahn and Strassmann. But from first to last that interest remained primarily scientific.

Competent physicists did call the attention of civil and military authorities to the operational possibilities, and these authorities, although generally divided against themselves, did make efforts to develop a coordinated research program. But the physicists themselves often resisted these bureaucratic efforts. A compelling example, and one which contrasts notably with what eventually happened in the United States, was the failure of a War Office plan to bring all the scientists concerned to Berlin. Although war had begun and the authority of the War Office was nominally complete, the plan "collapsed against the obstinacy of almost all the scientists." They refused to move from their universities, and while they agreed to help the project, their motives were those of scientists, not war makers. The scientific problems themselves were of first-class interest, and the military sponsorship of the research was helpful because it offered protection against the call-up of their young men.[19]

Under this military protection the separated German scientists kept individual control over the directions of their work on uranium. In 1939 it was like that in every country; no one who was not a scientist knew enough to make decisions or give orders, and in any case no high authority in any country was yet interested in more than a modest exploration. But unlike their counterparts in Britain and the United States, the German physicists were never brought into a coordinated war effort. Those with the highest prestige made their own choices of topic, and their choices defined the whole shape of the German uranium effort. Germany was a totalitarian state but its nuclear scientists remained far more detached from political authority than their colleagues in Britain and the United States.

Some of the best of them simply continued with their work, choosing subjects with no regard for any possible wartime result. Thus Otto Hahn himself continued to examine and analyze the various fragments produced by fission. Given the modest size of his laboratory, his results were impressive, though much less extensive than those produced by Glenn Seaborg and others in the course of the American effort. But what Hahn was doing was completely unrelated to any concerted German effort to produce anything at all for wartime use. He wanted it that way. "We ourselves . . . were able to continue our experiments in the Kaiser Wilhelm Institute unhindered." Indeed his colleague Heisenberg later remembered Hahn as "loud in his warnings and counsels against any attempts to use atomic energy in war."[20]

Yet Hahn, like other uranium scientists, retained his protected position and his access to needed materials. His work was designated as "decisive for the war effort," although in reality it was nothing of the kind. And while in 1939 it could well have been argued that such pure science was a proper target for protected support, at least on a modest scale (and Hahn's work, at its height, was receiving only sixty thousand dollars a year), by the latter part of the war it was plain to everyone who knew what was going on that the object of work like Hahn's was the preservation of German science, not the prosecution of Hitler's war. The German effort never went beyond the level of laboratory experiments.[21]

At the laboratory level the German scientists, independent and divided as they were, made much progress. They understood early both the importance of separated U-235 and the possibility of what others found and named plutonium—they thus identified the two major sources of a nuclear explosion. Yet they never thought either one was obtainable within the constraints of wartime urgency and difficulty. Like the French they thought the production of power was a more likely practical result, and they focused their chief attention on achieving a chain reaction which might lead to a "uranium engine." In this work they made important mistakes that might have been corrected by a larger and more collegial effort; thus they accepted a wrong experimental conclusion that graphite would not work in a reactor and so became wholly dependent on heavy water, which was much harder to get. But they also made rapid advances in the understanding of the basic physics of uranium fission.[22]

The most important figure in this effort was Werner Heisenberg, still only forty in 1941. He had been twenty-five when he formulated the principle of uncertainty—an extraordinarily subtle statement of what can and cannot be known about physical phenomena, and a productive one because it set physicists free from "asking questions to which there was no physically meaningful answer."[23] A Nobel Prize winner, his country's leading nuclear theorist, a known defender of Einstein's contributions to science, and a leading member of the German aristocracy of talent and intelligence, Heisenberg had unmatched standing among the German uranium scientists; only his relative youth was against him. To understand his course of action in 1941–42 is to understand why German scientists never pressed their government to make a nuclear weapon.

Heisenberg was brought into direct work on the uranium problem by military orders at the outbreak of the war. Like all atomic physicists he had recognized the importance of the Hahn-Strassmann discovery, but he had told Enrico Fermi in 1939 that he did not think there would be weapons in time to affect the coming war. In accepting the call to work on uranium he was comforted from the start by this belief, and he saw himself as working to give his country a leading role in future peaceful uses of atomic energy. Until Hiroshima he found no reason to doubt that this objective had been achieved; he hoped and believed the German uranium scientists were still ahead.[24]

As early as December 1939 Heisenberg had made major progress in the analysis of the uranium problem. He reported to the War Office that the fission process "can on present evidence be used for large-scale energy production" and that the surest way of "building a reactor capable of this will be to enrich the uranium 235 isotope"—thus foreshadowing by twenty years the character of the first commercial reactors the Americans would build. Heisenberg, like Hahn, thought the separation of uranium 235 in usable quantities was beyond the wartime capacity of Germany, and he was content to leave that effort to others. But he also reported that for the generation of energy the chain reaction in natural uranium was the easier road: "even ordinary uranium can be used," if used with the right moderator. His own work was devoted to that easier and, he thought, less dangerous road, and over the next two years he made progress that he found satisfactory. "Toward the end of 1941 our 'uranium club' had, by and large, grasped the physical problems involved in the technical exploitation of atomic energy." Heisenberg was confident that the road to a chain reaction—and so to nuclear power—was open, and he was equally confident that there was no prospect of making a bomb in wartime Germany. "Hence we were happily able to give the authorities an absolutely honest account of the latest development, and yet feel certain that no serious attempt to construct atom bombs would be made in Germany . . ."[25]

We should not overstate the self-restraint of this position; it rested in part on failures of scientific understanding. Heisenberg himself is an example of one such weakness—a separation of the theoretical physicists from their experimental colleagues. Even in his work on the chain reaction for nuclear power, Heisenberg made mistakes that can be traced to his habit of keeping his distance from the experimental side of physics. Gerald Holton has made an illuminating comparison between Heisenberg's style and that of Robert Oppenheimer, who had been an experimentalist before he turned to theoretical physics: At Los Alamos "the interlacing of the theoretical and experimental aspects was complete under Oppenheimer's influence and natural for all who worked with him." It was not so in Germany.[26]

In 1945 the leading German physicists were rounded up and held in custody in England, where they learned of Hiroshima and shared their reactions with hidden British microphones. Some held that they had not made a bomb because they never wanted to try, while others thought they had simply failed to discover any promising way to go about the job. Even Heisenberg later concluded that he had overestimated the difficulty of the task. Certainly the Germans never produced the quantity and quality of analysis, on the bomb as a specific objective, that became decisive in London and Washington in 1941. Their ignorance thus contributed to their indifference.[27]

But their indifference also helped to keep them ignorant. When we come to consider what led to the British and American conclusion of 1941 we shall find physicists of many sorts who were stirred by a combination of scientific insight and political concern; repeatedly the two will reinforce each other and even so it will take time to get a decision. This set of reciprocally reinforcing impulses is exactly what never existed among the German physicists. Heisenberg himself, because of his extraordinary distinction, is a crucial example. If he did not see just how to make a wartime bomb, it was in part because he did not choose to look.

In 1941 Heisenberg had a quite different concern, one that he had picked up largely from his close friend and colleague Carl Friedrich von Weizsäcker. Was there not a danger that the current situation could change, so that the German work might indeed lead on to a bomb? And what if colleagues in America, with a quite understandable view of Hitler, were going at full speed for a bomb? Considering these hazards, and believing that the physicists of the world were in a position to have a decisive influence on these events, Heisenberg decided in October 1941 to go to Copenhagen and talk with Niels Bohr.[28] His later explanation of his thinking is remarkable:

> We were convinced that the manufacture of atomic bombs was possible only with enormous technical resources. We knew that one could produce atom bombs but overestimated the necessary technical expenditure at the time. This situation seemed to us to be a favorable one, as it enabled the physicists to influence further developments. If it were impossible to produce atomic bombs this problem would

not have arisen, but if they were easily produced the physicists would have been unable to prevent their manufacture. This situation gave the physicists at that time decisive influence on further developments, since they could argue with the government that atomic bombs would probably not be available during the course of the war. On the other hand there might be a possibility of carrying out this project if enormous efforts were made.[29]

Heisenberg's probable intent—though he does not state it plainly in this account or any other—was to explore the possibility that the physicists of the world might hold back from a wartime bomb; specifically, might the British and Americans hold back if they could be sure the Germans were not in the race? Even to himself he may not have formulated these possibilities sharply, but if he had no such thought at all we have no good explanation for his effort to open an inescapably difficult and dangerous conversation.

We need not assume here that Heisenberg's purpose was purely humanitarian. As Hans Bethe heard the story after the war, he hoped for a German victory, after which "the good Germans would take care of the Nazis." Obviously that hope could not be realized if others got the bomb and used it on Germany first. His widow has written that "he was constantly tortured by this idea," and she believes that "the vague hope" of warding off such an attack "was probably the strongest motivation for his trip."[30]

Whatever his exact purpose, by his own admission he failed to carry it out. The master and a former favorite student were now separated by Hitler's war, and in more ways than one. Bohr the Dane was wary of Heisenberg the German, who, he was told, had defended the Nazi invasion of Poland, and who was in German-occupied Denmark to give a German-sponsored lecture that the Danish scientists did not attend. Heisenberg was equally constrained; the exploratory discussion he sought could be read by any Nazi as an attempt to strike a secret bargain with the enemies of Germany. His recollection continues:

> I tried to conduct this talk in such a way as to preclude putting my life into immediate danger. This talk probably started with my question as to whether or not it was right for physicists to devote themselves in wartime to the uranium problem—as there was the possibility that progress in this sphere could lead to grave consequences in the technique of war. Bohr understood the meaning of this question immediately, as I realized from his slightly frightened reaction. He replied as far as I can remember with a counterquestion. "Do you really think that uranium fission could be utilized for the construction of weapons?" I may have replied: "I know that this is in principle possible, but it would require a terrific technical effort, which, one can only hope, cannot be realized in this war." Bohr was

shocked by my reply, obviously assuming that I had intended to convey to him that Germany had made great progress in the direction of manufacturing atomic weapons. Although I tried subsequently to correct this false impression I probably did not succeed in winning Bohr's complete trust, especially as I only dared to speak guardedly (which was definitely a mistake on my part), being afraid that some phrase or other could later be held against me. I was very unhappy about the result of this conversation.[31]

Heisenberg is right about his "mistake," and he understates its consequences. Bohr was a man he could and should have trusted further, if only to break through the natural wariness of a deeply civilized man now living under Nazi occupation. As it was, the conversation failed entirely, and worse. Bohr heard no proposal for international scientific restraint, and instead he formed the quite erroneous impression that the Germans were trying hard to make a bomb. When he reported this impression, in 1943, it only gave new fuel to the fears of the English-speaking Allies—an ironic result, for until he learned firsthand of the Allied effort, Bohr himself remained doubtful of the practicability of a wartime bomb.[32]

But the perverse result of Heisenberg's expedition to Copenhagen does not diminish the fact that he and those he consulted appear to have been the only scientists of standing in any country who entertained a wartime impulse to explore the possibility that scientists of all countries might hold back from the bomb. Very likely even a much more explicit demarche would have failed. If Bohr could conclude, as he apparently did, that Heisenberg's vague exploration and a possibly more explicit one later by a younger German physicist were no more than "a German attempt at demolishing the feared American supremacy in nuclear physics," what would have been thought by physicists in England and the United States, then just reaching their own conclusion that there must be an all-out Allied effort?[33] Yet Heisenberg at least tried to try, and perhaps a more searching question is to ask what might have happened if any such inquiry or exploration had come to him from the Allies. Might he have found effective ways to give them confidence in what was, after all, the truth: that the Germans had no plan to make a bomb?

In the unwillingness of senior German physicists to press their master for support in making an atomic weapon there was a certain prudence. If they should persuade Hitler to back them in going after a wonder weapon, they would have to produce results that matched his sense of urgency or face his wrath. It was better not to attract his attention.

If the German physicists were not seeking an atomic bomb, neither was Adolf Hitler. The Führer, in one part of his wild-and-crafty mind, was a believer in wonder weapons, but most of the time he trusted only what he had learned to trust as a corporal in World War I: tanks, U-boats, and within limits the aircraft that Göring pushed for. Albert Speer remembers him as "filled with a fundamental distrust of all innovations which, as in the case of jet aircraft or atom bombs, went beyond the technical experience of the First World War generation and presaged an era he could not know." In this respect, if no other, he was of conventional mind. He was also profoundly wary of experts of all sorts and still more mistrustful of academic people. His view of nuclear physics, in particular, was hopelessly confused by his pathological and murderous anti-Semitism; Jewish physics, he called it.[34]

Hangers-on did push the atomic possibility at Hitler; oddly, it was his postmaster general who tried hardest and who seems to have earned the almost predictable cheap sneer: Look who's trying to win the war![35]

Those who had to deal with the leader more seriously were more circumspect. The most important was Albert Speer, the overlord of German war production, who tells us with cool satisfaction that among all the twenty-two hundred entries in the protocols of his official meetings with Hitler, the question of nuclear fission appears only once. Speer was not eager to stir up his master: "I was familiar with Hitler's tendency to push fantastic projects by making senseless demands."[36]

Speer knew his man; Hitler could indeed go from suspicious skepticism to absurd overexpectation. He did exactly that in the case of the V-2 rockets, which were used against London in 1944. But in that case he was the target of intense advocacy from two men who had a complete and passionate devotion to the future of rockets—for whatever purpose. For Walter Dornberger and Wernher von Braun the liquid-fueled rocket had been the center of life ever since 1932, and with Speer's assistance they had persevered, in spite of Hitler's own early skepticism. By the time Hitler was desperate for a new weapon, in 1943, they were ready to impress him. Twice that year at critical moments Hitler listened to them. Von Braun in particular he found persuasive. Here was a ten-year rocket veteran and an admirably Germanic young man of twenty-nine. By 1943 Von Braun had movies of a spectacular rocket launching, and Hitler loved movies and spectacles. Von Braun made the Faustian bargain with Hitler that no German nuclear physicist ever attempted. His project went forward, to technical success and military inconsequence, as the Third Reich was crumbling. For him it was the technical success that mattered.[37]

The uranium project was another matter. Both Speer and the scientists wanted to keep it away from Hitler's unpredictable attention, and they succeeded. There is only the one "very brief" official protocol; what it reports, in the middle of 1942, is that while there is no wartime value in the uranium project, Speer plans to give its scientists the small amount of research money they are asking for. Speer wanted no reaction, and he arranged his report so as not to get one. He tells us that Hitler had talked about the matter sometimes, "but the idea quite obviously strained his intellectual capacity." Speer found Hitler content to be confirmed in his view that "there was not much profit in the matter."[38]

Speer's decisive recommendation followed a long meeting with Heisenberg and other physicists early in June. Heisenberg and Speer have given somewhat different accounts of this crucial meeting, but they agree on its importance. Heisenberg: "Following this meeting, which was decisive for the future of the project, Speer ruled that the work was to go forward as before on a comparatively small scale. Thus the only goal attainable was the development of a uranium pile producing energy as a prime mover—in fact, future work was directed entirely towards this one aim."[39] Speer: " . . . I asked Heisenberg how nuclear physics could be applied to the manufacture of atom bombs. His answer was by no means encouraging. He declared, to be sure, that the scientific solution had already been found and that theoretically nothing stood in the way of building such a bomb. But the technical prerequisites for production would take years to develop, two years at the earliest, even provided that the program was given maximum support." Speer asked the scientists to make a list of what they needed for further research and was "rather put out" by the modesty of their requests. He suggested that they take "one or two million marks"—they had asked for some hundreds of thousands— "but apparently more could not be utilized for the present, and in any case I had been given the impression that the atom bomb could no longer have any bearing on the course of the war."[40]

Thus the two principals, Speer and Heisenberg, struck a non-Faustian bargain of their own. The physicists were given overriding priorities, but only for work at the research level. The postwar estimate was that expenditures on all aspects of the German uranium project were less than one thousandth of the American effort. From 1939 onward the dominant motive of most German physicists had been to assure the protection of both their science and their scientists from Hitler's war. With Speer's knowing help they succeeded. There is a certain decency in what they did and did not do.

By 1942 any other course would have been plainly foolish in the strictest military terms. Even if they had persuaded Hitler that nuclear weapons were the only road to victory, and even if he had given them a kind of sympathetic and patient support that was foreign to his nature, they could never have done the job in time. They were already well behind the Americans, and at the very best they would have been much slower to get the job done. They were weaker in every critical respect: in numbers and quality of scientists and engineers; in the availability of large research instruments (they had no cyclotron to help them learn about plutonium); in breadth and depth of industrial resources; in organizational flexibility; and most obviously of all, in their vulnerability to air attack. After the war, with an eye on defending himself against possible German criticism of "failure," and with no desire to emphasize his own lack of enthusiasm for a weapon-centered effort, Heisenberg summarized the situation persuasively:

> We have often been asked, not only by Germans but also by Britons and Americans, why Germany made no attempt to produce atomic bombs. The simplest answer one can give to this question is this: because the project could not have succeeded under German war conditions. It could not have succeeded on technical grounds alone: for even in America, with its much greater resources in scientific men, technicians and industrial potential, and with an economy undisturbed by enemy action, the bomb was not ready until after the conclusion of the war with Germany. In particular, a German atomic bomb project could not have succeeded because of the military situation. In 1942, German industry was already stretched to the limit, the German Army had suffered serious reverses in Russia in the winter of 1941–42, and enemy air superiority was beginning to make itself felt. The immediate production of armaments could be robbed neither of personnel nor of raw materials, nor could the enormous plants required have been effectively protected against air attack. Finally— and this is a most important fact—the undertaking could not even be initiated against the psychological background of the men responsible for German war policy. These men expected an early decision of the war, even in 1942, and any major project which did not promise quick returns was specifically forbidden. To obtain the necessary support, the experts would have been obliged to promise early results, knowing that these promises could not be kept. Faced with this situation, the experts did not attempt to advocate with the supreme command a great industrial effort for the production of atomic bombs. . . . In the upshot they were spared the decision as to whether or not they should aim at producing atomic bombs.[41]

The German vulnerability to bombing is in itself decisive. Let us assume zealous, unified, and accurate physicists, a wholly enthusiastic Hitler, and a different approach to the whole idea of military victory. Let us also assume a full-scale effort starting in 1939. It is extraordinarily unlikely that such a German effort would have succeeded in the face of Allied air attacks. Processing plants of the necessary size, whether for uranium 235 or for plutonium, could never have been hidden, nor their purpose effectively disguised. Attacks on such plants would have had an absolutely overriding priority. Even without compelling evidence of any large-scale German nuclear effort, the Allies made the small heavy-water plant in Norway the target of repeated and largely successful attacks by both bombers and commandos. The vulnerability of large production plants would have been very great indeed; by comparison to oil refineries or ball-bearing plants, nuclear installations are fragile.

Because their best physicists were not zealous for weapons, because they made uncorrected mistakes, because Hitler was Hitler, and because men like Speer always had more urgent production priorities, the Germans never really tried to make an atomic bomb, but if they had, they would have failed. Their country was in the wrong place at the wrong time.

The British

So far we have been considering activities that did not lead to an atomic bomb—now we turn to activities that did. The United Kingdom made almost no effort, beyond the elaboration of theory and the conduct of laboratory experiments, to construct an atomic bomb of its own in World War II. But work done in England between 1939 and the middle of 1941 was decisive in its influence on the United States. As we cross the Channel, therefore, and insofar as the construction of a bomb is our measure of achievement, we are moving from what did not work—indeed could not work—to what could and did. The British story also engages two other great themes—the way countries deal with one another on nuclear matters, and the relation between wartime and postwar activity—but for our immediate purpose what matters is the nature and quality of the British contribution to Franklin Roosevelt's decision.[42]

British scientists in 1939 were well placed in two respects: They had eminent nuclear physicists in considerable numbers, and those physicists were capable of effective communication with government. Scientists of distinction were official advisers to ministers, and the informal channels of the British establishment, to which men of science had belonged since Isaac Newton's day, were numerous and active.

The scientific events of early 1939 that immediately followed the Hahn-Strassmann discovery of fission took place mainly outside the United Kingdom; no British scientist elected to test for neutron emissions, or to work on the design of a reactor, or indeed to engage in large-scale speculation in the manner of Niels Bohr. But the British scientists knew what was going on, and they acted on that knowledge.

Well before the outbreak of war it was agreed that uranium research should go forward, and a simple but effective organization was set up to encourage that process. Avoiding a German error, the British centered governmental responsibility in one ministry (although they did not always remember they had done so), and responsibility for further experimentation was promptly entrusted to Professor G. P. Thomson of Imperial College, London.

Nonetheless in the words of the admirable official history, "The outbreak of war in September 1939 did not speed the uranium experiments—rather the contrary." The senior government scientist, Sir Henry Tizard, continued to believe that "it was in the highest degree improbable that any practical form of bomb could be made with uranium," and these sentiments were widely shared (for example by Winston Churchill and his "pet scientist," Professor Frederick Lindemann—later Lord Cherwell). More immediate and practical undertakings had priority, not only for British physicists as a class but even for those with a direct and personal interest in the uranium problem. If only native-born British physicists had been available to work on nuclear matters, the probability is high that the magnetic force of the immediate, coupled with the skepticism of the men at the top, would have kept the British effort well below the level of decisive impact.[43]

But Britain had been hospitable to Hitler's refugees, and early in 1940 two of them wrote a paper which ranks in importance and singularity with the Hahn-Strassmann experiment. In this paper Otto Frisch and Rudolf Peierls presented an elegant theoretical demonstration that an explosion of great power would result if pure metallic light uranium—U-235—in small amounts were brought rapidly together to make a sphere "of critical size." They thought this process might work at a level as low as 1 kilogram, and they thought that a bomb of 5 kilograms would produce an explosion "equivalent to that of several thousand tons of dynamite." It would also emit fatal radiation on a large scale. In essence Frisch and Peierls had taken an early insight of Niels Bohr—that U-235 was probably the fissile isotope of uranium—and applied their combined mathematical skills and physical intuition to the problem of its behavior in a pure form. It is hard to fault the judgment of Margaret Gowing, the British official historian:

> Indeed the Peierls-Frisch paper with its grasp of principles and properties is a remarkable example of scientific breadth and insight. It stands as the first memorandum in any country which foretold with scientific conviction the practical possibility of making a bomb and the horrors it would bring. The two scientists had performed one of the most important and difficult tasks in the development of science— they had asked the right questions. They had asked themselves what would be the cross-section for the collision of a neutron of various energies with a nucleus of U235? What fraction of such collisions would lead to fission? What was therefore the critical size of a mass of pure U235? What would be the consequences of a chain reaction

in pure U235? What would be the military value of such a weapon
in relation to the very large effort of separating the uranium isotopes?
Peierls and Frisch had not only posed these important new questions:
they had also answered them correctly from theory without any
experimental aid.[44]

Even where they went wrong, Frisch and Peierls erred constructively.
They made isotope separation sound easier than it turned out to be,
and their estimate of the amount of U-235 that would be needed was
too small, but these errors only encouraged immediate attention to
their work.

The Frisch-Peierls memorandum was secret, so secret that for over
a year no one outside the United Kingdom knew its contents. The
French and Germans had their secrets too, of course, but those secrets
never became part of any large-scale wartime success. The Frisch-
Peierls memorandum is the first large secret step toward the bomb, and
it invites a pause for reflection on secrecy. We shall have ample occasion to brood over the consequences of keeping, or trying to keep,
secrets, but it is hard to quarrel with the decision of early 1940, wholly
unanimous among all concerned, that the Frisch-Peierls memorandum
should be tightly held. The memorandum itself explained that its
analysis could easily encourage the Germans to try to make an atomic
bomb. It is hard to imagine a government choosing to share this sort
of information with an enemy, and genuinely inconceivable that one
would have wished to share it with Adolf Hitler. Even the mutually
wary relations between German physics and German power that we
have described, let alone the partnership in nationalism that many
perceived, might have been galvanized into a competitive effort by
such a paper as this. One good way to understand the force and
originality of the Frisch-Peierls memorandum is to consider what
might have happened if Frisch and Peierls had composed it in Germany and delivered it to a German government.

But when you set out to keep a secret from an enemy or potential
enemy, you are also required to keep it from most of your own people,
and you tend to be careful about sharing it with foreigners, even good
friends. So the British in the spring of 1940 held on tight to the ideas
of Frisch and Peierls. They referred them to a committee.

The British in World War II were good at cover names. I remember my own delight, as a junior staff officer, in learning that the name
Overlord had been chosen for the invasion of Normandy, and my
admiring recognition that the British and Canadian beaches—Juno,
Gold, and Sword—had names that rang out better than the American
Omaha and Utah (except of course for residents of those places). But
in naming the committee to consider this awesome matter they outdid
themselves; it was called the Maud Committee, and while some seem

to have thought the word was fraught with meaning, all it really stood for was the first name of a nurse in Kent who had worked with the family of Niels Bohr.

But if its name was more whimsical than dramatic, the work of the Maud Committee was the opposite. Over a period of fifteen months, through the successive shocks of the invasion of Norway, the fall of France, the Battle of Britain, the London blitz, the fall of Yugoslavia and Greece, and the attack on the Soviet Union, the Maud Committee tested the Frisch-Peierls conclusion. By the middle of 1941 the brief suggestion of the two refugees had become the settled conviction of a larger group of senior scientists widely known for brilliance and good judgment.

Committees also are a persistent element in our story, and as it is useful that we can begin with a real secret, so it is good that our first committee is one of the best ever. The Maud Committee was composed of distinguished scientists who understood also that they were not all qualified specialists in nuclear matters; they supplied themselves with a technical subcommittee whose members were the best specialists they could find—and thus more than incidentally they found a way to include a number of refugee scientists who could not easily have been appointed to the committee itself. They supported those specialists in all the further technical analysis that time and small amounts of money would permit; they took the problem apart, examined it together, and reached firm conclusions on all the subjects within their scientific competence. They reported in clear and effective prose; they allowed minority comments; they endorsed the brilliant insight of the Frisch-Peierls memorandum with the authority and depth that were indispensable to the task of persuading a government to make a bomb. It is not to their discredit that the government they helped to persuade was not their own.

If we allow for the fact that the British word *scheme* translates to the American *plan* or *proposal* or both, the language of the committee's first conclusion has a sharpness that committee prose seldom attains: "The committee considers that the scheme for a uranium bomb is practicable and likely to lead to decisive results in the war." U-235 could be separated, and pure U-235 could be made to explode dramatically. It was estimated that the material for the first bomb could be ready by the end of 1943. The committee also discussed the German interest in uranium and remarked with the force of understatement: "It may be mentioned that the lines on which we are now working are such as would be likely to suggest themselves to any capable physicist."

This decisive conclusion led to two recommendations: "that this work be continued on the highest priority and on the increasing scale necessary to obtain the weapon in the shortest possible time" and that "the present collaboration with America should be continued and extended especially in the region of experimental work."[45]

But who would do "this work"? Should Great Britain do it? And if so how? These questions were not answered by the committee. In the nature of things only governments could answer them.

The Maud report was finished in July and went upward in August—informally to Lord Cherwell, now the prime minister's personal adviser on science, and formally to the cabinet's Scientific Advisory Committee. Cherwell had been a skeptic; now he became a believer, at least in making the try—and in particular in making that try through an independent British effort. At the end of August he had his recommendations ready. While less optimistic than the Maud enthusiasts, at least about the time it might take, he said, "I am quite clear that we must go forward." Moreover the work should be done in Britain if at all possible. Cherwell not only opposed reliance on the United States, but even encouragement of the Americans. Professor Gowing describes his thinking:

> Whoever possessed such a plant would be able to dictate terms to the rest of the world. "However much I may trust my neighbour, and depend on him," he wrote, "I am very much averse to putting myself completely at his mercy and would therefore not press the Americans to undertake this work: I would just continue exchanging information and get into production over here without raising the question of whether they should do it or not."[46]

Cherwell's view became Churchill's, at least for a while. Without waiting for the report of the Scientific Advisory Committee he sent a note to his chiefs of staff. Like some other documents in nuclear history it has become famous beyond its real meaning: "Although personally I am quite content with the existing explosives, I feel we must not stand in the path of improvement, and I therefore think that action should be taken in the sense proposed by Lord Cherwell: and that the Cabinet Minister responsible should be Sir John Anderson. I shall be glad to know what the Chiefs of Staff Committee think." The chiefs of staff agreed; they met with the prime minister on September 3 and urged that "no time, labour, materials or money should be spared in pushing forward the development of this project" and "in Britain and not abroad."[47]

In appearance, then, the prime minister had decided to get a British atomic bomb just as rapidly as possible, and in appearance his senior military advisers had agreed to an overriding priority for a wartime effort to this end. This is the legend, and very good scholars have concluded that Britain was the first country to decide to build an atomic bomb. But in fact the decision was neither clear nor firm, as events quickly showed.

Churchill entrusted the undertaking to Sir John Anderson, lord president of the council and a member of the War Cabinet. Anderson was an unusual minister in two ways: He had been a scientist in his youth and a career civil servant most of his working life. He had even studied the chemistry of uranium. He was able and could be determined, but he had none of Churchill's own flair for galvanizing an undertaking, and in any case he himself had doubted from the first that there could be any practical use of uranium during the war. He had seen the Maud reports very early, and while they had impressed him deeply, they did not change his view on this critical point: " . . . I am bound to say that my critical skepticism [on wartime use] has only been confirmed by the extremely interesting details now supplied." Precisely because he had been both a chemist and a civil servant, he understood the distance between a brilliant analysis and a working result.[48]

Anderson's interest was great; he understood "the exciting and indeed sensational possibilities revealed" by the reports.[49] But he was thinking about the long run. He was in favor of going ahead, in Professor Gowing's words, "so that Britain and her associates might keep command of the enormous potentialities." He volunteered to take a leading role in it, and his offer was happily accepted. But there is no evidence at all that he ever supposed he had a mandate to produce a bomb in time to affect the war.

In his wariness Anderson was in good company. A number of leading skeptics were unswayed by the Maud report. The Scientific Advisory Committee reviewed the matter; during September it heard from skeptics as well as from the Maud enthusiasts; it produced a carefully balanced report. The bomb project was "of the very highest importance." Estimates of the time required varied from two to five years. "We expect that the lower estimate will be found to be too short." But for this very reason the work should be pressed "as rapidly as possible." The committee listed six heads for the work to be done, but not one of them included large-scale construction of anything, and the committee explicitly recommended that no final decision of this sort should be taken until there were results from a pilot plant and from further development of chemical processes.[50]

In itself this recommendation was no more than common sense. When the Americans came to make their decision, they too went ahead in stages, from research and development to construction, with a decision at each stage. But what was being deferred in the British case was not just the decision to build a full-scale plant, but a decision as to what country such a plant should be in. Both scientists and others were sharply divided on the point. At first Lord Cherwell and Sir James

Chadwick—the latter by now preeminent among British nuclear physicists—thought the whole project could and should be kept in Britain; the chiefs of staff agreed. Other scientists, notably Tizard and P.M.S. Blackett, thought it was wholly impracticable to build a large separation plant in the United Kingdom; it would interfere drastically with other war work, and it would get bombed. This was also the conclusion of the Scientific Advisory Panel and of Sir John Anderson.[51]

Thus the British decision of September was never a decision to make a bomb in Britain; it was a decision to go ahead as fast as possible with research and development, and then, if the work was promising, to get a production plant built in North America. Politically the more attractive site was Canada, but technical considerations favored the United States. In either case the main effort of technical support and production of components would have to be American.

That any such effort could not be under British control alone should have been obvious, but the conclusion was an unpleasant one, and in any case no immediate decision was required. The general purpose was agreed: There should be an effort to make a bomb somewhere, and as far as possible that effort should be British. Best not to borrow trouble by asking what the Canadians or Americans would say. The scientific advisers did not think it their business to address that obviously political question. Churchill and Anderson, the only two politicians with full knowledge of the matter, made their own choice to avoid it. Neither the politicians nor the scientists understood at the time that by their earlier decision to share their scientific findings with the Americans they had already played a decisive role in setting loose an effort in North America that would make any mainly British bomb project a wartime impossibility. The supporting American base that any British project would require was about to be preempted by its owners.

The Americans

The Americans decided to make atomic weapons if they could, and they succeeded. Both in 1945 and after, the primary attention of both participants and observers has been given to the extraordinary process by which success was achieved. Much less attention has been paid to the events that led to the basic decision, in 1941, to go ahead. Yet of all the political decisions of the nuclear age this one is the first, not only in time, but quite possibly in importance. It was in no sense automatic. With different persons in high places it would surely have happened differently, or not at all. The physics and politics of the United States in 1939 and after were different from those of any other country, and their interconnections, both effective and ineffective, were entirely unique.[52]

The United States was, of course, unique in one other way. In the circumstances of the war it was the only country with uncommitted and protected resources sufficient to this extraordinary purpose. Unlike the United Kingdom and Germany, it was immune to severe air attack. Unlike the Soviet Union, it was free of invasion and occupation, and its advantages over desperate Japan and quickly defeated France were even more overwhelming. Alone among the nations of the world it was so placed that it could in fact hope to make nuclear weapons during the war. This unique American situation has made it easy to assume that there is nothing remarkable about the American decision to try, but the American advantage in location and resources does not of itself explain the decision.

As in other countries, the story necessarily begins with the physicists. By 1938 American physics had come of age. Americans had shared increasingly in the great atomic adventures of the years between the wars. Already in the 1920s the transatlantic traffic of physicists became a two-way affair. In the expanding world of American universities there was room for many physicists, and some were of the highest class. American philanthropy, primarily that of the Rockefeller Foundation, reinforced the natural expansion of both American physics and of international traffic in excellence. By the beginning of the 1930s, according to its best historian Daniel Kevles, American physics was a self-confident world of opportunity and quality whose members "had virtually closed the historic gap in quality between European and American research." It is a fundamental error to suppose that the rise of American physics toward the front rank had to await the great migration after Hitler.[53]

Yet it would be an equal error to neglect the impact of that migration. Between 1933 and 1941 about a hundred refugee physicists came to the United States, mostly from Germany and Austria. They did not go to any one place, but rather to nearly all of the departments that had gained strength in the previous decade. What is more important, they were mostly young, and many of them were in the very front rank of the physicists of their generation; in physics, especially in nuclear physics, one of the very best is worth dozens of the second best. So it is not wrong to celebrate the arrival of such men as Hans Bethe, Felix Bloch, Enrico Fermi, James Franck, Leo Szilard, Edward Teller, Victor Weisskopf and Eugene Wigner. Men of this caliber became a permanent enrichment to science in America, and it is no trivial matter that most of them found themselves quickly and happily at home. It is never easy to migrate, and not every American scientist or department was warm to Jewish foreigners. But the dominant chord was one of welcome, compounded of both political and scientific fellow feeling. Weisskopf, a man of extraordinary human sensitivity, remembers that "within the shortest time one was in the midst of a society that was extremely appealing and interesting and active." And by the time war came the refugee physicists were "fully immersed in the scientific community and . . . were making major contributions . . . they were rapidly assimilated into and helped to transform the field of activity which opened itself to them in the United States."[54]

"The country was dotted with well-appointed laboratories and had more cyclotrons than the rest of the world combined"; strong departments of physics in a dozen places included nuclear physicists who "stimulated students and colleagues alike into significant lines of research." In the largest laboratory, that of Ernest Lawrence at Berkeley, the team research of "big physics" was already a fact of life; the cyclotron was a formidable invention, offering great experimental advantages for the exploration of the nucleus, but at least as important was what his colleague Luis Alvarez later called Lawrence's greatest invention, "not the cyclotron, but the modern way of doing physics in cooperative teams." There would surely be more "big physics" soon, and it too was hospitable to the migrants; their theoretical and even philosophical sophistication often complemented the experimental energy—the try it and see—that marked the zestful cyclotronists. The physics of the United States in 1939 was easily the strongest in the world. What Robert Oppenheimer later called "a rather sturdy indigenous effort" had been formidably reinforced by the refugees; there is no need here to sort out how much of this general strength was there already, and how much was Hitler's contribution. The president of the day had remarked, after all, that we were nearly all immigrants to begin with.[55]

The news of the fission of uranium caused a splendid stir in this lively and varied American world. That the great Niels Bohr himself should be the messenger was a happy and reinforcing accident, and the excitement spread from him rapidly, first in Princeton and New York, and then through the wider audience assembled at the fourth annual Washington conference on theoretical physics—an event originally organized by Edward Teller. Rapidly and repeatedly the phenomenon of uranium fission was experimentally verified, along with its release of very high energies. Physicists across the country were stirred. One of the leading theorists of the younger generation was thirty-four-year-old Robert Oppenheimer. As he often did later, Oppenheimer found words to fit the occasion; even to laymen the letter he sent a friend conveys a sense of the complexity and fascination of the "U business" and the questions it opened; the letter was written at the end of January, only two days after Oppenheimer heard the news of fission.

The U business is unbelievable. We first saw it in the papers, wired for more dope, and have had a lot of reports since. You know it started with Hahn's finding that what he had taken for Ra in one of the U activities fractionally crystallized with Ba. And then the recognition that the ekauranium series was chemically compatible with a series starting with Ma, running on through Rhe and Os and Pd. And then understanding suddenly why there were such long chains of beta decay, to get rid of the neutron excess with which half a U nucleus would start; and why one had "isomeric" chains that were really isotopic; and then remembering how a drop when it is charged up elongates, becomes less and less stable to longitudinal oscillations, final[ly] ruptures. At that point there were a lot of experimental things done here: recording the pieces when U is slow neutron bombarded on a differential chamber; seeing them, with about 2 cm maximum range and unbelievable ionization, in a cloud chamber at reduced pressure, and only during the neutron bombardment; measuring their range by the activities left in foils behind the bombarded U; measuring their energy by collecting ions, with a maximum of about 60 mv, as one could expect from the Coulomb field; showing that the 72 hr activity goes chemically with Te, leads to an X ray which is the K alpha and beta of Iodine, is followed by an Iodine activity. Many points are still unclear: where are the short-lived high energy betas one would expect? Are there strong gammas as one would think from the big dipole moments of the pieces? In how many ways does the U come apart? At random, as one might guess, or only in certain ways? And most of all, are there many neutrons that come off during the splitting, or from the excited pieces? If there are then a 10 cm cube of U deuteride (one would need the D to slow them without capture) should be quite something. What do you think? It is I think exciting, not in the rare way of positrons and mesotrons, but in a good honest practical way.[56]

These questions do not lead straight to a bomb, and Oppenheimer did not make the "U business" his main concern until 1942, but in the range of the letter and the "good honest practical" excitement of its writer, there is more than a hint of the spirit that later animated Los Alamos.

The strongest working American response to the news of fission came at Columbia University. The two principal general lines of worldwide inquiry in 1939 were whether there might be a road to a chain reaction in natural uranium and whether, as Niels Bohr was arguing, the fission so far observed was due to the uranium isotope 235. There were excellent scientists at Columbia with an interest in both. The inquiry into the chain reaction quickly led to the first significant contacts between physics and politics, a set of encounters as remarkable for the good intentions of all concerned as for their modest results.

The moving spirit was Leo Szilard. At forty-one, Szilard was in New York when he heard the news of fission; he had left his native Hungary for Berlin, Berlin for London, and London for New York, always a jump ahead in his political perceptions. Hungary would not be a good place to do science; Berlin in 1933 was no place for a Hungarian Jew; there would be war or anarchy in Europe after the Munich appeasement, and a foreign scientist would not be encouraged to do war work in Britain (although on this last point one cannot help wondering what might have happened if Szilard had stayed in England and found himself talking in 1939 with men like Frisch and Peierls). So he was in New York, unattached except by an uncommonly wide and various set of ties to physicists and other friends—he had always been gregarious and he had been making Americans at home in Europe since the 1920s. He was also a friend of Albert Einstein.[57]

The news of the Hahn-Strassmann experiment hit Szilard with multiple force. He had remained a physicist, resisting the temptation of biology, precisely because of a deep and double interest in the mysteries of the atom: It was fascinating as a scientific possibility and it was also a possible source of enormous energy—and specifically of bombs. Szilard had read and never forgotten the dramatic fantasy that Wells had made out of the physical intuition of Soddy. And now this vision was revived in his mind, at the very moment when he had been so deeply shocked by Hitler's triumph at Munich that he no longer felt able to do ordinary physics at all, feeling that the claims of the international crisis must come first. The news of fission fused his energies: To work on this problem was to attend to all his concerns at once. It was scientifically at the center of his own interest and ambitions; the practical consequences might be enormous; and nothing could be more important politically than to guard against the danger that Hitler's Germany might get there first.

If Szilard, with these concerns and capabilities, had been a part of the American scientific establishment, he would not have attacked the matter as he did. But he was one of nature's born irregulars. In a borrowed laboratory at Columbia he performed a brilliant experiment with radium that he rented with a borrowed two thousand dollars. He undertook a one-man campaign to establish self-censorship in the laboratories of the democratic countries. And he launched the first effort to engage Franklin Roosevelt's attention and support.

Szilard was an irregular but not at all a loner. He shared his concerns with his friends. To one of the greatest he was unpersuasive. Enrico Fermi, newly established at Columbia as a professor of physics, was as passionate about the chain reaction as Szilard, but much more patient. He was also deeply skeptical about the prospect for any early practical application, and while he had recently abandoned Italy for political reasons and was in every way a man of democratic temper, he was also uninterested in the process of political action. If those in authority wanted his help, they had only to ask, but they had to ask. Szilard's account of his underlying difference with Fermi is engaging and persuasive. Szilard wanted Fermi's support for his proposal of a benevolent conspiracy of secrecy; he visited the Pupin Laboratory at Columbia and finding Fermi out, he visited their common friend I. I. Rabi to relay his proposal. A few days later he came back and saw Rabi again.

> I said, "What did Fermi say?" Rabi said, "Fermi said 'Nuts!' " So I said, "Why did he say 'Nuts!'?" and Rabi said, "Well, I don't know, but he is in and we can ask him." So we went over to Fermi's office, and Rabi said to Fermi, "Look, Fermi, I told you what Szilard thought and you said 'Nuts!' and Szilard wants to know why you said 'Nuts!' " So Fermi said, "Well . . . there is the remote possibility that neutrons may be emitted in the fission of uranium and then of course perhaps a chain reaction can be made." Rabi said, "What do you mean by 'remote possibility'?" and Fermi said, "Well, ten per cent." Rabi said, "Ten per cent is not a remote possibility if it means that we may die of it. If I have pneumonia and the doctor tells me that there is a remote possibility that I might die, and it's ten per cent, I get excited about it."
>
> From the very beginning the line was drawn; the difference between Fermi's position throughout this and mine was marked on the first day we talked about it. We both wanted to be conservative, but Fermi thought that the conservative thing was to play down the possibility that this may happen, and I thought the conservative thing was to assume that it would happen and take all the necessary precautions.[58]

This temperamental difference did not prevent fruitful scientific collaborations, but for political encouragement Szilard turned elsewhere, to fellow Hungarians and then to Albert Einstein. Eugene Wigner had come to Princeton in 1933 and Edward Teller to George Washington in 1935; both were Szilard's friends and both shared his belief in the danger and promise of uranium. Through the winter and spring Szilard was busy with his unsuccessful effort to establish international secrecy and with two notable experiments, one as Fermi's friendly competitor and one as his partner. In the early summer, with these efforts behind him, with his status as a guest of Columbia ended, and with Fermi gone to Michigan to work on cosmic rays, Szilard, steadily more persuaded that a chain-reacting system could be designed, approached a friend in the Navy Department for help and was turned down; the navy of 1939 had no way to respond to a single-handed appeal from an unconnected refugee scientist.

Szilard then talked to Wigner. The two found that they shared a common concern; if the chain reaction was as likely as Szilard's calculations and confidence would suggest, they asked themselves "what would happen if the Germans got hold of large quantities of the uranium which the Belgians were mining in the Congo?" Shouldn't the Belgians be warned? Szilard had a flash of zany inspiration: "It occurred to me that Einstein knew quite well the Queen of the Belgians, and so I suggested that we visit Einstein . . . and ask him whether he might not write to the Queen."[59] So off they went to Einstein on Long Island, getting lost on the way (which in eastern Long Island is in no sense a purely Hungarian problem). Einstein, who had not heard about the chain reaction, understood its implications at once, agreed to write not the queen but a Belgian cabinet member, and dictated a draft of such a letter. It was also agreed that the State Department in Washington should be consulted before the letter was sent. Wigner went to California, leaving Szilard to carry on, and in particular to carry out the consultation with Washington.

At this point Szilard, who later remarked engagingly and accurately that "we were all green," decided that he needed "to talk to somebody who knew a little bit better how things were done." Through a friend he was introduced to Alexander Sachs of the Lehman Corporation, a man with access to Roosevelt.[60]

Sachs was an imaginative economist and political observer; he was aware of fission, understood the seriousness of what Szilard told him and reached the instant conclusion that the matter should be taken up with the president. After other intermediaries were considered, Sachs himself was settled on, and by the middle of August he was provided with a new letter from Einstein—drafted by Szilard—and he set about seeing the president. He was competing with the outbreak of war in Europe and the urgent need for legislation to allow the sale of arms to Britain and France; he did not see Roosevelt until October 11.

We have no account of this meeting from Roosevelt's side—no minute and no resulting order in writing; it is a difficulty that presidents often present to historians, and none more often than FDR. Because of the drama attached to a letter on this subject from the greatest of twentieth-century scientists to the greatest of twentieth-century American politicians, there has been a natural tendency to assume that the Einstein letter was decisive. The tendency has been reinforced by the testimony of Sachs that the president concluded the meeting by telling his aide Major General Edwin "Pa" Watson: "This requires action."

But what was "this," and what action was taken? Neither Einstein's letter nor a covering memorandum by Sachs was entirely clear on the first point. The letter described the probability of a chain reaction, the prospect of "vast amounts of power" that could be achieved "in the immediate future," and the much less certain possibility of powerful bombs of a new type that could be "carried by boat and exploded in a port." Szilard was apparently thinking not of an atomic bomb as we now know it, but of some sort of exploding fast neutron reactor of great size. Soon the Americans would be the first to learn that there is no such animal, but just such a concept had been borrowed by H. G. Wells from Soddy in 1913. The letter made only one concrete recommendation for action: that the president might appoint a person having his confidence to maintain contact "between the Administration and the group of physicists working on chain reactions." Such a person might keep government departments informed, help in securing uranium, and reinforce the experimental work—Fermi's and Szilard's were clearly intended—by helping, if necessary, to get money and equipment from *private* persons or industry. No suggestion is made for any large-scale *government* action.[61]

So the action requested turns out to be the action the president took. He set up a small committee under Lyman Briggs of the Bureau of Standards and through Watson, orally, he asked Briggs to deal with the matter. There is no record that he ever spoke to Briggs directly.

There is nothing in this encounter or its aftermath to suggest that it led Roosevelt to start a governmental program; he was not asked to start one, and he did not do so. He set up an arrangement for continuing communication with the interested scientists, and when Briggs sent him a memorandum in November, with quite specific findings and recommendations, Watson reported to Briggs that the president was most interested, but in fact Roosevelt took no new decisions; he did not even tell Briggs to go ahead. When Sachs pressed him again in March, with a letter enclosing another signed by Einstein and drafted by Szilard, Roosevelt replied by referring the matter back to the Briggs Committee and had Watson prod Briggs a bit by asking for suggestions "so that this investigation shall go on." Twice in early 1940 Sachs proposed further meetings with the president, but Roosevelt apparently did not receive him again on this subject until 1944.[62]

One can guess why. Sachs was a long-winded and even sententious expositor. By his own 1945 account he read the president not one but two memoranda of his own on October 11; each was longer than Einstein's letter, and one of them was a vaporous exercise in geopolitical pontification. Moreover, he was no master of the subject or of the exposition of science to laymen; one of his memoranda wrongly attributed the discovery of fission to Fermi and Szilard. Roosevelt could be a good listener, but only with people who got quickly to the point; it seems at least possible that the president never really understood what Sachs was talking about. In earlier years FDR had often had time for unofficial talkers like Sachs, but as presidents will, he talked more and listened less as he grew older. On this hard subject, in this season of danger, he needed a different kind of counselor.[63]

Nor can it be said that in Lyman Briggs he had picked a dynamic man of action. Briggs at sixty-five was indeed a trained physicist, but his scientific work had been in soil physics decades earlier. He was now a senior scientific administrator with thirty-nine years in the federal service. He was wary of enthusiastic amateurs and foreigners, and content to await the step-by-step progress of experiments designed by the brilliant but cautious Fermi. Nor did he see himself as under orders to proceed at forced draft. He helped a little to get supplies for the most important immediate experiment; he consulted a little with experts at Columbia and Princeton; by June 1940 he had developed a set of proposals for the support of research on both isotope separation and the chain reaction in natural uranium. It was a sensible program, and it went at least as far as Roosevelt's indirect oral instruction had told him to go.[64]

But Roosevelt almost surely knew his man; Briggs had been kept on by his own decision in 1933, and there had been no friction in their relationship. If in October 1939 Roosevelt had wanted much more than he got from Briggs in the months that followed, he could have said so or turned to someone else. In June 1940 he did.

Szilard, who knew what did and did not happen, was deeply disappointed by the failure of that first demarche. Einstein came later to regret his first letter for its supposed effectiveness, but as he later wrote, Szilard knew better. "The Washington meeting [with Briggs and others on October 21] was followed by the most curious period in my life. We heard nothing from Washington at all." And nothing happened on the chain reaction: "It is an incredible fact, in retrospect, that between the end of June 1939 and the spring of 1940, not a single experiment was under way in the United States which was aimed at exploring the possibilities of a chain reaction in natural uranium."[65] Szilard is right, but he does not seem to have understood where the trouble was: He was expecting the government to take the lead on a scientific matter in a country whose customs were then quite different.

Arthur Compton was a senior American physicist with a Nobel Prize and long experience of the national scientific scene. While his own primary current interest was in cosmic rays, he was well aware of the potential importance of the fission problem. He watched without a sense of direct engagement as the Briggs Committee went slowly about its work, and indeed so did most other American physicists. This was unfortunate, because what men like Compton knew, and Szilard did not, was that at least until there had been a much more powerful demonstration of its immediate military relevance, "preliminary work [on an atomic program] would progress much faster with private backing."[66] The president was for "action," and Briggs believed from the first that some government support was justified, but by the spring of 1940 the Briggs Committee had actually put out only six thousand dollars, for the graphite Fermi and Szilard needed. In the same season the Rockefeller Foundation was granting a million dollars for Ernest Lawrence's newest and largest cyclotron. If Fermi and Szilard had been Lawrence and Compton, they would have known how to get the amount of support they needed at first by very little more than a phone call. Conversely if Briggs had been the kind of facilitator and middleman that Sachs and Szilard had in mind, he would have known how to open private and corporate doors for them. But he was a government man through and through; anything he did would be done through official channels. Channels for action beyond what he did in these nine months did not then exist, and he was not the man to dig them.

The progress that did occur in late 1939 and the first half of 1940 owed little to the Briggs Committee. At Columbia University, John R. Dunning demonstrated that U-235 was indeed the isotope that fissioned with slow neutrons, but the problem of separating it was still thought to be formidable, and no one in the United States made the terrifying calculation of the Frisch-Peierls memorandum, written in just that season. Some physicists understood that in theory fast fission in U-235 might produce a big bang, but the dominant attitude was that it was not much good to speculate on that until more was known by direct evidence; for that enriched samples were needed, and for them more progress on isotopic separation. The Americans were proceeding experimentally, and in 1940 they never received the jolt of a quantitative theoretical calculation on what U-235 might do if you could get it. The bomb, as a specific objective, was far from the center of their thinking. The Briggs Committee would wait and learn, one step at a time. It did gradually work out a clear and accurate understanding that the two most important experimental problems were isotope separation and the chain reaction. By June 1940 it was ready with proposals for research in both fields, at a combined level of $240,000. At that point Briggs found himself for the first time with someone to report to who might pay him more attention, and frighten him less, than the distant great man in the White House.[67]

In the spring of 1940, moved primarily by the danger they saw in Hitler's progress, a small group of leaders in science and technology decided that the time had come to get better connections between American science and technology and the American government. One of them was an engineer named Vannevar Bush, who had come to Washington from the Massachusetts Institute of Technology a year earlier, to be president of the Carnegie Institution of Washington. Because Bush was in Washington, as he tells it, and because of his extraordinary capacity for persuasive initiative, as others report, Bush took the lead. He persuaded Harry Hopkins, and through Hopkins Roosevelt, that there must be a new group reporting directly to the president. On June 12, 1940, Bush went to see Roosevelt, whom he had never met before; he took with him a single-page memorandum of four paragraphs (which has been lost), and in less than ten minutes, he said, "I came out with my 'OK—FDR' and all the wheels began to turn." Bush was appointed chairman of a new organization called the National Defense Research Committee (NDRC), and a revolution began in the relations among American scientists, politicians, and soldiers.[68]

To most of those who had a part in the revolution it became a truism that Vannevar Bush was its indispensable man. His closest colleague, President James B. Conant of Harvard, called him "a great mobilizer of scientists," and so he was. His roots were in the university, and he began in 1940 with a basic operational innovation. Instead of working toward the establishment of government laboratories or the mobilization of scientists in uniform, he established a pattern of contract work at universities and research centers; the contracts were not with individuals but with institutions, and they thus allowed for activity at any desired level of magnitude and complexity. In the end the Radiation Laboratory of MIT had a staff of four thousand people, and the Los Alamos Laboratory itself was—and is—a unit of the University of California.

Bush knew what scientific research was. He also knew how to assemble and direct a staff of strong associates. But there were other remarkable scientific entrepreneurs in the country; what made Bush unique was his understanding of Roosevelt's Washington. Washington was not just his place of academic business; it was a place for whose own business he had a natural aptitude. He knew how to testify before congressional committees. He was usually an impeccable witness, even-tempered, straightforward, and as informative as possible. He understood the military and their departments, respecting the ways of generals and admirals and forming effective relations with those like Secretary of War Stimson and his staff who understood what he was about. To Stimson, who saw Bush and Conant correctly (and especially on nuclear matters) as a partnership, these two men and their associates "set a standard of effort which in its combination of soundness and daring left open . . . no intelligent course but full and hearty collaboration."[69]

We have been in other capitals—in Paris, where Joliot and the Curies had ample and excellent connections; in Berlin, where the best men of science wanted only to keep a safe distance between themselves and final power; in London, where there was easy discussion, formal and informal, among scientists and ministers. Washington in 1940 was like none of them. It was the city of politics, not the national metropolis. The nation's scientists did not look to it for leadership; its political leaders did not easily look beyond the government for counsel. The stuttering and mutually uncomprehending relationship called into being by the Einstein letter was the result of a vast gap between one world and the other; Briggs had done more than the average bureaucrat of the day to reach across it. But now the gap was to be closed, and for good and evil it has not been reopened since.

Most of all, Vannevar Bush understood that in a capital moving toward war, everything turned on getting and holding a direct relation of confidence with the president himself. "I knew that you couldn't get anything done in that damn town unless you organized under the wing of the President." This did not mean that one should impose on his time; ten minutes were plenty if they led to "OK—FDR." Even before that first meeting Bush sought an introduction to Harry Hopkins and explained his ideas at length to that extraordinarily quick-witted and time-saving servant of the president. When he saw the president, Hopkins was there and surely had been there ahead of him. In the five years that followed, Bush never put anything ahead of his "obligation to tell the President what he needed to know—and no more."[70] He whittled his memoranda to the sharpness that came naturally to a man who had always insisted that "even engineering students had to master the art of writing crisp, clear, precise sentences." He learned to respond quickly when the president asked him questions well outside his special competence—as presidents often do with those they trust—and correct himself later if necessary. He learned to joke with the president. He took no public credit, and the White House liked that too.[71]

When he established the National Defense Research Committee, Roosevelt put the Briggs Committee under its jurisdiction. No one seems to know whether this was his own idea or Bush's recommendation. Roosevelt had been getting pressure from Sachs to move things along faster, and Bush had some direct knowledge of the difficulties in the problem. We get an inkling of Bush's own attitude in Roosevelt's letter to Briggs, which Bush drafted: "I appreciate the thought and effort which you are devoting to this baffling and intricate matter." Bush did not know just what to make of the uranium problem, and his uncertainty continued for a year. He had more than enough to do with matters that seemed more urgent. He reorganized the Briggs Committee to strengthen it scientifically and also approved supporting expenditures, though less than Briggs asked for. Beyond that, he was, like Briggs, content to wait for more light.[72]

Light was slow to come. Research proceeded on the chain reaction and on isotope separation. Briggs also made a first effort in the field of fast fission, but here he made an unfortunate choice; he asked for help from Gregory Breit. Breit was a distinguished physicist, but sometimes inclined "to go straight past the point without recognizing it."

He was also obsessed by the need for secrecy. The combination was not fruitful. Understanding of the fast-fission process—a necessarily theoretical effort at a time when fissionable material was unavailable—was absolutely essential to any full-fledged effort to make a bomb; events two years later were to show that the subject was not easy even for a group of enormously powerful minds kept in constructive tension with each other by Robert Oppenheimer at his best. The selection of Breit was a way of getting nowhere in the dark.[73]

It may have been even worse than that. Because the Briggs Committee existed and because its doings were ever more secret, it was assumed among interested scientists that the work was in hand and that those who were wanted would be called on. Already in the spring of 1940 the two senior Americans in nuclear physics—Ernest Lawrence and Arthur Compton—had exchanged doubts about the progress of the project and promised each other to keep their eyes open. But in fact neither of them did anything on the uranium problem that year. Meanwhile Szilard was now effectively excluded from anything but an auxiliary experimenter's role; after the appointment of Bush the Sachs channel to Roosevelt was inoperative, and the Briggs Committee, as its concern for security intensified, became wary of foreign advisers. It never resolved this difficulty, as the Maud Committee had—and as Bush would in another context later—by the device of having two levels of work, one for policy, manned by nationals who might not all be expert, and one for technical questions, manned by experts who might not all be nationals. All in all Compton's retrospective conclusion is persuasive: Things would probably have gone faster if Einstein had never written and Sachs had never talked to Roosevelt.[74]

Yet we can have no certainty that an alternative approach would have been better. Bush did not seek his job because of the uranium problem, and with or without the Briggs Committee the first priority in physics would have gone to radar in 1940. Lawrence himself, at the urgent request of Bush and Alfred Loomis, put it first, although he refused to be the director of the new Radiation Laboratory for radar at MIT. Instead, he said, "I assured Loomis and Bush I would find them a better man for that job, which I did in the person of Lee DuBridge . . . and spent the fall of 1940 and a good part of 1941 helping recruit men . . . and assisting DuBridge and Co. in any other way I could." Among the first people he recruited was Edwin McMillan, of his own laboratory, who was then right at the edge of the discovery of plutonium.[75]

The emphasis on radar was not wrong: Rabi, Fermi's friend, who became DuBridge's deputy, said, "It was where you could do something good and quick against Hitler." By the end of 1940 there was still no American paper, open or classified, that took account of the possibilities that were before the Maud Committee. Sometime that winter (neither the records nor the official histories say just when) copies of minutes of that committee were sent over to the Briggs Committee, but they were not circulated, and Maud did not become important in America until the spring.[76]

By that time Lawrence himself was thoroughly aroused; he had done his bit for radar, and he had turned his attention to the uranium problem. During the winter two events in his own laboratory struck him: One was the discovery, by Glenn Seaborg, of plutonium, and the other was his own sudden realization that his thirty-seven-inch cyclotron might be converted into an instrument for the separation of U-235. Not surprisingly, Lawrence responded most vigorously when he could see a way to engage his own skills and resources. To Lawrence, Briggs was "slow, conservative, methodical, and accustomed to operate at peace-time government bureau tempo"; he was "still further inhibited by the requirement of secrecy." Something should be done, and perhaps Lawrence was the one to do it. He talked to Karl Compton (the brother of Arthur), and Compton called Bush.[77]

Bush was loyal to those who worked with him and he hated end runs. Yet Karl Compton was a very old friend and his former boss at MIT. Bush saw Lawrence and put him in touch with Briggs as a temporary adviser. But he was still defending Briggs two months later: "Briggs has done exceedingly well to keep his balance. . . . I have backed him up to the best of my ability, and I intend to do so in the future." But the same letter begins: "This uranium matter is a headache," and ends with a half-comical Yankee lament: "As I have said many times, I wish that the physicist who fished uranium in the first place had waited a few years before he sprung this particular thing upon an unstable world. However, we have the matter in our laps and we have to do the best we can."[78]

Bush knew that Lawrence was an enthusiast by temper, but he also must have known that Briggs really was a bit slow, for he was already beginning to hear of the Maud results. In April he had a visit from Kenneth Bainbridge, a young physicist just back from Britain, where he been included in a Maud meeting. Bainbridge was a careful and judicious witness; he had been impressed by the Maud meeting; he was in channels; it was a report Bush would not have ignored. Later that month Bush arranged for the appointment of a review committee of the National Academy of Sciences. What were the prospects? Could something serious be done in time to help with the war?[79]

The National Academy committee had a curiously hard time talking to the Briggs Committee; neither side was blunt or searching about the prospect of a bomb. The report supported "a strongly intensified effort" of research, but it was far from optimistic or clear about the ways and means of getting a bomb; its focus was on the need to learn more, not on the opportunity to do something decisive. It was cool about the prospects for large-scale separation of U-235. It placed the prospect of atomic bombs third in military importance, behind "radio-active materials to be used as missiles" and "a power source on submarines or ships." Prophetically, it set 1945 as the probable earliest date for atomic bombs, but its prediction was tentative, and in any case Bush and Conant were not convinced. They asked for a second report, with more engineering input, and on July 11 the second report reinforced the first, but it still did not tell Bush what he wanted to know. Should he be supporting a much more intense effort, in a situation in which funds were tight and other claims growing?[80]

Probably there was a real failure of communication here. Arthur Compton and Lawrence were both members of the National Academy committee and Compton was its chairman. Both of them by now believed that the uranium work was truly urgent, but it appears that both Conant and Bush were discounting their advocacy. Conant's recollection is characteristically dry and trenchant:

> To me, the defense of the free world was in such a dangerous state that only efforts which were likely to yield results within a matter of months or, at most, a year or two were worthy of serious consideration. In that summer of 1941, with recollections of what I had seen and heard in England fresh in my mind, I was impatient with the arguments of some of the physicists associated with the Uranium Committee whom I met from time to time. They talked in excited tones about the discovery of a new world in which power from a uranium reactor would revolutionize our industrialized society. These fancies left me cold. I suggested that until Nazi Germany was defeated all our energies should be concentrated on one immediate objective.[81]

The physicists were suspected of unrealistic enthusiasm for their own subject; they were much less intent than Bush and Conant on the simple single standard of defeating Hitler; they had not understood that in this context there was only one question: Was there a workable road to a bomb? The two reports addressed that question only cautiously, briefly, and abstractly, and the accurate prediction of 1945 did not persuade men obsessed by a closer danger.

But the reports from Maud kept coming. Early in July Bush heard another impressive witness. Charles Lauritsen of the California Institute of Technology had been in London, had listened to discussion of the draft Maud report, and came home convinced of its importance. Engineer and physicist, deliberate and brilliant, Scandinavian in sobriety but puckish in wit, Lauritsen would not have come to Bush without something serious to say; he said it: The Maud Committee believed a bomb could be made in two years. A few days later Bush had the draft

Maud report in hand, forwarded officially through his NRDC office in London. Fortune favors the prepared mind; he understood it at once.[82]

On July 16 Bush submitted a report on the year's work of 1940. He gave twelve pages to radar, and two to uranium, but the shorter passage is highly significant in showing his thought in flux.

> Early in the war the question arose whether it might be possible to obtain large sources of power from atomic fission, or even to create an explosive of tremendous power in this manner. The subject is highly abstruse, but one thing is certain: if such an explosive were made it would be thousands of times more powerful than existing explosives, and its use might be determining. . . .
>
> For some time it appeared that the possibility of a successful outcome was very remote. The Committee was faced, on the one hand, with the responsibility of expending public money on what might eventually appear to have been a wild search. On the other hand, it was known that much work on this subject had been done on the continent of Europe, and it was felt to be highly unsafe not to acquire knowledge concerning the underlying physics of the process. The Committee did not feel justified, in view of the apparently remote chance of success, in diverting to the work the efforts of scientists in considerable numbers, in view of the scarcity of highly qualified physicists for its other important work. It has therefore carried on a careful, but not an elaborate or expensive program. . . .
>
> There has appeared recently, however, new knowledge which makes it probable that the production of a super-explosive may not be as remote a matter as previously appeared. A program to determine this adequately would be extensive, and expensive in the time of scientists and in direct costs. The subject is being intensively studied in England. The Committee is now making a reexamination of the matter. It is of sufficient importance so that the whole matter should be placed before the President, if this present study indicates any probability that super explosives are possible.[83]

Bush's change was not complete, but through the summer the evidence and the pressure mounted; he responded more to the former than the latter. He was impressed when Conant was converted. Having been deeply skeptical, Conant changed his view completely when he learned (probably in September) that a Harvard friend and colleague, the physical chemist George Kistiakowsky, had reviewed the matter and fully accepted the feasibility of an explosion of U-235; in science as elsewhere one's personal estimate of a witness often determines the weight of the testimony.[84]

By the end of summer Bush was convinced. The possibility of a wartime bomb was strong enough so that there must be every effort, as fast as possible, to find out if it could be made. On October 9 he went to see the president.

There is no record of this crucial meeting on Roosevelt's side, nor on that of Vice President Henry Wallace, the only other man in the room. Even Bush made no complete record of Roosevelt's decisions, nor does it appear that he took any papers with him to show the president. The one document that survives is a memorandum that he sent the same day to Conant.[85] This memorandum makes it clear that Bush based his report on the Maud results. Although he could not be sure an attempt would be successful, he recommended an expanded program of research and analysis to test the British conclusions. Short of a production decision, he wanted authority to press ahead with this work at a new level of intensity, committing millions of dollars where tens of thousands had been spent before and enlisting the best physicists he could find in a concerted effort to see what special lines of effort were most likely to succeed. As far as we can tell, from the memorandum to Conant, from Bush's recollections, dictated years later, and above all from what these two highly disciplined men did next, the president agreed both immediately and completely. He did not call for a further separate study; he did not ask to read the Maud report himself. Bush was undoubtedly supported strongly by Wallace, who was less ignorant of the nature of science than Roosevelt, but what Wallace knew came mostly from earlier talks with Bush. As Bush wrote to Roosevelt the following March, he left the meeting understanding that he was to expedite the matter in every possible way.[86]

THE SECOND WORLD WAR is marked by many lonely decisions—decisions made by the dictators Hitler and Stalin, by the defiant democrats Churchill and de Gaulle, by Roosevelt himself, and by a host of lesser commanders. But in its speed, its loneliness, and the magnitude of its eventual consequences, Franklin Roosevelt's decision of October 9 stands alone. It is true that the president reserved the right to make a further decision when and if the project reached the production stage, but when that question did come back to him in the atmosphere of full-scale war some five months later, the progress that Bush reported made his affirmative response almost a formality.

Bush was well aware of the extraordinary loneliness of his own situation. At the same meeting he proposed to the president the establishment of a sort of board of directors to which he could report on matters of policy. Roosevelt readily agreed and named the committee: the three of them present, and three more: Conant, as Bush's deputy in the matter; and the civilian and military heads of the War Department, Henry L. Stimson and George C. Marshall. It was also agreed that when the matter came to large-scale production it would necessarily have to be administered by either the War Department or the Navy. Bush much preferred the War Department, and the naming of Stimson and Marshall in October shows that the president already concurred. But having named this committee, and having instructed Bush that "consideration of policy" should be restricted to these six individuals, Roosevelt continued to deal directly, and almost always one-to-one, with Bush. Bush consulted other members of the committee individually as he went forward, and Wallace called one meeting without the president, but all six men never once met together. The "top policy committee" was a committee that its creator never called into session. It was Bush, not Roosevelt, who was worried about loneliness.

Roosevelt's decision to keep policy decisions in his own hands was not only acceptable but agreeable to Bush in 1941. It gave him by delegation the authority he needed in dealing with strong-minded scientists like Ernest Lawrence, who were predisposed to believe that anything in physics should be run as they recommended. Obviously physicists must play a central role in the undertaking, but equally clearly, to Bush, this was not a matter for part-time committee management. A presidential decision to go ahead was a decision he could execute. There were years of hard work ahead, and the questions of policy could wait. As we shall see, Roosevelt let them wait too long.

In his impressive study, *The Making of the Atomic Bomb,* Richard Rhodes takes note of the importance of Roosevelt's reservation of policy to himself and five others. "Thus at the outset . . . scientists were summarily denied a voice in deciding the political and military uses of the weapons they were proposing to build. Bush accepted the usurpation happily."[87] The choice of the word *usurpation* is striking, suggesting as it does that scientists had a basic political right to a share in these decisions. Rhodes is here reflecting and representing a widely held feeling, strongest among such men as Leo Szilard, that they did indeed have a right to share in any decision about what they had made possible. We have seen parallel sentiments in Paris, and there is relevance also in the deliberate restraint of some German physicists. Yet *usurpation* is clearly the wrong word. Who but the president himself could make the political and military decisions for the United States on this enormous subject? The intimate and inescapable responsibility of the chief political officer for nuclear policy has been recognized in every country and in every decade throughout the nuclear age. In Roosevelt's immediate acceptance of this responsibility there was no usurpation, nor were he and Bush mistaken in believing the undertaking must be managed from the top down.

Yet there is indeed a mistake here—or the seeds of a mistake.

Roosevelt's reservation of policy responsibility to himself, powerfully reinforced by the intense secrecy on which he insisted to the end of his life, did indeed create a situation in which there was no arrangement for the orderly and timely consideration of questions that went beyond making the bomb as fast as possible. One of the consequences of this situation was that important questions were put off or neglected, and many sorts of advice not sought. Not all of those neglected were scientists—students of the Soviet Union were just as relevant and just as much cut out. The difference, of course, is that many scientists were "in the know," and some of them did indeed think hard about the enormous political implications of what was put in train on October 9. Those questions became urgent only as the project came close to its technical triumph, but by then the habit of lonely secrecy was deeply engrained. It is wrong to call the man with the final responsibility a usurper, but it is right to take note when by his own choice he cuts himself off from the advice of people who can help.

The consequences of secrecy and loneliness lay far ahead on October 9, and we should return to Roosevelt's basic decision to go ahead. That was lonely too, and yet surely it was right. Moreover Roosevelt must have been deeply certain that it was right, or he would not have moved so fast. Those who distrusted Franklin Roosevelt found him impulsive and unpredictable, and he himself delighted in the art of political surprise. But in large matters he was usually wary, and he had developed the habitual resistance to quick approval of one-man proposals that is essential for American presidents, besieged as they are by zealous partisans of this and that particular interest. In this very season Roosevelt was engaged in what may have been his most extraordinary demonstration of the art of gradual action as opportunity arose. More and more he and his leading advisers were convinced that the country must join in the war against Hitler. Less and less was he willing to have this happen by a clear and open decision of his own.

So the instant and sweeping approval that Bush was given on October 9 is far from typical of the man or the time. Though the records are thin, though we do not have his own voice or words to guide us, though the memoirs of his associates do not directly discuss his thinking, and though there had been no consultation on this question with his new friend Winston Churchill (they had met for the first time in August), we must do our best to estimate his reasons.

To make a decision of this sort in one morning a man with the experience and political acumen of Franklin Roosevelt in 1941 would have to reach several rapid conclusions: first, that there were urgent affirmative reasons for acting; second, that there were no compelling reasons for not acting; and third, that there was no reason in domestic politics for caution or consultation or waiting upon public opinion.

The urgent affirmative reasons are not hard to identify. First and foremost, if the thing could be done, it was vital that Hitler not do it first. Bush had little to tell his chief of just what the Germans were and were not up to; American understanding on the point was primitive in 1941 and remained so for three more years. But in such a case no news was bad news. The Hitler that men like Roosevelt and Bush had in mind in 1941 was not the man that we have seen, reliant mainly on the weapons he already trusted, slow to support real novelty, scornful of Jewish physicists, and fearfully avoided by physicists themselves. He was rather the brilliant practitioner of military and political surprise, the victor on all fronts not yet clearly stopped on his new road to Moscow, and the apparently unchallenged master of the resources, material and human, industrial and scientific, of most of Europe. Why would he not be well ahead in this matter, if he had chosen to be? Why would he not so choose? The British were too modest, but not at all irrational, when they said that what they had learned of the prospects would suggest itself to any competent group. In October 1941 it was natural to the point of inevitability that Roosevelt should decide that Hitler must not be first. So much, indeed, he had decided already. In his very first encounter with the subject, when even its advocate Sachs was talking more about energy than weapons and more about the possible than the prospective, FDR had been persuaded to do what little he did by the argument that we must not let the other fellow blow us up. The plausibility of that threat had been multiplied in the meantime by a still unbroken string of sharp and overwhelmingly successful Nazi surprises.

But if the controlling motive was not to be second to Hitler, the immediate catalyst of the decision was the Maud report, with its effect on Bush and Conant. British science had won admiration in the Washington of 1941. Roosevelt knew the story of radar, and he had warmly supported both Bush and Conant in their early commitment to close collaboration with British war science. He had been delighted in the previous winter when Conant proposed himself as leader of the first American scientific mission to London. A powerfully affirmative set of conclusions from "the best men" in Britain was bound to have great impact, and all the more when it came with the strong endorsement of two former skeptics, Bush and Conant. These were two men he trusted. Bush had been with him for only sixteen months, but his service in that time had been outstanding. As for Conant, Roosevelt had the Harvard man's traditional view of the Harvard presidency as a very high office indeed, and his personal relations with Conant had been cordial ever since the two of them had worked together to ensure that Roosevelt's appearance at the Harvard Tercentenary in 1936 was appropriate to his office rather than to the feelings of former president Lowell and other conservatives.[88]

The technical difference between the Einstein letter and the Maud report is great; one talks of vague possibilities, and the other says a bomb can probably be made in time to help win the war. But the difference between the witnesses of 1939 and 1941 may be even greater: Franklin Roosevelt was both adventurous and traditional; he had listened to Sachs and his account of the fears of distinguished refugees; he had politely thanked Einstein. But what he had now was not an expression of general fear but a clear proposal for action; it came with the combined authority of British science and the two American scientific leaders he trusted most. He accepted it.

We must put the British influence even higher than that of the two Americans. The work of Maud was persuasive not only to Bush and Conant, but to many others. The formal reports were closely held, but what Bainbridge and Lauritsen reported to Bush they also told others "in the know," and in August and September the Australian Marcus Oliphant, himself a member of the technical committee of Maud, crossed the United States like a nuclear Paul Revere. Oliphant was one of those who believed that the job would have to be done in North America and mainly by the Americans. He was especially effective in stirring the already enthusiastic Lawrence, and by mid-September Lawrence was urging action on the already persuaded Conant.[89] So if Bush, with Conant, had not been converted and had not sought out the president in October, it is certain that others would have done so before long. To I. I. Rabi, looking back forty years later, it seemed clear that the controlling element in the American decision of 1941 was the scientific judgment and counsel of the British. British science then had the commanding prestige that was necessary to give credibility to anything then so implausible as a twenty-five-pound device with an explosive force of some two thousand tons.[90]

We speak of British science here, not British politics. A year earlier the British government had taken the political decision to share most of its technical secrets with the Americans. In the spring of 1941 this practice was extended to the work of Maud; what Bainbridge and Lauritsen learned in London, and what Oliphant explained across the United States, was no more than what the British government's policy allowed. Yet by the time the basic message reached Roosevelt in October, the British government, as we have seen, was no longer sure that it wanted to urge the Americans onward. At the political level the British were silent on Maud. But neither the preference of Cherwell nor the wariness of John Anderson was passed back to men like Oliphant, who remained free to act on their own conviction that if the job was to be done in time, the Americans must be won around. This bifurcation in British policy was remarkably exemplified in a visit that George Thomson, chairman of the Maud Committee, paid to Washington at the beginning of October. Thomson carried a copy of the final Maud report to Conant. He also discussed its substance freely with two scientific committees, but he avoided telling them that the British scientists were pressing their government "to take up uranium in a big way." Thus Thomson confined himself to the physics of Maud, but he cannot have been blind to the implication of that physics for American policy. The permitted candor of British scientists accelerated an American decision that the British government was not sure it wanted.[91]

So Roosevelt had powerful reasons for acting, and there is no evidence to suggest that either he or Bush or Wallace thought of any reasons not to. Yet it is not hard now to think of worries they might have had, and the exercise may help us to understand them better.

Should they have asked themselves about the consequences of opening this box? Plainly they could not foresee what we now live with. The bomb that the Maud report described, and that they could not let others get first, had about one fifth of the explosive force of what was dropped four years later on Hiroshima; it was less than one part in a million of what is at the ready now in the forces of the Soviet Union and the United States. It might decide a great war; how it might lead on to the arsenals of the 1980s they could not know.

We have posed the question as if every nuclear weapon made since then were the consequence of one morning's work at the White House in 1941. Of course it is not so simple. As we review the decisions of men and nations in the years that followed, we shall find a large measure of the inescapable in what happened; if the American bomb was triggered by Hitler, the Soviet bomb was triggered at least as certainly by the Americans. We shall learn how it has usually been harder to have less than more. The three men at the White House could hardly have foreseen all that. Yet they did know this would not be just one more weapon; Bush told Conant they had discussed the problems of postwar control.

What they do not seem to have explored is the degree to which the course they were planning was essentially irreversible. It was only a plan for an energetic effort of research; they would look again when they knew the research results. But could they really stop if the results of the research were promising? If the struggle against Hitler was to get worse in the months ahead, as they quite correctly expected, would they not move to rapid production as readily as now they moved to rapid research? And if it was made might it not be used? And made by others? And made more destructive?

Here at the true political beginning such questions clearly had no deterrent weight. They did not arise in the White House on October 9. It is not in the American temper to assume that "events are in the saddle," and in this respect Roosevelt was supremely American. If this terrible new weapon was makable, he must not lose the race to make it. He would deal with other questions as they came along.

After October 9 an enormous effort lay ahead, but first Bush had to get the American physicists to give him their own judgment on the basic conclusion of the Maud report—that a U-235 bomb could be made quickly. On the same October 9, right after his meeting with the president, he set that process going by telling Arthur Compton's newly reinforced Academy committee what he wanted in a third report. "Bush spelled out for Arthur Compton just what he wanted. Most important was information on a uranium 235 bomb, particularly its critical mass and its destructive effect."[92] In order to get an independent review, Bush withheld the Maud report from Compton (although Maud's informal messengers were already having their individual effects on Compton and his colleagues). After a review that was far deeper and more searching than the two previous efforts, the third Compton committee duly reported on November 6 that *"a fission bomb of superlatively destructive power will result from bringing quickly together a sufficient mass of element U-235,"* that *"the separation of the isotopes of uranium can be done in the necessary amounts* [original emphasis]," and that while time estimates must be very rough, "if all possible effort is spent on the program, one might however expect fission bombs to be available in significant quantity within three or four years." The report was more conservative on time and cost than the Maud report had been.[93]

Bush had what he wanted. He passed the National Academy report to the president—for information, not for action—and went ahead. He reorganized the whole effort, drew in Compton, Lawrence, and Harold Urey to take charge of different parts, and on December 13, with Pearl Harbor one week behind him and a united war spirit to anneal both the president's instructions and his own convictions, he issued marching orders to all concerned.

The Americans never looked back. They could have moved faster, as many of them knew and more acknowledged later.[94] Both their scientists and their administrators had found it hard to get a clear understanding of the problems and also of each other. But by December 1941 they had laid the basis for a solid and mutually confident effort; to their unmatched location and resources they could now bring a unity between politics and physics that was equally unique—though it depended on a very narrow channel of power and confidence running to and from just one man. The circle of actors would widen enormously, but the special loneliness at the top would last the life of Franklin Roosevelt.

It is a truly extraordinary coincidence that the Bush recommendation of October 9 and the transforming events of December 7 were so near in time. Let us grant the important connection between one event and the other—the war that expanded at Pearl Harbor was the same one that had stimulated Frisch and Peierls, led to Maud, and put

Bush and Conant where they were. But nothing in this connection implied that Roosevelt would be presented with both a crucial choice and a virtually free hand in the very same autumn. We have said that his choice on October 9 was decisive, but of course if war had not come, it would not have been so simple. If he had been offered conclusions like those of Maud as much as two years sooner, say in the fall of 1939, his way of responding would have been different—he would have faced the question of money for production plants well before he had the war to justify a secret and solitary choice. And conversely, if the conclusions of the scientists had been delayed by two years, say until late 1943, this enormous effort would have faced a very different set of obstacles. It would then have been a great deal harder to make adequate room for the program in the fierce competition for men and resources as the war approached its "conventional" but unprecedented climaxes across two oceans. Even as it was it took energetic bureaucratic diplomacy to assure the necessary top priorities in 1942.[95] An effort begun even one year later would not have been complete in time for wartime use. At the very most, the opportunity to make a wartime bomb by one man's secret solitary choice lasted less than two years. It was accident as much as necessity that made possible the great unified secret adventure of the Manhattan Project.

The general question of timing is important in more than one country. A different order of political and physical events might in fact have given Hitler the head start that men feared. If fission had been discovered five years earlier might not the Germans, then just beginning their military buildup, have recognized its long-run promise as a weapon? Different relative timing would also have made for a different and more complex process of choice and action in the United States, and would quite probably have produced results less likely to give Americans a collective swelled head. The Manhattan Project was indeed a wondrous achievement, made possible by a remarkable partnership of science, industry and government, but the unique opportunity to make that effort under the stimulus of large-scale war and on a continent safe from attack was hardly the product of American genius.

Most important of all, if the first bomb project had not happened in war, it could not have happened in secret, certainly not in the United States, and probably not in Western Europe. Let us consider a discovery of fission as early as 1930 or as late as 1950 or 1955. Either way, the issues presented could not have been settled in silence. Certainly physics and politics would have met in both cases, but the dynamics of the encounter would have been dramatically different. Unless we suppose the very special and intrinsically improbable case of a set of discoveries confined to one closed society alone—the Soviet Union of the 1950s may be the least unlikely candidate—the prospect of a bomb will be openly discussed as research results are announced, and governments that seek to enforce any early secrecy in the manner of 1939 and 1940 will be openly opposed, first by physicists and then by others. The prospects and dangers will become a part of politics, both domestic and international, in an entirely different and probably a more gradual way. One can imagine both good and bad results from such a different process—it might have fostered a fierce and open international race to get there first, or it might have led to some sort of mutual restraint, or even to enforceable agreement, because no one yet had won a clear and therefore unacceptable monopoly. We do not need to decide how it would have come out; all we must do is recognize that the way it did happen was extraordinary, the product of a highly improbable conjunction in time between technical understanding of the most remarkable physical discovery in the history of destruction and a moment of uniquely solitary freedom of choice and action on the part of the president of the United States.

The Japanese

There was also a Japanese nuclear effort during World War II. It was small and divided, and wartime understanding in Japan of the right pathways to a nuclear weapon never reached the levels attained in Washington before Pearl Harbor. The Japanese enterprise is remarkable primarily for its very existence, which some Americans have understandably but wrongly taken as providing justification for American bombing decisions in 1945. There is also a recurrent temptation among American writers to fill in our admittedly limited understanding of the Japanese program with speculative suggestions that Japanese investigators came somewhere near making a bomb of their own, or even that they may have had a successful test in Korea. These speculations all break down under critical examination, and we are left with the reality that the Japanese program was always a small one with a low priority, handicapped by shortages, rivalries, and bombing attacks, never vitalized by any insight like that of Frisch and Peierls, and above all hopelessly outweighed and outclassed by the unimpeded and unified effort that went forward in the United States. That effort led to weapons whose use against Japan we must now consider.[96]

II

The Decision
to Drop Bombs
on Japan

I N AUGUST 1945 American aircraft dropped two atomic bombs
on Japan in the space of three days. That they should do this was
the decision of President Harry S. Truman, and there is no evidence that Truman found the judgment a hard one. Yet no single
decision ever made by an American president has aroused more discussion and debate. Truman's assurance and the unresolved debate are
equally real parts of this enormous event, and the tension between the
two is typical of many later debates on the politics of nuclear weaponry.
The matter has resisted any agreed judgment, and not surprisingly,
because the question ultimately turns on what is right in war.

The Adventure of Learning How

When Truman became president on April 12, 1945, the effort to
produce atomic bombs was reaching its climax. There had been no
looking back after Pearl Harbor, and the effort had gone forward with
unwavering presidential encouragement. Franklin Roosevelt had
faced sensitive and difficult questions on some international aspects of
the effort, and we will come back to them, but he had readily and
rapidly approved each successive step in the main effort of design and
production, insisting only on the utmost in speed and secrecy. These
two principles, and their occasional conflict with each other, governed
the enterprise throughout. Gradually the focus shifted away from the

notion of a race with Germany. By the end of 1944 direct evidence obtained in Strasbourg showed that the Germans were not close to a bomb.[1] The accelerating enterprise was now governed, from the top down, among scientists, engineers, production people, and military officers alike, by the driving commitment to get usable bombs in time to help shorten the war. For a very few, the end of a Nazi atomic threat marked the end of their own commitment. For many more, mainly at the University of Chicago's Metallurgical Laboratory, where direct contribution to the bomb project had crested early, attention shifted toward a concern with plans for long-run research and for international understanding. But the temper of the project as a whole was still one of growing intensity and single-minded commitment. Each new entrant into the effort, from October 1941 onward—scientific, industrial and military—had learned to live by the code of speed and secrecy that the commander in chief had established.[2]

From the beginning, the rule was to go for every option that might prove to be the fastest. All the possible roads to U-235 were kept open, and although neither Maud nor the National Academy reports had mentioned it, the plutonium prospect was also included from the first, thanks to Lawrence and Compton.

We need not linger over the complexity and magnitude of all this, except to remind ourselves that it was unlike anything that had ever happened before, in science or in war. One way of understanding the difficulties is to recall how very hard it was then to get the necessary understanding of the relations among these extremely small objects— nuclei and neutrons—and the extremely large results that would follow if the theory could become practice. One nucleus of a uranium atom is to its atom as a small marble is to the earth; a neutron is ten thousand times smaller. To measure the behavior of these infinitesimal objects is a matter of indirection and inference at best; and to build a coherent theory of that behavior was necessarily a process of testing and thinking, in a situation in which, to begin with, only the smallest amounts of the most relevant substances were available. The unpleasant characteristics of these substances were another powerful obstruction. To separate the uranium isotopes was to have to cope with the least manageable of uranium compounds, uranium hexaflouride—the infamous hex. And the intense toxicity of plutonium presented a new and daunting problem in action at a safe distance for those who first proposed to fashion it so that it would detonate on their command.

Paradoxically, moreover, it turned out that the plants required for producing, separating, and purifying mere kilograms of these precious and terrible materials were very much larger than anyone had thought in 1941. If the predictions of that year had been more accurate, the recommendations of Bush might have been less strong. But from October 9 onward, and still more sharply after Pearl Harbor, faith in success became a conscious policy. As Conant wrote in 1943, "Someone has well said that only optimists would have willingly entered this Alice in Wonderland area of exploration!"[3]

Optimism was matched by determination. As objectives were clarified and as the sense of urgency steadily sharpened, the strongest men came to the fore. It happened scientifically; thus the work on the chain reaction centered more and more on Fermi—the best man of all when both theoretical range and experimental precision were required. It happened in the civilian leadership in Washington, where Conant gradually assumed the senior role that Briggs had at first, and steadily pressed for whatever in his best judgment would help get there fastest. It happened in the leadership of the Manhattan Project, the military operation that took over in 1942 as the enterprise grew beyond what Bush and Conant could manage from the Office of Scientific Research and Development (OSRD). There Leslie A. Groves, a driving executive who understood more about getting the job done than about its meaning, replaced a less determined man in whom Bush and Conant sensed a lack of the necessary drives. In the most crucial assignment of all, that of learning how to make a bomb that would work, Robert Oppenheimer took over from Gregory Breit and went on to become the moving spirit of the great laboratory at Los Alamos.[4]

If any part can stand for the whole of this adventure, it is Los Alamos, and if anyone had the right to say what the place was like, it was Oppenheimer. Ten years afterward, to a board examining his eligibility for continued access to the secret of the bomb, he explained a part of his role in terms whose accuracy no one then or later has questioned. What is crucial in this account is its exposition of what it was that drew and held a great company of outstanding scientists to a most unlikely place and an unprecedented style of work:

> We needed a central laboratory devoted wholly to this purpose, where people could talk freely with each other, where theoretical ideas and experimental findings could affect each other, where the waste and frustration and error of the many compartmentalized experimental studies could be eliminated, where we could begin to come to grips with chemical, metallurgical, engineering, and ordnance problems that had so far received no consideration. We therefore sought to establish this laboratory for a direct attack on all the problems inherent in the most rapid possible development and production of atomic bombs. . . .
>
> The program of recruitment was massive. Even though we then underestimated the ultimate size of the laboratory, which was to have almost 4,000 members by the spring of 1945, and even though we did not at that time see clearly some of the difficulties which were to bedevil and threaten the enterprise, we knew that it was a big, complex and diverse job. . . . We had to recruit at a time when the

country was fully engaged in war and almost every competent scientist was already involved in the military effort. . . .

The prospect of coming to Los Alamos aroused great misgivings. It was to be a military post; men were asked to sign up more or less for the duration; restrictions on travel and on the freedom of families to move about to be severe; and no one could be sure of the extent to which the necessary technical freedom of action could actually be maintained by the laboratory. The notion of disappearing into the New Mexico desert for an indeterminate period and under quasi military auspices disturbed a good many scientists, and the families of many more. But there was another side to it. Almost everyone realized that this was a great undertaking. Almost everyone knew that if it were completed successfully and rapidly enough, it might determine the outcome of the war. Almost everyone knew that it was an unparalleled opportunity to bring to bear the basic knowledge and art of science for the benefit of his country. Almost everyone knew that this job, if it were achieved, would be a part of history. This sense of excitement, of devotion and of patriotism in the end prevailed. Most of those with whom I talked came to Los Alamos. . . . It was a remarkable community, inspired by a high sense of mission, of duty and of destiny, coherent, dedicated, and remarkably selfless. . . . I have never known a group more understanding and more devoted to a common purpose, more willing to lay aside personal convenience and prestige, more understanding of the role that they were playing in their country's history. Time and again we had in the technical work almost paralyzing crises. Time and again the laboratory drew itself together and faced the new problems and got on with the work.[5]

The same thoughts were at work in the continuing involvement of men like Bush and Conant—and in the engagement of Du Pont and other large companies. Like the scientists who answered Oppenheimer's call, the senior administrators were essentially volunteers. Bush and Conant continued throughout the war to be the responsible heads of the Carnegie Institution and Harvard University; they served the government without pay. Du Pont, painfully aware of its reputation after World War I as a greedy munitions maker, insisted on a profit-free contract—for legal reasons the contract called for a fee of one dollar but because the job was done in a shorter time than expected the government in the end paid only sixty-seven cents.[6]

By March 1945 the leaders of the project were convinced that it was within months of successful completion. Difficulties expected and unexpected had been overcome; in doubtful cases alternative methods had been explored simultaneously; wide margins of safety had been built in; if one plan was good, two were better, and neither money nor material had been spared. Estimates of cost had doubled and redoubled, but the probability of eventual success had become very high.

Franklin Roosevelt died knowing that his bold and solitary gamble was at the edge of technical triumph.

The Imperative of Shortening the War

The effort to get a bomb was coming to a head in the middle of 1945 just as the war in the Pacific was coming to the home islands of Japan. A series of great battles had marked the preceding months. In October 1944, in the battle for Leyte Gulf—the largest naval battle ever fought—the U.S. Pacific Fleet had "destroyed the Imperial Japanese Navy as an offensive force."[7] On March 9, 1945, flying from the Marianas, B-29s commanded by Major General Curtis LeMay had made a low-altitude incendiary raid on Tokyo, burning out a major fraction of that city by fire storm and setting a pattern for further massive fire raids on other large cities. And on April 1, 1945, there began the three-month battle for Okinawa, the last stop before Japan itself on the brilliantly conducted but bloody island-hopping campaign that had led, over three years, from Guadalcanal through Iwo Jima. The Okinawa campaign would claim the lives of 12,000 Americans, 110,000 enemy troops, and 75,000 civilians. The next large landing would be on Kyūshū, the southernmost of the four main islands of Japan.

That the bomb would be ready at this climactic moment was essentially a coincidence; there was no necessary connection between the time it took to make bombs and the time it took to bring Japan to the brink of defeat by other means. In the case of Germany there had been no such match; if bombs had become available a few months earlier, the Hitler who was ordering resistance to the end from his Berlin bunker in March and April 1945 would have seemed the perfect target. The first detailed schedule offered by Bush or Conant, in the spring of 1942, had called for the production of a few bombs by July 1944, and as late as the eve of Yalta, according to Groves, "if the European war was not over before we had our first bombs he [Roosevelt] wanted us to be ready to drop them on Germany."[8] But it did not work out that way. The German war ended on May 8, a week after Hitler had died by his own hand. He never learned of the imminence of the weapon whose creation owed so much to the dreadful and unfounded fear that he might get it first.

The new president had no difficulty whatever in connecting the climax of the war against Japan with the climax of the Manhattan Project. It had been plain from the very beginning that he must make the ending of the war his first and principal business. One hour after taking the oath of office on April 12 he had made his first statement as president, a one-sentence declaration: "The world may be sure that we will prosecute the war on both fronts, east and west, with all the vigor we possess to a successful conclusion." Four days later he addressed the Congress face to face, and the country by radio, and enlarged on this commitment. He reaffirmed the demand for unconditional surrender; he underlined the need for speedy victory: "Every day peace is delayed costs a terrible toll." He affirmed his commitment to the grand strategy of "the United Nations' war," and he promised that the direction of the war by the admirals and generals Roosevelt had chosen would continue "<u>unchanged and unhampered!</u> [original emphasis]." He separated the need for "complete victory" from the need "to maintain the peace"; the latter was a great task too, and in the same first hour on the job he had expressed his support for the coming San Francisco conference of the United Nations. But the first task—the great immediate unfinished business left by FDR—was to win the war. "So much blood has already been shed for the ideals which we cherish, and for which Franklin Delano Roosevelt lived and died, that we dare not permit even a momentary pause in the hard fight for victory."9

Victory—complete victory—as soon as possible; there was nothing new in these themes. They were what any successor of Franklin Roosevelt would have been expected to affirm, and the Congress gave them a warm welcome. When he said *unconditional surrender,* Truman banged the table before him, and "the chamber rose to its feet."10

Nine days later, on April 25, Truman met with Stimson and Groves to get his first detailed account of the bomb project. Stimson's primary purpose at that meeting was to introduce the new president to the international aspects of the matter, but it was necessary also to inform him on the progress of the project and on military plans, so he took with him General Groves, the man in charge. Groves had with him two copies of a full report, and for three quarters of an hour the new president listened and read. It was all there. Two kinds of bombs were being prepared; one would need to be tested and the other not. The test would come in July. Bombs would be ready by August. A special bombardment group was already in training and was about to be deployed to the Pacific. The explosive power of the two weapons was not certainly predictable, but it would probably be extraordinary: perhaps five thousand tons for one and ten thousand for the other.11

As far as we know from the accounts of the three men who met at this first major discussion, not one of them expressed any doubt that when the bombs were ready, they should be used. Formal consideration of that question, such as it was, came later, and so did formal decisions and orders. But the absence of any discussion on this crucial point on April 25 strongly suggests that in Mr. Truman's first major encounter with this awesome subject he found himself talking with men who took it for granted that if there was no hitch—if the July test worked and other arrangements went forward as they now quite confidently hoped—the new weapons would be used just as soon as they were ready. There is no reason to doubt that Mr. Truman fully agreed with this view, and no reason to question his later judgment: "Let there be no mistake about it. I regarded the bomb as a military weapon and never had any doubt that it should be used."[12]

So Groves went about his business after this meeting as he had before it, with the purpose of getting bombs completed and dropped on Japan just as fast as he could. In operational terms he now had responsibility for every phase of the undertaking short of the bombing missions themselves: the delivery of finished material to Los Alamos, the work under Oppenheimer to conduct the first test and complete the operational weapons, the training of the special bombing unit, and the initial selection of targets. This concentration of responsibility was the result of General Marshall's desire to keep the number of those involved just as small as possible.[13]

Throughout the vast project those who had direct responsibility for its completion shared Groves's sense of urgency. The pressure and tension may have been greatest at Los Alamos, where the crucial steps would be taken to make the fissionable material into weapons, but Groves asked and received the unstinting support of others: from the vast factories full speed in delivery of the material; from General Arnold of the air force the latest and best in bombers; from his direct superiors approval of a timetable set for the earliest possible combat use of the bomb. It is no wonder that in retrospect he saw Mr. Truman's eventual decision as "one of noninterference—basically, a decision not to upset the existing plans."[14]

Thus the great effort rushed forward unchecked, driven by an inner logic shaped by over three years of wartime speed and secrecy. The race with the Germans had been transformed into a race to help shorten the war, and as the mass and momentum of the effort grew, so did the desire of those in charge to win that race. If anything the end of the war in Europe increased the pressure. All accounts of life at Los Alamos testify to the rising intensity of effort through the spring of 1945. As Robert Oppenheimer recalled ten years later, "We were still more frantic to have the job done and wanted to have it done so that if needed, it would be available."[15]

In this sentiment the team at Los Alamos was at one with many others eager to make their contribution to victory. The air force would contribute fire raids; the navy would engage in blockade, air attack, and amphibious support for invasion; the army and marines would land and finish the job. Strategic planning for all this was hardly more than traffic control, and the only contested military decision of early 1945 was the judgment that it was better to go straight to Japan than to land in China first. Everyone who had a blow to strike would be encouraged to strike it, the harder and faster the better. Only the most senior commanders of the European victory—men like Eisenhower and Bradley—were untempted by a further search for glory in the Pacific. British and French Allies were eager for their own share of the work. Joseph Stalin had given his word at Yalta in February that he would come in against Japan two or three months after the end of war in Europe.[16]

The pursuit of final victory was legitimized for most Americans by the intensity of continuing Japanese resistance and the continuing sense of outrage over the attack on Pearl Harbor and the infamous Bataan Death March. Against Japan as against Nazi Germany, the national mood was implacable: Sink ships, bomb cities, kill Japs—this was the mood of the commanders, the mood of the men and women in the street, and the mood of the Congress.[17]

The mood of the combat forces themselves was not quite the same; by now it was at once harder and less self-righteous. The war must be ended, indeed; it must also be won. But most of those afloat, most aircrews, and nearly all marines and infantry soldiers would be delighted to see it won without more sacrifice from them. This state of mind had its parallel at home in the continuing and increasing anxiety of those whose sons and husbands were—or were thought to be—at risk. This mood too was known to the men at the top; the new president knew what he was doing when he measured the anguish of the continuing war by the "terrible toll" of every single day it lasted.[18]

The defeat of Japan was inevitable, but how long would it take? In considering this question the American government was heavily affected by the fanatical tenacity of the Japanese on Okinawa and the demonstration of willingness to die that was inherent in the kamikaze tactics newly adopted by Japanese fliers. What if this spirit, and not any rational calculation of the odds against them, were to govern the decision of Japan's rulers? The question gained in intensity from the prospect of still larger and more ferocious battles as the home islands were attacked. To Truman and Stimson—both World War I artillery-men—that nightmare was strong, and the prospect that it might in fact come true was intensified by the experiences of the Allies with the Germans. The outcome of the war in Europe was never in doubt after Patton had swept across France the summer before, but Hitler's armies had fought on; they had briefly shaken Allied self-confidence in the Battle of the Bulge at the end of the year, and surrender had come only when Germany was physically overrun.

The possibility of a long and bloody contest of ground forces was a matter of particular concern to George Marshall and Henry Stimson in the War Department. In postwar assessment many observers have concluded that this prospect was unreal, in the light of the damage already done in Japan and the increasing breakdown of both capability and will in Tokyo. But such assessments after the fact do not tell us much about what responsible American leaders were thinking as the readiness of the bomb drew near. As it happened, the men who would matter most on the military side were men advised by officers whose primary charge, in the first half of 1945, was to ensure effective planning for great ground battles in Japan. Already in 1944 the invasion of the Japanese home islands had been formally accepted by the Joint Chiefs of Staff as necessary, and indeed urgent, unless a satisfactory surrender could be achieved before the invasion forces were ready. Stimson and Marshall got their staff support from the operations division (OPD) of the War Department general staff, and OPD, which had a well-earned reputation for sound strategic thought, steadily emphasized the need to prepare for large-scale ground warfare in Japan and perhaps also on the Asian mainland, unless the war could be ended in other ways. It was not the assignment or the mental habit of OPD to give cheerful estimates of what might be expected from the actions of navy blockaders or air force bombers. The sights of this staff were set on the only operation in which large armies would be needed—the only operation, by general agreement, that could *surely* end the war—the conquest by invasion of Japan itself. If that operation were to become necessary, the two men short of the president who must recommend it were Stimson and Marshall, so they felt a special concern to neglect no promising means of ending the war before it became necessary to launch the invasion. I remember very well Colonel Stimson's awareness of this connection from my own talks with him in 1946 and 1947, and the point is made in his 1947 defense of the decision to use the bomb. Reinforcing evidence has recently been declassified from the papers of George A. "Abe" Lincoln at West Point. Abe Lincoln was the senior planner in OPD in 1945, and the declassified document is a 1946 history of the military use of the bomb based on OPD records, with a comment by Lincoln. What it shows is that while OPD recognized the possibility of collapse from within, and the possibly decisive effect of Soviet entry, and while its top men, including Lincoln, knew about the bomb, its own principal concern was to plan for the "decisive operation" against the Tokyo plain. "They always came back to the conclusion that invasion was the only way to certain victory." This was the great lesson of the European theater, and the settled conviction of the professionals advising Marshall and Stimson.[19]

By the spring of 1945 the imminent prospect of a great new secret weapon gave hope of ending the whole business quickly. Should we be surprised that its use was hardly questioned by the men with command responsibility? The decision itself may have been right or wrong for other and wider reasons, but it is hard to doubt that for the American president and his top War Department advisers, in June of 1945, this was an extraordinarily elemental matter: The bomb might help decisively; it should be used.

Moreover, the specific use to which the weapon should be put was regarded as a primarily military question. When General Groves was given responsibility for planning the military use of the bomb as well as its construction, he attacked the problem in a military way:

> I had set as the governing factor that the targets chosen should be places the bombing of which would most adversely affect the will of the Japanese people to continue the war. Beyond that, they should be military in nature, consisting either of important headquarters or troop concentrations, or centers of production of military equipment and supplies. To enable us to assess accurately the effects of the bomb, the targets should not have been previously damaged by air raids. It was also desirable that the first target be of such size that the damage would be confined within it, so that we could more definitely determine the power of the bomb.[20]

Taken together, as American military men were thinking in the spring of 1945, and measured against the expected yields of the new weapons, these requirements called for dropping the bombs on cities. Nothing was more natural and even inevitable to those who made the plans. But nothing is more shocking to a later generation, and it is important to understand why the use of this new weapon against cities was an almost automatic recommendation at the time.

The Bombing of Cities[21]

As World War II began, the bombing of innocent civilians was generally held by American leaders to be both moral wickedness and military folly. On September 1, 1939, Franklin Roosevelt addressed an "urgent appeal to every Government which may be engaged in hostilities publicly to affirm its determination that its armed forces shall in no event, and under no circumstances, undertake the bombardment from the air of civilian populations or of unfortified cities." Later in the year he attempted to extend his previously announced "moral embargo" against munitions shipments by urging manufacturers and exporters of airplanes and airplane parts not to sell them to belligerents who bombed civilians. As late as 1941 two rising stars of the Army Air Force, Major General H. H. "Hap" Arnold and Colonel Ira C. Eaker, made clear their conviction that on military grounds "bombing attacks on civil populace are uneconomical and unwise." In principle American bombers were designed to be able to achieve high degrees of accuracy, and the public posture of the air force was, and remained, one of insistence that only military targets would be hit. If civilians suffered, it would be either "poor bombing" or the result of "decided tactical errors."[22]

Of all the changes in war making wrought by experience and felt necessity in World War II, none is more remarkable than that which reversed both official and public attitudes toward the area bombing of cities. In part it was a spirit of revenge, aroused by the Germans at Rotterdam and the Japanese at Pearl Harbor. The dead at Rotterdam were relatively few, about a thousand, and Pearl Harbor was a truly military target if ever there was one, but it had been attacked without warning on the "date that will live in infamy." There was also a steady widening of ideas as to who was the enemy and what was military; "vital war supplies" had meant food for civilians as early as World War I, and as the second war grew longer and more terrible, any thing or person that reinforced Hitler or Tojo came to be seen as a fair target.

But the main cause of the revolution in the concept of targeting was the determination of believers in air power to design and execute whatever kinds of attacks would maximize their own contribution to victory. This way of stating its mission was common to every service and every advocate of this or that weapon or tactic, but there was a special missionary zeal among the believers in air power. In Great Britain urban obliteration raids became established practice as early as 1942, and by 1943 Churchill was boasting that the "havoc wrought is indescribable" and explicitly emphasizing its effect not only on "war production in all its forms" but on "the life and economy of the whole of that guilty organization."[23]

For a time the Americans tried to act differently. But the original *military* justification for "precision" bombing was that it would be more effective than area attacks, and it did not turn out that way. Bombers attacking a defended objective were not as accurate as advertised, and in daylight attacks on specific targets losses were high. Increasingly it was thought necessary to saturate an urban area in order to be sure of hitting specific factories, and as early as July 1943 British and American aircraft joined in a series of raids against Hamburg with the clearly understood purpose of overwhelming the defenses of the city as a whole and creating general devastation.

Both military and political leaders gradually came to think of urban destruction not as wicked, not even as a necessary evil, but as a result with its own military value. Distinctions that had seemed clear when the Germans bombed Rotterdam were gradually rubbed out in the growing ferocity of the war. Commanders continued to speak of great military results, but they were also increasingly proud of urban devastation for its own sake.

The British and American people supported this approach. A few determined pacifists and moralists protested in each country; they found little support. In the spring of 1944, when a British pacifist attacked the obliteration bombing of German cities, the public reaction in the United States was strongly negative—readers of *The New York Times* sent the paper what the editors described as "unusually heavy mail" with the proportion of letters 50 to 1 against the protest. Stephen Early, the White House press secretary, answered less angrily for Franklin Roosevelt. The president who had distinguished sharply between tenements and factories in 1943 now let his spokesman explain that, while he was "disturbed and horrified" by the killing of civilians, "the bombing is shortening the war, in the opinion of an overwhelming percentage of military authorities."[24] The objective was speedy victory, and the authoritative judgment on effectiveness must be military. The generals had become their own judges.

A major element in this shift was the intense concern of all Americans for the minimization of American losses. To shorten the war was to save American lives, and to widen target areas was to decrease the danger to American bomber crews. Saturation bombing was designed initially for overcoming defenses and reducing the attacker's losses, and as it developed a life and rationale unencumbered by earlier moral constraints, men readily engaged in such calculations of relative cost as those in the following account, written just after the war by W. H. Lawrence, a respected senior correspondent of *The New York Times:*

> Gen. Carl A. Spaatz, commanding general of the United States Army Strategic Air Forces, reported . . . that Superfortresses operating from the Marianas, India and China flew 32,612 sorties against the Japanese and dropped 169,421 tons of bombs in their fourteen months of war operations. The B-29's destroyed the major portion of the industrial productive capacity of fifty-nine Japanese cities, laid 12,049 mines in enemy waters and destroyed or damaged 2,285 Japanese planes.
>
> Total combat losses to the American forces amounted to 437 B 29's, of which the crew members—usually eleven to a plane—of 297 bombers were not rescued. About 600 airmen from downed B-29's were saved. . . .
>
> General Spaatz's figures made it clear that never in the history of warfare has so much been accomplished by one arm of a fighting force at so small a price.[25]

This report does not discuss civilian casualties. What it does instead is to praise a campaign in which heavy civilian casualties were simply taken for granted or ignored. The focus of the report is on military results and military losses—a *military* balance sheet.

What contributed most to this gratifying military balance was the use of saturation incendiary raids. It was largely in consequence of increasing dissatisfaction with costly and inconclusive "precision" raids that General LeMay was ordered, in February 1945, to give high priority to incendiary raids against major cities.[26] In executing those orders on the night of March 9–10, LeMay adopted radically new tactics of delivery. His bombers would go in low by night, not high by day; they would drop most of their defensive armaments; these changes would greatly increase their capacity to carry incendiaries, and they would aim those incendiaries not at aircraft factories but at a major part of downtown Tokyo.

As an exercise in unbounded destruction LeMay's innovation was a brilliant success. Attacking a densely populated area with closely spaced buildings of bamboo, wood and plastic, his bombers set fires that merged into a conflagration that burned out 15.8 square miles of Tokyo. Losses to the attackers were moderate—14 out of 334 planes (at the time only two of these losses were announced). Japanese dead were later listed at 84,000. More than 250,000 buildings were destroyed, about a quarter of the total in Tokyo.[27]

This attack on Tokyo remains today one of the two most destructive conventional operations in history.[28] The other, the bombing of Dresden, had taken place less than a month earlier, on February 13–14. There tens of thousands (the numbers are still disputed) were killed in a series of British and American raids that produced an enormous fire storm. The order for a heavy attack on a German city near the eastern front had come from Winston Churchill, eager to impress Stalin at Yalta. For operational reasons the attack was executed after that meeting, and Churchill never sought credit for it. Bitter questions were asked in the House of Commons, but the full character of the catastrophe was not grasped at the time. The highly accurate denunciations of the German radio were understandably discounted, and the Dresden raids do not appear to have had much impact, either way, on American thinking about the air war in Japan.[29]

As fast as he could, LeMay attempted to repeat his Tokyo raid, there and elsewhere, and by the time the committee established by General Groves began to look for suitable targets for the new weapon, in May and June, one of its concerns was the limited number of cities that seemed sufficiently free of damage to guarantee that the power of a single atomic bomb would be clearly demonstrated. The great fire raids were applauded not only by LeMay's superiors but by the press and the public. Highly favorable accounts appeared at the time, for example, in *The New York Times, Time,* and *Newsweek,* the latter remarking with satisfaction that the Tokyo raid had made a million people homeless.[30] In an unashamedly admiring four-part series in *The New Yorker* in June, St. Clair McKelway, home on leave from his post as LeMay's public relations officer, described the new technique in self-contradictory terms as "pin-point, incendiary bombing" designed

to start "one great conflagration." McKelway reported that while waiting for his flyers to return LeMay had explained, "If this raid works
the way I think it will, we can shorten this war," and he made the
general's purpose his own judgment: "LeMay and his people . . . are
shortening the war."[31]

It continued to be the argument of the air force that the targets
attacked were military. The one senior official who questioned the fire
raids was the secretary of war. Stimson had a long-standing aversion
to urban area bombing, and he thought he had assurances from his
undersecretary for air, Robert Lovett, against its use in Japan. He
questioned the head of the Army Air Force:

> I had in General Arnold and discussed with him the bombing of the
> B-29s in Japan. I told him of my promise from Lovett that there
> would be only precision bombing in Japan and that the press today
> had indicated a bombing of Tokyo that was very far from that. I
> wanted to know what the facts were. He told me that the Air Force
> was up against the difficult situation arising from the fact that Japan,
> unlike Germany, had not concentrated her industries and that on the
> contrary they were scattered out and were small and closely con-
> nected in site with the houses of their employees; that thus it was
> practically impossible to destroy the war output of Japan without
> doing more damage to the civilians connected with the output than
> in Europe. He told me, however, that they were trying to keep it
> down as far as possible.[32]

This last assurance had little basis in fact. Saturation incendiary bombing had proved so destructive that it was now the dominant method
of attack on Japan. The difficulty of "precision" bombing and the
demonstrated destructive power of massed incendiaries had made cities themselves the target of preference.

When Groves laid down his requirement for military targets big
enough to show the power of the weapon, he clearly meant cities, and
in his first instructions to his Target Committee he underlined the point
by remarking that General Marshall was especially interested in the
Japanese ports facing China. No one on the Target Committee ever
recommended any other kind of target, and while every city proposed
had quite traditional military objectives inside it—like an army headquarters, or harbor installations, or factories producing military supplies—the true object of attack was the city itself. The planners placed
the aiming point, in every case, at the center of the built-up area.[33]
Every target recommended, and every one approved by Truman, was
a city.

As with the targeting of cities, so with the schedule; it was determined by the general and overwhelming purpose of speed that had
been laid down years before. The attacks were executed on August 6

and August 9 with the clear authorization of the president and the secretary of war, but the timing was determined by readiness and weather, and neither man ever attempted to change it one way or the other. The dates were the earliest that could be achieved by the Manhattan Project and the air commanders in the Pacific; the targets were cities that met the requirements Groves and his Target Committee had used, and the number of attacks was as large as the supply of bombs then allowed.

This strictly military process of decision was interfered with at only one point, when Henry Stimson successfully prevented any nuclear attack on the city of Kyōto. We must come back to the decision to spare Kyōto, but what deserves emphasis here is that Stimson's intervention was wholly exceptional. The main line of decision making on the use of the bomb was the military line to the commander in chief. The object was military—to make the largest possible contribution to the earliest possible victory. The targets and the timing were those that military men thought best for this purpose. As we turn to consider the thin attention given by others to other possibilities, we will do well to keep it in mind that this basic process of decision and choice was squarely within the tradition of American war making. That does not make the choices and decisions right, but it does remind us that the animating motivation, along the line of command which was decisive, was to contribute to victory.[34]

The Interim Committee and the Decision

The inertial momentum behind the targeting of cities is plain not only in the proceedings of the Target Committee but also in the treatment that was given to the few and faint voices that raised questions about using the weapon this way. In the main these questions arose in, or were referred to, a special committee that was established in early May to advise on future atomic policy. This Interim Committee—so named because it was already clear that legislation would be needed to establish any lasting organization to deal with the national atomic program—was the product of months of pressure on Stimson, primarily from Bush. Its assignment was to get forward with all the planning and thinking that would be necessary in anticipation of the time when the bomb would be used and its existence thus made public. The most serious question for Bush and Stimson was that of international policy toward the atom, but there were other matters on which answers would be needed. What would be said when the bomb was first used? How much of what had been learned should be made public? What should be done about postwar research, development, and controls? These sorts of questions took up most of the committee's time.[35]

These assignments were based on the common assumption of Truman, Stimson, Marshall, Bush, Conant, and Groves: that the bomb would be used against Japan just as soon as it was ready. The committee members were appointed on the recommendation of Stimson from within the government. He was the chairman; his deputy, and the man who saw to it that the committee's work got done, was George L. Harrison, who was serving him as a consultant. Harrison, who had been successively chairman of the New York Federal Reserve Bank and president of the New York Life Insurance Company, had a remarkable reputation for practical sagacity and discretion, but he was no boat rocker. He was not at all likely to question the clear-cut assumption of the creators of the Interim Committee that it would address itself primarily to the questions that were posed by the general expectation that the bomb would be used as soon as it was ready— probably in August. The other members of the committee were Bush and Conant, both passionate believers in using the bomb to shorten the war, Ralph Bard of the Navy Department and William Clayton of the State Department, chosen from their departments by Harrison as men with his own kind of practical experience and common sense, and finally, James F. Byrnes, proposed by Stimson and approved by the president as Truman's personal representative. It was already known, though not formally announced, that Byrnes would soon be Truman's secretary of state. He had been Roosevelt's "Assistant President" for domestic matters (an informal press-bestowed title that Byrnes liked better than Roosevelt did). His past and prospective rank, and still more his relation to Truman, made him at least as important in the committee's counsels as Stimson himself.

Though most of its work was on other matters, the Interim Committee did consider the use of the bomb against Japan. The subject came up first informally, at lunch on May 31, during a joint meeting of the committee and its Scientific Advisory Panel. That panel had been established by the committee on the strong recommendation of Bush and Conant, who were well aware that many of the nuclear scientists most troubled about future policy would not regard the two of them—one an engineer, one a chemist, and both tight-lipped managers—as well-chosen spokesmen for the participating scientists as a whole. The panel members were Arthur Compton, Enrico Fermi, Ernest Lawrence, and Oppenheimer, men whose seniority and distinction as nuclear physicists were unquestionable. The morning of May 31 had begun with a fascinating but also terrifying seminar in which the scientists explained how the bombs currently in prospect, with a yield (conservatively estimated by Oppenheimer) of 2,000 to 20,000 tons, could certainly be followed by a second generation with yields of 50,000 to 100,000 tons. There had followed a wide-ranging discussion of the need for lively research, the prospects and problems of international control, and the problem of Russia.[36]

At lunch, almost by accident, conversation turned to the use of the bomb against Japan. The best account we have is by the official historians, pieced together from a letter that Lawrence wrote in August 1945 and an account that Arthur Compton wrote in 1956:

> At lunch . . . Byrnes asked Lawrence about a suggestion the physicist had made briefly during the morning: give the Japanese some striking but harmless demonstration of the bomb's power before using it in a manner that would cause great loss of life. For perhaps ten minutes, the proposition was the subject of general discussion. Oppenheimer could think of no demonstration sufficiently spectacular to convince the Japanese that further resistance was futile. Other objections came to mind. The bomb might be a dud. The Japanese might shoot down the delivery plane or bring American prisoners into the test area. If the demonstration failed to bring surrender, the chance of administering the maximum surprise shock would be lost. Besides, would the bomb cause any greater loss of life than the fire raids that had burned out Tokyo?[37]

After lunch the discussion continued. Changing the agenda, Stimson now directed discussion to the use of the bomb on Japan. The best account of that discussion is in the contemporary committee minutes:

> After much discussion concerning various types of targets and the effects to be produced, the Secretary expressed the conclusion, on which there was general agreement, that we could not give the Japanese any warning; that we could not concentrate on a civilian area; but that we should seek to make a profound psychological impression on as many of the inhabitants as possible. At the suggestion of Dr. Conant the Secretary agreed that the most desirable target would be a vital war plant employing a large number of workers and closely surrounded by workers' houses.[38]

On the following day the Interim Committee, in Stimson's absence, reached a somewhat more formal advisory conclusion: The bomb should be used as soon as possible; the target should be a war plant surrounded by workers' homes; and it should be used without warning.

Ten days later, on June 12, the question was reopened, for Harrison, by the submission from Chicago of what became known as the Franck report. The report was brought by Arthur Compton and James Franck; they came in person because Franck, in particular, and Compton as his willing intermediary, were eager to get the report to Stimson himself, as the highest accessible civilian. But Stimson was "not available," and the report was left for Harrison's attention.[39]

The Franck report urged that instead of making an attack on Japan without warning, it would be better to begin with a demonstration "before the eyes of representatives of all the United Nations, on the desert or a barren island." The argument was that such a course might greatly improve the prospect for effective postwar international control, although "after such a demonstration the weapon might perhaps be used against Japan."[40] Harrison appears to have concluded that the immediate requirement was to consider the practicability and effectiveness of a demonstration in the context already so firmly established: that of using the new weapon to end the war as quickly as possible. He referred the matter to the Scientific Panel, which was meeting at Los Alamos. It does not appear that the Franck report itself was put before the panel, although one member, Arthur Compton, had read it. As he recalled it in 1956, he and his colleagues were not asked to review the Franck report's argument that using the bomb might damage the prospect for international agreement. "We were asked to prepare a report as to whether we could devise any kind of demonstration that would seem likely to bring the war to an end without using the bomb against a live target."[41]

The question was considered by Compton, Fermi, Lawrence, and Oppenheimer on or about June 16 at Alamogordo. The conclusion they reported was unhappy, Compton recalled, but it was also clear, and it shows that whatever Harrison's exact question, the members of the Scientific Panel were aware of the wider concern animating the authors of the Franck report:

> The opinions of our scientific colleagues on the initial use of these weapons are not unanimous: they range from the proposal of a purely technical demonstration to that of the military application best designed to induce surrender. Those who advocate a purely technical demonstration would wish to outlaw the use of atomic weapons, and have feared that if we use the weapons now our position in future negotiations will be prejudiced. Others emphasize the opportunity of saving American lives by immediate military use, and believe that such use will improve the international prospects, in that they are more concerned with the prevention of war than with the elimination of this specific weapon. We find ourselves closer to these latter views; we can propose no technical demonstration likely to bring an end to the war; we see no acceptable alternative to direct military use.[42]

We have no full account of the discussion that produced this conclusion. What seems likely is that the four men will have gone back and forth over the difficulties that had been discussed at lunch on May 31. A demonstration in a barren area could not be counted on to make the necessary impression; a dud was possible. These were ingenious men, and humane, but they found no escape from their previous conclusions. They could not propose a demonstration "likely to bring an end to the war."

This conclusion ended the internal discussion of a demonstration. The difficulty of designing an event that would be both harmless and persuasive was not overcome, and indeed those who have argued for such a demonstration in later years have seldom been specific as to the kind of event that might have been both practicable and effective. Some definitions of "demonstration" have been pretty sweeping. Szilard himself, looking back, took a different view from the one he had strongly supported in the Franck report:

> I think it is clear that you can't demonstrate a bomb over an uninhabited island. You have to demolish a city. So a demonstration would have meant approaching Japan through a diplomatic channel, proposing a demonstration, say, over Hiroshima with the inhabitants removed from Hiroshima.[43]

Perhaps unimpressed by the practicality of this later notion, Szilard went on to say that the whole concept of a demonstration had been overemphasized: The Japanese were already beaten, and the real need was to end the war politically.

Curiously, the idea of a demonstration appears to have been considered at greater length than the notion of an explicit warning, and indeed the difficulty of devising a persuasive demonstration appears to have made the notion of a warning less attractive as well—if a demonstration was not likely to bring surrender, why should a warning? But this line of argument overlooked the fact that a warning, unlike a demonstration, involved no necessary delay in the actual military use of the bomb.[44]

Moreover at least one way of presenting such a warning might have been very persuasive indeed. In its essence it would have been a demonstration, but without the expenditure of an additional scarce and precious weapon, and without any advance warning that might be made foolish if the demonstration should be a dud. Were there not ways to use the first American test, on July 16 at Alamogordo? In the event the test was overwhelmingly impressive to its American and British audience, even to those who had a well-developed sense of what might be expected. The first official account, written by Groves, remains persuasively terrifying even now: the blinding flash of light, the enormous ball of fire, the mushroom cloud, the steel test tower vaporized, and the estimated yield in excess of 15,000 to 20,000 tons.[45] No extra bomb would have been needed; there would have been no delay in the schedule so remorselessly driven by the four-year insistence on speed. These effects could have been observed and reported by diplomats, soldiers, and scientists specifically selected for their reputation and standing in Japan. Such a delegation could have had members not only from the United States and Britain, but also from such neutral countries as Switzerland and Sweden. In short, a delegation of great reputation and persuasiveness could have been assembled and given the firsthand experience of the Alamogordo test—not at all to report on any durable atomic secret, but only to tell the government of Japan ahead of time what the whole world learned at Hiroshima. All this could have been done quickly, well within the three full weeks between Alamogordo and Hiroshima.

No one close to the Alamogordo test ever came close to examining such a possibility. In the Interim Committee General Marshall did suggest that two prominent Russian scientists might be invited to the test. The proposal was blocked by Byrnes, but his reason—that such an invitation would open the door to Russian pressure for more and more information—was not only unimpressive in itself but entirely inapplicable to diplomatic and neutral observers. The effectiveness of his opposition came from his rank as the president's representative, not from his logic. Was there a failure of imagination here?

It is not surprising that no such suggestion came from Los Alamos. To make a demonstration and a warning out of a first test is almost fanciful to the scientific mind. The Alamogordo test worked, but its extraordinary success was no foregone conclusion. In its design it was an experiment, not a demonstration, and to ask its hard-pressed scientific leaders to let it play both roles at once might well have struck more than one of these remarkable men as tempting the fates: They might well have been wary lest chivalry be wrecked on hubris. But if it had been proposed from above, would they have opposed such a plan? I doubt it; they would have respected a political judgment on the point and honored its generous purpose. And General Groves, though he would probably have been strongly opposed, would certainly have followed orders.

The only member of the Interim Committee who came anywhere near such a recommendation was Ralph Bard. Twice, on June 1 and again on June 24, he concurred in recommendations by the committee that the bomb should be used without warning, but by June 27 he had changed his mind. He had had a feeling from the beginning that Japan should have two or three days "warning," he wrote, and that feeling was based on his view of the "position of the United States as a great humanitarian nation and the fair play attitude of our people generally. . . ." He now proposed that after the coming meeting in Potsdam American emissaries make private contact with Japanese representatives and "give them some information regarding the proposed use of atomic power." Bard's advice was quite tentative in tone, and he coupled his suggestion with additional proposals on Russia's position and on the future of the emperor, thus entering other contested ground. But he cared enough to press his case face to face with the president in a farewell interview in early July (he was leaving the government for other reasons), and Truman assured him that the whole matter of a warning had been very carefully considered.[46]

Insofar as the president's assurance referred to the question of a new and general warning to Japan, it was at least partly accurate. But if he was referring to the possibility of explicit disclosure of the existence of the bomb, he was engaged in overstatement. We have seen the incompleteness of the examination in the Interim Committee, and the only other high-level discussion we know about was still more limited. On June 18 at the White House there was a meeting whose central subject was plans for the invasion of Japan. Its operational purpose was to secure Truman's authorization for the invasion plan, and the primary presentation was made by Marshall, who argued a powerful brief for the probable insufficiency of bombing and the imperative of deciding to invade Kyūshū and Honshū if necessary. The president listened and approved, characteristically limiting his approval to one landing at a time. Stimson and McCloy were there, and they had been talking in the preceding two days about other ways of ending the war. Now Stimson said little, and in accordance with the normal rules for an assistant secretary whose boss was present, McCloy would have kept silent, but Truman called on him: "We haven't heard from you, McCloy, and no one leaves this meeting without standing up and being counted." McCloy fired both barrels, saying that we ought to have our heads examined if we did not seek a political solution in preference to an invasion. He thought we had two instruments at hand: First, we could give an assurance on the future of the emperor, and second, we could give an explicit warning of the existence of the atomic bomb. On the first point Truman himself was sympathetic, but he told McCloy to consult Byrnes, who was not. On the second point military objections were strong, and Stimson himself was not enthusiastic. In the Interim Committee he had already heard and approved the argument against such advance warning. The two ideas McCloy had briefly bound together were separated and diluted as the days passed. Over the next two weeks Stimson and McCloy worked hard on designing an effective message of hope and threat to the Japanese, but specific advance warning of the bomb was not part of what they were free to work with. Only the most general warning of impending destruction survived to be included in the Potsdam Declaration, and American assurance on the emperor came only after the Japanese had offered surrender on that one condition.[47]

How careful, then, was the whole study of possible alternatives to the sudden and secret use of the bomb against cities, and how much difference might a different process have made? The answer depends on one's premises. It seems possible that for Groves the quantity of attention given was excessive. To him cities with major military installations were clearly proper targets; a demonstration might fail and would lack the persuasiveness of a direct attack; a warning would be still less persuasive and would run against the powerful tradition in favor of maximizing the shock effect of surprise when unveiling a new secret weapon. Groves always found it hard to understand "how anyone could ignore the importance of the effect on the Japanese people and their government of the overwhelming surprise of the bomb."[48] But in retrospect it is not at all obvious that accurate advance warning would in fact have reduced the shock of actual use. No doubt it would have been more impressive to some than to others among the divided Japanese, but if it had been necessary to go ahead with the actual attack, the existence of the explicit warning might well have accelerated and deepened understanding of what had happened.

The natural military resistance to any direct advance disclosure of a new secret weapon was almost surely one reason for the lack of sustained attention to it. No one ever pressed the idea on the operating military commanders, and it is a safe assumption that any proposal for a specific prior warning of the existence of an atomic bomb would have met strong military objection. If the Japanese were told of the existence of a new weapon of extraordinary destructive power, would they not, to the degree that they believed the warning, take extraordinary measures to attack any aircraft that might be its carrier? To add any such risk for any such purpose to a mission already unusual in its complexity and danger would have seemed quixotic to the military professionals. But they could certainly have been overruled, and there were men among their most senior brother officers who well understood that this was a special case. Two of the most important were Admiral Leahy and General Eisenhower; their published regrets over the use of the bomb make it at least plausible that they would have been sympathetic to a carefully worked-out plan for warning in advance. General Marshall himself favored some explicit warning as late as May 29. Though he later concurred in a different course, it seems certain that he would have supported a political decision to give warning.[49]

What blocked the development of any such plan, I believe, is not any intrinsic difficulty such as those surrounding a demonstration on a desert island. Just as there could have been neutral observers at Alamogordo, there were ways to protect the eventual attack against any risks created by warning. Decoys, feints, and fighter protection were all practicable. The sustained consideration that might have led to a serious warning plan was missing. Such studies were blocked by two ways of thinking that were deeply ingrained by 1945. One was the general disposition to separate military from political questions; the war must be won by winning it, and that was the business of military professionals. So a matter like the use of the bomb was primarily a military matter—the Interim Committee's examination was brief and relatively general; no specific targets were ever reviewed there. In no forum was there any sustained and serious back-and-forth argument between men like McCloy and Bard and men like Groves.

The second obstacle to careful staff study was even more formidable; like the proposal of outside observers at Alamogordo, serious and sustained staff work would have required a reversal of the most deeply ingrained of all the behavior patterns of the Manhattan Project, the commitment to secrecy. It was true, and even obvious, that if the test at Alamogordo succeeded, it would be the last large event before secrecy ended; the press releases for Hiroshima were already being drafted. But for the men at the top of the project it was also the climactic *secret* event of their great *secret* adventure. The Alamogordo test was off limits not only to everyone outside the project, but to many within it. The people at Chicago appear to have been particularly suspect; Szilard remembered that he knew the test was imminent when he found that members of the Chicago group were no longer allowed to telephone to Los Alamos.[50]

The secrecy that had begun with a proper concern not to arouse Hitler's interest had become a state of mind with a life and meaning of its own, so deeply ingrained that anyone who had asked the most experienced members of the Interim Committee just *why* it was a secret now, in May 1945, might have had to wait for the answer. It was a secret now because it had been a secret throughout the war (a poor answer, surely), or because it might bring victory (but so might the B-29s or the blockading fleets, and men boasted of them daily), or because the enemy did not know about it—but would it really be better or worse, now, if he *did* know? That question went so deeply against the grain, even for the most farsighted men in the undertaking, that they never examined it thoroughly. It is no accident that the two men to raise the question of warning directly with Truman were Bard of the Navy Department and McCloy. The Navy Department was not really in on the secret, and until relatively late McCloy was not at the center of the little group around Stimson on this topic. So these two did not begin with any ingrained assumption that continued secrecy was somehow vital to success. Part of the cool response to McCloy's sudden suggestion of June 18 came from shock at his audacity in proposing a disclosure of the bomb in a meeting on another subject, the invasion of Japan—never mind that what he was saying was directly connected to the possibility of making that invasion unnecessary.[51]

Among those closest to the project, exactly that state of mind continued, and perhaps more sharply than ever as the climax approached, for the tension over any secret is highest just before it is revealed. It was a fateful legacy from the project's origin, and from Franklin Roosevelt.

SO THERE WAS to be no demonstration and no explicit warning. If the Japanese did not surrender before the first bombs were ready, they would be used. They would be used against cities. Let us look once more at the way men satisfied themselves that cities were military targets.

The military targeters never considered any other target than cities. The Interim Committee's minutes speak of a major factory surrounded by workers' homes; Stimson enlarged on that conclusion in two ways— we could not hit civilian targets, and we must try to maximize the psychological effect. But what was a major factory surrounded by workers' houses if not a city—or at the very least a large town? Thus it became clear that the Interim Committee was subject to the same way of thinking that had governed both the military approach and the public response to the fire raids. Since cities with military targets in them were themselves seen as military targets, an attack on such cities did not violate the prohibition of attack on civilians, and once an attack on factories was justified, the almost inevitable presence of workers' homes in the neighborhood (certainly in the Japan of 1945) would have the value of increasing the shock effect so greatly desired. Not its civilian population as such, but only some other commanding claim to immunity could override the presumption that *any* city, as a contributor to the war effort, was a fair target.

One recommended target was in fact forbidden by high civilian authority, and the exception proves the rule in a most illuminating way. The best witness to what happened is Leslie Groves:

> With these selections in hand, I prepared a plan of operations for General Marshall, recommending his approval. This report was in my office when I went to see Secretary Stimson about another matter. In the course of our conversation, he asked me whether I had selected the targets yet. I told him that I had and that my report was ready for submission to General Marshall. I added that I hoped to see the General the next morning.
>
> Mr. Stimson was not satisfied with this reply and said he wanted to see my report. I said that I would rather not show it to him without having first discussed it with General Marshall, since this was a military operational matter. He replied, "This is a question I am settling myself. Marshall is not making that decision." Then he told me to have the report brought over. I demurred, on the grounds that it

would take some time. He said that he had all morning and that I should use his phone to get it over right away.

While we were waiting, he asked me about the targets. When I went over the list for him, he immediately objected to Kyoto and said he would not approve it. When I suggested that he might change his mind after he had read the description of Kyoto and our reasons for considering it to be a desirable target, he replied that he was sure that he would not.

The reason for his objection was that Kyoto was the ancient capital of Japan, a historical city, and one that was of great religious significance to the Japanese. He had visited it when he was Governor General of the Philippines and had been very much impressed by its ancient culture.

I pointed out that it had a population of over a million; that any city of that size in Japan must be involved in a tremendous amount of war work even if there were but few large factories; and that the Japanese economy was to a great extent dependent on small shops, which in time of war turned out tremendous quantities of military items. . . . I pointed out also that Kyoto included 26,446,000 square feet of plant area that had been identified and 19,496,000 square feet of plant area as yet unidentified. The city's peacetime industries had all been converted to war purposes and were producing, among other items, machine tools, precision ordnance and aircraft parts, radio fire control and gun direction equipment. The industrial district occupied an area of one by three miles in the total built-up area of two and one-half by four miles.

Mr. Stimson was not satisfied, and without further ado walked over to the door of General Marshall's office and asked him to come in. Without telling him how he had got the report from me, the Secretary said that he disagreed with my recommendation of Kyoto as a target, and explained why. . . .

After some discussion, during which it was impossible for me discreetly to let General Marshall know how I had been trapped into by-passing him, the Secretary said that he stuck by his decision. In the course of our conversation he gradually developed the view that the decision should be governed by the historical position that the United States would occupy after the war. He felt very strongly that anything that would tend in any way to damage this position would be unfortunate.

On the other hand, I particularly wanted Kyoto as a target because, as I have said, it was large enough in area for us to gain complete knowledge of the effects of an atomic bomb. Hiroshima was not nearly so satisfactory in this respect. I also felt quite strongly, as had all the members of the Target Committee, that Kyoto was one of the most important military targets in Japan. Consequently, I continued on a number of occasions afterward to urge its inclusion, but Mr. Stimson was adamant. Even after he arrived in Potsdam, Harrison sent him a cable saying that I still felt it should be used as a target. The return cable stated that he still disapproved, and the next day he followed it with another which said that he had discussed the matter with President Truman, who concurred in his decision. There was no further talk about Kyoto after that.[52]

Although Groves acknowledged at the end of this tale that Stimson had been right, what shines through his account, second only to his embarrassment at being caught apparently "out of channels," is his astonishment at the secretary's attitude. A civilian was intruding on a military matter; the factories in Kyōto defined its importance as a target; its large size and its topography made it an ideal proving ground; its cultural and historical significance had simply not been considered by the planners, or by Groves. Stimson's intervention was exceptional, for him or for any other civilian, including the president. And it was not his concern with Kyōto as a city full of people that was at work here; it was clearly Kyōto as a great historical and cultural monument that mattered.

Yet in defending his bold and quick personal decision Stimson too used split-level thinking. Compton remembered him as arguing on May 31 that Kyōto was "exclusively a place of homes and art and shrines."[53] It was not so, as General Groves had argued from his target folders. No city of a million could have been irrelevant to the Japanese war effort. But in his passionate determination to spare Kyōto, Stimson simply swept the military argument aside. It was more comfortable to look at only part of the truth at a time: The industrial heart of Tokyo was military; ancient Kyōto was civilian; to admit that the distinction was artificial, *in both cases,* came hard.

Harry Truman was even more categorical in insisting on artificial distinctions. After he had approved a target list that included Hiroshima and Nagasaki, and also supported Stimson in the protection of Kyōto, he made the following note in a journal he kept at Potsdam:

> ... I have told the Sec. of War, Mr. Stimson, to use it so that military objectives and soldiers and sailors are the target and not women and children. Even if the Japs are savages, ruthless, merciless and fanatic, we as the leader of the world for the common welfare cannot drop this terrible bomb on the old capital or the new.
>
> He & I are in accord. The target will be a purely military one . . .[54]

What is striking here, in addition to the curious notion that Tokyo, already so ravaged by fire, was being spared for humanitarian reasons, is the president's belief that capital cities, old and new, are somehow off limits. This notion recurs for other reasons in later and more sophisticated analyses of targeting policy, but one wonders if somehow, to Truman, there was a human content in the word *Tokyo* that he did not find in *Hiroshima*—was one a great city he had heard about for years, and the other only a place name for an army headquarters?

Truman never chose, then or later, to grapple with this self-deception; indeed he repeated to the end of his life that it was a purely military action against military targets. Stimson, in reviewing and defending his own position a year and a half later, found it best to confront the dilemma head on; he believed as firmly as ever that the choices made were the best available, but he recognized the human costs: "the destruction of Hiroshima and Nagasaki" and "death to over a hundred thousand Japanese." He still found no other kind of target that could believably have achieved the desired shock.[55]

In truth other targets have not been easy to propose. No much smaller target—no single fortress or airfield or factory—would have served; the danger of missing it was too great—by Groves's account the Nagasaki bomb fell a mile and a half from its original aiming point. Any target large enough to be thoroughly and shockingly destroyed by a single inaccurate bomb was also a target full of men, women, and children.[56]

Thus the dilemma that military targeters found irrelevant and that most civilians preferred not to face was all too real. Cities had proved themselves "rewarding" targets for B-29s in massed incendiary raids, and in choosing cities as the targets for the first atomic bombs the military targeters were true to their assigned mission. Given the overriding objective as Roosevelt and Truman had repeatedly stated it—to end the war as fast as possible in total victory—this could well be seen, in Stimson's later words, as the "least abhorrent choice."[57]

It would have been possible, of course, to instruct the targeters to find built-up areas of adequate size with *relatively* small populations, but no one was thinking in such selective terms, and anyway unpredictable happenings would probably have dominated any such attempt at "fine tuning." Consider the actual events that were not foreseen when the targeters began their work in April. No one foresaw that the attack on Hiroshima would take place without so much as an air raid alert to send people into shelters; the absence of such an alert was the largest cause of the difference between Oppenheimer's advance estimate of 20,000 deaths and the actual toll of some 130,000. No one guessed that the three attacking aircraft—one with a bomb and two with instruments—would be too few to cause orders for alert. No one foresaw that a single determined old civilian would veto the most wanted target of all, and Stimson himself did not act on a calculation of human suffering. But Kyōto was both larger and more densely populated than either of the cities that were hit; unless its broad avenues had limited the effects of fire—still another variable not fully pondered at the time—the death toll from an attack on Kyōto might well have run far higher. And at Nagasaki no one foresaw the overcast or the resulting bombing error which greatly and providentially reduced the casualties there (60,000 to 70,000 dead), perhaps by a factor of two.[58]

I offer these notes on unanticipated consequences intending neither condemnation nor apology for what happened, but rather a reminder that right here, at the very beginning of the atomic age, we encounter two fateful characteristics of nuclear weapons. Intrinsically and almost inescapably they are weapons of mass destruction, and their effects must always be extraordinarily dependent on the uncertain behavior of defenders, of weather, of targeters, of pilots, of statesmen, and of possibly contested processes of attack.

So deliberations in May and June in Washington served only to confirm the assumptions of April. If the war was still going on in August the atomic bomb would be used against Japanese cities; there would be no prior warning of its existence, and no demonstration on a desert island or anywhere else. These decisions were indeed no more than decisions not to interrupt a process whose momentum had grown inexorably over years of complex effort, compulsive secrecy, and growing hope that the new weapon would be ready in time to help shorten the war. What required further consideration, by the middle of June, was not the use of the weapon, but the way that use should be related to the achievement of Japanese surrender.

In one sense, the events from the middle of June to the Japanese surrender on August 14 are quite simple. It was agreed in early June that the bomb would be used when ready. It was agreed later that month that before such use the Japanese should receive a generally phrased last-chance warning of total destruction unless they should surrender. It was expected that such a warning would probably be rejected. It was hoped that the use of the bomb, promptly thereafter, might break the impasse. There was readiness, if that happened, to give assurances, in some form, that the emperor might keep his throne. And all this is what happened: The last chance warning was given in the Potsdam Declaration of July 26; it was dismissed by the Japanese; two bombs were dropped, and the Russians entered the war. The Japanese then accepted the Potsdam offer, with the proviso that the emperor's position not be compromised; the Americans replied on this point in a fashion that the emperor himself found acceptable; the war ended. The American people cheered on V-J Day as they had not cheered three months earlier when only half the war ended, in Europe. Two Japanese cities, Hiroshima and Nagasaki, had suffered atomic attacks, and *the war was over.* It is not surprising that to Truman, Byrnes, Stimson, and Marshall, as to Bush, Conant, and Groves, this result seemed a full and indeed overwhelming return on the whole long effort to make a bomb and on the detailed set of actions that made it a decisive force in the Japanese decision to surrender.[59]

Some Questions

There were questions at the time, and there have been more later. Two of them fall outside the premises on which Truman and his advisers were working: that the proper first object of policy was to win the war just as fast as possible, and that the use of the atomic bomb against cities was a legitimate instrument to this end. Some have argued that such use was intrinsically a moral wrong, and some have argued that it was not really to shorten the war that the bomb was used. These arguments deserve attention, but it is better to begin with two other lines of argument which begin from the same premise as Truman, Byrnes, and Stimson. One is that precisely in order to end the war more rapidly, *with or without the bomb,* there should have been an earlier assurance on keeping the emperor, and the other is that for this same purpose there could have been a better use of the readiness of the Soviet government to enter the war against Japan, as it actually did on August 8, two days after Hiroshima.

To understand the importance of these questions we must consider the ending of the war from the standpoint of Japan. The desperate situation of Japan in July 1945 was at least as well known to the Japanese government as to the Americans. But there were three things that the Americans knew and the Japanese did not: that Japan would soon be hit by atomic bombs, that the Soviet Union was going to attack, and that the Americans would let the Imperial Dynasty continue if it proved to have popular support. These three realities produced prompt surrender as they became clear to the Japanese government between August 6 and August 12. What deserves attention is why none of them was made clear sooner. We have already seen what forces, in the case of the bomb, stood in the way of any prior demonstration or warning. There were parallel difficulties with the other two realities, and still greater obstacles to the consideration of all three together.

Until the spring of 1945 there was little direct discussion at the highest levels in Washington on the question of the retention of the emperor. For Franklin Roosevelt one of the advantages of his doctrine of unconditional surrender was that it allowed the postponement of decisions on such questions. But with the end of the war in Europe and the battering of the Japanese enemy by land, sea, and air, thinking turned to this question. The acting secretary of state, in the absence of Edward Stettinius at the San Francisco conference, was Undersecretary Joseph C. Grew; he had served ten years as ambassador to Japan and was deeply convinced that a public decision to allow the survival of the Imperial Dynasty would be both right on the merits and helpful in encouraging early surrender. He believed that in the aftermath of the great fire raids on Tokyo, now three in number, it would be well to include such an assurance in a major appeal for prompt Japanese surrender. Grew presented this case to President Truman on May 28; the president said he was thinking along the same lines but asked Grew to discuss the matter with Stimson, Marshall, Forrestal, and King. At a meeting the next day Grew found general support for the principle of keeping the emperor but general opposition to the early public statement he wanted. In part the objection was based on fear that such a concession might be taken as a sign of weakness while the fighting in Okinawa was unfinished, but Stimson at least had an unstated additional reason: He thought any last-chance warning should come later, at a time when, if rejected, it could be followed promptly by the use of the bomb. Grew had won on the principle, but not on the timing.[60]

During June discussion of this issue continued. The White House meeting of June 18, at which McCloy surprised the company by mentioning both the bomb and the notion of an explicit warning about it to Japan, produced a rejection of that specific idea but also gave a new impetus to the framing of a more general last-chance warning to Japan, this time for possible use at Potsdam. On July 2 Stimson presented to Truman a draft of such a warning supported by a powerful memorandum on the importance of giving the Japanese hope as well as warning. He added, "I personally think that if in saying this we should add that we do not exclude a constitutional monarchy under her present dynasty, it would substantially add to the chances of acceptance." Stimson, like Grew, found the president generally sympathetic.[61]

But the role of senior adviser to the president on this question passed on the following day to James Byrnes, newly sworn in as secretary of state. Byrnes found his department divided. Grew's opinion was emphatically not shared by all his colleagues. Divisions of opinion in that department were reflected in the ambiguity of planning papers that Byrnes probably never read. But as Byrnes prepared to leave for Potsdam he heard directly from Assistant Secretary Archibald MacLeish. Speaking for himself and his colleague Dean Acheson, MacLeish argued that the notion of agreeing to keep the emperor seemed incompatible with unconditional surrender and also dangerous, because "the institution of the throne is an anachronistic, feudal institution, perfectly adapted to the manipulation and use of anachronistic, feudal-minded groups within the country."[62] Antipathy to the emperor was also rampant in the country and strong in the Congress. Franklin Roosevelt himself had not been above coupling "Hitler and Hirohito" as objects of scorn. A Gallup poll of June 29 asked persons who knew Hirohito was the emperor of Japan, "What do you think we should do with the Japanese emperor after the war?" Thirty-three percent responded, "Execute him"; 17 percent, "Let court decide his fate"; and 11 percent, "Keep him in prison the rest of his life."[63]

Byrnes found himself in no mood to hurry forward with public assurances on the emperor's future, and he and Truman agreed, probably during their sea voyage to Germany the following week, both to delay the "last-chance" warning and to omit any specific assurance on the emperor. When he got to Potsdam Byrnes found powerful reinforcement of his position in a cable reporting the views of Cordell Hull, whom he had consulted before leaving Washington. Hull shared with Byrnes both strong political standing and great sensitivity to possible criticism. He said he recognized the force of the argument for assurances on the emperor, but he feared they might bring no response, and that then "the Japs would be encouraged while terrible political repercussions would follow in the U.S." Byrnes replied that he agreed.[64]

On July 26, with the extraordinary news of Trinity in hand, and with Hiroshima in early prospect, the last-chance warning was issued from Potsdam over the signatures of Truman, Churchill, and Chiang Kai-shek. It contained both threats and promises, but no mention of the bomb and no assurance on the emperor. While the statement was already being cleared with Chiang, Stimson made one last effort with Truman to get such an assurance into that declaration and found he was too late, but he came away with what he understood as Truman's assurance that if the problem of the emperor became the only impediment to surrender, he would "take care of it." Mr. Truman did just that, but not until August 10.[65]

On that day, driven to decision by the use of atomic bombs and the sudden Soviet declaration of war, the Japanese government announced its acceptance of the Potsdam Declaration, subject only to the understanding "that the said declaration does not comprise any demand which prejudices the prerogatives of His Majesty as a Sovereign Ruler." With victory in plain sight the issue was forced in Washington, and in a single day it proved possible to reconcile the concept of unconditional surrender with the retention of the emperor. The American reply did not explicitly accept the Japanese condition; it simply stated the American view that "the authority of the Emperor and the Japanese Government to rule the state shall be subject to the Supreme Commander of the Allied powers" and that the "ultimate form of government of Japan shall, in accordance with the Potsdam declaration, be established by the freely expressed will of the Japanese people."[66]

There was no backlash at home, and if there had been, it would have been outweighed by the instant reaction of the troops in the field. *The New York Times* report from Guam on August 11 appeared under the headline GI'S IN PACIFIC GO WILD WITH JOY: "LET 'EM KEEP EMPEROR," THEY SAY. The report of unconditional jubilation that followed made it clear that anyone in Washington who thought differently could expect to hear from the armed forces in no uncertain terms. The story reported that on Guam men already believed that the emperor had not been bombed "because he was the one single force that could be counted upon to control all Japanese troops if he decided to surrender." And on the same day the stately *Times,* which only ten days earlier had harshly criticized the emperor and compared him directly with Hitler, took editorial note of the difference between abstract debate and concrete opportunity. The editorial avoided a direct recommendation, but its preference for accepting the Japanese surrender offer, proviso and all, was clear: "The United Nations must decide whether they will continue the war, with its cost in the lives of Americans and of our allies, merely to decide the status of the Emperor alone."[67]

When the Japanese government accepted the American response and announced its surrender, on August 14, the few remaining critics were drowned out by general delight. Nothing in the subsequent history of Japan has called into question the wisdom of the decision to let the emperor stay. Those with honest fears of the imperial institution have been proven wrong, and there has never been any doubt that its continued existence has the strong support of the people of Japan—a support intensified by respect for the courage and wisdom the emperor displayed in August 1945.

We know now that in the whole process of the Japanese surrender the emperor himself was the decisive force. At least twice his personal intervention was crucial—in the decision of August 10 to surrender with a single proviso, and in the decision of August 14 to accept the American response. In the second case he astonished Lord Privy Seal Kido Kōichi by his acceptance of the American insistence that the eventual form of government of Japan must be determined by the will of the Japanese people; he said that he would not want to be emperor on any other basis. This judgment was decisive for Kido and then for the prime minister. The emperor also made full use of his own personal prestige and of his royal relatives as personal emissaries to ensure that the men commanding his army and navy would faithfully execute his decision to surrender. No one in the American government understood at the time how deeply and directly the emperor was engaged, and this failure of understanding is itself understandable, since there was no precedent whatever for such direct intervention. But without the emperor, and the oblique but effective assurances on his position issued from Washington on August 11, peace could not have come when it did.[68]

Indeed if it were not for the deeper questions presented by the nuclear bombing of Hiroshima and Nagasaki, it is doubtful that the course pursued by Harry Truman on this issue would have aroused much retrospective comment. It is not self-evident that because the

assurance on keeping the emperor brought peace on August 14 it
would have done so in June or July. The governmental stalemate that
the emperor broke that day was the same as it had been before the
assurance was given, and what appears to have moved the emperor in
both of his interventions was not the matter of his own standing, but
the simple imperative of surrender in the light of the bomb and the
Soviet declaration of war; both were also important in reinforcing
military acceptance of his decision.[69] A public assurance offered in
June or July might well have been rejected as the Potsdam Declaration
itself was rejected; the total set of forces operating for surrender at the
top of the Japanese government might not yet have been strong
enough to prevail; no one can say. No one can tell, either, how much
divisive debate there might have been in the United States, but certainly that debate was minimized by waiting until the assurance could
be seen as a sure last step to victory. Grew and McCloy always thought
an earlier statement might well have brought victory without the use
of the bomb, and Stimson later came to think that judgment might be
right.[70] But at the time the partisans of that earlier assurance never tied
their argument to the question of not using the bomb. Stimson, the one
man with a direct and intense awareness of both the emperor and the
bomb, did not truly expect that an assurance on the emperor would
in fact bring a quick surrender before the bomb was used; the "substantially improved" chances that he thought such an assurance would give
were still small.[71] Here, as in the case of the planning on the use of
the bomb itself, the way Stimson and others thought about these
matters was conditioned by a deep-seated expectation that until
heavier shocks were administered, the war would almost certainly go
on.

It is true that at Potsdam the Americans had access to intercepted
messages between Tokyo and the Japanese ambassador in Moscow that
showed the urgent Japanese desire for Soviet mediation and repeatedly referred to unconditional surrender as the only obstacle to peace.
We know now that what Foreign Minister Tōgō Shigenori had in
mind, in this formulation, was that for him and other civilians the only
obstacle to peace was the absence of assurance on the emperor. But
what *we* now know is not what *he* then said, and to reread all these
messages today and fit them into the mind's eye of the men at Potsdam
is to understand very well why neither Stimson nor Byrnes read them
as relevant to the issue that divided them.[72]

At the most the intercepts might have led to some thought of a
private diplomatic message to Japan. But it would have been quite out
of character for Truman to have authorized any such process while he
was preparing and concerting with allies a major public declaration,
and in any case a private assurance on the emperor, offered in advance
of any knowledge that it would be decisive, would have carried the risk

that it might be rejected and revealed; its furtiveness would then have been the target of explosive criticism. Stalin was quite straightforward in describing the Japanese feelers to Truman, but to send serious messages back through Moscow would not have been easy; Stalin was getting ready for war, not mediation. To go secretly around the Russians would have been more tricky still. In any case Truman and Byrnes were saying everything they were ready to say to Japan in the Potsdam Declaration; the intercepts of Tōgō's instructions were much too vague to change that. If indeed they read the whole set of exchanges, they must have agreed with the cable sent home by the Japanese ambassador in Moscow: ". . . YOUR SUCCESSIVE TELEGRAMS HAD NOT CLARIFIED THE SITUATION. THE INTENTIONS OF THE GOVERNMENT AND THE MILITARY WERE NOT CLEAR EITHER REGARDING THE TERMINATION OF THE WAR."[73] I conclude that only a strong and settled determination to make a major effort to end the war *without* using the bomb could have led to any change in the Truman-Byrnes position in July. We already know that no such determination existed, and if it had, then probably other measures also, like explicit warning, would have been considered.

There remains one other possibility—advance notice that in the absence of surrender the Russians were coming. Stalin's pledge in February at Yalta, that he would join in the war against Japan, was sought and given in a context very different from that of July at Potsdam, but in his first meeting with Truman on July 17 he confirmed his pledge and set the date of his readiness at August 15. Truman noted the assurance in his private journal and remarked, "Fini Japs when that comes about."[74] Thus Truman received on the first day, and essentially without argument, a reassurance that was one of his main objectives in attending the two-week meeting, and his pungent comment reflected not only the slang of a World War I artillery captain but also the careful judgment he had heard on June 18 from George Marshall, that either alone or in combination with new American actions, Russian entry "may well be the decisive action."[75]

No one at Potsdam had any intention of warning the Japanese of all this. The Russians, while they had played hard to get in the past, were now clearly looking forward to getting into the war and to obtaining by their own actions at least as much as they had already been promised at Yalta: special rights in the Manchurian railway and at Dairen and Port Arthur, and outright cession of the Kuril Islands and southern Sakhalin. It would have been quite out of character for them to betray their intentions by a warning. Stalin might in fact have increased his overall influence in the area by demanding surrender *before* he attacked, but we have no evidence that he thought about it that way. Nor could the Americans give this warning on their own. They had secretly sought Soviet help, and to tip the Soviet hand to the

Japanese without Soviet agreement would have been unthinkable.

In any case Truman learned of Stalin's renewed pledge just as he was about to lose interest in it. When the full report from Alamogordo arrived in Potsdam on July 21 he asked for Marshall's opinion and found that the general, whom he greatly respected, no longer thought it urgent to have Soviet help. Byrnes was even more emphatic; fearing Soviet intentions in Asia, he somewhat naïvely hoped that he could keep Stalin out of the war by encouraging Chinese delay in negotiations with the Russians on the execution of the Yalta terms. Stimson, more realistic, saw no way to prevent Russian entry, but he now hoped for an early surrender, induced by the bomb, that would limit the weight of the Russian claim to a share in the occupation of Japan itself.[76] These emerging opinions made it entirely natural for the Americans not to consider using the Soviet plan to attack as a means of inducing Japanese surrender. No one asked Stalin to join in issuance of the Potsdam Declaration, nor did the Russians choose to subscribe to it until they were ready to make war.

So the Soviet intention remained secret, and the Soviet and American military staffs went forward at Potsdam with detailed plans for meshing their prospective operations—always excepting the new weapon, which was mentioned only briefly and with carefully staged casualness by Truman in a private exchange with Stalin. Stalin's reply was equally casual and equally staged: he was glad to hear about it and "hoped we would make 'good use of it against the Japanese.'"[77] For both men, as we shall see, the true meaning of this conversation lay elsewhere than in the quest for Japanese surrender.

IN THE DECADES since Hiroshima a number of writers have asserted a quite different connection between the American thinking on the bomb and the Soviet Union—namely that a desire to impress the Russians with the power of the bomb was a major factor in the decision to use it. This assertion is false, and the evidence to support it rests on inferences so stretched as to be a discredit both to the judgment of those who have argued in this fashion and the credulity of those who have accepted such arguments. There is literally no evidence whatever that the timetable for the attack was ever affected by anything except technical and military considerations; there is no evidence that anyone in the direct chain of command from Truman to Stimson to Marshall to Groves ever heard or made any suggestion that either the decision itself or the timing of its execution should be governed by any consideration of its effect on the Soviet Union.[78]

What is true—and important—is that these same decision makers were full of hope that the bomb would put new strength into the American power position. As we shall see, they were in some confusion as to how this "master card" (Stimson's term) should be played, but they would have been most unusual men if they had thought it irrelevant. It is also true that Byrnes in particular was eager to get the war in Japan over before the Russians came in, thinking quite wrongly that their moves on the mainland might thus be forestalled. In May he also argued with Leo Szilard on the question whether the use of the bomb in Japan would make the Soviet Union harder or easier to deal with—but this was merely an argument with a scientist who was presenting a contrary view, not a statement of basic reasons for the decision. That decision belonged, by all the accepted practices of wartime Washington, in the hands of the commander in chief and the Pentagon; Byrnes supported it, but he did not originate it or modify it in any way. At the most the opinions of Byrnes deprived Truman of the different advice that he might have heard from a different secretary of state. But the name of a man who would have been ready and able to sway Truman from the course so powerfully supported by Stimson and Marshall, and so deeply consonant with the wartime attitudes of the American people and with his own, does not leap to mind. Ending the war in complete victory just as fast as possible was a totally dominant motive in its own right. This preemptive purpose, along with the compulsive secrecy of the whole business, certainly made men slow to attend to other considerations, one of which could well have been a more thoughtful look at the real effect the use of the bomb would have on Moscow. But this is a totally different point well made by later and more careful critics.[79]

Each of the realities that produced the Japanese surrender was purposely concealed from Japan, and each of these concealments was governed on the American side by the conviction that for use against Japan the bomb was indeed *a military weapon like any other,* if more so. Keep the value of surprise and do not give warning; use it to bring your enemy to the very brink of surrender *before* you make a concession on the emperor that might otherwise seem weak or embarrass you at home, and use it right on schedule if its use can help to minimize the role of an increasingly troubling ally.

What you do not think of separately, you seldom think of all at once, so it is not surprising that no one fully examined the possibilities of a triple demarche: warning of the bomb, warning of Soviet entry, and assurances on the emperor. Obviously Potsdam was no place for such thoughts; by then the basic decisions had been made, and no senior American at Potsdam was in a mood for reversing them. A more interesting question is what might have happened in May and June, in Washington, if there had been a group charged with the duty of considering the bomb, the emperor, and the Soviet pledge, all together, in the context of achieving early surrender, and if that group had been charged to consider also the possible advantages of *not* having to use the bomb. Or better yet, what might have happened if the same questions had been examined even earlier, by Roosevelt and a few advisers?

There are several tantalizing hints that Franklin Roosevelt was troubled about the basic question of using the weapon against Japan in a way that his successor never was. In a most secret private memorandum that no other senior American saw until after he was dead, Roosevelt agreed with Churchill, at Hyde Park on September 18 or 19, 1944, that "when a 'bomb' is finally available, it might perhaps, after mature consideration, be used against the Japanese . . ." Four days later he asked Bush, in a long and general exchange, whether the bomb should actually be used against the Japanese or tested and held as a threat. The two men agreed that the question should be carefully discussed, but Roosevelt also accepted Bush's argument that it could be "postponed for quite a time" in view of the fact that "certainly it would be inadvisable to make a threat unless we were distinctly in a position to follow it up if necessary." So twice in less than a week Roosevelt thought about *whether* and *how* to use the bomb.[80]

Six weeks later, in a fireside chat on the eve of the election, he made his one public reference to the bomb. It was cryptic and not much noticed at the time, but its meaning is plain enough now. Speaking of the need to put a lasting end to "the agony of war," he warned of terrible new weapons:

> Another war would be bound to bring even more devilish and powerful instruments of destruction to wipe out civilian populations. No coastal defenses, however strong, could prevent these silent missiles of death, fired perhaps from planes or ships at sea, from crashing deep within the United States itself.

The records at Hyde Park show that this extraordinary forecast was the product of the president's own changes in the speechwriter's draft, and it takes no great leap of imagination to suppose that a man facing a decision on the use of just such a "devilish" device would have thought about it pretty hard. Yet in the same speech Roosevelt called it an all-important goal to win the war "at the earliest moment." In 1944 he said to his secretary Grace Tully, without telling her what the Manhattan Project was about, that "if it works, and pray God it does, it will save many American lives." He also told his son James in January 1945 that there was a new weapon coming along that would make an invasion of Japan unnecessary. It would therefore be wrong to conclude that Roosevelt would not have used the bomb *in some fashion.* Nevertheless the joint memorandum with Churchill and the conversation with Bush do give the impression that the question of actually dropping an atomic bomb on a Japanese target was for Roosevelt a real question as it was not for Truman, or indeed for Stimson and Byrnes. The men at the top when the time came had the rapid ending of the war as their wholly dominant purpose.[81]

Sometime in December Roosevelt heard a recommendation for an international demonstration from Alexander Sachs, the friend who had brought him Einstein's letter back at the beginning. But he did not follow up on this conversation with anyone else; indeed he never again pressed his September question to Bush. Here, as on still larger questions of long-run atomic policy, he kept his counsel. In his last few months a posture that had been established by the combined force of his passionate concern for secrecy and his desire not to be crowded by advice was reinforced by the dreadful weight of his own growing fatigue. If something did not have to be done now, he would not do it. In the winter of 1944–45 both the first nuclear test and the final climax of the war on Japan still seemed far away. Given the orders for secrecy that he had given so explicitly in October 1941 and reinforced so strongly ever since, his own delay meant delay by everyone.[82]

But what was too far away in the winter was also too near in the spring. Consider the case of Ralph Bard: In early May he joins a committee whose first business is to plan the actions required by an expected use of the bomb. He is exposed to the problems and possibilities of warning and demonstration only on May 31; both the soldiers and the physicists, well ahead of him in both exposure and expertise, argue that sudden surprise use is more likely to work. Nowhere in this meeting or in a second discussion on June 18 is he asked to relate this problem to that of the emperor, or to that of Russian entry. Is it surprising that it takes him until June 27 to work out those connections for himself, probably helped by talks with McCloy? But by then it is really too late; his committee has long since been recorded the other way, and in any case Bard has no standing on two of the three questions he has correctly pulled together; even his second thoughts on explicit warning about the bomb have an air of indecisiveness.

Or consider the effort of McCloy. He gets his one big chance on June 18 almost by accident. He is present and prepared because Stimson, feeling unwell, has not initially intended to come. But when he does speak, at the president's direction, one part of his proposal, for an explicit warning on the bomb, is not supported by his own secretary or indeed by the president. They have already decided the matter the other way two weeks earlier. His proposal on the emperor is referred to the unenthusiastic Byrnes. McCloy impressed the president; on August 14 Truman called him up and ordered him over to the White House to attend the announcement of the Japanese surrender. After the ceremony, the president told the assistant secretary that he had given more help than anyone else. But what Truman clearly meant was help in ending the war before an invasion, not in ending it before using the bomb. Helping Harry Truman to be ready to "let 'em keep the emperor" was not trivial, but it was not the same as a full study of the fateful choices on the use of the bomb, and no one knew that better than McCloy himself. Like Bard, but with the advantage of a direct order to speak his mind, he did what he could. Through no fault of his, it was too little and too late.[83]

It is hard to avoid the conclusion that the real opportunities had been missed earlier. Let us suppose Roosevelt himself had established a council not unlike the Interim Committee, but with an earlier start and a wider charge. Might not all these possible ways to peace have been examined, at least, and possibly tried? The use of Alamogordo for demonstration and warning could have been imagined more easily before its imminence made men tense. The role of the emperor, which divided the government so sharply when stated in terms of its effect on the Japanese political future, might not have been so divisive if considered in the context of trying to start the atomic age the right way. I find it relevant that two of those most wary of the emperor, Acheson and MacLeish, later showed themselves intensely aware of the magnitude of the issues presented by nuclear weapons. In July 1945 they were not authorized parties to the secret.

In earlier months, with Soviet participation still clearly desired, it might not have been impossible to think through a pattern of combined action that was at least worth consideration—and quite possibly action. The inclusion of the Soviets is difficult; it inevitably engages wider questions about the bomb in relation to the Soviet Union that we have yet to consider. Yet American decisions to give assurances on the emperor and to demonstrate the bomb, if announced in time to Moscow, might in themselves have produced prompt Soviet action of a sort that would help bring surrender from Tokyo. Moreover the later fear of an unwanted Russian role in the main islands of Japan was not a fear of what the Soviets could insist on, but rather of what the Americans themselves might unwisely concede. The forces occupying these islands would always be those allowed ashore by the United States Navy, and in any case a Russian claim to an occupation zone in the main islands would have failed by the precedents already established in Europe. Certainly the Russians wanted such a zone, but there was no good reason, still less any need, to let them have it.

All these possible means of ending the war without using the bomb are open to question; they remain possibilities, not certainties. It remains remarkable that nothing remotely like them was ever even considered, by any senior body, or by any single individual except Ralph Bard. After the war Colonel Stimson, with the fervor of a great advocate and with me as his scribe, wrote an article intended to demonstrate that the bomb was not used without a searching consideration of alternatives. That some effort was made, and that Stimson was its linchpin, is clear. That it was as long or wide or deep as the subject deserved now seems to me most doubtful. Franklin Roosevelt, the great man who himself had the earliest recorded doubts of use without warning, was probably also the principal obstacle to such consideration.

Yet if Stimson claimed too much for the process of consideration, his basic defense remains strong, within his own assumption that in the context of the war against Japan the bomb was a weapon like any other. Its use did surely help to end the war. The attack on Hiroshima, by the persuasive evidence of the Japanese best placed to know, provided a shock of just the sort the peace party and the emperor needed to force the issue. It also served to accelerate the Soviet entry (a point that Stimson and I, among other defenders of the decision, later failed to emphasize). Stalin at Potsdam had said he would be ready by August 15, but after Hiroshima, on August 6, he decided on an earlier date and thus provided a second and nearly simultaneous shock. When the Soviet Union broadcast its declaration of war, before dawn on August 9, three Soviet armies were already invading Manchuria. The Japanese decision for surrender came less than twenty-four hours later. Efforts to measure the two shocks against each other are futile; both were powerful, and different Japanese advisers weighed them differently.[84] The two together brought a Japanese response that led in turn to the American assurance on the emperor. So in the event the use of the bomb did catalyze the rapid convergence of the three actions that both forced and permitted surrender.

Even today we cannot know *by how much* this extraordinary set of events shortened the war—whether by days, weeks, or months. None of the retrospective estimates, long or short, is entitled to high credibility; in particular one should be skeptical of the estimates of officers who thought their own preferred weapons had almost finished the job. No such guesswork, in advance, could be a basis for action or inaction at the time. I have argued my own present belief that there were things that might have been done to increase the chance of early surrender, but I have also had to recognize how hard it was to decide to do those things as matters actually stood in May, June, and July.

And if perhaps, or even probably, there were better courses, we must also recognize that we are measuring a real decision against might-have-beens. The bomb did not win the war, but it surely was responsible for its ending when it did. To those who cheered at the time—and they were the vast majority—that was what mattered most. The bomb did shorten the war; to those in charge of its development that had been its increasingly manifest destiny for years.

Moral Questions

There remain two questions of morality, one specific and one general: Even if Hiroshima was necessary, or at least defensible, what of Nagasaki? Long before Alamogordo and Potsdam it was agreed to seek authority for more than one attack in a single decision, and Truman accepted that arrangement. This decision was defended later on the ground that it was not one bomb or even two, but the prospect of many, that was decisive.[85]

But Hiroshima alone was enough to bring the Russians in; these two events together brought the crucial imperial decision for surrender, just *before* the second bomb was dropped. The news of Nagasaki arrived during a meeting that had been called by Prime Minister Suzuki Kantarō after the emperor had told him expressly that he wanted prompt surrender on whatever terms were necessary.[86] There can be little doubt that the news of a second terrible attack strengthened the peace party and further shook the diehards, but the degree of this effect cannot be gauged. It is hard to see that much could have been lost if there had been more time between the two bombs. If the matter had not been settled long since, in a time when victory seemed much less close than it did on August 7, or if the authority to order the second attack had simply been retained in Washington, one guesses that the attack on Nagasaki would have been delayed for some days; the bomb in actual use was a shock in Washington too.[87] Such a delay would have been relatively easy, and I think right.

More broadly, what if the notion of dropping the bomb on a city was simply wrong—not just hasty because there should have been warning, or gratuitous because assurance on the emperor could have done the job, or excessive because a smaller target could have been used just as well, or even dangerous because of its impact on the Russians (an argument we have yet to consider)—but just plain wrong? This fundamental question has been addressed most powerfully by Michael Walzer, and his argument deserves respectful attention, although—or perhaps because—*no one* put it forward before Hiroshima.[88]

All of the alternatives to surprise attack on a city that were proposed or considered by anyone who knew about the bomb, in 1944–45, were put forward in terms that allowed for such possible use if other alternatives failed. Roosevelt asked Bush about a demonstration and a threat, but he recognized in the same conversation that you do not make a threat you are not able to carry out if necessary. The Franck committee proposed a demonstration, and George Marshall at one point considered a uniquely military installation (as distinct from a city full of such installations), but both recognized that it might be necessary to go on to urban targets. Bard, with all his desire for a complex diplomatic demarche, never argued against using the bomb if the demarche failed, nor did McCloy. No one ever went beyond the argument that we should use up other forms of action—warnings, demonstrations, or diplomacy—before an urban attack. Szilard came closest; in a petition Truman almost surely never saw—he was already at Potsdam when it was signed on July 17—Szilard and sixty-seven colleagues asked Truman not to decide on use "without seriously considering the moral responsibilities which are involved." Yet even this petition conceded that "the war has to be brought to a successful conclusion and attacks by atomic bombs may very well be an effective method of warfare."[89] No one ever said simply, do not use it on a city *at all*.

That is what Walzer says, and he says it powerfully. To underline the strength of his conviction he accepts in its strongest form the contention that the bomb was less terrible than the kinds of warfare it helped to end. His reply is that the attack on Hiroshima was still wrong, because it violated a fundamental rule of war—that the rights of noncombatants must be respected. The citizens of Hiroshima had done nothing that justified the terrible fate that overtook them on August 6; to kill them by tens of thousands merely in order to shock their government into surrender was a violation of the great tradition of civilized warfare under which "the destruction of the innocent, whatever its purposes, is a kind of blasphemy against our deepest moral commitments."[90] Walzer grants an exception for "supreme emergency"—for the British, perhaps, when they were embattled alone against Hitler. But where, he asks, was the supreme emergency for the United States in August 1945? Even if Hiroshima was less murderous than continued firebombings and blockade, it was wrong, and all that the comparison can demonstrate is the equal wickedness of the existing "conventional" unlimited war. You might justify any one of these kinds of war against civilians if it was all that stood between you and a Hitler: If we don't do X to him, *he* will do Y (much worse) to us. But it is quite another matter to say, "If we don't do X, *we* will do Y."[91]

Walzer's is a powerful argument, but it runs as forcefully against incendiaries as against nuclear bombs. His moral argument against the use of the bomb requires an equal moral opposition to the whole long, brutal tendency of modern war makers to accept, and sometimes even to seek, the suffering of civilians in the search for victory. He may well be deeply right, but we have seen already the enormous distance between this view of war making and what Americans actually thought in 1945. To reject the climactic act as immoral Walzer must reject so very much else that his judgment becomes historically irrelevant. The change in strategy and tactics required by his argument is one that no political leader could then have imposed. By requiring too much he proves too little.

The war against Japan that had such momentum by the summer of 1945 may well have involved much immorality and in more ways than Walzer had space to catalogue. But that was the war that needed ending, and so much the weapon did. To those who were caught up in that war on both sides, it was no small service. I should declare a personal interest: If the war had gone on to a campaign in the main Japanese islands, the infantry regiment of which I was then a member would have been an early participant, and I do not to this day see how that campaign could have been readily avoided if there had been no urban bombing and no threat of an atomic bomb. If as a company commander I had ventured to take Walzer's view, with officers or men, I think I would have been alone, and even to reach the question of taking such a lonely view I would have had to have more understanding than I did.

There remains a final question: Was not the nuclear weapon, in and of itself, morally or politically different from firebombs and blockades, and in ways that should have required that it not be used? Cannot Walzer's argument be amended and strengthened, by remarking that even these "primitive" nuclear weapons were so terrible, not only in their explosive and incendiary effect but also in their radiation, that it was morally wrong to be the first to use them? And especially because the American effort had uncovered, as early as 1942, the still more terrible prospect of thermonuclear weapons, was there not also a political imperative to set an example of restraint? Although none of them ever presented such an argument in categorical terms, thoughts like these were strong among men like Franck, Szilard, and Bard. But since they all agreed that the bomb might be used on an inhabited target if all else failed to bring surrender, they accepted the terms of debate that in fact were followed. When their proposals were judged unlikely to end the war as quickly as direct military use, they could not fall back on a claim that there was a moral or political imperative against killing civilians in this new and terrible way. Even the doubters were in some measure prisoners of the overriding objective of early victory.

Yet it is right for us all to ponder these more absolute questions. I do not myself find Hiroshima more *immoral* than Tokyo or Dresden, but I find the *political* question more difficult. The nuclear world as we now know it is grimly dangerous; might it be less dangerous if Hiroshima and Nagasaki had never happened? If so, a stretchout of the anguish of war might have been a small price to pay. No one can make such an assessment with certainty: as we move on to later events we shall encounter evidence that weighs on both sides. All that we can say here is that the Americans who took part in the decisions of 1945 were overwhelmingly governed by the immediate and not the distant prospect. This dominance of clear present purpose over uncertain future consequences is a phenomenon we shall meet again.

Historically almost predestined, by the manner of its birth and its development, made doubly dramatic by the fateful coincidence that it was ready just when it might be decisive, and not headed off by any carefully designed alternative—of threat, assurance, demonstration, or all of them together—the bomb dropped on Hiroshima surely helped to end a fearful war. It was also the fierce announcement of the age of nuclear weapons. To the men who made and used it, or at least to many of them much of the time, this double meaning of what they were doing was evident, and we shall soon be looking at what they did and did not do about its import for the future. In the summer of 1945 their overriding present purpose was to shorten the war, and in that they succeeded.

Given this overriding purpose it was natural for most of them to accept the argument for using the new weapons by surprise just as soon and just as impressively as possible. The president with doubts never acted on them or set others free to work them through. The president without such doubts never looked behind the assumptions of April, the recommendations of June, or the final approvals of July, nor did anyone close to him ever press him to do so. Whether broader and more extended deliberation would have yielded a less destructive result we shall never know. Yet one must regret that no such effort was made.

III

The Americans
and Their
Wartime Allies

English-Speaking Difficulties

Although the political decisions to make a bomb and to use it were quintessentially American and were made by two presidents easily and rapidly for American reasons, these decisions and the American nuclear enterprise built around them were affected from the beginning by an international setting larger than the two controlling judgments—that Hitler must not be first and that a weapon that could shorten the war should be used. At their decisive meeting of October 9, 1941, Roosevelt and Bush "discussed at some length after-war control," and one of the major decisions of that meeting was that Roosevelt should propose a cooperative effort to Churchill.[1] No one knows what was said on that day about international control, and the question stayed well in the background for three more years. But the nuclear relation between London and Washington was already important in 1941, and its ups and downs over the four secret years before Hiroshima are full of irony and instruction.

We have seen that the extraordinary quality of the British Maud report greatly accelerated the assessments that led Bush to seek a decision from Roosevelt on October 9. It would be natural to suppose that this great contribution led on easily to harmonious Anglo-American cooperation. In the first postwar accounts, and especially in Churchill's magisterial memoirs, that is how the story was told, and in fact British scientists, few in number but high in quality, did make great contributions to the Manhattan Project. What became known only much later, primarily through the work of outstanding official historians, was that in the first two years of the full-scale American effort there was mutual incomprehension, open disagreement, and a breakdown in cooperation that resisted repeated efforts at resolution by Churchill and Roosevelt. To understand what these leaders eventually achieved, we must consider the difficulties they encountered, including some of their own making.[2]

As far as we know Roosevelt and Churchill had never mentioned the nuclear question to each other when Roosevelt made his own decision of October 9 to proceed. Two days afterward he wrote to Churchill to propose that efforts in the field be "co-ordinated or even jointly conducted," and Churchill in December sent a reply that expressed "readiness to collaborate." There seems not to have been time for this subject when the two men met in Washington after Pearl Harbor, but in June 1942 at Hyde Park they reached an oral understanding which Churchill took to include agreement that there would be a joint undertaking with equal sharing of the results. Roosevelt wrote to Bush that there had been "complete accord" in that conversation, but there is no evidence that he ever told anyone just what he thought had been settled. More than a year passed before agreement was reached and registered in a way that ensured action, and in the meantime disagreement and mutual distrust at lower levels led to the end of almost all cooperation in early 1943. On neither side did negotiators have a clear understanding of what Roosevelt and Churchill had said to each other at Hyde Park, and each of them, at different points, approved proposals from subordinates that proved strongly unacceptable to the other government.[3]

One important obstacle to understanding was that in June 1942 neither Roosevelt nor Churchill knew how much the relative positions of the two countries had changed since each government had learned of the Maud conclusions. The Americans had gone full speed ahead, while the British had wrestled indecisively with the question of where and how to proceed. Only with great reluctance did the prime minister's advisers recognize, as he put it in his description of the Hyde Park meeting, that "it seemed impossible to erect in the Island the vast and conspicuous factories that were needed." Churchill was "very glad when the President said he thought the United States would have to do it." Roosevelt was able to make this statement because just before the Hyde Park meeting he had approved a recommendation from Bush for the construction of a "four-horse" program of pilot plants, with a clear expectation that the survivors in this race would be carried into full-scale production.[4]

There is no evidence that Churchill understood in this meeting how fast the Americans had been moving, and in his memoirs he mixed things up in a highly revealing way. "I have no doubt that it was the progress that we had made in Britain and the confidence of our scientists in ultimate success, imparted to the President, that led him to his grave and fateful decision." This sentiment, as we have seen, is entirely accurate as applied to Roosevelt's basic go-ahead decision of October 9, 1941. It is entirely wrong as applied to Roosevelt's production decision of June 1942. Moreover, the British government had no direct connection with either decision; it had not encouraged the former, and the prime minister's talk with the president came after the latter. Between October and June the American project had taken on a life of its own in a way that Churchill did not understand until more than a year later.[5]

Neither Churchill nor Roosevelt appears to have reported the Hyde Park conversation of June 1942 to subordinates at the time. My own guess is that Roosevelt believed that he had said nothing that went beyond the generalities already exchanged in letters, while Churchill, to whom the matter was much more important, became heavily beset by more immediate issues. On the day after the Hyde Park meeting, back at the White House, he learned that in North Africa the entire British garrison of Tobruk had fallen to Rommel, and in the following weeks he was preoccupied successively by the resulting parliamentary debate, by the threat to Egypt, by plans for the landing in North Africa, and by preparations for his first meeting with Stalin. Compared to these pressing realities, the nuclear project, however portentous, was remote and hypothetical.

In this situation the question of the ways and means of nuclear cooperation was left to subordinates with conflicting concerns. For Bush and Conant the central purpose was to get a bomb in time to help win the war, and they were already hard pressed to get the allocation of resources, and above all the overriding priorities for scarce materials, that their explosively expanding enterprise required. The British, on the other hand, were now hoping for a pilot plant essentially their own, to be built with American resources in the United States. When this proposal came forward with Churchill's approval from John Anderson in August, Bush and Conant concluded at once that there was no room for a British horse on their already crowded track. If such a British proposal had been made in quick response to Roosevelt's letter of October 1941, Bush and Conant would probably have reacted differently, but in the ten months required to produce this proposal, the Americans had moved so fast that they now had all they could do to manage an American effort that had accelerated beyond their expectations. A program of research and experiment running at a level of less than one million dollars a year had expanded more than a hundredfold. Nonetheless the Americans still wanted cooperation wherever it would help to get a bomb faster, and Bush invited Anderson to send an emissary to Washington to discuss "the best method of utilizing to the full scientific resources of both countries in this important undertaking."[6]

There followed, in November and December, one of the least successful negotiations in the history of Anglo-American relations. The two principal negotiators were W. A. Akers for Britain and James B. Conant for the United States, both honest believers in Anglo-American cooperation but with different views of the purpose of such cooperation. For Conant cooperation was important only insofar as it could contribute to winning the war. That interest is demonstrated in his initial skepticism about the wartime utility of nuclear fission, his later commitment to the most rapid possible development of the weapon, and his untroubled acceptance of using it against Japan.

Akers wanted cooperation not for winning of the war as such, but to advance the British interest in having a postwar weapon. Like Anderson and Cherwell, he had at first wanted a made-in-Britain bomb, but a long visit to the United States in early 1942 had persuaded him that a joint project in the United States offered the only path to wartime British progress. He had come now to get the largest possible British role in the American enterprise; he proposed unlimited British access to the whole American effort.

Conant saw no contribution to winning the war in this proposal and correctly understood that Akers was moved by a British postwar interest; he further suspected quite wrongly that this British interest was primarily commercial. Akers had been the research director of Imperial Chemical Industries, and Conant thought he was showing an especially intense interest in the very facilities—separation plants and production reactors—that might have most to do with the postwar position of British industry. Akers's real interest was political, not commercial, but his American listeners did not hear him so.[7]

As the negotiations continued, Conant came to be more concerned with limiting British access than with devising means of cooperation. His concern was intensified by a heavy sense of responsibility for the secrecy of the program and by his personal support for the principle of "compartmentalization" now being enforced by General Groves throughout the project. Why should British experts have rights of general access that were being denied to Americans? He continued to believe that a British presence would be welcome but only where that presence would be a contribution to the pursuit of a wartime bomb. He also thought it would be wrong to grant access to any part of the project simply for the purpose of strengthening the British postwar position.

Conant shared his concerns with Bush, and Bush took the matter to the president, proposing an American policy of "limited interchange" that would be governed by the already established general principle that technical sharing would be authorized whenever it would help the war effort. Bush carefully provided Roosevelt with a paper from Akers that showed the British position, and he warned that restriction of interchange would bring British complaint, but he made Conant's recommendation his own. Roosevelt approved the recommendation in writing on December 28, and Conant moved rapidly to execute it, preparing a memorandum that he shared informally with Akers in early January. This Conant memorandum has a harsh sound even today, much more so than the memorandum he had written two months earlier as the negotiations began.[8] Where the British had no present programs, as in plutonium, bomb making, and all production processes except gaseous diffusion, they were to be excluded completely. Exchange on the permitted subject of diffusion would be under the control of General Groves, and basic scientific information would be exchanged only with Conant's direct approval, except for exchanges on the use of heavy water in chain reactions (where the British knew more than the Americans).

The British in London found Conant's position wholly unacceptable. Akers himself recommended an attempt to live with the new rules in the hope that they would be relaxed as British help proved its value, but Anderson sharply disagreed. The new American position, he reported to Churchill, "has come as a bombshell and is quite intolerable." Most of his senior scientific advisers agreed, and their reaction was the exact reciprocal of Conant's: Where the Americans had seen an unjustified British attempt to get access to the fruits of American effort and expenditure, the British scientists, after a review of the American proposals, "felt sure that they were designed to give the United States a position of control in the Tube Alloys [atomic energy] field and to ensure to themselves the sole use of the results of the work both as a military weapon and for industrial purposes." There must be an effort to "restore" complete collaboration, and this effort should be undertaken by the prime minister with the president; the two were about to meet at Casablanca. Meanwhile it would weaken the British bargaining position to continue limited cooperation on the terms Conant offered, so communication stopped, except for a few scientists on both sides, in Canada and Chicago, who did not get the word and kept on as before. There followed an eight-month breakdown of communication that was good for neither the wartime effort nor the postwar British program.[9]

At Casablanca in January Churchill returned to the charge. He spoke to both Roosevelt and Hopkins and received assurances that matters would be put right. But back in Washington Hopkins discovered that Bush and Conant strongly defended their position, and he passed their argument back to London. At the end of February Churchill replied with a detailed historical claim for Roosevelt's original notion of "a coordinated or even jointly conducted" effort, but Hopkins had not responded further when Churchill came once more to Washington in May. There he renewed his direct appeal to Roosevelt and reported the result to Anderson as he had not done after Hyde Park in 1942:

> The President agreed that the exchange of information on Tube Alloys should be resumed and that the enterprise should be considered a joint one, to which both countries would contribute their best endeavours. I understood that his ruling would be based upon the fact that this weapon may well be developed in time for the present war and that it thus falls within the general agreement covering the interchange of research and invention secrets.[10]

This message suggests that the president and the prime minister, consciously or unconsciously, had successfully squared the circle of the arguments of their advisers. They had agreed that cooperation would be resumed, but not on the ground that anyone's postwar position was at stake; it was justified because of the wartime possibilities. In effect the two men had supported the principles of Bush and Conant and the practices desired by Anderson and Akers. Churchill must have been well pleased with this result.

Yet still no order came to Bush from the White House. Instead Bush had two conversations there, one on May 25 with Hopkins and Cherwell and one on June 24 with Roosevelt. He came away from both with no change at all in his December orders to limit interchange. Of these two talks we have only Bush's accounts, and they shed a puzzling light on Roosevelt's decision making.[11]

On May 25, reporting that "the Prime Minister had formally raised the question of interchange on S-1" (the American name for atomic energy), Hopkins asked Bush to come and "confer with Lord Cherwell in his office to see if there could be a meeting of the minds." There followed a conversation which showed Hopkins "for the first time" just where the real issue was. In response to questions from Bush, Cherwell agreed that the central British interest was to be able to develop the weapon quickly *after* the war. There was a wartime element in the problem, he insisted, because if the Americans would not provide the information needed for the purpose, including manufacturing information, the British "might have to divert some of their war effort in order to get it." Cherwell insisted that it was not commercial advantage the British wanted, but prompt access to a weapon, and the reason he gave was that the British needed to protect their own security as against "some other country" that might be far along in development.

Bush left the meeting believing that Hopkins would report this conversation to FDR; he told Hopkins he "would sit tight and do nothing unless and until I heard from him further on the matter." He did not hear from Hopkins, but one month later, on June 24, the president invited him to lunch. In the course of a general review of the project he asked Bush "how relations with the British now stood." Bush replied by asking the president if Hopkins had reported the conversation with Cherwell. Roosevelt said he had not and professed himself astounded when Bush explained that "Cherwell had placed the whole affair on an after-the-war military basis." The president returned to the matter several times and "seemed to be amazed that they could take such a point of view." He also "nodded rather vigorously" when Bush said "we might as well sit tight on British relations." Bush concluded that he clearly had "no instructions to do anything except to proceed as we are."

What Roosevelt was doing in this conversation we cannot know for sure, but we can be clear on one point: He was not dealing openly with Bush. He knew that he had made a fresh agreement with Churchill; he almost surely knew that Bush would have objections, and he probably raised the question as a means of finding out just what those objections might be. He had certainly talked to Hopkins—although not necessarily about Cherwell's views—if not back on May 25, then in the days before he sent for Bush. On June 17 Hopkins had cabled to Churchill that he expected the question to be "disposed of completely" in a few days, and it seems probable that the continuing delay came from some lingering concern in Roosevelt's own mind. He did not dispose of the matter, and he did send for Bush. Possibly, as the official historians surmise, he intended to tell Bush of the new agreement with Churchill and held back when he heard of Cherwell's argument and Bush's view of it. But we do not know.[12]

What we do know is that after this lunch nothing happened at the White House until Churchill pressed the president yet again, on July 9. Roosevelt asked Hopkins to prepare an answer for dispatch on the same day. Ten days later Hopkins told him he had no choice but to "go through with" his "firm commitment to Churchill," and on July 20 the president signed a letter instructing Bush to "renew, in an inclusive manner, the full exchange of information with the British Government regarding tube alloys." This instruction was not limited to wartime purposes. But by then Churchill himself had raised the matter with Bush in London, with remarkable and quite different results.[13]

In the middle of July Bush went to London on anti-submarine business, and Churchill sent for him to talk about tube alloys. Bush told Churchill he should discuss the matter with Stimson, who was also in London and already engaged in a series of fierce but friendly arguments with Churchill over plans for the invasion of Europe. Churchill pursued this suggestion at once, during a daylong visit with Stimson to troops in the Dover area. Then on July 22 he convened a full-dress parley—Churchill, Anderson, and Cherwell on the British side, and

Stimson, Bush, and Harvey Bundy for the Americans; Harvey Bundy, my father, was Stimson's special assistant and Bush's point of contact to the secretary. None of those present had yet heard of the decision Roosevelt had made two days before. "Now at last in London," remarks the British historian Margaret Gowing, "the right people seemed to be meeting." The meetings led to a new level of understanding on both sides and laid the basis for a formal written agreement between Roosevelt and Churchill at Quebec the next month.[14]

The British learned that Bush and Conant had quite wrongly concluded that the British were aiming largely at postwar commercial advantage. There were certainly British technical people who cared deeply about the prospects for atomic power, but at the policy level it was not the prospect of postwar energy but the need for a postwar British weapon that was decisive. Churchill drove the point home by proposing that in view of the relative size of the two efforts any decision on postwar commercial advantages should rest with the president alone.

The British also showed their understanding of the American desire to justify any continued cooperation in terms of the search for a wartime weapon. What Cherwell had rejected as a matter of principle in May they now explicitly accepted. Churchill told Bush in their first meeting that he did not "give a damn" about postwar matters, and this position was maintained in later meetings. Bush and, still more, Stimson were prepared to respond generously to this renunciation.

But at the same time the Americans were left in no doubt of the deep British interest in having a strong position with respect to making weapons at the end of the war. Churchill spoke to Bush about "the threat from the East," and he made it clear on July 22 that his basic concern was that Britain be able to maintain its independence in the future. "Unless Americans and Britons worked together, Germany or Russia might win the race for a weapon they could use for international blackmail," and "unless the Americans agreed to full interchange," he threatened, "Britain would launch a parallel development."[15] This threat was weak—the prospects for a separate British effort had been canvassed in the grim months between the Conant memorandum and the May 25 talk with Roosevelt, and they were not promising. British technical and economic resources were already stretched too thin by the war.

But Churchill's appeal was not in vain; it was almost perfectly designed to appeal to Stimson's sense of fair play. The secretary of war understood the strain on British resources; by pressing ardently for the great cross-channel attack he was himself adding to that strain. He understood why the British could not ignore their postwar interest in a weapon that might indeed be decisive, and he did not believe war and postwar concerns could in fact be separated as sharply as Bush argued. So he was sympathetic to Churchill's argument, and both Bush and the British felt that sympathy. The meeting adjourned with an agreement to work on a paper that might be signed by Roosevelt and Churchill.[16]

Reports of Roosevelt's decision of July 20 reached the British on July 27 and Bush on July 28. They had a healthy and encouraging effect on both sides, especially as no one in London knew that the president's decision had no relation to the Churchill-Stimson-Bush conversations. Roosevelt told Churchill, "I have arranged satisfactorily for tube alloys" and suggested he send his "top man . . . to get full understanding."[17] His instruction to Bush, "to renew" full exchange, was garbled in decoding and came out "to review," which Bush was now quite ready to do. Even if there had been no garble the renewed cooperation would probably have taken essentially the form foreshadowed in the meeting of July 22. Bush would have seen no reason to give up what had already been agreed. Early in August Anderson arrived in Washington with a Churchillian draft, and in four days he and Bush worked out the final language of an agreement that Churchill and Roosevelt signed later in the month at Quebec. Insofar as it related to the terms of wartime cooperation the agreement was acceptable even to Conant.

What made the Quebec Agreement satisfactory to the British was its promise of an extensive renewal of "full and effective collaboration," a promise reinforced in their eyes by the appointment of Stimson as the chairman of a new Combined Policy Committee. What made it satisfactory to the Americans was that the stated purpose governing all forms of collaboration was to bring "the Tube Alloys project to fruition at the earliest possible moment." Moreover commercial advantage to the British was forsworn, except as the president might later determine. A further protection was the provision that with respect to large-scale plants, interchange of information would be regulated by "ad hoc arrangements" governed by the criterion of their contribution to "earliest possible fruition." In addition Hopkins persuaded Churchill to accept Bush's stipulation that a respected scientist, not Akers, should be the senior British professional in Washington. The appointment fell to Sir James Chadwick, and all went well in the two years that followed before Hiroshima. The Manhattan Project was reinforced by British scientists and engineers, few in number (about fifty) but high in quality. They went where they were wanted, to the gaseous diffusion headquarters in New York, to Lawrence's electromagnetic effort in California, where Oliphant became Lawrence's deputy, and most of all to Los Alamos, where British scientists were full participants in most aspects of the work of bomb design. It was under British auspices that Niels Bohr himself visited Los Alamos in early 1944 and gave to the enterprise not only the direct support of his active participation in several aspects of bomb design, but also the deep encouragement of the sympathetic presence of the greatest living nuclear physicist.[18]

No one can tell just how much help the British scientists brought— the only important measure is time, and in the nature of the enterprise no one can say how much time was saved by this or that contribution. One senior British scientist estimated that "the British contribution at Los Alamos may possibly have hastened by two or three months the time when the first bombs were ready." Even one month would be a lot, given the value the Americans placed on speed and the timing of events in the summer of 1945. If we add in the earlier influence of the Maud report, it is not at all unreasonable to accept the estimate of an unnamed American scientist that is reported by Margaret Gowing: "The British share in the work of producing the first atomic bomb had certainly shortened by at least a year the time which would otherwise have been required." Even if we cut that estimate in half, there would have been no bomb in 1945 without the British.[19]

Chadwick understood from the first that the way for the British to get the largest return in knowledge and understanding was quite simply to make the best contribution they could to the project as a whole. Not all of his offers of help were accepted, and there were large areas like plutonium production in which the British never did participate, but Chadwick earned the full confidence of Groves, and by the end of the war the British participants had a vastly greater understanding of the field than they could have obtained in separate efforts at home. Early in 1944 Chadwick recommended the transfer to America of all the nuclear physicists wanted by the Americans. As zealous in the execution of the Quebec Agreement as he had been in its creation, Churchill approved: "Act as proposed forthwith."[20]

Thus in the event large-scale cooperation served the interests of both countries: The Americans got the bomb faster, and the British learned more. This was not at all a case in which one side's gain was the other's loss. Why was it so hard to work out for so long, and then so easy? One can offer answers at the levels of personality, of process, of perception, and of high policy. If the British had sent Chadwick and not Akers in October 1942 the breakdown might never have occurred. If Conant had been Stimson, or even Bush, it might also have been better; the Harvard president was curiously stiff in this matter. And if matters had not been held in so tight a circle in both countries, differences and misunderstandings would surely have been resolved more rapidly. By the end of 1942 the senior British residents in Washington—Lord Halifax the ambassador and Sir John Dill the soldier—had an extraordinary understanding of Americans and were themselves deeply trusted. No one asked for their help.

Another easy target is the process of decision making on both sides. In approving restrictions on exchange in December, Roosevelt almost surely intended nothing as draconian as Conant's memorandum of January 7, and his new decisions with Churchill on May 25 would have been more rapidly executed if he had talked to Bush beforehand, not a month later. Here as on many other matters Roosevelt was handicapped by his own distaste for due process, and in this case he made matters worse by explicitly reserving all decisions of policy to himself. For this reason Churchill's direct appeal to the president was powerful but uncertain, and it was no accident that Churchill succeeded in getting an operational agreement only after he himself brought Bush and Stimson into the negotiations.

Roosevelt was disorderly, but the British were excessively deliberate. It was a long way from the immediate perceptions of a Chadwick or an Akers through committees in London to the prime minister. The realities of attitude and activity in America were not well understood through these channels. Moreover the British at the political level were slow in understanding the difficulties experienced in their own program during the year that followed the great intellectual achievement of the Maud report. The vast disparity of late 1942 was the product of delay and indecision in Britain as well as speed and forcefulness in the United States, and neither phenomenon was quickly reported to Churchill. Cherwell, his closest adviser, appears to have grossly misunderstood what was and was not practicable—the contrast with the extraordinarily clear technical channel that Bush provided to Roosevelt is striking.[21]

Between the submission of the Maud report and the arrival of Chadwick in Washington, over a period of two years, the British program was essentially directionless, and only in the latter part of that time was the primary problem that of relations with the Americans. The program expanded rapidly, by ordinary standards, from an expenditure of 20,000 pounds over the eighteen months of Maud to over 400,000 a year in early 1943.[22] But it is impossible to read Professor Gowing's scrupulous account of what went on in that program without concluding that in the main the scientists concerned were doing what interested them as individuals. Relations with industrial contractors were loose; priorities were much too low to ensure that schedules were met; there was no active commander—and indeed, no clear mission. This failure was not the fault of the Americans.

Nor was it, at the root, a failure merely of personalities or process. It was the result of reluctance to make a profoundly difficult choice. It is easy to see in retrospect that there was really no way at all for Britain to produce a wartime bomb. Equally there was no way for the country that had produced the Maud report to abandon the enterprise. To find the right middle course was a much harder matter than any of the quick command decisions that Bush sought and got from Roosevelt. FDR had only to say yes to repeated recommendations of full speed ahead; that took courage, trust, and self-confidence. The British had to face a much more subtle set of questions. They could not make a wartime bomb; they were determined not to drop out of the field. What should they do? It is no wonder that sharp answers were slow to come.

By ordinary standards of national behavior the wonder is not that the British government took some time to find and set its course, but rather that in only two years it found the most effective course of action available, and successfully negotiated its acceptance by the United States. The initial wariness of Chadwick, the persistent and self-deceiving national pride of Cherwell, the overambitious initial bargaining of Anderson and Akers, and above all the deep sense, shared by all of them, that somehow a distinctly British enterprise must be preserved—all this is far more usual in the affairs of nations than the boldness that infused the British approach after Churchill himself took charge. It is unfortunate that he did not take charge sooner and more completely. It seems doubtful, for example, that the prime minister himself would ever have chosen the tactic of rejecting specific proposals for technical discussion that Sir John Anderson imposed to protect the British bargaining position in early 1943. This tactic had no great impact on the American effort, but if Bush, Conant, and Groves had been less cool and confident than they were, it might have had truly damaging results; it was certainly inconsistent with the principle of putting the wartime effort first. More important, it was intrinsically narrow and ungenerous—at least as narrow as the Conant memorandum itself—and thus inconsistent with Churchill's whole approach to the issue. No less than his countrymen was he concerned with long-run British interests, but what he understood all the way—it had been the guiding star of his grand strategy since 1940—was that the right way to deal with the Americans was to win their trust and then rely on it. That understanding was the key to the Quebec Agreement and to Chadwick's masterly conduct of the ensuing British effort. It was no small step to have carried this political insight from the affairs of a wartime alliance into the first international agreement on the production and use of nuclear weapons.

Compared to Churchill's leap of imagination, the decision required of Roosevelt in 1943 was much smaller, but still not trivial. His own basic course was set; he had only to accept the proposition that exchange of information with the British—which he favored instinctively—was justified and politically defensible because it would help in the great American wartime effort. That it took so much time to work out this proposition was the result of his failure to deal early and openly with Bush; it was not the consequence of any basic difficulty. The fifth paragraph of the Quebec Agreement, which defined the terms of this wartime cooperation, was the product of rapid but careful negotiation between Anderson and Bush in early August and rested on what both sides had suggested along the way. It was much more generously worded than the Conant memorandum of January, but it left operational decisions on the ways and means of cooperation just where they had been before—in the hands of the Americans. The Combined Policy Committee it established never came close to a decision that its American members did not support, and at the operational level Chadwick never appealed upward from a decision by Groves. Some of the British had hoped that the Combined Policy Committee might play a general supervisory role over the whole enterprise, but the notion was fanciful, and Bush had obtained Anderson's explicit agreement that the committee's existence would not "interfere with the control of the American programme by the Corps of Engineers of the United States Army."[23] Roosevelt—and quite separately Stimson—had responded to the spirit of Churchill's appeal, and this response eventually came to be understood and loyally supported by all concerned; so the spirit that began with Churchill came to inform the substance of wartime cooperation.

Indeed as Churchill grappled with this vast question his political imagination carried him far beyond the particular bargain of the fifth paragraph and even beyond the commercial disclaimer embodied in the fourth. The really startling paragraphs of the Quebec Agreement are its first three, and all three had sprung full blown from the head of the prime minister on July 22.[24]

These three paragraphs of the Quebec Agreement constitute the strongest assurances that any political leaders have ever given to each other in the age of nuclear weapons:

> We will never use this agency against each other . . . we will not use it against third parties without each other's consent . . . we will not either of us communicate any information about Tube Alloys [atomic energy as a whole, not just bombs] to third parties except by mutual consent.

All three undertakings were equal, reciprocal, and sweeping. Although governed, at least loosely, by a "whereas" clause describing wartime objectives, these clauses were not in themselves limited in time, and it is clear that Churchill wanted no such limitation. A year later he sought and got from Roosevelt an explicit agreement to full postwar cooperation.[25]

The limitation Churchill did want was that this club should have only two members. The intensity of his conviction on this point was to grow over the following two years, but already in July 1943 his governing motive was his fear that Britain might somehow be overtaken by Germany or Russia; against that threat he wanted first to share in what the Americans were learning, and second to keep the secret from all others. In Churchill's mind, from the beginning, this was to be a private Anglo-American partnership with a friendly but secondary Canadian participation, and it is most unlikely that he was blind to the most important consequence of the provision that neither government would inform a third party except by mutual consent: Roosevelt had forsworn any independent decision to open the subject with the Soviet Union. This was a first step in a fateful direction.

Yet what deserves equal notice is that the language of these three paragraphs did not require a permanently wary view of third parties. On the contrary, precisely these propositions, if they had endured into the postwar world, could have been the central elements of a multilateral agreement among victorious nations determined to have nuclear weapons for themselves: The three or four parties would never use these weapons against one another; they would never use them against anyone else without unanimous agreement; there would be no nuclear assistance—no information even—for outsiders unless all the insiders agreed. So enlarged, these three propositions could have been a multilateral postwar agreement among states with nuclear weapons: a treaty against the common dangers of nuclear war and nuclear proliferation. Principles so accurately fitting a possible wider alliance against nuclear danger compel attention, and even admiration, across forty years.

Admiration must promptly be tempered by an awareness that in their Quebec form—secret, bilateral, and personal—these principles had shallow roots and a short life. They were Churchill's, and by quick consent Roosevelt's, but neither man moved to enlist further support even within his closest circle of advisers, and both neglected difficulties that would be presented later. The largest of these was whether the Russians were to be partners or adversaries, but other troubles appeared. When Churchill promised not to give information to third parties he was neglecting an existing British agreement on patents with the French. When Roosevelt agreed that the weapon would be used only by common consent he was neglecting the danger that both Congress and the country might be skeptical of any purely presidential pledge of this sort—a skepticism that was predicted in May 1945 by the first man of congressional temper who learned of this clause, James Byrnes.[26] Yet Churchill was not receiving a pledge of decisive value: When bombs were ready, two years later, it was clearly understood on both sides that British approval was hardly more than a formality. Only the pledge never to use the weapon against each other was free of difficulty, and after all it simply asserted the self-evident.

Roosevelt appears to have accepted these three paragraphs without much reflection. They came from Bush as part of the document worked out with Anderson, but in his covering note Bush took care not to offer advice on them—or indeed on the commercial disclaimer.

Of these four points he said only "I have encountered some strong opinions concerning them, but you will undoubtedly wish to consult on this broad aspect of the matter directly rather than through me."[27] Here Bush was reflecting a conviction which he and Conant shared at the time that neither of them had any standing to advise on such political matters. Still there was an element of warning in the sentence and a suggestion that Roosevelt might wish to consult others—Hopkins and Stimson would have been in Bush's mind. But if FDR took this hint, we have no record of it.

Reflecting on these matters nine years later in a lecture at the London School of Economics, Conant offered what he called "a cautious word" on the way they were handled. The question was still "delicate"; indeed the Quebec Agreement was still secret. He took note of what we have neglected here, the significant role of the Canadians as a friendly third party with uranium mines, and he went on to suggest, correctly, that "troubles, misunderstandings, and bad feeling might have been avoided by greater frankness at the outset." He also thought things would have gone better "if at least a committee of the Senate of the United States had been apprised of the U.S.-British wartime negotiations when they took place." Then he went on to the heart of his criticism:

> As a very humble observer from a distance of what occurred at high levels in 1943, I thought then and I still think that a treaty should have been drawn between the three nations involved [the United States, Great Britain, and Canada], a treaty dealing with everything even distantly related to atomic energy.[28]

The sentence is both sweeping and cryptic. A treaty could have been "drawn," but could the Senate have considered it in secret? And was not the secrecy of the enterprise still absolutely essential, to Conant just as much as to Roosevelt, in 1943? It is doubtful whether this sentence was intended to mean that a treaty should have been completed in 1943. What we know of Conant's views suggests rather that he wanted the matter pursued on two quite different levels: The one right wartime goal should be a wartime weapon, and postwar considerations deserved separate attention at a higher level. So it seems likely that what he wanted in 1943 was not a treaty, but preparation for a treaty; a two-man exchange of secret but sweeping pledges going far beyond wartime needs may well have seemed exactly the wrong way of pursuing that larger goal.

But we do not need to know Conant's exact meaning, or precisely what he thought in 1943, to know that he is struggling here with an absolutely crucial question—the question of the legitimacy and durability of international arrangements on nuclear weapons—and that exactly this question got short shrift from Roosevelt in 1943. Neither then nor later did the president discuss any clause of the Quebec Agreement with another American in a way that has left a record. For Churchill the agreement was vital; he regularly tested all nuclear proposals against its terms. Roosevelt took no such pains and probably gave little thought to the long-term possibilities and problems that were latent in its first three provisos. In effect the agreement became not a basis for the careful construction of a long-term policy but a substitute for any such effort. Of all Franklin Roosevelt's nuclear decisions the gravest, after his basic decision to make bombs, may have been his constant refusal to examine such questions of policy—or let others examine them—one step further than was immediately necessary. Nowhere is the result of this attitude more obvious than in the unexamined, fragile and ambiguous grandeur of the first three paragraphs of the Quebec Agreement.

Shall We Discuss It with the Russians?

We draw near the end of the story of the secret secret. Only one part of it remains to be retold and reconsidered—we need to look at something that did not happen. The government that was making the bomb never discussed the undertaking or its prospects with its most powerful wartime ally until July 25, 1945, nine days after Alamogordo and twelve before Hiroshima, and the discussion on that day, as we have already seen, was minimal—a very few sentences exchanged between Truman and Stalin at Potsdam. Neither the nuclear nature of the weapon nor its postwar significance was mentioned by either man. "We have a new weapon of great force"—"Glad to hear it, I hope you'll make good use of it against Japan." The exchange is so short and so far from the true importance of the matter that it amounts to deliberate trivialization, certainly by Truman and probably by Stalin too. Why did it happen this way, and what difference does it make? The first question is less difficult than the second.

The two central figures in most of this story, once again, are Roosevelt and Churchill. No member of either government (spies excepted) would have dreamed of talking to any Soviet official on this matter without direct instruction from the top; more than that, the conditioned expectation of all who were privy to the secret was that any such initiative must come essentially from Roosevelt to Stalin; in their different ways both American and British advisers recognized the decisive role of the American president with respect to any disclosures about an overwhelmingly American undertaking. The undertaking against disclosures to third parties was reciprocal, but not evenly so.

The man responsible for Roosevelt's first serious encounter with the problem was Niels Bohr, who had been at once impressed and profoundly disturbed by what he learned on his arrival in London and what he saw when he came to the United States at the end of 1943.[29] He had no trouble, then or later, with the wartime effort and its wartime purpose; to that effort he made his own contribution. What engaged him much more deeply was the great opportunity for new international cooperation and the great danger of a new arms race. The best chance for a good result was for the United States and Great Britain to open early private discussion with the Russians, looking toward effective international controls. Bohr recognized—indeed he insisted—that a safe world would have to be an open world, and he understood the profound change in Soviet behavior that would be necessary for that, but in his view this obvious difficulty only increased the urgency of making the effort.[30]

It was not Bohr, but Justice Felix Frankfurter on his behalf, who first presented Bohr's concerns to Roosevelt. Frankfurter and Bohr had known each other before the war, and when Bohr renewed their acquaintance, Frankfurter made it clear that he knew of the nuclear enterprise. Bohr seized the opportunity to express his concerns, and Frankfurter decided to discuss the matter with the president. As usual we have only Frankfurter's report of this conversation of February 1944, and unfortunately that report was written fifteen months later, after Bohr himself had come under unjustified suspicion of indiscretion, partly because of his talk with Frankfurter. The Frankfurter memorandum thus has a faintly defensive tone, but there is no reason to doubt its essential veracity. The president and the justice talked for an hour and a half. Frankfurter was an authentic intimate, but even for him that was a long time, and he came away with a strong impression that Roosevelt had welcomed his approach. He vividly remembered Roosevelt's remark that the whole thing "worried him to death." Roosevelt agreed to see Bohr at some later date; he agreed that "the solution of this problem might be more important than all the schemes for a world organization," and he agreed that Bohr should be told that "he, Bohr, might tell our friends in London that the President was anxious to explore ways for achieving proper safeguards in relation to X [atomic energy]."[31]

Both Roosevelt and Churchill set great store by the privacy and directness of their communications, so it is highly unlikely that Roosevelt intended this authorization to constitute a new channel from himself to the prime minister. But to Bohr and his British advisers Frankfurter's report had a different ring. Lord Halifax, the British ambassador in Washington, had taken the time to get a clear understanding of Bohr's concerns and had come to share them, but he had warned Bohr that "any initiative would almost certainly have to come from President Roosevelt."[32] In this context, what Roosevelt said to Frankfurter assumed high importance. It could be taken as just the triggering expression of interest that was needed. Halifax and Anderson agreed that Bohr should carry Roosevelt's "message" to London.

In April and May Bohr tried, and except at the summit he succeeded. Anderson promptly agreed with him, persuaded at least in part by a report from Halifax; he listened to Bohr and was spurred to further efforts. Bohr also talked to Cherwell, and to South African Field Marshal Jan Smuts, whose standing among the statesmen of the empire was such that Churchill in this period agreed to include him among the knowledgeable. Like Anderson, Cherwell and Smuts came to believe that there should be talks with Russia. All three, in their ways, urged this course on Churchill.[33] They also persuaded him to receive Bohr, who had come to put a very high value on the direct personal delivery of his message from Roosevelt.

The meeting between Churchill and Bohr, on May 16, 1944, is one of the first and most famous failures in the arduous process by which scientist and statesman seek to understand each other on nuclear dangers. Bohr was taken to Number Ten by Cherwell, and the prime minister promptly derailed the discussion. First he picked a quarrel with Cherwell for having arranged the meeting in an irregular way and then went on to accuse his adviser of wanting to reproach him for concessions he had made to get the Quebec Agreement. All this was meaningless to Bohr, who never got started on his carefully prepared formal statement. "All that Churchill seemed to gather was that [Bohr] was worried about the likely state of the post-war world and that he wanted to tell the Russians about the progress towards the bomb." Bohr walked away feeling that "he scolded us like two schoolboys."[34]

But the meeting did not fail merely because Churchill was in a bad temper or even because Bohr's extraordinary methods of exposition required a sympathetic and patient listener. The difficulty of listening to Bohr was legendary among physicists; he had a tendency to mumble in a low voice, and even his written English often had wonderful Danish convolutions. In a formal memorandum to Roosevelt, dated July 3, 1944, Bohr described the German nuclear effort thus:

> Although thorough preparations were made by a most energetic scientific effort, disposing of expert knowledge and considerable material resources, it appeared from all information available to us, that at any rate in the initial for Germany so favourable stages of the war it was never by the Government deemed worth while to attempt the immense and hazardous technical enterprise which an accomplishment of the project would require.[35]

The paragraph is accurate and shows how well informed Bohr had made himself, but are we to believe that Roosevelt read it easily—or at all?

But Churchill was not held up by difficulties of language; when he wanted to overcome those he could. Nor did the meeting fail because Churchill, in the pressure of the last weeks before Normandy, thought the subject unimportant. It failed because the prime minister had already made up his mind and did not want to hear further argument. He thought that atomic energy was very important indeed, and he thought it would be wrong to discuss it with the Russians. He had said so already in at least three pungent minutes to his closest associates, and he did not want to hear further discussion.

The basic argument for Bohr's position had been put to Churchill by Anderson in a powerful and tactful memorandum about two months earlier: It was time to think about international control; to think about international control was to think about the Russians; there was much to be said for telling them the bare fact of our expectation that we would presently have a "devastating weapon." There was danger in not taking this course, and little risk in taking it. The prime minister vehemently disagreed; he "peppered the minute with disapproving comments and wrote at the end simply 'I do not agree.' " Anderson tried again in a different mode a month later: He again asked for study of the problem of control and argued that it would be useful at least to "break the ice" on the subject with the Americans. Here, though he did not say so, Anderson was acting directly on Bohr's report of Roosevelt's interest. Churchill refused to "widen the circle" so as to study the problem, or to send any message to Roosevelt. When Cherwell, much more circumspectly, asked him to let Smuts consider the problem of international control, he agreed, but only with warnings; the secret must be preserved and the centerpiece of everything must be the preservation of the American connection.[36]

Bohr returned to Washington and eventually, on August 26, he had his long-sought interview with Roosevelt.[37] The president showed both courtesy and understanding. He agreed that there must be an approach to Stalin, and he thought Stalin, as a realist, would understand the meaning of this new scientific revolution; he had heard—probably from Frankfurter—of Churchill's attitude, but Churchill had changed his mind before. Roosevelt said he would be meeting soon with Churchill and would then discuss an early invitation to the Russians. He invited Bohr to keep in communication with him and said he would like to see him again after the meeting with Churchill. Bohr was understandably delighted, but not for long.

Roosevelt and Churchill met at Quebec on September 11 and continued their talks more privately at Hyde Park on September 18–19. At the end of this meeting they initialed an astonishing memorandum, which no other American above the rank of filing officer saw until after Roosevelt's death:

TUBE ALLOYS

*Aide-mémoire of Conversation Between the President
and the Prime Minister at Hyde Park,
September 18, 1944.*

1. The suggestion that the world should be informed regarding Tube Alloys, with a view to an international agreement regarding its control and use, is not accepted. The matter should continue to be regarded as of the utmost secrecy; but when a "bomb" is finally available, it might perhaps, after mature consideration, be used against the Japanese, who should be warned that this bombardment will be repeated until they surrender.

2. Full collaboration between the United States and the British Government in developing Tube Alloys for military and commercial purposes should continue after the defeat of Japan unless and until terminated by joint agreement.

3. Enquiries should be made regarding the activities of Professor Bohr and steps taken to ensure that he is responsible for no leakage of information, particularly to the Russians.[38]

This agreement was still more casual in origin, sweeping in commitment, and fragile in effect than the Quebec Agreement. It is clearly Churchillian in three vital respects: its commitment to full postwar collaboration, its rejection of any change from "utmost secrecy," and its totally unfounded suspicion of Bohr. There is no problem in understanding Churchill's position; the difficulty is in understanding how far Roosevelt shared it, in the light of what he had told Bohr less than a month before.

The best guide we have on this question is a well-reported discussion at the White House a few days later, on September 22. Roosevelt called Bush to a long meeting with Admiral Leahy, newly admitted to the secret, and Lord Cherwell.[39] Leahy had been at Hyde Park, Cherwell only at Quebec. The president did not mention the Hyde Park memorandum, but his remarks shed much light on his view of it. They show that Roosevelt was indeed wary of both his old friend Frankfurter and his new acquaintance Bohr. How did Frankfurter know about it? Was Bohr trusted? Both Cherwell and Bush warmly defended Bohr's integrity and discretion, and Bush explained how Frankfurter might quite innocently have acquired some general sense of the project. The president may have been reassured but in fact he refused to see Bohr again, referring him to Bush. These worries appear to have been Roosevelt's own, taken with him to Quebec; combined with Churchill's own unfavorable view of Bohr, they amply explain the foolish paragraph three. The secrecy of the secret clearly mattered to Roosevelt just as much as ever.

But his larger and stronger interest was in the postwar economic strength of Great Britain. In the aftermath of Quebec he made this point in various contexts also to Hull and Stimson.[40] In making it to Bush he put special emphasis on the commercial value of nuclear energy, thus leading Bush and Cherwell to explain both the dangers in commercial development and the fact that important use was perhaps ten years away.

But if this economic argument was farfetched, the general concern behind it was wholly authentic. Roosevelt's long-standing conviction that there could be no peace in Europe without a strong United Kingdom was vastly more important than his irritation with the remaining pretensions of Empire; moreover he had shown his willingness to bend his policy to Churchill's felt necessities on many great and small occasions through the long years of war. At Quebec, in discussions of the future of lend-lease, in exchanges on the wisdom of a harsh policy toward Germany, he had come face to face with the extraordinary bleakness of the British economic outlook—"The British are broke," he told Stimson twice, in earnest if irrelevant extenuation of his temporary love affair with the plan for a pastoral Germany put forward by Treasury Secretary Henry Morgenthau. There is no reason whatever to doubt that this concern was deep and real. And he had heard nothing from anyone that would have led him to resist an appeal from Churchill that connected this danger, and this need, to the bright promise of atomic energy. Why not convert the nuclear partnership for winning the war, sealed at Quebec in 1943, into a partnership for winning the peace?

To Bush, as he heard the president on September 22, the question had a sharp answer: Any postwar partnership with Britain would gravely endanger the prospect of understanding with Russia. But Roosevelt had heard no such argument, from anyone, when he went to Quebec. Bush and Conant were convinced—and many have shared their conviction since—that too close an association with the United Kingdom would endanger the prospect of understanding with Russia. But this was not Bohr's view—he came to Roosevelt with a deep awareness of his own enrollment as an honorary member of the *British* nuclear team, and he was at great pains to do nothing that was not approved by his British friends short of Churchill; Sir John Anderson, the most important of them, was at once a strong believer in Anglo-American partnership and a strong proponent of an early approach to the Russians. As for Frankfurter, who was the first to raise these questions with Roosevelt, no more passionate Anglophile was to be found among all Roosevelt's associates. Neither Bohr nor Frankfurter, by their own reports, ever presented the question of discussion with the

Russians as one requiring any restraints in Anglo-American relations; it would have been quite out of character for either man to take this view. Roosevelt's embrace of cooperation with Churchill does not of itself imply any desire *on his part* to exclude the Russians.

But what of paragraph one, which rejects "the suggestion that the world should be informed . . . with a view to an international agreement"? This is of course not what Bohr proposed; it comports much better with the suggestions that Churchill had received from Anderson.[41] It was Churchill, not Roosevelt, who had seen all such notions as conflicting with his understanding with the president. On balance one is led to guess that here Roosevelt acquiesced, without much thought, in a sentiment pressed upon him by his friend. It is notable that in his long talk with Bush he said nothing, either way, about planning for international control, and nothing at all derogatory about the Soviet Union. Nor did Roosevelt criticize Bohr's ideas as such; Bush records him as calling them "very striking."

Roosevelt will of course have been in no doubt about Churchill's view of the great Anglo-American secret or about Churchill's sense that counterweights would be needed against Russia; already in 1943 that Churchillian sentiment had been part of the dialogue. Whether Roosevelt himself put to Churchill any of the points he had discussed with Bohr we cannot know; he did not repeat them—either affirmatively or negatively—to Bush. But clearly in some degree the meetings with Churchill had cooled his interest in early talks with the Russians.

Probably that result was related to a long telegram of September 9 from Averell Harriman, his ambassador in Moscow, which arrived at the start of the Quebec meeting and which Roosevelt shared with Churchill. "Now that the end of the war is in sight," Harriman reported, "our relations with the Soviets have taken a startling turn evident during the last two months. They have held up our requests with complete indifference to our interests and have shown an unwillingness even to discuss pressing problems." Soviet demands, on the other hand, "are becoming insistent . . . The general attitude seems to be that it is our obligation to help Russia and accept her policies because she has won the war for us." In Harriman's view, "Time has come when we must make clear what we expect of them as the price of our good will."[42]

Roosevelt was wary of sweeping conclusions about the Russians, and both at Quebec and later he recognized that Stalin might have his own reasons for suspicion.[43] Nonetheless the Harriman message, coming on top of Stalin's cynical lack of support for the Warsaw uprising of Poles against Hitler, following shortly after an egregious Soviet demand for sixteen votes in the United Nations General Assembly, and arriving at a time when Roosevelt and Churchill shared a growing concern over expanding Soviet power in Europe, probably helped to create an atmosphere in which the president could well hesitate to press on Churchill the need for early talks with Stalin on the bomb.[44]

All this shows no more than that for Roosevelt September 1944 was a time for cheering up Churchill, not one for talking about the secret with Uncle Joe. It gives us no ground whatever for concluding that Roosevelt had made a clear and durable decision against an approach to the Russians. The Hyde Park memorandum, with all its fascination, is too frail a document to carry that heavy conclusion. It was initialed, after all, by two men who in the same week also accepted the Morgenthau argument and initialed another short memorandum declaring their interest in "converting Germany into a country primarily agricultural and pastoral in its character."[45] This preposterous paper died young; Roosevelt shared it with Hull, Hull with others, and someone with the newspapers. In the resulting hullabaloo Roosevelt promptly began to assert that he had no such plan, and when Stimson responded by reading back to him what he had initialed, he was "frankly staggered . . . and said he had no idea how he could have initialed this." Roosevelt's troubles with this memorandum on Germany may have helped to persuade him that there was no reason to court trouble by sharing the Hyde Park memorandum with anyone. No one since then has supposed that the memorandum was Roosevelt's last and best thought on the subject. A similar if less drastic fate overtook other Quebec agreements—on the future of lend-lease and the issuance of a cautionary message to Stalin on political problems in Europe. In preparation, conduct, and execution, this set of Roosevelt-Churchill meetings may well be the messiest and least conclusive of all.[46] No single page that came out of these meetings is entitled to massive weight; at the very least it begs for corroboration. For keeping the secret, and for making the British full partners, the corroboration is excellent. But for any conclusion that Roosevelt had made a firm decision never to include the Russians, corroboration is exiguous in the extreme. It is true that at the end of December, when Stimson told him of his own view that "it was not yet time to share it with Russia," Roosevelt said "he thought he agreed." But is the emphasis in this diary entry on not sharing or not sharing *yet*? And how firm is "he thought he agreed"? Usually if Roosevelt fully agreed with a visitor he took pleasure in expressing himself. And if Roosevelt was really so sure, what are we to make of the fact that six weeks later, at Yalta, he spoke "in a casual manner" to Churchill "of revealing the secret to Stalin," giving as his grounds "that de Gaulle, if he heard of it, would certainly double-cross us with Russia." While we have no record of Churchill's response, we can make a good guess at it, and we know that Roosevelt did not in fact speak to Stalin. But does not this episode suggest a man in two minds?[47]

Roosevelt took no further action on this subject. He and Stimson did have one more talk about the bomb, at lunch on March 15. Stimson's diary tells us that he described two schools of thought about the postwar future, one in favor of secret control "by those who control it now," and the other for "international control based upon freedom both of science and of access."[48] Stimson's diary entry shows no expression of preference by either man, and I conclude that neither was ready to choose. Both were near the end of their strength, and the president, unlike Stimson, had heard much more from Churchill than he had yet heard from Americans like Bush and Conant. None of his advisers had ever asked him to reconsider the ideas in the Hyde Park memorandum, because none of them had ever seen it. Stimson evidently did not urge a choice in this last meeting; he was not ready to choose himself. Four weeks later Roosevelt was dead.

The approach to the Russians that Bohr had pressed in vain while Roosevelt was alive did not occur until the Potsdam meeting of July 1945, and then in a form so different that it did not come close to meeting Bohr's standard. Bohr himself did not stop trying. He successfully enlisted Bush in a new effort (though Bush had been wary in an earlier conversation while Roosevelt was alive). In response Bush pressed again for action by Stimson, and one result was the appointment of the Interim Committee. But that committee did not look initially with enthusiasm on any serious approach to the Russians. Part of the trouble was Stimson, and more of it was Byrnes.[49] Stimson in April 1945 was weary and troubled and still not settled in his mind about the relation between the bomb and the Russians. He knew that Bush and Conant believed in open communication and respected both of them. Partly he agreed with them. However deeply he—like them—was committed to using the new weapon promptly if it would help to end the war, he was also increasingly aware that the bomb in the postwar world would be no ordinary weapon, and that the crucial question was that of the relation between such a weapon and Soviet power and purpose. We shall come back to Stimson's thinking as it developed after Hiroshima; here it is enough to say that until after that event he did not reach Bohr's conclusion.

Still more cautious was the new secretary of state. As late as March Byrnes had thought the whole project might be a longhair's boondoggle, and indeed the first topic of Stimson's last meeting with Roosevelt was the secretary's refutation of a memorandum to this effect from Byrnes to Roosevelt. When he learned more, in May, as Truman's representative on the Interim Committee, Byrnes quickly changed his mind, but in those same deliberations he made it clear that he did not begin with a trustful view of Moscow. His prompt and strong opposition put a stop to General Marshall's tentative suggestion that Soviet observers might be invited to Alamogordo. From the beginning he was set on keeping a long lead over the Soviet Union. He heard the scientists argue that the Soviets could make a weapon of their own in three or four years, but he also heard industrialists say it would take longer, and he heard Groves's estimate: twenty years. Characteristically and illogically he split these differences and concluded that "any other government would need from seven to ten years, at least, to produce a bomb." He was not disposed to do anything that would reduce this time advantage, and like Churchill he feared that to open the subject with Moscow was to invite technical questions it would be hard to fend off.[50]

The successful initiative for a different conclusion came from nuclear scientists and found its effective expression through the Scientific Panel. The panel's discussion was set off by Harrison's request for its opinion on the Franck report; even as it confessed itself unable to propose a technical demonstration "likely to bring an end to the war," it also recommended that "Russia, France, and China be advised that we have made considerable progress in our work on atomic weapons, that these may be ready to use during the present war, and that we would welcome suggestions as to how we can cooperate in making this development contribute to improved international relations."[51]

This recommendation was received by the Interim Committee on June 21. Stimson was absent but Byrnes was there. So were Bush and Conant, and they seized the opportunity to press their own strong belief in opening the subject with the Russians.[52] The committee concluded unanimously that there was considerable advantage in informing the Russians at the coming Postdam meeting of the Big Three. Harrison reported the conclusion to Stimson on June 26. Stimson passed it on to Truman on July 2, and Truman, after further discussion with Byrnes and with Churchill, duly spoke to Stalin on July 24.

In this process, however, much of what moved the scientists was lost. As Harrison reported, they felt "great concern for the future if atomic power is not controlled through some effective international mechanism." Granting that the ways and means were "a problem of the future," they nonetheless believed that the general prospect of such an effort at control should be held out to the Russians. As Harrison put it, the statement informing the Russians of the work on the weapon and the plan to use it against Japan "might well be supplemented by the statement that in the future, after the war, we would expect to discuss the matter further with a view to insuring that this means of warfare will become a substantial aid in preserving the peace of the world rather than a weapon of terror and destruction."[53] But Stimson's diary entry does not indicate that he made this point to Truman, and Truman certainly did not make it to Stalin.

Churchill and Byrnes would hardly have pressed him to do so. Both were afflicted by the curious nightmare that Stalin would respond by asking to discuss the secrets of bomb production, and both recorded in their memoirs their relief when he did not. Churchill's fear and relief are particularly vivid: "Nothing would have been easier than for him to say 'Thank you so much for telling me about your new bomb. I of course have no technical knowledge. May I send my expert in these nuclear sciences to see your expert tomorrow morning?' " But nothing of the sort happened; Truman told Churchill, "He never asked a question."[54]

Churchill's fear and relief are ill considered but illuminating. There could have been extensive technical exchanges at Potsdam without going one word beyond what the United States would publish less than a month later in its official Smyth report on the whole wartime project, and in any case, as Byrnes later acknowledged, the Russians were not at all in the habit of pressing their allies for a private peek at technical secrets.[55] Churchill's state of mind on the matter plainly reflects the depth and strength of his conviction that there was an English-speaking head start here that could easily be endangered by conversations with the Russians.

More broadly, the notion of international control had, as yet, no substance; there had been no technical examination of the conditions for success, and no one had studied the central question of connecting the requirements of any such system with the expectations of sovereign, and especially totalitarian, states. Given the persisting ambivalence of Stimson, the wariness of Byrnes, and the outright insistence on keeping the English-speaking lead that governed Churchill, it is not at all surprising that Truman was not urged to open the postwar control question with Stalin, for these were the only three men who discussed the matter with him. As far as we know Truman had never heard of Bohr.

So what survived of the recommendation of the scientists was hardly more than a negative point: For Truman to conceal such a weapon from Stalin, less than two weeks before using it against a common enemy, would be a flagrant act of mistrust. In Churchill's retrospective words, Stalin "had been a magnificent ally in the war against Hitler, and we both felt that he must be informed of the great New Fact which now dominated the scene . . ."[56]

If the object was indeed to share a "great New Fact," Truman went about it with less than his usual directness. He did not even say that the new weapon was nuclear. Churchill, watching from across the room, thought that Stalin "had no idea of the significance of what he was being told. Evidently in his intense toils and stresses the atomic bomb had played no part." Stalin knew much more than that, but Churchill's judgment is important here for what it tells us about his own view. He had been informed, from American reports passed on by Anderson, that there was Russian intelligence interest in the American effort, but he apparently did not suppose that this interest necessarily implied significant understanding at Stalin's level; the Americans were equally ignorant. Neither government then had any idea of the extent of Soviet penetration of the Manhattan Project or of the serious research effort already begun under Igor Kurchatov.[57]

It was indeed Harry Truman who executed the brief informal act of informing Stalin, but his responsibility for the fact that no more was said is small. He certainly could have told what kind of bomb it was, and the ceiling would not have fallen if he had offered a preview of the Smyth report. But Truman did not even know about the Smyth Report until after he got back to Washington. As in this specific instance, so in general, Truman had to pick up the nuclear problem where Franklin Roosevelt had left it when he died. Everything was in hand for the earliest possible test and use of the new weapon, and postwar Anglo-American partnership had been privately agreed with Churchill, but not one thing had been done, by Franklin Roosevelt or by anyone else, to deal with the question of relations on this subject with Russia. I have argued that Roosevelt had simply not decided—but indecision implied inaction. Given Roosevelt's insistence on the deepest secrecy, and his reservation of all policy matters to himself, there was little thoughtful preparation by anyone else. Not because he reached conclusions on the subject, but because he pushed it almost unexamined ahead of him, Franklin Roosevelt was the largest single cause of the absence of any serious communication with Russia before Hiroshima.

The one man who could almost surely have persuaded Roosevelt to take a different course was Winston Churchill, and the notion of such advice from London is not as fanciful as our account so far makes it appear. In later years Churchill himself was to show a perceptive and even magnanimous awareness of the inescapable role of the Soviet Union in the atomic age; his sharp and repeated wartime insistence on refusing to open the subject with Stalin was not his last argument, and my own impression is that it was much affected by his belief in his own almost talismanic relation to Roosevelt. On this subject above all, what was done by the two of them was good, and no third party was needed; Roosevelt was his one and only way to a right British role. But in their varied ways his senior advisers all counseled a different approach. The most thoughtful of all was Smuts, writing—in longhand for the sake of secrecy—from South Africa House in Trafalgar Square on June 15, 1944—just nine days after the Normandy landing.

Smuts wrote with a full and face-to-face understanding of Churchill's resistance to the suggestion of disclosure to Stalin. He began soothingly. There was no need to talk to Stalin immediately; in any case the initiative must come from the president. But then he moved to the heart of the matter:

Of course the discovery is both for war and peace, for destruction and beneficent use, the most important ever made by science. I have discussed its possibilities with the scientific expert [Bohr] who saw you also, and it is clear that it opens a new chapter in human history. Something will have to be done about its control, but exactly what is at present far from clear. While it may be wise to keep the secret to ourselves for the moment, it will not long remain a secret, and its disclosure after the war may start the most destructive competition in the world. It would therefore be advisable for you and the President once more to consider this matter, and especially the question whether Stalin should be taken into the secret. There must of course be the fullest trust and confidence between you as a condition precedent of any such disclosure. But the matter cannot be allowed to drift indefinitely.

If ever there was a matter for international control this is one.[58]

Smuts went on to talk of the need for steps "of the strictest character" in this direction "immediately after the war." He thought a "small committee of foremost physicists should advise the Powers responsible for maintaining world Peace," and it is evident from the context and from his earlier exchanges with Churchill that this class, in his mind, included the Soviet Union. The letter ended very gently, "You may decide to discuss the matter once more with the President and this note is to remind you . . . ."

Churchill did not reply, and in fact his next discussion with Roosevelt went quite the other way, to the wary bilateralism of the Hyde Park memorandum with its gratuitous meanness about Bohr. But we are now considering not what Churchill did but what another British prime minister might well have done in the situation. Here the evidence of the Smuts letter is heavy. Except for Churchill, no one in the British commonwealth then had a higher reputation for farsighted statesmanship; none, indeed, was valued more highly by Churchill himself, who wrote in another context that he always "found great comfort in feeling that our minds were in step."[59] In later years more than one British prime minister of the nuclear age has set himself the task of presenting to the American president the case for breadth and moderation of view, for seeking reasonable agreement with Moscow, and for weighing the general danger more heavily than any immediate or narrow advantage. It could well have been so here.

It is not quite so easy to hypothesize different and more effective advice to Roosevelt from his American associates. Nothing as searching and thoughtful as the Smuts letter reached an American president until Stimson briefed Truman on April 25, 1945, and even that important document did not reach a clear conclusion on whether or how to open the subject with Stalin. The earlier paper of Bush and Conant, of September 30, 1944, was still less explicit on this aspect, and in any case it never reached Roosevelt. Weariness, respect for the president's closely guarded policy prerogative, and the press of other business all contributed to that result, and we have seen how Frankfurter, even with old friendship as his shield, aroused the president's suspicion.

Probably the simplest way to imagine a different result is to suppose that Roosevelt, Stimson, and Hopkins had all been five years younger and stronger in the year after D day. If we make that assumption it becomes quite easy to believe that Roosevelt might have come to a view like that of Smuts.

So let us suppose that by listening to a different voice from London, or more deeply to Bohr, or by stimulus and response in his own circle, or all three, Roosevelt had sought to address the question of the bomb and Russia, and to open it in some fashion with Stalin. What might he have done, and what difference might it have made?

To many students of these matters, the largest question has been whether a wartime approach based on Bohr's analysis of the future danger would have produced a favorable response of some sort from the Russians. Most careful students recognize that there is very little in the Soviet record that justifies optimism on the point. My own belief is that what the Soviet government would and would not do about the control of nuclear weapons was only marginally related to the timing of any American diplomatic communication on the subject. We shall have more to say on this question when we come to consider the failure of the postwar effort to get international control, but the most that we can say about the absence of any serious wartime communication with Moscow is that it may well have made a hard prospect even harder.

IT REMAINS to consider the difference it might have made in *American* behavior if there had been more thought about these things before Alamogordo. What if Roosevelt had relaxed his tight personal control over all matters of policy related to his great secret? What if he had recognized that the fear of German competition which had made the very existence of the American program a proper secret in 1939 was wholly irrelevant after intelligence discovered in 1944 that there was no serious German effort? What if he had recognized further that no secrets of know-how or even of physics were necessary for an initial understanding that nuclear weapons would be a phenomenon of the first political and military importance? What if he had sought the kind of counsel on these nontechnical questions that he sought from his planners on military choices and from advisers whom he trusted on relations with Moscow?

I find it hard to doubt that if in his own mind the secret of the bomb's existence had ever been sharply separated from the quite different matter of knowing how to make it, Roosevelt would have been quick to see the advantage of widening the circle of those free to consider it. Since the secret of its existence was sure to end soon, and since it had lost its major sensitivity with the end of any danger that the Germans might get there first, there was no reason why it should not have been shared with as many persons as were needed to think seriously about the full range of the implications of nuclear weapons for national and international policy, and the product of such thinking could have been available to Roosevelt well before Yalta, to Truman well before Potsdam and Hiroshima.

One subject that would have required, and repaid, careful study in any such review is the Anglo-American connection, and my own belief is that any such study would have had two major results. First, it would have confirmed the need for some new arrangement extending into the postwar period. The arrangements of the Quebec Agreement, reinforced in the field of raw materials by a more specific agreement of 1944, were explicitly wartime arrangements; should they be continued, modified, or ended? It sets no very high standard to suggest that careful study could have led to a policy more thoughtful than that of the Hyde Park memorandum.

In particular I believe that under careful analysis one crucial assumption made by Bush and Conant would have been questioned and quite probably overturned: the assumption that there was conflict between a continuing close connection between London and Washington and a possible agreement with Moscow. We have seen that Niels Bohr himself made no such assumption. Neither did the senior British scientists and politicians, always excepting Churchill. As early as the spring of 1943, during the breakdown of Anglo-American cooperation, Akers and his deputy M. W. Perrin had put the point powerfully: It was Anglo-American *competition,* not cooperation, that would be most dangerous to the prospect of postwar control. "The carrying out of this project competitively by Britain and America can only make almost impossible a postwar control problem which from its nature will be difficult enough even if the two Governments are working in the closest cooperation."[60] Akers and Perrin were probably not then thinking about the problem of including the Soviet Union among the participants in control, but I think their proposition applies to that hard question too. I have already suggested that when Churchill invented the first three paragraphs of the Quebec Agreement—(1) no use against each other, (2) no use against others, and (3) no nuclear aid to them without agreement—he was sketching, all unconsciously, major elements of an understanding that might also, at the beginning, have been negotiable with the Soviet Union. Compared to what happened, this notion seems farfetched, but it is not as far from the mark as the idea that understanding with the Soviet Union required distance from Great Britain.

One can make a quite different point about the bomb and the Soviet Union with even more confidence: Careful reflection would have made it plain, anytime after 1943, that the one absolutely indispensable partner in any successful effort for postwar control of atomic energy was the Soviet Union. Studied from the aspect of war-conferred power and prestige, the point was obvious. Studied in terms of access to uranium it was equally plain, although General Groves got that point wrong both during the war and later. It was also clear in terms of scientific and technical capability. Most important of all, it was evident in the answer to this question: When the Americans get it first, who will have the greatest interest in getting it second? I believe that these considerations would have had overwhelming force for anyone who accepted Bohr's argument that nuclear energy required some form of international control. They would have meant what they meant to Bohr: the key to international control is in Moscow. I believe that any such process of consideration would have led the American government to place this topic firmly on the agenda of great-power diplomacy. This in itself would have been no trivial achievement, as we shall see when we have to consider what happened when the issue was put into the fledgling United Nations.

This argument assumes a belief in the importance of international control. It is a large assumption. It was not Churchill's belief. He wanted rather to stay ahead—he thought that an achievable goal, and he put it first. What Roosevelt believed we do not know; I think he had not decided. But I believe that any group giving sustained attention to the prospects for nuclear weapons as they were already understood by 1944 would indeed have emerged with a strong conviction that Smuts had it right: "If ever there was a matter for international control this is one." We shall see, in the event, how all sorts of men, in different ways and at different times, gave eloquent endorsement to this proposition, and how no government, either in its acts or its proposals, ever came near to any such firmness of purpose. All that I wish to suggest is that more and earlier thought might have moved our government—the one that was then so plainly in the "lead"—some distance in this direction.

Early and careful study of this merely political "secret" would have gained time for the American government. Whatever the president concluded, or advisers counseled, they would have had a chance to move beyond first reactions, to hear and weigh contrasting estimates, and to get accustomed in advance, at least in some slight measure, to the enormous reality announced by Hiroshima. We cannot be sure that the time so gained would have been time well used, but as we go on to see what actually happened, we shall find plenty of evidence of events running ahead of thought. We have already seen how it was probably so at Nagasaki and quite possibly at Hiroshima itself. It will be so also in the nuclear "New World" that those events made public forever.

IV

The Failure of
International Control

I N THE YEAR AND A HALF that followed Hiroshima, the
three powers that might have made and enforced a worldwide
agreement on the control of atomic weapons took a different
course. By early 1947 it was cruelly plain that there was no prospect
of any such agreement. Each of the three powers, in its own way, was
acting on the settled assumption that a nuclear arms race had already
begun and would not be ended, or even limited, by any early international agreement. No effort to reverse this prospect, except at the level
of propaganda, was made by any of the three powers over the ten years
that followed. When negotiations of some seriousness were at last
undertaken, in the context of worldwide concern for the consequences
of fallout from nuclear tests, the visible reality of nuclear weapons,
already terrible beyond precedent in the ruins of Hiroshima, had been
transformed twice over—by the development of the hydrogen bomb
and by the imminence of long-range ballistic missiles. Ever since, as
people have struggled with the complexities, both technical and political, of arms control, we have lamented our failure to control these
weapons at the beginning—when it would, we tell ourselves, have
been so much easier.

The Americans Get the News

The explosion over Hiroshima told the world what H. G. Wells
had foreseen, what the Hahn-Strassmann discovery had made possible,

what had been Franklin Roosevelt's greatest secret, and what could never be undone: that human beings had learned how to make atomic weapons. The first announcement came in the name of Harry S. Truman:

> Sixteen hours ago an American airplane dropped one bomb on Hiroshima, an important Japanese Army base. That bomb had more power than 20,000 tons of T.N.T. . . . It is an atomic bomb. It is a harnessing of the basic power of the universe. The force from which the sun draws its power has been loosed against those who brought war to the Far East. . . .

The president's announcement continued in this grand manner to outline the "marvel" of the vast enterprise, "the greatest achievement of organized science in history." It also threatened the Japanese with "a rain of ruin" if they did not now surrender, and it promised further messages on control of atomic power in the United States and on how it "can become a powerful and forceful influence towards the maintenance of world peace." The message was accompanied by a longer statement from Stimson, giving details of the project and a graphic account of what had happened at Alamogordo. Both documents, drafted in the Interim Committee, were triumphant but sober in tone.

A parallel announcement from London explained the British role in Churchillian prose:

> By God's mercy British and American science outpaced all German efforts. . . . The whole burden of execution . . . constitutes one of the greatest triumphs of American—or indeed human—genius of which there is record. . . . We must indeed pray that these awful agencies will be made to conduce to peace among the nations. . . .

Reinforced within days by first reports of the bomb's effects, by the surrender of Japan, and by the publication of the extraordinarily careful and extensive Smyth report, these announcements made the menace and promise of atomic energy an instant public reality. The awe that had been shared in secret by a few became in some degree the common property of all within reach of these announcements. The bomb had gone public with a bang.[1]

The government most immediately involved in this instantaneous transformation was that of the United States. For the present the bomb was an American monopoly; the cooperative roles of Canada and Great Britain were acknowledged in the formal statements, but these acknowledgments did not obscure the fact that in manufacture, design, delivery, and present possession the weapon was under the exclusive control of the Americans. The politically incendiary fact that under the Quebec Agreement any use of the weapon required British consent remained carefully hidden. But though the existence of the weapon was no longer a secret, the sense that *some* great secret remained in American hands spread almost as widely and deeply through the American public as the news of the bomb itself. The fundamental secret—that this thing could be done—had been published to all the world at Hiroshima, but the mystique of secrecy endured.

Politicians and publicists expressed themselves promptly and loudly; there must be a world government, or a new American vigilance; the very nature of war had changed, or it had not; others would soon catch up, or they would not.[2] But even the boldest and most energetic of those who spoke up were also waiting for the next step from the president. The man in the White House was no longer shut up in the peculiar privacy of exclusive command over an enormous enterprise whose very existence was unknown to most of his fellow countrymen and almost all his fellow politicians. The final choices remained largely his to make; in particular he would decide what course the United States government would take in coming to terms with the international meaning of nuclear energy. His decisions would now be directly affected by public sentiment and political comment. The test of congressional approval would have a weight and meaning quite different from the secret assent of a few leaders to large secret funds for a wartime project. What he decided would be in the papers, and he would need continuous public support. Still it was to him that others now looked for a lead. Franklin Roosevelt had decided to make it. Harry Truman had approved its use. Now he must choose what to do next.

Truman Begins to Choose

What now had to be faced was not merely a promising project or even a desert-tested device, but a weapon whose power had been made evident in the destruction of two cities, a weapon that had been used deliberately by a great government, an enormous act that had met with the overwhelming approval of its own people. A few religious leaders protested, as did some individual citizens, but the public as a whole strongly supported the decision so many have questioned since.[3] No significant public protest was made by any organized group; no national political leader criticized the decision. There was no large-scale protest abroad. The hostile reaction predicted in the Franck report did not occur. The doubting scientists themselves kept their counsel on the question; when they began to speak out a few months later, their immediate concern was with the issues of the future, not the past.

The president, in his own early reactions, reflected the sentiments of his countrymen. In one part of his mind and spirit, he was delighted that the great effort had succeeded and that the war was over. When he was handed Stimson's first flash telegram that the attack on Hiroshima was a "complete success," he was having lunch with the crew on the cruiser *Augusta,* on his way home from Potsdam. He reports in his memoirs that without explaining what was in the message, he told them, "This is the greatest thing in history. It's time for us to get home." He then announced to cheers the use of "a powerful new bomb which used an explosive twenty thousand times as powerful as a ton of TNT." But "the greatest thing in history" was not the attack on Hiroshima; it was rather the enormous denouement of the adventure Roosevelt had launched almost four years earlier, and it was the resulting prospect of early victory that made it time to get home. As Truman said plainly three days later in a radio address devoted mostly to Potsdam, he recognized "the tragic significance of the atomic bomb" and the "awful responsibility which has come to us."[4]

The president expressed publicly his thanks to God that this responsibility "has come to us, instead of to our enemies." At Potsdam two weeks before he had made a more blunt and inclusive diary entry: "It is certainly a good thing for the world that Hitler's crowd or Stalin's did not discover this atomic bomb." Now he asserted a consequent obligation: "We must constitute ourselves trustees of this new force— to prevent its misuse, and to turn it into the channels of service to mankind."[5] In all this, still, he was in tune with his countrymen; only Hitler, not yet Stalin, was a hated enemy, but Stalin and his crowd were not the sort of people you would want getting this kind of weapon first.

But what would the trustees do? The president in August did not say because he did not know. There is no record that he had thought much about this question or received any solid recommendation about it from anyone in the months since his meeting of April 25 with Stimson. Only on the question of informing Stalin at Potsdam had he received definite advice, and we have seen how that approach was attenuated in execution. The Potsdam meeting and the sea voyages it required had removed the president and his secretary of state from Washington for a critical month, and on his return he was caught up at once in the rush of the events that immediately followed Hiroshima. It is not surprising that he was not ready, on August 9 or for some time after, to say what he would do next about the bomb.

Yet one position he *had* reached: there was a secret, and for the present those who had it would keep it; the radio address was blunt on the point:

> The atomic bomb is too dangerous to be loose in a lawless world.
> That is why Great Britain, Canada, and the United States, who have
> the secret of its production, do not intend to reveal that secret until
> means have been found to control the bomb so as to protect ourselves
> and the rest of the world from the danger of total destruction.[6]

In this very early public statement Truman aligned himself tempera-
mentally with Churchill. By the overwhelming authority of the American president, what Churchill called "marvelous secrecy" would now
be maintained as the obligation of "trustees." The "secret" of the
bomb's production existed and would be kept.

Truman's position was not quite that simple. Earlier on the day of
his report to the nation, he had approved a proposal that a thorough
account of the scientific principles of the business should be published.
On the unanimous advice of Bush, Conant, Groves, Harrison, Byrnes,
and Stimson, he had authorized the prompt publication of the Smyth
report, a document that had been in preparation for more than a year
by agreement between Groves and Conant and one that is still today
an excellent introduction to the story of atomic energy from Otto
Hahn to Hiroshima.[7]

The Smyth report contained the most important single set of technical disclosures in the history of atomic weapons. It discussed the
essential roles of U-235 and plutonium, the problems of purity, critical
size, and speed of assembly. It gave full weight to the requirement of
separating or producing the two crucial materials. It was silent on all
sorts of details; it was intended as a citizen's introduction to this "New
World," not as an engineering handbook. But it is impossible to disagree with the conclusion of Bertrand Goldschmidt, himself both a
pioneer in the subject and its foremost French historian:

> The details revealed in the Smyth report were invaluable for any
> country launching into atomic work; for nothing is more important,
> when undertaking technical research over a wide field than knowing
> in advance which lines of approach can or cannot lead to success,
> even if this knowledge relates only to basic principles.[8]

Yet Goldschmidt considers the decision to publish sensible—the
information given was general and hard to keep secret for long. The
British leader, Chadwick, initially wary about the scope and detail of
the report, finally concurred in its publication on similar grounds—he
told Groves that it might save a competitor three months, hardly more.
Groves and Conant took a still stronger view; they believed that the
Smyth report was a reinforcement to the security of the enterprise as
a whole. Unless an authoritative and reasonably forthcoming basic
account was published, they believed, it would be impossible to pre-

vent "serious breaches." As Conant put it to an initially skeptical Stimson, "publication will help us defend against the inevitable cry for more information about the project." It was these arguments that were persuasive. As Stimson put it, "The subject was so vast and the scientists' report was so voluminous that we had to rely upon the opinions of our scientific advisors." He thought Truman showed great courage and skill in reaching a prompt and affirmative decision.[9]

The Smyth report was a sensational success and deservedly so. It was fresh, accurate, clear, and comprehensive, and it told a story of extraordinary achievement. Yet it also served the purpose that Groves especially had in mind, of restricting any discussion beyond its own limits. In a foreword he had stated the position flatly and frankly:

> All pertinent scientific information which can be released to the public at this time without violating the needs of national security is contained in this volume. No requests for additional information should be made to private persons or organizations associated directly or indirectly with the project. Persons disclosing or securing additional information by any means whatsoever without authorization are subject to severe penalties under the Espionage Act.[10]

Thus the Smyth report was both revelation and security fence, and in the months that followed those who had worked on the project proved generally respectful of the fence. Much was excluded: The Smyth report says nothing concrete about the prospect of thermonuclear weapons; it is brief and speculative on the chances for nuclear power; it keeps its distance from technical details that might allow a layman to make the beginning of a judgment of his own on such a critical question as the length of time it might take some other country to make a bomb. It was, as it was designed to be, a better guide to the past than to the future.

Broad expression of opinion on the future was not constrained. Physicists could and did say that much more powerful bombs might be developed. Physicists and managers could and did argue on the length of time it would take the Russians to get a bomb of their own. But precisely where such arguments might have been joined on questions of fact, the curtains remained drawn. One of the critical questions governing estimates on the Soviet timetable, for example, was whether and when the Russians could get enough high-grade uranium ore. Groves quite wrongly thought the Americans and their friends had achieved a near monopoly, but both the magnitude of this effort and its dependence on special arrangements with other countries were treated as deep secrets; so, officially, was the little that was known about sources of uranium inside the Soviet Union. Indeed officials would not publicly discuss what outsiders readily did. The large deposits in Soviet-occupied Czechoslovakia were well known because of their long service as a major source of radium.[11]

But if the Smyth report did not end secrecy, or even diminish its aura, it did provide important protection in 1945 and 1946 for scientists who might otherwise have been in trouble for expressing their own views on the future and their own judgments on the technical prospects. Even further, "whenever scientists were accused in the coming months of wanting to give atomic secrets to the Russians, it was easy to retort that after the Smyth report there was not much left to give."[12] That argument may be overstated, but the Smyth report did show the strength of the proposition that at the level of basic science secrecy was neither practicable nor desirable. At the urging of Bush, Truman soon accepted this principle quite explicitly; two months later he put it with characteristic simplicity and force: "There isn't any reason for trying to keep the scientific knowledge covered up, because all the great scientists know it in every country."[13]

The Smyth report met the test of openness on matters of basic science, and few voices were raised at the time to criticize it for what it left out. So it appeared in August that Truman had quickly established a solid and defensible position. Production "secrets" would—and inferentially could—be protected. Basic scientific information could and should be shared. It turned out to be harder than that, and many of the difficulties showed themselves in the next month, when Harry Truman was called on to give his first sustained attention to the problem of the bomb and the Russians.

Stimson's Last Charge

Public speculation on the connection between the atomic bomb and foreign policy began right after Hiroshima, but here we encounter a particularly strong initial disposition to await the president's lead. In four extended press conferences in August and early September he received no questions on the matter.[14] The man from whom he first heard directly was Henry Stimson. What Stimson urged was a major effort, led by the president, to work out directly with the Soviet Union and with Great Britain a three-power covenant "to control and limit the use of the atomic bomb as an instrument of war."

Stimson had come slowly to his September conclusions. A year had passed since Bush and Conant had first called his attention to the inescapably international character of the problem and the crucial importance of the Soviet Union. He had not been immediately persuaded and had never pursued the matter seriously with Roosevelt. Later he had agreed to the advice of the Scientific Panel that Stalin should receive some forewarning at Potsdam, and he would probably have handled that exchange less elliptically than Truman. But at the same time he had been shocked at Potsdam "by his first direct observation of the Russian police state in action." In a memorandum the president read and said he liked, Stimson had stated the difficulties of dealing with a state so differently organized and led. He thought this basic difference could not be accepted as permanent, and he did not find it consistent with effective international control of atomic energy. Yet the need for such control had been pointed out "in no uncertain terms" by his Interim Committee. What he thought at Potsdam was what he had also thought in somewhat different terms in one of his glancing talks with FDR—that "before we share our new discovery with Russia" the Americans should think hard about what they might get in return. Earlier he had hoped for progress on such disputed questions as Poland. Now what he thought might be needed was nothing less than the beginning of a constitutional transformation of Russia.[15]

But in the month after Hiroshima the old gentleman came to a very different view. He had time to think. Physically at the end of his rope, he had left Washington on August 12 for three weeks of rest; he already had an understanding with the president that the victory now in sight would be followed by his retirement. He retreated to a deeply loved cottage at the expensively simple Ausable Club in the Adirondacks, and as he rested he thought again about the atom. I draw on the account I wrote more than forty years ago:

> Stimson was worried. Granting all that could be said about the wickedness of Russia, was it not perhaps true that the atom itself, not the Russians, was the central problem? Could civilization survive with atomic energy uncontrolled? And was it practical to hope that the atomic "secret"—so fragile and short-lived—could be used to win concessions from the Russian leaders as to their cherished, if frightful, police state? A long talk with Ambassador Harriman persuaded Stimson that such a hope was unfounded; the Russians, said Harriman, would regard any American effort to bargain for freedom in Russia as a plainly hostile move. Might it not then be better to reverse the process, to meet Russian suspicion with American candor, to discuss the bomb directly with them and try to reach agreement on control?[16]

One other element strongly influenced Stimson in these weeks: his growing belief that Secretary of State Byrnes was choosing an opposite and profoundly mistaken course, that of maintaining a conspicuous silence on atomic weapons while negotiating with Moscow on the treatment of defeated enemies and the future of disputed territories. Byrnes appeared to believe that the existence of the American weapon might make the Russians more tractable on other issues. Stimson and his associates, most notably McCloy, disagreed. Talking to each other after a cabinet luncheon on September 4, the two secretaries learned how far apart they were. Byrnes had decisive advantages. He was a newly installed secretary of state dealing on a diplomatic question with a secretary of war who was about to retire. And on the general need for political firmness with an expansive and demanding Moscow he had the president's unhesitating support.

To Byrnes the meaning of his many troubles with Moscow was that this was no time to think of sharing atomic trumps. In August Harrison had showed him a letter from Oppenheimer to Stimson urging international control; he had reacted strongly and negatively, sending word to Oppenheimer that "for the time being his proposal about an international agreement was not practical and that he and the rest of the gang should pursue their work full force."[17] But Stimson and his colleagues had lived longer than Byrnes with the meaning of the new weapon and, in the long war years, with the difficult but massively effective Russians as well. By the time he went to see the president on September 12 Stimson was clear on his priorities. The memorandum he took with him is the first, and almost the last, that directly urged on Truman a direct approach to Stalin. To read it all, as Truman and Stimson did together, is to get a solid grip on the way the President heard the argument. I follow Colonel Stimson's underlining of the two pairs of sentences which he then and later thought most important:

> Those relations may be perhaps irretrievably embittered by the way in which we approach the solution of the bomb with Russia. For if we fail to approach them now and merely continue to negotiate with them, having this weapon rather ostentatiously on our hip, their suspicions and their distrust of our purposes and motives will increase. . . .
>   I emphasize perhaps beyond all other considerations the importance of taking this action with Russia as a proposal of the United States—backed by Great Britain but peculiarly the proposal of the United States. Action of any international group of nations, including many small nations who have not demonstrated their potential power or responsibility in this war would not, in my opinion, be taken seriously by the Soviets [original emphasis].[18]

This argument impressed the president. He told Stimson he agreed that such an approach was needed. There was a part of Harry Truman which understood very well that the bomb was not merely another weapon. Truman raised the matter with others in the week that followed and scheduled a full-length cabinet discussion on September 21, Stimson's last day in office. In that meeting and still more in its aftermath the question that was central to Stimson—a prompt, direct approach to Moscow—became fatally entangled with the quite different question of "sharing secrets."

There are many accounts of the cabinet meeting of September 21, and taken together they justify the dry comment of Dean Acheson: "The discussion was unworthy of the subject." Few of those present had read Stimson's memorandum. He himself, asked to lead off the discussion, was near exhaustion from a morning of emotional farewells and a surprise presentation of the Distinguished Service Medal. His argument appears to have been focused less on the urgency of direct discussion than on its lack of danger; he had found Robert P. Patterson, who was to succeed him, responsive to the argument that there really was no secret to protect; he made the same point now. But in consequence the discussion that followed was directed mainly to the question of "secret sharing." Forrestal, secretary of the navy and the future secretary of defense, characteristically saw the secret as "the property of the American people" and expressed his doubt that the "essentially Oriental" Russians could be trusted any more than the Japanese. Henry Wallace, also characteristically, argued strongly for full scientific exchange, though not for any "sharing of factory technique or 'know-how.' " But the good and decent Wallace, in his own long account, shows plainly why Dean Acheson wrote his daughter that Wallace had "soared into abstractions." Acheson himself, present as acting secretary of state, strongly supported Stimson, whose main point he correctly understood as advocacy of direct discussion with the Russians. Others divided more or less evenly, mainly on the basis of their degree of mistrust of the Soviet Union. Bush, present at Stimson's request, supported the full exchange of scientific information. The president found the intense but inconclusive discussion stimulating and asked for further comments in writing.[19]

The next morning the story hit the front page of *The New York Times*. The distance from the original Stimson memorandum to the story written by Felix Belair, Jr., tells a lot about Washington then and now:

PLEA TO GIVE SOVIET ATOM SECRET
STIRS DEBATE IN CABINET
No Decision Made on Wallace Plan
to Share Bomb Data as Peace Insurance
Armed Forces Opposed . . .

WASHINGTON, Sept. 21—A proposal sponsored by Secretary of Commerce Henry A. Wallace that the United States, Britain and Canada reveal the secret of the atomic bomb to Russia was discussed at President Truman's Cabinet meeting today and brought about a pointed debate that ended with no decision after having caused the longest Cabinet session of the present Administration.

It is understood that the question as to what should be done with the atomic bomb secret was brought up by President Truman and evoked from Secretary Wallace ardent advocacy of the proposal that Russia be let in on the secret, and soon. Secretary of War Henry L. Stimson, who was present for the last time at the two-and-a-half-hour meeting, is said to have suggested that disposition of the question be put up to a world body to be established at some future date. . . .

It is known that the Army and the Navy are determined in their opposition to revealing the secret to any but the nations that participated in its perfection. The two services are prepared to resist the proposal to the hilt, at least until such time as an antidote has been perfected by the United States.

Mr. Wallace, it is understood, argued in support of his proposal that now is the time to make a real start toward a working world union through a demonstration of good faith to the Soviet Union. . . .

The proposal, understood to have been discussed in President Truman's official family for the first time today, is based on the further and major premise that any nation as far advanced scientifically as Russia will learn the secret of the bomb in the not far distant future anyway.

It is the contention of the Wallace adherents that since this is inevitable, the United States, Britain and Canada should move quickly to bring the Soviet Union into full play as a force for perpetual world peace rather than as a continuing question mark in all United Nations discussions. Now is the time, it is insisted, to end the suspicions with which the Russians are known to regard the intentions of Britain, if not of the United States.

Against these considerations are the tough-minded strategists and not a few scientists in the War and Navy Departments, who have told President Truman that Russia would be so long in developing the atomic bomb that this country and Britain would by that time have discovered an antidote.

Strengthening their arguments, understood to have been laid before the President during the Cabinet meeting, was the statement in New York today by Maj. Gen. Leslie R. Groves, who was in complete charge of the "Manhattan Engineer District," as the Army atomic bomb project was designated, that the United States should closely hold the secret of the bomb until all other nations have demonstrated their anxiety for peace.[20]

There followed the usual denials—Truman was firm in defending Henry Wallace—and the usual tut-tuts about a "lying leaker." In his memoirs Truman praised this meeting for its "frank and open argument," but he never again held a full cabinet discussion on the subject.[21]

Internal argument continued in other ways. Most of those who had been present at the meeting responded to Truman's request and sent him thoughtful memoranda. At least four were supportive of the Stimson proposal, as the writers understood it. Patterson, the new secretary of war, wrote straightforwardly that his former chief was right; we should approach the Russians. He thought the secret would not last in any case and the main purpose must be to "exert our best efforts to prevent an armament race." Wallace repeated his agreement with Stimson, but he described it as a proposal "for the free and continuous exchange of scientific information . . . between all of the United Nations." Bush wrote most specifically about scientific exchange—its lack of danger and its possible value—but he also underlined the need to lose no further time in offering the Russians an alternative to competition.[22]

It was Dean Acheson who picked up most strongly on what had been Stimson's central concern: the political need to address the Russians soon and directly. His memorandum argued that "what we know is not a secret which we can keep to ourselves," that "this scientific knowledge . . . relates to a discovery more revolutionary in human society than the invention of the wheel," and that "if the invention is developed and used destructively there will be no victor and there may be no civilization remaining." Further, "the joint development of this discovery with the U.K. and Canada must appear to the Soviet Union to be unanswerable evidence of an Anglo-American combination against them." His conclusion was somber: "It is impossible that a government as powerful and power conscious as the Soviet Government could fail to react vigorously to this situation. It must and will exert every energy to restore the loss of power which this discovery has produced. It will do this, if we attempt to maintain the policy of exclusion, in an atmosphere of suspicion and hostility, thereby exacerbating every present difficulty between us. For us to declare ourselves trustee of the development for the benefit of the world will mean nothing more to the Russian mind than an outright policy of exclusion." This last sentence showed a certain courage, in the light of Truman's public assertion of August that "we must constitute our selves trustees."[23]

The Acheson memorandum concluded that an immediate approach to the Russians was needed and that the administration should begin to clear the way, by advance discussions with the British, by explanations to Congress, and by encouraging "informed and extensive public discussion." Without such discussion "the public and Congress will be unprepared to accept a policy involving substantial disclosures to the Soviet Union."[24]

Evidence on this last point was already plentiful. Congressional reaction to the report of the "Wallace plan" had been immediate and fierce. Senator Connally of Texas, the chairman of the Senate Foreign Relations Committee, spoke the clear sense of the Senate when he said, on the day the story broke, that "complete secrecy should be maintained regarding the atomic bomb." From within the cabinet Truman was getting similar advice from such members as Anderson of Agriculture and Vinson of the Treasury, who were closer to him at the time than Bush or Acheson. It is not surprising that Acheson, like Bush and Patterson, reinforced his argument with the point that the discussion with the Russians could in fact begin without any great secret sharing: "It need not involve at this time any disclosures going substantially beyond those which have already been made to the world."[25]

By now the president was under heavy pressure to state his own atomic energy policy, both domestic and international. The most urgent questions were those relating to the management of the existing American enterprise. The Manhattan Project was a wartime creation resting purely on presidential authority. Something must take its place, and the administration must make proposals. Where was Truman's plan?

The president's message on atomic energy went to Congress on October 3. It dealt with both domestic and international policy, and the story of its international section clearly indicates how Truman reached his first conclusion on the question Stimson had opened.

The international paragraphs were initially drafted by Acheson's assistant Herbert Marks, who had already had a large hand in his boss's memorandum of September 25. Marks wrote in the Stimsonian vein, and most of his draft survived into the final Truman statement:

> In international relations as in domestic affairs, the release of atomic energy constitutes a new force too revolutionary to consider in the framework of old ideas. We can no longer rely on the slow progress of time to develop a program of control among nations. Civilization demands that we shall reach at the earliest possible date a satisfactory arrangement for the control of this discovery in order that it may become a powerful and forceful influence towards the maintenance of world peace instead of an instrument of destruction.
>
> Scientific opinion appears to be practically unanimous that the essential theoretical knowledge upon which the discovery is based is already widely known. There is also substantial agreement that foreign research can come abreast of our present theoretical knowledge in time.
>
> The hope of civilization lies in international arrangements looking, if possible, to the renunciation of the use and development of the atomic bomb, and directing and encouraging the use of atomic energy and all future scientific information toward peaceful and humanitarian ends. The difficulties in working out such arrangements are great. The alternative to overcoming these difficulties, however, may be a desperate armament race which might well end in disaster.

Discussion of the international problem cannot be safely delayed until the United Nations Organization is functioning and in a position adequately to deal with it.

I therefore propose to initiate discussions, first with our associates in this discovery, Great Britain and Canada, and then with other nations, in an effort to effect agreement on the conditions under which cooperation might replace rivalry in the field of atomic power."[26]

Control is urgent—it cannot wait on the United Nations; scientific knowledge cannot be monopolized. Discussion must start, first with "our associates" and then with others; it was evident, if unspoken, that the Soviet Union would be the first of those others.

Acheson had cleared this statement with Byrnes in London and with the War Department officers concerned. He had alerted the British. Only at the White House had there been amendment; either Truman or his senior draftsman Samuel Rosenman took out a reference to the advantage of offense over defense in these weapons, and cut the words "comparatively short" from the sentence about others catching up "in time." Acheson had good reason for his hope "that the road had been kept open" for discussion on the Stimson model.[27]

In one sense, the road was never open at all. To the degree that Stimson's approach required any early or unrequited disclosure of nuclear know-how, the president never did accept it. Tutored by Bush, Truman accepted the proposition that the basic scientific principles were already generally known, but he fully shared the aversion of congressional leaders to sharing the secrets of American know-how, and he apparently accepted the assurances of all Stimson's supporters that no such disclosures would be required in any initial approach. A few days after the message he showed his mind plainly and publicly. On the porch of Linda Lodge, on Reelfoot Lake in Tennessee, he held an impromptu press conference. The day before he had spoken without a prepared text at a county fair in Missouri and his emphasis had been on the promise, not the menace, of atomic energy. "That great force, if properly used by this country of ours, and by the world at large, can become the greatest boon that humanity has ever had." For that to happen the nations would have to decide that "the welfare of the world is much more important than any individual gain which they themselves can make at the expense of another nation." When they did that, "then we can take this discovery which we have made and make this world the greatest place the sun has ever shone upon." It was an early example of the rhetoric of hope that has so often served statesmen of all nations as a substitute for thought, and it invited the probing question that opened the press conference. Did the president mean, by his call for such a high standard of international behavior, "that the atomic secret would not be shared, unless and until we had positive assurance that the world had progressed to that point?"

Truman's initial answer was "No," because "the scientific knowledge that resulted in the atomic bomb is worldwide knowledge already." But his real answer was yes: "It is only the know-how of putting that knowledge practically to work that is our secret; just the same as know-how in the construction of the B-29," and indeed as in the mass production of cars. That know-how he was not planning to share with anyone; "If they catch up with us on that, they will have to do it on their own hook, just as we did." He thought the British and Canadians, "our partners," would agree with this view (he was right), but in any case it was an essentially American problem because "we have all the information so far as the practical know-how is concerned."

The questioning continued, and the president took his distance clearly and sharply from a major premise of the whole Stimson-Acheson approach:

> Q. . . . Mr. President, if we can return to the atomic bomb subject for just a minute, sir—
> THE PRESIDENT. Sure.
> Q.—have any of these other countries that are our allies asked for the secret of the know-how?
> THE PRESIDENT. No.
> Q. Mr. President, in that connection, I have read that one of the causes for the lack of accord between this country and Russia—or on Russia's part, at least—grows out of the fact that we have the atomic bomb, and Russia doesn't.
> THE PRESIDENT. It isn't true—it isn't true at all. The difficulty, I think, is a matter of understanding between us and Russia. There has always been a difficulty, principally because we don't speak the same language. It is a most difficult matter to translate the meaning of what I am saying right now into Russian, so it will mean the same thing in Russian as it means in English. The same thing is true when you translate Russian into English. When I was at the conference with Stalin at Berlin, he had an interpreter and I had one, and it took the four of us to be sure that we each understood the meaning of the other; and when we did, there was no difficulty in arriving at an agreement.[28]

These critically important answers, as Gregg Herken has persuasively argued, are from the real Harry Truman. The president was not about to share American know-how; he really did not think anyone else was going to catch up soon, and he saw no reason for anyone in Moscow to be upset by the position. In all this he was nearer to the senators than to the scientists, and nearer to Groves than to Stimson, Bush, and Acheson.[29]

In his memoirs Truman recorded that as he considered his position in this period he was aware of the view of the Joint Chiefs of Staff that for the present the United States should retain "all existing secrets with respect to the atomic weapons." The chiefs, prodded by Robert Lovett, also recorded their belief that political initiatives should be promptly and vigorously pressed. "The possibility that other nations may succeed in developing atomic weapons in the not too distant future," they argued, "suggests that the question of political controls is a matter of immediate importance."[30] In their hearts the chiefs were more concerned about keeping the secret, and Truman understood their view; it had all been reported in Belair's *Times* article of September 22, and the president had almost surely learned it from Leahy before that. Truman, like the chiefs, saw no inherent contradiction between secrecy about the weapon and a search for political control.

Moreover the president did not think any such "giveaway" plan was necessary to get down to brass tacks with the Russians. He had agreed with Stimson, and then with Acheson, that direct talk was needed—he was proud of his own directness at Potsdam, and he remembered himself as more candid than he really was. He was not himself eager for another meeting with Stalin, but he had a man he currently trusted to do his straight talking for him. A reporter asked him who would conduct the initial conversation with Britain and Canada. He replied that it would be the secretary of state. Would there be special advisers? "No. That's what I have the Secretary of State for."[31] That is how Byrnes learned of his new assignment.

Byrnes Turns to the UN

The secretary of state to whom the president thus passed the chief role in nuclear negotiations was far from delighted, at first, with the assignment. Byrnes had been absent in London throughout the weeks between Stimson's memorandum of September 11 and the president's message of October 3, attending a most frustrating meeting of the three-party Council of Foreign Ministers that had been established at Potsdam. In his view the meeting had shown the Russians to be most intransigent and demanding. They were eager to discuss control over Japan and over Italian colonies; they resisted all efforts to question their control of Eastern Europe. They were stubborn on procedures. Molotov was Molotov. Revisionist historians have accused Byrnes of practicing atomic diplomacy in this session, but the records do not bear them out. Byrnes did not mention the bomb; he left the crude joking to Molotov, and any hope that the unspoken reality of the weapon would make the Soviet delegation responsive proved wholly wrong. Byrnes may well have gone to London with the bomb "ostentatiously on his hip," as Stimson thought, but he did not find it useful there. We shall come back to this large question of the diplomatic value of nuclear weapons. All we need to know now is that Byrnes returned to Washington with a grim view of Soviet diplomacy.

Though he had not opposed it from London, Byrnes did not like the promise of international consultation in the American message of October 3. He told his cabinet colleagues Patterson and Forrestal, on October 10, that before his departure in September he had begged Stimson not to recommend such a statement. He now feared Molotov would use the message to raise "the whole question of the control of the atomic bomb," and he thought that "before any international discussion of the future of the bomb could take place we must first see whether we can work out a decent peace." In a later meeting he advanced other doubts: He thought the key issue was inspection, and he had no confidence the Russians would ever allow it. "He said that we can't get into Rumania and Bulgaria much less Russia and that it is childish to think that the Russians would let us see what they are doing." Obviously any diplomatic effort led by Byrnes would be different from what Stimson and Acheson had urged.[32]

An initial meeting with the British and Canadians was now essential. Truman had promised discussions, and for Prime Minister Clement Attlee it was vital, both politically and as a matter of his own direct concern, that the discussion should be led by heads of government. A meeting was arranged, to begin at Washington on November 11. Truman had publicly given Byrnes the responsibility for the U.S. side of the discussion. What would the Americans have to say?

As he faced this question Byrnes did not turn to Acheson, who played no part in the meeting. The secretary was slow in addressing the matter and did not begin to take it seriously until he was visited by Bush on Saturday, November 3. As a result of this meeting Bush prepared a memorandum over the weekend that reflected his own conviction, and powerfully shaped the following events, although its central point was never accepted.

Bush told Byrnes that there would be two basic questions before the meeting: the future of the Quebec Agreement and the approach to Russia on the future of atomic energy. On the first he recommended, in a single page, that the meeting limit itself to an understanding that a new and public agreement should be negotiated. His main interest was the approach to Russia, and his recommendations were fateful.

Bush was a scientist, not a diplomat (though he possessed great personal diplomatic skills). His way of approaching the Russian question was not to ask what the Russians would or would not be willing to negotiate—he probably knew of the doubts Byrnes had expressed, but his memorandum did not address them directly. Instead he led from his own strong suit and set forth a three-stage proposal for increasing technical cooperation with Russia, matching technical inducements with protective safeguards, mainly inspection. He proposed starting with scientific exchange and moving on as confidence developed to technical exchanges, and finally to an agreement that no one would have bombs. The inspection system when "mature" would give protection against surprise atomic attack. An "appalling" threat "would be largely removed." "Certainly," said Bush, "we do not wish to be in a position to make such an attack, if we are sure no one else is." All this would take many years, but "the important point now is to make it clear to the world that this is the way in which we would like to proceed."[33]

The technical ways and means of international control were to be studied much more carefully in the months that followed than Bush could manage in his weekend paper, but his notion of going at the problem from its technical side was adopted at once. So was another suggestion: that both the technical process and the work of setting it up should be entrusted to the United Nations. Bush later reminisced that in making his proposal he was "following what had in my judgment been the President's plan for going to the United Nations," but his proposal gave new concreteness to that notion. Truman's various statements in October had said only that "other nations" must be drawn in after talks with Britain and Canada, and that the United States would give its full support to the UN. What Bush did was to transform those vague assertions into a real proposal. His object was to work toward cooperation with Russia; in this respect he remained a Stimsonian. But his one specific and immediate proposal for discussion with Russia was that "she join Britain and the United States in suggesting the establishment under the UNO"* of a body that might get started on the long, hard, three-stage road toward control, by promoting full scientific exchange. Byrnes and Truman agreed.[34]

But for Byrnes, and also for Truman, the idea of a United Nations commission was a way of moving forward without having to confront hard questions, now strong in both their minds, about the Russians. Byrnes fell in with Bush's argument, but their purposes were not the same. When Bush pointed out that the United States could safeguard its know-how until Russian attitudes had been tested in other ways he was writing from hope, but Byrnes was reading from fear. It was

---

*UNO, standing for United Nations Organization, is the shorthand of 1945 for what we now call the UN; curiously the "O" was dropped as the organization gradually came into existence.

entirely practicable to couple a proposal for sweeping measures of international control with a clear-cut assurance that secrets would be protected until such measures were agreed—as long as the hard questions of negotiation and terms of agreement could be put off. Yet it seems unlikely that any one understood at the time how readily the idea of "going to the UN" could become a substitute for action.

So the proposal for a UN commission became the centerpiece of the American position when Attlee came to Washington but what that commission was really going to do was left for later consideration. The establishment of this commission and the formulation of American proposals to present to it became the main purpose of American policy. What to say to the Soviet Union became a question to be addressed in this context and for this purpose, and thus it happened that the direct approach to Russia on substantive questions that Stimson and Acheson had urged simply never took place. As Acheson put it, "a series of leaks and pressures, and responses to both, had brought the Administration to the opposite pole from Colonel Stimson's position."[35]

This result was the opposite of what Bush intended. His memo called the approach to Russia "the great question before the conference," and he put forward his ideas for UN action in terms of what might induce Russian participation and of agreements framed "in such manner that it will be in Russia's interest to keep them." It is one of the major ironies of the history of atomic energy that Vannevar Bush should have been the author of a proposal which allowed the question of direct and substantial negotiation with the Russians to fade away.[36]

In fairness we must remember that in 1945 the United Nations was very young and hopes for its effectiveness high. To many more Americans then than now, it was a sign of seriousness and high international purpose to take an issue to the UN. The thoughts of scholars and scientists that fall were full of the need for international control. Appeals for such control came, in the weeks before the meeting with Attlee, from Los Alamos and Chicago, and from national gatherings of chemists, physicists, and engineers. Moreover scientists talking on this subject with friendly senators found them insistent that the basic effort be launched through the UN. As one reported, "It soon became evident . . . that the Senators would refuse to sign a document which did not contain a statement about the UNO. . . . After extensive talks . . . I have the very definite conviction that one must work through the UNO. The UNO is the Senators' baby . . . , any attempt to circumvent it in general falls on deaf ears in Washington."[37]

Byrnes had believers of this same sort in his own staff. At this time his assistants Benjamin Cohen and Leo Pasvolsky were both closer to him—though not to each other—than Acheson; Pasvolsky especially had worked hard for the charter. Both were believers in international organization as such, and while neither was unaware of the need for direct discussions with Moscow, both were content—as Stimson and Acheson had not been—to have the discussion of substance remanded to a larger, more "international" forum.

Further reinforcement to this approach was supplied, as soon as the Truman-Attlee-King meetings began, by both the Canadians and the British. The principal Canadian draftsman for the meeting—counterpart in this sense to Bush—was Lester B. Pearson, then the young Canadian ambassador in Washington. Pearson, who was to become his country's foreign and then prime minister, was then and throughout his later career a man of the United Nations; in 1957 he was to win a Nobel Peace Prize for his work in its behalf in the Middle East. Now his powerful memorandum was clear-cut in its recommendation: For the same reasons as the scientists, Stimson, and Bush, he saw no answer except international control, no course but a lead in this direction from the three English-speaking partners. He also saw no instrument but the United Nations, and indeed in his memoirs he tells us that although he was by far the junior official present when the three heads of government met, "I could not resist the opportunity [given by Truman, who asked every one to speak] to plead for a deep and broad international effort through the United Nations to control this new and final threat to human survival." In the UN, moreover—and the consideration escaped no Canadian—Canada could expect to play a role that she had never sought in direct dealings with Moscow, or even, for that matter, in the nuclear relations between London and Washington. The Canadian voice was not heavy in the November meetings, but it was clear.[38]

The role of Canada in the history of nuclear weapons is unique, and it seems appropriate here to remark that Canadian good sense and moderation are visible at many points in the nuclear age. The issues presented were usually both complex and relatively minor, so that it would be hard to treat them effectively except at disproportionate length. This is a difficulty which turns up elsewhere in the relations between Canada and the United States. The real wonder is not that Canadians occasionally get annoyed when Washington fails to pay fair attention to problems that are large in Ottawa, but rather that the Canadian government, more often than not, makes allowances for its large neighbor and goes on to do at least its share in resolving differences. Certainly that has been the overall record in nuclear matters.

Canada played a significant role in supporting a basically American effort in 1942–45 and also in moderating Anglo-American differences. Canada was the first country to decide clearly that it would not itself become a nuclear weapons state, reaching that conclusion openly, and with no voice on the other side, in 1945. The Canadians had everything at hand—the uranium, the science, and the technical head start—everything but the desire. In 1946 Canada became a member of the

UN commission that eventually became the forum for debate on international control, and an American reviewing that debate can hardly avoid the conclusion that the basic case for international control would have been more widely persuasive—though not in Moscow—if it had been made not by Bernard Baruch but by the Canadian member, General A.G.L. McNaughton. There have been differences between Washington and Ottawa over the years. They have usually been resolved, and on balance what is impressive is that on this troubling subject the habit of self-respecting cooperation between Canadians and Americans has endured.

Attlee Joins Byrnes

Of the three countries in the meeting in Washington, the one whose path to the United Nations, and away from Moscow, is most interesting is the United Kingdom, and the central figure in that story is Prime Minister Clement Attlee.

August for Attlee was at least as hectic as for Truman; he had the same enormous transition from war to peace to cope with, and in circumstances vastly harder. The British were weary and their economy more "broke" than ever. Attlee had a new government to organize; that process was still on his mind as he flew to Washington three months later. Among his problems the future of atomic energy could not have the urgency it had for Truman, nor did the world look to him as it did to the man in the White House. In Britain of course he must lead—but he must also keep a wary and respectful eye on Churchill, and he had wisely and generously let Churchill's draft become his country's statement after Hiroshima. Many powerful realities stood between Attlee and any effort to take a major international initiative on the nuclear question. Only two forces argued the other way: the overriding magnitude of the issue and his own conscience.[39]

On August 25 Attlee received a copy of a cabinet office memorandum on "the international policy to be followed on the use of atomic energy." This paper had been prepared in June by "a group of officials" stirred to action by reports from Washington that the American Interim Committee was at work and would probably welcome consultation. In the tumultuous events of the summer such consultation between London and Washington had been occasional and fragmentary; Attlee himself had come late to the game and had only the most general notions of the enterprise before the Labour victory put him in Churchill's place at Potsdam. It seems likely that the anonymous official memorandum, which came to him as background for the start of work on the matter in a small and secret committee of his cabinet, was the trigger for his first determined effort to confront the nuclear future. Sometime in the next three days—the typed version bears the date of August 28—he wrote in longhand an extraordinary memorandum.

First, and starkly, he noted that "a decision on major policy with regard to the atomic bomb is imperative." Without it neither civil nor military departments could plan. The new weapon had already made much earlier planning out of date.

Then Attlee seized on what has been crucial for British governments ever since. The bomb had made one and only one reality central to the situation of Britain. Men might chatter at Potsdam about river boundaries, and planners might talk of dispersal and other defenses against ordinary bombs, but with the atomic bomb in the world, "the vulnerability of the heart of the Empire is the one fact that matters." He foresaw that the answer "to an atomic bomb on London is an atomic bomb on another great city." But he did not like that conclusion: "Duelling with swords and inefficient pistols was bearable. Duelling had to go with the advent of weapons of precision. What is to be done about the atomic bomb?"

Attlee saw no hope in merely "banning" the bomb; it was too strong a weapon. He thought that to attempt an Anglo-American hegemony "to enforce a worldwide rigid inspection" was neither desirable nor practicable. "We should not be able to penetrate the curtain that conceals the vast area of Russia. To attempt this would be to invite a world war."

Just one answer remained: "The only course which seems to me to be feasible and to offer a reasonable hope of staving off imminent disaster for the world is joint action by the U.S.A., U.K. and Russia based upon stark reality." So his conclusion:

> *I can see no other course than that I should on behalf of the Government put the whole of the case to President Truman and propose that he and I and Stalin should forthwith take counsel together.* . . . Only a bold course can save civilization [emphasis added].[40]

It took a month for Attlee to put his case to Truman, and when he did, that case had radically altered. His proposal of prompt direct talks with Stalin had been successfully resisted by his own foreign secretary, Ernest Bevin, and his rejection of an Anglo-American partnership had been fiercely questioned by Churchill. Bevin argued that it would be unwise to raise the subject with Truman and Stalin in isolation from the whole set of political issues with which he was wrestling all through September.[41] Wariness of summitry comes naturally to foreign ministers and their professional advisers.

Churchill's concern went deeper. For him the key to the nuclear future lay in Anglo-American cooperation. He was mistrustful of woolly schemes from scientists and of arguments for cooperation with the Russians on the subject. When Attlee shared with him a draft of his letter to Truman, he cabled sharp questions.[42] He took particular exception to a passage that spoke of accepting risks in the interest of an agreement, and of "an act of faith justified only if the risks of not so proceeding are in fact greater." Although the draft contained no mention of the Soviet Union, Churchill read the passage with suspicion and responded with a question and a threat: "Do you wish them [the Americans] to tell the Russians? Is this what is meant by 'an act of faith'? If so I do not (not) believe they will agree and I personally should deem them right not (not) to and will certainly have to say so, if and when the issue is raised in public."* Attlee cut out the offending passage.[43]

Shorn of its reference to "an act of faith," Attlee's letter went forward on September 25. Compared to his longhand memorandum of the previous month it was pallid. It had been drafted by his officials, and the changes of substance—no word of Russians, or of Stalin, or of direct discussions—were matched by changes of style. Attlee's own prose—the terse and rapid argument of a man in the grip of a great concern newly perceived—was replaced by the smoothly flowing and almost deferential language of Whitehall addressing an American president on a subject in which the Americans held a commanding position.[44]

The letter did include a careful and extended rendering of Attlee's point that strategic reality had been revolutionized, and it addressed, gently but clearly, the probability that the American lead might be only temporary. While omitting any direct reference to the Russians, it picked up and expanded a somewhat different thought from Attlee's first memorandum—that the work done at San Francisco on the United Nations "must be carried much further." But it did not say how. Indeed it carefully described its own analysis as "tentative" and intended primarily to elicit from Truman a knowledge of "how your mind is moving." Its most concrete comment was "later on, . . . it may be essential that you and I should discuss this momentous problem together."[45] Arriving in the same week as the memoranda from his own advisers that were generated in the aftermath of the Stimson presentation to the cabinet, this letter does not appear to have stirred Truman in any perceptible way. He sent a friendly but noncommittal reply three weeks later, but his real answer was given by Acheson to Halifax on October 1; the president was going ahead with his message to Congress, and that message would propose discussions with Britain and Canada.[46] There would indeed be a meeting, and to Attlee that

---

*Parenthetical *not*'s are cabled emphases.

was now the main point, but he had to press once more before the November date was set.

The British preparation for Attlee's trip to Washington produced a remarkable internal paper that further weakened Attlee's initial interest in a meeting with Stalin. On October 29 a group of senior officials led by Sir Edward Bridges presented a report entitled *International Control of Atomic Energy*. Nothing of this report was made public at the time, and even in the admirable official history published almost thirty years later it is only briefly noticed. Yet it is one of the most powerful, prophetic, and imperfect documents of the early atomic age.[47]

The officials concluded, as Stimson and Acheson had a month earlier, that American monopoly could not be maintained for long. But their next conclusion was more portentous: No scheme of control and inspection that was technically reliable would be politically practicable. Given the nature of Soviet Russia, any such plan would lead to obstruction, evasion and rising suspicion; the countries observing the agreement would have placed themselves at a strong disadvantage. "A system of inspection of the Big Powers is thus bound to develop into a highly dangerous sham, productive of endless suspicion and friction."[48]

Reinforcing this conclusion was the officials' conviction that the Russians were already determined to have a bomb of their own; their statement was bold and unargued: "There can be no doubt that her scientific and industrial resources are sufficient to enable her within, say, not less than five years to produce atomic weapons and that she will do so."[49]

The officials also expected that France would be among the "principal competitors" and in a separate section they pressed for a decision that Britain too should produce bombs as quickly as possible. They reached a prophetic conclusion: "No international agreement is likely to be successful which attempts to restrict the freedom of any of the major Powers to produce atomic weapons." The officials added that this conclusion applied also "to a proposal that the production of atomic weapons should be confined to an international organization."[50]

Having reached these sweeping conclusions, the officials then gave only cursory attention to the conclusion that seems obvious as one reads their paper four decades later: that the major powers had better think together, and talk together, about the world they were separately determined to create—a world of major states with bombs. Read with hindsight their argument powerfully supports Attlee's immediate judgment of August, that he and Truman and Stalin had better talk. But that was not the conclusion of the officials. They recognized as a possible policy "that the production of atomic bombs should be confined to the Big Five," a glancing and still more prophetic inclusion of China, but they did not recommend it. Instead they concluded, with almost no explanation, that it was better "to leave all nations free to make bombs if they can," and to seek control of use, not production, by a pledge never to use atomic bombs except against someone who had used them first—what we would now call "no first use," with a further pledge to use the bomb against any country that did go first. This proposal drew Attlee's immediate and vehement disapproval and so reinforced his own growing preference for seeking salvation in the United Nations.[51]

Attlee's argument against the officials was not feeble. Their proposal, he noted, assumed that other nations would gang up even against a victim of aggression if *in extremis* such a victim used the bomb. It assumed that the United States would accept a reversion to the power balance of the preatomic age. It neglected the fact that because of their peculiar vulnerability the British would be in extraordinary danger if they took any pledge to use bombs against a violator. "To accept this obligation would be to expose London to annihilation. Could any Government accept such a risk?" Attlee held that if major war broke out between Great Powers, in a world of atomic weapons, those weapons would be used. The remedy was not in implausible pledges of nonuse, or of retaliation, but in a recognition of the reality that the advent of the atomic bomb had made war itself obsolete. "The only hope for the world is that we should all lay aside our nationalistic ideas, and strive without reservation to bring about an international relationship in which war is entirely ruled out."[52]

To Attlee the instrument for this transformation must be the United Nations. Seizing upon a quite routine endorsement of the UN made by Truman on October 27 in a speech that included strong statements opposing Soviet behavior in Eastern Europe, Attlee told his cabinet that in Washington he would put the reinforcement of the UN at the head of the agenda. He agreed with his officials that "no attempt should be made to restrict the development of atomic energy by any other country." The right role for atomic weapons was that they should be "available to restrain aggression" and "the best way of achieving this is not by any special convention, but rather by the determination of all those who develop atomic energy to live up to the principles and purposes of the Charter, and to back up its authority by using their atomic weapons against an aggressor if the occasion arises."[53]

With this conclusion of November 5 Clement Attlee had come a long way from his August judgment that the only course offering hope was "joint action by the U.S.A., U.K. and Russia based upon stark reality." The stark reality of his November position was that there was to be no proposal of "joint action" with Russia—not even a proposal for talks.[54]

A still more stark reality was that the United Kingdom was preparing to make its own atomic bombs. The fears that had moved Attlee in September had been overtaken two months later by a purely British concern for a program to make a British bomb. Attlee had not formally accepted the recommendation of his officials to make bombs as quickly as possible and also tell Truman of his intention, but his own gentler language had the same intrinsic meaning: "I should tell the President that we are naturally interested in the development of atomic energy, both as a means of self-defence, and as a source of industrial power." And that expression of interest would be accompanied by an attempt to ensure continued cooperation under which the British effort would benefit from preferred access to American knowledge. Attlee in Washington would be no ardent voice for international control.[55]

Agreement to Go to the United Nations

And so by different paths the three heads of government came to their meeting on November 10 with a single shared objective: to take the problem of the control of atomic energy to the United Nations. They met alone that morning at the White House, and by lunchtime they had found themselves in essential agreement. The problem was grave; international control was needed; this control "should be lodged in the United Nations," but only when there was assurance that "the confidence of each nation in the good faith of the other was well founded." The way to begin was with a "free interchange of scientific knowledge." If the specific problem of Soviet Russia was mentioned that morning, there is no record of it.[56] Truman and Attlee agree that the first conversation on nuclear control came the first day, Saturday, November 10. The essential agreement was reaffirmed on Saturday afternoon with principal advisers present; it was discussed again Sunday. On Monday morning Byrnes sent for Bush to say that the American position had been endorsed and to ask for a draft communiqué.

There ensued three days of drafting rendered complex by the fact that Bush, the principal draftsman, had not been present at the crucial meetings and also by the divergent considerations that had led the great men to their common conclusion. But summits, with all their faults, are good forcing beds for communiqués, and within the limits of what had been settled the resulting document was balanced and respectable. The three leaders recognized the central reality of a "means of destruction . . . against which there can be no adequate military defense, and in the employment of which no single nation can in fact have a monopoly." They recognized that the situation imposed responsibility on all civilized nations but also that their three countries were in a special position, and they proposed, "as a first contribution," to proceed with full exchange of scientific fundamentals with any nation ready to reciprocate. They were "not convinced" that spreading technical information before safeguards were established would be constructive but (a Canadian addition) they were prepared to share such information as soon as effective safeguards "against its use for destructive purposes can be devised."

Their specific proposal was that a commission should be set up under the UN to make recommendations for preventing the destructive use of atomic energy and promoting all its "industrial and humanitarian purposes." In particular the commission should formulate proposals for scientific exchange, for control adequate to ensure only peaceful uses, for the elimination of atomic weapons and for effective safeguards against the risk of violation. This agenda came mainly from Bush.

The declaration concluded with Attlee's main point. These new dangers made it imperative "to banish the scourge of war," and that could be done only "by giving wholehearted support to the United Nations Organization."[57]

Much else happened in this meeting. More time was spent on the secret tangle of Anglo-American nuclear relations than on international control, and Truman and Attlee, with many counselors, proved no more effective in setting a clear and steady course on this question than Roosevelt and Churchill had been alone, fourteen months earlier, at Hyde Park. But our concern here is with the effort for international control, and on this front the meeting did serve to get the American government, at last, in motion. More than a year had passed since Bush and Conant had written to Stimson to try to start the process. Now the United States government was publicly committed to take the matter to the United Nations. The declaration did not constitute a substantive proposal, and as some critics noted it did not directly mention the Soviet Union. But it created a situation in which Washington would have to make decisions on both its own policy and its way of talking to Moscow.

Byrnes tackled the Moscow problem first. The secretary of state appears to have been stirred by the discussions at the Washington meeting. Even before it ended he seized on a speaking engagement in his native South Carolina to speak for the first time of the awesome danger and promise of the atom. While he continued to balance the need for boldness with the need for caution, his dominant tone was one of determination to press ahead with "what is certain to prove a long and difficult journey." Less than a week later, alone in his office on Thanksgiving Day, he decided that the next step should be taken in Moscow. The following day he sent a message to Molotov: The three foreign ministers had consulted one another at the UN Conference at San Francisco in May and at the foreign ministers' meeting in London; was it not time to meet again, and Moscow's turn? Molotov was warmly responsive even before he consulted Stalin, and after a week of delay resulting from Ernest Bevin's understandable annoyance that no one had consulted him (he also had not been in Washington with Attlee) the meeting was set for mid-December.[58]

Byrnes had other motives for proposing the Moscow meeting. The general political impasse reached at London had endured through the autumn, and Byrnes was ready for a new effort to break it. Still he put atomic energy at the head of his agenda, and he underlined the importance of the problem repeatedly in his exchanges with Bevin before leaving. He wanted Soviet agreement to join in sponsoring the idea of a United Nations commission.

The Russians proposed that this question come last: Byrnes readily agreed. In consequence his scientific adviser—Conant on this occasion—had a chance to watch for a week as the three foreign ministers reviewed their almost worldwide differences—on the procedure for peace treaties, on Eastern Europe, on Japan, on China and Iran.

During the days before the last item was reached there was almost no mention of atomic energy. Molotov did remark informally to Conant that the president of Harvard should speak on atomic energy at the University of Moscow, but when Byrnes followed up by telling Molotov that Conant would be glad to make such a speech Molotov said he had no authority in the matter and had only meant to be pleasant. Toward the end of the meeting, on Christmas Eve, when Molotov offered a crude jape about Conant having "an atom bomb" in his pocket, Stalin rebuked him, offering a generous toast to the achievements of the Western scientists. Conant continued to hope that scientific exchange over time might produce constructive results and made a careful proposal on the subject to Byrnes, which went nowhere. Conant's own comment on his hopes for scientific exchange is illuminating: "I was never asked by Secretary Byrnes to discuss my proposals. I did not realize that the decision to place the problem of the control of atomic energy before the United Nations had already precluded the development of any arrangement involving only two or three nations."[59]

When at last it was time for formal discussion of atomic energy, the discussion was entirely on procedure in the UN commission; no one made any statement or asked any questions about the atomic energy policy of the three parties or any other country. Both Molotov and Byrnes had said more about atomic energy in public speeches than they said to each other in Moscow. The American proposal, which rested firmly on the Washington declaration, was accepted with only one material change. At the insistence of the Russians, it was agreed that while the proposed commission should be established by the General Assembly, it would report to the Security Council and be accountable to the Security Council "in matters affecting security." There was some sparring over this change, but Molotov, and Stalin on appeal, stood firm. Molotov correctly argued that security was the most important aspect of the problem, and if he also had in mind that in the Security Council the interests of the Soviet Union were protected by its great-power veto, he was merely demonstrating anew a point that should have been self-evident from the beginning—that there would be no "UN solution" that included the Soviet Union without Soviet consent. To take the matter to the United Nations would change the location in which the question would be raised and it might also change the way it was addressed. It would not change the question itself.

The Acheson-Lilienthal Report

Before the Americans could approach the new UN commission, they had to know what they themselves wanted. The principles agreed in Moscow were not a program. So now at last, at a level capable of action, it came home to the American government that it did not have a policy. It was only at the end of ten days that he spent in Washington between his return from Moscow and a departure to London, that Byrnes did what Bush and Conant had urged on Stimson fifteen months before. He appointed a committee to formulate American policy on the international control of atomic energy. Acheson was chairman, and the other four members were Bush, Conant, Groves, and McCloy. Four of the five could have played their parts fifteen months earlier, though Groves would not then have been considered a man with a strong sense of policy.[60] The composition of the committee strongly suggests consultation between Byrnes and Bush: These were people that both were ready to trust.

The new boy on this subject was the chairman. We do not know precisely how Acheson came to be chosen; one may guess that it was a combination of his rank, second only to Byrnes in the State Department, and of his own interest, already displayed to Truman in September over Stimson's proposal, and probably shown also to Byrnes in his ten days back on the job. Acheson was also the natural candidate of others in the State Department, close to Byrnes but themselves not sufficiently senior for the assignment. It was in many ways a happy choice. Acheson had three qualities which gave him extraordinary advantages in the execution of his assignment: He believed in its importance, he disbelieved in his own omniscience, and he had an experienced respect for both committee process and staff support. He also had as his assistant Herbert S. Marks, a young lawyer who had understood the urgency of the problem better than most nonscientists. It was Marks who made the decisive suggestion that the committee Byrnes had appointed was too grand to work the problem through for itself.[61] Let there be a board of consultants with the necessary time and technical skills, and let its chairman be David Lilienthal, then the chairman of the Tennessee Valley Authority, where Marks had worked for him. Lilienthal had made the TVA a symbol of effective public enterprise; at forty-five he was able, articulate, energetic, optimistic, ambitious, and decent. With Lilienthal's assistance and the advice of his committee, the other members of the panel were soon chosen: Chester Barnard, an elder statesman of the business world and theorist of executive decision making, Charles A. Thomas of Monsanto Chemical, and Harry A. Winne of General Electric, the first a plutonium chemist and the second a proven manager, both veterans of the already legendary Manhattan Project, and finally, as the board's physicist, J. Robert Oppenheimer.[62]

Oppenheimer, the genius of Los Alamos, became the decisive force behind the Acheson-Lilienthal report of March 1946, a document whose completion, publication, and warm public reception was the high-water mark of the American effort to grapple with the issue of international control. All of the participants, especially Acheson and Lilienthal, have emphasized that the whole enterprise was a group effort, but the record also demonstrates the truth of Acheson's further conclusion that "the most stimulating and creative mind among us was Robert Oppenheimer's."[63]

It was Oppenheimer whose natural intelligence, physical understanding, prolonged exposure, and practical imagination allowed him to formulate what became the central proposition of the report: that there should be an "Atomic Development Authority" with a worldwide monopoly of control over the dangerous elements of the whole field of atomic energy, from mining through manufacturing, and with the affirmative duty of keeping at the forefront of all forms of nuclear research and development.

The report gave both negative and positive reasons for this recommendation. Most of the other proposals that had been made in the aftermath of Hiroshima were designed to deal with the problem either by some agreement to "outlaw" atomic weapons or by some system of inspection, or both. But the very nature of a world of nations was such that merely to "outlaw" decisive weapons would be ineffective (this had been Attlee's instant judgment)—and as long as the nations remained free to conduct their own atomic activities, no system of inspection could hope to give confidence. "So long as intrinsically dangerous activities may be carried on by nations, rivalries are inevitable and fears are engendered that place so great a pressure upon a system of international enforcement by police methods that no degree of ingenuity or technical competence could possibly hope to cope with them."[64]

But if a single international authority were the only legal participant in dangerous activities, these difficulties would be greatly eased. To make atomic bombs one would require uranium—let uranium sources be controlled, and for additional safety thorium sources too, since with only a little uranium one could use thorium too. To make bombs one must either separate fissile isotopes or make plutonium in reactors; let the sources of the two metals and all reactors and separation plants beyond laboratory size be under the control of the authority. International in its staff and management, the authority would be immune to internal subversion, and any illegal undertaking large enough to lead to weapons would be discoverable by methods of inspection much more rough and ready, much less intrusive, than would otherwise be required.

Moreover, an international authority could promote, and be reinforced by, energetic research and development in the constructive application of atomic energy. Here was an idea deeply resonant to Oppenheimer's own spirit. He did not think an authority with merely preventive functions would be durably effective, however wide its formal process. "Only a unit that was organic and alive could keep abreast of the changing technology and attract an able, imaginative staff. . . . It would exercise certain controls, to be sure, but its emphasis would be on positive, not negative, responsibilities."[65]

The board of consultants began its work on January 23, 1946. After waiting through a week whose main highlight was his own "short course in nuclear physics"—his colleagues were awestruck—Oppenheimer made his basic proposal; his idea "had immediate appeal," and the panel never looked back. Under Lilienthal's guidance it continued to work as a group; every member had a part in its drafting and redrafting. It also spent a week visiting the secret atomic empire and returned with a stronger sense of mission than ever.[66]

That mission was to win its own government and people to the cause of the international authority. Immediately, it needed the agreement of the Acheson committee. The board of consultants was going well beyond its initial charge—to ascertain the facts on inspection and control. It was pursuing these facts to a strong conclusion. It kept in touch with Acheson, and he did not discourage it from presenting its own judgment, but when the consultants and the full committee met at Dumbarton Oaks on March 7 no one knew how it would go. It went well. Groves and Conant thought the draft made inspection seem too easy; Bush thought it important to reassure the American people that they were not going to be asked to entrust everything to the authority all at once; he still believed in "stages." In one sense, as Lilienthal told the committee and his own journal, that was a basic difference: "They were committed to a 'step-by-step' program, in their earlier statements; our plan is integral."[67] But in a wider sense these were differences within agreement. For Acheson, Bush, Conant, and McCloy this was the best plan they had seen for doing a job they strongly believed in, and for Groves it was, if incomplete, at least endurable, for if he did not himself believe the Russians would ever agree to a workable plan of control, he did at least believe that such a plan must be offered, and he was willing to concur in this one. He was not in the habit of open disagreement with Bush and Conant and McCloy.

The committee's approval in the end was enthusiastic. The revisions it required were made quickly and deftly. The board shortened and softened its argument on the limited value of inspection: It was not in itself sufficient, and too much would be unacceptable and even unworkable, but some would surely be necessary, especially for the control of raw materials. It also added to its report a section on the way the new institution might be built, concluding sensibly enough that some steps—like the sharing of the "theoretical information" necessary for discussion and planning—would be required at an early stage, and that others, like the transfer of physical control over raw materials and production facilities, would depend on negotiations and decisions "in the domain of highest national policy in international relations." With these revisions the Acheson committee in effect endorsed the report, sending it on to Byrnes with a letter of transmittal describing it, in the board's own language, "not as a final plan, but as a place to begin, a foundation on which to build." But the letter also called it "the most constructive analysis of the question of international control we have seen and a definitely hopeful approach to a solution of the entire problem." The consultants had won the backing of the committee.[68]

Bernard Baruch

On the same day that this agreement was reached, Sunday, March 17, President Truman asked Bernard Baruch to be the principal United States negotiator at the United Nations, and Baruch accepted. The appointment produced a second and more protracted internal debate, this time between Baruch and his advisers and the backers of the Acheson-Lilienthal report. The idea of appointing Baruch apparently originated with Byrnes; none of the ten men involved in the report was consulted. Most of them were shocked. Bush told Baruch to his face that he was hopelessly unqualified; Oppenheimer later recalled that the day he heard of the appointment—March 18—was the day he gave up hope. By the time Baruch was finally ready to speak at the United Nations Byrnes himself had confessed to Acheson that the choice was "the worst mistake I have ever made."[69]

Like many "elder statesmen" before and since, Bernard Baruch at seventy-five was the object of sharply divided opinions. To his admirers—among whom most members of the Senate were proud to be counted—he was the wonderfully practical counselor to presidents, the organizer of the home front in World War I, the man who had solved the rubber crisis in World War II and could have done much more if Roosevelt had been less wary of him. For leading senators in both parties he was a most reassuring choice, and Byrnes wanted reinforcement in the Senate.[70]

But to his critics this wise and farsighted Baruch was largely the invention of inspired public relations work, lavish hospitality, and skillfully spread political gifts from his speculator's fortune; his serious work, if any, was well behind him. To Lilienthal, the choice was the opposite of what was needed. "We need a man who is young, vigorous, not vain, and whom the Russians would feel isn't out simply to put them in a hole. . . . Baruch has none of these qualifications." Later when he and Baruch had become friends, Lilienthal called this judgment "brash"—but it accurately reflects what he thought at the time. Even Baruch's admirers seldom denied either his vanity or his low energy level.[71]

As for Truman, he shared the opinion of Byrnes that Baruch was needed to help hold the Senate and the public, but his private opinion was tart. On the day he formally offered the appointment, he noted in longhand on his appointment sheet: "Asked old man Baruch [by telephone] to act as U.S. representative. . . . He wants to run the world, the moon and maybe Jupiter—but we'll see." On the substance of the matter, and especially in their attitudes toward the Russians, the two men would turn out to be in close agreement, but Truman's personal distaste for Baruch eventually separated them in later years.[72]

Even a man with less vanity than Baruch might have been troubled by one element in the situation into which he had been called. The Acheson-Lilienthal report, though initially intended as a paper designed to assist the American negotiator in his work, became a public document, and indeed an apparent statement of policy, before he ever had a chance to comment on it. McCloy had warned against the embarrassment in such publication, but neither Acheson nor Lilienthal agreed with him—to Lilienthal indeed a major purpose of the report was to assist in the rational democratic process in which he deeply and somewhat simplistically believed. When the predictable leaks occurred after the inevitable early congressional briefing, those in favor of publication had their way, even though neither Byrnes nor Truman had yet decided to approve the report. It was published on March 28, and while it promptly drew fire from the right, the response of moderates and liberals was so strongly favorable as to make it quite understandable for Baruch to feel, with some resentment, that his hand was being forced.

Baruch pressed Truman for clarification of his role, and Truman, characteristically, told him not to worry: The president would make final decisions, but the draftsman of the formal U.S. proposals would be Baruch himself. By early April Baruch had finally and somewhat loftily agreed to let himself be confirmed by the Senate and had begun to prepare himself. But there was already a strain on his relations with the creators of the report, and in the next two months Baruch jockeyed for position, trying to take his distance from the parts of the Acheson-Lilienthal report he disliked and yet gradually drawn by Acheson and Byrnes into substantial acceptance of its argument. Baruch's vanity was expensive in terms of the time it took to do this work, and the members of Lilienthal's board also showed some pride and prejudice. When Baruch asked them to carry on as *his* consultants, they refused; they feared entrapment, and they were fiercely and collectively loyal to the one true plan. So the process of defending their work before Baruch, Byrnes, and finally Truman fell largely to Acheson, supported throughout by Marks.[73]

Fortunately for Acheson and also for Baruch, the latter had, in John M. Hancock, a colleague of flexible sagacity (if we except his exaggerated concern for the protection of the private property of mine owners). Hancock and Acheson succeeded in working effectively together. Baruch himself was able to focus strongly on only one issue of substance, the problem of enforcement, but Hancock set himself to understand not only the argument of the Acheson-Lilienthal report, but the personal views of Byrnes and Acheson. In the end the policy guidance that Truman approved in early June reflected the view of Baruch on enforcement and the views of the Acheson-Lilienthal report on nearly everything else. As Acheson and Hancock traded memoranda, their differences steadily narrowed and the essentials of the proposal endured.

Indeed the memoranda thus exchanged were essentially revised versions, one after another, of a paper that Baruch himself requested from the Lilienthal board at the end of the one occasion that he met with them. What he asked for, almost plaintively, was a summary of what the board itself thought it was recommending: "Give him a chart, he said, and he could steer his way."[74] Working until after midnight that evening, May 18, the board did just what he asked. There followed two counterdrafts by Hancock and parallel replies or revisions from Acheson, but a line-by-line comparison of what the Lilienthal board drafted on May 18 and what Truman approved on June 7 shows plainly that what Truman approved—always excepting the issue of enforcement—was in essence the proposal of the Lilienthal board. The argument was shortened and tightened, but it was all there: The development authority with wide powers, both affirmative and negative, the worldwide activity of control and development, the successive stages and even the technical disclosures required in the process of negotiation. Of the words that Truman initialed 90 percent were written by the Lilienthal board in one evening's work. When Lilienthal saw the presidentially initialled memorandum he was understandably delighted: "It was our Report to the 'T.' "[75]

Baruch's one big change was on the question of enforcement. He insisted on swift and sure penalties for violation of the plan. On this point the Acheson-Lilienthal report had been silent, by the deliberate choice of its authors. The Lilienthal board had decided to make its argument in terms of the hope and confidence that a strong international authority would create; it did not want to argue in terms that implied mistrust of the Soviet Union. Two members of the Acheson Committee, McCloy and Acheson himself, had seen at first hand the difficulties presented in framing the United Nations Charter by the issue of international action against a great power. The Soviet Union had insisted on a veto over such action; so had the United States. This plain political fact was matched by a problem of logic: What would be meant by international action against a great power, or by "swift and sure penalties" in so grave a case as illegal work on atomic bombs? War? The committee did not disagree with its consultants; this was a good subject to stay away from. The best solution was to be sure that the plan provided for adequate early warning of large-scale violation; then other nations would have time to act as they chose.[76]

Baruch took the opposite view. He could not advocate a proposal that did not honestly confront the need for a system of enforcement—of "immediate and certain punishment" subject to no veto. Anything less would be fraud, offering safety where none could be assured. The subject was hotly debated on May 17, but neither side moved the other. Baruch stuck to his guns, and when Byrnes and Truman successively reviewed the question they both agreed with him. The United States would insist, in the careful words of the memorandum Truman approved, on a clear statement of the consequences of "violations . . . including . . . the penalties and concerted action which would follow." Truman and Baruch agreed that there should be no veto on enforcement, and Baruch knew that on this issue he could state the case his own way.[77]

Truman's decision came easily. On other issues he had supported

Byrnes while Byrnes supported Acheson through May and early June. He was no expert on the Acheson-Lilienthal report, but he understood its basic recommendation, and he agreed with it. He never publicly endorsed the report at the time, but that was a tactical avoidance of confrontation with Baruch; in his memoirs it is "a great state paper."[78] His respect for both Acheson and Lilienthal was great; one would become his secretary of state and the other his first chairman of the United States Atomic Energy Commission. But on the veto he simply agreed with Baruch. It was not a new preference for him; back in November he had told Attlee and King of his belief that reliable UN control "might make it necessary to abandon the veto power." In expressing this agreement now he explained that he had always believed in sanctions against aggression; if Stimson had been backed up on Manchuria there would have been no World War II. This was hypothetical history of doubtful validity, but there is no reason at all to doubt that Truman believed it; it was a popular view at the time. The president signed a basic policy paper that was clearly derived from the Lilienthal board's own summary of its views, while he also approved a memorandum from Baruch that was full of the old man's doubts of that particular week: Warning time would be dangerously short; secrets were leaking out; denaturing, as a means of safeguarding nuclear materials, had been overplayed, but above all, "penalization," "punishment"—in their talk Baruch said "war"—must be visited on violators.[79]

This difference over the veto seemed important to the participants at the time, but in retrospect it is not easy to see why the issue raised such strong feelings. Lilienthal later asserted that he and his colleagues "agreed completely with the 'no-veto' principle," but "felt that the injection of this issue prematurely would endanger consideration of the affirmative basis of the plan itself." To Acheson the issue was unreal. He shared Baruch's view that effective "punishment" of a great power meant war, and he thought a general agreement to go to war on such an issue would mean little. Moreover, if the Russians thought it was aimed at them, as they almost surely would, they would certainly use the veto to prevent any agreement to get rid of it. "Provisions for paper police sanctions . . . were only an illusion."[80]

After one more week of drafting and redrafting, Baruch was ready, and on June 14, at the opening session of the Atomic Energy Commission of the United Nations, in the Hunter College gymnasium in the Bronx, he set forth the American plan in an address of one hour, crafted by his friend Herbert Bayard Swope and intended for immortality. "We are here to make a choice between the quick and the dead," he began, and he went on in overblown eloquence to describe the absolute weapon, to plead for an end of war itself, to propose an authority, to insist on the indispensable abolition of the veto in this one issue, and at last to set out the main points of the Acheson-Lilienthal report. The Baruch plan lay before the world.

Impasse Without Negotiation

Within weeks the plan, as a real possibility, was gravely ill, and in less than six months it was dead. On June 19 Andrey Gromyko, then only thirty-six, spoke for the Soviet Union. Instead of international control he wanted a flat prohibition on the possession, production, and use of atomic weapons, and he announced that the Soviet Union would never accept any change in the veto. On July 24 he repeated his proposals, repeated his insistence on the veto, and added a root-and-branch denunciation of the Baruch proposals: The Soviet Union could not accept them "either as a whole or in their separate parts." No American could accept this position; even if there had been no issue of veto-free punishment the gap between the two positions was enormous, and as time passed it grew wider. Truman told Baruch he should "stand pat."[81] The old man did just that. He continued for a little while to hope that when the Russians really understood the plan they would take more interest, but during August the balance of his concern shifted. Losing hope of Russian agreement, unwilling to bend on what he saw as basic, he now set out to win the propaganda battle; he would wait a while longer, but only for the purpose of making it entirely clear that it was the Soviet government that stood in the way of agreement. By December he had run out of patience and forced a vote. The language of the resolution was moderated in deference to other friendly delegations, but in essence it endorsed the American position. Gromyko remained adamant. The resolution was passed by a vote of 10 to 0, the Russians and Poles abstaining. To Baruch the vote was a resounding endorsement. But to him and to his government it was also the end of the road for any real hope that the plan would be accepted. Baruch resigned in early January, and there is no record that from that day forward anyone near the top of the Truman administration had any hope, or made any effort, for agreement.

The bitter truth is, moreover, that what we have just reviewed was not at any time a serious negotiation on either side. The discussions in the United Nations continued throughout 1947 and 1948, but with steadily decreasing hope of any substantive result. The record of those later years is helpful mainly in demonstrating, more clearly in each successive session, the depth and strength of the Soviet rejection not only of Baruch's position on the veto, but of the basic idea of the Lilienthal board. What we do not find is any effort, by either side, to narrow the difference by negotiation.

Indeed there is almost nothing of this kind even in 1946. Only one private diplomatic discussion of any substance is recorded in *Foreign Relations of the United States,* and that one discussion led to gloomy but correct American conclusions on Soviet rigidity. What the Americans heard that went beyond public Soviet statements was that the Soviet government would accept no limitation of any sort on its own atomic program. In response to an American assertion that "the American Proposals would apply equally to both nations," the Soviet official, who came alone to the meeting, replied that "the Soviet Union was not seeking equality, but, rather, freedom to pursue its own policies in complete freedom and without any interference or control from the outside." When this conversation was reported to the political officers of the American embassy in Moscow, they remarked that this position was "a Stalinist truth." They also noted that no American concession such as an end to American bomb production would induce the Soviet Union "to abandon its own gigantic atomic research project."[82]

There is no report of any other serious exchange. Whatever else it was, Baruch's diplomacy was open and unchanging. His position did not alter between June 14 and the December vote. Neither did Gromyko's. We have here a fact of some importance: In the forum to which, by agreement, they had referred the question—the largest threat to the human future ever known—the representatives of the two greatest powers in the world never undertook any direct negotiation. Why not?

We have seen already that the American choice of the United Nations as a forum was dictated in part by public belief in the United Nations as a body to be reinforced by use. That choice certainly did require formal public statements. But there is nothing about the United Nations that requires its use *only* for public diplomacy; in the years since 1946 American and Soviet diplomats in New York have often said important things to each other in private. As early as 1949 the United Nations provided the site for the meetings that put an end to the blockade of Berlin. The public forum did not preclude private negotiation; what forces did?

Let us begin with Baruch, the man on the spot. He had come to the UN to make a real proposal, and with some real hope of a positive response. But he also came with a conviction that what the president had authorized him to put forward must be presented not merely as "a basis of negotiations but a formula of a secure peace."[83] He would be flexible on details but adamant on fundamentals. Let a government accept the fundamentals and Baruch could be accommodating; as a result the documents produced by the majority in the UN Atomic Energy Commission are often more persuasive than the initial American proposals.[84] If the Soviet government had given a yes, even in principle, to the two basic ideas—an Atomic Development Authority and the end of the veto in atomic matters—Baruch and his colleagues would have been as eager for negotiations as any Wall Street operator within striking distance of a deal. Even if only one of the two had been accepted, with fuzzy noises about the other, there would have been much incentive for serious talk. Baruch wanted an agreement. But if there was to be unrelenting Soviet insistence on "the principle of unanimity," together with a total absence of support for control and inspection by an international authority, then Baruch saw nothing to negotiate. As early as August 1, although he was not ready to give up, he was getting ready to accept the reality of Soviet intransigence on both points, telling the Canadians that "ultimately we must face the facts," that "the United States would not trade" and that "this problem was far too important to do any trading about."[85]

Baruch's sternness here was more than a tactical difference with the Acheson-Lilienthal group, but perhaps his tactics might have been different if the publicity given the group's report had not led him to put an early public stamp of his own on the problem. If Acheson had proposed a firm and inflexible opening position, it takes no great imagination to think of Baruch advising the president that his vast experience of affairs led him to doubt the wisdom of making one's first position one's last in a big negotiation. Indeed one of his initial complaints about the Acheson-Lilienthal report was that it looked like an effort to lock him in with no room for maneuver.[86] Baruch had shown considerable openness on the subject of relations with the Soviet Union. In the last half of 1945 he had had on his payroll Professor D. F. Fleming, later the father of cold war revisionism, and he had hoped for "a two-way street" of cooperation with Russia. In early 1946 he had been drawn toward Churchill's sterner view, and a year later he made the first public use of the phrase *cold war,* but as he took up his work on atomic energy he was not rigidly hostile to the Soviet Union.[87] He had a deeper and more specific reason for his wariness; he did not think an agreement on so great an issue could rest on trust alone, so he was not going to settle for anything less than solid guarantees. He took this position so often, and repeated it with such emphasis, that there is no reason to doubt that it reflected both his own convictions and an equally firm judgment that most of his countrymen agreed with him.[88]

In a sense everyone who struggled with the problem of international control, in 1945 and 1946, had to come to terms with the question whether a less-than-perfect agreement was better than none at all. The answer to that question depended heavily on the way one weighed the Soviet threat against the threat inherent in the atom itself. At extreme positions like those of General Groves and Henry Wallace, the tensions in this balance would disappear: To Groves, in his inmost being, the right answer was to hang on to the secret, build the best, the biggest, and the most, and challenge the Russians to catch up, or even tell them flatly not to try.[89] To Wallace it was the intransigence of Washington, not Moscow, that prevented a good agreement. But in between, where most of the actors and most of the public were, the problem was one of balance, and Baruch stood at the wary end of the scale: He thought the bomb was a "winning weapon," and he was for holding on to it unless and until he got firm guarantees.

At the other end of the scale were most of the atomic scientists. To them it was the bomb itself that was the final enemy. This might be a necessary weapon; if no agreement could be reached one might have to keep it for deterrence. But it was not a winner, in the long run, in any acceptable sense, because others would have it too, and in any atomic war all would lose. This, in essence, was the decisive argument in the deliberations that produced the Acheson-Lilienthal report: The common enemy of mankind was the atomic bomb as a widely held weapon; the common interest of mankind, and of the nation too, was to get that potential enemy under control. If men and nations could be brought to see that common interest, they might act on it, in spite of all their other differences. And one should set forth on that effort in hope not fear.

This conviction did not make the scientists automatic supporters of a serious negotiation. The Acheson-Lilienthal report was in its own way a considerable obstacle to realistic bargaining with the Russians. Lilienthal, as he later explained, had seen it as his duty to start from the facts, rather than the political problems, "to analyze what is called a political problem in a scientific spirit." And indeed the Acheson-Lilienthal report does reflect, even today, a remarkable respect for the facts of the atom and the innate requirements of effective international control. Those requirements were strongly, if only inferentially, supported by the searching review of the Scientific and Technical Committee of the UN commission, and they have never been seriously challenged by Soviet critics or by Western revisionists. If you wanted to sweep the bomb off the international board—and that is exactly what Lilienthal and his colleagues were trying to do—then an Atomic Development Authority was the right way to go about it.

But once "the facts" had led you to this conclusion you could not settle for less. To its creators, their proposal was, in political terms, the most modest that would do the job. They thought it much less intrusive in its requirement for inspection than what would be needed if dangerous activities remained in the hands of individual states. They saw it as nonpolitical in design, and they would not have supported any rigidly self-serving American position on the order of the stages leading to its establishment. But at the time it did not occur to them—any of them, as far as the records show—that the basic concept should be abandoned or even compromised. In that fundamental sense Oppenheimer's concept was not intended to be negotiable; it was intended to be fair, and to be in the common interest, but it was also seen as *required.* If it was rejected, there would be nothing left to discuss.

Those who framed the report did not underestimate the difficulty of winning Soviet support for their proposal. Lilienthal publicly said it might be "something like insisting that a fellow who never in his life has broad-jumped more than ten feet must jump twenty feet." Hancock understood Oppenheimer to say, in private, that "the proposed system is entirely incompatible with the present Russian system." But both men put their hopes in the eventual persuasiveness of "the facts."[90]

Oppenheimer in particular did everything he could to get the facts across. It was with that purpose that he eventually joined Baruch's delegation in New York. With the utmost frustration he discovered that very little could be done there. He thought part of the problem was that Baruch and his team did not truly understand the plan; in addition, he thought that "Baruch's preoccupation with 'punishment' and 'veto' has done great harm so that there is little or no discussion of the essentials of the plan." But a deeper trouble was that there was no one to talk to. "Gromyko does not have any authority, and the men who do have are unknown, no one can talk to them, no one can have any assurance that they know, firsthand, what this is all about."[91]

There was another difficulty in making the facts persuasive: secrecy. In one sense the reality of the bomb was adequately declared by Hiroshima and Nagasaki. Although those terrible events may not be fully understood even now, after forty years of awareness and study upon study, culminating in a massive report commissioned by the two cities themselves, it was not hard to know from the start what an enormous difference these events made.[92] The problem was rather to express the difference persuasively. In its immediate human dimension there was no problem of secrecy; as it happened, in this same summer of 1946 John Hersey's *Hiroshima,* appearing all at once in a single issue of *The New Yorker,* brilliantly demonstrated by a careful account of what happened to six survivors how catastrophic this single primitive bomb had been. Hersey was a master of reporting, but no scientist, and he had no access to secrets.[93]

Yet secrets still existed, or at least secrecy did, and its effect on the persuasiveness of "the facts" was great, if hard to measure. The crudest and perhaps the most important impact had been registered at the turn of the year, when Senator Arthur H. Vandenberg had forced the administration to give sweeping assurances against any revelations before agreement. As Lilienthal was quick to recognize, those assurances were in danger of creating a catch-22: "We would not supply facts until safeguards had been established. And yet without supplying facts to other countries how could they know enough to discuss safeguards?" Formally the difficulty had been repaired by the president's direction of June 7: "The United States must be prepared to make available the information essential to a reasonable understanding of the proposals which it advocates."[94] But in reality every scientist, and Oppenheimer more than most, felt an oppressive constraint in what he was free to say.

There was a deep and powerful difference between what the atomic scientists, and Oppenheimer in particular, could say in secret and what they could say in public. The members of Lilienthal's board had felt that difference listening to Oppenheimer on January 28 in New York. Lilienthal, not easily impressed by ordinary military notions of secrecy, had suspected "that in the real sense there are no secrets," but he found out at least enough to change the way he thought:

> No fairy tale that I read in utter rapture and enchantment as a child, no spy mystery, no "horror" story, can remotely compare with the scientific recital I listened to for six or seven hours today. . . . I heard more of the complete story of the atomic bomb, past, present, and immediate future, than any but a few men have yet heard. It was told well, technically, dispassionately, but interspersed with stories of the decisions that had to be made . . . [in] this utterly bizarre and, literally, incredible business. There were things that have never been even hinted at that are accomplished, or virtually accomplished, facts, that change the whole thesis of our inquiry, and of the course of the world in this generation.
>
> None of this can be written down. These are the very top of the top secrets of our country . . .[95]

In his memoirs Acheson recorded a somewhat lighter view of his exposure to Oppenheimer:

> When later I achieved a wholly undeserved reputation for expertise in nuclear matters, no one knew better than Robert Oppenheimer how fraudulent this was. At the beginning of our work he came to stay with us and after dinner each evening would lecture McCloy and me with the aid of a borrowed blackboard on which he drew little figures representing electrons, neutrons, and protons, bombarding one another, chasing one another about, dividing and generally carrying on in unpredictable ways. Our bewildered questions seemed to distress him. At last he put down the chalk in gentle despair, saying, "It's hopeless! I really think you two believe neutrons and electrons *are* little men!" We admitted nothing.[96]

What Lilienthal and Acheson and their colleagues learned did include things that were then real military secrets: how many bombs there were—or how few—and how much—or how little—would give a critical mass. They were told of the process of implosion that had been developed, under such pressure of time, for the plutonium bomb; they were told about the eventual prospect of thermonuclear weapons. But most of all, they were *told*. They did not have to take the resulting sense of awe and fear on someone else's say so, and the direct exposure that they thus obtained was of the greatest value in convincing them of the magnitude of the danger they were asked to deal with.

There also resulted from this access and from their collective experience a considerable aura of authority. In his lavish praise of everything in Baruch's speech except the attack on the veto, Walter Lippmann paid particular tribute to the special knowledge of the members of the committee and the board:

> The proposal which Mr. Baruch has made for the United States is in all its essentials the work of the ten men who produced the Acheson-Lilienthal Report and its covering letter. These ten men know more about the atomic bomb than any other body of men in the whole world could possibly know. They include the leading men who conceived it, invented it, designed it, manufactured it, and played a responsible part in the military and political planning to use it. No other collection of men, in any country, or in this one, could possess the same theoretical and practical, the same intimate and detailed, knowledge. For while the theoretical science is generally known to nuclear physicists everywhere, there is no other group of men who combine all the practical experience of actually making and using a weapon.
>
> Their conclusions require a very special kind of respectful attention, a little like that which an ancient geographer, who knew in theory, but in theory only, that the world was round, would have to pay to Columbus and Magellan.[97]

There is hyperbole here—Acheson and Lilienthal themselves had been neophytes in January, and information about atomic reality was not nearly as much the private preserve of any man as Lippmann argued. But the significant point is that a man with more than thirty years of experience in the study of politics, with doubts already expressed about the durable significance of "the secret," could attribute a very special understanding to insiders.[98]

It was just this sense of special understanding, so impressive to Lippmann from outside and Lilienthal from inside, that neither Oppenheimer nor anyone else could convey to any Russian because of the American obsession with secrecy. No one can say that a lecture on atomic reality from Oppenheimer would have changed Gromyko's words or Stalin's mind—we shall see that Soviet policy was based on deeply set convictions about political reality that would not have been easy to shake—but the fact remains that the kind of extended discussion of the new reality that Bush and Conant had envisioned, that Lilienthal had experienced, and that Lippmann respected, simply never occurred with the Russians. Under warning by Vandenberg, under watch by Groves, and channeled through Baruch and the unresponsive Soviet delegation in New York, the scientific effort to talk to the Russians about "the facts" and the conclusions they "compelled" was very much weaker than what had gone on in the open intimacy of the board of consultants.

Ideas about secrecy had another and still more baleful effect in a different quarter. The concept that the United States was ahead and could stay ahead by keeping its know-how to itself took deep root in this year. It was constantly nourished by Groves, and most of the politicians found his message persuasive. There is a striking difference, for example, in the way that senators received Groves with approval and Bush with skepticism when the former spoke of fifteen or twenty years of American monopoly and the latter of the prospect of a foreign (obviously Russian) bomb in three to five years. By a process of thought not easy to explain those who were most wary of the Russians tended also to believe that by protecting secrets and by energetic effort the United States could be sure of staying ahead, and that staying ahead was what mattered most.

We are here face to face with one of the most powerful and durable tensions in the whole long story of the American experience with nuclear weapons: the tension between fear of the atom and reliance upon its protection. That tension reappears in every debate and in every judgment that political leaders have made. In 1946 it was what finally divided a Baruch from an Oppenheimer. Much deeper than any difference over the details of the American proposal or the tactics of debate was the difference over the nature of nuclear reality. To both men that reality had more than one face. Oppenheimer knew the value of getting there first from intense and direct experience, and Baruch had spoken of choosing between life and death. But in the end what Baruch saw first was the "winning weapon," and right at Alamogordo what Oppenheimer had seen more clearly was "the destroyer of worlds." So one was serene and the other despairing in the face of the emerging impasse at the United Nations.

It is not so easy to tell just where Byrnes and Truman should be placed along this scale, or how their own attitudes affected their view of this issue. Byrnes was impatient with scientists in October, and still earlier he had briefly hoped the bomb would reinforce his diplomacy. But once he listened to Bush in November his position became, and remained, more balanced; his speech of November 16 showed a real understanding of the atomic danger. Yet his conversion, while genuine, was not passionate, and in any case, as he understood very well by 1946, the final decisions rested with the president. In the spring, as he sought to reconcile what he heard from Acheson and what he heard from Baruch, he does not appear to have been hampered by any overwhelming convictions. If Byrnes never practiced atomic diplomacy neither did he ever practice the diplomacy of atomic agreement.

We are driven back to Truman. What balance of concerns governed the man who spoke of "the greatest thing in history," who said he understood its tragic significance, who planned to hang on to secret know-how but repeatedly put his name to papers declaring no monopoly would last, who approved the substance of the Acheson-Lilienthal report, but who also backed Baruch on the veto?

With Harry Truman it is dangerous to attempt complex explanations; he was an extraordinarily downright man. So let us start by supposing that he meant all the things he said and did what he did because he thought it right. Let us assume that he really does agree with the principles of the Acheson-Lilienthal report and also with Baruch on the veto. Let us also assume that he really does understand the danger of the bomb—there will be more evidence of that in later years—even while he is glad to be ahead and has no intention of sharing know-how except in the context of a solid agreement. It is not really very hard to hold all these views together if you add one more: that in this field the Russians could present no early threat.

The evidence that in 1946 Truman saw no imminent danger of a Soviet bomb is indirect but persuasive. There is no evidence that anyone with direct access to him ever said that the Russians would soon have a bomb. Both Leahy and Groves took the opposite view.

Those with gloomier estimates were mainly scientists, and Truman's interest in the political views of scientists was low. He had a strong belief that the American system of enterprise had a lot to do with the American success. He believed that the production miracles of the war confirmed the superiority of that system, especially over the "slave labor" of the Soviet system.[99] The most striking and disquieting confirmation of this attitude comes from later years. In early 1953, shortly after he left the White House, Truman casually told reporters that he did not think the Russians had the bomb: "I am not convinced the Russians have achieved the know-how to put the complicated mechanism together."[100] He had acted on a different assessment while in office, but he was convinced against his will. In 1946 there was neither evidence nor direct counsel to run against this conviction. Even Stimson had never told him that the Russians would get the bomb fast—only that they would get it sooner or later and it didn't matter which.

There was a failure here in the work of the Acheson committee and the Lilienthal board. Part of the initial mandate to those groups had been to make "a judgment (on the basis of all the facts, including top secrets secured by our military intelligence) of the industrial and scientific potential of other nations (really meaning Russia) for the development of atomic bombs; in other words, the relative hazards to us."[101] But this part of the job was never tackled by either Acheson's committee or Lilienthal's board. The board quickly became engrossed in its work on the testing and elaboration of Oppenheimer's basic idea, and the committee conducted no separate inquiries of any kind. It does not appear that anyone was troubled by the omission; probably the board thought the question unimportant, considering that the realities that made international control imperative were independent of the number of years of grace that might precede a Soviet bomb. And certainly the committee had its hands full in deciding what it thought of the board's bold proposal. So the question of the capabilities of others was addressed only glancingly, in the committee's letter of transmittal, which reported that the disclosures required to get international agreement might save one year for a country that might otherwise have the ability to get a bomb in five years, and went on somewhat gratuitously to say that "Whether any nation—we are excluding Great Britain and Canada—could achieve such an intensive program is a matter of serious doubt."[102] The Acheson-Lilienthal report thus did nothing to tell Truman what he could expect of the Soviet Union, and when, and no other agency moved to fill the gap. He heard only the optimistic guesses of the complacent.

In a wider sense, while Truman believed that it was right to advance a serious proposal for international control, he doubted that the world was ready. There is obvious conviction in his private remark to an old friend back in October 1945 that "maybe we could get world government in a thousand years or something like that, but that it was nothing more than a theory at the present time."[103] His support for the proposals in the Acheson-Lilienthal report was probably not accompanied by high hope.

There is some doubt also as to how far Truman (or Baruch or Byrnes for that matter) really understood the analysis of the report. There is no evidence that he read it with care, nor did he ever discuss its argument with any of the ten men who had a hand in it. He approved its essential conclusions, but it seems doubtful that he ever fully accepted its essential message that an international authority was what the common danger insistently required.[104]

Truman by the spring of 1946 mistrusted the Russians. He had been impressed by Stimson in September, no doubt, but he had not been durably persuaded, and as his troubles with Soviet behavior continued to grow, his interest in a policy of trust declined. His own appetite for direct negotiations had been oversatisfied by Potsdam; from then on negotiations were what he had the secretary of state for. Moreover, his one serious substantive disagreement with Byrnes came in December when he thought the secretary of state was soft on Moscow, and when he himself was "tired [of] babying the Soviets."[105] To approve the Acheson-Lilienthal proposal was one thing; to take a lead in using it as a basis for intense direct negotiations would have been quite another.

All this was Truman, not his advisers. But Truman's policy, on any subject, seldom went beyond the counsel he had to choose from. He was not an initiator but a chooser; the buck stopped here, but he waited for the buck to arrive. Not one of his counselors ever pressed him to go further than he did on this matter. By July, Walter Lippmann might wish out loud that we would talk more seriously with the Russians; Oppenheimer might be in despair because he could not do so. But no one that Truman trusted on such matters raised the question with him. He had gone to the limit of what he thought was wise in what he had authorized Baruch to say in June. It would have been hard, I think, to change his mind, and no one with a solid claim on his attention tried. Those who had his ear were divided; some were fearful of diplomatic softness and others had dared to hope that hope was the right starting point. The fearful thought he might have gone too far; the hopeful thought he had gone as far as they could fairly ask. Neither one nor the other urged him on.

It might have made a difference if they had. Harry Truman had his imperfections, but neither indecision nor hesitation was among them. With a single exception he may have been, among all the statesmen facing nuclear decisions at the end of World War II, the one least troubled by doubt.

The exception was Stalin.

Stalin's Choice

The second country to make a firm decision to make atomic weapons was the Soviet Union. This decision is at once easy and hard to explain—easy because there is a rare and solid agreement among Soviet and non-Soviet students on its basic cause, but hard because we cannot penetrate beyond what official sources tell us of the internal process of the decision. This difficulty will be much more serious as we examine other and more complex Soviet decisions.

The Soviet decision to build a bomb was made by Stalin and communicated to those concerned in the middle of August 1945. The leading Western student of the matter, David Holloway, has found only one "brief and cryptic" account of the decisive meeting. Those present were People's Commissar of Munitions Boris Vannikov, his deputies, and a forty-two-year-old nuclear physicist, Igor V. Kurchatov.

"A single demand of you, comrades," said Stalin, "provide us with atomic weapons in the shortest possible time. You know that Hiroshima has shaken the whole world. The equilibrium has been destroyed [*ravnovesie narushilos*]. Provide the bomb—it will remove a great danger from us."[106]

There is no reason to doubt this account. Stalin had known of the Manhattan Project through intelligence reports. He had probably understood that Truman at Potsdam was telling him about an atomic bomb; Marshal Gyorgy Zhukov tells in his autobiography that he heard Stalin report Truman's remark to Molotov and say, "We'll have to talk it over with Kurchatov and get him to speed things up." But it is most unlikely that Stalin got a full understanding of what the new weapon was like from Truman's short comment, and it does not appear that he received any independent intelligence on the Trinity test before August 9.[107] Moreover Zhukov's account does not square with that of another Soviet general, Sergey Shtemenko, who was in the Soviet delegation and heard an account of the Stalin-Truman conversation from his superior Aleksey Antonov, chief of the Soviet general staff. Shtemenko reports that Antonov, and "Stalin himself apparently," did not get the impression that Truman was discussing a weapon "new in principle." The difference is striking, perhaps especially for what it may suggest of Stalin's lack of interest in discussing possible atomic weapons with a mere chief of staff. David Holloway suggests that there may be some truth in both accounts: perhaps "Stalin knew that Truman had the atomic bomb in mind, but did not appreciate the full significance of the weapon." Adam Ulam, in his brilliant *Stalin,* finds Shtemenko more believable than Zhukov, though he does not tell us why. But any lack of understanding on the point lasted less than a fortnight. Hiroshima told Stalin not only that the Americans had the bomb but that they had made use of it (as he had told Truman he hoped they would). To let this new weapon remain an American monopoly was unthinkable if he could do anything about it—and he believed he could.[108]

Stalin knew in August 1945 that the Soviet Union had both excellent nuclear scientists and a formidable capacity for doing what it had to do industrially. The performance of his munitions makers during the war had been extraordinary; no doubt the atomic bomb was more complicated than tanks and aircraft, but his scientists had told him long before 1945 that these difficulties, though great, could be dealt with. At the end of 1942 he had authorized a serious if small-scale uranium project, moved by evidence that both Germans and Americans were already at work. That he should take this step at the height of the war, in a situation in which he knew he could not expect wartime results, is an ample demonstration of his early determination not to be left out of a race already begun. The project was led by Igor Kurchatov, a nuclear physicist of Oppenheimer's age whose energy and talent had been recognized early, and whose enthusiasm for the undertaking was like that of Ernest Lawrence in the United States. By the end of 1944 there were one hundred research workers in Kurchatov's laboratory, and in the spring of 1945 his effort was reinforced by a number of German scientists who had offered their services to the Soviet Union. Kurchatov and his project were well known to Stalin, and once Hiroshima had "shaken the world" the next step was entirely obvious.[109]

Stalin's decision to end the American monopoly as soon as he could was not kept secret. On November 6, Molotov, as principal speaker on the occasion of the twenty-eighth anniversary of the revolution, announced to tumultuous applause and a rising audience, "We will have atomic energy, and much else." And during the following month both the American and British ambassadors in Moscow reported their belief that the Russians had just that sense of the disruption of a satisfactory balance which is reported in the Soviet account of Stalin's demand for atomic weapons.[110]

What the ambassadors did not report, because they did not know it, was the ground for confidence behind Molotov's boast and the considerable head start the Kurchatov group had made. The Soviet scientists told their government they could do the job in five years if they got full support, and in the end they beat their promise by a year. That such speed was possible was what American scientists were warning. That the Russians would make a most serious effort was the shared prediction of Kennan and Acheson in September—each writing in the aftermath of Stimson's last cabinet meeting. Acheson warned that the Soviet government "must and will exert every energy to restore the loss of power which this discovery has produced."[111] Kennan was just as emphatic: "The Soviet Government will undoubtedly endeavor with every means at its disposal to learn the secrets of atomic energy." But both men focused their attention less on this basic point than on what the American attitude should be, Acheson urging a proposal for cooperation and Kennan warning against any foolish gestures of trust—to reveal any knowledge that might be vital without guarantees "would constitute a frivolous neglect of the vital interests of our people." Kennan's paper did suggest a new and stronger program to obtain information on Soviet progress; in a note on that paper Acheson urged a follow-up—but apparently no such follow-up occurred.[112]

At the working level at least one American observer made a remarkably accurate assessment of Stalin's commitment. Thomas P. Whitney, an attaché at the embassy in Moscow described by Ambassador Harriman as "an extremely competent economist with an excellent command of the Russian language," had concluded in September that the Russians certainly had the will, and probably the resources, to do the job; his report was the trigger of Kennan's own September assessment. In December, in a general economic review, Whitney was more explicit and he identified one formidable advantage of the Soviet system:

> The USSR is out to get the atomic bomb. This has been officially stated. The meager evidence available indicates . . . that super-priority will be given to the enterprise. . . .
>
> The Soviet Government is able to mobilize all the resources of the Soviet Union *in peace as well as in war* for the fulfillment of economic plans. If the primary problem at the present time is the manufacture of the atomic bomb everything else will be sacrificed for that end [emphasis added].[113]

Whitney's assessment does him credit, but even he could not know or report the depth and quality of the Soviet effort, or its roots in earlier decisions. There is little reflection of what he did report in what we know of the thinking of Harry Truman, James Byrnes, or the ten wise men of the Acheson-Lilienthal report during the following year.

Lacking a full appreciation of the firmness, clarity, and confidence of Stalin's decision to make bombs of his own, Americans of all sorts in Washington were ill placed to estimate with accuracy the probable Soviet response to the Acheson-Lilienthal proposal and its presentation by Baruch. The basic offer—to give up the bomb in return for a workable international authority with a monopoly of dangerous activities—seemed generous to most Americans in and out of government. Very few understood at the time that to the Soviet government this proposal, with its requirements for early disclosure and inspection, would mean the exposure of a critically important and deeply secret effort of self-defense at a stage when the Americans still had their own bombs and a large manufacturing head start. The general judgment that the Russians would want a bomb of their own was not accompanied by recognition of the speed and energy of the Soviet effort, nor of the way an intense commitment to that effort might affect Soviet thinking about an international authority.

Hindsight is easier. The Soviet decision to break the American monopoly was immediate and unhesitating, and conversely the American position on international control was seen as an effort to maintain that monopoly. One virtue of the long process in the UN was that gradually Gromyko laid out on the record the full depth of Soviet opposition.[114] The notion of an effective control system—whether by international inspection or by establishment of an operating authority or both—was absolutely unacceptable to the Soviet Union and was routinely described by Soviet spokesmen at all levels as a device for protecting the American monopoly. As the weary debate went on into 1948, Gromyko made the position entirely clear:

> The USSR Government has no intention of permitting a situation, whereby the national economy of the Soviet Union or particular branches of that economy would be placed under foreign control. The Governments of some other countries may look at this question in a different light; that is their affair.[115]

What the Acheson-Lilienthal report saw as a technological imperative the Soviet government saw as a plan to violate its political authority.

Gromyko also rejected Baruch's stand on the veto. Here the Soviets had an easier task polemically, since there were many in other delegations who thought Baruch was unnecessarily insistent on the matter. Gromyko made the Soviet position clear right from the start: the requirement of unanimity among the great powers for action by the Security Council was a fundamental principle without which the UN would not have come into existence; it must not be abandoned. Molotov, late in the year, suggested that there need not be a veto over day-to-day operations of an international authority, but Soviet rejection of any enforcement that lacked its approval was total.[116]

The rest of the Soviet position was equally well attuned to Stalin's fundamental policy. While protecting its atomic energy program from inspectors and dismantlers, the Soviet Union did all it could to limit any advantages the Americans might seek to gain from their temporary monopoly. Gromyko's proposal that bombs should be outlawed was certainly not advanced in any naïve hope that the Americans would promptly accept, but equally certainly the Russians were not blind to the usefulness of making the bomb itself an object of obloquy while only the Americans had it. Soviet propaganda steadily minimized the military and political weight of the bomb; it was the Soviet intervention, not the bomb, that had ended the Japanese war; no one weapon could replace the power of combined arms as demonstrated especially by the Red Army in defeating the Nazis; the bomb would kill civilians, but it would not settle matters at the front. As time passed the United States also came under increasingly strident Soviet criticism for attempting to practice "atomic diplomacy," while at the same time Soviet leaders were careful never to show any concern about atomic weapons during the increasingly bitter disagreements over the making of postwar settlements.[117] All of this fits perfectly with Stalin's decision to have Soviet bombs as secretly and as rapidly as possible; it does not fit at all with any desire to negotiate seriously for effective international control. The Soviet government had no such desire. Recognizing the wide popularity of international control, Soviet leaders from time to time gave lip service to the idea—thus Stalin told an American reporter in October 1946, "It is necessary to have a strict international control of atomic energy." But whenever this onion was peeled in the UN debates, it always turned out that any such control would be managed by each state separately in the territory under its authority.[118]

So the USSR showed no interest whatever in finding any common ground with the Americans or in supporting any proposal even remotely resembling an Atomic Development Authority; there is no record that any Soviet official, at any level, ever tried to suggest ways and means by which specific Soviet objections to the proposal could be met. The sustained efforts of non-Soviet diplomats to elicit such comment were steadily resisted. We have seen that Baruch made little effort to negotiate. Gromyko made none.

A particularly interesting Soviet show of indifference to discussion and *a fortiori* to negotiation was offered in the field of scientific and technical information. American scientists had set great store by such exchanges, believing, as Bush wrote to Byrnes in November 1945, that this was a relatively cost-free way to test Russian willingness to cooperate, and hoping that such exchanges would be attractive to the Russians.[119] But the idea worried Vandenberg and Groves more than it ever attracted the Russians. Right at the start Molotov had backed away from his own suggestion that Conant might give a public lecture. Neither Kurchatov nor any other Soviet physicist who worked on the Soviet bomb project had any contact whatever with Westerners. The scientists attached to Gromyko's delegation were courteous but not communicative and still less inquisitive. Their main concern was to see to it that technical findings were not used to determine what they called political questions; the kind of control that "the facts" might require was the quintessential question of this sort. No Soviet scientist ever conceded that the technical realities required control by an international authority, and none showed any interest whatever in strengthening international scientific exchange. While obviously the Russians were aware that as early as August 1945 Truman had made it clear that production secrets would not be shared, this almost ostentatious lack of interest in scientific exchange is still significant for what it shows of Soviet priorities. Better to keep one's counsel and prosecute one's secret program than to expose one's leading scientists to the perilous process of open communication. Better to show the world, and especially the Americans, that "we will have atomic energy," and by our own work.

The Soviet authorities were thus never directly exposed, as American politicians were, to the process of thought that had led Oppenheimer first, and then so many others, to the central idea of the Acheson-Lilienthal Report. Gromyko emphatically and repeatedly denied that technical studies could ever require a particular political solution, and Soviet scientists were carefully kept away from exactly the kind of communication that Oppenheimer craved. These choices are entirely understandable from the standpoint of Soviet politics and ideology; Soviet leaders might not share all of Byrnes's ideas, but they were with him, or well ahead, in their unwillingness to let scientists decide political questions.

A fateful consequence of this state of mind was that Soviet political leaders were wholly cut off from the process of thought which in the United States finally convinced Truman and Byrnes that the technical realities had persuasive political meaning. No doubt Stalin's xenophobia, along with his belief in raw power, made him an unlikely target for the conclusion of Bohr that in this case the power of nature was itself the enemy. He would have been a hard man to persuade. Yet it would be wrong to conclude that the task was impossible. There is nothing intrinsically inconsistent with the principles of Marxism or the interests of the most ruthless Soviet ruler in a judgment that nuclear weapons are so terrible that they simply cannot be controlled on a worldwide basis without some trespass upon such other interests as that of running one's own atomic enterprise. The question is political all the way through; the danger in the weapons is itself a political reality of the first importance. If you think that danger great enough, and if you see no other way to avoid an inherently expanding and enormously dangerous arms race, then the negotiation of some control arrangement becomes not a technical but a political imperative. We know of no one who ever came to this view in the Soviet government led by Stalin; we know indeed of no one who ever urged it on Stalin himself. There is no known Soviet counterpart to Americans like Stimson, Oppenheimer, Acheson, and Lilienthal. No doubt any such process of persuasion, hard and imperfect enough in Washington, would have been even harder, and more deeply resisted, in Moscow. But we do not know that it was impossible; we only know there is no sign that anyone tried.

When the Soviet Union and the United States are not negotiating with each other, the United States usually begins to negotiate with itself. The first such episode, in the field of nuclear weapons, began even before Gromyko had been instructed to reject the Baruch plan. On July 23 Henry Wallace, who had been Roosevelt's vice president from 1941 to 1945 and who was now secretary of commerce, had a talk with Truman and left with him a long letter. The letter was in essence an extended argument against the views of Americans whom Wallace saw as believers in an inevitable war with Russia. Wallace believed that a cooperative relationship with the Russians was not only possible but indispensable and feared that "some of the military men and self-styled 'realists' " would get their way and try to keep peace by building "a predominance of force." At the same time the American public was being led into a deep and exaggerated distrust of the

Russians, ignorant of the strong grounds for Russian distrust of the United States and the Western world. But the central problem was the control of atomic energy, and while applauding Truman's wisdom in urging enforceable atomic disarmament, Wallace argued that there was "a fatal defect" in the American plan to proceed by stages, in that, as generally understood, it required the Russians to disclose their resources of uranium and thorium and stay away from military research while the United States still kept its bombs and its secrets. No step-by-step process would work; there would have to be a single package. "We must be prepared to reach an agreement which will commit us to disclosing information and destroying our bombs at a specified time or in terms of specified actions by other countries, rather than at our unfettered discretion. If we are willing to negotiate on this basis, I believe the Russians will also negotiate seriously . . ." Wallace also thought the issue of the veto was irrelevant.[120]

Wallace's letter remained private for two months, but it found its way into the press in the aftermath of a more sweepingly critical Wallace speech in September. The September speech led quickly to Wallace's resignation, in a brouhaha that showed neither Wallace nor Truman at his best. The president had casually agreed to the speech without reading it, and Wallace had given his boss only faint warning of what he was up to. But it is Baruch's reaction to the July letter that is interesting. He was untroubled by the comment on the veto, but he was furious over the assertion that the American position on stages was fixed and unfair.

At Baruch's request Wallace came to New York on September 27 for an extensive discussion. Baruch and his people asserted that they too were in favor of a simple comprehensive agreement, that stages, in terms of different actions at different times, were in fact inescapable, but that the order and timing of the stages were matters for negotiation. They argued that the United States was not seeking unilateral advantage, and that it was the Soviet proposal that called for a big separate first stage: a prohibition of use, production, and possession before there was any agreement on long-term control. When asked what else should be done by the Americans, Wallace first proposed a halt in bomb production but later agreed that the time was not right. Wallace was not fully persuaded by what he heard, but he was sufficiently impressed to admit that "It's obvious that I was not fully posted." Even on the veto the two had reached a measure of agreement, at least temporarily.[121]

This measure of agreement did not persist. Baruch wanted a public retraction, not a political reconciliation, and Wallace, fired by Truman one week earlier, was now launched beyond recall on his crusade against what he saw as Truman's cold war. Presently Baruch put out documents detailing his view of Wallace's errors, while the latter continued to use the arguments of his July letter. Yet the fact remains that Baruch and Wallace, supported by their associates, came closer to serious negotiation on that September 27 than Baruch and Gromyko ever did. Wallace might have got his facts confused (though he was not all wrong about some of the strong preferences of the Baruch group). Still he had posed some of the right questions, and Baruch had eagerly responded. What Baruch did for Wallace I believe he would have done much more readily for Gromyko, but Gromyko had no instructions to ask. His government did not want an international development authority, so why should it strengthen the appearance of the American proposals by negotiating improvements in them?

What then did Stalin really think of the bomb? The evidence is circumstantial, but it is clear and strong. He thought it was dangerous enough so that the Americans must not be allowed to have it alone, but not so dangerous that *no* country should be allowed to have it. For himself, he wanted it. His government's proposals for banning the weapon were obviously not serious; not even the most severe noncommunist critic of the Western position has ever suggested that a mere paper prohibition was acceptable, and Stalin never offered anything more. Stalin, in other words, accepted an atomic arms race. He was never interested in the argument that this race was in itself so dangerous that it was worth some pain and cost to avoid it. The technical realities never translated, for him, into any such political imperative, and indeed one of Gromyko's most interesting complaints was that the Americans and their friends showed a tendency "to subordinate the political tasks of control to considerations of technical detail." The bomb must accommodate to Soviet political imperatives, not the other way around.[122]

Suspicion and Fear

With the real positions of the Soviet and American governments so very far apart, it hardly seems necessary to adduce still further causes for their failure to agree or even to negotiate, but the unhappy reality is that at least two such causes existed in 1946, and we should note them not only because of their relevance at the time but because they turn up repeatedly in the later relations between the two countries on nuclear weapons. One is less important in 1946 than in later years, and I note it here only in passing: Their disagreements over other matters and their growing suspicion of each other's basic intentions made it increasingly difficult for the two to deal with the atomic problem as a special case or a matter apart. How can we ever trust people like that? The question was posed in different ways by leaders and spokesmen in both countries, and no judgment on the relative merits of the arguments is here required: In 1946 and 1947 its existence was another and steadily growing obstacle to real negotiation.

More immediately pertinent and strongly present at least from Hiroshima onward, is the tendency to read the words and acts of others in a light colored heavily by fear. This phenomenon occurs in other kinds of international rivalries—one side's fair economic competition is another's trade war, and a great power's need for friendly neighbors is imperialist expansion to its rivals. But I believe the distance between what one party really means and what the others may take it to mean tends to be larger in the case of atomic weapons, simply because the weapon is so dreadful that there is a deep imbalance of feeling between having it and having it to fear. I think the American monopoly gave more fear to the Soviet Union than comfort to the United States, and conversely I believe the fear of Soviet trickery was deeper, among Americans, than was justified by any real Soviet hope or intent. Thus an observer as acute as George Kennan, writing in July 1946, explained the Soviet proposal to outlaw the bomb as designed "to effect the earliest possible disarming of the United States with respect to atomic weapons."[123] This explanation imputes a seriousness to the Soviet effort that is not reflected in the record.

But that the Soviet government feared the American bomb more than most Americans then supposed seems highly probable. This opinion is not subject to historical proof, but it is not from thin air. Consider the American attack on Hiroshima: We have already examined closely the way that decision was made, and we have rejected, as wholly unsupported by the evidence, the conclusion that the bomb was dropped primarily—or even secondarily—to frighten the Russians. But it would be quite another matter to conclude that because it did not have that intent it did not have that effect, nor should we be surprised if Stalin believed that effect was intentional. Even before the awful effect of Hiroshima was apparent, there was suspicion. It seems likely that Zhukov is telling the truth in his account of Molotov's first reaction to what Truman told Stalin of the new weapons: They're raising the price.[124] And while prices did not in fact change, unwillingness to lower them was certainly strengthened; Alamogordo stiffened Truman's already firm spine. Acheson was right in September when he noted that while we might call ourselves trustees for the world, we could hardly expect Moscow to find that formulation comforting. What were necessary safeguards of control and inspection to Americans only too easily appeared as a proof of monopolistic intent to Soviet spokesmen, and there was much more than Marxist cant and cynical propaganda—though there was plenty of both—in their arguments. We should not exaggerate Soviet fears—Stalin showed plenty of firmness and even daring in the years of the American monopoly—but it is hard to avoid the conclusion that those fears were stronger and deeper than most Americans recognized.

Some Second Thoughts

The fact that Stalin's position was so firm, from Hiroshima onward, does not mean that it could never have been changed, so it is pertinent to consider what might have been done better. Communication on this subject remains critically important today, and also deeply difficult, and it is useful to look at some of the things that went wrong in 1946.

The first was delay. If we treat what Truman said to Stalin at Potsdam as essentially trivial, at the best a show of manners, there is an interval of almost two years between the day in February 1944 when Niels Bohr first spoke to Felix Frankfurter about the need for "East-West" contact and the days in Moscow when Byrnes sought and got Soviet agreement that the matter should be discussed in the UN. Most of this delay must be charged directly to the account of Franklin Roosevelt, with lesser charges to Winston Churchill, who energetically disagreed with the idea of including Stalin, and to Henry Stimson, who was himself uncertain what to do and not quick to pass on the ideas of Bush and Conant. Nor is it merely that Roosevelt himself chose not to communicate with Stalin. As with the decision on using the bomb against Japan, what Roosevelt left to Truman on the question of international control was an absence of thought and study. The situation was not quite as bad in this case, because at least there was not a full-scale process of operational planning and preparation already far advanced, with all the expectations that such a process tends to create. Instead there was nothing at all except the gradually growing conviction of Stimson, pushed by Bush and Conant, that the new weapon would have enormous postwar implications that needed attention.

Truman's Interim Committee, in its short life, paid only marginal attention to the postwar problem, so that when the question became public in August there was very little that anyone could offer for the president to say—no more than that the discovery must be used for peace, the know-how would be safeguarded, and the United States would be a reliable trustee. Not until October could he add that we would consult our friends in Great Britain and Canada about plans for "international arrangements."

To the absence of planning we must add the confusion attendant upon changes in the cast of characters at the top of the government. The largest such change is from Roosevelt to Truman, and I am one of those who think the change truly fateful. That Roosevelt was seriously mistaken in holding his secret so very close seems evident, and his way of dealing with Churchill in one vein and Bush in another, both on the future of Anglo-American cooperation and on the question of dealing with Russia, was irresponsible and disingenuous, as well as unnecessary. But the larger question is whether Roosevelt had it in him to grasp the political meaning of the weapon and apply his own best efforts to the quest for a workable international agreement; here it seems right to be hopeful. At the very least we must suppose that in the end he would have made the matter his own most pressing business, which is precisely what Harry Truman never did.

The sudden transition from Roosevelt to Truman at the top was followed over the next six months by sweeping changes at the next level of government. Only one major change, Byrnes for Stettinius, came before the war ended, but with victory most of those who had joined for the duration were as eager as any GI for prompt discharge. Stimson and Conant are only the most conspicuous examples in the nuclear field. The Interim Committee itself faded away, and Byrnes, preoccupied by London and Moscow, was slow in finding an effective way to search for a policy. That he moved as he finally did in January was the product less of his own strong concern than of the urgent advice of associates in the department like Cohen and "holdover" advisers like Bush. These senior counselors, in turn, were often responding to the efforts of such younger men as Oppenheimer and Carroll Wilson.[125] Compared with Franklin Roosevelt's secretive and forbidding loneliness, this effort was substantial and collegial. The process that eventually led to the Acheson-Lilienthal report was too slow, but it included remarkable personal efforts by remarkable men.

Yet these efforts were both fragmentary and flawed. As we have seen, the Lilienthal board directed its attention, in tune with Lilienthal's temper and in response to Oppenheimer's imaginative insight, to what "the facts" required—but the facts it addressed were the facts of nuclear energy, not the facts of American or Soviet political life. Neither the board nor its parent committee, nor anyone else in a position to advise the president, addressed with adequate care two inescapably central questions:

> 1. What was the real and right connection between American "secrets" and the effort for international control?
> 2. What Soviet requirements would need to be met if the object of the negotiation was to get the best available agreement and not simply to make the best possible case for the plan "the facts" required?

The confusion over secrecy had begun with the efforts of the very man who first understood the urgent need to abandon it—Niels Bohr. When Bohr sought to talk with Roosevelt and Churchill he had no intention of proposing to transfer nuclear know-how. He wanted to get a political dialogue started, and the dangers that immediately leaped into Churchill's mind were, as far as Bohr himself was concerned, entirely nonexistent. Yet Churchill's fears, shared with Roosevelt at Hyde Park, helped to delay action, and even thought.

The same thing happened in a slightly different way to Bush and Conant. When they initially proposed sharing scientific information in 1944 they were probably not thinking of anything much beyond what was in fact published in the Smyth report. Even later, when they urged the specific value of scientific exchange as part of the process of communication with the Soviet Union, they were not talking about an early need to share information beyond that report. Bush, indeed, is almost surely the source of Truman's early and entirely reasonable distinction between basic scientific understanding, which was open to all, and the know-how of bomb making, which was not.[126] Yet at the same time Bush, like Bohr, persistently connected the notion of an approach to the Soviet Union with the idea of exchanges of scientific information, and Churchill was not the only one to understand the proposal as involving the sharing of dangerous, and in some sense keepable secrets.

The most dramatic instance of confusion between the claims of secrecy and the case for seeking international agreement is the cabinet discussion of September 21, 1945. Some of the confusion was already present in Stimson's original memorandum: "It is true if we approach them now . . . we may be gambling on their good faith and risk their getting into production of bombs a little sooner than they would otherwise."[127] But surely this was wrong; any such risk would come not in seeking an agreement, but only in the process of putting it into effect. Certainly any agreed plan for control would eventually require sharing know-how as well as basic science. But Stimson's sentence sounds as if the initial approach necessarily involved some secret sharing; in the cabinet discussion both friends and opponents made that assumption, and the public debate touched off by the immediate leak followed the same course. It was a false trail.

There was no logical requirement for any early disclosure of genuinely sensitive information in the process of seeking agreement on international control. The most important information had been disclosed with literally blinding clarity at Hiroshima, and within weeks the Smyth report provided more than enough technical exposition to make clear the crucial roles of uranium and thorium, of reactors and separation plants, and of organized large-scale scientific and technological effort. To understand these things deeply, and to draw out their implications for international control, was not easy for anyone, and obviously the decisive contribution made by Oppenheimer to the Acheson-Lilienthal report grew out of his own experience. His capacity to persuade his fellow consultants obviously owed much not only to his own understanding but to the fact that they in turn had been admitted behind the secret curtain; they knew that nothing was being kept back from them. We have seen how this fact gave them persuasiveness to such a layman as Lippmann. Yet the basic argument of the report did not depend on secrets; reading it in 1946 and again forty years later, I have found the argument extraordinarily clear and self-sustaining, without ever really understanding the basic physics of the matter.

So the logical persuasiveness of the basic argument did *not* depend on secrets; its exposition required no disclosure of "know-how." At a few points there was indeed some technical uncertainty. The issue of the effectiveness of denaturing—a method of making nuclear material usable for power but not for bombs—was probably the most significant, but this issue was decisive for no government and few individuals. Nor was technical information required for understanding the essential menace of the bomb itself. To most men the evidence of Hiroshima and Nagasaki was amply persuasive.[128] Those who refused to follow the argument of "the facts"—who wanted freedom to keep or get these weapons for themselves—were not ignorant of their revolutionary power; they were only resistant to the idea of a common danger requiring a common answer.

This failure of understanding, whenever it occurred, was indeed in some measure a failure to understand the full meaning of what the scientists were now able to do. But it was not so much a failure of scientific understanding as of political imagination. It was not caused by a lack of technical information, nor was it always subject to repair by even the most brilliant exposition of the technical secrets of the Manhattan Project. When Oppenheimer spoke of the need for an international development authority he obviously spoke with greater persuasiveness because of his evident scientific understanding, but the argument itself was not scientific; it was merely consistent with a scientific reality whose essentials had already been announced.

Certainly physicists, and Oppenheimer in particular, did carry with them an aura of special authority in those early months. They did know the nuclear reality in a way that others had to accept at second hand. Moreover scientists could talk to each other across all sorts of political and ideological frontiers; this was one reason for the foresight of Bohr, first citizen of the world's physics and so in his own mind and conscience a citizen of the world. But neither of these realities made the transfer of technical know-how a necessary part of either public education or international dialogue.

Oppenheimer himself always believed that the constraints of continuing secrecy deeply impeded understanding both among Americans and in international discourse. Eventually in 1952 this conviction led him to take the lead in what came to be known as Operation Candor (see Chapter VI), and by that time there was indeed a deep and destructive difference between the public and the classified levels of discourse. But with a single exception I do not find any technical secret remaining after the publication of the Smyth report that was crucial to an understanding of the menace of the atom.

The exception is an important one: the possibility of moving from uranium to hydrogen, from fission to fusion, from kilotons to megatons. The discovery of this possibility, back in 1942, had sent Oppenheimer across the continent by train to report it in awe to Arthur Compton, and no one who had heard about it in secret had ever failed to be amazed.[129] But it did remain a secret, at least in the sense that there was no public discussion of it by public authorities, or by the scientists who knew about it, in the first year after Hiroshima. There were vague references to the possibility of much more powerful weapons; right at the beginning Stimson's statement of August 6 referred to "the possibility that another scale of magnitude will be evolved" and distinguished this possibility as "more important" than the short-term prospect of increasing "by several fold the present effectiveness." But there is a wide difference between this general warning and a concrete statement of the scientific reasoning behind it. The spreading menace of nuclear weapons, in later years, has come to be described as both horizontal and vertical, where horizontal means the spread of the weapons to more and more countries and vertical means the multiplication in the destructiveness and the sophistication of national arsenals, particularly those of the United States and the Soviet Union. The horizontal risk was recognized, at least in principle, from the first; to ward it off was the governing purpose of everyone involved in what became the Baruch plan. But the calculated vagueness of the references to the thermonuclear prospect effectively concealed from those "not in the know" the terrifying nature of the prospect of vertiginous "vertical" escalation.

It is not easy to estimate the effectiveness of this obfuscation or to judge its wisdom or folly. Some of those who learned about it thought, like Byrnes, that it was simply something to go ahead with and develop "full force," but others took the matter much more seriously. I find it hard to avoid the conclusion that if the American government had spoken of this prospect publicly as it did privately, the sense of urgency that moved the authors and sponsors of the Acheson-Lilienthal report would have been more widely shared both inside the United States and internationally.[130]

The argument against any such concrete disclosure, of course, was that it might alert an adversary to this possibility and stimulate his effort. The possibility (though not much more) must have been mentioned by Klaus Fuchs to his Soviet spy masters, and there is evidence that published reports of a possible "superbomb" did stimulate Soviet studies in 1947–48.[131] So a full-scale, high-level announcement of this prospect in 1945 might have had a similar but stronger earlier effect (as indeed it might have stimulated the pressure for an American superbomb effort that developed only four years later after the Soviet explosion). So there were reasons for reticence. Still it might have been better, on balance, if this gigantic vertical risk had been more explicitly discussed.

What remains entirely clear is that except for this difficult question of discussing the H-bomb, the general confusion about secret sharing was both avoidable and highly inhibiting. That confusion began in the context of the intense wartime secrecy of the project, and it survived by a momentum of its own well after that kind of secrecy had entirely vanished. Throughout 1945 no one looked hard at what would really need saying in even the most direct and purposeful negotiations with the Russians, and so no one really noticed that neither giving nor withholding information still considered secret was of immediate importance. Only when it came time to talk about the Baruch plan in the UN did detailed work disclose that there were no large problems in meeting the needs of interested governments that wished to be confident of their own technical judgment on the merits of the proposal.

By then the waters were permanently muddied with misunderstanding; suspicion of all scientific and technical exchange had become deep-seated in Congress, and the very idea of serious discussion with the Russians was suspect as necessarily involving risk to secrets. It was an unnecessary confusion, and it undoubtedly contributed to both the caution and the rigidity of Baruch, as indeed it contributed to the congressional environment that made his appointment so attractive to Byrnes.

No one, of course, could neglect the reality that *if* there were an agreement, then indeed information would have to be shared. A central element in the American plan was that the Atomic Development Authority should become the world's leading center of nuclear knowledge of all sorts. The problem of deciding when and how such information should be shared would have been complex, part of the broader question of timing and stages that was never reached between Gromyko and Baruch, only between Baruch and Wallace. But there was no great opposition from Congress to the idea of sharing secrets in the context of a real agreement. Such opposition might have developed later. There was latent congressional suspicion of the American plan even after Baruch had stiffened it; Senator Robert Taft, in opposing Lilienthal's confirmation as first chairman of the Atomic Energy Commission in 1947, felt free to say that the Acheson-Lilienthal plan had amounted to a proposal for "putting atom bomb plants in Russia . . . the limit of all asininity on our part."[132] But in 1946 it was the notion of sharing secrets early, as a cost-free inducement to agreement, that aroused suspicion. This notion represented an entirely avoidable misunderstanding.

What Might Have Been Agreed

We have seen that there was no negotiation with the Russians and that those who prepared the way for what did happen at the United Nations, as well as those who conducted the process there, did not understand their assignment as one which required them to consider what proposals would be necessary to get agreement. To address that question is at once difficult and essential. It is essential because if we do not consider what possible agreement may have been missed because it was not sought, we have no basis for a final judgment on what actually happened. It is difficult for all the obvious reasons: Who can ever say that what was not tried would or would not have worked, and are not such speculations doubly uncertain when we are asking about the responses of a government that conceals its internal process as fiercely as does the Soviet Union? Recognizing the risks, let us yet make the attempt.

We can start from at least one plausible and powerful hypothesis: the Soviet government could never have accepted any agreement that did not give it the right to make and keep some numbers of atomic weapons and so to have, in the language of a later day, parity with the United States. This was the clear object of Stalin's peremptory command of August: "Provide us with atomic weapons" to "restore the balance." That this would be the Soviet objective was plain to embassies at the time; that the Soviet effort was well in train was plain to them a few months later. That this *must* be the reaction of a Great Power did not escape other astute observers.

Consider the view from Whitehall, where the behavior of Great Powers (the phrase was regularly capitalized) had been the object of study and action for generations. When British officials concluded in October that the Soviet Union surely had the resources "to produce atomic weapons and that she will do so," they had not only their general sense of Great Powers' behavior to guide them, but also the additional evidence of their own deep determination that the United Kingdom itself must have such weapons "on a large scale." When we return to the British story we shall see how strongly held this position was. If any major country had reason to be untroubled by the American monopoly it was Britain, and indeed it was not any American threat, but rather the uncertainty of American protection against a certain Soviet bomb that was troubling. But what one senses at a deeper level in the officials' view of October is a simple and governing conviction that Great Powers, not less than three and perhaps as many as five, simply cannot be prevented from having these weapons. Indeed the officials themselves, as we have seen, went further. While they thought "a possible policy . . . might be to seek agreement that the production of atomic bombs should be confined to the Big Five," they themselves preferred simply to outlaw the use of the weapon and "leave all nations free to make atomic bombs if they can." Thus they mentioned and discarded what seems in retrospect the one line of action that might have led to a solid agreement with Moscow.

Suppose it had been accepted in Washington that as a matter of intrinsic Great Power necessity the Soviet Union would have to have nuclear weapons of its own, and suppose that this understanding had been accepted as part of "the facts," a reality as worthy of respect as the fission of uranium itself. Is it possible to imagine an agreement that would have allowed for this reality and yet provided for controls or limits of the sort that were not even attempted for another generation, after the weapons had multiplied far beyond the worst expectations of 1945, in numbers, power, and speed of delivery?

Let us put aside the question of sharing secrets here and assume an essentially political proposal. Could we have agreed with Moscow that Great Powers and only Great Powers should have nuclear weapons? Could we then have agreed that these Great Powers should limit themselves to some finite number of such weapons? Could we have addressed the question of limits on technological advance, by all the means of control that have been thought of since, especially limits on testing? The prize might have been very large: a much less dangerous nuclear world.

To raise these political questions is to understand at once how difficult it would have been, in 1946, for Washington, London, and Moscow to address them effectively. Those who were most committed to an effort for international agreement were trying to get rid of the terrible new weapon, not license it on a limited scale. The problem of confidence in any agreement, which has bedeviled the arms control process in all later negotiations, would have been large and new and hard for all in 1946. A limited nuclear regime would have been much harder to manage than the Atomic Development Authority envisaged in the American plan. In real terms it would be no better for either side; if Russians and Americans were to have equal numbers of weapons surely zero was the best number to agree on. Moreover, zero has an interesting property that gives it particular value in negotiations of this sort: It allows parity both among individual nations and between any nation and any group of others, and this property is important when a balance may be needed between one nation—the Soviet Union—and two or three others—Britain, France, and the United States—and when those two or three also need some balance among themselves. If the agreed number is zero, both conditions can be satisfied because zero equals zero, and also zero equals zero plus zero plus zero. No other number or combination of numbers can meet this test. For this reason it is much easier to prohibit a given dangerous weapon than to ration it "fairly." So for the Americans to give up their technically excellent proposal, they would have had to be convinced of two propositions at once: first, that their proposal, however well presented and however sensitively redesigned, would *never* win Soviet agreement, and second, that without *some* agreement the clear and early prospect was one of open-ended nuclear competition in which, whatever skill and energy either side might demonstrate, both would be losers.

These two propositions were unpalatable, and those disposed to believe one were usually indisposed to believe the other. Thus it was not just Baruch who believed that the American plan should be defended through thick and thin. This was the view of its true authors, the Lilienthal board, and its first sponsors, the Acheson committee. No member of either body ever urged a retreat. Repeatedly they and their supporters argued that the basic concept of the Atomic Development Authority was intrinsically right. Reviewing the whole effort in a melancholy mood at the end of 1947, Oppenheimer still concluded that the United Nations Atomic Energy Commission had established one point: "Through many months of discussion, under circumstances of often dispiriting frustration, and by delegates not initially committed to it, the basic idea of security through international cooperative development has proven its extraordinary and profound vitality."[133] Those holding this conviction might be ready for compromise on all sorts of details. They might, as many did, think Baruch at least tactically wrong in his rejection of the veto, and at the tactical level Baruch may have come to agree with them. They might think, with Wallace, that the Soviet government was ready to be reasonable, or with Oppenheimer that it was not. But they did not believe the basic concepts should be abandoned. Someday, somehow, the Russians might understand the implications of "the facts."[134]

Even among those who most clearly perceived that the Soviet government was determined to break the American monopoly just as fast as possible, there arose no cry for a change in the basic American proposal. Arnold Wolfers of Yale, then perhaps the dean of American students of international relations, wrote in 1946 that the Soviet Union must and would have bombs of its own. His conclusion did not lead him to recommend an approach different from that of the Acheson-Lilienthal report.[135] Later in the year Walter Lippmann pointedly noted that Baruch's rigid position seemed to take no account of Stalin's obvious determination to have a bomb of his own. But he then failed to deal with the difficulty he had so clearly perceived, calling not for any desertion of the basic principles of the Acheson-Lilienthal report, but only for greater flexibility in "the strategy and tactics of the approach to it." Lippmann himself still saw the bomb as requiring precisely the new "project and design of world organization" that held no interest whatever for Stalin.[136]

While the believers in the effort for international control thus remained firm in their devotion to an unattainable goal, more skeptical and nationalist leaders showed little fear of a nuclear arms race with the Russians. Baruch and Groves—and Truman most of all—believed firmly that the United States could remain decisively superior for years, long enough to make the prospect of a nuclear arms race quite undaunting. They might not believe, after the first flash of hope, that international control was achievable, but they saw no reason to seek any less satisfactory form of agreement.

Both the firm adherents of international control and the optimistic believers in American atomic leadership had the strong support of public opinion. There was no serious public attention to the notion that the right course of action might be to accept both the firm purpose and probable capability of the Soviet Union and reach the best available agreement on that basis. Not even the most zealous defenders of Moscow made any such suggestions. They confined themselves to support of the Soviet propaganda position: The Baruch plan was a scheme for American monopoly, and the right course was simply to ban the bomb. The reality that was almost self-evident to British officials never penetrated the political consciousness of Americans.

Any lead on this question would have had to come from the top, from the president himself. It would also have been much more likely to attract support if it had come early, and if the unlimited danger of fusion in the lighter elements had been clearly stated. It would have required a recognition that the scientific facts alone were not decisive and that policy must also respect political realities, above all the realities defining the purposes of, and the relations between, the Soviet Union and the United States. It would have required, as all subsequent serious efforts for arms control have required, the persistent participation of the president, and it would have required an immediate and enduring insistence that the primary object of policy must be to get the best achievable agreement, not to state the best unobtainable plan. None of this is compatible with the character of Harry Truman.

How far might it have been different with Franklin Roosevelt alive and well? He would have had many advantages, not the least of them his own preeminent role in the success of the vast and quite personal gamble that he had taken in the beginning. That he would have attempted direct negotiations seems almost certain, but it is much less clear that he would have sought an agreement that recognized and accepted the prospect of Soviet weapons. Roosevelt died without resolving his own deeply ambiguous view of the world of the future. He had led his country into the new United Nations with all the rhetoric of the four freedoms and collective security, but equally he had taken the lead in Great Power diplomacy and had never resolved, only deferred, the innate conflict between the two, a conflict deriving primarily, though by no means uniquely, from the intrinsic nature of Stalinist Russia. The legacy of this unresolved contradiction was a major element in the stressful process by which the United States slowly came to terms with itself as wartime sympathies grew dim and the reality of Soviet power displaced the illusions of wartime hope in Eastern Europe.

The evocation of Franklin Roosevelt tells us only how very hard it would have been to take the course of organizing and legitimizing nuclear oligopoly among the great powers. Roosevelt himself had allowed the secret to achieve its mythic magnitude; he himself had blocked all forms of planning for the future; he had planted the seeds of misunderstanding among the closest of allies at Quebec and Hyde Park; he had managed the unresolved ambiguity of his own postwar policy in growing loneliness. Could he or anyone have broken through the apparent imperative of international control to accept the reality of what the Soviet Union was *bound* to do? It seems unlikely.

So the best became the enemy of the good. As their differences on every subject grew sharper month by month, Moscow and Washington continued to make speeches in favor of their incompatible proposals for a world without the nuclear weapon, as they both continued to count on having it, each in its own way, as an indispensable equalizer.

V

To Have Thermonuclear Weapons—and Other Truman Choices

ATE IN THE SUMMER OF 1949, probably on August 29, the Soviet Union conducted a successful test of a nuclear device. Within days American aircraft detected atmospheric evidence of this event, and within weeks the accumulated evidence had been pronounced conclusive by experts led by Bush. On September 23, the president announced the Soviet explosion. Four months later, on January 31, 1950, he announced that the United States would proceed with the development of "the so-called hydrogen or superbomb." His announcement was only 125 words long, and he refused to go one word beyond it in public until the very end of his presidency. Harry Truman's decision is second in importance only to Franklin Roosevelt's commitment of October 1941; it led straight on, with no second thought by the president, to the world's first full-scale thermonuclear explosion, on November 1, 1952. For the human race there was no turning back. The first Soviet device was tested less than a year later.[1]

Let us note at the outset that Truman's decision was only half of what produced this result. There was a parallel decision by Stalin, and the Soviet decision probably came first. Certainly there is no evidence of any delay by anyone on the Soviet side; Soviet accounts give no hint of any debate or dissent over thermonuclear development, and the impression left both by official accounts and the recollections of such a crucially important scientist as Andrey Sakharov is that there was a unanimous determination in August 1949 to go forward promptly to the "second stage of the atomic epoch."[2] There is no reason to believe that the Russian effort was caused by Truman's January decision or indeed by any other American action. Nor was there any change in the dreary emptiness of Soviet propaganda for an uninspected ban on all nuclear weapons, or any sign of even the most modest Soviet effort to find some way of reaching agreement not to go on to the next stage. No one from Stalin to Sakharov appears to have harbored any doubt at any time that the right course of action was to get a Russian H-bomb just as fast as possible. The responsibility for this second great step in the nuclear age is thus shared by two governments. When Franklin Roosevelt told Vannevar Bush to go ahead in 1941, he was acting out of fear that there was a rival in the race. That rival was a phantom, but Harry Truman in 1950 was choosing to engage in a competition that was entirely real.

Fission weapons in themselves are terrible enough, but the potential destructiveness of thermonuclear weapons is different. After the world's first multimegaton explosion, on November 1, 1952, the terror and awe that followed Hiroshima were renewed and intensified, perhaps especially among those who had been closest to the earlier enterprise. Here is Winston Churchill in 1955:

> There is an immense gulf between the atomic and the hydrogen bomb. The atomic bomb, with all its terrors, did not carry us outside the scope of human control or manageable events in thought or action, in peace or war. But [with the publication of the first comprehensive review of the hydrogen bomb], the entire foundation of human affairs was revolutionized, and mankind placed in a situation both measureless and laden with doom.

In this same speech Churchill went on to speak of the possibility that safety might be "the sturdy child of terror," and "survival the twin brother of annihilation." The comfort was and is cool. In deciding to make hydrogen bombs if they could, the governments of the United States and the Soviet Union were making no small choice, both for themselves and for the world. Yet neither government held back, and no representative of either government ever raised a question with the other as to whether there was any alternative.[3]

In this inescapably two-sided matter we can look closely at only one side. We shall return to the Soviet program, and we shall have to speculate on what Stalin might and might not have done if the Americans had chosen a different course of action. But the only government whose process of decision is open to direct consideration is the government in Washington. In seeking to understand its actions we must remember that while things were happening in Washington, things were happening—or had already happened—in Moscow too.

The Soviet Test and Harry Truman

The first Soviet test was a shock to official Washington. Although scientific advisers from Bush and Conant on down had believed from the beginning that the Russians could have a bomb in about five years if they chose to make the necessary effort, people had tended, as I. I. Rabi later explained, to push that five-year estimate ahead of them: "If you had asked anybody in 1944 or 1945 when would the Russians have it, it would have been five years. But every year that went by you kept on saying five years." So although Rabi was always certain they would get it, when it actually happened, he said, "It was a stunning shock." Rabi may have exaggerated; in July 1949 Secretary of State Acheson reminded a large meeting of senior officials, senators, and congressmen that "the best intelligence estimates available indicated that the Soviets might have a bomb by mid-1951 and, in three or four years' time thereafter, a fairly serious quantity." A two-year error, in a matter so readily concealed, was not enormous. Nonetheless Rabi's sense of shock was widely shared.[4]

The government in Washington that had to consider its response to the Russian bomb was not the government that had faced the question of international control four years earlier. Harry Truman was still president, but nearly all the other leading players had changed or taken new roles. The president himself was different. He had now been through decisions that he always considered larger and harder than these: He had launched the Truman Doctrine and the Marshall Plan; he had replaced Byrnes with Marshall and Marshall with Acheson. Above all, he had fought and won an election in which he beat Henry Wallace and Strom Thurmond as well as Thomas Dewey. He had successfully defended Berlin by airlift, and the blockade of that city had been lifted in May. He correctly estimated himself as stronger and wiser than any of his election opponents, and he was president now in his own right. He thought himself well and truly in command of the executive branch, and one thing he understood clearly about nuclear weapons: They were presidential business.

"Only the President . . . can authorize the use of an atomic bomb," he wrote in his memoirs. "Only the President can decide the nature of the weapons to be made . . . can decide whether a weapon can be detonated for test purposes . . . where and when the weapons may be shipped or stored . . . The President even sets the annual goal of the number of bombs and the quantity of material to be produced." In the three years since the establishment of the Atomic Energy Commission Truman had been making such decisions briskly and easily, guided by four clear and simple standards. First, in the absence of international control (and he had been an early pessimist on that subject): "Our country had to be ahead of any possible competitor." Truman never rejected a recommendation from the AEC for expanded production.[5] Second, the stockpile should remain under civilian control; he had firmly rejected occasional Defense Department efforts to obtain military control of the weapons. Third, these were not ordinary weapons. Although Truman had also been willing to let B-29 bombers go to Britain as reminders of American power at the time of the Berlin blockade, he had not allowed any nuclear weapons to leave the country or to go out of the custody of the Atomic Energy Commission, explaining to eager Pentagon officials that "you have got to understand that this isn't a military weapon . . . it is used to wipe out women and children and unarmed people, and not for military uses."[6] Fourth, he firmly believed that the bomb was "all he had" to counterbalance the Russians in Europe. He must be ready to use it, and he assured his defense officials that he would never hesitate if necessary. But any such decision would be his own, and he prayed he would never have to make it.[7]

By 1949, as the number of bombs on hand and on order increased, he recognized that the air force had begun to make contingency war plans, and in April he asked to be informed about them. But the only policy paper he had approved on the use of atomic weapons, while it recognized that the armed forces must indeed be ready to employ them, explicitly reserved any decision on use to the president.[8] Since August 1945 Truman had not come close to using these weapons. He had not threatened Stalin with them, nor had anyone presumed to do so in his name. There is a myth that he made such a threat in 1946 over Iran, but that is a product of his own later imagination, as we shall see.

Truman took prompt personal control of the problem of responding to the first Soviet test. When he reluctantly agreed that there had indeed been such an event, he made his own wise decision that it should be announced to the world, and he controlled the timing and content of that announcement, holding it up for a few days to avoid entangling it with an already planned British announcement of the devaluation of the pound; the Russian achievement must not wrongly appear to be the cause of the British difficulty. Ignoring the reality that official Washington had been both surprised and shocked, he adopted a tone of undisturbed confidence: "The eventual development of this new force by other nations was to be expected. This probability has always been taken into account by us."[9] Then he allowed the various elements of the government to go to work on their own responses to the new situation, secure in the conviction that when the time came for a decision he would be the one to make it.

What Truman expected was secret advice secretly concerted. It had been that way with nuclear matters through all his years as president, and by now the habit was deeply ingrained. The president himself strongly supported a policy of secrecy and indeed insisted on it at every opportunity. He believed that everything connected with the know-how of the bomb, and still more everything connected with the changing size and shape of the American stock of nuclear weapons, should be held as closely as possible. Access to restricted data outside the Atomic Energy Commission was extraordinarily limited. Some of the secrets deserved all of the protection they could get: "How to make an H-bomb" was then unknown in the United States, but the exact character of the American ignorance was a subject that it was proper not to discuss in public. Unfortunately secrecy went much further, even at very high levels in the executive branch. In 1949 George Kennan was the head of the Policy Planning Staff in the State Department, the senior adviser to the secretary of state on the policy aspects of this subject. He never knew, and never asked to know, how many fission bombs his country then had, how many it would or could have before any nation could have thermonuclear weapons, or what the power of existing and prospective American fission weapons might be, compared backward to Hiroshima or forward to a hydrogen bomb. A similar (and less characteristic) respect for the secret had kept the formidable congressional Joint Committee on Atomic Energy from asking for stockpile information. In this and many other ways most of those who were asked to help in thinking about this awful decision were flying blind.[10]

Secrecy—and also awe—constrained even those with an obvious right to know. The president himself was careful not to discuss stockpile numbers, and beyond that he had no deep curiosity about nuclear questions. The subject, for everyone, was surrounded by taboos. The result was enormous ignorance, even at the top. Until October 1949, Truman was himself apparently unaware of the possibility of thermonuclear weapons. In the aftermath of the Soviet atomic test the matter came to his attention.

Advisers' Advice

The strongest early reactions naturally occurred among those most directly concerned with atomic energy. They were in three places, each interconnected with the other two: among nuclear physicists, in the Atomic Energy Commission, and in the Joint Committee on Atomic Energy. In these three small circles, during the weeks immediately after the president's announcement, individuals of ability, energy, and conviction determined that the necessary answer to the Soviet explosion was an all-out effort to develop a thermonuclear weapon, also called a hydrogen bomb, or more simply, the super.

On the other side was the General Advisory Committee of the AEC.

It had been recognized since 1942 that a thermonuclear weapon was theoretically possible. Its energy would come from fusion in the lightest elements, and in principle there would be no limit to its explosive force. The conventional statement, among the few who were informed, was that this weapon could be up to a thousand times more powerful than the Hiroshima bomb. But it was apparent that no such explosion could occur unless it were triggered by a fission device—it would take an A-bomb to provide the high temperatures necessary for detonation, and even then it would not be easy. The development of the fission weapon remained the overriding wartime priority. Thermonuclear theory was studied, but development was not undertaken, and the possibility of such weapons was kept secret even after Hiroshima. It was not discussed in the Smyth report, and many physicists (in and out of the official circle of those who were cleared for "restricted data") joined in what they saw as a benign conspiracy of silence on the subject. Public speculation did occur outside the United States, notably in a book published in 1946 by the Austrian physicist Hans Thirring. With no access to secret information Thirring offered a technically sophisticated discussion of the possibilities that was sufficient to alert knowledgeable readers in other countries. But in the United States public references to the topic were few and cryptic; they did not set off any debate.[11]

Nor was there any surge of thermonuclear activity after 1945. With victory the Manhattan Project came apart in much the same way as the wartime armies and armadas. Americans in uniform went back to civilian life, and most of the leading scientists returned to the universities. A further obstacle to sustained progress was the need to move from an organization created entirely by secret presidential wartime decision to one with a basis in peacetime law. When the new Atomic Energy Commission finally took over from General Groves at the beginning of 1947, it found that its first and most urgent task must be to attend to the quantity and quality of its fission weapons. On April 3, 1947, the first chairman of the commission, David Lilienthal, informed President Truman that there were no nuclear weapons available for immediate use, only a few sets of components ready for final assembly, and no competent assembly teams at the ready. This remarkable situation has many explanations and no villain, but it does demonstrate that in the first year and a half after the end of the war there was no concerted American effort whatever to build powerful nuclear forces, one further indication of the superficial and temporary character of the flirtation of James Byrnes with atomic diplomacy. In August 1945, when Byrnes had urged Oppenheimer to go ahead "full force," he had indeed been thinking of the super, but no one had paid any attention to him.[12]

In April 1947 the attitude was different. By then the United States had had almost two years of disillusioning experience with steadily rising Soviet hostility. While the government had reached no solid consensus on the exact role of nuclear weapons, it was already apparent that with Western Europe economically prostrate and politically in danger, and with conventional forces demobilized, any revelation of American atomic impotence would be profoundly shocking, most of all to the American people. Keeping the figures deeply secret, the new commission set about getting a stockpile. No one who knew the numbers, from Truman on down, disagreed with this effort. As Lilienthal explained in June to the Joint Committee, the commission recognized that the country and the Congress expected it to "maintain and increase the preeminence of this country in atomic energy development and atomic weapons." The weapons came first. As Robert Oppenheimer later put it, "Without debate—I suppose with some melancholy—we concluded that the principal job of the Commission was to provide atomic weapons and good atomic weapons and many atomic weapons."[13]

By the summer of 1949 progress had been made. The nonexistent stockpile had been replaced by a substantial supply of warheads— perhaps 200. The exact number is still classified forty years later. Secrecy on early stockpile figures was intense, even mystical, at the time, and declassification officers are still loyal to the mystique. The best assessment I know of stockpile sizes in this period is by David Alan Rosenberg, who believes that there were about 50 bombs in mid-1948. Rosenberg also notes that by May 1949 the Atomic Energy Commission was confidently projecting a stockpile of 400 by the end of 1950. So an estimate of about 200 in mid-1949 does not seem wild, and I remain untroubled by any small error in this matter. In counting nuclear warheads it is mainly orders of magnitude—factors of 10—that are important. There are critical differences between 10 and 100 and 1000 and 10,000, but not between 150 and 200. In this respect nuclear weapons are different from armored divisions and ships.[14]

As the stockpile grew, so did the technical sophistication of Los Alamos. By the middle of 1949 the explosive power achievable in individual weapons had been multiplied by a factor of five or more, and plans for a further expansion of productive capacity were well advanced. The first practical effect of the Soviet test was to speed up an agreed recommendation to the president for such expansion and for a general acceleration of the atomic energy program. This proposal had originated in the Joint Chiefs of Staff early in the summer, and the process of review it underwent in a special committee of the National Security Council—the secretary of state, the secretary of defense, and the chairman of the Atomic Energy Commission—had been regarded by Lilienthal in July as a major step forward. In principle it recognized the role of the commission and the State Department in setting production requirements.[15] In fact, however, this military request was almost routinely approved. The finished report of October 10 began with the firm recommendation of the Joint Chiefs and continued with straightforward endorsements from both the commission, on feasibility, and the State Department, on political acceptability. No one questioned the judgment of the Joint Chiefs that "when the USSR attains a stockpile of atomic weapons, overwhelming superiority of our own stockpile and production rate will be necessary if our atomic weapon posture is to continue to act as a deterrent to war."[16] The bureaucratic meaning of this recommendation was almost the opposite of what Lilienthal supposed. Always before, the military had been content to set requirements at whatever level the production schedules of the AEC could meet. Now the Pentagon had taken a first successful initiative in changing those levels.

The real question after the Soviet test was whether even this enlarged program would be enough. At least three important people thought not: Edward Teller at Los Alamos, Ernest Lawrence at Berkeley, and Lewis Strauss at the Atomic Energy Commission. Soon many others came to agree with them and to agree also with their prescription.

The first clear statement of this position came in a memorandum of October 5 from Strauss to his fellow commissioners. Noting "a tendency in my own thinking to resort to the prospect of increased production of fissionable material" for A-bombs as the logical response to the Soviet test, Strauss went on to argue that this prospect was not enough: "The time has now come for a quantum jump in our planning . . . we should now make an intensive effort to get ahead with the super. . . . That is the way to stay ahead."[17] This memorandum, both in its argument and in some of its precise language, such as "quantum jump," was the result of a remarkable handwritten letter from William Golden to Strauss, dated September 25. Golden had been a staff assistant to Strauss at a dollar a year since 1947, but had spent the summer on leave in Europe. His letter was written in Florence the night after he learned of Truman's announcement of the first Soviet test.[18]

Strauss knew from discussion with his fellow commissioners that his memorandum would not find immediate and unanimous support, but he had other ways of expressing his opinion. His memorandum was delivered to his colleagues on the afternoon of October 5; at lunch on the same day he shared his thoughts with his good friend Sidney W. Souers, the executive secretary of the National Security Council. Souers was the man who saw Truman most often and most intimately on matters of intelligence and national security. Strauss explained the possibility of the super, his belief in its vital importance, and the lack of interest he had already found among his fellow commissioners. Souers seemed impressed; he "urged Strauss to prod the Commission toward a report to the President," and after checking with Truman he reinforced this advice. Souers found that "Truman seemed to know nothing about the super, but showed an immediate interest. Truman wanted Strauss to force the issue up to the White House and to do it quickly."[19]

Strauss soon found other allies. On October 10 he had a visit from Lawrence and learned that both Lawrence and Teller strongly favored a crash program to develop the super. Lawrence had already found his enthusiasm shared by Senator Brien McMahon, whom he had seen earlier on the same day. It was obvious that the super would have powerful friends. Two days later Lawrence was back in Washington, where he sought the additional assistance of Major General Kenneth Nichols "in initiating in the Joint Chiefs of Staff a requirement for the superweapon." Nichols had been deputy to Groves and was now the senior military expert on nuclear weapons; he agreed with Lawrence at once. Thus by October 12 a number of the principal advocates of the super had identified one another, agreed on their objective, and set to work.[20]

It was not a trivial group. Edward Teller had been the leading scientific enthusiast for the super since 1942; with Oppenheimer's agreement he had made the study of it his principal concern in wartime Los Alamos, and he had hoped that it would be pursued with high priority after the war. When it was not, he accepted an invitation to the University of Chicago, but he returned regularly to Los Alamos in summer, and in the autumn of 1949 he was there on a full year's leave. When Lawrence and Luis Alvarez came to consult him on their way east, he was already well along toward his own decision that the Soviet explosion made the super urgent. He pointed them toward the need for tritium, a heavy isotope of hydrogen not found in nature and essential for the super; it would require special production facilities such as a heavy-water reactor that might well be built under Lawrence's leadership. He pointed himself toward missionary work with fellow physicists.[21]

Senator McMahon, chairman of the Joint Committee on Atomic Energy, had made himself the Senate's foremost authority on atomic energy. He had first won attention by fighting the battle for "civilian control," successfully opposing a bill drawn in the War Department that was thought to leave too much room for military influence. But McMahon himself had come to believe strongly that a greatly increased emphasis on atomic weapons was vital to American security. Quick to share the enthusiasm of Lawrence, energetic in seeking out scientists and military men of parallel conviction, and supported by a staff director, William Liscum Borden, whom it is moderate to call zealous, McMahon argued formidably for the super, most importantly in letters to the president himself.[22]

Ernest Lawrence, in 1949, had lived for a decade at the summit of entrepreneurial physics. His laboratory at Berkeley was the largest, his Nobel Prize one of the earliest among American physicists, his Americanism the most obviously robust, and his energy unfailing. He was an optimist about himself, about large-scale physics, and about his country. Difficulties existed to be overcome. In the super he saw a national need, a new role for his own team, and a cause that required his leadership. In the end Lawrence had little to do with the technical development of thermonuclear weapons, but he helped to plead the case for them when it counted. His standing was particularly high among military men and politicians.[23]

But the most formidable of all the friends of the super was Lewis L. Strauss. He had worked as a young man for Herbert Hoover in World War I, and had made himself rich as an investment banker between the wars. He had been called up from the Naval Reserve in 1941 and had risen by energy, brains, and favor to the rank of rear admiral (as had his friend Souers). He had been chosen by Truman as a member of the five-man Atomic Energy Commission established by the McMahon Act, and it was largely his force and foresight that had led to the timely establishment of the monitoring system that detected the first Soviet test. In the commission he had established himself as an occasional dissenter—the only one so far. He was trusted by those who mistrusted the liberal New Dealer Lilienthal, and vice versa. An early and single-minded cold warrior, he had hoped that his friend James Forrestal would become the Democratic candidate for president in 1952. He himself, as he had told Truman at the time of his appointment to the commission, was "a black Hoover Republican."[24]

To these active and energetic supporters of enlarged thermonuclear effort, we may also add two other important figures who were already persuaded by mid-October. One was Sidney Souers, whose influence was as great as his work was quiet. From his first meeting with Strauss, with no disloyalty to a president still undecided, Souers appears to have believed that Strauss was on the right track. Certainly the friends of the super counted him a friend.[25] Similarly, by the middle of October the chairman of the Joint Chiefs of Staff, General Omar Bradley, briefed by Kenneth Nichols, had reached a conclusion from which he never shifted: If a thermonuclear weapon was possible, the Soviet Union must not be allowed to have it first; such a result would be "intolerable." Speaking not only for himself but for the Joint Chiefs of Staff as a body, Bradley expressed this opinion at a secret session of Senator McMahon's committee in mid-October. While this statement did not represent a full and formal JCS recommendation on the course to be followed, it did constitute a formidable counterbalance to any possible recommendation against a program of development. Just such a recommendation was about to be made, and by another redoubtable group.[26]

As Strauss had recommended on October 5, the proposal for a much expanded effort on the super was referred by Lilienthal to the commission's General Advisory Committee. Most advisory committees in Washington are more for show than for use, but this one, in 1949, was an exception. Since 1947 it had established itself as the most effective and influential source of policy guidance to the executive branch on the development of atomic weapons. From the beginning its chairman had been Robert Oppenheimer, chosen unanimously by his colleagues.[27] Oppenheimer's extraordinary performance as the wartime director of Los Alamos had been followed by his decisive contribution to the Lilienthal report and then by a continuing readiness to give relevant technical counsel to Baruch at the UN, to Acheson in the State Department, and to members of Congress. Working first from a double university base in California, and after 1947 from his new post as director of the Institute for Advanced Study in Princeton, Oppenheimer had become the central figure in the network of scientists who continued to concern themselves with atomic energy, inside and outside government. The principal forum for his exercise of this role was the General Advisory Committee.[28]

The General Advisory Committee was not a one-man show. In Enrico Fermi, I. I. Rabi, and Glenn Seaborg it had three other nuclear scientists of the first rank whose sound practical judgment matched their scientific talents. Seaborg made brilliance out of tenacity and opportunity out of every unoccupied moment. He also had the sober sense of reality that is often found among excellent chemists.[29] Rabi had the practical common sense of a man who had first learned to take care of himself as an immigrant boy on the streets of New York and who had moved from chemistry to nuclear physics—not an easy change—because he was determined to work on what he found most interesting. Fermi, who had known when, why, and how he must leave fascist Italy, had established himself in the United States, among all the nuclear physicists of his generation, as the one whose combination of practical and theoretical insight was most deeply respected. When Oppenheimer was asked to convene the General Advisory Committee to consider the super, he delayed the meeting for weeks until Fermi could be present, and in all the ensuing controversy no one ever questioned that decision.

In addition to its working physicists, the committee had, in James B. Conant and Lee DuBridge, two of the leading scientists-turned-college-presidents of their time, a time in which such leadership had wider impact than now. Conant of Harvard held a particularly commanding position. He was older than most of his colleagues—"Uncle Jim" to Oppenheimer. He had been second only to Bush in the high command of the wartime project, and he had turned down the job that Lilienthal had eagerly taken. Conant had decided to accept Truman's offer, making the single condition that he would not serve with Lewis Strauss, but Truman told him there was a commitment to appoint Strauss that he could not break.[30] The three remaining members of the committee were strong men too. Cyril Smith as a metallurgist and Hartley Rowe as an engineer had played distinguished parts in the Manhattan Project, while the most recently appointed member, Oliver E. Buckley, was president of the Bell Laboratories, the most distinguished scientific establishment in the world of American business.

When the General Advisory Committee met in Washington on October 29, most of its members already knew that the largest question before them would be the future of the super. Over an intense two-day period, members of the committee talked with George Kennan, with General Bradley, and with a number of other military officers. They also had a series of discussions with the commission itself. At the end of their meeting the eight members present (only Seaborg was missing) reached some unanimous conclusions:

> We all hope that by one means or another, the development of these weapons can be avoided. We are all reluctant to see the United States take the initiative in precipitating this development. We are all agreed that it would be wrong at the present moment to commit ourselves to an all-out effort toward its development.[31]

The committee divided, 6–2, on one issue. The majority favored an unqualified commitment not to develop the weapon. A minority, Fermi and Rabi, felt that this commitment should be "conditional on the response of the Soviet government to a proposal to renounce such development." This different view is critically important, but in immediate effect it was marginal, compared to the committee's unanimous opposition to any present commitment to development. Moreover, the expressions of revulsion in the majority and minority reports were equally strong: "The extreme dangers to mankind inherent in the proposal wholly outweigh any military advantage that could come from this development . . . a super bomb might become a weapon of genocide" (majority). "The fact that no limits exist to the destructiveness of this weapon makes its very existence and the knowledge of its construction a danger to humanity as a whole. It is necessarily an evil thing considered in any light" (minority).[32]

The General Advisory Committee's report went to the five commissioners and immediately sharpened the divisions that had already begun to separate them. To Lilienthal the report was both reinforcing and puzzling. He agreed that the super should not be developed. He thought there was too much reliance on atomic bombs already, and he had noted that the only military justification put forward by General Bradley was the "psychological" advantage of having something so powerful. But he could not see how to translate an opposition to crash development into a defensible public position, and he knew that McMahon and other members of the joint committee were already organizing support for a strong development program. Lilienthal reached some quick conclusions that did much to shape the next step in the executive branch: First, if the president wanted to make his own decision free of public pressure he did not have much time; second, this was not a case in which Lilienthal himself could hope to do what he had done so often before (notably in the framing of the Acheson-Lilienthal report): work to find a common ground on which he and his colleagues could stand. This was a time for "a pretty clear line," and the best way to proceed was for each of the commissioners to reach his individual answer.[33]

Lilienthal's final conclusion was that the issue involved was not "merely, or chiefly" one for the commission. It was a matter of foreign policy for the president and the secretary of state. On Tuesday, November 1, he went to Acheson and told him so. Acheson, who had known of the thermonuclear possibility since 1946 but had believed that research made it look unpromising, at once understood the gravity of the issue: "What a depressing world it is." Within three days Acheson had spoken to Truman and persuaded him that this was an important and complex matter with the broadest ramifications that should not be rushed into without great thought.[34] He had also begun to think about it himself, notably in a two-hour session with State Department planners led by Kennan, who had been charged one month earlier with a general review of the American position on atomic energy in the light of the Soviet test.[35]

Truman Decides

Truman prided himself on firm and orderly administration. On November 7 he told Lilienthal that he knew he had a serious question to decide, and when Lilienthal spoke of his fear that McMahon and his committee might try "to put on a blitz" the reassuring answer was "I don't blitz easily." Lilienthal went ahead to prepare and present a report from the divided commission. He himself, joined in different ways by Sumner Pike and Henry D. Smyth, recommended a decision against development of a super "at this time." Strauss, joined by Gordon Dean, dissented. Lilienthal had the advantage of presenting the report in person and pressing his own view face to face. He thought that an immediate decision for development would undermine the president's "strategy for peace," that an effort "to produce something capable of almost *unlimited* destruction" would alienate a large part of the world, that such a decision would serve to confirm and intensify "the already serious overvaluation placed upon atomic weapons by the American people," and that the existing stockpile of atomic weapons constituted an adequate deterrent against the Russians.[36]

All members of the commission recognized that the president would wish the views of others with more direct responsibility for both foreign policy and defense. To reread their report today is to understand why the president sought further advice. Not only were they divided, but their analysis of military and diplomatic issues was so brief as to be casual. Even if they had been unanimous the president would have wanted further counsel.

Such counsel was promptly sought. On November 19, following the precedent he had established in July, Truman referred the matter to "the Secretary of State, the Secretary of Defense and the Chairman of the Atomic Energy Commission as a special committee of the National Security Council to advise me on this problem."[37]

It is rare that cabinet-level committees do their own work, and this committee of three was no exception. It did not even meet for more than a month, until December 22, and its first session persuaded Acheson, its chairman, that the temperamental differences between Lilienthal and Secretary of Defense Louis Johnson were so wide that there should be no further sessions until he had done what he could to work out an agreed recommendation by "shuttling" between the two. Nor was the staff work much more impressive. The members of the interdepartmental working group behaved as representatives of their individual agencies, not as a unified staff. The resulting effort was both slow and fragmented. The men from the Pentagon, as usual, kept their own counsel until an agreed departmental view had been expressed by their superiors; indeed their own main labor was that of preparing the internal papers that presently led to written positions of the Joint Chiefs. The representatives of the Atomic Energy Commission, themselves of differing views, were interested primarily in finding out from the Pentagon what the military uses of thermonuclear weapons might be. Failing to extract any clear-cut answer, the members of the commission's staff wrote papers of their own on the subject. The State Department staff also held its hand until it could learn from Acheson what he himself wanted. In effect the personal incompatabilities in the committee of three and the departmental loyalties of the members of the working group insured that the real work of the next two months was done in other ways.[38]

Formally the president waited upon the report of his three-man committee, but informally he continued to be aware of the secret debate, and most of what reached him after Lilienthal's visit of November 7 came from those who disagreed with the General Advisory Committee's report. Even before Truman established the committee of three he had received a letter from President Karl Compton of the Massachusetts Institute of Technology, arguing that development must proceed. Compton believed that the Russians must not be allowed to get ahead, and that unilateral American renunciation would not stop them.[39] Compton was expressing his own strong opinion, but his letter was probably stimulated by Strauss or Louis Johnson, or both, in an effort to demonstrate that not all academic statesmen were of the same opinion as the luminaries of the General Advisory Committee.

A fortnight later the president received a formidable letter from Senator McMahon. Drafted by Liscum Borden, this five-thousand-word document was a fierce root-and-branch attack on the "false, horror-inspired logic" of the GAC report. The weapon could not be at once enormously powerful and militarily unnecessary; there were obvious military uses for very large explosions, notably as insurance against inaccuracy—"a Super might miss its target by ten miles or more and still serve the purpose intended"; there was no "moral dividing line" between one big explosion and many smaller ones; "modern warfare," not the super, was "the real instrument of genocide." Above all we must assume that the Russians were already racing ahead, and "if we let Russia get the Super first, catastrophe becomes all but certain." McMahon was also allowed to press his case in person.[40]

Truman had no great opinion of Brien McMahon, but soon the argument was put forward by people that he respected more. On November 25 he received a long letter from Strauss, who stated a series of conclusions in support of his recommendation to proceed "with all possible expedition to develop the thermonuclear weapon." The most powerful conclusion was his first: "Its unilateral renunciation by the United States could very easily result in its unilateral possession by the Soviet government." Truman had now heard a clear recommendation from the very man whom he had urged to force the matter forward.[41]

At about the same time, in all probability, the president learned of the opinions of a man he respected still more, General Omar Bradley, chairman of the Joint Chiefs of Staff.[42] On November 23 Bradley signed a memorandum from the Joint Chiefs to Secretary Johnson which stated flatly that it would be "intolerable" to let the Russians get the weapon first, and further that American restraint would not prevent such a result. This memorandum was the product of a staff process in which major roles were played by the men who were serving as Pentagon representatives on the working group of the three-man committee, men who knew and shared the views of Lawrence and

Strauss.[43] We do not know that Truman read it, but it is most unlikely that he was unaware of its tenor. He saw Souers and Johnson regularly, and either one could have told him. Both of them must have known that Truman enjoyed keeping on top of the state of play within his administration. Earlier in November he had startled Lilienthal by remarking with satisfaction that he saw "Johnson's copy" of one important report before Johnson did.[44] But whether Truman learned Bradley's opinion then or later is less important than that he found it persuasive. Two months later, in mid-January, Johnson sent him a longer but essentially parallel report from the Joint Chiefs, again over Bradley's signature, and this time Souers promptly reported to Acheson that Truman had said it "made a lot of sense." This later report concluded that while a "crash" program was not necessary, research and development must go forward "as a matter of top priority." Acheson learned that Truman "was inclined to think that was what we should do," and he replied that he had about reached the same conclusion. He had listened to leading members of the General Advisory Committee, but they had not persuaded him; he saw no alternative to going ahead as the Joint Chiefs proposed. Truman and Acheson were now eager to get the decision made before rising concern in McMahon's committee forced a public debate in which an undecided president would be on the defensive.[45]

By his own standards the president had waited a long time. The first major press account of the problem appeared in mid-November in *The Washington Post,* when Alfred Friendly picked up a speech that Senator Johnson of Colorado had made on November 1. Yet in a fashion quite unfamiliar to present-day readers the story then lay fallow until it was further developed by Stewart and Joseph Alsop, and then by James Reston, in January. The president, still a true believer in secrecy, was furious at the Alsops, whom he described to McMahon as the "Sop Sisters," and "lying scoundrels."[46] But on January 19 a question about the H-bomb appeared in his weekly press conference, and it was plain that time was short.

Acheson moved quickly to concert a report from the three-man committee. He saw to it that a draft was prepared which recommended a prompt decision to go ahead. On January 31 the three-man committee held its second and final meeting. Acheson presented his draft; it adopted the essence of the Joint Chiefs' position, but it also contained a concession to Lilienthal, in that it called for "a reexamination of our objectives in peace and war," a reexamination that Lilienthal had hoped might precede, not follow, any decision on thermonuclear weapons. During the discussion, in a concession to Johnson, Acheson agreed to drop a paragraph that would have explicitly reserved any final decision on production. It was masterful management of a process of formal recommendation that was not central to the president's own process of decision.[47]

Immediately after this meeting, the committee of three took its recommendations to the president, and he approved them at once. He liked Lilienthal, but he cut short his speech expressing "grave reservations." The meeting lasted seven minutes. The president did not read the supporting analysis. Lilienthal wrote in his journal that the president was "clearly set on what he was going to do before we set foot inside the door." The governing considerations had been well stated by the Joint Chiefs of Staff in the paper that Truman had already found persuasive: "Possession of a thermonuclear weapon by the USSR without such possession by the United States would be intolerable" and "a unilateral decision on the part of the United States not to develop a thermonuclear weapon will not prevent the development of such a weapon elsewhere." In the seven-minute meeting Truman sharpened the point. "Truman asked, 'Can the Russians do it?' All heads nodded, 'Yes, they can. . . .' 'In that case,' Truman said, 'we have no choice. We'll go ahead.' "[48] The formal recommendation that Truman approved derives from the recommendation of the Joint Chiefs:

> That the President direct the Atomic Energy Commission to proceed to determine the technical feasibility of a thermonuclear weapon, the scale and rate of effort to be determined jointly by the Atomic Energy Commission and the Department of Defense; and that the necessary ordnance developments and carrier program be undertaken concurrently."[49]

Nothing in Truman's papers or in reports of conversations with him suggests that this judgment ever seemed to him anything but the right and inescapable consequence of the basic argument of the Joint Chiefs.

Truman's decision was easily made, but it was not small. However limited the authorization—to determine "technical feasibility"—all concerned were aware that in effect it was a decision to make H-bombs if possible. Acheson took pains to spell the point out in a brief covering memorandum. While the president did not take time to read the memorandum, he almost surely understood the point for himself, and he certainly did not miss the four-column headline in the next day's *New York Times,* which began, TRUMAN ORDERS HYDROGEN BOMB BUILT.[50] In March the military backers of the bomb obtained his immediate approval of a still more categorical position, that "the thermonuclear weapon program is regarded as a matter of the highest urgency." So it remained from then on. The rapid development of thermonuclear weapons became unchallenged official policy, although enthusiastic supporters of that policy believed that the work would have gone faster if the General Advisory Committee, and Oppenheimer in particular, had given more support. At first no clearly promising path to success was found, until in early 1951 a major new concept was developed at Los Alamos. All this, important and interesting as it is, took place far from the White House. At Truman's level the matter was settled. He never reconsidered it; no one ever asked him to.[51]

The Neglected Alternative

Both the intrinsic importance of this decision and the need to get a better understanding of what did and did not happen in its making invite us now to consider what other course Truman might have followed, why he did not, and whether a different president might have made different choices. The most interesting proposal open to study, the one that offered the best single chance of avoiding a world of thermonuclear weapons, was the one suggested in the minority report of Fermi and Rabi. They sketched it in a single paragraph:

> For these reasons we believe it important for the President of the United States to tell the American public, and the world, that we think it wrong on fundamental ethical principles to initiate a program of development of such a weapon. At the same time it would be appropriate to invite the nations of the world to join us in a solemn pledge not to proceed in the development or construction of weapons of this category. If such a pledge were accepted even without control machinery, it appears highly probable that an advanced stage of development leading to a test by another power could be detected by available physical means. Furthermore, we have in our possession, in our stockpile of atomic bombs, the means for adequate "military" retaliation for the production or use of a "super."[52]

The proposal here, as the full report stated explicitly and as Rabi later confirmed to Herbert York, was "to couple American forbearance with a Soviet pledge to do the same." The means of verification would be the detectability of any advanced thermonuclear test by what in a later age are called "national technical means"—in those days mainly offshore aircraft testing for debris in the atmosphere. The safeguard against violation would be in the existing and growing stockpile of fission weapons. In effect, then, Fermi and Rabi were proposing something very much like a thermonuclear test ban agreement. The distance from their recommendation to such a proposal is nothing more than a matter of analysis and draftsmanship that one more discussion might have bridged. No such discussion took place.[53]

When the General Advisory Committee completed its report it agreed to maintain the most complete secrecy about its recommendations. There is no record that anyone ever sent for Fermi or Rabi to seek an elaboration of their thoughts. Nor did they press their views with anyone on their own account, and Rabi later remarked with regret that the General Advisory Committee had left the lobbying to those on the other side.[54] There was no lobby at all for a test ban.

Nor did the staff work done for the committee of three produce any study of this idea. We have already remarked that those assigned to this staff were people who stuck to the concerns of their own agencies, and in 1950 the idea of a test ban was too large to be contained within such bureaucratic boundaries. It combined technical and political considerations. It matched the technical feasibility of test detection and the technical reality that no one could really know he had this weapon without tests with the Soviet political reality that no intrusive means of inspection could be accepted and the American political reality that without some means of confidence in an agreement there was no way of answering Truman's basic question—can the Russians do it?—with any other conclusion than the one he reached: that we must do it too.

To a later generation these realities and their interconnection are familiar. We have lived with the uninspected atmospheric test ban of 1963 for a quarter of a century. But they were not at all clear in 1949. No one spelled them out to any member of the committee of three or to the president.

The narrowness of the staff work was not accidental. The original proposal for the three-man committee went to the president from his naval aide, Rear Admiral Robert Dennison, who suggested that the committee should be invited to consult with a working staff of such members as: "Mr. Kennan, Mr. Oppenheimer, Mr. Conant, General Norstad—and others of similar caliber." The staff that actually served did not meet that standard of eminence or independence. Truman or Souers or Acheson must have wanted a safer, more controllable process.[55]

The habit of obsessive secrecy may be as significant here as any conscious intent to restrict the range of analysis and advice. Truman plainly thought it crucial that he should make his decision ahead of any wave of public debate. But this secrecy had its cost: To keep ahead of public debate he needed a decision in January, whatever the state of the staff work, and when the government decided to conduct that work through in-house, departmentally-based officials, it was in effect turning away from the exploration of unfamiliar suggestions.

As a consequence the Fermi-Rabi suggestion was never seriously examined in the executive branch. In one meeting Acheson came somewhere near. On November 3, in a meeting with his policy planning staff, he sketched the notion of "an agreement to take a two-year vacation on development of the super-bomb," possibly without inspection, "on the general theory that they can't develop this thing during that time and we don't want to." But this sketchy notion was never elaborated. The only direct comment I have found on the Fermi-Rabi proposal is a strong rejection in Senator McMahon's long letter to Truman of November 21. McMahon found it "surprising" that an uninspected Russian pledge should be suggested when we had been trying since 1946 to persuade the world that these weapons were so dangerous as to require far-reaching international controls. He granted that if a full-fledged super were tested, "the gigantic blast effect could hardly help but make itself known to us," but he thought other kinds of tests might not be detectable, and in any case "I fail to see the special advantage of knowing when Russia has nearly acquired supers if we were so far behind that she would achieve them first regardless." Within the executive branch the issues between McMahon-Borden and Fermi-Rabi were never argued out.[56]

Yet the most important reason for failure to give adequate attention to the Fermi-Rabi proposal was not Truman's narrow staff process or even his insistence on the maintenance of secrecy. The decisive difficulty was that their idea was eclipsed in the debate by the more categorical position of the majority of the General Advisory Committee. The majority's flat recommendation against *any* American development of the H-bomb was what enraged the opposition, what attracted Lilienthal, and what Acheson could never persuade himself to accept. This recommendation was particularly impressive in having the strong support of Conant and Oppenheimer, both of whom were as well known to Acheson and Lilienthal as Fermi and Rabi were not. Acheson tried to understand the position of the majority; he talked to Oppenheimer and to Conant, and the position that he finally found unconvincing was theirs. He is surely thinking primarily of Oppenheimer, Conant, and Lilienthal in his summary recollection:

> Enough evil had been brought into human life, it was argued by men of the highest standing in science, education, and government, through development of atomic weapons without adding the super-horror of thermonuclear ones. If the United States with its vast resources proved that such an explosion was possible, research would be bound to press on to find the way for themselves. If no one knew that a way existed, research would be less stimulated. Those who shared this view were, I believed, not so much moved by the power of its logic (which I was never able to perceive—neither the maintenance of ignorance nor the reliance on perpetual good will seemed to me a tenable policy) as by an immense distaste for what one of them, the purity of whose motive could not be doubted, described as "the whole rotten business."[57]

So we must ask why the General Advisory Committee's majority rejected the Fermi-Rabi idea in favor of a broader opposition to development. We have no answers to that question; it was not directly posed in any of the later inquiries. One reason, probably, is that Oppenheimer and Conant, like many others, by now deeply doubted the prospect for any agreement with the Soviet Union. Like Acheson and Lilienthal, they had shared in the great effort to frame a workable scheme of international control, and they had shared also in the disappointments of the following years. Moreover, Oppenheimer in particular was clearly aware of the fact that in those later years opinion in Washington had hardened. In mid-November he warned his new friend George Kennan that for many people "the notions of safeguards and of effective control have attained a kind of rigid and absolute quality," and that the presumption against any less binding arrangements could not possibly be overcome "even within the executive branch of the Government in the present climate of opinion, and in a time short enough to conform to the necessities for a Presidential decision on the 'Super.'" On this analysis the Fermi-Rabi idea would have been a loser.[58]

We must remember here the enormous difference, especially for those with final responsibility, between the devil one knew—the Soviet Union—and the devil one did not—a weapon no one yet knew how to make. By the time of Truman's decision the cold war was raging. The Soviet menace was everywhere; the dream of a cooperative postwar world was long dead; the iron curtain was solid; the Berlin blockade was a recent and instructive memory; the captive nations were not a slogan but a vivid reality; Soviet hostility and duplicity were taken for granted. China had "fallen," and "Who lost China?" was the question of the hour. Alger Hiss had been convicted of perjury early in January, and Klaus Fuchs confessed his treason just four days before Truman's final decision (his confession came too late to influence Truman's action, but it would have had a quite different weight if the president had been leaning the other way). Whatever the retrospective judgment may be on the responsibility for the cold war (and I would still pick Stalin for the lion's share) there can be no doubt whatever of the mood of the American executive branch. Truman and Acheson had learned not to trust the Russians, and both of them now had more critics on the right than on the left.

Even the advisers who most feared the H-bomb sometimes seemed to be moved less by the opinion that it was necessarily an evil thing than by a conviction that it was the wrong weapon for dealing with the Soviet threat. Conant was explicit about it: A false reliance on this excessive weapon would lead to neglect of what was really needed in reply to the Russian bomb: conscription, a conventional buildup, and a move away from heedless reliance on a vanished atomic monopoly.

Conant found the crash program for the H-bomb repellent, in part indeed on straight moral grounds, but also, and perhaps more, because he thought it was strategically wrong. It was not a state of mind that would readily lead him to think of striking a bargain with Stalin to ward off thermonuclear weapons as the common enemy of mankind.

The Fermi-Rabi idea probably had another serious weakness for Conant and Oppenheimer and others in the majority. The proposal clearly implied that if no agreement could be reached with Moscow, the United States would proceed with development and eventually with testing. But the majority simply did not wish to endorse that course. The thermonuclear weapon was not the right answer to the Soviet fission test; "the extreme dangers to mankind inherent in the proposal wholly outweigh any military advantage that could come from this development," said the majority.[59] This unconditional opinion would not have mixed easily with a proposal that would probably require a decision to go ahead if it were rejected by the Kremlin. Conant and Oppenheimer and their colleagues in the majority, reinforcing one another and reacting against Lawrence and Teller, determined that the important thing to say was that the all-out development of this weapon was not the right answer to the Soviet test. That is exactly what they and their colleagues were heard as saying, but neither of them could ever give to Acheson, or to anyone else, any persuasive answer to the immediate question: Won't the Russians try for it, and if so, must not we? Reading Russian intentions was a question for the diplomats, not the scientists, and one of the few points of unanimity among Acheson's advisors, right from the start, was that "we would have to start with the assumption that the Russians were working on it also."[60] That point alone made a flat decision against development unacceptable, and it made Acheson quite unresponsive to what he heard from his friends about the desirability of a good American example.

Even if the Fermi-Rabi idea had not been overshadowed by the more downright position of the majority, its requirement of a negotiation with Stalin would have fallen on stony ground in Acheson's State Department. Oppenheimer was right about the lack of enthusiasm for uninspected agreements. I know of no State Department document explicitly reviewing the Fermi-Rabi idea, but the general conclusion reported to Acheson and passed on to the president was that any proposal for an agreement to forgo work on thermonuclear weapons would require "safeguards necessarily involving an opening up of Soviet territory" and thus "unacceptable to the Soviet Union." And without such safeguards no agreement would give "sufficient assurance . . . to make it worth while."[61] The implied dismissal of the Fermi-Rabi concept is either unwitting or cavalier in the extreme, but it went unchallenged.

Acheson himself in these matters was a pessimist on the value of negotiation with the Russians. The Soviet test might lead others to urge new efforts of understanding; he found their arguments unpersuasive. When Lilienthal made a general statement to this effect, Acheson simply reminded him that dealing with the Russians was a problem for the secretary of state, not the chairman of the Atomic Energy Commission. "This was a field in which I would be supposed to know more than David. I pointed that out to him . . ."[62] And when the public announcement of the president's decision on the H-bomb produced calls for new discussions with Moscow from leading senators and even from Winston Churchill, Acheson commented firmly that "no good would come from our taking the initiative in calling for conversations at this point. . . . Only the Russians would benefit from such a step." To him the record showed that the Russians preferred to exploit outstanding issues "for their own objectives of world domination."[63]

On this question, as usual, Acheson was in full harmony with his president, who had expressed himself still more briefly and clearly at an even earlier stage. On January 19, the same day that Souers told Acheson of Truman's reaction to the analysis of the Joint Chiefs, the president held a news conference where for the first time he was asked a question about the H-bomb.

Q. Mr. President, are you considering direct negotiations with Russia on the hydrogen bomb?
THE PRESIDENT. No.[64]

Polarization

One important cause and effect of the recommendations of the General Advisory Committee was the polarization of opinion on nuclear weapons policy. Members of the committee were more certain of what they were against—what they called a crash program of development—than about what they were for, just as their critics were more certain of the dangers of letting the Russians win the race than they were of the advantages of an American program of development. Polarization of this sort is so important to the later history of these matters that this early instance deserves a closer look.

With the single exception of the Fermi-Rabi minority report, the documents sent forward by the General Advisory Committee in October took little account of options between a full-scale development program and doing nothing. It is not surprising then that the majority opinion was generally read by its opponents as a flat declaration of opposition to development. In reality the individual members of the committee were not opposed to all exploration of the problem; in

December Oliver Buckley of the Bell Laboratories wrote a supplementary memorandum explicitly urging "a thorough and detailed study" of thermonuclear reactions and weapons design, and neither he nor Oppenheimer regarded this recommendation as conflicting with the October 30 report. Yet the notion of a program of careful and even intense exploration as an alternative to any immediate decision "to order the H-bomb built" was never carefully considered by anyone. Though Truman's January decision "to continue" the thermonuclear work sounded minimal, in reality it was, and was understood to be, a rejection of the basic GAC position.[65] The middle ground of research without commitment to development had been turned into a no-man's-land by polarization.

In its opposition to developing the weapon, the General Advisory Committee was not only saying that the hydrogen weapon was the wrong answer to the Soviet test, but it was also opposing the zealous advocacy of such men as Teller and Lawrence; thus the issue became polarized, and the other side acted accordingly. Preoccupied with this broader issue, both sides were disinclined to examine complex intermediate courses.

Polarization may have come earliest in Oppenheimer. On October 21 he wrote Conant to warn him that Teller and Lawrence were pushing for the super, and he called them "two experienced promoters." It was not unreasonable to call Teller and Lawrence "promoters"; neither was ever bashful in advancing his views, and both were proud of their energetic advocacy of thermonuclear development; nonetheless there is some personal feeling in the term. But what is more serious than "who started it" is the possibility that polarization may have blinded Oppenheimer, the most influential and persuasive member of the committee, to the one line of action that might have served his own objective of keeping thermonuclear weapons out of the world.[66]

The most obvious point that was missed is that there was no intrinsic contradiction between the recommendation the president accepted on January 31, for accelerated work "to determine the technical feasibility of a thermonuclear weapon" and a proposal to ban large-scale thermonuclear tests. There were undoubtedly powerful psychological barriers to such a course of action; it would certainly not have satisfied the enthusiasts. In their hearts, then and later, they preferred an unlimited technological contest to any agreement that did not force an opening of Soviet society. But the progress of thermonuclear research did not require that the enthusiasts be pleased on all counts. If an accelerated research program had been coupled with a test ban proposal, would Teller have refused to join in? And if he had, was there no one else to do the work? My own reading of the temper of the Los Alamos laboratory, where the negative attitude of the General Advisory Committee was not generally shared, is that if feasibility studies had been authorized while a test ban was pursued, Los Alamos under Bradbury could and would have pursued studies more than ample to safeguard the U.S. position. This particular failure of perception in Oppenheimer and Conant is surprising, and it must be attributed, I think, to their preoccupation with blocking the enthusiasts. Oppenheimer had recognized at the outset, as he wrote to Conant on October 21, that "it would be folly to oppose the exploration of this weapon. We have always known it had to be done; and it does have to be done." Then he added: "But that we become committed to it as the way to save the country and the peace appears to me full of dangers," failing to recognize that Fermi and Rabi had an idea that might allow the necessary exploration without the dangerous commitment.[67]

The connection that Oppenheimer did not make was also missed elsewhere, notably by Acheson and the president when they rejected the idea of negotiation. It was understandable that they should consider themselves the right men to judge the practicability of negotiation; they were the ones with both responsibility and experience on that issue. But in their self-confidence they neglected the possibility that in the new situation the technical realities might permit a different and more acceptable approach.

There is one other element in this situation whose impact is not easy to estimate. While there was agreement, from 1942 onward, that the thermonuclear explosion was theoretically possible, there was also no clearly promising way to make it happen. Those who believed most ardently that the weapon was needed were still quite unable to explain how it could be made to work. Those advocating a thermonuclear program had no motivating insights comparable to the Frisch-Peierls memorandum. The decisively promising ideas came only in 1951 from Edward Teller and Stanislaw Ulam. For some, like Oppenheimer, the absence of any promising idea was one element in their opposition, and indeed Oppenheimer later argued that if the Teller-Ulam insight had been at hand in 1949 it would have been hard to argue against the super: "When you see something that is technically sweet, you go ahead and do it."[68] Oppenheimer recognized that not all his colleagues would agree with this view, but it is nonetheless an important part of the background of the debate, as it did take place, that the ways and means to a man-made thermonuclear explosion were not at all clear when the question came before Truman. This difficulty did not concern Truman or those whose advice he accepted, but it deserves note because the technical obscurity of the undertaking was one element in the readiness of Oppenheimer to oppose it. Yet it seems right to doubt that in these matters technical sweetness should always be a license to go ahead.

With a Different President?

It remains to consider how the matter might have been resolved on different assumptions about the president's position and the process of deciding. Let us make assumptions that are optimal from the standpoint of avoiding a world of hydrogen bombs. What chance is there that the result could have been different?

The first requirement is that the president should understand the danger, as Truman did not at the time, and as not many others did either. The meaning of thermonuclear weapons that Churchill so dramatically described in 1955 was only a sickening foreboding in 1949, not a fully articulated analysis, not even in the minds of the members of the General Advisory Committee and still less in its report. Mindful that the primary source of its influence lay in its technical preeminence, the committee presented its main report in technical terms, leaving its deeper moral and political concerns to the shorter majority and minority opinions, where they were expressed dramatically but almost cryptically. These opinions never attracted Truman's attention.

They might have attracted another man's. My own view is that the chances would have been much better with Roosevelt or Eisenhower or Kennedy, each of whom one can imagine reading the fierce short phrases—"extreme danger to mankind," "an evil thing considered in any light"—and concluding that he simply would not choose to cross this ghastly Rubicon if he could help it.

Any of these presidents might have asked himself how to do better, and he might then have done at least three things that Truman did not do. First, and most important, he could have insisted upon, and taken part in, a process of inquiry much more searching and serious than the one we have examined. The arguments that mattered most—"it is evil" but "a Russian monopoly would be intolerable"—could have been tested against each other by direct and extended discussion between Conant and Bradley. A president impressed by both arguments could have insisted on a search for further alternatives. It is not fanciful to suppose that a president with such concerns, served by such a process, would have had his attention drawn to the possibilities of the Fermi-Rabi idea.

In this process our different president would have had to begin to think hard (if he had not begun before) about the ways in which he would explain and defend a policy of restraint. We must not make his problem unrealistically easy by removing from the scene all friends and advocates of the super. There would always have been men like Strauss, McMahon, and Teller. A president wanting to hold back would require a position strong enough to satisfy, or at least to contain, such forces, and that position would have to be public. Given the state of mutual mistrust prevailing between Moscow and Washington, the shock of the successful Soviet test, and above all the emotional engagement of the advocates of rapid development—there is a quantum jump in sight, and we can be first if we will—a president moved by a larger vision of common danger would have had to share that vision with the American public and so with the world.

The very idea of going public in this fashion would have been alien to Truman, who wanted as little public debate as possible. But it was not alien to others, and another president would have found initial encouragement toward such a course in the General Advisory Committee's report. It explicitly urged a prompt disclosure of what it regarded as the fundamentals of the problem:

> The Committee recommends that enough be declassified about the super bomb so that a public statement of policy can be made at this time. . . . In one form or another, the statement should express our desire not to make this development. It should explain the scale and general nature of the destruction which its use would entail.[69]

This passage bears the imprint of Oppenheimer, whose concern over the lack of public understanding found other expressions later. No one in the administration supported the recommendation, but no one in the administration was in need of greater public understanding of the new order of menace in the nature of the proposed development. Truman had wanted the matter secret partly because he wanted to avoid public debate, but for a president who shared the basic judgment of the General Advisory Committee a wholly different prospect would have opened: He could not hope to avoid a debate, so he must find a way to launch it and win it.

In such an undertaking our alternate president would have had great advantages. First, he could have had as his supporters and defenders the overwhelming majority of those who had done most to put the United States first in nuclear weapons. Truman took great pains to keep the General Advisory Committee silent; another man could have encouraged them all to speak out. There can be little doubt that with presidential leadership and support the most notable figures in American science and higher education would have been overwhelmingly on the side of restraint. The arguments only sketched by the General Advisory Committee could have been spelled out in powerful detail. A later generation, familiar with what physicians tell us about the consequences of a one-megaton weapon, can readily consider for itself the impact of a parallel (if necessarily less sophisticated) campaign in 1950.

In the same way, especially after approving the expanded fission effort in October, a president choosing to hold back from the H-bomb could have expanded on another theme foreshadowed by the General Advisory Committee and much more familiar today: that the weapons already developed and already planned for production were quite sufficient for basic deterrence. In 1950, because the ground had not yet been trampled in extended and increasingly arcane debate, this proposition would have had even greater psychological force than it has today. The president could have decided to describe the stockpile already in prospect, and he could have revealed that the United States was already arming itself with weapons having a total destructive power thousands of times greater than what was used at Hiroshima, weapons that could inflict in a day death and destruction on a scale vastly beyond all of what was done in World War II by both sides to each other. Moreover, all these propositions could have been quantified by the simple say-so of the president. That Truman thought these numbers a vital secret tells us much about the way his mind had been shaped by the real secret of real scarcity in 1946. It tells us nothing about what another mind could have concluded. A president who wanted to propose restraint would have had extraordinary advantages in taking his case to the American public.

Such evidence as we have suggests that a president making these arguments would have found strong public support. Barton Bernstein has pointed out that even as Truman was deciding to go ahead, just over half of those voting in a poll preferred to try negotiations first, while in March, after a "peace offensive" from scientists and senators (including McMahon) the balance in favor of negotiation was three to one. Surely this shift would have been even more striking if the president himself had been leading the way. Most people thought the negotiations would fail, but most people wanted to try.[70]

Even with the public on his side, our president would have had two flanks to guard: He must avoid a head-on conflict with the great military heroes of World War II, and he must have an answer to the danger of a Russian effort to get ahead. Both of these problems are familiar today, when we have seen many proposals for restraint discounted by fear that the Russians would get some advantage and many presidential initiatives constrained by the prospect of public opposition from the Joint Chiefs of Staff. In 1950, however, the two problems could have been reduced to one: The senior military leaders of that time were both moderate and sensitive, especially Omar Bradley, the chairman of the Joint Chiefs. While pressure for ever-larger "air-atomic" forces was not trivial, especially in the air force itself, it had none of the pervasive mystique that was to surround the nuclear triad twenty-five years later, and in fact when the Joint Chiefs made their formal comments on the need for an H-bomb, it was not any clear military requirement that governed their argument or persuaded Truman; it was rather what the Russians might do. If he could find an answer to that one, the president could keep the Joint Chiefs with him.

It is just here, I think, that we are entitled to hope that our president would have been drawn to the Fermi-Rabi idea. It offered a way out of the difficulty in which Truman, with his very different approach, took refuge—the flat refusal of the Russians to have any part of the Acheson-Lilienthal-Baruch proposal, with its intrinsically intrusive process of control over all major nuclear installations. What Truman and Acheson did not see, a different leader could have understood and chosen to emphasize: that in the particular case of the thermonuclear weapon, no one could truly possess it without conducting tests that would surely be detectable. Thus the kind of insurance provided by a comprehensive plan for an international development authority was not necessary here. An agreement that could be monitored by existing national means of detection would serve. Nor should we be led astray on this point by the remarkable later case of Israel, which does appear to have developed thermonuclear devices without testing them. The Israelis have had the experience of others to guide them.

The argument, of course, would not have stopped there. It would have been necessary to demonstrate that Senator McMahon was wrong when he argued that skillfully conducted experiments might not be detectable and that in consequence the Russians might acquire a decisive lead in secret.[71] But even McMahon admitted that a full-fledged test would be detected, and there were two strong supporting arguments available that our president would not have neglected: first, insurance was supplied by the greatly superior American fission stockpile—this point was clear to all members of the General Advisory Committee and could have been driven home by facts and figures; second, the president could and surely would have authorized the program of research and exploration that even Oppenheimer had recognized as inevitable in mid-October.

How far a serious program of research could be pursued while full-scale tests were prohibited was debatable and therefore would have been debated. The debate, moreover, would have taken place within the fog of ignorance that then surrounded the whole question of the design of a workable thermonuclear device. These uncertainties would have reinforced the enthusiasts for full-scale development in their opposition to unwelcome limitations. One does not need to know exactly what combination of scientific passion and political concern moved Edward Teller to know that he would have protested in this situation. Indeed the General Advisory Committee's report itself argued at one point that exploration would require testing.[72] But in fact there was plenty of room, as events demonstrated, for an intermediate course of the kind we are now considering. The scientific authority available to support such a course would have been great, and the inhibitions that later led many first-rate physicists to choose not to participate in the thermonuclear program would hardly have been applicable in this situation, where the basic policy was one of restraint and the program of research no more than a form of prudent insurance. As it turned out in 1951 the decisive advance was conceptual, not experimental, and that conceptual work would have gone forward.

The recognition of thermonuclear danger, the prospect of a new kind of unintrusive international agreement, the protection afforded by a large fission stockpile, and the explicit encouragement of scientific exploration could have been developed and presented together as a rational response to the double danger of thermonuclear weapons themselves and of some secret Soviet success in their development.

The strength of this case, both technically and logically, has been persuasively demonstrated by the physicist Herbert York in *The Advisors*. Having worked on the H-bomb after Truman's decision, York asked himself, twenty-five years later, what would have happened if there had been no U.S. thermonuclear program whatever in 1950 (a much more demanding condition than we have set with our proviso for extensive explorations), and if the Soviet program had followed the exact course it did—also a strong condition, since it is likely that the Soviet program got some help and stimulus from U.S. announcements and what could be learned from U.S. tests. After careful comparison of the important tests on each side as they actually occurred, York concluded that if the Americans had launched no new programs until after the first Soviet thermonuclear test, and if they had then gone forward no faster than they actually did after Truman's decision of 1950, the United States would still have had time to develop thermonuclear weapons in a fashion essentially equal to the Soviet program. York found it much more likely that the United States would have quickly overtaken the Russians in such a situation, and obviously that likelihood is increased by our own assumption of a lively program of exploration from 1950 onward. Not all of York's argument, based as it is on what is now understood, can be fairly made available as a part of the initial case put forward by our hypothetical president, but what it does tell us is that anyone who took the opposite view would in the event have been wrong.[73]

Now let us add explicitly to our argument the advantage that has been implicit so far—the advantage of being president. We have seen how both the awesome character of nuclear weapons and the history of their development combined from the beginning to put unusual authority in the hands of the president. That authority had been used mainly for choices that had relatively strong public support, but the special role of the president in these matters was generally acknowledged. It was the *president* that men like McMahon were trying to persuade, and an appeal beyond him to the public would have been a last resort. In the event the pressure of the joint committee did speed up Truman's decision to do what his own convictions were leading him to do in any case, and in later years members of that committee took much pride in that role, but in fact they were pushing an open door. They would have found it much less easy to put pressure on a president who disagreed with them. The only truly daring assumption we have made is that of a president sharing the basic approach of the members of the General Advisory Committee. If that assumption is granted, the course we have sketched becomes not only plausible but likely. No one can say finally just how strong the position would have been, but I think it requires no great act of faith to conclude that it could have been strong enough to support a serious effort at agreement with Moscow.

Once we assume a serious American effort at negotiation, the focus of our doubts and uncertainties must necessarily shift to the Kremlin. Without some response from Stalin, not even the boldest and strongest American president would have been able to sustain a policy of restraint forever. But at least we have brought the Americans to a hypothetical starting line. What can we speculate about possible Soviet responses?

The fragments of evidence that have allowed us to give some substance to the shape of an alternative American policy are not available on the Russian side. We do not know, for example, to what degree Russian perception of the problem was clouded by theoretical and technological uncertainty, as it was in the United States. We do not know how far the remarkable achievements of the preceding four years and bright expectations for the future may have created, either among scientists or among their political superiors, a confident expectation of special advantage in a thermonuclear race. We do not know to what degree the continuing American lead in fission weapons, which would have been so helpful to an American president, might have been inhibiting on the Soviet side, creating fear of an inferiority that might be permanent if no technological break-out were attempted. We do not know to what degree there may have been men on the Soviet side sharing the same sense of foreboding that moved the members of the General Advisory Committee in Washington.

What we know, and it is almost all we know, is that the decision would have been Stalin's. And what we know of Stalin is not immediately encouraging. He would have suspected an imperialist trick in any American proposal. He would have found it hard to turn away from any avenue to greater Soviet power, and he would have found unfamiliar the notion of a danger shared by all mankind. Suspicious, obsessed with power, supremely cynical, hardened in ruthlessness, Stalin does not fit easily into a speculation about shared and mutually confident restraint. It may be right to conclude that the best intentioned and most carefully developed American proposal would have found him unresponsive and even hostile. In speculating on this question with friends I have found that those who have a cool view of his character and intentions are inclined to believe that no opportunity was missed in this great case, simply because Stalin was Stalin. Yet the same Stalin was capable of astonishing flexibility when confronted with unexpected new situations, and I think it wrong to take him as predictably and totally hostile to a direct and serious American approach.

Moreover, in considering Soviet reactions we are not limited to Stalin alone. As matters actually developed, the Americans did cross the thermonuclear Rubicon while he was still in command. The full-scale test of November 1, 1952, ended the practical prospect of a thermonuclear test ban, since no one could expect the Soviets to forgo a weapon that the Americans had already developed. But it is not at all certain that the different president of our speculation would have conducted that test. Even if his more moderate program of development had produced the necessary readiness, he might well have listened to arguments for postponement. The reasons would have been basically the same as those that might have led him to the Fermi-Rabi idea. Just such a postponement was in fact urged, in 1952, principally by Vannevar Bush. The argument at the time was that so large a decision should be left to a new administration, but if that argument had been accepted, the next proposition, made to that new president, would have been that no test should take place without one more effort to reach agreement with the Russians. Stalin died in the seventh week of Eisenhower's first term. So it is relatively easy to reconstruct events—always assuming a president different from Truman—in such a way that the matter would have been open for discussion with the quite different Soviet leaders of the first post-Stalin period. It is wrong to push aside the lessons of this great case by supposing that because Stalin was Stalin, the result was inevitable.

But certainly Truman was Truman, and it is time to return to that reality. Acheson was also Acheson, Souers was Souers, Bradley was Bradley, and Truman agreed with them all: If the Russians could do it, he must go ahead. He chose not to reach beyond this inner circle to Lilienthal, Conant, Oppenheimer, Fermi, and Rabi. These men could have made their case more strongly, but Truman remains Truman, and in the end I find it impossible to avoid the conclusion that the decision he actually made is the only one that fits him as he was by 1950.[74]

A Fermi-Rabi test ban treaty would have been a great achievement, but certainly not a panacea. It would hardly have been enough by itself to ensure a permanent avoidance of thermonuclear weapons. Continuing research would over time have strengthened belief in the certainty of "success" and also produced ideas for particular weapons that would have been highly attractive to commanders. The thermonuclear weapon, along with its capacity for hideous and unmilitary overkill, has had the real military value of permitting relatively lightweight warheads, and it seems likely that heavy pressure to make it would have developed over time, in one government or the other. We must also take account of the attraction that the thermonuclear weapon has had in later years for every other nuclear weapons state. The Fermi-Rabi idea offered a prospect of reliable delay, not a sure promise of permanent escape. But such delay would itself have been a large prize, and an agreement of this sort would have encouraged a continuing process based on a growing understanding of nuclear danger as a common problem. The insight of these two great men cannot be put aside because it is not in itself enough. That objection applies to every achievable improvement in our perilous position.

NSC 68 *and Expanded Production*

Truman's decision on the hydrogen bomb, because of the way it was made, had consequences wider than the decision itself. As Lilienthal had feared, it both marked and encouraged a pronounced shift away from the principle of civilian control to which he had believed (as the president did himself) that Truman was strongly committed. Obviously Truman and Acheson—and Louis Johnson and Lewis Strauss and Brien McMahon, for that matter—were civilians themselves. But all of them, in the process of the H-bomb decision, had shown great respect for, and even reliance on, the judgment of the Joint Chiefs of Staff, and none of them had responded to Lilienthal's passionate argument that a decision of this magnitude must be considered in a perspective larger than that of a competition in destructive power with the Soviet Union.[75]

Significantly, when Acheson finally conceded the necessity for such a wider study, to be undertaken after the decision, he explicitly excluded members of the Atomic Energy Commission from any direct participation. The study that resulted, the famous document called *NSC 68,* which was presented to the president on April 7, 1950, simply took for granted the truth of the very proposition which Lilienthal had so passionately questioned: the imperative of a comprehensive all-out effort to retain qualitative and quantitative nuclear superiority. *NSC 68* took the gloomiest possible view of the prospect of any agreed and verifiable bilateral limitation on such weapons. It fully endorsed the major efforts of nuclear expansion already in progress. It also strongly urged a rapid and massive conventional rearmament, and this was indeed its major departure from existing policy. It contained nothing that was construed by any part of the government as a limitation on the military role of nuclear weapons. It explicitly considered and rejected a proposal that George Kennan had put forward in January, at the end of the debate on the H-bomb, for adoption of a policy of no first use of nuclear weapons.[76] In effect this study hardened the "military" approach to nuclear weapons which was so influential in the H-bomb decision itself. When *NSC 68* came under critical interdepartmental review in the months after its initial submission, many questions were raised about others of its conclusions, but not about its view of nuclear weapons.[77]

A still more striking and still less debated demonstration of Truman's decisive turn from his original concept of civilian control is to be found in the series of decisions he made to enlarge capacity for the production of weapons-grade material. Three times between the summer of 1949 and the end of his administration he received requests originating with the military for major increases in productive capacity, and each time he approved the request without hesitation. On the first occasion he referred the recommendation to the same committee of three—Acheson, Johnson, and Lilienthal—that later reviewed the question of the hydrogen bomb, and we have seen that at the time Lilienthal took this referral as a recognition of the role of others than "the military" advising the president on such matters.[78] But in reality Truman had already decided that "since we can't obtain international control we must be strongest in atomic weapons" and "the military" knew it.[79] When the three-man committee reported to the president, on October 10, the military request was untrimmed, and the main burden of the argument in its favor was presented directly by the Joint Chiefs of Staff. Lilienthal was right in principle when he was outraged earlier that year by the opinion of Louis Johnson that "a unanimous military judgment of the Joint Chiefs is something the President *has* to follow."[80] But what he left out of his account in his optimism of July was the reality that when the president and the Joint Chiefs were in agreement, no other force in the executive branch would have much weight. Only Congress could effectively resist that combination, and in 1949 Congress was two decades away from seriously questioning any proposal from the executive branch for greater nuclear strength.

So on October 19, without a debate or even a face-to-face discussion, Truman formally approved what was in essence a military recommendation. Twice more in his time as president he approved further large-scale proposals for expanded nuclear production capacity, and the capabilities thus authorized were sufficient to support the extraordinary increase in the size and destructiveness of the nuclear stockpile that marked the 1950s. It is impossible to improve on the authoritative summary offered in 1983 by David Rosenberg:

> The three approved increases in nuclear production may well have been the most substantive actions taken by the Truman Administration in the area of strategic nuclear policy during its last three years. By January 1953, a construction program was under way which would add eight plutonium production reactors and two gaseous diffusion U-235 production plants to the five reactors and two gaseous diffusion plants operating in mid-1950. These plants and reactors were capable of supporting an enormous expansion of the nuclear weapons stockpile. According to recent authoritative unclassified estimates, the stockpile grew from approximately 1,000 weapons in the summer of 1953 to nearly 18,000 by the end of the decade. No subsequent administration found it necessary to authorize any further expansion of nuclear production facilities to meet weapons requirements."[81]

Truman Keeps Clear of Further Use

Truman's acceptance of military advice on building more and better bombs was not accompanied by any relaxation of his own determined personal control over questions of custody, deployment, and use. He never departed from his insistence on complete presidential control of the weapons whose multiplication he supported. After Nagasaki he never came close to the use of even one against an enemy.

In particular Truman never came close to the use of nuclear weapons in Korea, where war broke out on June 10, 1950, and continued through his time in office. Once, at the height of the general anxiety over the Chinese advances of November 1950, he seemed to suggest serious consideration of such use in incautious replies to press conference questions. His slip promptly led to such a series of disclaimers and clarifications—complete with a summit visit from Clement Attlee—that the real situation was plainly revealed: This president and his advisers saw no good role for nuclear weapons in Korea. And while the military argument was at least in part that the weapons were too scarce and valuable for use in a secondary theater, Truman's own view was simpler. In the very answer that caused the furor, he made this view clear and showed in so doing that he now understood the weapon better than he had before Hiroshima:

> THE PRESIDENT. We will take whatever steps are necessary to meet the military situation, just as we always have.

Q. Will that include the atomic bomb?

THE PRESIDENT. That includes every weapon that we have.

Q. Mr. President, you said "every weapon that we have." Does that mean that there is active consideration of the use of the atomic bomb?

THE PRESIDENT. There has always been active consideration of its use. I don't want to see it used. It is a terrible weapon, and it should not be used on innocent men, women, and children who have nothing whatever to do with this military aggression. That happens when it is used.[82]

The real meaning of this exchange is in the president's last two sentences. What Truman had thought about using the bomb to end World War II was not what he thought about using it in later years.

The Myth of a Nuclear Ultimatum over Iran

There remains one myth about Harry Truman and the bomb that is his own fault—the notion that in March 1946, during a crisis over a temporary Soviet failure to honor an agreement on troop withdrawal from Iran, Truman sent Stalin an ultimatum that produced a Soviet withdrawal. Truman used the word *ultimatum* in a number of later comments on the episode (though not in his memoirs), and the most graphic version of the myth came from Senator Henry Jackson in 1980, in the context of nationwide frustration over the American hostages held in Teheran. Jackson told *Time* that he had heard from Truman himself in later years how Truman had told the Soviet ambassador that if Soviet troops were not withdrawn in forty-eight hours, the United States would use the bomb, and how the Soviets then withdrew in twenty-four hours. The trouble with this tale is that nothing of the sort ever happened. Truman did not see the Soviet ambassador. Soviet troops were withdrawn only slowly, after complex negotiations between the Soviet Union and Iran. Truman did indeed send messages of real diplomatic importance, but not one of them contained anything remotely like an ultimatum, or any reference to the bomb. In the strongest of these messages, on March 8, the American chargé in Moscow, George Kennan, said that the United States "can not remain indifferent" to the continuing presence of Soviet troops. Truman also sent a personal message to Stalin through his new ambassador, Bedell Smith, but Smith's talk with Stalin came eleven days after his conversation with Truman and ten days after the first Soviet announcement that the troops would be withdrawn, and it contained no ultimatum. Smith did tell Stalin that if the United States were faced by "a wave of progressive aggression on the part of any powerful nation or group of nations, we would react exactly as we have in the past," but the comment was phrased in conditional terms, and the other part of Smith's message was an invitation to Stalin to visit the United States.[83]

Truman's faulty recollection here was doubly unfortunate. Not only did he invent an explicitly nuclear threat that never happened, but his account obscured a diplomatic intervention that was entirely creditable and almost surely influential in the process by which Stalin did in the end carry out the withdrawal of his troops from Iran. American concern, expressed both privately and publicly, and conspicuously lacking in the sort of crude pressure suggested by the word *ultimatum,* certainly helped Iranian leaders to resist Soviet pressure for concessions, and the Americans also encouraged close attention in the Security Council of the United Nations in a way that plainly embarrassed Moscow. There is little reason to doubt that these actions were helpful in persuading Stalin that keeping troops in Iran would give him more trouble than it was worth. The Truman administration's response was prompt, intelligent, and effective—and all the more so because it did *not* take the form of atomic diplomacy.

Truman's Final Message

As his term drew to an end, Harry Truman showed a much better understanding of the thermonuclear world into which he had led his countrymen. He had been president from before the first explosion through the ten-megaton thermonuclear test that took place on November 1, 1952, at Eniwetok Island in the Pacific. In his final message on the state of the union, he discussed the nuclear future in a fashion which at once sums up his own hard-earned understanding and sets the stage for our examination of the labors of his successor:

> . . . The stakes in our search for peace are immensely higher than they have ever been before.
>
> For now we have entered the atomic age, and war has undergone a technological change which makes it a very different thing from what it used to be. War today between the Soviet empire and the free nations might dig the grave not only of our Stalinist opponents, but of our own society, our world as well as theirs.
>
> This transformation has been brought to pass in the seven years from Alamogordo to Eniwetok. It is only seven years, but the new force of atomic energy has turned the world into a very different kind of place.
>
> Science and technology have worked so fast that war's new meaning may not yet be grasped by all the peoples who would be its victims; nor, perhaps, by the rulers in the Kremlin. But I have been President of the United States, these seven years, responsible for the

decisions which have brought our science and our engineering to their present place. I know what this development means now. I know something of what it will come to mean in the future. . . .

The language of science is universal, the movement of science is always forward into the unknown. We could not assume that the Soviet Union would not develop the same weapon, regardless of all our precautions, nor that there were not other and even more terrible means of destruction lying in the unexplored field of atomic energy. . . .

The progress of scientific experiment has outrun our expectations. Atomic science is in the full tide of development; the unfolding of the innermost secrets of matter is uninterrupted and irresistible. Since Alamogordo we have developed atomic weapons with many times the explosive force of the early models, and we have produced them in substantial quantities. And recently, in the thermonuclear tests at Eniwetok, we have entered another stage in the worldshaking development of atomic energy. From now on, man moves into a new era of destructive power, capable of creating explosions of a new order of magnitude, dwarfing the mushroom clouds of Hiroshima and Nagasaki. . . .

Inevitably, until we can reach international agreement, this is the path we must follow. And we must realize that no advance we make is unattainable by others, that no advantage in this race can be more than temporary.

The war of the future would be one in which man could extinguish millions of lives at one blow, demolish the great cities of the world, wipe out the cultural achievements of the past—and destroy the very structure of a civilization that has been slowly and painfully built up through hundreds of generations.

Such a war is not a possible policy for rational men.[84]

Truman continued by expressing his doubt that Soviet rulers understood this fundamental truth, along with his belief that once they did, the American response would be warm. But he saw no early prospect of this change, and meanwhile he expected "a long, hard test of strength and stamina." This test would take place at levels of conflict well short of nuclear war; the examples Truman cited were those most obvious at the time: the continuing war in Korea, the struggle for political and economic strength in Western Europe, and new patterns of change in the decolonizing world of Africa and Asia.

It would be wrong to suppose that in this long written message every word originated with Harry Truman or that all his thoughts about the bomb and the Russians were included. He had a belief in American know-how and a disbelief in Soviet ingenuity that are not reflected here. But there remains no reason to doubt the depth and seriousness of his basic conclusion about atomic war; he repeated it one week later in a much more personal farewell broadcast to the country:

"Starting an atomic war is totally unthinkable for rational men."[85] As he left office, the first and only American president to order the use of nuclear weapons was fully aware that in only seven years such changes had been wrought that it would now be madness to make nuclear war.

VI

Eisenhower:
Theory and Practice

D WIGHT EISENHOWER was the first American president to come to office with significant previous knowledge of nuclear weapons. Indeed he knew more about them, in every respect except the direct experience of final authority and responsibility, than Harry Truman ever learned. Moreover, something in him had led him to a quick and humane response when, as the victorious Allied commander in Europe, he first learned about Alamogordo from Henry Stimson at Potsdam—he hoped "we would never have to use such a thing."[1]

Yet like other military leaders, Eisenhower was forced in successive postwar assignments to consider how the weapon might be used. Explicit attention to this question was small in the first years after the war. As chief of staff of the army during demobilization and military occupation, between 1946 and 1948, Eisenhower had much else on his mind. The few bombs that then existed were not in the hands of the services but in the custody of the Manhattan District and later the Atomic Energy Commission. The Manhattan District reported to Eisenhower until it was phased out with the creation of the Atomic Energy Commission late in 1946, but Groves remained the primary manager, and the secretary of war the primary spokesman on policy. Eisenhower watched with sympathy but not with close attention the effort of his friend Baruch for international control. His own view was that thorough international inspection would be necessary and that Soviet agreement would be unlikely, but he understood the importance of the effort and roundly disagreed with a proposal by the journalist Dorothy Thompson that the United States should itself enforce a *pax Atlantica* while it held a monopoly.[2]

When Harry Truman made his quick and unexamined decision to develop the H-bomb, Eisenhower was president of Columbia University and disengaged from this particular issue. When the North Korean attack of June 1950 produced a new sense of danger and urgency in the year-old Atlantic alliance, he was recalled to active duty by Truman to be the first allied supreme commander. He held that job for sixteen months. In the spring of 1952 he returned to seek the presidency, convinced that it had become his duty to beat first Robert Taft and then the Democrats, and skillfully finding the middle way between ineffective passivity and an unbecoming chase for office.

There is no better or harder way to learn the paradoxes of nuclear weaponry than to be the supreme allied commander in Europe (SACEUR). When he returned to the United States, Eisenhower had firsthand experience of three propositions of cardinal importance: first, no one in authority saw a viable way to defend the free nations of Europe without the threat of the bomb; second, no military commander, not even SACEUR, could suppose for a moment that any president would give up his own final responsibility for any actual use of the weapons; third, while in one part of the European mind the American bomb remained the great equalizer, in another part the notion of actually using these weapons in Europe was an abomination. Eisenhower renewed his acquaintance with Winston Churchill, who returned to office late in 1951 and remained the most eloquent and the most quoted of those who held that only American nuclear strength, now superiority not monopoly, stood between the Stalinist hordes and the Atlantic Ocean. But arriving in Europe just after the short but intense spasm of anxiety caused when Harry Truman seemed to say that if atomic bombs were needed in Korea they would be used, Eisenhower could not fail to recognize that it was one thing to rely on the bomb for deterrence and quite another to speak in public about using it. In his time at NATO he made no such error.

At the same time, however, his work required him to think continuously about these questions. Oppenheimer exposed him to the new possibilities of tactical weapons, and Dulles to the emerging concept of massive retaliation. He had enthusiasm for the first notion but reservations about the second: Could you really use these weapons "if Soviet political aggression, as in Czechoslovakia, successively chips away exposed portions of the free world?" He was unconvinced: "Here is a case where the theory of retaliation falls down." His own sense of his mission to Europe was not that it was his business to plan for a nuclear war; he did not believe the Russians either wanted or planned any large-scale military aggression. He placed great emphasis on the capacity of NATO's developing forces to "convey a feeling of confidence to exposed populations, a confidence which will make them sturdier, politically, in their opposition to Communist inroads."[3]

This task of creating confidence he carried out, as far as one man could in the time he had, and he did not do it by brandishing nuclear weapons. There were none in his command at any time. He successfully managed the central paradox of NATO: In one sense the supreme commander, as an American officer, was the representative of the nuclear strength of the United States; in another and much more active way he must encourage capacity, resolution, and self-confidence by leadership on less apocalyptic matters. To play this role—indeed to create it—was not the worst preparation for the nuclear responsibilities of the presidency.

The Korean Armistice

The first major nuclear issue to come before the new president in January 1953 was the question of the relation between these weapons and the continuing war in Korea. That question had been dormant for two years, Truman's careless comment of late 1950 having driven it out of circulation. In the truce negotiations, carried on since July 1951 with intermittently severe fighting, neither the American government nor its critics had talked of nuclear weapons. But Eisenhower had come to office with a pledge to do his utmost to bring the war to an early and honorable end. His campaign promise to go to Korea was the tactically brilliant expression of that purpose—persuasive, because of his spectacular military reputation, as no pledge from the civilian Stevenson could have been. As the new president came to consider what he would do, it was inescapable that he should reexamine the possible role of nuclear weapons, and in this study his closest associate would be his secretary of state, John Foster Dulles.[4]

American history is full of remarkable relationships between presidents and secretaries of state, and none is more puzzling than the relation between Eisenhower and Dulles. Nowhere was that relation more complex, or more frustrating to some of the president's own purposes, than on nuclear weapons policy. But on the Korean question no difference arose between them. Both believed that clear indications of a greater readiness to use nuclear weapons would increase the chance of an acceptable truce; both agreed that these indications should not be conveyed by explicit public threats; both believed, then and later, that their messages were received and respected, and that, as Eisenhower later said to his assistant Sherman Adams, it was "danger of an atomic war" that brought the July agreement. "We told them we could not hold it to a limited war any longer if the Communists welched on a treaty of truce. They didn't want a full-scale war or an atomic attack. That kept them under some control." We have the authority of Eisenhower himself for the view that a deliberate threat of nuclear warfare was decisive in ending the Korean War.[5]

While the general caution inspired by nuclear arsenals is a pervasive element in the history of the nuclear age, the number of cases where a nuclear threat can be said to have caused a specific result is small, so we must look closely at this case. The most comprehensive assertion of what Eisenhower and Dulles did is given by Eisenhower in his memoirs:

> The lack of progress in the long-stalemated talks—they were then recessed—and the nearly stalemated war both demanded, in my opinion, definite measures on our part to put an end to these intolerable conditions. One possibility was to let the Communist authorities understand that, in the absence of satisfactory progress, we intended to move decisively without inhibition in our use of weapons, and would no longer be responsible for confining hostilities to the Korean Peninsula. We would not be limited by any worldwide gentleman's agreement. In India and in the Formosa Strait area, and at the truce negotiations at Panmunjom, we dropped the word, discreetly, of our intention. We felt quite sure it would reach Soviet and Chinese Communist ears.
>
> Soon the prospects for armistice negotiations seemed to improve.[6]

There was one other action, and Dulles underlined it as particularly important when he explained the truce agreement to British and French allies at Bermuda in the following December:

> The principal reason we were able to obtain the armistice was because we were prepared for a much more intensive scale of warfare. It should not be improper to say at such a restricted gathering that we had already sent the means to the theater for delivering atomic weapons. This became known to the Chinese Communists through their good intelligence sources and in fact we were not unwilling that they should find out.

The reference here is probably to the movement of aircraft or warheads or both to Okinawa, whence either B-29 or B-36 aircraft could have delivered attacks against targets in North Korea or China.[7]

To all these signals we should add a simpler one: On returning from his visit to Korea, on December 14, 1952, Eisenhower had publicly promised that henceforward the enemy would be impressed by deeds "executed under circumstances of our own choosing."[8]

We know, therefore, what Eisenhower and Dulles believed about the nature and effect of their signals, but it is not at all clear that their belief was correct. One major difficulty is with dates. It seems probable that the most important Chinese decisions came before the most important American signals. The first indication of a new Chinese seriousness came at the end of March, when the Communist negotiators accepted a six-week-old proposal from General Mark Clark, the UN commander, for an exchange of sick and wounded prisoners. Clark's proposal was routine—in Eisenhower's words "almost a common practice"—but this time it led to acceptance and to a renewal of truce negotiations that had been suspended since October. Then on March 30 Zhou Enlai, returning from Stalin's funeral in Moscow, announced a major Chinese concession on the largest single point of disagreement in the truce negotiations. With North Korean concurrence he reversed the previous Communist insistence that all Chinese and North Korean prisoners in UN hands must be repatriated, by force if necessary.[9]

At the time of this March decision it is most unlikely that the Chinese knew of the movement of nuclear-capable forces, which is reliably reported to have occurred sometime "in the spring." They could not have heard of the warning expressed "in India," because Dulles did not go to New Delhi until May 22. And no warning had been expressed at Panmunjom because no meetings had occurred there. Thus in all probability what the Chinese had in mind before their critical decision was little more than the general determination and impatience expressed by Eisenhower on his return from Korea and before that by himself and by other Republicans during the election campaign. The only clearly visible action Eisenhower had taken in office before the Chinese decision was the announcement in his State of the Union speech on February 2 that the Seventh Fleet would no longer screen the mainland from attacks by Chiang Kai-shek's forces. But in reality this announcement was hardly more than a bit of bravado, because in fact, as the Chinese Communists knew well, the U.S. Navy had never interfered with Formosan raids. Even if Beijing paid it more attention than it deserved, this particular signal had no specifically nuclear meaning.[10]

When the Chinese changed their stand on prisoners, the largest recent event was not any nuclear signal from Eisenhower or Dulles but the death of Stalin on March 5. That the observer Stalin may have found the stalemated but costly war more acceptable than the participant Mao is at least possible. Certainly the dates are impressive if we are to accept inferences based on timing, and we have nothing much better. There was no official statement, at the time, from any responsible Chinese or North Korean authority on what produced the decisive change of March, and such statements could not be accepted uncritically in any case. In the 1980s, when responsible Chinese experts are communicative in a way that would have been unthinkable in 1953, some of them say in private conversation that Stalin's death was the turning point. A Chinese friend of high professional standing told me in 1983 that he had heard from three separate individuals that they had been told by Zhou Enlai himself that Stalin's death was what made the armistice possible. That is hearsay of hearsay, but it is worth notice.

Moreover we should not neglect the possibility that the costs of the conflict in Korea, even without a threat of nuclear escalation, were becoming excessive to Beijing. Insofar as it had been defensive in purpose, to prevent a hostile presence at the Yalu River, the original Chinese objective had long since been achieved. The two years of stalemate had caused growing strains on the Chinese economy, and ferocious Chinese propaganda campaigns, including totally fabricated charges of American biological warfare, had notably failed to win foreign hearts and minds.

Certainly Chinese estimates of the new administration must also have been important, and by March it must have been clear that Eisenhower and Dulles and their colleagues and supporters would probably be less restrained, over time, than their predecessors. Certainly also the springtime move of nuclear-capable forces to Okinawa and the hints dropped in New Delhi in May are likely to have reinforced Chinese readiness for a truce. But taken altogether the evidence that such signals were decisive is thin.

Beijing must also have understood, as Eisenhower certainly did, that a resort to nuclear weapons would have had great costs for the United States. The point was made strongly in an early meeting of his National Security Council, on February 11, 1953. The president himself touched off the discussion. He "expressed the view that we should consider the use of tactical atomic weapons on the Kaesong area," which had been exempted from UN attack because it was the first site of the truce negotiations; General Clark now asserted that it was "chock full of [enemy] troops and matériel." The suggestion produced a lively discussion. General Bradley argued that even to mention this possibility to our allies would be unwise; he knew from direct experience how unenthusiastic they would be. His comment led the secretary of state to assert that this difficulty should somehow be removed. "Secretary Dulles discussed the moral problem and the inhibitions on the use of the A-bomb, and Soviet success to date in setting atomic weapons apart from all other weapons as being in a special category. It was his opinion that we should try to break down this false distinction." Eisenhower seemed at first to be attracted by this idea. "The President added that we should certainly start on diplomatic negotiations with our allies. To him, it seemed that our self-respect and theirs was involved, and if they objected to the use of atomic weapons we might well ask them to supply three or more divisions needed to drive the Communists back, in lieu of use of atomic weapons." But at the end of the discussion he pulled back. "In conclusion, however, the president ruled against any discussion with our allies of military plans or weapons of attack." This decision was not reversed until well after the armistice. Whatever intentions Eisenhower may initially have had, and however strongly he wished to indicate to Beijing that he might use nuclear weapons, he never even began the process of winning the consent of other participants in the war.[11]

It would be wrong to conclude from this record that no whiff of nuclear danger reached or influenced Beijing, or that in making its signals the American administration was merely bluffing. During the spring there was an intensive review of the military options available if the armistice negotiations broke down. The Joint Chiefs of Staff reviewed a set of six. They strongly recommended the adoption of a combination of the three largest and most vigorous and added their own clear view that these operations should include "extensive strategical and tactical use of atomic bombs." Eisenhower reviewed this recommendation with care and instructed that the record should show that "if circumstances arose which would force the United States to an expanded effort in Korea, the plan selected by the Joint Chiefs of Staff was most likely to achieve the objective we sought." This was not a binding decision to act, because any decision that an expanded effort in Korea was needed could come only from the president. Eisenhower had made it clear that such a decision would be one of great gravity. Earlier in the same meeting, after noting his understanding that in the view of the Joint Chiefs it would be necessary to expand the war beyond Korea and also to use the atomic bomb, he had made an interesting comment: "His one great anxiety, said the President, with respect to this proposal was the possibility of attacks by the Soviet Air Force on the almost defenseless population centers of Japan."[12]

The armistice negotiations did not break down, and Eisenhower was never forced to decide whether to expand the war. The military plans of the Joint Chiefs were referred to the Department of State for a political annex setting forth "the foreign policy implications" of the proposed course. The resulting paper cannot have added to Eisenhower's happiness with the prospect. It predicted attempts by European friends to exert the strongest pressure against any such action and estimated that in the end the United States "would be faced with choosing directly between Allied and neutral support and the pursuit of the proposed course of action." The Soviet Union would do its utmost to exploit this split in the alliance, and might well be tempted to mount "serious new pressures against the Western position in Germany, particularly in Berlin." Once the offensive began, the Soviets would be strongly influenced by the fact that the operations would be near Soviet frontiers and by the existence of a treaty of mutual assistance with the Chinese. As to nuclear weapons, the State Department's language was less colorful than that of the president, but not comforting: "It is believed the Soviets would not consciously decide to embark on general war. However, their reaction would undoubtedly be sufficiently vigorous to create a major risk of initiating a spiral of action and reaction which could result in world-wide conflict." If he read this analysis—and he may not have, because it was delivered to the NSC when the attention of senior officials was fixed on making the armistice negotiations a success, not planning for their failure—it is unlikely that Eisenhower found his own basic anxiety relieved. The impact of this paper can only have been to increase its readers' interest in a successful negotiation.[13]

Returning to what principal officials really thought as they discussed the matter in the months of their muffled warnings, I conclude that Dulles might well have favored the actual use of nuclear weapons, that Bradley would not have, and that Eisenhower had no intention of deciding before he had to. The moment of choice never came, and he had taken great care not to say anything that might in the end require him to carry out a nuclear attack or else be exposed as a nuclear paper tiger. He allowed the movement of relevant equipment to speak for itself, and whatever verbal warnings he sent were less specific, and probably less numerous, than his memoirs suggest. When Dulles went to New Delhi in May, according to his own report, he spoke not directly of nuclear weapons but of the possibility of "stronger" military action that "might well extend the area of conflict." Neither the formal instructions to American negotiators at Panmunjom nor the formal reports of meetings there show any warning at all in the renewed meetings of April, May, and June. The strongest passage in the "basic instructions" for these meetings says simply that "The U.S. will not countenance prolonged and inconclusive negotiations." The possibility that Eisenhower sent some stronger personal message cannot be excluded, but it is significant that the likely recipient of any such private message, the commander in the Far East, General Mark Clark, himself always believed that any wider action after a breakdown of negotiations would not have involved nuclear weapons. Most important of all, Eisenhower never started the diplomatic effort that would have been required for even grudging allied approval; the relevant passage of his memoirs suggests that he never decided firmly whether the use of atomic weapons would "have to be . . . agreed to by our allies" or would be simply "an American decision." In a single paragraph he seems to endorse one view at the beginning and the other at the end.[14]

After the truce this ambiguity persisted. The nations that had joined in assisting South Korea issued a declaration of warning that if there should be renewed Communist aggression, "in all probability it would not be possible to confine hostilities within the frontiers of

Korea." This declaration was generally assumed in the United States to include the possibility that such a wider response would include nuclear weapons. But at the December meeting with the British and French, Eisenhower learned again that there would be British resistance. Dulles explained that in the event of a "deliberate Communist offensive" in Korea "we would feel free to use the atomic bomb against military targets, whenever military advantage dictated such use." Churchill expressed "definite opposition." "Britain, he argued, was a small crowded island; one good nuclear bombing could destroy it, and recklessness might provoke such a catastrophe." Eisenhower replied that he had no intention of acting rashly, but he also indicated his unwillingness to be hobbled by any veto by any ally. "I merely wanted our friends to know that past limitations on our actions, in the event of a heavy attack on us, would not necessarily be observed." Churchill persuaded Eisenhower on one point—that a public announcement of this new plan would be unfortunate in the context of his forthcoming "Atoms for Peace" speech. The president told the National Security Council at a meeting shortly after that speech that "he felt that the small nations of the free world had been greatly bucked up by his speech, and he did not wish, if he could avoid it, to let them down" by talking about the possible use of these weapons. Dulles, characteristically, had earlier expressed a quite different view. He told the council he was not impressed by Churchill's conviction that there would be a worldwide revulsion "if the United States took the initiative in the use of such weapons." To Dulles the prime minister's opinion "indicated that our thinking on the atomic weapon was several years in advance of the rest of the free world."[15]

Eisenhower himself remained firm in his non-Churchillian view. In January 1954 he reviewed his defense policy with congressional leaders, and when one of them questioned the wisdom of his decision to take two army divisions out of Korea, he replied that this was a sign of strength, not weakness—of confidence in new weapons and air power. If the Communists reopened the war his plan was to "hit them with everything we got." Although everyone at this meeting agreed not to talk, the remark was reported by the United Press. There was no major public reaction, and no questions were asked in following press conferences. Meanwhile a policy of "employing atomic weapons" if the Communists renewed hostilities was formally approved in a meeting of the National Security Council on January 8. Eisenhower insisted, however, that the actual decision to authorize such action would be made by him. Until that decision was made, any immediate response to Communist attack must be limited to conventional weapons. One of Eisenhower's comments showed the impact of his meeting with Churchill. "Our people, continued the president, have understood the atomic weapon, but we must be a little patient with our allies, who had not as yet fully grasped the import of atomic warfare."[16]

This whole episode constitutes a comprehensive overture to the large and varied nuclear history of the Eisenhower administration; a number of its themes reappear. The Korean War itself has persisting influence. Here it must be ended; later it must not be repeated. Whatever else the administration must plan for, it will not be another three-year conventional stalemate in a single remote area. A second recurrent theme will be the counterpoint engaging Eisenhower, Dulles, and the military. The positions of the men in uniform will change, most notably as Admiral Arthur Radford succeeds General Bradley as chairman of the Joint Chiefs of Staff, but the parts played by the other two will be interestingly constant. As in this case the secretary of state, a civilian, will wish to make it clear that the nuclear option is real and legitimate; the president, a military man, will agree in principle, while in practice he looks around to see what major allies think and reminds himself that the hard question is not what these things may do to strictly military targets, but what they may do—as he had foreseen they would at Hiroshima—to everything else nearby. Both the probable reactions of allies and the mixed character of most targets will continue to weigh on the side of caution. The allies will want the weapon's protection but not its use. Plans of nuclear attack that are at once militarily rewarding and otherwise innocuous will not prove easy to find, and the president himself will not be found looking for them.

Other themes visible in this case will show major variations in later episodes. The Russians are just offstage here, and their nuclear strength is still marginal, but the first Soviet thermonuclear test will come on August 12, 1953, scarcely two weeks after the signing of the truce at Panmunjom. That explosion will be the signal for new attention to the central problem of finding the right response to a new kind of direct American vulnerability. To Eisenhower general nuclear war will soon be no better than suicide; eventually it will be like that for Dulles too. In broad political terms the truce in Korea will lead on to a gradual but powerful easement of tension, comforting to Eisenhower, troubling to Dulles. A whole set of somewhat separate themes will enter later, when Eisenhower begins to struggle with the unyielding problem of effective arms control.

There remains a final and more important theme which has been plainly sounded here. The Eisenhower administration will not be slow to threaten, but it will not be fast to act, and between the threat and the act—and also between the desires of subordinates and the decisions of the United States government—will stand the enigmatic but self-commanding president. That is exactly where we shall find him as we turn now to consider the nuclear meaning of the modifications of defense policy that were called the "New Look."

The New Look and Its Nuclear Import

On October 30, 1953, Eisenhower formally approved the following sentence as part of a statement of the basic national security policy
of the United States: "In the event of hostilities, the United States will
consider nuclear weapons to be as available for use as other munitions." The president authorized this statement with full awareness of
its importance; unlike many other parts of the ten-thousand-word document, it was the product of argument in which he had taken a direct
part, and its language was what he himself wanted. He also approved
an accompanying sentence: "This policy should not be made public
without further consideration by the National Security Council." The
origins and consequences of these two sentences are the nuclear part
of the story of Eisenhower's initial review of the defense posture of the
country.[17]

This New Look was not a quick look. Eisenhower had come into
office with many ideas of his own about the right military posture for
the country, and these ideas were generally shared by his senior civilian advisers, but he took his time about putting them into effect. In
their first months in office he and his secretary of defense carried out
a clean sweep of the Joint Chiefs of Staff and then devoted several
months to an effort to obtain military agreement to the change of
emphasis which they were planning. The basic national security policy
of October 30 (NSC 162/2) was one part of this process, and the
decisions on nuclear policy which it embodied were a direct reflection
of the views of Eisenhower and his most trusted associates.

The most important factor in shaping the New Look was not military but economic. The incoming president strongly shared what were
then prevailing Republican views: that the federal budget was far too
big and that the most promising place for large-scale savings was the
Department of Defense. Long before he entered politics Eisenhower
had been convinced that economic strength was as important to national security as military strength, and that military budgets must not
be expanded beyond what a prosperous economy could be expected
to support; moreover his interpretations of these two propositions
were those of a fiscal conservative. As army chief of staff in 1946–47
he had warned his colleagues of the need to respect the requirements
of the nation's economy, and in 1948, as an adviser to Secretary
of Defense Forrestal, he had held that a total defense budget of
$15 billion was as much as could be asked for (it was more than
Truman would then approve). Now, only five years later, he found
that the departing administration had left him a proposed military
budget of $45 billion, together with a carefully prepared paper, signed
by the secretaries of state and defense and the mutual security adminis-

trator (Acheson, Lovett, and Harriman) proposing further increases in defense expenditures that Eisenhower estimated at $20 billion.[18]

Neither the Truman administration's budget nor its parting advice was acceptable to the new president. He discarded the advice, ordered modest cutbacks in the 1954 budget, and set about his own inquiry. What he wanted, fundamentally, was less. He had already found this position passionately supported by his secretary of the treasury, George Humphrey, a man of his own open temper and conservative convictions, and one with whom he found it highly comfortable to agree. Defense planning must be based on what the country could afford over what Eisenhower soon called "the long haul," and $45 billion was much too much.

At the outset Eisenhower was careful not to be explicit about the particular military choices that he himself would prefer in effecting the savings he sought. He respected the processes of the Joint Chiefs of Staff, of which he had been a leading member only five years before. He confined himself to a firm request, in July, that the new chiefs should bear in mind the "great equation" between military and economic requirements and come forward not with split opinions but with unanimous conclusions. It was only when their recommendations proved both insufficiently economical and incompletely unanimous that the president made his own choices.

The first of these choices confirmed a priority set in Truman's time: There was a commanding requirement for a persuasively deterrent strategic nuclear force. In 1953 this requirement led to a primary role for the long-range bombers of the Strategic Air Command. In budgetary terms this priority had been recognized for several years, but Eisenhower personally intervened in the final discussions of 1953 to insure that this force should be recognized not as "*a* major deterrent" to Soviet aggression, but as "*the* major deterrent [emphasis added]." In the Eisenhower years such small changes in the language of formal documents were often significant beyond their appearance. The president's change in this case signaled his refusal to accept a Pentagon compromise which was intended to recognize the general contribution of the army and the navy to overall deterrence. To Eisenhower the indefinite article "failed to meet a primary objective, which was to establish a clear priority among the various kinds of military force."[19]

Eisenhower's insistence on the central role of strategic nuclear forces was reinforced by his conviction that there would never be another full-scale conventional war. As the man who had commanded the largest American expeditionary force in history, he felt that he was entitled to be his own expert on this question, and he liked to point out what two atom bombs would have done to the two great artificial harbors on which the early logistic support of the Normandy landing had been dependent. He was not impressed by military arguments for

the maintenance of large forces "ready to sail at a moment's notice."
He would defend Europe as firmly as General Matthew Ridgway, the
army chief of staff, but he would do it another way. As he explained
in his memoirs:

> I could not help being sympathetic. The safety of United States
> troops and their dependents in Europe was my concern as well. I
> stressed to General Ridgway that I had no intention of allowing
> Europe to be overrun, as it had been in 1940. But we knew that the
> Soviets maintained something in the neighborhood of 175 divisions
> active in Europe at all times. The United States had twenty divisions,
> only five of which were in Europe. Therefore, in view of the disparity
> in the strengths of the opposing ground forces, it seemed clear that
> only by the interposition of our nuclear weapons could we promptly
> stop a major Communist aggression in that area. Two more divisions
> or ten more divisions, on our side, would not make very much
> difference against this Soviet ground force.
>   But I was not pessimistic. My intention was firm: to launch the
> Strategic Air Command immediately upon trustworthy evidence of
> a general attack against the West. So I repeated that first priority must
> be given to the task of meeting the atomic threat, the only kind of
> attack that could, without notice, endanger our very existence.[20]

The answer to any large-scale attack in Europe would be strategic
nuclear attack on the Soviet Union. Eisenhower never wavered from
this position. Strategic nuclear strength was the key, not only to ensuring "our very existence," but also to the safety of Europe.

And just as he did not want massive conventional forces for a new
version of World War II and was skeptical of the tendency of Army
officers to think in such terms, so also he did not plan to allow a
repetition of Korea: "I saw no sense in wasting manpower in costly
small wars that could not achieve decisive results under the political
and military circumstances then existing." So there were two kinds of
conventional war that the president saw no need to prepare for.[21]

The new Joint Chiefs of Staff, by what they did and did not recommend, played a major role in Eisenhower's final decision. They believed that in the aftermath of Korea the armed forces were
overextended and they wanted to rely less on large conventional forces
deployed overseas, notably in Europe and in Korea. (The exception
among them was Ridgway, who had been the allied commander in
both places.) The necessary balance to such redeployment must be a
clear commitment to the use of nuclear weapons wherever they could
do the job. At the same time the Joint Chiefs were unable to produce
as large a reduction of the defense budget as the president wanted. The
result was a series of meetings in which all concerned made their
opinions clear.

Many of those who sat in the back rows of these discussions, or heard about them from colleagues, believed at the time that the language which made it "basic policy" to consider that nuclear weapons were "as available for use as other munitions" was obtained by the Joint Chiefs in return for their own acceptance of budget reductions. Excellent scholars have accepted that interpretation, but documents made public in 1984 show that the reality was more complex. Sentiment in favor of an increased reliance on nuclear capabilities went well beyond the Joint Chiefs and was most briskly expressed by Humphrey of the Treasury and Dulles of the State Department. Humphrey thought that great savings could be obtained by relying on nuclear weapons, and he insisted that "the military ought to be so damned dollar conscious that it hurts." When he heard of the new views of the new chiefs, with their proposed new reliance on atomic weapons, he found their report "terrific." Dulles was more reserved because of political dangers he found in redeployments, but on atomic weapons policy itself he repeatedly expressed his view that "somehow or other we must manage to remove the taboo from the use of these weapons."[22]

Sentiments such as these, expressed in a meeting of the National Security Council on August 27 missed by the vacationing president, led to the first draft of the paragraph that gave nuclear weapons their new status. That paragraph was strengthened after a meeting in which Eisenhower himself took an active part, on October 7. Yet in that meeting the president expressed views less affirmative than the language of the new paragraph might suggest. In his insistence that the new policy not be made public, he said that "nothing would so upset the whole world as an announcement at this time by the United States of a decision to use these weapons." He also expressed serious concern about the views of allies. And he made one further comment that was not obviously consistent with the paragraph he approved. In their war plans, he said, the Joint Chiefs should count on the use of nuclear weapons "in the event of general war," but they should not "plan to make use of these weapons in minor affairs."[23]

All three of the president's reservations were in conflict with Admiral Radford's convictions. Radford saw the problem of public opinion as one to be dealt with firmly, not avoided by secrecy. In his view, "we had been spending vast sums on the manufacture of these weapons and at the same time we were holding back on their use because of our concern for public opinion." He thought it was "high time that we clarified our position on the use of such weapons if indeed we proposed to use them." As for allies, while he did not dispute their right to a role in what was done from bases on their territory, he saw no reason for their concerns to affect a decision to use nuclear weapons not so based, and he "thought it vital that we should be able to make this decision." Among possible "minor affairs," the one that currently concerned him most was Korea, and there he wanted a clear readiness to use the new weapon if aggression was renewed.[24]

It is not surprising, then, that after hearing the president's concerns Radford found the new language inadequate. Far from accepting it as an authorization that would justify a smaller budget, he asserted, in the meeting on October 30 in which it was finally approved by the president, that the statement "was regarded by the Joint Chiefs as insufficient guidance to enable them to effect any real change." The president disagreed and then rejected a suggestion that Radford should be asked to propose language of his own, saying that "we could not hope to do better than the presently agreed language on this point." Humphrey and Radford immediately responded to this ruling in ways which showed their shared understanding that the president was not wholly of their opinion:

> Secretary Humphrey said that he thought it absolutely essential to settle this issue of the use of atomic weapons. Only their use on a broad scale could really change the program of the Defense Department and cut the costs of the military budget.
>
> Expressing agreement with the Secretary of the Treasury, Admiral Radford commented that unless we could use these weapons in a blanket way, no possibility existed of significantly changing the present composition of our armed forces.[25]

These two men, and particularly Humphrey, were seeking greater clarity on the availability of nuclear weapons largely because of a desire to accelerate the redeployment of other forces, especially out of Europe. But for Eisenhower and Dulles the question of troops in Europe had a political sensitivity and importance that quite outweighed any immediate budgetary consideration. Both were well aware that any such unilateral withdrawal would have a damaging effect at a time when American policy in Europe was focused on the need for a much stronger allied military defense. In one part of his mind Eisenhower believed that "the stationing of American troops abroad was a temporary expedient," but he fully agreed with Dulles that any hasty change would be most imprudent. After several sessions of debate, Dulles summed up the matter in a fashion which the president promptly endorsed as stating his own position "with greater clarity than he himself had been able to." Dulles said that any operation to redeploy American forces from overseas stations would be delicate. It would take time to accomplish, and the decision to try it must first be made "at the very highest levels of government." The establishment of a new emphasis on "retaliatory capability" might take two or three years. Dulles favored the change, because "if we do not decide now . . . no change will ever occur." But he was against any immediate move because of the overriding importance of maintaining the alliance. No redeployment out of Europe happened in his time.[26]

A deeper difference between the president and his senior military advisers emerged a year later when the basic policy paper was reviewed. In the course of that review the Joint Chiefs presented a paper arguing that *NSC 162/2* had led to a policy of defensiveness characterized "by continued emphasis on reactive-type security measures and continued growth of the threat to the free world." The Joint Chiefs recommended no specific change with respect to nuclear weapons policy, but they did recommend that the paper be revised "with the purpose of providing a basic U.S. security policy of unmistakably positive quality." The ensuing debate demonstrated that the president did not agree, for reasons that were directly related to nuclear weapons.[27]

Here as in the debate over redeployment, the first response to the proposal of the military came from the secretary of state. Dulles denied that the preceding year had been one of growing danger or of reverses caused by a weak basic policy. Conceding economic difficulties, he asserted that the political and military situation was "in pretty good shape." As the secretariat heard him, he argued that "our basic policy on the whole was pretty good, even [speaking sarcastically] if it hasn't got us into war, and he was not sure [again sarcastically] that not getting into war was a bad thing." He found only one respect in which the position was deteriorating, "namely, the forthcoming achievement of atomic plenty and a nuclear balance of power between the U.S. and the USSR." But how, he asked, "were we to prevent the Soviet Union from achieving such a nuclear balance of power without going to war with the USSR?"[28]

The debate precipitated a clear-cut decision by Eisenhower that the concept of preventive war must be rejected. He himself had raised the matter more than once in the preceding twelve months. In September 1953, in a memorandum for Dulles alone, he had noted the prospect of an arms competition so intense and costly that over time it could "either drive us to war—or into some form of dictatorial government." He had gone on to note that in such circumstances "we would be forced to consider whether or not our duty to future generations did not require us to *initiate* war at the most propitious moment that we could designate [original emphasis]." There is no evidence that this grim thought was pursued, but Eisenhower raised the question again in the summer of 1954, this time in the context of a possible breakdown of allied resistance to the Soviet Union. "If this were indeed the situation," he said, "we should perhaps come back to the very grave question: Should the United States now get ready to fight the Soviet Union?" Eisenhower noted that he had raised this question before, and "that he had never done so facetiously." Available documents do not show that the question thus raised in June was sharply debated in the months that followed, but what they do show is that, one after another, all of the president's advisers expressed themselves plainly as opposed to preventive war. This was the position of the Joint Chiefs in their November memorandum; it was endorsed by Dulles and Humphrey, both of whom opposed not only preventive war but the kind of aggressive policy that would lose allies and run unwarranted risks. In Humphrey's words, the right course was to practice "a policy of co-existence." The rejection of preventive war (but not the endorsement of co-existence) was formally written into the new basic policy paper: "The United States and its allies must reject the concept of preventive war or acts intended to provoke war."[29]

It would be a mistake to read Eisenhower's speculations as an indication that he ever came near to a decision accepting the concept of preventive nuclear war. He thought that the question required consideration, but the result of this consideration was an unqualified and undivided rejection of the concept. In the summer of 1954, when he was questioned on the subject in a press conference, he had no trouble making his rejection clear:

> All of us have heard this term "preventive war" since the earliest days of Hitler. I recall that is about the first time I heard it. In this day and time, if we believe for one second that nuclear fission and fusion, that type of weapon, would be used in such a war—what is a preventive war? . . .
>
> A preventive war, to my mind, is an impossibility today. How could you have one if one of its features would be several cities lying in ruins, several cities where many, many thousands of people would be dead and injured and mangled, the transportation systems destroyed, sanitation implements and systems all gone? That isn't preventive war; that *is* war.
>
> I don't believe there is such a thing; and, frankly, I wouldn't even listen to anyone seriously that came in and talked about such a thing.[30]

And when Chalmers Roberts asked him whether he was opposed to preventive war only for such "military reasons" he made his full position clear:

> Well, let me make it this way: if you remember, I believe it was Conan Doyle's *White Company,* there was a monk that left the church; he said there were seven reasons, and the first one was he was thrown out; they decided there was no use to recite the other six.
>
> It seems to me that when, by definition, a term is just ridiculous in itself, there is no use in going any further.

> There are all sorts of reasons, moral and political and everything
> else, against this theory, but it is so completely unthinkable in today's
> conditions that I thought it is no use to go any further.[31]

This comment reflects not only Eisenhower's general view of nuclear weapons, but also an understanding of the capabilities of the
Soviet Union which he had shown as early as July 1953, soon after he
was first exposed to evaluations of what could be done by each side
to the other in general nuclear war. What he thought, he said to a large
group of advisers, was "that the only thing worse than losing a global
war was winning one." This conviction was reinforced in August by
the first Soviet thermonuclear test, and in September he underlined the
importance of that test in response to a question at a press conference,
where he made a cautious revision of his earlier private comment,
saying that "the only possible tragedy greater than winning a war
would be losing it." In his own mind this Soviet nuclear strength was
a reason for being prudent about recommendations for a more asser-
tive policy. Shortly after the Soviet H-bomb test, he remarked to his
assistant Robert Cutler that even before that, he had been doubtful
"about how much we should poke at the animal through the bars of
the cage." Eisenhower was determined not to provoke a nuclear war
with the Soviet Union. He told the NSC in December, 1954, "We are
not going to provoke the war, and that is why we have got to be
patient. If war comes, the other fellow must have started it. Otherwise
we would not be in a position to use the nuclear weapon, and we have
got to be in a position to use that weapon if we are to preserve our
institutions in peace and win the victory in war."[32]

At the same time, and insistently, Eisenhower held to the view that
any war between the Soviet Union and the United States would in fact
be a nuclear war, and if that war ever came, he knew what he intended
to do. His position was made very clear in March 1954 during a
discussion of a staff paper entitled *United States Objectives in the Event of
General War With the Soviet Bloc.* When Admiral Radford reported
diverse views on the conduct of such a war among the Joint Chiefs, the
president listened but then responded "with considerable vehemence
and conviction." These matters, he said, "came pretty close to the area
of prerogatives of the Commander-in-Chief," and he expressed "his
absolute conviction that in view of the development of the new weapons of mass destruction . . . everything in any future war with the
Soviet bloc would have to be subordinated to winning that war." On
this particular occasion he seemed to accept a limitation which was not
in reality a part of his policy—that we would use these terrible weapons
only if the Soviets used them first. After admitting that his point of
view might seem brutal, he added that "in view of the fact that we
would never enter the war except in retaliation against a heavy Soviet

atomic attack, he simply could not conceive of any other course of action." Dulles made the same self-comforting adjustment at least once in public, telling a meeting of Republican women in April 1954 that "our main purpose" in having a capacity for atomic retaliation was "to deter the use of that weapon by our potential enemies." They are not the last statesmen to have comforted themselves with the inaccurate assertion that their policy was to use nuclear weapons only in response to nuclear attack.[33]

Eisenhower did not at any time grant to his commanders the kind of discretionary authority to make their own decision on the use of nuclear weapons that most of them would have preferred. He permitted a pronounced and growing transfer of warheads from the control of the Atomic Energy Commission to that of the Pentagon, but he retained for himself the sole authority to authorize the actual use of such weapons, and such delegations as he made were limited to the cases in which a commander might have no time to seek guidance in the face of unprovoked attack. All the military leaders of the Eisenhower years understood that their authority to plan on using nuclear weapons—and to save money that way—was not an authority to use them unless and until the president said so. Moreover, if they listened to the president in private meetings, or read the newspapers, they must have had very little doubt that in reality this particular president believed that nuclear weapons, taken as a class, were not the same as other munitions.

Eisenhower might talk of seeking victory when he spoke of the required readiness to reply to aggression, but he fully understood the limited meaning of "victory" in any large nuclear exchange. He made the point publicly over and over again, both in the elevated rhetoric of his speechwriter Emmett Hughes and in the more direct language of his press conferences. At the General Assembly of the United Nations in 1953, only six weeks after the decision of October 30, he discussed the "hideous damage" that nuclear war could bring and said: "Surely no sane member of the human race could discover victory in such desolation. Could anyone wish his name to be coupled by history with such human degradation and destruction?" Talking to White House reporters a little more than a year later, in the course of a long and deliberately imprecise comment on a question about when these things might or might not be used, he allowed himself a clarifying outburst of feeling: "The concept of atomic war is too horrible for man to endure and to practice, and he must find some way out of it." There is nothing that rings false in either comment. Dwight Eisenhower did not have an eager finger on the nuclear trigger.[34]

Yet there was occasional public evidence of a different view in other comments, in which the president seemed to reject, in detail, the very distinction he so emphasized in general. Thus in early 1954, in a special message to Congress, he gave a glowing description of "mighty increases in our assets" in nuclear weapons, and he noted that "a wide variety of atomic weapons—considered in 1946 to be mere possibilities of a distant future—have today achieved conventional status in the arsenals of our armed forces." These words were probably sent forward by Chairman Lewis Strauss of the Atomic Energy Commission, but they were accepted by Eisenhower. A year later he said it for himself in a press conference: "Now, in any combat where these things can be used on strictly military targets and for strictly military purposes, I see no reason why they shouldn't be used just exactly as you would use a bullet or anything else."[35]

But this last assessment was not as definitive as it seemed. In the very next sentence the president entered a major qualification. "I believe the great question about these things comes when you begin to get into those areas where you cannot make sure that you are operating merely against military targets. But with that one qualification, I would say, yes, of course they would be used." The qualification was more serious than it may have sounded, and it had been in Eisenhower's mind since 1945. The "great question" was not about military utility, but about unmilitary side effects. Just as he had hoped in 1945 that Hiroshima might be spared, so in the early stages of the Korean War, as a private citizen, he had distinguished between airfields and warehouses—targets to be considered—as against attacks on human beings—targets to be rejected. "We're trying to stand before the world as decent, just, fair people, not as judges to exterminate those who oppose us." There is no reason to doubt that these varied public musings, like his private remarks, represented real and contrasting considerations in the president's own mind.[36]

"Massive Retaliation"

The man who tried to put it all together in public was Dulles, and the results were not happy. On January 12, 1954, the secretary of state, speaking on the record to his old friends at the Council on Foreign Relations in New York, announced the decision of *NSC 162/2* in a form which became known inaccurately but indelibly as the doctrine of massive retaliation.

> We need allies and collective security. Our purpose is to make these relations more effective, less costly. This can be done by placing more reliance on deterrent power and less dependence on local defensive power. . . . We keep locks on our doors, but we do not have an armed

guard in every home. We rely principally on a community security system so well equipped to punish . . . that, in fact, would-be aggressors are generally deterred. . . .

What the Eisenhower administration seeks is a similar international security system. . . . Local defense will always be important . . . [but] must be reinforced by the further deterrent of massive retaliatory power. . . .

The way to deter aggression is for the free community to be willing and able to respond vigorously at places and with means of its own choosing.

Dulles went on to explain that the new administration had learned that in the absence of such a policy defense costs would be intolerably high:

If an enemy could pick his time and place and method of warfare— and if our policy was to remain the traditional one of meeting aggression by direct and local opposition—then we needed to be ready to fight in the Arctic and in the Tropics; in Asia, the Near East, and in Europe; by sea, by land, and by air; with old weapons and with new weapons.

That in turn involved, for 1954 alone, a projected deficit of $11,000,-000,000. So "the president and his advisors . . . had to take some basic policy decisions. . . . The basic decision was to depend primarily upon a great capacity to retaliate, instantly, by means and at places of our choosing."[37]

This speech, which caused great commotion, was a curious mixture of Dulles the individual and Dulles the loyal spokesman for Eisenhower. It was Dulles who believed in "a community security system" and in the homely but ill-judged analogy to deterrent police protection. Dulles was also the author of the phrase "massive retaliatory power," which Eisenhower had disliked when he first met it in a Dulles paper of 1952. Much more than the president, the secretary of state believed that there should be no squeamish constraints on nuclear weapons. He had no irresponsible desire for their instant use, but he wanted nothing to inhibit the *threat* of such use; that inhibition was what Soviet propaganda was trying to achieve, and what Soviet propaganda sought Dulles reflexively opposed. There is more than a hint of relish in his repeated emphasis on the nuclear threat, and in his warnings that a potential aggressor "must know that he cannot always prescribe battle conditions that suit him."[38]

Yet in its central message the speech was faithful to the president's own convictions; its decisive sentence was drafted mainly by Eisenhower himself: "The basic decision was to depend primarily upon a great capacity to retaliate, instantly, by means and at places of our choosing."[39] The trouble with the sentence was that it tried to do too much; it gathered into twenty-two words a number of thoughts that should have been—already had been—separately expressed.

The first and simplest of the president's convictions was that the country must be ready for an instant and large-scale reply to any sudden nuclear attack on the United States. By 1954 there was nothing new in such a conviction; that it was uppermost in his mind is suggested by the answer he gave when he was asked to comment on the crucial sentence the day after the Dulles speech. The great danger, he said, was surprise attack—Pearl Harbor multiplied—and "about your only defense is the knowledge that there is a strong retaliatory power." Eisenhower's preoccupation with this requirement was deep and continuing, and on this point there was no disagreement.[40]

As for the possibility of actually using nuclear weapons in other situations—and what else could be meant by means "of our own choosing"?—that point had been made months before in the aftermath of the Korean War, and Eisenhower himself had made it again less than a week before the Dulles speech, in his State of the Union Message: "We take into full account our great and growing number of nuclear weapons and the most effective means of using them against an aggressor if they are needed to preserve our freedom." He had gone on to say that these weapons would permit economies in manpower while requiring reinforcement of air power. No one outside the Army had expressed alarm.[41]

It was not retaliation for an attack on the United States or Europe that was startling; nor was it an increased reliance on tactical nuclear weapons or on air power. It was two other things: two adverbs, *primarily* and *instantly.* Did *primarily* mean that the preferred American military response to any challenge would be nuclear? Did *instantly* mean that neither allies nor Congress would be consulted? Might the two words together mean that the American government would henceforth be nuclear-trigger-happy in any confrontation anywhere? Questions like these were raised, though generally less sharply, both at home and abroad.[42]

As criticism increased, both Dulles and Eisenhower were pressed for clarification, and Eisenhower did the better job of it. Dulles, in an article in *Foreign Affairs,* published in March 1954, explained that "massive atomic and thermonuclear retaliation is not the kind of power which could most usefully be evoked under all circumstances," that the new policy "does not mean turning every local war into a world war," and that its object was simply to prevent such wars by making them "too risky." There was special value in "air and naval power and atomic weapons which are now available in a wide range, suitable not only for strategic bombing but also for extensive tactical use." What methods would be used when? "That is a matter"—the relished threat reappears—"as to which the aggressor had best remain ignorant."[43]

Eisenhower was strenuous in his personal support for Dulles, but his own way of argument was almost the opposite. Of course there was no intent to bypass Congress; as we shall see case by case, Eisenhower strongly believed that military engagement required congressional authorization. Of course there was an exception that explained the adverb *instantly:*

> Let us take an extreme case: suppose, while we are sitting here, right at this minute, there came a message flashed over the United States that coming up from the south somewhere were a great fleet of airplanes, and we had positive evidence that they were intent upon spreading destruction in the United States.
>
> Now, if there is anyone here or any citizen of the United States who would hold me guiltless if I said, "We will sit here and try to get in touch with Congress," well, then, I don't know who they are.[44]

The president was equally firm in defusing the explosive issue of turning a local war into a big one:

> Q. . . . Mr. Dulles has outlined the policy of retaliation, and in some quarters that has been interpreted as meaning that if you have a local war or a local situation that the retaliation might be against Moscow or Peiping or some major point. Could you discuss that question of the local warlike situation?
>
> THE PRESIDENT. Mr. Wilson, there is one thing I can tell you about war, and almost one only, and it is this: no war ever shows the characteristics that were expected; it is always different. What we are trying to say now is to express a generalization that would apply in an infinite variety of cases, under an infinite variety of provocations, and I just don't believe it is possible. . . . Foster Dulles, by no stretch of the imagination, ever meant to be so specific and exact in stating what we would do under different circumstances. . . . So no man, I don't care how brilliant he is, would undertake to say exactly what we would do under all that variety of circumstances. That is just nonsense.[45]

We may perhaps ask ourselves just which brilliant man may have been in Eisenhower's mind as he made this last comment. The president, with equal vigor, is supporting his secretary of state and rejecting the most alarming interpretations of his speech. Dulles might wish to keep "the aggressor" in ignorance; Eisenhower preferred to attend to his countrymen's fears.

If there remained any doubt on this preference, Eisenhower removed it three weeks later. On April 5 he made a television speech—an informal fireside chat from notes, and one of the very few such appearances that was not related to a specific crisis such as Suez or a formal occasion like a State of the Union Message. Eisenhower addressed American fears, and his object, characteristically, was reassurance. Beginning with a fervent affirmation of American spiritual strength, he went on to address certain specific fears. Only one, "the possibility of depression and the loss of jobs," was domestic. The other four were the "Atomic Age" and three different aspects of the Communist menace—"the men in the Kremlin," "the loss of our international friends in exposed areas," and "Communist penetration of our own country."[46]

The last phrase was a roundabout but obvious reference to the worries exploited by Senator Joseph McCarthy, and the next to last referred in particular to the situation of the French in Vietnam. As for McCarthy, the fears to which he played were exaggerated; the FBI could be trusted to handle the "dangerous" but "minute" problem of Communist penetration, and any congressional abuses would surely be straightened out by public opinion "wherever and whenever there is real violence done to our great rights." On the danger to weaker countries the president was less optimistic, and with good reason, for in the "exposed area" of Vietnam the French were under heavy pressure, and it was already becoming clear that there was not much that the United States could do about their fate.[47]

The largest fears, the two that Eisenhower put first, were the hydrogen bomb and the Soviet threat. The Soviet danger came first of all. "That is the struggle of the ages," and it was what made nuclear weapons dangerous. "The H-bomb and the Atomic Age . . . are not in themselves a great threat to us. Of course not. The H-bomb is a threat to us only if a potential aggressor, who also has the secrets of the H-bomb, determines to use it against us. And against that, then, we have to make our provisions." Once again the emphasis was on the prevention of a nuclear attack by Moscow.[48]

The most important passage of all was the next one. Eisenhower turned to the good news, and he found most of it in what an attentive listener to John Foster Dulles might have thought a most unlikely place: in the Kremlin.

> Now let us take the first of what I would call the counteracting or counterbalancing factors. The very fact that those men, by their own design, are in the Kremlin, means that they love power. They want to be there. Whenever they start a war, they are taking the great risk of losing that power. They study history pretty well. They remember Mussolini. They remember Hitler. They have even studied Napoleon very seriously. When dictators over-reach themselves and challenge the whole world, they are very likely to end up in any place except a dictatorial position. And those men in the politburo know that.[49]

Eisenhower adduced other considerations that must lead to caution in the Kremlin: the risks from "captive satellites" in time of war, the risk of making war from economic weakness, and, above all, the risk of retaliation. He concluded that the Soviet leaders were unlikely to run high risks of general war. Insurance was needed against catastrophe, and the possibility of insanity must be granted, but Eisenhower was confident that the men in the Kremlin would hold back from any adventure that might threaten their own survival in power: "They want to be there." Nothing that happened in his eight years as president ever shook his conviction on this crucial proposition.[50]

What Eisenhower understood about the men in the Kremlin he also understood about himself: that a decision which brought nuclear war would itself be disastrous. He would rely on these weapons to keep peace because he saw no better course. He would resist attempts to cut into his own lonely responsibility to decide. He would repeatedly cut short debate on policy language by saying that matters would have to be decided case by case, and at the end of one particularly frustrating discussion he said that "he was tired of abstractions; they got him down."[51]

Dien Bien Phu and the Bomb, 1954

The first operational test of the Eisenhower administration's new policy on the use of nuclear weapons came in the climactic months of the French effort to defend against Communist insurgency in Vietnam. The result cannot have been encouraging to those who truly believed that these weapons were the same as others. There are nuclear threads in the story, but their color is not that of "other munitions."[52]

The critical period began on March 13, 1954, with the launching of a major Communist attack on an encircled French outpost at Dien Bien Phu, two hundred miles west of Hanoi. It continued until July 21, when the new French government of Pierre Mendès-France concluded an agreement that ended the war, partitioned Vietnam, and set the stage for the further Indochinese struggle in which direct American combat engagement began more than ten years later.

The attack on Dien Bien Phu quickly produced a sense of alarm in Paris and Washington. The two governments had joined over the preceding year in an awkward but seriously intended partnership under which the Americans were paying most of the bills while the French did most of the fighting, weakly supported by ill-trained and far from zealous Vietnamese units. The French General Henri Navarre had developed an ambitious two-year victory plan that was already in difficulty. In February the French government, under heavy pressure from a war-weary people, took the lead in placing the Indochinese question on the agenda for a Great Power conference that would begin in Geneva on April 26. Through January and February Eisenhower fretted about what more the Americans could do to help. He expressed concern about "the evident lack of a spiritual force among the French and the Vietnamese," but he also made it clear that the one result he was determined to avoid was the large-scale commitment of American ground combat troops to Indochina. Publicly on February 10 he said "I cannot conceive of a greater tragedy for America than to get heavily involved now in an all-out war in any of those regions, particularly with large units." He had made the same point privately to the National Security Council one month earlier: "I can not tell you, said the President with vehemence, how bitterly opposed I am to such a course of action. This war in Indochina would absorb our troops by divisions!"[53]

But the Communist threat to Southeast Asia was seen as extraordinarily serious. On January 16 the president approved a policy paper whose first sentence stated that "Communist domination, by whatever means, of all Southeast Asia would seriously endanger in the short term, and critically endanger in the longer term, United States security interests." Vietnam was the immediate point of danger. The United States must do what it could to strengthen French will and capability, and to help arouse the non-Communist Vietnamese to their own danger. To his skeptical friend George Humphrey the president explained: "What you've got here is a leaky dike, and with leaky dikes it's sometimes better to put a finger in than to let the whole structure be washed away." In other metaphors Eisenhower publicly referred to Vietnam as a domino whose fall might topple a whole set of other countries in the region and as the "cork in the bottle."[54]

Eisenhower would not put major ground forces in, but he was in favor of many other kinds of action, overt and covert. Repeatedly, as he tried to make sense of the confusing reports that reached him— "almost as many judgments as there were authors of messages"—he pressed his advisers to find better ways to strengthen the dike, keep the cork in the bottle, and prop up the domino. Once he went so far as to ask if anyone could find "a good Buddhist leader to whip up some real fervor" and was reminded, amid laughter, "that, unhappily, Buddha was a pacifist." His deep concern over the danger to all of Southeast Asia did not translate readily into effective action.[55]

The attack on Dien Bien Phu sharply raised the level of attention. Would the French defense hold? What should the United States do now, and on what condition? In particular, would it make sense to use American air power to attempt a relief of the besieged outpost? In the discussion of this last question the first nuclear threads appeared.

The possibility of American air support at Dien Bien Phu was put forward in the course of a visit to Washington by Radford's French counterpart, General Paul Ély. While General Ély made no direct request for American flyers, he did argue that increased air support was the crucial requirement at Dien Bien Phu, and he turned American attention toward the possibility of such support. On March 24 Dulles spoke with the president about the danger there, and reported Eisenhower's reply: "The President said that he agreed basically that we should not get involved in fighting in Indochina unless there were the political preconditions necessary for a successful outcome. He did not, however, wholly exclude the possibility of a single strike, if it were almost certain this would produce decisive results." On the same day Eisenhower received a long memorandum from Admiral Radford arguing that if the loss of all of Southeast Asia was to be avoided, "the U.S. must be prepared to act promptly and in force possibly to a frantic and belated request by the French for U.S. intervention." The president and Radford had already discussed this possibility in a more hypothetical way at an NSC meeting in January, even before Dien Bien Phu was first surrounded. Radford had speculated "that if we could put one squadron of U.S. planes over Dien Bien Phu for as little as one afternoon, it might save the situation. Weren't the stakes worth it?" The president's response was sympathetic. He thought of "a little group of fine and adventurous pilots . . . we should give these pilots U.S. planes without insignia and let them go . . . from the aircraft carrier, and this all could be done without involving us directly in the war, which he admitted would be a very dangerous thing." Radford's idea aroused strong opposition from such men as Humphrey and Cutler, and no action was authorized, but the president was plainly interested.[56]

In the first days of April the matter came to a head. On April 1, according to James Hagerty's diary, the president had lunch with Roy Howard and Walker Stone of the Scripps-Howard newspapers and told them that he might have to make an immediate decision to "bomb Reds at Dien Bien Phu—'of course, if we did, we'd have to deny it forever.' "[57]

What the president said to his luncheon guests accurately reflected one half of a crucial meeting from which he had just come. A small session called by Eisenhower *after* a meeting of the full NSC, it was the president's way of continuing discussion of a comment by Radford in the larger meeting that help could be given to Dien Bien Phu "as early as tomorrow morning if the decision were made." Radford's assertion was neither accidental nor out of character. In April as in January he believed in American air action to relieve Dien Bien Phu. On March 26, in a final private session with General Ély, he had left the Frenchman convinced that if the government in Paris should ask for such support, Radford would strongly support the request. Radford was doing what he could to arouse the "frantic and belated request" he had predicted to Eisenhower two days before. On March 31, on the eve of the NSC meeting, he called a highly unusual meeting of the Chiefs of Staff, including the marine commandant, and asked his colleagues if the Joint Chiefs should propose an offer of air support to the French. Undaunted by finding himself in a minority of one in favor of such a recommendation, he was now trying his luck with the president himself. Eisenhower knew that Radford stood alone among the Joint Chiefs, and in the NSC meeting he acknowledged the "very terrible risks" in any air strike, but he still thought the issue was one for "statesmen."[58]

Certainly it was the statesman Eisenhower who took charge in the smaller session. We have no record of it, but we know its result: the president ruled that there could be no intervention without congressional approval, and he instructed Dulles and Radford to consult promptly with the congressional leaders. In this decision Eisenhower was true to both a long-standing conviction and a public pledge. The conviction was that it had been a mistake not to get explicit congressional support in 1950 for the intervention in Korea, and the public pledge had been given only three weeks before. On March 10, three days before the beginning of the attack on Dien Bien Phu, he had been asked whether the presence of air force technicians created a risk of involvement in war and his answer had been blunt: "I will say this: there is going to be no involvement of America in war unless it is a result of the constitutional process that is placed upon Congress to declare it. Now, let us have that clear; and that is the answer." Two weeks later he had been just as plain in private: "In any case, said the President, he was clear that the Congress would have to be in on any move by the United States to intervene in Indochina. It was simply academic to imagine otherwise."[59] The president as cold warrior might be momentarily attracted by the thought of a sudden secret air strike, but the president as statesman would not move the American armed forces into battle without congressional authorization. The notion of a covert attack by regular U.S. air units was lunchtime fantasy.

Radford would have to take his campaign to the congressional leadership, and he would have to go as junior associate of a secretary of state who had his own ideas on what was needed. Dulles agreed with Radford and with Eisenhower on the magnitude and imminence of the threat to all Southeast Asia, but he had never been attracted by the notion of saving the situation by saving Dien Bien Phu. His own response to the events of March had been quite different. What he wanted was a demonstration of unity and determination among all concerned, and he wanted that demonstration not to support specific military action, but rather to deter the monolithic Communist enemy from further aggression in Southeast Asia. He had launched his own effort in this direction, with the president's line-by-line approval, in a major speech on March 29. The critical sentences of this speech, to which he insistently drew the attention of diplomats and journalists, were strong but cryptic: "Under the conditions of today, the imposition on Southeast Asia of the political system of Communist Russia and its Chinese Communist ally, by whatever means, would be a grave threat to the whole free community. The United States feels that that possibility should not be passively accepted but should be met by united action."[60] Writing "on the highest authority" the next day, James Reston began this way: "The Eisenhower Administration has taken a fundamental policy decision to block the Communist conquest of Southeast Asia—even if it has to take 'united action' with France and other countries to do so."[61]

On April 2 Dulles and Radford went back to the White House to concert the plans for their meeting with the congressional leadership. They saw the president with Charles Wilson of Defense and Robert Cutler of the NSC. One guesses that the same men had been in the small meeting the day before. Dulles showed the president a draft resolution authorizing air and naval action; the president found it satisfactory but suggested that it not be submitted until after the leaders had a chance to express their own thinking. Dulles agreed, and then, to his credit, he went on to spell out to the president the difference between his view and Radford's. He saw the proposed congressional authorization as part of a policy of deterrence, an element in the general effort to build international readiness for "united action" that he had launched on March 29. He thought that on the other hand "perhaps Admiral Radford looked upon this authority as something to be immediately used in some 'strike' and irrespective of any prior development of an adequate measure of allied unity." Radford said that while he had indeed thought of a "strike" in relation to Dien Bien Phu, he now thought its fate would "be determined within a matter of hours." He did not exclude a need for some direct action at some later stage, but he "had nothing specific now in mind." If the president said anything to indicate his own judgment between the two views, Dulles did not record it. Nor had Radford in fact lost his interest in action to save Dien Bien Phu.[62]

The next day Dulles and Radford spent two hours discussing the crisis with eight senior congressional leaders at the State Department. The consequences of the meeting are clearer than its content; the State Department record and the findings of excellent contemporary reporting are different.[63] We know that Radford gave an extended account of the critical situation at Dien Bien Phu, but we do not know whether he was pushing for an air strike or not. At least some of the congressional leaders thought so, but the State Department record has him saying that he thought it was too late. He certainly described the kind of operation he had also suggested to Ély: air strikes executed by hundreds of carrier-based light bombers and supported by air force heavy bombers from the Philippines. He said enough to arouse complaints that air action would lead to ground action. But the principal focus of congressional concern was on the need to avoid *any* lonely American effort. There was much questioning about British and French resolution, and all accounts agree that by the end of the meeting the reaction of the congressional leadership was unanimous: "There should be no Congressional action until the Secretary had obtained commitments of a political and material nature from our allies."[64]

Dulles reported immediately by telephone to Eisenhower at Camp David, and the two men promptly found themselves in basic agreement with the congressional leaders. Their brief conversation covered three requirements that were discussed further on the following day and formally stated by Dulles to the National Security Council on April 6: Any American military intervention in Indochina would require (1) support of other allies, especially Britain; (2) clear and complete independence for Vietnam, Laos, and Cambodia; and (3) assurance that the French would agree "not to pull their forces out of the war if we put our forces in."[65] Events quickly demonstrated that not one of these conditions could be met in time to affect the fate of Dien Bien Phu. Eisenhower's determination to insist on these conditions marked the end of any real prospect for the use of American air power at Dien Bien Phu or anywhere else in support of the French in Indochina. The British never moved away from a firm and nationally popular opposition to making any new commitments before the impending effort to get peace at Geneva. The French continued to resist American suggestions that their grant of "independence within the French Union" was insufficient. Most of all, as Dulles had foreseen, the French were unwilling to commit themselves, before the Geneva Conference, to any continued and internationalized military effort. What France wanted, and got under Mendès-France in July, was peace at the necessary price, not "united action." There were avoidable misunderstandings in the course of Dulles's frantic effort to build his deterrent coalition, and questions can be asked about his diplomatic methods, but for our purposes the central point is that from April 3 onward Eisenhower's three prerequisites for united action were a solid barrier to Radford's dream of saving Dien Bien Phu. Both Eisenhower and Dulles understood this result.

Two direct appeals from the French were promptly rejected. Late on April 4, just after Eisenhower had confirmed the three decisive conditions in a Sunday evening meeting at the White House, the State Department received a cable from Ambassador Douglas Dillon in Paris reporting the first French appeal. The French had told him that "for good or evil the fate of Southeast Asia now rested on Dien Bien

Phu," that immediate armed intervention of U.S. carrier aircraft was necessary, and that they now requested such action. The French told Dillon that they were encouraged to make this request by Ely's report of Radford's personal promise of support. The urgency and seriousness of the request were underlined by the fact that Dillon had been summoned to the office of Prime Minister Joseph Laniel at eleven o'clock on a Sunday evening.[66]

Dulles received Dillon's telegram at 10:30 P.M. Washington time; at 8:27 the following morning, in a telephone conversation less than four minutes long, Eisenhower and he agreed that the French request must be rejected. The president thought Radford had been imprudent, but Dulles reported that the admiral was now "quite reconciled" to the fact that air action was a political impossibility. The president said that such a move was impossible without congressional support—it would be "unconstitutional and indefensible." One hour later the cable of rejection went out.[67]

On April 23, with the position still more desperate, the French appealed directly to Dulles, then in Paris on his way to Geneva. Because of the press of other business and the need to clear his response with Washington, it took Dulles two days to answer formally, but no time at all to know what the answer would be. Nothing could be done without Congress and the British, and in any case his military advisers thought it too late to save Dien Bien Phu. Dulles did keep alive the prospect that if the British would join in united action, the Americans would be able to give direct military support "within the next few weeks," but in making this assurance he fully understood that the British were unwilling to act. Rightly or wrongly he believed that the British had let him down after leading him on, and he was quite willing to take shelter behind them now. No one was surprised when Churchill and Eden were not moved, except to greater firmness in their own position and greater irritation with Dulles. On April 24, without waiting for the final British response, Dulles told C. L. Sulzberger of *The New York Times* that the French request had been rejected.[68]

Since Eisenhower never came close to approving any action to save Dien Bien Phu, it follows that he never came close to approving any use of nuclear weapons there. Nonetheless there were others who harbored the idea, and their thoughts and actions are instructive. The central figure is Radford, and his attitude is best captured by his colleague Nathan Twining, the chief of staff of the air force, in oral reminiscence eleven years later:

> I was Chief then, but as I recall this—and I might be a little wrong—it came to a final showdown, and we were told—The State Department said to us, "We must save Dien Bien Phu at all cost."

There was only one way to save it that late and Radford and I were the only ones that agreed. We didn't want to bomb the mainland of China—the whole area. But what we thought would be—and I still think it would have been a good idea—was to take three small tactical A-bombs—it's a fairly isolated area; Dien Bien Phu—no great towns around there, only Communists and their supplies. You could take all day to drop a bomb, make sure you put it in the right place. No opposition. And clean those Commies out of there and the band could play the "Marseillaise" and the French would come marching out of Dien Bien Phu in fine shape. And those Commies would say, "Well, those guys may do this again to us. We'd better be careful." We might not have had this problem we're facing in Vietnam now had we dropped these small "A" weapons. . . . I don't think that three small A-bombs placed properly would have caused too much trouble or set a precedent, but it would have taught those Chinese a good lesson, we would have saved the French and perhaps our present difficulties in Southeast Asia could have been avoided.[69]

Twining is here describing a possible nuclear action at Dien Bien Phu for which a study existed. There were no leaks on this possibility at the time, and no question about the relation of nuclear weapons to Indochina was ever raised in Eisenhower's weekly press conferences. But a proposed plan did exist. Nixon refers to it briefly in his memoirs,[70] and Radford raised it discreetly not only with Twining but with others who might be sympathetic. On April 7 Radford's assistant, Captain George Anderson, asked to see the counselor of the State Department, Douglas MacArthur II, on a "delicate matter." It was the day after Dulles had formally stated in the NSC the three conditions which barred any early action at Dien Bien Phu. Correctly understanding that the effort to organize a coalition was now the centerpiece of the administration's policy for Southeast Asia, Radford had instructed Anderson to present a suggestion. MacArthur reported at once to Dulles:

> The "advance study group" in the Pentagon has been making an estimate of whether atomic weapons could be used to clean up the Vietminh in the Dien Bien Phu area. It has reached the conclusion that three tactical A-weapons, properly employed, would be sufficient to smash the Vietminh effort there.
>
> This study in turn raised in Admiral Radford's mind the question of whether in the event of establishment of a coalition in Southeast Asia, in which the US participates and commits forces, we could use atomic weapons on the Vietminh if this seemed the best means of smashing them and cleaning up Indochina.
>
> In the event we are successful in forming a coalition in Southeast Asia, Admiral Radford wondered whether we could not go to the

French and get their approval for using atomic weapons in Indochina if this became necessary when the coalition was participating in operations. His feeling was that if we could get French acceptance of the principle of the use of such weapons, the whole conception of gaining acceptance of their use would be assisted. Furthermore, if we got French approval in principle after the coalition was formed but before we actively committed forces to Indochina, we could later use such weapons when our forces (air) were engaged.

Two days later Dulles sent back word that he and Radford would undoubtedly have a chance to talk about this possibility "some time."[71]

We do not know when or even whether they did discuss it, but if they did, the likely moment is a lunch Dulles had on April 20 with Radford and Defense Secretary Wilson.[72] My own belief is that they probably did discuss it then. It was a suggestion of great seriousness on a purpose—making the use of atomic bombs internationally acceptable—that Dulles and Radford shared. By connecting this idea to the "united action" Dulles so highly prized, Radford had been characteristically calculating.

What finally persuades me that such a discussion took place is that without it we have only the MacArthur memorandum as explanation for the remarkable fact that Foreign Minister Georges Bidault, only a few days later, reported to trusted junior officers that in a private conversation Dulles had suggested that atomic bombs might be made available to the French. In the following August, one of these officers, Roland de Margerie, described the episode to an officer at the American Embassy in Paris, and Ambassador Douglas Dillon at once reported to Dulles: "He said you had made this offer to Bidault during a private conversation . . . during your visit here en route to Geneva."[73] Dulles promptly replied that he was "totally mystified," that he had "no recollection whatever of alleged offer," that the law itself forbade any offer, and that perhaps Bidault had misunderstood what Dulles had indeed said on April 23 in a restricted NATO meeting, namely that "such weapons must now be treated as in fact having become conventional." The secretary's reply falls short of a categorical denial, but when this explanation was reported back to de Margerie by his American contact, the two men readily agreed that there must have been a misunderstanding. De Margerie volunteered that Bidault himself had been "ill, jittery, overwrought, and at his very worst" on April 23, the probable day of the misunderstanding. Others had similar recollections of his condition on that day.[74]

Did Dulles say nothing whatever to Bidault about nuclear weapons for possible use in Indochina? I find it improbable. It was a tense time.

On April 22 Bidault had renewed his appeal for help at Dien Bien Phu. On April 23 during the NATO meeting he gave Dulles a copy of a message just received from General Navarre, saying that massive U.S. bombing was now the only hope for the outpost. Dulles had in his head the Radford idea and was telling NATO, that very afternoon, that nuclear weapons must be seen as conventional. Did Bidault, unaided, connect all this into one thought? Or was he correct in telling his staff that Dulles had raised the subject? I find the latter the likelier conclusion. In talk—though never in action or in formal recommendation—Dulles was a bit of a nuclear swordsman.[75]

Bidault never doubted that he had been sounded out, but his own memoirs—bitter and polemical—are not convincing in detail. There he places the conversation back on April 14, which does not fit the mood of that earlier one-day meeting or the recollections of his own staff. Nor is his direct quotation of Dulles—"What if we give you two atomic bombs?"—to be taken as precise, any more than we can be sure of his own recollection that he promptly rejected the suggestion. All the memoirs allow us to conclude is that what he told his staff at the time was what he still believed in 1965: Dulles had made some sort of suggestion of help with nuclear weapons.[76]

We can set limits to what Dulles had in mind and how he expressed it. At the very least he said enough to create a misunderstanding. At the most he was tempting Bidault as Radford had tempted him, suggesting that one possible advantage of "united action" might be the availability of a few atomic bombs. Given the different preoccupations of the two men—Bidault obsessed with Dien Bien Phu, on which Dulles had given up, Dulles zealous for a broader plan of deterrence by a show of united determination, a scheme for which Bidault barely concealed his scorn—it seems likely that any direct connection to Dien Bien Phu comes more from what Bidault thought he heard than from what Dulles meant to say. There can be no certainty to these speculations, but it is hard to believe that nothing at all was said.[77]

After this strange and murky moment, the question of the possible use of nuclear weapons in Indochina sank quickly back into the hypothetical world of staff analysis. At the end of April the Policy Planning Staff of the NSC discussed nuclear weapons briefly in the context of the new possibility—never realized—of a decision to join the French in Indochina without Great Britain. The planners asked themselves whether "new weapons"—their polite phrase for nuclear bombs—should be used in the event of such intervention, once again conceivably at Dien Bien Phu, which against earlier expectations was still holding out. If that was the intent, should allies be told, or would the effect of that be "to frighten them off"? Could a weapon be "loaned to France for this purpose"? Would using a weapon in Indochina tend to deter the Chinese from joining in? Were the Soviets and the Chinese eager to avoid a "new weapon" war? The discussion is significant primarily because it led to a response from Eisenhower and Vice President Nixon when Robert Cutler discussed it with them the next day:

> Note: Ro [Cutler] had opportunity to discuss generally the foregoing with the President and Vice President this morning. Their opinion was (1) that the regional grouping should be formed without announcing our intention about the "new weapons"; (2) that the U.S. would unquestionably be asked by its associates what its attitude was toward the use of "new weapons"; (3) that it was very unlikely that a "new weapon" could effectively be used in the jungles around DBP [Dien Bien Phu], and that well piloted Corsair strikes with HE [high explosive] bombs and Napalm bombs would be more effective; (4) that we might *consider* saying to the French that we had never yet given them any "new weapons" and if they wanted some *now* for possible use, we might give them a few; (5) that the declarations which we had already made relative to what we would do if China overtly intervened in Indo-China was the important deterrent to Chinese intervention, rather than whether or not we used the "new weapon" in Vietnam; (6) that the important thing was to get a regional grouping together as rapidly as possible [original emphasis].[78]

Here we have the same rather casual notion of giving a few to the French that Bidault was sure he had heard from Dulles, together with a clear military judgment that Dien Bien Phu would be the wrong place. We also have a lack of enthusiasm for using the weapon as a deterrent against the Chinese, and an evident understanding that discussion of such a possibility would not help in "the important thing," which is still, even without the British, "to get a regional grouping together." Eisenhower kept a stronger recollection of his feelings on this occasion. Years later he told his biographer Stephen Ambrose that he had turned on Cutler and said: "You boys must be crazy. We can't use those awful things against Asians for the second time in less than ten years. My God."[79]

In the available records the subject does not come up again, and other difficulties proved more than enough to prevent the establishment of any regional grouping that might allow American participation in "united action." The Geneva Agreements of July brought partition and armistice to Vietnam, and early French withdrawal from Indochina. The conditions for united action, as the British and the French had intended from the first, did not come into existence before the French phase of the war ended.

The Bomb at Geneva

The distance we have found between Radford and Eisenhower does not in itself complete the story of the relation between nuclear weapons and Indochina in 1954. A much more subtle but equally important question is that of the relation between nuclear fears and the diplomacy of the powers concerned. To Dulles, for example, it appeared at the time that at least one major friendly government was severely inhibited by the emerging menace of thermonuclear weapons. After visiting Churchill in early May he reported to Eisenhower that he "found the British, and particularly Churchill, scared to death by the specter of nuclear bombs in the hands of the Russians."[80]

As Dulles admitted, part of Churchill's concern was caused by Radford's apparent belligerence, but it had deeper origins. Profoundly affected by the fifteen-megaton American test at Bikini on March 2, the prime minister reported to the House of Commons three weeks later that the subject filled his mind "out of all comparison with anything else."[81] This concern was not unreasonable, but it did not take the hydrogen bomb to make Churchill and his colleagues unenthusiastic about supporting the French in Indochina. What Churchill said to Radford was sufficient: "Since the British people were willing to let India go, they would not be interested in holding Indochina for France."[82]

A more impressive estimate of the relation between nuclear weapons and the agreement on Indochina at Geneva is that of Anthony Eden: "This was the first international meeting at which I was sharply conscious of the deterrent power of the hydrogen bomb. I was grateful for it. I do not believe that we should have got through the Geneva Conference and avoided a major war without it." In Eden's view, this deterrent power heavily affected the Soviets and the British, but the Chinese less, because "they probably count life cheaper than any other people," and the Americans least of all, because they were not yet heavily threatened. Eden does not make any attempt to trace cause and effect directly, but his opinion is entitled to respect—no one at Geneva had a longer experience of international meetings. How did the hydrogen bomb help, if it did? Certainly it reinforced an already ample British caution, but what is more significant is Eden's judgment that it had a similar effect on the Communists.[83]

The great surprise of the conference was the readiness of Molotov and Zhou Enlai for a compromise that fell short of what the balance of forces on the ground had led the allies to expect. In the month of negotiations before the deadline that he had publicly declared, Mendès-France achieved agreement on a dividing line in Vietnam close to the seventeenth parallel—much closer to the French opening proposal than to that of the Vietminh. Mendès-France won more than half of what he asked on most other points and achieved his political objective, a settlement acceptable to his own countrymen. Evidently both Molotov and Zhou preferred that result to the alternative of a breakdown and a possible return to the uncertainties of open conflict. Of those uncertainties the most important were the possible reactions of the Americans. A breakdown in Geneva would have led to—what, from Washington? No one knew (certainly not the Americans themselves), but within that uncertainty, if only at its far edges, the possibility of the hydrogen bomb must at least be considered. To Eden its particular importance was in what the Soviet leaders must be thinking. He believed that like the British they recognized real danger in a spread of the Indochina conflict. "Soviet Russia would have the grim choice of leaving her ally to her fate and half the Communist world to its destruction, or plunging herself into the abyss of nuclear conflict. We can argue as to which would have been her choice, had she been compelled to make it. It was certain that she would at least consider a compromise arrangement to avoid it."[84]

This was Eden's thought from the start of the conference, and Dulles in a different way came later to have a similar view. Although his schemes for "united action" were blocked, and although he regarded the Geneva Conference with grave misgivings from its start almost until its end, he came to argue that the Communists did get a message from his "policy of boldness," and that in consequence, as a friendly interviewer reported, "Mendès-France and Eden found themselves able to bargain from Dulles' strength."[85]

Eden and Dulles came to their conclusions at different times, and their thoughts were not quite the same. What Dulles eventually claimed as a conscious and intended threat was to Eden more a matter of the very existence of danger. The difference is critical, and not least in the degree to which it is easier for an opponent to acknowledge an objective danger than to give way to a direct threat. Moreover Eden, unlike Dulles, saw the hydrogen bomb as an encouragement to negotiations, not as a substitute.

Eden's conclusion remains remarkable. It is not beyond challenge, because no one can be sure what would have happened at Geneva without the new weapon in the background. Given the intrinsic weakness of the French position, the relative moderation of post-Stalin Soviet diplomacy, and Eden's own skills, it seems plausible to suppose that another settlement, possibly less favorable, would still have been found. Certainly Mendès-France himself would have accepted less than he in fact obtained, and quite probably the Soviets and the Chinese had their own concerns with the balance of power within the Communist world.[86] But it seems likely that Eden's conclusion is right, and that the existence of thermonuclear weapons in the hands of the Americans increased the appeal of a peaceful result for the Russians and perhaps also the Chinese.

We thus emerge with the conclusion, superficially paradoxical, that the very weapon whose real availability seems quite uncertain, given the hesitancy and secretiveness surrounding suggestions for its use, was still a force in the process by which a temporary settlement is reached. It is a difficulty we shall encounter again. But from this cloudy case we can at least reach the firm conclusion that whatever temptation nuclear weapons presented to Radford and a few others, and whatever restraint their existence induced in Geneva, there is no evidence that they were seen by anyone as having merely conventional status.

Quemoy and Matsu

Twice in Eisenhower's presidency, in 1954–55 and again in 1958, there were international crises over Chinese Communist attempts to take by force the small offshore island groups of Quemoy and Matsu, and each time Eisenhower had to contend with the possibility of a painful choice between embarrassing defeat and the use of nuclear weapons. The situation was different from the one at Dien Bien Phu, and the means by which the president successfully avoided the choice are instructive.[87]

To many critics at the time, and to most students in retrospect, what is most notable about these two crises is that Eisenhower and Dulles should have declared a major American interest in the defense of these islands. A lively prospect of open conflict with China, let alone a possibility of nuclear war, over these trivial bits of land struck many as preposterous. Each of the two island groups was within artillery range of the Chinese mainland, and together they contained less than one hundred square miles. Neither was a vital military asset from the point of view of the defense of Taiwan, whose real and ample protection was the combination of the American Seventh Fleet and the one-hundred-mile-wide Formosa Strait. In the early days of the second crisis Dean Acheson put the point with characteristic sharpness: "We seem to be drifting, either dazed or indifferent, toward war with China, a war without friends or allies, and over issues which the administration has not presented to the people, and which are not worth a single American life."[88]

In 1958 Eisenhower and Dulles emphatically disagreed. Only the day before Acheson spoke they had agreed on a private memorandum which reflected their shared—and hardened—conviction that "if Quemoy were lost either through assault or surrender" the probable consequences would include the loss of Formosa by "subversive and/

or military action," and then in a few years a fall of dominoes all through the western Pacific until "Japan with its great industrial potential would probably fall within the Sino-Soviet orbit." All in all, "the consequences in the Far East would be even more far-reaching and catastrophic than those which followed when the United States allowed the Chinese mainland to be taken over . . ."[89]

The weakest link in this astonishing chain of judgments is the first, connecting the fall of Quemoy to the fall of Taiwan. Here Eisenhower and Dulles allowed themselves to be prisoners of what Chiang Kai-shek and his spokesmen and supporters asserted. No doubt they were also influenced by Chiang's ardent American friends; not to help defend the offshore islands would be to expose themselves to exactly the kind of domestic political assault by the "China lobby" that had gravely weakened their Democratic predecessors in the wake of Chiang's defeat on the mainland. Yet a cool reading of Chiang's own self-interest and of the intrinsic unimportance of the offshore islands might have led them to a different judgment. Senator John F. Kennedy and many others reached that judgment; they would defend Formosa, but not by defending the offshore islands. It is hard in hindsight to believe that such critics were wrong, but Eisenhower and Dulles had a different conviction. In their view a decision to stand aside from the defense of Quemoy and Matsu might well be fatal to the morale of the Chinese on Taiwan. During the first crisis Eisenhower explained to Churchill, who was in eloquent dissent, that a retreat from Quemoy and Matsu, with "the coercion we would have to exert to bring it about, would so undermine the morale and the loyalty of the non-Communist forces on Formosa that they could not be counted on."[90]

Given this conviction, Eisenhower was determined to help Chiang hold Quemoy and Matsu. At the same time he recognized in both crises that if a full-scale Communist assault were launched against the islands, successful resistance could not be assured without a possible recourse to nuclear weapons; he knew that this would be the insistent recommendation of his own commanders, and he himself agreed with Dulles that once the battle was joined, the islands must be saved at any cost. Yet use of nuclear weapons would produce "revulsion against the U.S." that "would be particularly intense in Asia." It would be vastly better not to let the matter come to this point. The islands should be saved by other means. Given their location, it was a testing enterprise.[91]

The first crisis ran from September 1954 to May 1955. Eisenhower's task was complicated by the fact that not one of his senior military advisers initially saw the situation as he did. General Matthew Ridgway of the army thought the disputed islands unimportant, while his colleagues were disposed to respond promptly by air attacks on the mainland; Chairman Radford indeed made no secret of his own desire to use the occasion for "a showdown with the Mao regime."[92] Eisenhower agreed with none of these positions and took his own time in finding a middle ground. In his first major decision, on September 12, he rejected the advice of the three more belligerent chiefs of staff and accepted Dulles's proposal to take the matter to the United Nations—an enterprise that led nowhere but did no harm. For the remainder of 1954 Eisenhower's position was cautious. When the Chinese Communists announced prison terms for thirteen American fliers captured toward the end of the Korean hostilities and the Republican Senate leader William Knowland called for a blockade of China, Eisenhower made a detailed public argument against such a course and was heartened by strong support from other senators of both parties. He allowed Dulles to negotiate a bilateral security treaty with Formosa, and the price extracted from Chiang was a pledge that there would be no attempt to return to the mainland without American approval. The Communist harassment of the offshore islands continued sporadically—heavier in September and November than in the month between—and Chiang, for his part, with American logistic support, replied in kind against local Chinese Communist installations. No showdown was forced by either side. The low level of tension is indicated by the absence of a single press conference question to Eisenhower on the subject in the last three months of 1954.

The new year brought a new level of action and a need for new American decisions. On January 10 one hundred Chinese Communist airplanes attacked the Tachen Islands, still another offshore group well to the north and much less important politically than Quemoy and Matsu. On January 18 the single small island of Ichiang, just north of the Tachens, was taken by 4,000 Chinese Communist troops who overwhelmed 1,000 Nationalist irregulars in a two-hour battle. Meanwhile airfield construction continued opposite Quemoy and Matsu, together with occasional air and artillery harassment, and Eisenhower concluded that "the time had come to draw the line." Strong public reactions to the increased Chinese Communist pressure made it clear that he could now make a firm choice with ample support from Congress.[93]

The basic position was worked out in a single meeting on January 20, 1955. The United States would no longer seek to defend the unimportant and relatively distant Tachen Islands, and would instead insist on their evacuation by the Nationalists. But it should fight to defend Formosa and should include in that determination a readiness to fight also for Quemoy and Matsu if their defense were judged necessary to the defense of Formosa. This judgment would rest with the president, and explicit support for this policy would be sought from the Congress. Every effort would be made to explain the American position to friends and allies, but in setting policy toward China the administration faced no such political need for allied company as it had in Indochina the year before. In the American view, policy toward China, as friend or enemy, was a matter for Americans alone.[94]

On January 24, in a message to the Congress, Eisenhower presented his case: The mounting artillery and air attacks, together with insistent Chinese Communist announcements of a determination "to fight for the liberation of Taiwan" made it clear that the United States must show its "readiness to fight, if necessary, to preserve the vital stake of the free world in a free Formosa." To this end, moreover, the nation must be ready to engage in whatever actions were necessary in "closely related localities." While the necessary authority for many such actions was inherent in the powers of the commander in chief, and while the president would not hesitate to act in any emergency which might occur before Congress could respond to his message, much the best way to show the united will of the nation would be the adoption of an appropriate congressional resolution. The House approved the resolution 409–3 on January 25, and the Senate 85–3 on January 28; a Senate amendment withholding protection from Quemoy and Matsu was beaten 74–13.

Eisenhower did not get what he asked for quite as smoothly and easily as these statistics (and his memoirs) suggest. The belligerent views of Radford and others had not escaped diligent reporters in the autumn. Chalmers Roberts in particular had broken the story of the September recommendation which Eisenhower had overruled.[95] Gravely concerned about the location of decision-making power under the authority requested by the president, influential senators pressed their concern with Dulles, and in response the president readily agreed to a "clarifying statement" in which the White House announced the president's assurance that "any decision to use United States forces other than in immediate self-defense or in direct defense of Formosa and the Pescadores would be a decision which he would take and the responsibility for which he had not delegated."[96] On the floor of the Senate the manager of the resolution, Walter George of Georgia, clarified the meaning:

> Do Senators want anything . . . more? What does this statement say? It says that Chiang Kai-shek will not make the decision. . . . What does this statement mean? For one thing, it means that neither the President of the Republic of China nor any of the officers of that Government will start the war, if one is started. But it means infinitely more than that. It means that no admiral here and no line officer off the coast of China, in the Formosa Straits or elsewhere, will start it. It means, in explicit terms, that the decision will be made here, that it

will be a personal decision of the President of the United States, and that he has delegated no authority to anyone else to make that decision.[97]

Both the overwhelming vote in Congress and the senatorially inspired clarifying statement strengthened Eisenhower's position. He now had the reinforcement of the Senate for his own clear insistence on retaining control of the level and character of American participation in the defense of Quemoy and Matsu. Against the advice of a majority of the chiefs of staff, he at once gave orders for the evacuation from the Tachen Islands.

In the month of February there was increasing tension. Forces on both sides were built up, and international pressure for a peaceful resolution increased. Dulles took a two-week swing through the Pacific to encourage friends and send a signal of determination to Peking. When he returned in early March he brought a somber report: In his view Quemoy and Matsu must be held, and if they were subjected to a full attack, only nuclear weapons would provide an effective response.[98]

Eisenhower reports in his memoirs that he agreed with this estimate, but he promptly took steps to find a better way out: On March 11 he met with a number of senior advisers, Foster Dulles, his brother Allen, director of CIA, "most of the Chiefs of Staff," his assistants Robert Cutler and Colonel Andrew Jackson Goodpaster, "to discuss the Chinese Nationalists' capacity to defend Formosa during the coming weeks without active American help or without the American use of the atomic bomb." After this meeting Eisenhower sent Goodpaster to Hawaii to learn the judgment of the commander in chief, Pacific, Admiral Felix Stump. Goodpaster's report, delivered on March 15, provided a critically important estimate: The immediate danger period would last only another ten days. After March 25 the Chinese Communists would be able to overcome Nationalist opposition "only by an all-out coordinated amphibious attack against Quemoy and Matsu, with artillery and air support . . ." Since Eisenhower believed the Communists had no appetite for the risks of such prolonged large-scale combat, he turned his attention to the period immediately ahead and joined with Dulles in issuing deterrent warnings of nuclear danger.[99]

On March 8 Dulles spoke of "new and powerful weapons of precision, which can utterly destroy military targets without endangering unrelated civilian centers." He warned against the Chinese effort to portray the United States "as being merely a 'paper tiger' " and insisted on U.S. readiness "to stand firm and, if necessary, meet hostile force with the greater force that we possess." Four days later Eisenhower was asked whether the United States would use tactical weapons in a general war in Asia and gave the reply we have already noted in our discussion of his basic policy on nuclear weapons—that while he could not "foresee the conditions of any particular conflict" he did think that "in any combat where these things can be used on strictly military targets and for strictly military purposes, I see no reason why they shouldn't be used just exactly as you would use a bullet or anything else." He tells us in his memoirs that he hoped this answer "would have some effect in persuading the Chinese Communists of the strength of our determination."[100]

It is surely not accidental that this unusual warning—the last public statement by Eisenhower that matches his formal policy of treating nuclear weapons as having achieved conventional status—was made only one day after Goodpaster's report from Stump. The statement was intended for stop-gap deterrence, not as a prelude to expected action. The main reliance of the commander in chief was on the report from his theater commander of the growing conventional capability of Nationalist forces on and around the threatened islands.

What Eisenhower really wanted here has recently become clear beyond doubt with the publication of Robert Cutler's careful minutes of the meeting of March 11. The president listened to Admirals Radford and Carney on the tactical situation; he heard Dulles warn of the bad impact in Europe of U.S. intervention, and he stated his own position with great clarity:

> The President summed up by saying that the U.S. should do every practical thing that could be done to help the Chinats [Chinese Nationalists] to defend themselves; that if it was necessary later for the U.S. to intervene, it should do so with conventional weapons; . . . that if we had to intervene with conventional weapons, such intervention might not be decisive; that the time might come when the U.S. might have to intervene with atomic weapons, but that should come only at the end, and we would have to advise our allies first. He said that, if we possibly could, we should avoid involvement during the next sensitive weeks, because any U.S. direct involvement might critically damage us in Europe. Radford replied that Stump understood the point of view expressed by the President.[101]

So the president who joined his secretary of state in a public warning of nuclear danger had already made it entirely clear to his own government that his real object was not to have to face any such choice. The warning was intended to deter; it was not a declaration of intent to act.

The difficulty, of course, was that the warning so publicly delivered must also be overheard by fellow citizens and foreign friends. The shock wave was considerable, and a week later the president retreated behind a deliberate smoke screen: He was not trying to predict when or how such weapons might be used, and he believed that if the man with the responsibility for the decision should predict "what he is going to use," he would merely "exhibit his ignorance of war." Eisenhower told his press secretary Hagerty beforehand that "if that question comes up, I'll just confuse them." Yet his concluding comment was not confusing at all: He fell back on the same mystique of lonely presidential responsibility and the same assurance of his own peaceful purpose that had served him earlier in obtaining congressional support: "So I think you just have to wait, and that is the kind of prayerful decision that may some day face a President. We are trying to establish conditions where he doesn't."[102]

As he spoke the president was on the brink of success. The ten-day danger period that Stump had described passed without incident, and in April the crisis abated. Whether the Chinese were affected more by the nuclear threat or by the rising cost of pressing their attacks against the reinforced islands, we cannot know. What we do know is that on April 23, on the eve of the first great third-world conference in Bandung, Indonesia, Zhou Enlai made a speech protesting his government's desire for peace and for negotiations. The president responded with parallel assurances. The eventual meetings were unfruitful, but the shooting stopped.

The second crisis over Quemoy and Matsu was shorter but sharper. On August 23, 1958, the Chinese Communists opened an intense artillery bombardment of Quemoy, and less than two weeks later, on September 4, at Newport, Eisenhower reviewed, edited, and approved the secret document we have already quoted; here the possible use of nuclear weapons was explicitly discussed and accepted.[103] This time the president did not wait to make his determination visible. Believing, as his memoirs report, that only clear-cut American firmness would discourage the Chinese from enlarging their attack, he now accepted more clearly than before the connection between the safety of Quemoy and that of Taiwan, and authorized Dulles to make this position publicly visible at once. Dulles, as usual, was at least as ready to give warning as Eisenhower, and he already had nuclear weapons in mind. On September 2, preparing himself for the meeting with Eisenhower at Newport, he had talked on the telephone with General Twining, now Radford's successor as chairman of the Joint Chiefs, and the notes of his secretary record a remarkable exchange:

> Sec. said he did not know where we now stood on use of nuclear weapons. There was no use of having a lot of stuff and never being able to use it. The Sec. asked if the weapons were usable and T. said yes. Twining said it was not the place to use conventional ones.[104]

The announcement Dulles made at Newport was much less explicitly nuclear than this talk with Twining. The president, Dulles announced, had full authority under the Formosa Resolution to decide when force was needed to defend Quemoy, and circumstances made such a determination more likely now than before, because "the securing and protecting of Quemoy and Matsu have increasingly become related to the defense of Taiwan." Moreover, "a Presidential determination, if made, would be followed by action both timely and effective." In a press briefing Dulles went still further, remarking that "if I were on the Chinese Communist side, I would certainly think very hard before I went ahead in the face of this statement . . ." He also made it clear that the serious question about intervention to help the Nationalists save the islands was not whether but when. If Chiang's forces could do it for themselves, so much the better, but if not, the United States would act. The headline in *The New York Times* was only a little more flat than reality: U.S. DECIDES TO USE FORCE IF REDS INVADE QUEMOY.[105]

One week later the president himself reinforced the warning in a television broadcast. Noting that the Chinese Communists continued to insist on Taiwan itself as their main objective, he declared that the Formosa Resolution clearly applied. If Quemoy were subjected to "a major assault, with which the local defenders could not cope," the United States would face precisely the situation the resolution had envisaged. The warning against Chinese escalation could not have been more emphatic.[106]

Neither Eisenhower nor Dulles made any public reference to nuclear weapons, except in response to press questions, and then to emphasize that this question remained a matter for the president alone. Nonetheless the inclusiveness of their warnings was underlined by major deployments whose visibility the president explicitly encouraged. Eight-inch howitzers that could have been supplied with nuclear warheads at Eisenhower's choice were landed at Quemoy. The number of attack aircraft carriers in the area was raised from two to four. Destroyer patrols in the Formosa Strait were increased. The air units on Formosa were reinforced, and it was well known that the air and naval forces so assembled had nuclear weapons. The recognized presence of those weapons made it accurate to say that during the crisis the United States assembled in the area "the most powerful air-naval striking force in its history."[107]

Backhanded confirmation that this nuclear capability was not being neglected by opponents was provided as early as September 7 by Nikita Khrushchev. In an extended and earthy letter, the chairman complained to Eisenhower about American air and naval movements, and explicitly noted that "in the USA there are still people who do not want to part with the policy of threats and atomic blackmail . . ."

Khrushchev was at pains to ridicule both nuclear threats and naval movements, and he was not above a landsman's verbal flourish: "In the century of nuclear and rocket weapons of hitherto unheard of power and speed of action, these once threatening naval vessels are fit, in essence, only for paying courtesy visits, giving salutes, and can still serve as targets for appropriate types of missiles. Perhaps this will wound the self-esteem of people who are closely connected with fleets but what can you do, it is impossible not to reckon with indisputable facts."[108]

This denigration of nuclear threats and sea power was good theater but bad analysis, and on two counts. First, there seems little doubt that the warnings orchestrated by Dulles and approved by Eisenhower on September 4 had a powerful effect. A day and a half later, on September 6, the Chinese, in a statement by Zhou Enlai, reaffirmed their preference for a peaceful settlement and proposed a renewal of ambassadorial talks for whose suspension each government had been blaming the other; the offer was promptly accepted. This Chinese reaction, combined with the absence of anything in Khrushchev's letter that was comparable in any way to the American warnings of September 4, made it clear that only one superpower stood ready to escalate for the sake of Quemoy, and that Beijing knew which one it was. The American warnings effectively ended any threat of a full-scale Chinese invasion of Quemoy, and it is hard to suppose that the visibly deployed presence of nuclear-armed naval and air forces was irrelevant to this result.

By 1958 Nikita Khrushchev had himself become a practitioner of atomic threat making, and we should regard his comments on this aspect of Eisenhower's position as a way of dismissing a danger that he was not himself prepared to match with any firm nuclear guarantee to China. His letter of September 7 contained no such guarantee, and by the time he issued a more clear-cut statement, he was well aware that his assurance was risk free. On September 19 he did indeed assert in a new letter to Eisenhower that if an attack should be delivered on the Chinese, "the aggressor will at once get [a] rebuff by the same means." But neither the Americans nor the Chinese were deceived by this empty assurance. As the Chinese explained in 1963, after the public split between Moscow and Beijing, "Although at that time the situation in the Taiwan [Formosa] Strait was tense, there was no possibility that a nuclear war would break out and no need for the Soviet Union to support China with its nuclear weapons. It was only when it was clear that this was the situation that the Soviet leaders expressed their support for China." Eisenhower's nuclear threat was real, and Khrushchev's belated assertion of a readiness to reply was not.[109]

In this situation Khrushchev's general sneer at naval forces was demonstrated to be a mistake, indeed the same mistake that Mao had already made in planning his attack on Quemoy. What turned out to be decisive was precisely the naval power of the United States. The tactical issues presented in 1958 were interestingly different from those of 1954–55. The second time the primary question was resupply, not gaining time for fortification. By now Chiang had put almost one third of his troops on the offshore islands and had built them formidable defenses. If they could be supplied, they would not be easy to defeat. But what permitted assistance of all sorts to these small islands, which had no significant capacity for handling airlift, was sea power.

It is hard to doubt that Mao had hoped and believed his massed artillery would produce an effective blockade. The first attempts to break that blockade were not successful, but by the middle of September the Chinese Nationalists and the Americans together had found effective ways of moving supplies past the artillery barrages—by increasing the number of landing areas, increasing the speed of unloading, and providing air drops. In the same way local air superiority was established; both the American aircraft and their Chinese Nationalist pilots proved superior to their opposite numbers. While the administration used threats to discourage whatever thought of large-scale escalation Mao may have had, it used conventional air and sea power to break the attempted artillery blockade.

Eisenhower's summary judgment seems exactly right: "But while speeches were made, statements issued, and resolutions passed, the crisis was really eased by the success of the Nationalist Navy, with the help of United States advisers, in defeating the Red interdiction of Quemoy." Eisenhower's excellent account of "this rather tiny military action" carefully sets it in context, and that is not surprising because it was Eisenhower himself who established that context. He ruled that as far as possible the resupply effort must be handled by the Nationalists, but he also relaxed that ruling to allow convoy by the Seventh Fleet (up to the three-mile limit) and technical assistance on the beaches. He refused to become "frantic" when Chiang did, and he steadily rejected repeated requests for advance delegation of authority for the engagement of U.S. forces in response to this or that specific escalation: "I insisted that I would assess developments as they occurred. Therefore, I kept to myself the decision to employ U.S. forces."[110]

The second Quemoy-Matsu crisis, then, shows first a clear threat that at some point nuclear weapons were to be feared; second, a clear presidential determination that any American engagement whatever, even at the lowest conventional level, would require his own explicit authorization; and third, an energetic effort to use effective local superiority—air and naval in this case—to win by conventional means the "tiny" battle that was all the adversary chose to risk. The immediate result was success. The attack on the outposts gradually subsided, after passing through a bizarre phase of announced alternate-day barrage.

Different though they are in tempo and level of tension, the two crises in the Formosa Strait have the same fundamental structure: a probe repelled at its own level, while any possible larger effort is deterred by evident readiness to escalate if necessary. In the first crisis the president, before he speaks or acts strongly, seeks and gets a congressional resolution that explicitly authorizes him to decide by himself whether and how far to commit U.S. forces of any sort. In the second crisis he has the authority from the start because the resolution is still in place, and he quickly issues a warning, which he believes will be respected, meanwhile supporting a most determined exploitation of air and naval strength just short of the direct engagement of U.S. combat forces. Both times, in the varied ways dictated by the situation, the president relies on nuclear threats, but no more than he thinks he must, and never in such a way that any decision to execute the threat can be taken by others or forced by events. We do not know—he may not have known either—exactly what Eisenhower might have done if a Chinese invasion of Quemoy or Matsu had seemed about to succeed in either crisis. We do know that he took with the utmost seriousness his own interest in not having to face that choice, and that in both cases he succeeded in avoiding it.

No one boxed him in. When in 1958 he allowed Dulles to harden the connection between Quemoy's defense and that of Taiwan, he was acting on his own conviction, not in ill-considered reliance on an overassertive cold warrior. When he found himself "continually pressured—almost hounded" by Chiang and his own commanders for delegation of authority to widen the battle in response to any increased attacks, he simply refused. In both crises he combined reassurance of Chiang with visible and effective insistence that there must be no attempt to return to the mainland without U.S. approval. When allied statesmen and Senate leaders complained that the risks of confrontation exceeded the value of the offshore islands, he patiently and repeatedly explained his own view that much more was at stake.[111]

This last process had its costs. It was obvious in both crises that from the point of view of every friendly government but Chiang Kai-shek's, matters would be much easier if the line of defense were drawn in the Formosa Strait, not at the offshore islands. In each crisis Eisenhower drew successfully on his own personal prestige, but the second time around there were more questions. Already in 1955 it was clear that the president would have preferred a Nationalist redeployment reducing the commitment at Quemoy and Matsu; after the crisis ended he tried to get it and failed. That Chiang was not persuaded is understandable, because his natural hope was that the contest over the islands might somehow produce direct American support for his struggle against his Communist enemies. But as Eisenhower wrote in a remarkable ten-page, single-spaced memorandum to Dulles on April 5, 1955, it was entirely clear that any direct American intervention in defense of Quemoy and Matsu would be divisive at home and deeply unpopular abroad. Moreover the memorandum shows Eisenhower's understanding that these troubles would be aggravated if "we felt compelled to use atomic weapons." The lonely president had not enjoyed the risky days of March. Now in 1958, critics at home and abroad were stronger than before. The president kept his self-control under press questioning that was much more active than in 1955, but he granted that the failure of allies to see things as he saw them—a failure, from his standpoint, to see appeasement in retreat—was "a very heavy weight" on mind and spirit.[112]

The best answer to this concern, in both crises, was success—success in conventional defense and success in making escalation unattractive—but in both crises, the president, fully aware of the intrinsic awkwardness of risking war for useless rocks, sought to reduce both public and international concern by visibly urging moderation on Chiang Kai-shek. These efforts produced much less than he had hoped for, and, characteristically, the man who so actively watched over the tiny battles was a relatively passive observer of relatively passive diplomacy after the danger subsided. If there had been yet a third crisis over these intrinsically irrelevant islands, this diplomatic passivity might well have had costs.

But it cannot be said that Eisenhower wore out his public support on this issue. Three years later, in his presidential campaign against Nixon, John Kennedy spoke eloquently of the folly of fighting a war for Quemoy, and soon found himself driven back to the very position of ambiguity that had been Eisenhower's starting point five years before: the importance of any threat to Quemoy would depend on its relation to the safety of Formosa. Kennedy was not unhappy when the issue died, and in 1962 when the matter reappeared for a few days in an exchange of threat and counterthreat between Taipei and Peking, he readily adopted a position that left no space between himself and his predecessor.[113]

As crises in their own right, these two were not very large even at the time, and they are smaller still in retrospect. That these small islands were not worth the fuss still seems a reasonable judgment. They remain in the hands of the government on Taiwan as I write, and with no visible anguish in Peking, which probably never did want them for their own sake alone. Eisenhower accepted a task of deterrence that he could have declined without catastrophe. But he took a different course, and we must find the lessons we can in what actually happened. The problem of assessment is not simple, but I draw four broad conclusions.

First, there were nuclear threats, and within their limited terms they cannot be called unsuccessful. They were aimed to deter, not to compel—to prevent some larger Chinese action, not to force a change in existing behavior. It may be argued that such larger action was never intended by Mao in any case, and certainly the sweeping domino-theory assessment so swiftly agreed on by Dulles and Eisenhower at Newport in 1958 has a look of feverish unreality in retrospect. Still the American leaders did have real weapons readily available for use, and there were real, if controlled, deterrent intentions behind them. It is hard to doubt that in these two cases the "winners" were reinforced in their belief that nuclear deterrence had helped, while the "loser" was reinforced in the conviction that he must press on to get such weapons of his own.

Second, and on the surface paradoxically, the offshore-island crises show a pronounced evolution away from any eagerness to brandish the bomb or any public assertion that it will be treated like any other weapon. While readiness to use nuclear weapons was prominent in the secret analysis on which Eisenhower and Dulles agreed at Newport in 1958, there were no parallel public statements. It was Khrushchev who made the public noises that year about nuclear danger, and he surely knew what he was doing. By 1958, public discussion of the use of the bomb was highly disquieting to Eisenhower's own public, and both the president and Khrushchev knew it. In a single presidential press conference of 1955, the bomb was just like a bullet, but only for a week and only for interim deterrent purposes. In 1958 there was no such assertion.[114]

Within the government the president's behavior showed his real view. His principal concern with respect to nuclear weapons, in both crises, was to manage matters so that he would never have to decide whether to use them. His willingness to let the possibility of their use carry some deterrent weight did not extend to any readiness to tie his own hands in advance by an explicit commitment. The consequence of his retention of tight control in both crises was to make it plain to senior military commanders that whatever formal assertion he might have made, he did not treat nuclear weapons as having achieved conventional status. This conclusion was registered with particular clarity in the mind of the commander in chief of the U.S. Pacific Fleet, Admiral H. G. Hopwood. In a letter report on the operation, his first conclusion was that the operation had shown the Pacific Fleet to be capable of "rapid emergency contingency action," though not without difficulties and strains. His second was that "plans for emergency action are deficient in that too much dependence is placed on the employment of nuclear weapons."[115]

A third and perhaps still deeper conclusion is that the real contests in these two crises took place at the level of small-scale conventional encounter. The limits set by each side are not identical in the two cases, and not as clearly defined in 1955 as in 1958, but in both cases they fall several levels short of the kind of engagement that might have involved nuclear weapons. The American leader may be a little more ready to raise the stakes than the Chinese, but his readiness does not reflect desire for a wider war—only Chiang wants that. So Eisenhower's nuclear weapons become a kind of umbrella over both sides as they contest the future of the little islands by gunfire, landing craft, fortification, air drops, and dogfights. The one man closely engaged who can press the nuclear button becomes the man most interested in doing well enough in the "tiny" war to avoid the choice between nuclear weapons and defeat. The bomb, present in the wings, makes both sides focus on the lesser onstage battle. Admiral Hopwood reached this conclusion too. "The capabilities of, and plans for the use of conventional weapon systems should be reviewed to provide for greater flexibility of action under various contingency situations short of nuclear war."[116]

Fourth and finally, as in the Indochina conference at Geneva in 1954, the bomb had a diplomatic role in these crises. It was the embodiment of the worst that might happen and thus a powerful force inclining both parties toward an appearance of being reasonable. This role is not quite the same as the one played earlier at Geneva. There the long shadow of recent thermonuclear tests inclined both sides to a serious negotiation in which serious concessions were exchanged. What happened over Quemoy and Matsu was rather that in different ways both Washington and Peking were driven to show at least an appearance of good sense—in the Chinese case by an announced readiness for peaceful settlement, and in the American case by a decision to be seen discouraging adventurism by Chiang. Wherever there is an international sense of nuclear danger, there is also an incentive to make it appear that one is not the more militant party to the dispute.

The role of the nuclear weapon, as seen at Quemoy and Matsu, is varied. It helps to deter, by the threat that it might be used; its actual use is nonetheless an option so highly unattractive that other means of defense are eagerly sought; the real determinant is conventional sea power; yet the bomb in the background encourages both sides to show public moderation. These four characteristics cannot be given exact weight as against one another. They were not coherently experienced by the participants, and still less completely explained. It is not for the historian to give them a clarity they did not have at the time. Moreover, not every actor learned the same lesson from these events, and some learned nothing. Yet the effect of the contest over Quemoy and Matsu on the international perception of nuclear danger was not small. At the very least it showed that one president of the United States did not confuse a readiness for threat with an eagerness for use. As he worked to avoid any agonizing choice between accepting defeat and launching a nuclear attack, he observed the work of his landing craft with much more care than he counted his bombs.

International Initiatives for Limiting Nuclear Danger, 1953–56

Eisenhower, before, during, and after his presidency, put the pursuit of peace at the top of his agenda, and at the top of his agenda for peace he put nuclear danger. The same man who could repeatedly say that these weapons had achieved "conventional status," and who could repeatedly use the express or implied threat of their use as a means toward ending hostilities or preventing them, fully understood the terrible and increasing danger that nuclear weapons presented, by their existence and their prospective multiplication, to all the peoples of the world. From his first inaugural to his farewell address, his public papers reflect a passionate concern for the issue. In his inaugural he noted that he was speaking at a moment "when man's power to achieve good or to inflict evil surpasses the brightest hopes and the sharpest fears of all ages . . . Science seems ready to confer upon us, as its final gift, the power to erase human life from this planet." In that speech he emphasized the need for unity in the West and for determination and self-confidence among the people of his own country, but it was not long before his attention was drawn to the possibility of progress toward international understanding—toward taming the nuclear danger by agreement among nations not allied. In his first term Eisenhower made two major proposals aimed in this direction. The first was his "Atoms for Peace" proposal, and the second was for "Open Skies." It is no accident that the names were as striking as the results in reducing nuclear danger were small.[117]

ATOMS FOR PEACE
On December 8, 1953, before the General Assembly of the United Nations, Eisenhower proposed that the nations should join in an attack on nuclear danger by turning from the existing focus on the development of nuclear weapons toward the peaceful uses of atomic energy. Specifically he proposed that the governments principally involved should begin to make joint contributions "from their stockpiles of normal uranium and fissionable materials" to a new international atomic energy agency. Surrounding the proposal in high hopes and higher language, the president held out a vision of peace in the nuclear age. "It is not enough to take this weapon out of the hands of the soldiers. It must be put into the hands of those who will know how to strip its military casing and adapt it to the arts of peace." He concluded

on a still grander note: "The United States pledges before you—and therefore before the world—its determination to help solve the fearful atomic dilemma—to devote its entire heart and mind to find the way by which the miraculous inventiveness of man shall not be dedicated to his death, but consecrated to his life."[118]

The applause was thunderous, wave after wave, and the president responded with the grin which so marvelously combined modesty, pleasure, and pride. The response around the world was equally affirmative. In the end, moreover, the speech did have consequences of considerable importance. Yet its eventual effect on the central arms race between the two superpowers was either zero or negative. Throughout the Eisenhower years, against all the hopes held out in this speech, the number and destructiveness of the nuclear weapons on both sides continued to grow apace, and this growth may have been sheltered in part by the very professions of peaceable purpose that stirred the General Assembly.

Probably no single utterance in Eisenhower's eight years as president was the product of longer or more intense consideration. The deliberations began with the review of a paper left on the White House doorstep by the departing Democrats. During Truman's last year a panel of consultants under the leadership of Robert Oppenheimer had prepared and presented to Dean Acheson a report called "Armaments and American Policy." With Robert Oppenheimer as its chairman and Vannevar Bush and Allen Dulles among its other four members, the panel had a combination of experience, knowledge, and access to information which gave its report sufficient standing to attract early attention in the new administration.[119]

The Oppenheimer Panel's report painted a stern picture of the nuclear world its members foresaw: very rapid expansion of stockpiles on both sides, to a point where both sides could have many thousands and neither side could hope to have any usable superiority. It rehearsed with authority the explosive growth of the American program over only seven years and elaborated on its wider meaning. A similar pattern could be expected in the Soviet Union. A thousand Soviet bombs might be only a few years away, and five thousand only a few years further. "Any sensible forecast must assume that within our time Soviet atomic weapons may be numbered in five figures." In this situation each great power would be able to do enormous damage to the other, but only "at the gravest risk of receiving similar terrible blows in return." And this situation was not likely to be affected by the fact that "one side"—the panel was thinking of the Americans—might always have many more weapons than the other. Both would have "enough." It was conceivable that "a world of this kind may enjoy a strange stability arising from general understanding that it would be suicidal to 'throw the switch,'" but "a world so dangerous may not be very calm," because "it will be necessary for statesmen to decide against rash action not just once, but every time."[120]

In the world of the 1980s, when we have lived with thermonuclear stalemate for a generation, this analysis is familiar. At the time it was both startling and chilling. It was presented when no Soviet thermonuclear explosion had yet occurred and when American superiority was overwhelming. In this situation it was daunting to be required to recognize the absence of any reason whatever for future complacency. Nor did the panel find early hope in old or new proposals for nuclear disarmament. In the history of the Baruch plan it noted the absence of "any genuine negotiation," the demonstration of deep-seated differences between the "free world" and the Soviet Union, and the obstacles presented to agreement and even to serious discussion by obsessive Soviet secrecy. It concluded bleakly that "no real progress is at present likely in the field of arms regulation."[121]

Constrained by these somber conclusions, the Oppenheimer Panel made only modest recommendations. The one which stirred prompt consideration within the new administration called for "a policy of candor toward the American people"—candor in explaining the realities of "the size and shape of the growing destructive power of atomic weapons" and candor about "the fact that the atomic bomb works both ways."[122]

In explaining its recommendation the panel made a point that was particularly sharp to Oppenheimer, oppressed by the difficulty of arousing his fellow citizens to a danger that he could not fully describe in public:

> We think it difficult to overestimate the importance of such an act of candor. It has been our experience that without a direct and informed understanding of the rates of atomic development, most men are reluctant to give full value to warnings which they hear from others. The more responsible the citizen, indeed, the more he is likely not to pay full attention to the problem of atomic weapons as long as present security restrictions are enforced. A man who is in the habit of trying to think in rational terms will naturally hesitate to attempt a judgment on any matter on which he knows himself to lack important information; he will tend to leave the problem to those who know the facts.[123]

The initial responses of the new administration were sympathetic. On May 8 the Planning Board of the National Security Council agreed on a careful but affirmative interim report, which concluded that an active policy of candor could be executed without risk to the compromise of restricted technical data or intelligence sources and also that the release of the necessary information "need add but little to what the Kremlin already knows." In this same season Oppenheimer wrote an unclassified essay on the need for candor, and before deciding to publish it he took it to the president, with whom he had had friendly dealings since 1951. The president passed the paper to Robert Cutler, and Cutler encouraged its publication. It contained a fervent plea for authoritative governmental exposition of the realities.[124]

By the end of May Eisenhower had charged C. D. Jackson, his assistant for psychological warfare, with responsibility for the preparation of a speech. Jackson promptly dubbed the enterprise "Operation Candor" and there followed what he later called "many drafts on Candor through September—none satisfactory because they either told too much or too little and were uniformly dull." Eisenhower had a different objection to them; they were too gloomy. He told Jackson, "We don't want to scare the country to death." Characteristically he sought a message of hope.[125]

The notion that was to supply the necessary hope came from Eisenhower himself in early September, out of musings on vacation in Denver that were stimulated by the first Soviet thermonuclear test on August 12. As he later explained it to his brother Milton, "It all grew out of my original basic idea that as long as the more extensive Baruch plan had been rejected by the Soviets . . . that possibly a gradual approach would open up new possibilities, new lines of study, and bring some hope to replace fear in the world."[126] The idea was simple: "Suppose the United States and the Soviets were each to turn over to the United Nations, for peaceful use, X kilograms of fissionable material."[127]

The first reaction to the suggestion was skeptical. Replying for himself and Jackson on September 17, Strauss said that while the proposal was novel and "might have value for propaganda purposes," it was doubtful as a practical move. He recommended further study, but he feared that a joint action might help the Soviets more than the Americans. The way Eisenhower's question was transmitted by Cutler invited attention to this question of comparative advantage, since Eisenhower's original suggestion was followed by his thought that "the amount X could be fixed at a figure which we could handle from our stockpile, but which would be difficult for the Soviets to match." Right at its origin Eisenhower's idea thus had the double aspect that it was intended to open the doors to better understanding while doing so in a way that was to the net advantage of the already superior American stockpile. No one appears to have addressed the question of the likelihood of Soviet enthusiasm for such a bargain.[128]

Greeted skeptically, and duly referred to a committee for further study, Eisenhower's idea was overshadowed through most of October by the prospect of a much wider initiative. Early in September Dulles wrote Eisenhower suggesting the possibility of "a spectacular effort to relax world tensions on a global basis." He was troubled by strategic and political trends, especially in Europe, and he thought that "the present is a propitious time for such a move, if it is ever to be made, because we will be speaking from strength rather than weakness." Eisenhower responded promptly endorsing both points. What moved him most was the somber alternative—an endless contest for strategic advantage with an opponent stubbornly resisting all efforts to reach agreement. This was the paper in which he drew a picture of the future so gloomy that he raised the question of a possible future requirement "to *initiate* war." As we have seen, this notion was firmly rejected a year later, and the immediate meaning of the memorandum as a whole was its strong endorsement of Dulles's desire to seek a better way out. Eisenhower emphasized the need for "intensive study by the ablest group of individuals we can possibly assemble." But first and foremost he put the need for public understanding, particularly including public understanding of the bomb. The proposal for a new diplomatic initiative was thus tied in Eisenhower's mind to the continuing problem of executing Operation Candor.[129]

Another man who liked this tie-up was C. D. Jackson, a zestful cold warrior and a natural optimist who saw no conflict between winning propaganda points against the Russians and establishing a peace of good will and harmony. On September 21 he wrote Eisenhower listing the year's "important victories in the cold war" and asserting it was time "to grasp this moment as one during which the fly-wheel of history has slowly begun to turn in our favor." He wound up with a not very subtle but flattering challenge: "For a long time you have been one of the few who not only believed but understood that it would be possible to win World War III without having to fight it. It is now beginning to be apparent to other people, including the enemy, that you were right." Ten days later, after talking with the president about Candor and reviewing the matter for him with Dulles, Strauss, and others, Jackson's pitch was still higher: "This can not only be the most important pronouncement ever made by any President of the United States, it could also save mankind."[130]

The only trouble was that no one yet knew what the president should say. "What is missing," Jackson wrote, "is the 'package.' " The package he wanted was the one Dulles and Eisenhower had been discussing, and accordingly he suggested that Dulles be put in charge of producing it—"something much more than what is at the end of the current draft, namely, the withdrawal of Russian and Allied forces from Germany."[131]

On October 3 Dulles received this assignment from the president, and for the next twenty days he and his senior advisers wrestled with the problem of winning World War III by a peaceful package for a single speech. On October 23 the secretary wrote the president to say that it could not be done. First, any public proposals for new agreements between Moscow and Washington would "almost surely" undercut the current allied effort to get agreement among allies on a European Defense Community. Second, any broad atomic initiative would make it easier for the Soviets to pursue their own current effort to link the problem of the bomb with that of U.S. strategic bases. Third and more sweeping still, Dulles had been persuaded that "it is probably a mistake to try to make serious proposals by means of a public speech." He concluded by outlining the "atomic speech" he could still see "as acceptable, and perhaps desirable"; it would describe the danger and the American determination "to take the necessary steps to deter attack," and it would restate a general willingness to discuss both arms limitation and "present sore spots." It would, in short, repeat what Dulles had said one month earlier at the United Nations. There was not much of Oppenheimer's candor in this, and no war-winning package at all.[132]

Jackson now suggested that Eisenhower's own idea might provide the missing package. Strauss, this time, reacted much more warmly, and by early November he had produced more than one draft of a memorandum strongly endorsing Eisenhower's basic concept. He remained untrusting of the Russians, but he now believed that the risks were manageable and the benefits of a constructive proposal great. He had come to agree with his large-minded assistant, William Golden, that a small joint effort might be like "getting the first olive out of the bottle." Sharing with Eisenhower the conviction that any such effort should be so designed that its acceptance would be clearly advantageous to the United States, he was nevertheless hopeful that somehow real progress might be made.[133]

The president, not unnaturally, was happy to find his own idea newly supported, and as drafting continued he readily agreed to a suggestion from Henry Cabot Lodge that the speech should be made at the United Nations where Lodge was the American ambassador. The last month of work was marked by repeated breakfast meetings between Jackson and Strauss, and in honor of their choice of cereal Operation Candor was rebaptised "Wheaties." In due course the speech was written, approved, and delivered.

Judged by lesser standards than those of Eisenhower and Jackson themselves, the Atoms for Peace speech was not undeserving of the warm welcome it received and also not without its constructive long-range consequences. It set in motion the process by which new attention was given to the prospects for international cooperation in the peaceful uses of atomic energy. The long-run institutional result was the establishment of the International Atomic Energy Agency (IAEA) in Vienna, and along the way there also occurred the first open international conference on the subject, a triumph of science over secrecy and a welcome reminder of the fascination of nuclear physics as a subject with a wonderful and varied life of its own quite apart from military uses.[134] Good questions have been raised about the degree of skill and foresight that went into the drafting of the charter of the IAEA, and it can be argued also that in the 1950s men were not as attentive as they should have been to the risk that the promotion of peaceful uses might stimulate appetites for bombs.[135] Yet on balance it was clearly right to get the enterprise going, and this Eisenhower did. It was also entirely legitimate that at least in the short run these consequences of his initiative had the effect of increasing worldwide respect for the seriousness of American interest in peaceful uses and were therefore considered by sober observers "a success not only scientifically but also from the American political viewpoint."[136]

But while the Atoms for Peace speech had considerable constructive consequences in these other fields, it did nothing serious to cope with the need for candor that was its origin, or to advance the presidential hope for progress in arms control that animated its central proposal. Oppenheimer's basic thought, that a new public understanding of danger would lead to more serious efforts to deal with it, had been rejected by the president himself. Eisenhower understood the somber conclusions of Oppenheimer's panel, and in many later words and actions he showed his broad agreement with them, but he was not willing to "scare" people or to leave them without an upbeat message of hope. Parts of his speech did indeed address with eloquence the terrible dangers of a world with thermonuclear weapons in unfriendly hands, and in particular the risk that "two atomic colossi" might be "doomed malevolently to eye each other indefinitely across a trembling world," each able to threaten "the annihilation of the irreplaceable heritage of mankind." But having described this danger, he went on to assert that he had found a way to escape it. Recognizing that beginnings would be small, he yet spoke earnestly and ardently of the prospect of reducing the destructive power of stockpiles by giving them away for peaceful uses, moving from fear to hope, and helping to "solve the fearful atomic dilemma." Yet there was never any real prospect that his proposal could do any of these things. The small beginning that Eisenhower wanted most—"to get the Soviet Union working with us in some phase of this whole atomic field"—never happened.[137]

In part the difficulty here lay in the fact that Eisenhower had a notable tendency to overrate the power of a major formal address and to underrate the need for follow-up. His diary entry on this speech gives lip service to the proposition that words have only limited value, but its real theme is the opposite; the diarist gives the speech a range of objectives that no one utterance should have been required to meet—to engage the Russians, to awaken the understanding of small countries, to "improve our relative position in the cold war," to tell about the size and strength of American atomic capabilities, but in a comforting way, and so on. But once the speech was delivered, the president appeared to relax and to let his lieutenants carry on in their own ways. We do not find Eisenhower asking anyone to put to the Russians the point he makes to himself—that there might be good reasons from the standpoint of their own fears for them to find promise in his proposal. The speech has been made. It has been applauded with fervor and praised everywhere but in Moscow. It has done its job.[138]

It must be added that the Soviet responses were never encouraging. The first reply was correct in tone but argumentative, showing no hint of any sympathy for Eisenhower's declared purpose of finding common ground. Instead the Soviets held fast to their own long-standing insistence that the way to begin was by a joint declaration banning the bomb—precisely the preference for declaration over action that had been rejected by the West for seven years. This Soviet response encouraged each of Eisenhower's advisers to pursue his own agenda, and the president did not stop them. Jackson pursued the propaganda contest. Dulles developed a publishable diplomatic record that aimed to show U.S. decency and Soviet intransigence. Strauss, more slowly, labored to establish the new agency with or without Soviet cooperation. No one, from Eisenhower down, kept the president's own initial primary purpose at the forefront. If the Russians would not play, that was their fault, and the next objective must be to win lesser contests on points.

Though they held to their proposal for a purely verbal and unverified ban, the Russians made responses that deserved more attention than they received. Their first reply correctly observed that the American proposals "neither check the growing production of atomic weapons nor limit the possibilities of their use."[139] It was precisely this reality that had enabled Eisenhower to proceed without opposition from the Defense Department, the Atomic Energy Commission, or indeed himself, and it was this reality also that made his hopeful rhetoric deeply misleading. No one in the American government was ever forced to inquire into the hard choices that would have been presented if indeed there had been a significant conflict between contributions to peaceful uses and the claims of the growing American weapons stockpile. The Russians were right; in Washington—as in Moscow—building more weapons remained the top priority, and the stockpiles continued to grow unchecked. The propaganda battle was joined, and the diplomatic record was made. Eisenhower's notion that his original idea might help turn the corner

from danger to hope remained a mirage whose temporary persuasiveness was evidence not only of general respect for the president's
sincerity, but also of the degree to which his hearers found it comforting to share his optimism.

That optimism also buried the idea that had started the whole
process. Instead of awakening his countrymen to the realities of the
thermonuclear world, Eisenhower's speech allowed them to believe
that his proposal offered a way out. His references to danger became
the prelude for a message of hope, not for a sharing of knowledge and
a summons to concern. His own understanding of the danger he kept
to himself, writing in his diary that what underlay the whole speech
was his "clear conviction that as of now the world is racing toward
catastrophe." It cannot be said that the speech slowed that race or
changed its direction.[140]

OPEN SKIES

On July 21, 1955, at a four-power summit meeting in Geneva,
Eisenhower made his second dramatic public proposal for progress in
arms control. Putting into effect a decision reached only the day
before, he proposed first that each country should give the other "a
complete blueprint of our military establishments, from beginning to
end," and second, still more dramatically, that each country should
provide the other with "ample facilities for aerial reconnaissance."
The proposal, which quickly came to be known as "Open Skies," was
put forward, the president said, as a means of assuring both parties and
the world that neither side was engaged in preparations for a "great
surprise attack."[141]

In terms of general press and public reaction the proposal was an
immediate and overwhelming success. It was praised by Eisenhower's
British and French colleagues, and the nominal Russian leader, Niko-
lay Bulganin, approved its spirit and promised careful study.[142]

Yet it is plain in retrospect, and became plain to Eisenhower very
quickly, that his proposal had no significant chance of acceptance.
Right after his speech, in the cocktail lounge nearby, Eisenhower
found himself talking with Nikita Khrushchev: " 'I don't agree with
the chairman [Bulganin],' he said, smiling—but there was no smile in
his voice. I saw clearly then, for the first time, the identity of the real
boss of the Soviet delegation."[143] Eisenhower was right, and while the
Soviet rejection continued to be polite, it was never modified. As a
serious effort at agreement on a means of mutual reassurance, Open
Skies died the day it was born. Yet the man who made the proposal
and those who persuaded him to make it remained proud of what they
had done and were persuaded of the importance of their achievement.
This continuing affection for Open Skies would in itself be enough to

justify a look at what happened and why, and the story has other lessons.[144]

THE OPEN SKIES proposal was first put forward in the scramble to fill the vacuum created around a president when there is agreement that there will be a summit meeting without any agreement on what the United States government will say. The 1955 summit itself was not the product of any American desire for such a meeting. Since the beginning of his administration the president had been resisting proposals from British prime ministers—Churchill and then Eden—for such a gathering. But the British maintained their pressure and were presently joined by the French. Their case became overwhelming when in May the Soviet government gave its long-delayed consent to a peace treaty with Austria. A summit invitation issued by the three Western powers on May 10 was promptly accepted by the Soviet Union, and by the end of the month the American government was heavily engaged in discussion of what the American position should be.

John Foster Dulles knew what he wanted: a meeting in which problems would be identified and defined and then referred back to the foreign ministers. This basic preference rested on his fear that somehow in the processes of a summit meeting Eisenhower would be drawn into dangerous concessions amounting almost to appeasement. Dulles himself believed that the summit must be an exercise in the containment of damage—the Soviet leaders were bound to acquire international respectability when they gathered as equals with their Western counterparts, and he preferred the limitation of losses to the risk of a false step by the president. On the eve of the meeting he confided his worries to C. D. Jackson:

> ... what I am most worried about is the President ... he is so inclined to be humanly generous, to accept a superficial tactical smile as evidence of inner warmth, that he might in a personal moment with the Russians accept a promise or a proposition at face value and upset the apple cart. .... The President likes things to be right, and pleasant, between people. He tires when an unpleasantness is dragged out indefinitely ... this is something that I have never breathed to a soul, or even intimated, and I suppose there is not anybody else I could actually say it to. My big problem is a personal problem. I am afraid that either something will go wrong in Geneva, some slip of the allies, some slip of the President's, which will put me in the position of having to go along with a kind of foreign policy for the U.S. which could be described as appeasement—no, appeasement is too strong a word, but you know what I mean—or, on the other hand, I may

have to behave in such a way at Geneva that my usefulness as Secretary of State, both domestically and abroad, will come to an end.[145]

Nelson Rockefeller took a different view: Rockefeller had succeeded Jackson as a special assistant to Eisenhower and believed that Eisenhower must not limit himself to defining problems but must somehow make a splash at the summit. When it became clear in May that a summit meeting was probable, he organized a four-day conference of a dozen men in and out of government who had been concerned in various ways with American responses to the Soviet threat. They met on the marine corps base at Quantico, Virginia, where security and privacy could be assured. To Jackson, who attended some of the meetings, they seemed at first a gaggle of wordy academics. But to themselves they were serious and disinterested professionals who had been asked to advise on "courses of action for the president at the summit." They worked with a will. Their chairman was W. W. Rostow, then a senior member of the Center for International Studies of the Massachusetts Institute of Technology.[146]

The Quantico conference soon agreed on a grim proposition: evidence of growing Soviet military strength at all levels, conventional and nuclear, was so compelling that unless the summit should produce some demonstration of a new Soviet seriousness in the pursuit of peaceful agreements, the United States should promptly undertake major new military efforts of its own. Thus the purpose of the summit should be to test Soviet intentions, and the means proposed was the presentation of "a spectrum of proposals ranging from hard to soft" where "hard proposals" could be accepted only if the Soviet Union was ready to end the cold war, while "soft" ones might well be accepted merely as a matter of tactics and appearances.[147]

Accepting the standard negotiating priorities of the time, the Quantico panel made the reunification of Germany and graduated disarmament its two principal "hard" objectives, and in the case of disarmament it emphasized the problem of inspection. American officials were now united in believing that there could be no serious progress in disarmament unless there was a means of knowing that the other side was not cheating on any agreement. There was also a growing fear that unless in some fashion the iron curtain could be penetrated, the Soviet Union might well make secret deployments that could at some point lead to a dreadful surprise—even perhaps a surprise thermonuclear attack.

To advocate inspection was good, but it would be even better if such advocacy could be sharpened and even dramatized by some specific proposal. The proposal for mutual aerial inspection, first put forward by Max Millikan of MIT, met this requirement. It became a major element in the Quantico report, and it promptly entered the mind of Nelson Rockefeller as the right way of providing the president with an important initiative that he could put forward at the summit.

The Quantico panel report found interested listeners in Washington, but not initially at the highest levels. There is no evidence that Eisenhower himself read it. Dulles actively discouraged any show of interest by the State Department, and since he did not know at the time what the report contained, this reaction must be put down tô his own intense aversion to competition in counseling the president on foreign affairs. Rockefeller himself failed to attend an NSC meeting of June 30 at which the problem of disarmament policy was discussed and referred back to Harold Stassen, for a comprehensive review of the inspection problem that would not be ready for use at the summit. No one had yet overcome the argument of Dulles that the summit was no place for specific proposals, for what he called "quickies."[148]

Rockefeller persisted. On July 6 he saw the president face to face and presented a memorandum that argued directly for "a proposal for mutual inspection." Eisenhower was much taken with the idea and called Dulles to praise it as a good idea from Rockefeller. Rockefeller, sitting in Eisenhower's office and hearing one side of the conversation, came away believing that Dulles had thrown cold water on the idea. But it was now alive in Eisenhower's mind, and Rockefeller was not discouraged from pursuing it. In battles over presidential speech drafts in the following week he continued to propose language designed "to commit the president to making concrete proposals" and he won what Rostow calls "a limited but certainly not a decisive victory" when Eisenhower included in his opening statement in Geneva a ringing call for joint exploration of "the challenging and central problem of effective mutual inspection." He also persuaded the president to authorize a "rear echelon" of senior advisers to be deployed to Paris, and there he went with a small staff of his own.[149]

In the Hôtel Crillon on July 18, as the summit meeting opened an hour away in Geneva, Rockefeller made the decisive conversion of Admiral Radford. He had to tell his story twice, but presently Radford took the point that was basic for him: the proposal would be good for the United States if it was accepted and bad for the Russians if they turned it down. Acceptance would "give the U.S. a decided intelligence advantage," and rejection "a decided public opinion advantage." Radford's opinion was shared by Robert Anderson, the deputy secretary of defense (one of the four men in his administration that Eisenhower considered best equipped to succeed him as president), and Stassen too was converted in these discussions. Encouraged to keep up its work by Goodpaster from Geneva that evening, the rear echelon expressed itself on July 19 in telegrams to Goodpaster and Dulles. The reply was quick. They were ordered to Geneva and so was

General Alfred Gruenther, the supreme commander of NATO and one of Eisenhower's most trusted friends.[150]

Late in the afternoon of July 20 Eisenhower held a meeting with Dulles and all these visitors at which the Open Skies proposal was approved for immediate public use. He was for it himself by now, and he had also tested it that morning at breakfast with Anthony Eden, receiving an encouraging reaction. In this atmosphere the earlier reservations of Dulles disappeared and agreement was quickly reached on a clear-cut proposal for reciprocal overflights. Lesser matters were quickly sorted out, and Dulles, the great opponent of "quickies," now expressed his enthusiasm for the proposal as one which offered both "drama and substance." He insisted only on surprise: "If word got out in advance . . . much of the impact would be lost." The idea that had been unwelcome when it came from Rockefeller had a different value now that it was coming from the president himself with support from such men as Radford, Anderson, and Gruenther. But we should not suppose that Dulles was converted merely by deference to the president. The proposal he now heard was not presented or endorsed as a risk worth taking in the cause of disarmament, or even, in the words Eisenhower had used on the phone to him on July 6, as "an idea that might open a tiny gate in the disarmament fence." What Dulles now heard was a proposal presented as a no-risk proposition with immediate public appeal, and as such it met precisely the standard he himself had laid down in a strikingly candid private memorandum to Eisenhower three weeks earlier.[151]

This memorandum, written on the eve of the NSC meeting that Rockefeller missed, gives us the clearest exposition we have of the way Dulles thought about disarmament at the time. The argument marches firmly through fourteen numbered paragraphs. The first nine do indeed conclude that the United States must produce a good proposal for arms limitation:

> 1. The purpose of national armament is to defend the nation . . .
>
> 2. Under modern conditions, offensive capabilities have been developed to a point such that the most effective defense is massive retaliatory power . . .
>
> 3. The United States has greater ability to deter attack than has any other nation or any potential combination of nations. This is true now and for the foreseeable future. . . .
>
> 4. The Soviet bloc economy cannot indefinitely sustain the effort to match our military output . . .
>
> 5. The greater military potential of the United States . . . gives the United States its maximum bargaining power and this is a power which should not be cheaply relinquished. Even though it is not used in direct bargaining, it constitutes a strong pressure on the Soviet

Union to bring about the reduction of United States armament which would almost automatically follow from better international conduct by the Soviet Union . . .

6. While the United States can reasonably assure its defense by massive retaliatory power, no other free nation can do so. Therefore, our allies depend upon us. . . . a dependence which they naturally desire to see terminated if it can be done "safely." They are situated so that they are disposed to take more risks as regards "safety" than should the United States.

7. The frightful destructiveness of modern weapons creates an instinctive abhorrence to them and a certain repulsion against the strategy of "massive retaliatory power."

8. The result of Soviet disarmament propaganda; plus our allies' weakness and dependence on us; plus natural humanitarian instincts, combine to create a popular and diplomatic pressure for limitation of armament that cannot be resisted by the United States without our forfeiting the good will of our allies and the support of a large part of our own people . . . persistence in this course [of resistance] would endanger our system of foreign bases.

9. We must, therefore, propose or support some plan for the limitation of armaments.

But the desired proposal should not be one that would lead to any early change in the existing advantageous situation:

10. Since, however, the present and likely future position, in fact, gives greater protection than any plan that rested upon agreement and supervision, we should not seek quickly or radically to alter the present situation. We should proceed cautiously so long as the present situation gives us important bargaining power and so long as Soviet leadership continues basically hostile, autocratic and controlled by those who are not inhibited by any moral scruples.

11. . . . present steps to stabilize or curtail armament should be tentative and exploratory only until good faith and good will are demonstrated by the Soviet Union.

Any plan which implied the acceptability of the risks presently inherent in Soviet creed and conduct would involve giving up the greatest brake that there is against extreme emotional disarmament which would greatly endanger us and remove the greatest pressure that could be exerted on the Soviet Union to reform its ways.

The conclusion is sharp:

12. It is suggested that while any present plan could and should hold out promise of future agreed stabilization and/or reduction of armament . . . there should not be any effort to agree upon any over-all plan until first a measure of inspection has been tried out and found to be workable.[152]

The memorandum concluded with two final paragraphs in which Dulles urged "intensive efforts" to resolve outstanding political problems and granted that if and as inspection proved workable and political problems were solved, one might go on to accept the risks of some control of armaments. But since the political problems he listed included the unification of Germany in freedom and the end of Soviet control of the satellites, it is apparent that for John Foster Dulles in 1955 agreements on arms control were to be sought only after the cold war was won.

In essence what Dulles feared about proposals for disarmament in 1955 was simply that they might lead to agreement. He could imagine no situation that would be better under such an agreement than the one that already existed—unlike the Quantico panel he did not fear the nuclear arms race, because he had confidence the Russians could not keep up. What he feared much more was an agreement, because then the Americans would let down their guard, their pressure would come off the beleaguered Russians, and Soviet creed and conduct, unmodified, would pose grave risks. When we match these fears with the secretary's worry about his president's desire to be pleasant, and his bureaucratic suspicion of Rockefeller, it is only too easy to see why he was wary in Washington.

But the proposal he now heard in Geneva was for an agreed inspection that his friend Radford thought advantageous. Agreed inspection would give insurance against surprise and beyond that it could be a satisfactory public substitute for any proposal of arms limitation. Since it had no danger, it could be put forward for its "drama and substance."

So the proposal was approved and the dramatic presentation was made. When Khrushchev promptly showed both his final authority and his lack of enthusiasm, Eisenhower set about converting him, in more than one earnest conversation. But the most he could get was assurance that Khrushchev would not "kick the idea out the window." The Soviet leader insisted that the whole thing "was nothing more than a bald espionage plot against the USSR." It was almost as if he had been listening to Radford—to accept this proposal would be to give the United States "a decided intelligence advantage."[153]

As the months passed and further statements were exchanged, the Soviet position hardened, though Soviet language remained courteous. The Russians argued that aerial inspection of such large countries would be ineffective, that inspection should include many other countries than the two initially proposed, and above all that inspection without disarmament was insufficient. On this last point the Russians might as well have been responding directly to Dulles, whose insistence on the separation of inspection and arms control was duly reflected in the official presentations elaborating the initial proposal.

Assertions of commitment to disarmament were strong—"the United States is pledged to work for, earnestly desires, and energetically seeks a comprehensive, progressive, enforceable agreement."[154] But such agreement could come only after inspection had been tested and proved. It is not surprising that no agreement ever came in sight.

A further difficulty with inspection, as both Khrushchev and Eisenhower remark in their memoirs, is that in terms of narrow national advantage the proposal was indeed unbalanced. This difficulty, which still bedevils the negotiations between the two countries, is intrinsic to their different societies and has been present throughout the nuclear age. What Radford could see in a single session Khrushchev could see just as quickly: Eisenhower's proposal, taken by itself, was unbalanced. It is quite true that in a larger sense there was and is a Soviet interest in avoiding the kind of American response that fear and ignorance might generate.[155] But it is hardly surprising that leaders of a government still living in the shadow of the all-powerful and all-suspicious Stalin should have been slow to understand the wider advantage of Eisenhower's proposal and quick to observe its immediate one-sidedness. Khrushchev was acutely aware that he was an apprentice on the world scene, and mindful of Stalin's warning that "when I'm gone the imperialistic powers will wring your necks like chickens." If there was one thing he was not going to do, at Geneva or in its aftermath, it was to accept a one-sided American proposal.[156]

There is no evidence that anyone concerned with the Open Skies proposal ever addressed the question of finding a way to offer a balancing incentive in return for Soviet agreement to aerial inspection. Instead the Americans held to the view that since as a matter of logic inspection was essential to any reliable agreement, their proposal required no balancing concession. Seen from the vantage point of the common interest in limiting the arms race, the proposition is unassailable, but at least until the time of Gorbachev it has been a characteristic of all arms control negotiations between the Soviet Union and the United States that any Soviet agreement on means of verification is regarded by Soviet negotiators as a concession requiring some balancing American action. In his retirement Khrushchev took a different and broader view, but his immediate successors followed the example he set in office, not his advice from the sidelines.

Most of the Americans who supported the Open Skies proposal had no great expectation that it would be accepted, and in the first reactions in the United States praise of the initiative was accompanied by very low expectations for its success. Intending no dissent from the general chorus of congressional approval Representative James P. Richards, the chairman of the House Foreign Affairs Committee, praised the president's "bold challenge to the Soviet to put up or shut up," but added that he thought there was "about as much chance for a snowball in hell as there is for the Russians to say 'yes' to the plan." And what Richards said publicly was what most of Eisenhower's advisers also thought. The proposal had "drama and substance," but it was not put forward with any lively hope of its acceptance—except on the part of Eisenhower himself.[157]

Eisenhower's personal hope for real agreement and resulting progress on wider issues, with both Atoms for Peace and Open Skies, is beyond doubt. Yet it is equally clear that in both cases his serious purpose was obstructed by other preferences. He made both proposals publicly, by surprise, in speeches whose first object was immediate popular success at home and abroad. There was a conflict, as State Department advisers repeatedly warned, between such acts of "psychological warfare" and the conduct of serious negotiations. In preferring public applause to private exploration Eisenhower was reducing the prospects for what he himself most deeply wished.

Those prospects were reduced still more by his reliance on senior subordinates whose central purpose was not his own. Neither Strauss nor Dulles was truly hopeful of an affirmative Soviet response, and Dulles at least would have been alarmed if there had been one. Dulles wanted a good disarmament proposal as protection against criticism from impatient allies and a possibly gullible American public. In different ways both Dulles and Strauss managed in the end to use these two initiatives for their own primary purposes, not for Eisenhower's. Dulles was able to make the Soviet rejection of Open Skies one more reason for wariness about arms control, and he was reinforced in a resistance to major new efforts in the field which he successfully maintained for three more years.

From his own standpoint Strauss had an even larger success. Atoms for Peace, in his hands, became not only the occasion for a new emphasis on the peaceful promise of the atom, but also the starting point for a conscious and sustained policy of using that promise as a means of reducing attention to the dangers of nuclear weapons. By the autumn of 1955 he felt able to claim success in this effort, proudly announcing to an audience of enthusiasts for nuclear power that at his Geneva conference on peaceful uses, "the mesmerism of the bomb" had been cast off. "No other event that has occurred has done so much toward taking the horror—the terror—out of the atom." Strauss made no effort in this speech or anywhere else to explain how in fact the promise of atomic power, however great it might be, would reduce the danger in the steadily expanding thermonuclear arsenals.[158]

The uses to which his subordinates put his initiatives were not so much alien to Eisenhower as secondary. With Dulles he wished to avoid the trap of uninspected or unbalanced disarmament, though he did not share his friend's opinion that an agreement otherwise reasonable would still be dangerous because it might lead Americans to let down their guard. Like Strauss he wanted to encourage cooperation in advancing peaceful uses, though he never supposed that advancing these uses somehow made the weapons themselves less horrible or changed the prospect of a world racing toward catastrophe. Unlike both he persisted in the belief that there must be some way to get a start on ending that race, and with little help from either he did in fact make his own significant contribution to that end in his visit to Geneva. He impressed Khrushchev with the reality of his own opposition to nuclear war, and he was able to report in a television broadcast on his return to Washington that "there seems to be a growing realization by all that nuclear warfare, pursued to the ultimate, could be practically race suicide." To recognize that such a war would have no winners was the right first response to the increasing horrors of thermonuclear weapons.[159]

In observing how Strauss and Dulles carried things out in their own ways, we should remember also that they were acting as Eisenhower expected. He believed in the generous delegation of authority, and he disliked detailed supervision of his subordinates, both on principle and by temperament. He trusted both men, and both were zealous in their efforts to hold his trust. If he ever fully understood how different from his own their basic attitudes were on this particular question, he never showed it.

What Dulles once called "loyalty down" to subordinates was not his own most conspicuous quality, but it was one of Eisenhower's. In these two cases it helped blind him to the fact that with respect to his own principal purpose—to find some way of beginning a serious common effort with Moscow—he had field commanders who marched to a different drummer.

Ironies abound in these episodes. Oppenheimer's original purpose was to create an informed awareness of danger. Transmuted by Eisenhower into a message of hope, it was turned upside down by Strauss, into a way "to lift the darkest cloud overhanging humanity."[160] The original purpose of the Quantico wise men was to test Russian sincerity, which most of them did not expect to find, as a necessary first step in moving to a new and more demanding level of national effort in the cold war. Yet their central proposal became part of a temporarily soothing "spirit of Geneva," and in adopting their proposal neither Eisenhower nor Dulles ever came close to accepting their underlying argument. When Open Skies was rejected, Rockefeller attempted to press the case for greater cold-war effort through a second Quantico meeting, but he found Eisenhower flatly opposed and decided to leave the administration.

The deepest irony of all is that a generous and intelligent president, confident of his own good will and good sense, and intent on a serious contribution to limiting nuclear danger, allowed his attachment to speeches and subordinates to persuade him that these two short efforts were the best he could do in all of his first term.

Eisenhower and the Oppenheimer Case

On December 2, 1953, Eisenhower learned that the gravest charges had been made against the loyalty of Robert Oppenheimer. The next day he ordered that Oppenheimer be cut off from all access to classified information until the matter was resolved, and so set in motion a process which led seven months later to a formal ruling by the Atomic Energy Commission that Oppenheimer "should be denied access to restricted data." The central event in those months was a four-week hearing whose published record is one of the fundamental historical documents of the nuclear age, just as the findings unfriendly to Oppenheimer, and especially the final majority judgment of the Atomic Energy Commission, are classic demonstrations of the human capacity for error and deception. The commission's profoundly misguided decision was the consequence of many actions by many people, but the individuals who bear the heaviest burden of responsibility are Lewis Strauss and Gordon Gray, and the man who wrongly relied on the integrity of Strauss and the judgment of Gray was Dwight Eisenhower. The Oppenheimer case is perhaps the clearest demonstration we have of the degree to which the quality of Eisenhower's judgment on nonmilitary matters was affected by the quality of the men he trusted.[161]

The document that caused Eisenhower's initial action was a letter written to J. Edgar Hoover by the former executive director of the Joint Committee on Atomic Energy of the Congress, William L. Borden, which set forth his "exhaustively considered opinion . . . that more probably than not J. Robert Oppenheimer is an agent of the Soviet Union." Because of Borden's important connections with the Congress and his skill with words, his letter carried an appearance of authority which immediately sent tremors through the administration, and the requirement of immediate action was increased by the prospect of a public denunciation of Oppenheimer by Senator Joseph McCarthy.[162]

Eisenhower never quite believed Borden's charge, but he was immediately alert to its explosive character. He knew, as the whole country did, that Oppenheimer was the most famous of all Americans connected with the bomb—the presiding genius of the effort at Los Alamos, the most active and articulate of the scientists who continued to advise the government in the following years, a man who knew essentially all there was to know about American nuclear weapons. If such a man were a Soviet agent the public reaction would be horrendous. Eisenhower quickly recognized that if Oppenheimer were what Borden thought he was, the real harm was already done—the Russians would long since have had full access to his formidable knowledge. His diary entry on the day after he heard of Borden's letter is pungent: "If this man is really a disloyal citizen, then the damage he can do now as compared to what he has done in the past is like comparing a grain of sand to an ocean beach. It would not be a case of merely locking the stable door after the horse is gone; it would be more like trying to find a door for a burned-down stable."[163]

In this situation, Eisenhower's instant reaction was understandable. It was necessary that there should be a new and careful inquiry of some sort. Responsibility for that inquiry passed to the Atomic Energy Commission, and the dominant figure in the management of the ensuing process was Strauss, now its chairman. In particular Strauss was the trusted channel from the commission to the president. He and Eisenhower settled together on the choice of Gordon Gray to chair the board which would hold secret hearings and reach an initial judgement. Strauss himself selected Roger Robb to serve as counsel to the commission, and it is evident from his behavior in the hearing that Robb, who proved that he deserved his reputation as a powerful prosecutor, fully understood that his assignment from his client was to bring Oppenheimer down if he could.

Strauss gave Robb all the help he could. He had already enlisted the FBI to monitor all Oppenheimer's movements, tap his telephone, and provide daily summaries of his activities, including his conversations with his attorney. Strauss drew on these reports in his frequent guidance to Robb. This outrageous procedure was successfully concealed at the time, and has been fully revealed only in a careful, honest, and generally sympathetic biography of Strauss by Richard Pfau. Strauss not only concealed his enlistment of the FBI, but flatly denied at the time that there was ever any tapping of anyone on his initiative. Robb himself later told Pfau that he considered the wiretaps an unethical invasion of Oppenheimer's relations to his lawyer; he said he did not know at the time that his guidance from Strauss was based on such activity. If this arrangement had not been successfully concealed, Strauss would have been promptly and deservedly ruined, and the disclosure would have wrecked his effort to show "that the Government had acted in a considerate manner, as well as justly."[164]

Yet we must recognize that Strauss thought he had good reason for doing what he did. He was a passionate believer both in the gravity of the Soviet menace and in the strongest possible American nuclear armament as the only reliable shield of freedom. He was disposed to believe that men who disagreed with him on these points were not merely wrong, but evil or misguided or both. He saw Oppenheimer as the most powerful opponent of the American effort to get the H-bomb first, and in addition he had been deeply wounded in a public hearing when Oppenheimer effectively ridiculed his claim that the export of certain radio isotopes was dangerous. Such isotopes, said Oppenheimer, were less important than electronic devices, more important than vitamins, and essentially irrelevant to an atomic energy program. Strauss was furious, and he found it easy to look on Oppenheimer with suspicion.[165]

By the time the Borden letter forced the issue, Strauss had come to believe that Oppenheimer might be a Soviet agent; "several times in those December days he wondered aloud whether Oppenheimer might flee behind the Iron Curtain." He also argued privately that if Oppenheimer kept his clearance, "then anyone can be cleared, regardless of the information against them," and "the atomic energy program and all research and development connected thereto will fall into the hands of left-wingers." In Pfau's words, Strauss "would spare no effort to win."[166]

Quite aside from matters of atomic policy, his target had a vulnerable history. Oppenheimer's political past was not conventional. In the years before the Hitler-Stalin agreement of 1939 he had himself been an ardent fellow traveler closely connected to communists. His brother, his wife, and his former fiancée had all been communists at one time or another. He had changed his views, but only gradually. As late as 1943 he had foolishly substituted a "cock-and-bull story" for the truth in warning security officers about a man named George Eltenton. His object in this invention, whose details are as irrelevant as they were foolish, was to give the warning without disclosing the identity of his friend Haakon Chevalier, through whom Eltenton had expressed interest in "the possibility of transmitting technical information to Soviet scientists."[167]

In the years after Hiroshima, though his general view of the Russians had become steadily more realistic, Oppenheimer had made powerful enemies by his advocacy of particular nuclear policies. In the Pentagon and on Capitol Hill many believed that he had dangerously obstructed the national defense. The most fervent of these opponents were in the air force, whose single-minded commitment to the strategic offensive he had repeatedly challenged, but the issue that was foremost in the minds of the men at the Atomic Energy Commission, and in Borden's letter too, was his role in the hydrogen bomb controversy.

Logically these elements in Oppenheimer's past could be considered separately, but psychologically they readily flowed together, and Borden's fearful conclusion was only an extreme example of the result. For many this fear of Oppenheimer was intensified by a feeling that his war-won reputation and his extraordinary persuasiveness in face-to-face argument had given him an uncanny and dangerous influence over susceptible innocents like his colleagues in the General Advisory Committee.

As the hearing went forward in April 1954 each of these elements in his past was worked over by Roger Robb to demonstrate that Oppenheimer was not to be trusted. The issue of his honesty and candor, already an element in the formal charges against him, became the centerpiece of Robb's implacable cross-examination, and both Gray and Strauss, in quite different ways, relied strongly in their final opinions on the judgment that in his testimony Oppenheimer had been "less than candid" or had shown "fundamental defects in his 'character.' "168

Under Robb's cross-examination, Oppenheimer was unable to keep it clear that his attempt to protect Chevalier had been little more than a futile exercise arising from what General Groves described as a "typical American school boy attitude that there is something wicked about telling on a friend." Robb belabored the Chevalier episode until Oppenheimer had confessed his folly a dozen times and accepted the prosecutor's description of his story as "a whole fabrication and tissue of lies."169 Worse yet, Oppenheimer and his counsel too readily submitted to a process by which errors of memory were given the appearance of deception. Robb had files and records that were not made available to Oppenheimer until after he had given occasionally inaccurate accounts of events. Although Gray as chairman had an obvious distaste for what he called "entrapment" and repeatedly denied that it was intended, he was speaking for himself, not for Robb, and Strauss later explained to James Reston of *The New York Times* that Robb had only been doing what his client wanted. Since Oppenheimer's veracity was at issue, Strauss told Reston, "We felt it relevant to test his oral statements against the actual documents" without letting him know of their existence. Entrapment was repugnant to Gray but not to Strauss, and Gray did not hold Robb to his own high standard.170

Gordon Gray had other stern convictions that did not help Oppenheimer. He did not believe any man should set himself up as his own judge of what was safe in matters of security, so he was not only shocked by the original Chevalier incident, but also by the fact that Oppenheimer continued to see his friend in later years. Chevalier and Oppenheimer had met twice in Paris as late as the preceding December. For Gray, a man of great decency but highly conventional decorum, it was self-evident that continuing association with an impenitent fellow traveler was improper. He did not believe that a responsible man with secrets in his head should associate with a man like Chevalier. He recognized that Oppenheimer might believe Chevalier was not a Communist, but how could he be sure? All this was so obvious to Gray that although he questioned Oppenheimer carefully about his later meetings with Chevalier, he never asked why Oppenheimer thought the meetings proper, or whether any official of any sort had ever requested him not to have them.

Gray's second concern was with Oppenheimer's opinions on weapons, and again his conclusions were affected by strong personal convictions. He thought it beyond dispute that the United States must have "the strongest possible offensive capabilities," and he thought that advisers should base their counsel on this "genuine conviction." Though he earnestly tried, he plainly never understood how Oppenheimer could have thought it might be dangerous to emphasize offensive capabilities excessively at the expense of other needs. Gray also thought it obvious that the opposition to the hydrogen bomb had been misguided at best, and during the hearings he was clearly impressed by the testimony of Edward Teller, who then had great standing as the "father" of the H-bomb—the man who was thought to have overcome the technical and theoretical obstacles that Oppenheimer and others had considered so formidable.[171]

Early in his extensive and passionately hostile testimony, Teller was asked by Robb whether he thought Oppenheimer was a security risk. His answer was that Oppenheimer's "confused and complicated" actions on numerous issues where the two men had disagreed left him with "a feeling that I would feel personally more secure if public matters would rest in other hands." Toward the end of Teller's appearance Gray reminded him of this statement and asked if he also felt "that it would endanger the common defense and security to grant clearance to Dr. Oppenheimer." Teller's answer, together with a further answer to Oppenheimer's lawyer, showed that what worried him was neither Oppenheimer's intent nor his reliability as a guardian of secrets—on these two points he saw no danger. The danger was in his repeatedly bad advice: "If it is a question of wisdom and judgment, as demonstrated by actions since 1945, then I would say one would be wiser not to grant clearance." These responses cost Teller the respect and friendship of men whose high opinion he greatly valued and became an enduring self-inflicted wound to his own self-regard. But Gray's opinion would make it clear that they had a great effect on him.[172]

Gordon Gray had still a third predisposition that did not help Oppenheimer. He did not believe in special treatment for the very clever. In his view, the more a man was marked for preferment by his special talents, the more he should be held to a high standard of general behavior. When witnesses dwelt on Oppenheimer's extraordinary abilities, he was wary, and when some of them suggested that scientists should not be held to the same standards of routine behavior as others or that scientists as a class might be offended if Oppenheimer were not vindicated, his reaction was strongly negative. The opinion in which he joined reflects a clear irritation with those who had seemed to suggest that Oppenheimer's brilliance excused his peccadilloes, and still stronger resistance to the notion that scientists as a group had any special claim. Thus the very witnesses who seem strongest today in the written record, men like Rabi and Bethe and Bush, were probably not helpful to Oppenheimer with Gray. He was not looking at brilliance, loyalty, discretion, or past services; he was looking for affirmative enthusiasm, not only for offensive capabilities but also for security regulations and customs. He correctly found neither in Oppenheimer.[173]

Thinking as he did, Gray found himself driven to conclude that Oppenheimer's clearance should not be restored. Joined by Thomas A. Morgan, he wrote a majority opinion whose two central conclusions were that Oppenheimer had shown "a serious disregard for the requirements of the security system" and that his conduct in the hydrogen bomb affair raised "a doubt as to whether his future participation" in defense programs "would be clearly consistent with the best interests of security." Gray and Morgan firmly rejected Borden's contention that Oppenheimer was probably a spy, and unlike the rest of their opinion that rejection has stood the test of time. They found "no evidence of disloyalty" and "much responsible and positive evidence of . . . loyalty and love of country." They also reached a "clear conclusion, which should be reassuring to the people of this country, that he is a loyal citizen." They even noted, if somewhat grudgingly, that Oppenheimer "seems to have had a high degree of discretion reflecting an unusual ability to keep to himself vital secrets."[174]

But loyalty and discretion were not enough. To dine with Chevalier was "not the kind of thing that our security system permits on the part of one who customarily has access to information of the highest classification." And while Gray and Morgan in one place asserted Oppenheimer's right to his own convictions on the H-bomb, they did not really mean it, holding that these convictions had led him to actions that damaged "the security interests of the United States," primarily because they did not sufficiently respect "the protection of the strongest offensive military interests of the country."[175]

The next step in the affair was the publication by Oppenheimer's lawyers of the Personnel Security Board's opinions, together with a response. Oppenheimer and his counsel acted here to protect his reputation; they believed it certain that the adverse opinion would leak, and they found that opinion so vulnerable that they thought it in Oppenheimer's interest to insure that it should be printed with a simultaneous rebuttal. This they arranged with *The New York Times,* and within two weeks they also provided to the *Times* a brief dissecting the majority opinion.[176]

The consequences for Oppenheimer were both good and bad. There was indeed a strong public reaction against the notion that any man should be judged for his opinions. Every later defender of the verdict, right up to Eisenhower, was at pains to deny that Oppenheimer's opinions in the H-bomb dispute were relevant to the decision. But at the same time Eisenhower and Strauss were outraged by what they saw as an attempt to try the case in the newspapers. Eisenhower's comment to his press secretary Hagerty was sulphurous: "This fellow Oppenheimer is sure acting like a Communist. He is using all the rules that they use to try to get public sentiment in their corner on some case where they want to make an individual a martyr."[177]

The next judgment, Oppenheimer having waived an appeal to still another review board, came from the commission's general manager, Kenneth Nichols. Nichols was a professional soldier of high intelligence and considerable vanity who had been through deep disagreements and wounding encounters with Oppenheimer in earlier years.[178] Now he pulled out all the stops. To him Oppenheimer had been a Communist for many years, in all but formal membership. He had continuously and flagrantly offended against security regulations; his earlier contribution might have justified his earlier employment, but now he was of only marginal value to an enterprise in which many could serve as well as he. The long and detailed opinion ended with a flat recommendation against the restoration of clearance. It so deeply satisfied his superior Strauss that in his memoirs he reprinted it complete, the only document in the case to which he gave that doubtful honor.[179]

Now it was the turn of the commission itself. Its five members produced five opinions, but the only one with more than one signer was that written by Chairman Strauss. Two colleagues joined him in what became the majority opinion, and a fourth joined in the result. The majority opinion concluded that "concern for the defense and security of the United States requires that Dr. Oppenheimer's clearance should not be reinstated." But what is important here is the way Strauss reached this conclusion. Carefully read, his opinion tells more about him than about Oppenheimer.[180]

Strauss began with an assertion that was characteristically adjusted from the truth. "The Atomic Energy Act of 1946," he wrote, "lays upon the Commissioners the duty to reach a determination as to 'the character, associations, and loyalty' of the individuals engaged in the work of the Commission."[181] He then went on to accept in silence the Gray board's unanimous endorsement of Oppenheimer's loyalty, but to assert that "substantial defects of character and imprudent and dangerous associations . . . are also reasons for disqualification." This paragraph appears to assert that character and associations *as such* are what the commission is enjoined to weigh, but that is not what the law says. What it says is that the commission is to determine that permitting a person "to have access to restricted data will not endanger the common defense or security," and it is for that purpose and no other that the statute requires a report from the FBI as to "character, associations and loyalty." Moreover, this requirement is a part of Section 10 of the law, the part entitled "Control of Information," so it is obvious that what the law intends is a judgment on the danger that allowing access to sensitive information will lead to its disclosure. Strauss himself was later to assert quite falsely that the denial of Oppenheimer's clearance was "a measure taken to safeguard such information . . . and for no other purpose." But in his formal opinion, by this skillful rephrasing, he allowed himself to treat "character" and "associations" as independent hurdles, not indications for a reasonable judgment on reliability, and he compounded this distortion by deliberately neglecting the part of the Gray board report which was most relevant to the real question of risks—its ringing endorsement of Oppenheimer's discretion as well as his loyalty. This rearrangement of the language of the act allowed Strauss to go at once on the attack.[182]

The heart of Strauss's attack was the Chevalier connection. It was the centerpiece of his claim of fundamental defects of character, and also of his charge of persistent and continuing association with Communists. As to character he adduced the "tissue of lies" told in 1943 and went further (following Nichols) to suggest that things might be even worse. Perhaps Oppenheimer had told the truth the first time and his later story was the lie; if it were so, then Chevalier had approached three people, not Oppenheimer alone, and the possibility that he was dangerous would be increased. Here Strauss conveniently neglected the clearly contrary opinion of the men to whom Oppenheimer had eventually named Chevalier—Groves and his security officer. He further failed to mention the fact that in 1947 he himself had voted to clear Oppenheimer although an FBI report on the Chevalier incident was before him. All that was new was that his lawyer Robb had managed to get Oppenheimer to accept Robb's description of a single cock-and-bull story as "a whole fabrication and tissue of lies." Strauss approvingly noted in his memoirs that Robb's words were "ugly," but they did not change the reality he himself had accepted and excused seven years earlier. The Chevalier incident was by far his most important example of defective character. He named five more, which Commissioner Smyth readily reduced to their intrinsic triviality in a lonely but powerful dissent. Smyth also flatly denied an unsupported assertion by Strauss that his six examples were only samples from "a whole catalogue" of "falsehoods, evasions, and misrepresentations."[183]

On "associations" the chief charge made by Strauss was that Oppenheimer was still seeing Chevalier. This at least was something new since 1947.

Strauss used these continuing meetings, as Gray had, to justify the assertion of continuing "close association with Communists, ' but in making his case he offered at least three statements so exaggerated as to amount to falsehoods. First, his opinion cited these meetings with Chevalier as his only concrete illustration of what he called "imprudent and dangerous associations, particularly with known subversives who place the interests of foreign powers above those of the United States." But Chevalier was not a "known subversive"—certainly not to Oppenheimer, who saw him as a literary leftist and fellow traveler, and not even to Gray and Morgan, who with access to all the documents never made a finding as to whether he was a Communist or not. Second, Strauss described Chevalier as having been "intermediary for the Soviet Consulate in 1943," whereas there was no evidence that Chevalier had ever done more than describe an approach from Eltenton; there was not one word anywhere that linked him to any Soviet official. Third, Strauss twice implied that Oppenheimer wrongly helped Chevalier in dealings with the government, once by writing him a letter describing his innocent role in the incident of 1943, a letter which Chevalier used in seeking a passport, and once by referring him to an official of the embassy in Paris for advice. What we have in these two charges is a description of the mind of Strauss, not the character of Oppenheimer. Seen from Oppenheimer's position, as maintained steadily from late 1943 onward, Chevalier was innocent of wrongdoing and entitled to encouragement from his friends and advice from his country's embassy. No one had ever told Oppenheimer that Chevalier was dangerous, and he did not himself believe that he was. But to Strauss he was tainted, and to help such a man was to acquire the taint. There is still another irony here. From everything we know, even today, what made Chevalier look dangerous, if anything, was Oppenheimer's original silly story.[184]

That Strauss chose to take Chevalier's bad character for granted, and so to assert Oppenheimer's guilt by association, is suggested by the way he mixed the matter up in his memoirs eight years later. There he wrote that Oppenheimer himself "had informed on" Chevalier "as being involved in an attempt to obtain secret information . . . for the Soviet espionage organization." But that was exactly what Oppenheimer had never done at any time. No one ever heard him say, because he obviously did not believe, that Chevalier was trying to obtain information. Yet Strauss claimed that Oppenheimer was guilty of continuing and current association with a man against whom he "himself had made a grave accusation." Once again this is what Oppenheimer never did. Even in telling his original story of 1943 he had described the then-unnamed Chevalier as unsympathetic to Eltenton's suggestion of communication with the Russians, saying, as his security agents recorded at the time, "I think that the intermediary between

Eltenton and the project thought it was the wrong idea . . . I don't think he supported it. In fact, I know it." And later he said to Lansdale, "It's my overwhelming judgment that this guy isn't involved," and "I would regard it as a low trick to involve someone where I would bet dollars to doughnuts he wasn't involved." If one thing is more clear than any other from the whole record, it is that Oppenheimer never made any "grave accusation" against Chevalier. In his formal opinion Strauss avoided this outright falsehood, but in his memoirs he let himself go. On the most charitable interpretation he deceived himself.[185]

One must be less charitable about the fact that he deceived Eisenhower on precisely the same point. The evidence is compelling. On June 1 James Hagerty told his diary of a talk with the president—the same one in which the president found Oppenheimer to be acting like a Communist in taking his case to the press. At this point the hearings had not been made public, and what Eisenhower and Hagerty knew about them could have come only through Strauss. Unlike anyone else in the case, he had regular access to both men, and they to him. Here is what Hagerty reported: "The President and I agreed that one of the most damning things in the Oppenheimer testimony was his visit to Paris and his stay there with Chevalier after Oppenheimer had reported to the commission that Chevalier had tried to get secret information from him for the use of a foreign government. 'How can any individual report a treasonable act on the part of another man and then go and stay at his home for several days?' the President asked. 'It just doesn't make any sense to me.' " That the two men here confused a Chevalier visit to Oppenheimer's home in 1950 with two social meetings in Paris in 1953 is trivial, except insofar as it demonstrates a wholly secondhand knowledge of the record. What is decisive is that their garbled version of the original incident, a version so damaging to Oppenheimer and so far from reality, is the Strauss version. It was what he wanted everyone to believe, and it was quite simply false. Oppenheimer had never reported a treasonable act by Chevalier to anyone, nor had he ever reported that "Chevalier had tried to get secret information from him." The president of the United States, in the matter of J. Robert Oppenheimer, became the easy captive of Lewis Strauss, and in consequence he was decisively misled.[186]

Eisenhower was misled not only on Chevalier but also on the other decisive point—that of the relevance of Oppenheimer's opinions on policy. In his memoirs he was "sure" that the members of the Gray board had given no weight to Oppenheimer's position on the hydrogen bomb. This conclusion conflicts not only with the plain language of the majority opinion, but with the whole record of the hearings. The hundreds of pages devoted to the H-bomb controversy and to other contested questions of nuclear weapons policy are suffused with passion on both sides, and we have seen how deeply Gray was affected.[187]

A still stronger demonstration that Eisenhower was deceived when he asserted the irrelevance of the H-bomb issue can be found simply by asking if it is credible that the proceedings would ever have begun if Oppenheimer's position on the hydrogen bomb had been that of Teller, or if instead of arousing the fears of the air force on other matters, he had been its steadfast ally. Not only would Borden's letter to the FBI become impossible, but the interest of the very men who pursued Oppenheimer most ardently would be reversed. If he is their champion—and what a champion he would have been, with his reputation and his persuasiveness—it is they who become interested in minimizing his youthful indiscretions and explaining away his continuing association with Chevalier. At the very most such defenders might have urged him privately to be careful about Chevalier—perhaps to see him only after notice to security officers, perhaps not to see him in a foreign country. (The Paris visit, James Reston was told, was particularly dismaying to the commission because of the possibility that Oppenheimer might have been "forced at gun-point into a plane and taken behind the Iron Curtain." One does not know whether to wonder more at the willingness of grown men to entertain this notion or at their belief that it would somehow carry conviction to Reston's readers.) It is simply inconceivable that if he had been seen as a tested and powerful advocate of "the strongest possible offensive capability" he would have been pursued as Strauss, Nichols, and Robb pursued him in this proceeding.[188]

Yet it seems to me entirely believable that Eisenhower himself would have considered all the angry hostility aroused by Oppenheimer's policy positions to be irrelevant. There is a ring of authenticity in the account in his memoirs—not only in his recognition that a man could well believe "the world would be better off if this development was stifled before birth," but also in his recollection that back in July 1945 he himself had expressed "grave misgivings" to Stimson over the plans for using the bomb against Japan. He found no question of loyalty or security in such misgivings. I conclude that he did not read the Gray-Morgan opinion and once more trusted Strauss. It is hard to doubt that what he heard from Strauss was what the latter blandly and falsely asserted in his own opinion: that the Gray board attached no importance to Oppenheimer's view of the hydrogen bomb.[189]

It remains true that Oppenheimer's position on the hydrogen bomb was not in itself sufficient to damn him. The Chevalier matter was also necessary, and it took the two together to bring him down. Oppenheimer himself was fully aware of this danger, just as he was aware of his own continuing distress over the original Chevalier incident, but he relied for protection on his extraordinary record of service and on the testimony of his impressive supporters. Until he encountered the devious and determined hostility of Strauss, and the deceived passivity of Eisenhower, he was right. Oppenheimer and his counsel never appealed past Gray and Strauss to Eisenhower, believing that he would not overrule two men he trusted, and that to engage him directly in endorsing their opinion "would simply compound the injury." They were probably right; Eisenhower was indeed steadfast in the support of subordinates he trusted. Moreover, in what may have been a major tactical error, Oppenheimer's counsel had relied throughout on the fairness of their judges, and Garrison had expressed recognition and appreciation of such fairness. The defense was not now well placed to challenge the result.[190]

THE OPPENHEIMER CASE has many meanings. One can focus on the personal tragedy of Oppenheimer. No Shakespeare has yet treated that story, but talented writers have tried, and with good reason. Quite aside from Oppenheimer's extraordinary rise and fall in prestige and power, his character has fully tragic dimensions in its combination of charm and arrogance, intelligence and blindness, awareness and insensitivity, and perhaps above all daring and fatalism. All these, in different ways, were turned against him in the hearings. Relatively early in the ordeal he lost his self-confidence, and so he never showed his judges the underlying strength of mind and spirit and the intense dedication to the reduction of nuclear danger which had governed his life and work for almost a decade.

Or one might try to understand his persecutors better. Even the most obvious dishonesty, like that of Lewis Strauss, can have interesting causes. There are other tempting questions. Was Oppenheimer's counsel, Lloyd Garrison, too gentle for the task he generously undertook? Was there no way for the defense to reach past Gordon Gray's narrowness to his essential fairness? What would have happened if the hearings had been public from the start, so that the tactics of Robb, the character of the various witnesses, and the emphasis on policy debates could be exposed in the open air and not held within the stifling privacy of the small and guarded room?

But my concern with the case is different: It is to understand how Dwight Eisenhower himself came to be a party to a miscarriage of justice in which the name of an illustrious citizen was brutally if only temporarily blackened. What seems clear is that he relied on the wrong men. He did not know that Gray would wrongly allow policy differences to play a decisive role in his judgment, and he did not know that Strauss was an accomplished twister of truth with a passionate interest in securing the outcome he did. Eisenhower never reviewed the record for himself or looked behind what he heard from Strauss. He never sought out others who could have told him what Strauss left out.

Among the strongest and most persuasive witnesses for Oppenheimer, for example, were three men whom Eisenhower knew well and respected greatly.

John McCloy he had known for a decade and had wanted in his Department of State, possibly at the top; James Conant he had known as a fellow president of a great university and had chosen as his high commissioner for Germany; I. I. Rabi and he had become friends at Columbia, and Rabi saw him now from time to time as chairman of the General Advisory Committee in succession to Oppenheimer. There is no evidence that Eisenhower read their sturdy testimony, and not one of them appears to have mentioned the case to him. Rabi had a chance once, finding himself momentarily alone with the president at a White House reception, but the two men were joined by a publisher before he could speak.[191]

What Eisenhower could have learned in an afternoon with Conant, McCloy, and Rabi is what he never learned from Strauss: that Oppenheimer was held by all three in the highest regard; that all three had seen him repeatedly tested and repeatedly proven clear-headed on the subject of Soviet behavior; that none of them believed he would ever do again what he had done in 1943 over Chevalier; and that none of them had much respect for either the quality or the fairness of the Gray board's proceedings. At a minimum he would have learned that his reliance on Strauss was one-sided.

As it turned out, the Oppenheimer case only strengthened Eisenhower's respect for Strauss. Most of the public criticism of the proceedings came from people he mistrusted. The most powerful early public attack on the results was that of Joseph and Stewart Alsop in a magnificent broadside, *We Accuse*. Eisenhower had no use for the Alsop brothers—they were investigative reporters, and they found out much more than he liked. Criticism from them became armor for Strauss. As far as I can tell, it was not until 1958, during a later Senate battle over the confirmation of Strauss as secretary of commerce, that Eisenhower ever heard directly from someone he respected that Strauss might have failed him in the Oppenheimer case. Angered by the fact that many scientists opposed Strauss, the president asked his science adviser, James R. Killian, Jr., for an explanation. Killian replied that a large part of the scientific community thought great harm had been done by the unfairness of the Oppenheimer proceeding and its results, and that many held Strauss responsible. As Killian reports it, Eisenhower received this account in silence. In his memoirs, years later, Strauss had his unswerving support.[192]

There are many tragedies in this affair, in addition to Oppenheimer's. Teller, Strauss, and Borden later suffered in ways for which they were themselves responsible. Teller's attack cost him friends and self-respect. Strauss made enemies who later joined in the battle that denied him confirmation as secretary of commerce. Borden's prospect of a job in the Kennedy administration was blocked by recollection of his letter.[193] But the largest tragedy may be Eisenhower's. Under the surface that was all Strauss let him see, spread on the record that he never stopped to read, was compelling evidence that what had made Oppenheimer his most passionate enemies, what had led him to run the risks he understood so well, was a view of nuclear danger and nuclear reality that Eisenhower deeply shared. By trusting the wrong men and accepting their wrong result, the president tilted the balance of public reputation and influence against his own basic beliefs. To understand this deeper tragedy we must now examine nuclear issues larger and harder than those that any president had yet confronted.

VII

Into
the Missile Age

Which Weapons and How Many

Eisenhower was the first American president to confront multiple complex choices about the number and kind of nuclear weapons that the United States should have. He came to office less than three months after the first successful test of a thermonuclear device, at a time when no deliverable weapon of this kind had been made. The thousand fission warheads in the stockpile could be delivered only by aircraft, and their total explosive power was probably about one hundred megatons. The decisions he made and allowed others to make were so broad and deep that even in the middle of the 1980s the underlying structure of the nuclear armaments of the United States retains a shape that the Eisenhower of 1960 would recognize: three major classes of strategic systems based on aircraft, land-based missiles, and submarines, and a large variety of less-than-strategic weapons with shorter ranges and uncertain missions. By 1960 these systems were armed from a stockpile of eighteen thousand warheads.[1]

So wide and varied was this development that when the Kennedy administration, applying new and more centralized methods of analysis and decision, shaped the three-legged "triad" of Polaris submarines, Minuteman missiles, and B-52 bombers, a force that ensured strategic stability for the two decades that followed, it was in the main simply selecting and enlarging the best of many different weapons systems it found in different stages of development when it took office. The eventual triad was shaped by Kennedy's rejection of what was considered unnecessary, not by the design of any new force. Eisenhower's was an extraordinary legacy, both in its quality and in its excess.

Given the state of the cold war and the rapid advances in weapons technology, it is probable that a great expansion of both weapons systems and warhead destructiveness would have occurred in the 1950s under any president, but the particular course of events was determined by the choices that Eisenhower made about what he would and would not decide for himself, and by the further choices that he made about what he would and would not explain to the country.

His first and most significant choice was simply to support and expand two basic programs of the Truman years, the development of thermonuclear weapons and the continuing modernization of the bomber forces of the Strategic Air Command (SAC) under General Curtis LeMay. During his first term the technical promise of thermonuclear weapons was amply proved—most spectacularly by the detonation of a fifteen-megaton deliverable warhead at Bikini atoll in the spring of 1954. The first customer for these new weapons was SAC, and as the production authorized by Truman came on line, the stockpile of thermonuclear weapons expanded dramatically. The total megatonnage available was about 5,000 by 1955, 14,000 by 1956, and about 20,000 by 1960. Most of it was assigned to SAC. In his memoirs General LeMay himself relied on an even higher "unofficial public" estimate of 27,000 megatons.[2] In the same years, LeMay took delivery of the B-52 bombers, which in eight successive models developed over as many years became, as they remained for thirty years, the mainstay of the long-range bomber force; they were supported by more than one thousand shorter-range and smaller B-47s.

The United States may never have had a finer military unit, in terms of discipline, intelligence, readiness, and dedication, than the Strategic Air Command created by LeMay in the nine years of his service as its first commander. I shall be expressing differences with General LeMay, some of whose opinions I find neglectful of the nature of thermonuclear warfare. It is thus doubly appropriate to observe that in establishing exemplary standards of performance for this indispensable command, LeMay greatly served his country and the cause of nuclear peace.[3]

If the delivery of megatons and bombers to SAC was mainly, for Eisenhower, a matter of approving what was already well in train, we find him taking a far more active role in what may be a still more significant decision: the decision that if this enormous force should ever have to be used, its first and central mission must be to cripple the enemy in a single overwhelming blow. To Eisenhower it was always plain that any large-scale Soviet aggression against the United States or its major allies would require retaliatory nuclear reprisal. "My intention was firm: to launch the Strategic Air Command immediately upon trustworthy evidence of a general attack against the West."

From then on it would be up to LeMay. SAC was under his command and it was his responsibility to employ it effectively.[4]

To General LeMay there was only one proper target for SAC: the whole military power of the Soviet Union and its allies. Moreover, there was only one good way of attacking that power:

> When I led the Strategic Air Command I operated on the premise that we should have some warning of enemy preparations to attack us. Toward this end we spent a great deal of our energies learning what the opposition was doing day to day. Believing I could foresee an attack, I was prepared to beat him to the draw and attack all of his bomber and missile bases. In accordance with the Joint Chiefs of Staff my purpose was to destroy his war-making capability, particularly in the strategic nuclear area. Of course, I had no authority to order such attacks. All I could do was have the capability and hope that the orders would be given if necessary.[5]

LeMay's dedication to preemptive attack was not shared by Eisenhower, and it is interesting primarily as an indication of the intensity of LeMay's own conviction that once war was inevitable, his own job would be to fight and win. Eisenhower had no commitment to preemption, only to retaliation, and for him the purpose of the capacity to retaliate was deterrence. Yet he not only shared but actively endorsed the proposition that if SAC should ever have to be used, it must be used at once and to the hilt. The first retaliatory strike must indeed be massive. In 1960 the problem of strategic targeting became a matter of fierce debate because of disagreement over procedure for targeting the Navy's Polaris missiles, and the matter came to Eisenhower for decision. His comments in the crucial meeting are crystal clear and they show strong approval of the concept of a full-scale retaliatory strike. It must be executed "on a completely integrated basis"; it "must be simultaneous"; "if we put large forces outside of the plan, we defeat the whole concept of our retaliatory effort, which takes priority over everything else"; "there must be rigid planning, and it must be obeyed to the letter." At this showdown, the president backed the air force. The result was the establishment of a joint strategic targeting process under the commander of SAC.[6]

The establishment of a single unified planning command was a response to the deployment of Polaris, the first strategic nuclear system not controlled by the air force. Placing this planning command under the commander of SAC was a fateful decision, as both air and naval officers understood. For operational reasons, the recommendation that Secretary of Defense Thomas Gates made and the president accepted was hardly avoidable. Only SAC, in 1960, had the computer capability necessary for preparing the inescapably enormous operational plan. In part of Eisenhower's mind, the protests made by other services in this case were merely another reminder that it had been a mistake not to unify the military in a single service after World War II. But that mistake could not be repaired by a stroke of the pen in the waning days of his presidency, and so SAC was chosen.[7]

The plan that emerged in December 1960, the Single Integrated Operational Plan (SIOP), was a direct descendant of the plans LeMay had made in earlier years. It was a truly massive affair, aimed at the immediate destruction of the enemy's "war-making capability." In the particular targets chosen it owed much more to LeMay than to Eisenhower; the president did not get far into targeting. Like its predecessors, it was a "counterforce" plan in that it aimed at targets of military value. But like its predecessors, and in accordance with LeMay's own convictions, it did not omit military targets merely because they were in or near cities; to LeMay, mastermind of the bombing of Japan, cities were themselves sound military targets. Eisenhower himself did not like the targeting of cities. Early in his administration he had sharply questioned such targeting in discussions with senior military officers, asking, "If we batter Soviet cities to pieces by bombing, what solution do we have to take control of the situation and handle it so as to achieve the objectives for which we went to war?"[8] But he never insisted on an answer to his question. The targeting of SAC remained unaffected, and the later targeting of the SIOP was the targeting of SAC planners. At the end of his administration, prompted by his naval aide, Captain E. P. "Pete" Aurand, Eisenhower sent his science adviser George Kistiakowsky to Omaha to study the plan, and he was interested in Kistiakowsky's findings, one of which was that SAC's methods of planning would "lead to unnecessary and undesirable overkill." But this report came after the 1960 election, and Eisenhower's only action was to pass it on to his successor. The SIOP that Kennedy inherited was a plan for a single overwhelming attack on the USSR, on Eastern Europe, and on China, using many thousands of megatons, and it was the plan that Eisenhower's decisions and delegations had created.[9]

The president's next general choice, in the field of tactical weapons, was in the main a consequence of the way in which the New Look had been worked out. Once he had ratified the recommendation of Radford that nuclear weapons should be "as available for use as other munitions" he had no ready means of resisting the natural and steadily growing tendency of all services to look for appropriate nuclear missions for themselves. The most important case of unimpeded expansion was that of tactical nuclear weapons for Europe, but there was also a proliferation of systems for antisubmarine warfare, for air defense, and for less-than-strategic aircraft. By 1960 there may have been as many as ten thousand tactical warheads, with a yield of seven or eight thousand megatons, deployed in fifteen or twenty different systems in all three services.

As these tactical weapons multiplied, Eisenhower more than once expressed a sense of growing concern. In early 1959 he "wondered at the necessity of putting atomic weapons throughout ground forces and into the hands even of battalion commanders." More broadly, by early 1960 he found himself puzzled about the numbers of these smaller weapons, saying that "if we use thousands of small weapons we would be in a general war situation, in which the hydrogen weapon would be used, making the smaller ones insignificant." And in August of that year, according to the secretariat's report on a meeting on technology for limited warfare, he was more gloomy still; "The more the services depend on nuclear weapons the dimmer the President's hope gets to contain any limited war or to keep it from spreading into general war. This is the problem, the President said, which always nags him." But apparently he could find no way around it; "he did not intend to say that the possibilities for tactical weapons should be neglected." At a later meeting on limited warfare, he found fault with scenarios that assumed things might stay conventional, "saying that he thought the whole thing was very unrealistic and that we were unfortunately so committed to nuclear weapons that the only practical move would be to start using them from the beginning without any distinction between them and conventional weapons and also, assuming there was direct Russian involvement, mount an all-out strike on the Soviet Union." The logical consequences of the New Look might nag him, but he continued to accept them, at least in theory. Even a small war would be nuclear, and to limit even a small nuclear war would be hard—impossible if it involved the Russians.[10]

Yet since he retained complete presidential control over the use of such weapons, nuclear systems were more and more perceived by his commanders as supplementary forces, and not as integral elements of military units that would be used, if needed, as readily as an ordinary bullet or shell. Eisenhower did approve careful and complex arrangements for delegating emergency authority to others, but this delegation was no more than a precaution against the case in which the president himself might be unable to act.[11] In spite of the doctrine that came with the New Look, the services (always excepting SAC) came to think of all their forces in two quite different ways—in the modes of conventional and of nuclear war. In another administration, in Vietnam, these two separate modes of thought would become familiar even to commanders of strategic aircraft. Not so much by design as by the combined effect of his principle—that these weapons are like any others—and his practice—to be used only when I say so—Eisenhower led the three separate services to continue to think about six separate kinds of war, just as he had found them doing in the first year of the first term.

Eisenhower's worries about tactical nuclear weapons were matched by still stronger doubts about the enormous strategic forces he had authorized. In the early years he had readily approved the testing and construction of multimegaton weapons and the expansion of bomber forces, but by early 1959 his patience with such proposals had become thin. When John McCone, as chairman of the Atomic Energy Commission, asked for expanded reactor capacity to meet expanded military "requirements," the president was shocked; ". . . they are trying to get themselves into an incredible position—of having enough to destroy every conceivable target all over the world, plus a three-fold reserve. The patterns of target destruction are fantastic." The unrealistic attitudes of the military worried the president even more than the proposal for a new reactor, and McCone agreed that "they talk about megaton explosions as though they are almost nothing."[12]

A month later the president expressed still deeper worries in a conversation with Gordon Gray, who was then his national security assistant:

> In adverting to the question of targeting systems, the President said that if our plans contemplate targets in the thousands, this would involve tremendous numbers of weapons of megaton size. He said, for example, that if we were planning a thousand or more weapons averaging 3.5 megatons or even greater numbers of weapons he wondered what would be the cumulative effect of ground bursts of such a magnitude of megatonnage on the Northern Hemisphere. He asked me to seek to ascertain an AEC conclusion on this point. Also, he wondered what would be the effect if such megatonnage were exploded, say at 10,000 feet or whatever the optimum air burst altitude might be. An approach, he said, might be to base the study on what we have and immediately contemplate that we will have in stockpile, whether it be 5,000 or 7,000 weapons or what not. He expressed his concern that there just might be nothing left of the Northern Hemisphere. He felt that such a study might be useful in arriving at some of the major decisions.[13]

In the 1980s, when we have had before us the uncertain but previously unexamined possibility of a nuclear winter caused by much smaller wars than the one that SAC could have fought all alone in Eisenhower's last years, this expression of concern is so striking that we must pause to recall that Eisenhower's fear was of radioactive fallout, not of sky-blackening, earth-freezing soot and smoke. I have found no evidence that his suggestion for a study was ever followed up, and certainly his concern had no operational result. The president was aware of the profoundly excessive character of the strategic forces he had approved and aware also of the possibly catastrophic consequences of their use, but he did not act on his awareness.

Preventing Surprise Attack

On a different subject, in a strikingly different way, Eisenhower turned awareness into action. There are two great requirements for a strategic nuclear deterrent. The first is simply that deliverable weapons should exist in adequate quantity and quality, and we have just seen how for the Eisenhower administration the inertial momentum of the 1950s more than took care of that. Deliverability—getting the aircraft to their targets through Soviet defenses—was by no means an automatic capability, but the tradition of the air force and the superior command performance of General LeMay were such that no deep civilian concern with this problem was required in the 1950s. The question that did require and receive presidential action and attention was what Eisenhower always thought of as the prevention of surprise attack. It was this concern that led him in 1954 to one of the most important and constructive initiatives of his administration: the appointment of the Technological Capabilities Panel (TCP)—the Killian committee.

James R. Killian, Jr., in 1954 had been for six years the president of the Massachusetts Institute of Technology. Not himself a scientist, he understood the scientific process and scientists; he also had a sure sense of the relation between technical advice and political decision making, excellent judgment of people, and a natural discretion reinforced by his deep respect for Eisenhower both as a man and as president. Under his leadership, the Technological Capabilities Panel produced in early 1955 a two-volume report called *Meeting the Threat of Surprise Attack.* This report is one of the most influential in the history of American nuclear policy.[14] The TCP report decisively accelerated the development of ballistic missiles; it led to an important new departure in the collection of intelligence; it gave notice of the need to develop early-warning systems not only against bombers but against ballistic missiles; it gave Eisenhower an enduring respect for the value of independent technical advice.

The timely development of ballistic missiles during the Eisenhower administration is one of the best achievements of those eight years. Yet it is well to begin with a recognition that both the United States and the Soviet Union might be in much less nuclear danger today if these missiles had never been developed. Ballistic missiles move at a speed on the order of ten thousand miles an hour. They can reach from one homeland to the other in thirty minutes or less. Based on submarines or on land nearer the other side (West Germany and Cuba are examples) they can arrive in ten minutes. Once launched they cannot be recalled, and no system so far deployed by either side can be disarmed in flight. The decisions made in both countries in the 1950s created an enduring situation of reciprocal vulnerability to almost-instant devastation.

I am aware of no serious contemporary proposal, in or out of either government, that ballistic missiles should somehow be banned by agreement before they were ever deployed. The issue was never presented even in the limited and secret fashion of the Fermi-Rabi opinion on the H-bomb. Nor is it easy, even in hindsight, to know how such a ban could have been accepted by either government. The concept of banning the carrier rather than the nuclear weapon would have been new to both sides in the decisive years. For the Americans there would have been a most difficult problem of verification. H-bomb tests could have been detected with confidence from outside the Soviet Union, but would it have been easy to know about test flights of missiles? We must remember that later capabilities for verification of such tests, and of much else, depend heavily on reconnaissance satellites which reach their orbits in space precisely by riding up on ballistic missiles. It is remarkable, but on the whole not surprising, that a missile test ban was absent from the international agenda of the early 1950s.

When the Killian committee began its work, the future of ballistic missiles was uncertain, but at a level far below Eisenhower critically important steps had already been taken to move from noncommittal research to actual development. The decisive figure in this shift was Trevor Gardner, special assistant to Eisenhower's secretary of the air force, Harold E. Talbott. Gardner, a man of driving energy and conviction, believed that evolving technology, and especially the new prospect of lightweight thermonuclear weapons, made the possibility of strategic missiles much more hopeful than the air force then believed. He rapidly won authority to review all existing missile programs, and under that authority he organized an unusually strong committee of civilian scientists chaired by John von Neumann, a mathematician of the first rank who was already a believer in missiles. Von Neumann's Strategic Missiles Evaluation Committee produced in short order a report that Gardner used to get a firm decision making the development of an intercontinental strategic missile a matter of the highest priority within the air force, thus ending a period of years in which senior uniformed fliers had devoted themselves with equal energy to limiting the air force effort on ballistic missiles and opposing all efforts by other services to enter that field on their own. Gardner's performance was a classic instance of the effectiveness of a single resourceful individual acting with the full support of his immediate superior, and his success is the more remarkable in that it was achieved at a time when new projects of this magnitude were not expected in the Pentagon of the New Look.[15]

Responding to the same persuasive technical developments that had moved Gardner, and indeed owing its very existence in part to his earlier advocacy, Killian's panel made the energetic development of an intercontinental missile its very first specific recommendation. Its second, less to Gardner's taste, was a recommendation for the development of a shorter-range missile (1,500 nautical miles as against 5,500) with consideration of "both land-basing and ship-basing." The two recommendations were persuasive to Eisenhower. He never became an enthusiast for missiles as such—the first few were what he wanted, and not because he thought them a particularly good weapon. These early models indeed were not notably military; they had only enough accuracy for large unprotected targets like cities. Eisenhower wanted them because he understood their value as insurance against surprise attack; he also shared the Killian committee's view that "it is important that the United States achieve such a capability first."[16]

By December 1955 Eisenhower had accorded the highest national priority to no less than four missile programs. Two were intercontinental, Atlas and Titan, and two intermediate, Thor and Jupiter. Even more important, he had underlined his new convictions in the presence of his new chief of naval operations, Admiral Arleigh Burke, who heard the commander in chief say in a meeting of the National Security Council on December 2 that "the United States had to have a reliable missile system quickly, even if he had to run the project himself."[17]

If any one new weapons system is to be singled out as the best that emerged in the 1950s, it must, I think, be the Polaris submarine-based missile, and if any one man is to be given the principal credit for Polaris, it must be Admiral Burke. Even before hearing Eisenhower's avowal, he had become a strong advocate of the development of a fleet ballistic missile, recognizing that such a weapon could be a nearly invulnerable deterrent. Encouraged by the report of the Killian committee and himself determined that the navy should show a new awareness of technical opportunities, Burke had already established in November a special project office under Rear Admiral William Raborn. Initially the navy's effort was a partnership with the Army to produce the Jupiter missile—the two services needed each other's support in their shared effort to prevent an air force monopoly. But the requirements of a sea-based system drove the navy to seek a smaller solid-fueled missile, and late in 1956 it became clear, through the perceptive counsel of Edward Teller, that the weapons laboratories could now promise a warhead of the desired yield—more or less a megaton—with a weight of only six hundred pounds. As Teller pointed out, it made no sense for the navy to plan on using a 1958 warhead in a 1965 weapons system. When the hope held out by Teller was confirmed by the Atomic Energy Commission, the new and separate naval Polaris program was proposed and approved. By the summer of 1957 that program had "the highest priority of any project in the Navy." It is not easy to believe that Burke and Raborn could have produced this rapid evolution without the stimulus provided by the Killian recommendations and their warm endorsement by the president.[18]

Eisenhower's far-sighted concern with the risk of surprise attack had effects well beyond his acceleration of missile development and his decisive stimulus to Burke on Polaris. He boldly took the lead in opening Soviet skies by unilateral action instead of agreement. He encouraged the development first of the U-2 airplane and then of observation satellites. And while he did not take the advice of those who wanted a single unified management of all ballistic missile development (and later spoke once or twice as if that had been a mistake), the priorities he granted and the sense of urgency which he communicated allowed a rapidity of system development that is still astonishing. Polaris, to take the most important case, was begun late in 1955, and the first submarine, *George Washington*, was operational in 1960. Two years later there were nine.[19] Moreover interservice competition was stimulating as well as wasteful; the prospect of Polaris was an important element in the air force's move to its own solid-fuel Minuteman.[20] Eisenhower and his secretaries of defense may well have let too many systems get started, leaving politically hard choices to be made by their successors, but they opened the doorway to the rapid and timely deployment of the secure, survivable, and varied strategic systems that the possibility of ballistic missiles both required and permitted. Killian is quite right in his summary judgment of what happened in the missile competition in Eisenhower's last five years: "We started later than the Soviets and we overtook them."[21]

Negotiating on Nuclear Tests

Eisenhower's second term saw the first serious negotiations between Washington and Moscow on the limitation of nuclear danger. We have seen how neither in the great case of the Baruch plan nor in the substantively trivial cases of Atoms for Peace and Open Skies was there ever anything approaching a real negotiation. But in the question of nuclear tests, we find real efforts by each side to achieve its objectives in terms that may be acceptable to the other; we have a negotiation. The change is a great one, and as we have held Eisenhower accountable for earlier emptiness, so we must look with interest at his role in a new and deeply serious enterprise.

Neither Eisenhower nor any member of his administration was responsible for originating interest in a test ban. Where Atoms for Peace had been essentially an internally developed gimmick designed to give hope, and Open Skies a transparent attempt to achieve a one-sided advantage, the pressure for limiting or ending tests emerged from a widespread public fear of radioactive fallout. The first major political leader to call for an end of testing was not an American, but Jawaharlal Nehru of India, reacting in shock and alarm to casualties caused by an American test. In March 1954 twenty-three Japanese fishermen were showered with fallout borne by unpredicted winds from the unexpectedly large fifteen-megaton U.S. explosion at Bikini atoll.

The initial American reaction, dominated by Strauss, was to insist that danger from radioactive fallout was minimal, and the requirement for continued testing absolute. As American scientists took up strong positions on both sides of the question, there developed a public debate from which Eisenhower at first stood aloof. American tests continued, and the official position on disarmament continued to include a requirement for a comprehensive plan with clear-cut provisions for "effective safeguards and controls."[22]

As concern over fallout continued to grow, and as the debate widened, political leaders outside the administration were increasingly drawn to the issue. Eisenhower's personal enthusiasm for multimegaton weapons and tests was distinctly moderate, but until the fall of 1956 his role was limited to that of occasional internal expressions of hope that the need for such weapons and tests might be limited. Publicly the stern position stated by Strauss was maintained.

The first national political leader to take a clear-cut position for the limitation of testing was Adlai Stevenson of Illinois in the presidential election of 1956. Stevenson's position developed only gradually, but it began from his deep-seated conviction that further multimegaton nuclear tests were both unnecessary and poisonous, and that a proposal to end them made sense at every level of politics and morals. He believed that a ban on big bomb tests could be self-policing and that it would end the worst dangers of fallout; above all he thought it could create a new opening for disarmament. As he put it in the peroration of a full-dress speech on October 15, it offered a chance for "mighty, magnanimous America" to speak up for "the rescue of man from the elemental fire which we have kindled."[23]

Stevenson's repeated attacks hardened Eisenhower's heart. His own doubts about large-scale testing were put aside, and a discussion of alternative American policies which had begun inside the administration in September, in response to a new Soviet demarche, was overtaken by the perceived requirement to close ranks against Stevenson's assault. Campaign criticism tends to produce this reaction from the White House in any election year on any issue, and on this one Eisenhower appears to have had an additional reaction of anger, which he concealed at the time—anger at the injection of a complex and sensitive international question into a political campaign. This is a normal response of even the most consciously political incumbent, and Eisenhower, himself a skilled politician, had almost perfect double vision here: He thought politics was a game only other people played, and he believed it should stop well short of the nuclear issue. In 1956 this instinctive reaction served him well, at least in political terms.

On October 24 the president himself issued a comprehensive statement of a hard position which had been coordinated by his loyal friends Strauss, Dulles, Wilson of Defense, and Stassen (now his assistant on disarmament). The administration insisted that there could be no agreement without safeguards, that continuing tests were essential for our own nuclear strength, that the issue was the avoidance of war, not the avoidance of fallout, and that in any event the danger from fallout was trivial. Sober in tone, careful in language, and replete with reminders of Eisenhower's own unequalled experience in war and peace, the document was as powerful in politics as it was incomplete in logic.[24] And it was strongly reinforced in its impact by the fact that only five days earlier the Soviet government, in a new proposal by Bulganin, had effectively if unintentionally sideswiped Stevenson by referring with approval to his proposals. Praise from Moscow is bad medicine for critics of popular incumbent presidents.

Stevenson's proposal did not help him in the campaign, but it is not clear that it hurt him much; Eisenhower's ten-million-vote victory did not come from his defense of testing. Still Stevenson's effort showed the difficulty of an attack by a lonely candidate on an administration that skillfully exploited both the general authority of the executive branch as guardian of the atomic flame and the personal prestige of the soldier-statesman in the White House. The case was remembered by politicians as evidence of the danger to a challenger in seeming to be soft. A better lesson might have been that proposals of this sort should be made with great care. Stevenson did not understand at the outset the real (if limited) connection between H-bomb tests, which he would stop, and ballistic missile development, which he would accelerate. Nor did he initially recognize that no moratorium was likely to be durable unless both sides respected it. Finally, he complicated his position by also proposing an end to the military draft. The two proposals were not logically in conflict, and both foreshadowed what would eventually happen, but in 1956 the double-barreled attack increased the political vulnerability of each proposal.

Although he stumbled on lesser matters, Stevenson firmly expressed three fundamental truths: There was no lasting requirement for continued large H-bomb tests; an agreed moratorium could be sustained without the controls and inspection the Russians continued to resist; and the fallout from such large tests was well worth stopping. Eisenhower probably had the better of the argument in terms of votes affected, but events soon proved his opponent prophetic.

Within a year of his triumphant reelection, Eisenhower had begun to shift his ground, and in less than two years he had put in place the very moratorium he had denounced in the campaign. In 1957 and early 1958 the shifts were more cosmetic then substantive, because new American proposals for test suspension were regularly tied to Russian acceptance of a cutoff in the production of nuclear weapons materials; in that field the United States remained so far ahead that Russian agreement was predictably unattainable. Pressure for an end of testing continued to grow, both in the United States and internationally, and the president's belief in the urgency of particular tests continued to decline. The full-time presence of Killian, from late 1957 onward, gave Eisenhower, for the first time, continuous access to scientific advice less one-sided than what came to him through Strauss, and the growing success of Soviet propaganda for an unconditional test ban converted Dulles at about the same time.

Soviet proposals had great international impact, although they were often transparently self-serving, as when on May 1, 1958, Moscow announced a halt in all further tests just after completing a major series of megaton-level tests and just before a well-publicized American series was to begin. Since the Soviets reserved freedom to test again if others did, the proposal naturally struck Washington as cynical—I've had my tests, and if you don't abandon yours, I'm free to test again. But the impact on world-wide opinion was very different. So great was the international desire to get testing stopped that the question of who stopped first was not significant.

Recognizing this reality, Dulles himself would have preferred to preempt the Soviet move (which American intelligence had accurately predicted) by an earlier American announcement that the forthcoming American series would be Eisenhower's last. In a long meeting with the president on March 24, he made this proposal and lost the argument to Strauss and the Pentagon and Teller, saying in the end that in the light of all the arguments "we had better give up this proposal."[25]

But this was the last battle Dulles lost, and the record of the meeting shows that he had one ally—the president. Eisenhower intervened repeatedly in his support. Suspension might offer "hope for our own people and for world opinion." It was "simply intolerable to remain in a position wherein the United States, seeking peace, and giving loyal partnership to our allies, is unable to achieve an advantageous impact on world opinion. . . . Testing is not evil, but the fact is that people have been brought to believe that it is." And when Dulles withdrew his proposal, the president accepted his withdrawal but made it clear that he thought that under proper conditions a suspension of testing must be accepted. It was a critically important judgment, because the basic argument of Strauss and the Pentagon was that no suspension of testing under any conditions would be in the U.S. interest.[26]

Eisenhower's opinions on test limitation, even in 1956, were more moderate than his formal statements suggested, and his second term shows a steady and progressive shift in his position until it was only at the edges that it could be distinguished from what Stevenson had urged. In 1957 he allowed test suspension to become the first order of business for his senior negotiator Harold Stassen. Although he still insisted that it be connected to progress on a wider front, it was clear that he now thought it right to respond visibly to public concern about fallout. His new positions were more than enough to stir partisans of testing to new argumentation; their new argument was that testing itself was the best road to the production of clean bombs and thus the reduction of fallout in the event of war. At the end of April 1958 Eisenhower took the decisive step of separating the effort for a test ban from all other arms control objectives. He proposed an international conference of experts on the ways and means of making sure that a test ban agreement could be verifiably monitored, and Khrushchev presently agreed. When that summer conference seemed to go well, Eisenhower further proposed, on August 22, that negotiations on a test ban treaty should begin at the end of October, and he announced that the United States would at that time suspend all tests for a year, if the Russians also refrained from testing. After a last round of tests on both sides in September and October, and a final pair of small Russian tests in the first days of November, there began a moratorium not just on the large tests as Stevenson had proposed, but on all nuclear tests. In the spring of 1959, when it became clear that there were unresolved technical obstacles to a verifiable general test ban, Eisenhower proposed a limited ban, on tests in the atmosphere, which was a first cousin of what Stevenson had urged and still closer to what Kennedy achieved four years later. Khrushchev rejected this proposal—his objective at the time was to stop *all* U. S. tests—but negotiations for a broad agreement continued.

By the spring of 1960, Eisenhower and Khrushchev had made a record of proposal and counterproposal, joint technical inquiry, and serious argument, that was entirely without precedent in nuclear arms control negotiations. They had drafted a treaty banning tests at all

levels except that of small underground tests—for those there would
be an uninspected moratorium. Only two issues remained: how much
inspection would be allowed, and how long the moratorium would
last. The Americans were looking forward with hope to a summit
meeting in Paris as the place where Eisenhower and Khrushchev might
resolve these two remaining issues.

Then the whole process came to a sharp end, for Eisenhower's
time, when Khrushchev chose to use the U-2 episode to break up the
Paris summit and suspend negotiations until a new president was in
office. For Eisenhower it was a bitter disappointment. There is no
reason whatever to doubt his repeated assertion that nothing had a
higher priority for him than the cause of disarmament, and in the
spring of 1960 he had every right to hope for a crowning achievement.
Looking back on this second-term effort, it seems reasonable to view
it as at once less gloomy and more poignant, and certainly more
complex than Eisenhower's own conclusion that the failure was mainly
the result of the Soviet refusal to permit inspection.[27] These four years
emerge as a necessary bridge from the sterility of 1946–56 to the
restricted but real achievement of the Limited Test Ban Treaty in
1963. The record leaves me torn between admiration for what Eisenhower accomplished and regret for what he left undone. It recalls also
the crucial roles of the bitterly divided scientists, the competing military services, the Congress, and the public. Above all, it reminds us,
as Eisenhower learned to remind himself, that an agreement with the
Russians is by definition an agreement they will agree to.

Let us begin with what was achieved. The man who had settled for
looking good in 1953 and 1955 was interested, from 1957 onward,
primarily in results. He wanted to make proposals which would get
positive responses, and he wanted to make positive responses of his
own whenever he could. When his advisers were still skeptics, like
Strauss at every stage until his resignation in 1958, and Dulles until
after the departure of Stassen late in 1957, he showed a readiness to
go beyond them. When new advisers, especially Killian and then
Kistiakowsky, gave him new access to men who truly believed in a test
ban, he steadily backed them up. As his new purpose hardened, he
found Dulles also a convert. In spite of the breakdown of his own
effort, Eisenhower left to his Democratic successor an established precedent of serious commitment to a test ban, a well-blazed path of
diplomatic process to that end, and a specific proposal which Kennedy
would repeat until Khrushchev finally accepted it. Most important of
all, he left the commanding precedent that a Republican war hero with
eight years in the White House was a believer in this effort.

Could he have done more? Surely. He could have looked past the
nuclear scientists favored by Strauss—conspicuously Teller and Law-

rence—sooner than he did. He could have taken a more direct role in the process of negotiation or picked more energetic negotiators. Only in the short period between the conversion of Dulles and his terminal illness did the policy process go forward with executive energy. At other times policy was made from one tactical decision to another, as differences demanding resolution were passed up from a continuously divided set of second- and third-rank officials who came to be known, paradoxically, as the "Committee of Principals." The president did succeed—and it was no trivial achievement—in permanently reversing the fifteen-year-long presumption that tests demanded by the Pentagon were tests required by the nation; he regularly overruled the arguments for renewed testing of both the Pentagon and the Atomic Energy Commission from 1958 to the end of his term, supported in this process by his new access to independent technical advice. He decided firmly what came to him for clear decision, steadily keeping open the prospect of agreement, and steadily refusing, for more than two years, to shadow that prospect by a unilateral return to nuclear testing. He did not fully take charge, or assign anyone else to do so, but he set precedents that became highly important in 1963.

The So-called Missile Gap

Between 1957 and 1961, the nuclear weapons policy of the United States, and still more the state of public understanding on this subject, was affected by a phantom—the missile gap. The idea that the United States was faced by the prospect of a significant and possibly even a decisive Soviet advantage in long-range ballistic missiles persisted in one quarter or another until late in 1961. The actions that Eisenhower did and did not take in the face of this possibility are among the most interesting and instructive of all in the record we are reviewing.

The first and most powerful of the forces that produced the missile gap debate was the Soviet satellite *Sputnik,* which appeared in the skies of the world on October 4, 1957. The shock to assumptions about American preeminence in science and technology was profound. James Killian, whom Eisenhower appointed as science adviser in response to Sputnik, remembered his own first reaction:

What I felt most keenly was the affront to my national pride. . . .
    I was, of course, led at once to speculate about whether this country had grievously underestimated the technological capacity of our adversaries. . . . Undeniably the Soviets had actually accomplished, ahead of the United States, a technological feat to which we had both directed our efforts.

And this did violence to a belief so fundamental that it was almost heresy to question it: a belief I shared that the United States was so far advanced in its technological capacity that it had in fact no serious rival.[28]

Generally, then, Sputnik signaled high Soviet achievement. Specifically it showed the existence of a powerful ballistic missile, because nothing less could have placed in orbit so large an object. There followed additional spectacular Soviet launchings of larger satellites, one with a dog aboard. A belated American launching sputtered and failed.

Less than three months later there came a new shock, a powerfully written news report of the findings of a group apparently chosen by the president himself to advise on the strategic balance. Here is what Chalmers Roberts told the readers of *The Washington Post* on December 20:

> The still top-secret Gaither Report portrays a United States in the gravest danger in its history.
>
> It pictures the nation moving in frightening course to the status of a second-class power.
>
> It shows an America exposed to an almost immediate threat from the missile-bristling Soviet Union.
>
> It finds America's long-term prospect one of cataclysmic peril in the face of rocketing Soviet military might and of a powerful, growing Soviet economy and technology which will bring new political, propaganda, and psychological assaults on freedom all around the globe.
>
> In short, the report strips away the complacency and lays bare the highly unpleasant realities in what is the first across-the-board survey of the relative postures of the United States and the Free World and of the Soviet Union and the Communist orbit.
>
> To prevent what otherwise appears to be an inevitable catastrophe, the Gaither Report urgently calls for an enormous increase in military spending—from now through 1970—and for many other costly, radical measures of first and second priority.
>
> Only through such an all-out effort, the report says, can the United States hope to close the current missile gap and to counter the world-wide Communist offensive in many fields and in many lands.[29]

Compared to the actual language of the Gaither report (declassified and made public in 1973), the language used by Roberts is overheated. For example, what he calls "an almost immediate threat from the missile-bristling Soviet Union" appears in the report at first as an estimate that the Soviet Union has "probably surpassed us" in intercontinental missiles, and then as "the threat posed to SAC by the prospects of an early Russian ICBM capability." But the tone in which

Roberts reported was the tone he undoubtedly heard from informants who had participated in the Gaither study and who felt it urgent to describe their own grave concern to a member of the press. An earlier but less explosive account had come from Stewart Alsop, and the Alsop brothers later reported that William Foster, the codirector of the Gaither panel, had described his experience on the committee as that of "spending ten hours a day staring straight into hell." Moreover, the report itself did sound as if the *possible future* Soviet capability together with the *real and present* vulnerability of SAC presented a critical need for immediate action: "If we fail to act at once, the risk, in our opinion, will be unacceptable."[30]

A part of the difficulty that Eisenhower confronted in considering his response to *Sputnik* and the Gaither report was his own conviction that both events had little relevance to the real problem of strategic deterrence. He had not asked the Gaither committee to consider that problem, and he did not at first understand that his special assistant Robert Cutler had approved a committee request for authority to study and report on a wider field than civil defense. As for *Sputnik*, he had for years sharply separated the problem of satellites in space from that of ballistic missiles with warheads. The first, as he saw it then, was primarily a nonmilitary scientific question, and the second was a matter to which he had already given careful consideration and the highest possible priority. He was also wholly unaccustomed to the unauthorized use of a classified report from his own chosen advisers as an instrument for arousing the citizenry, and it is hard not to sympathize with his feeling that those who took this course were betraying a trust. He was thus wholly unprepared for the double-barreled shock that *Sputnik* and the Gaither report administered to American public opinion.

In the circumstances what is notable is the difference between what Eisenhower did and the way he felt and spoke. After *Sputnik* he took prompt action to meet not only the specific risks which most exercised the Gaither committee, but two general weaknesses which he himself had felt for some time, one in the management of strategic programs and the other in his own access to independent advice on the issues presented by technological change. While rejecting the broader budgetary recommendations of the Gaither committee, and indeed deploring what he thought its alarmist temper, he accepted and responded to its concern on the specific matters of warning and alertness for strategic forces. He publicly promised renewed attention to these matters in November, and in his January budget he proposed new resources for both undertakings.[31]

Most important of all, even before the Gaither report he had brought Killian to the White House as the first special assistant to the president for science and technology. This appointment led on to a reorganization of authority over defense research, and in the remaining Eisenhower years, Killian and his successor George Kistiakowsky, ably supported from the Defense Department by Herbert York as the first director of defense research and engineering, conducted a program which admirably served Eisenhower's own double objective: first to improve and safeguard the strategic deterrent, especially against surprise attack by missiles, and second to resist unnecessary programs pressed forward by interested parties as the answer to a new Soviet threat. The best of the new strategic programs were accelerated, so that already by 1960, as later evidence demonstrated, the United States had a clear lead in both land-based and submarine-based strategic missiles. At the same time such inferior programs as the B-70 bomber, the Dynasoar hypersonic glider, and the nuclear-powered airplane were rejected or delayed with increasing skill. Eisenhower's establishment of first-class analysis at a level that engaged the authority of both the president and the secretary of defense was a major positive consequence of *Sputnik*. [32]

The steps that Eisenhower took did not end public debate about the prospect of a dangerous gap. Most of those who joined in the Gaither report believed that the New Look defense program had been too small from the beginning. They suspected that one way or another the Soviet leadership would steal a strategic march if it could. As it happened a principal draftsman of the Gaither report was the same Paul Nitze who had described the monolithic Soviet threat with great force in 1950, in *NSC 68*. And while Eisenhower responded to the immediate issue of protecting the American strategic forces from surprise attack, the advocates of a larger effort were unsatisfied.

Their concerns were reinforced by the American intelligence estimates of 1958 and 1959. No one observed any Soviet intercontinental missiles in these years, but the CIA continued to project the early prospect of such missiles in hundreds; air force estimates were regularly higher, and the intelligence assessments of the Strategic Air Command were higher still. These estimates were regularly shared with interested reporters and sympathetic senators, and such men as Jackson of Washington and Symington of Missouri became continuous campaigners on the danger of the missile gap.

In repeated columns and magazine articles, the Alsop brothers among others estimated the forthcoming Soviet missile advantage as very large, and their conclusions were suggested by such titles as "After Ike, the Deluge," and "Our Gamble with Destiny." Drawing their numbers from different intelligence estimators at different times, the president's critics predicted a Soviet advantage of hundreds, or of thousands, in a year or two or three. Senator Stuart Symington was perhaps the most extreme, offering a flat prediction in early 1959 that "in three years the Russians will prove to us that they have 3,000 ICBM's."[33]

The main source of these continuing reports of imminent Soviet superiority was the estimating done in one part or another of Eisenhower's government, and as far as I can tell, the president never offered, either to the public or to his principal officials, a careful explanation of his own skeptical view of the intelligence estimates. He did make his own private inquiry, through his trusted assistant Goodpaster, and he knew, as historians now understand and as senators did not, that in essence the gloomier predictions were based mainly on what estimators believed about what the Soviets would decide to do and not on activities of which anyone had significant direct evidence. The basic argument of the pessimists was that the Soviets had sharply decreased their production of long-range bombers, and that since as a matter of basic conviction they must be committed to the best possible strategic striking force, the turn away from intercontinental bombers implied their replacement by intercontinental missiles. Thus, the bomber gap wrongly predicted in earlier years was transmuted into the prediction of a missile gap. There was no hard evidence. More than that, Eisenhower knew from the limited but enormously valuable photographic production of the U-2 flights, each of which he personally authorized, that these photographs gave no confirmation of ICBM deployment. Because flights were few and the Soviet Union enormous, there was no way to cover all possible target areas. Still the most likely sites (along railroad lines) were checked, and to a man with a long experience of estimating the enemy, the absence of any positive confirmation was significant. Eisenhower, in short, had good reason to believe that the gloomier predictions of intelligence officers rested on nothing more than their own sense of what they would do if they were Soviet decision-makers. He felt confident in downgrading such estimates in his own mind. In his memoirs he claimed that the U-2 "provided proof" that the "missile gap" and the earlier "bomber gap" were "nothing more than imaginative creations of irresponsibility." The word *proof* is too strong, in that the "missile gap" was mainly a prediction of what would happen soon, not a claim that it had already happened; moreover believers in the danger could and did claim that Soviet missiles might well escape the limited coverage of the U-2 cameras. There was also an asserted risk of successful camouflage. No intelligence adviser thought that the U-2 photography was positive proof of the absence of missiles, but it was certainly an important reinforcement of Eisenhower's own confidence on the matter. The fact that excellent photographs of the most interesting stretches of the Soviet Union showed nothing could not but have a generally comforting effect.[34]

In recognition of this comforting effect the possibility of a public announcement of this U-2 capability was put forward by Dulles early in the post-*Sputnik* period. But on this point Eisenhower never hesitated. He knew that the Soviet government was well aware of the U-2 flights—it had repeatedly protested them in private. But he also knew that a public boast about them could have destructive international diplomatic and political results. He kept the secret, and for this decision he was greatly admired not only by the operators of the program, but by such men as Killian.[35]

Beyond the specific and relatively clear-cut case of the U-2, Eisenhower was also held back by what had become a tradition of secrecy about nuclear capabilities. We have seen how Franklin Roosevelt treated the very existence of the project as a secret, for excellent reasons at first and by unexamined habit in later years. We have seen how for Harry Truman the inherited secret acquired special importance when he learned in early 1947 that in fact he had no ready bombs at all; *that* gap was a real secret, well worth keeping. From then on questions of numbers and capabilities were treated with the greatest reserve, and adjectives took the place of quantities in public discussion. Eisenhower never challenged this deeply rooted convention, and he therefore never considered sharing with the public in detail his own conviction that the only serious question about American nuclear capabilities, by 1957, was how far they might be excessive.

A powerful reinforcement to reticence was Eisenhower's own concept of the role and responsibility of the commander in chief in the field of nuclear weapons. Each of the presidents of the nuclear age has been aware of his final and lonely obligation here, but each in his own way. Eisenhower's way was that of a man already habituated to the role and responsibility of senior military command. He had been both planner and commander, and he had been listening to intelligence officers and technical assessors for decades. He knew from both ends the difference between planning and deciding. He had no reason to suppose that there was anyone in Washington whose final judgment he should prefer to his own, and in any case making the judgment was his job. He also believed that he had a right to expect the confidence of his countrymen. Eisenhower was modest in other ways, and indeed much of his first public discussion after *Sputnik* was devoted to his respect for the advice of persons with a scientific and technical competence he never claimed. As he explained it, his satellite program was the one scientists had recommended. His estimate of the scientific meaning of *Sputnik* was based on what such advisers had told him. His estimate of what the Soviet success implied was in the first instance that we must attend to the quality of our scientific education and our scientific research. But on military matters he could give assurances on his own authority, and he believed himself entitled to trust. Most of the time his expression of this view was careful and moderate, but in

January 1960 a journalist suggested that there might be partisanship in the debate, and Eisenhower reacted with a sharp expression of his own feeling:

> I don't take it very kindly—the implied accusation that I am dealing with the whole matter of defense on a partisan basis.
>
> First of all, I don't have to be partisan; and, second, I want to tell you this: I've spent my life in this, and I know more about it than almost anybody, I think, that is in the country, because I have given my life to it, and on a basis of doing what is good for the Government and for the country.[36]

So Eisenhower's reassurances, until very late in the game, were general and personal, not detailed and comprehensive. He regularly gave lists of the kinds of forces assigned to the strategic mission and assurances of general American superiority, but he never offered a specific and detailed account of the strategic nuclear balance as he himself understood it in his own mind. Nor did he spell out his own reasons for rejecting the intelligence estimates of Soviet capabilities and intentions. Because of these omissions, he soon found himself in an essentially defensive position in the public debate. It will help to consider more closely what he could have said.

He could have discussed directly and in detail the existing strategic deterrent forces of the United States. Whether or not there was a prospective gap in the numbers of intercontinental ballistic missiles on each side, there was no gap whatever in strategic deterrence, because there were United States forces of ample variety and strength which no Soviet force in sight could hope to eliminate in a single blow. The point was made plainly and publicly (though without the reinforcement of accurate numbers) by Admiral Arleigh Burke, Eisenhower's chief of naval operations, in early 1959:

> It is not saber-rattling to say that the Soviets know that the United States has the ability, right now, in being, to destroy the Soviet Union. We can do it in several ways, and several times over with our powerful Strategic Air Command of the United States Air Force, with carrier striking forces of the United States Navy, with tactical air, and with Intermediate Range Ballistic Missiles which are now being installed in certain European sites.[37]

When Burke left out the numbers here, he was following the existing rules, but Eisenhower himself could have changed those rules by his own single-handed decision. He could have made it clear that the hundreds of carrier aircraft were by themselves alone a daunting nuclear deterrent and that the extraordinary difficulty of a simultaneous salvo attack by liquid-fueled missiles against even a part of the forces

Burke described was one which any rational Soviet leader must respect. It was a point he fully understood. So Eisenhower could have said what Burke did: "The Soviet Union can not prevent our retaliatory strikes should the Kremlin leaders decide to initiate general nuclear war," and "therefore, the probability of general nuclear war is remote, for it would be suicide for the USSR." This basic assessment could have been explained right at the start of the controversy, and having presented it and repeated it as often as necessary, Eisenhower could then have gone ahead to deal still more directly with the problem of preventing surprise attack. He could have explained that he had made this question his own first concern as early as 1954 and that as a consequence forces with a new kind of invulnerability—Polaris and Minuteman missiles—were already far advanced in development. He could then have emphasized his own alertness to the importance both of adequate early warning and of maintaining alert elements in the massive bomber forces of SAC. In short, he could have accepted the responsibility of *showing,* and not simply asserting, the quality of his own performance.[38]

He could then have gone on to reinforce his argument by setting out once again the basic analysis of Soviet motives that he had offered in his first term. Unfriendly as the men in the Kremlin might be, their own survival was their own first interest—"They want to be there." Exactly on this point Eisenhower's assessment of the Soviet leadership differed decisively from the habitual mindsets of intelligence officers assessing the Soviet threat and of many strategic analysts assessing the stability of the nuclear balance. He was right and they were wrong, but in the years of the missile-gap debate he simply did not make his case. Even in meetings of the National Security Council he seems to have preferred not to press his own view. Kistiakowsky's diary reports a characteristically brief and sharp reaction in November 1959 to a gloomy assessment of the growing threat from the USSR: "The President quite suddenly stopped his usual doodling, raised a hand, and said: 'Please enter a minority report of one.' "[39]

Eisenhower seems never to have understood fully the shock that *Sputnik* administered to his countrymen, and while part of the problem was his failure to recognize promptly the dramatic impact of the first man-made satellite, I think there was a deeper reason. What *Sputnik* did, reinforced by the Gaither report and erroneous intelligence assessments, was to present the American public with a prospect of Soviet thermonuclear power and possible advantage that seemed genuinely new. But it was not new to Eisenhower. He had been through this shock years before. The prospect that American superiority would inevitably be eroded by growing Soviet capability had been a commonplace of the strategic dialogue inside the administration since 1954, and Eisenhower himself had been exposed at regular intervals to the terrible war games that drove the point home. He had also looked hard at what was needed to ensure continued deterrence and had made the necessary decisions. He had thus been through both the pain of the challenge and the hard work of the response, and he really did not understand that the reactions of his countrymen in 1958 were much more than a response to partisan propaganda, or that those whom he saw as merely partisan were often themselves genuinely—if wrongly—fearful. Because of his insufficient understanding of those fears, he responded in ways that made them grow. To his critics he seemed not to be taking the danger at its true value.

It is true that much of the difficulty that Eisenhower faced in the missile-gap debate was the consequence of real uncertainties in the available intelligence. When that debate began there was no one in the American government who could know for certain what the Soviets would produce in the coming years. The *possibility* of a considerable future Soviet numerical advantage in strategic missile deployments was real, and nothing that Eisenhower could have said—not even the direct account of U-2 photographic results which he refused to give—could have shown beyond argument that there was not going to be a gap of that sort. So an important part of what he had to contend with here was a fear of what *could happen.* It was what was *not* known that allowed the intelligence estimators and the Gaither panel's members to feed their fears. The missile gap, in this sense, is the largest example of the self-defeating effect of successful Soviet secrecy: The absence of solid information on Soviet activities greatly contributed to the creation of effective political pressure for new American deployments.

But it is too simple to blame the darkness here. The underlying and compelling argument, which Eisenhower fully understood and never fully explained, was that even if this possible missile gap should become real—even if the Soviet Union should develop a lead of several hundred missiles—there would be no increased risk of surprise attack, because it would still be impossible to make an attack so complete and sudden as to prevent a devastating reply. Survivable American forces would still present a wholly inescapable risk of wholly unacceptable retaliation, and the Soviet leaders would still be men who simply would not take such risks in the absence of immediate and catastrophic danger to themselves. I find it a large missed opportunity for leadership that the man with the rank, the record, and the personal understanding to make this argument fully and persuasively appears to have made it, as far as the record now shows, only to himself.

A more specific failure was the lack of effective control over the way in which the assessments of the intelligence community were presented to Congress over the years 1958–60. The most conspicuous and costly example of this failure came in the early months of 1960 when with the help of U-2 photography all the intelligence services sharply reduced their earlier estimates of what the Soviets would deploy, and when. Even the air force came down. The national intelligence estimate, which was essentially the CIA position, now predicted 35 Soviet missiles for mid-1960, and 140–200 for mid-1961. George Kistiakowsky, who was more worried about the Soviet missile threat than Eisenhower, wrote in his diary when he heard these estimates: "The missile gap doesn't look to be very serious." He was entirely right, in that missile forces of these sizes on these dates would have given no prospect whatever of a successful Soviet surprise attack against the American forces and defenses to be deployed by those dates. Yet he was also skeptical, as his parenthetical comment showed: "(I hope this estimate is not a political effort to cut down on trouble with Congress.)"[40]

When the administration set out to explain its new estimates, it made a series of blunders that fed the suspicions of senators much more skeptical than Kistiakowsky. The most serious mistake was made by the senior administration witness, Secretary of Defense Gates, who seemed to explain the new estimates as the result of a shift from predicting what the Russians could do if they chose to a prediction of what their "intentions" were. Gates did not mean what he seemed to say. As he eventually explained, what he really meant was that improved information made it possible to know more accurately what the Russians were in fact doing, and thus to make better estimates of what they would do next. But his explanation never fully caught up with the damage done by his initial statement. He made it sound as if the administration had simply changed its base of estimation from Soviet capabilities—what they could do if they chose—to Soviet intentions—what they would decide to do. Such a shift was bound to look like dangerous and muddle-headed trickery to men who thought it absolutely essential to assume the worst possible Soviet intentions and to judge the future balance only by what the Soviets were capable of doing.[41]

The suspicions aroused by these clumsy and mistaken references to intentions were sharpened when the commanding general of the Strategic Air Command, General Thomas Power, warned of an imminent Soviet capability to mount a missile attack that "could virtually wipe out our entire nuclear strike capability within a span of thirty minutes." The situation was further confused by Allen Dulles, director of the CIA, who not only seemed to defend estimates based on "intentions," but chose to submit estimates of his own that had not been shared with other witnesses.[42]

At a time when the real situation was favorable, when the intelligence estimates that had done so much to create the "missile gap" were dramatically lower because of improved information, and when any serious comparative assessment would have shown no present or future danger of a gap in strategic deterrence, the sloppy performance of Eisenhower's subordinates allowed his critics to have a field day. While none of these errors was specifically predictable, there is no record that the president himself took active steps to prevent them, or to rebuke those who committed them, or even to get matters quickly straightened out. The absence of any strong response from the president suggests a lack of effective concern with the handling of public statements by members of his administration on a matter of fundamental national importance in which his own final responsibility for public explanation was clear. The inescapable conclusion is that Eisenhower cared much more about what he himself thought of the intelligence reports than he did about what the country was told by others.

Yet this 1960 revival of controversy did at last persuade Eisenhower to make a stronger and more comprehensive statement on American strategic strength than he had ever made before. On February 22 he finally gave an account of the varied American forces almost as clear and strong as the one that Burke had offered a year earlier, and he was able to add that the first invulnerable Polaris submarine would soon be at sea. But he still left out any direct attention to the current issue of intelligence assessment. He never himself attempted to explain what Gates really meant, and he never directly refuted General Power, saying only that "too many of these generals have all sorts of ideas." The moderation of this reply was deliberate. He had told his staff earlier on the same day that he would "dismiss General Power's statement as unimportant."[43]

In terms of the choices that were actually made while he was president, Eisenhower, in the main, had his way, and that was what mattered most to him. Pressures from the Gaither panel and its supporters in the press and the Senate did not overcome his own insistence on the tight limitation of defense budgets. Increased effort was successfully limited to the cases he himself found persuasive: better warning, better capacity for aircraft dispersion and alert, greater speed but not larger programs in the deployment of missiles, not new airplanes (not one cent for the B-70 if he could help it), not new conventional forces, and no abandonment of the basic priorities of the New Look.[44]

Eisenhower also successfully prevented the missile-gap debate from spilling over into other major efforts of his second term, such as the resistance to Soviet pressure on Berlin and the effort to get an agreement ending nuclear tests. There is little evidence that the course of events on these matters was affected by any view that the Americans were weak or threatened by surprise attack. The missile-gap debate was narrow and its resonance limited.

Even in domestic political terms, the immediate effect of the debate was modest. Three Democratic senators who sought the presidency in 1960 made an issue of the gap—Lyndon Johnson, Stuart Symington, and John F. Kennedy.[45] In the final contest between Nixon and Kennedy, direct discussion of this specific issue was slight. When in its last days the election became a cliff-hanger, the only foreign policy issue that seemed to help Kennedy was the general claim that America had been losing prestige in the world. Every time he opened a specific attack, as on policy toward Cuba or the offshore islands, he wound up on the defensive. At this decisive stage he made only a single reference, in one sentence, to the "missile gap." It became entirely clear as the campaign ended that the most respected voice in the country on foreign issues still belonged to Eisenhower. What helped Kennedy most was no single foreign issue, but his effective showing against Nixon in debate. I cannot improve on the analysis of Irving Brandt, that insofar as the election was won on international questions, what was decisive was the following syllogism:

NIXON: I can handle Khrushchev.
TELEVISION VERDICT: Kennedy can handle Nixon.
CONCLUSION: Kennedy can handle Khrushchev.[46]

In terms of what actually happened, Eisenhower won the missile-gap debate, but his way of winning had costs. It was entirely unnecessary, for example, to have begun by pooh-poohing *Sputnik.* It was a sign of weakness, not strength, for Eisenhower's chief assistant Sherman Adams to say that the administration had no interest in getting "a high score in an outer space basketball game." Sensible people knew from their own reactions that the matter had the kind of impact which Killian records. Adams's comment was not an accident; it reflected a presidential desire to "play down the whole thing," not a desire to meet its impact with concrete and explicit reassurances. A similar defense by belittlement was Eisenhower's response, both publicly and privately, to the Gaither report, and the consequence was to stir the men who had worked on the report to greater public efforts. Eisenhower's response simply confirmed the conclusion they had reached during their studies, "that the top echelons of the government did not fully appreciate the extent of the Soviet threat as it was described by the Pentagon and the CIA."[47]

The administration's defense of tight budget limits, and its claim that everything was all right, became such fixed positions that even good and reassuring steps had to be taken quietly. Thus in early 1960 Herbert York found further ways of reinforcing the defense against any possible surprise attack by speeding up both Polaris production and the deployment of a second missile-warning installation. He promptly persuaded both the secretary of defense and Kistiakowsky, and the changes were readily accepted throughout the administration. Those changes had to be made, however, not by a public request for a modest new appropriation, but by a quiet internal reprogramming of defense funds. General Wilton Persons, successor to Sherman Adams, explained to Kistiakowsky that "the administration has gone so firmly on the record that we had enough deterrent that a request at this time would be a political catastrophe." If the president had established himself from the start of the debate as a man who had put the prevention of surprise attack at the head of his own agenda since 1954, as a man who had insisted on top priority for strategic missiles since the Killian report of 1955, and as the alert and well-staffed assessor of each new opportunity for improvement, then the recommendation that York made could have been publicized and not hidden, as one more proof of alertness and success. It would then be only a marginal irony that these prudent changes were stimulated by worst-case analysis, in York's office, of just the sort that had stirred the critics in the first place. York told Kistiakowsky that he was brought to his recommendation because "studies in his office indicate that if one is a pessimist and allows the Soviets the maximum capability that the national intelligence estimates suggest, in mid-1961 we will pass through a critical period when they may be able to destroy virtually all our retaliatory forces by a perfectly coordinated surprise attack." It is hard to reconcile this assessment with Arleigh Burke's.[48]

The fact that the administration remained on the defensive had another and wider cost, one that persists in some measure even to our own day. It allowed intelligent men to argue that the condition of the strategic balance was "precarious," and also that the predictable missile gap would lead to "nuclear blackmail." The most notable expositors of these two mistaken propositions were Albert Wohlstetter and Henry Kissinger, each already an important participant in discussion of nuclear weapons policy.

Wohlstetter's argument was presented in *Foreign Affairs,* in January 1959, under the title "The Delicate Balance of Terror." To many it remains a classic. It presented in general terms to a general audience an argument that Wohlstetter had been making in official quarters for years—an argument initially developed from a careful analysis of the vulnerability of U.S. strategic air bases—that nuclear deterrence was no better than the capacity of nuclear forces to survive and reply after the strongest surprise attack an opponent might make. It was not the presentation of these important propositions, however, that gave the article its immediate impact. It was rather the assertion that the strategic balance "is in fact precarious." Wohlstetter did not directly attack the Eisenhower administration; his horrible examples of people who made strategic deterrence seem easier than reality were drawn from journalists and publicists. But if there had been on the public record at the time a thorough account of Eisenhower's own understanding of the matter and of his performance, Wohlstetter's article would necessarily have been very different, and much less frightening. Instead of referring, without evidence, to "our deep pre-sputnik sleep," Wohlstetter would have had to take account of the fact that primary emphasis on a survivable second-strike capability had been settled presidential policy for four years, that choices and priorities of great importance had been settled by that criterion—though this was not always the case within the Strategic Air Command, whose ill-protected bases had been Wohlstetter's initial concern—and that the specific responses of the administration both to *Sputnik* and to the Gaither report had been precisely the ones his own argument supported: the dispersion of vulnerable assets, the improvement of warning and alert, and the more rapid development of modern invulnerable forces like Polaris. More broadly, if Eisenhower had made his full position so clear that it could not be ignored in such an article, it would have been impossible for Wohlstetter to argue, more by assertion than by demonstration, that adequately deterrent second-strike forces would be "extremely difficult to achieve."[49]

Moreover, there were fundamental differences between Eisenhower's Russians and Wohlstetter's. Wohlstetter, a quantitative systems analyst, assumed an opponent quite ready to run the unpredictable risks of general surprise attack. Wohlstetter's Russians were not only inclined to accept nuclear warfare as a lesser evil in many kinds of crisis, but they were seen as coldly prepared for losses in tens of millions, as they had shown in World War II. As we have seen, these were not the Russians in Eisenhower's mind, nor did he think the worst of World War II remotely comparable to what was likely in a general thermonuclear exchange. But he never made his case in compelling terms to the country, and Wohlstetter's overstated argument was an uncontested success.

There were many fine passages in "The Delicate Balance of Terror": a sound assessment of unhelpful intermediate missiles like Thor and Jupiter, a prudent argument that careful analysis was required to distinguish good systems from bad ones in the face of military and industrial salesmanship (but no recognition that Killian and York, and Eisenhower too, were already at work on just this task), and an intelligent awareness of the roles of communication, accident, and technological change. Nonetheless in its basic expression of alarm it was wrong. The balance of terror was not delicate in 1959, but the man in the White House had not made that clear.[50]

The notion that nuclear advantage permits effective political pressure is one which we have already encountered, in the mind of James Byrnes in 1945, in Truman's incorrect recollections about Iran, at the edges of the offshore island crises, and in Eisenhower's own mind over ending the war in Korea. But no case is more interesting than that of the threatened "missile gap," and no one stated the risk more sharply than Henry Kissinger. The young Kissinger had won a notable reputation as a student of nuclear policy with the production in 1957 of his book, *Nuclear Weapons and Foreign Policy.* There he had especially recommended reliance on tactical nuclear weapons as an additional deterrent in the face of growing Soviet strategic strength. In 1961 in a second volume, *The Necessity for Choice,* he was less enthusiastic about tactical weapons, noting correctly that no one had found a way to use them that did not carry a great risk of escalation to general nuclear war. But what is more notable in this second volume is a new and intense concern with the prospect of Soviet nuclear blackmail, and for Kissinger what would permit such blackmail was the missile gap. He dismissed entirely the possibility that no such gap would appear: "The missile gap in the period 1961–1965 is now unavoidable." In his view many risks were thus created, but the most serious was that in this period "the vulnerability of our retaliatory force will create major opportunities for Soviet nuclear blackmail—even to the extent of threatening direct attacks on the United States."[51]

Eisenhower did not believe in nuclear blackmail. Once both sides had thermonuclear warheads that could be used in retaliation, he saw no way in which one side could credibly charge a price for *not* dropping the bomb. The use of the weapon in response to aggression he thought a very different matter, and as we shall see, he consciously chose to defend West Berlin in these years by exactly that kind of possibility. But while he had no high opinion of Soviet behavior or intentions, he never believed for a moment that the Soviet government would deliberately choose a nuclear war, and so he saw no need for any American president to be moved by Soviet nuclear blackmail. He recognized, in his later years, Khrushchev's inclination to brandish his bombs, and at least once, in the Lebanon crisis of 1958, he noted publicly that some might call this tactic "ballistic blackmail." But while he denounced the practice as dangerous, comparing it to a cry of "fire" in a crowded assembly, he went on to say firmly that "pressures such as these will never be successfully practiced against America . . ."[52]

Eisenhower did not expect a significant missile gap, and Kissinger accepted much gloomier estimates. But there are other and more important differences. Kissinger, like Wohlstetter, was disposed to believe that nuclear advantage would translate into usable political pressure; the "weaker" side would find it prudent to give in to the "stronger." But Eisenhower believed that no marginal advantage would translate the shared catastrophe into victory for anyone; he also believed the Soviet leaders understood this too—this was the shared understanding that had been registered at Geneva in 1955—so he thought any threat could safely be treated as a bluff. Just as Eisenhower understood the operational uncertainties that Khrushchev must face and that Wohlstetter neglected, so he understood the cautious realism that pervaded the Kremlin and that Kissinger neglected when he talked of blackmail. But again, Eisenhower did not adequately explain himself. His failure to give a full explanation of his disbelief in a prospective missile gap was reinforced in its unfortunate effects not only by his failure to spell out publicly his view of the deterrent strength of the forces on both sides, but also by his failure to press on his countrymen the understanding he had expressed so clearly back in 1954, that in matters of this magnitude Soviet leaders would predictably be most cautious. So while he did sensible things and resisted foolish ones, he allowed the ensuing public argument to be led by men who did not understand matters as well as he did.

In this same episode there is a further difference between Eisenhower and the Gaither panel, not on the likelihood of nuclear blackmail by the Kremlin, but on the parallel question of the political utility of *American* superiority. While the primary emphasis of the Gaither report was on future dangers, it did identify one significant window of American opportunity in the period immediately ahead, "starting now and ending 1959/early 1960." In this period, while Soviet bombers were few and Soviet missiles not yet deployed, the United States could have clear strategic superiority if it would only ensure for the Strategic Air Command "an effective 'alert' status." Such a status, protecting the American second-strike capability, would insure that "the U.S. will be able to carry out a decisive attack even if surprised." That capability in turn could be used for political advantage: *"This could be the best time to negotiate from strength, since the U.S. military position vis-a-vis Russia might never be as strong again* [original emphasis]."[53]

The Gaither panel was telling Eisenhower to use his current nuclear strength to get a political settlement, and while it would certainly not have occurred to its members to think that they were recommending nuclear blackmail, a Soviet reader of these sentences would probably have reached that conclusion. What value would a present American nuclear advantage have, in any effort to get an early and general political settlement, unless Soviet negotiators believed that if they did not settle on American terms, the nuclear advantage might be used?

Eisenhower paid no attention to this suggestion, and it played no significant part in the public debate that followed. It deserves our attention here as the last known appearance of a responsible recommendation in an American governmental document for this kind of political use of nuclear superiority. It is a recommendation with ancestry. A similar but much more modest recommendation had appeared in the Killian report of 1955—the same transient military advantage had been predicted for approximately the same period, and it had been suggested that there should be "an intensive study" of the "diplomatic and political policies" that might turn this situation "to our best advantage."[54] Still earlier the Eisenhower administration had itself examined this position and found no good way to win political advantage from nuclear superiority. In September 1953 Dulles had suggested "a spectacular effort to relax world tensions," and had urged speed because "we will be speaking from strength rather than weakness"; part of that present strength was in the nuclear balance. Eisenhower noted beside this passage, "This, I think, is important!" But only Atoms for Peace emerged in that season, and a year later, when Dulles commented on military proposals for a "more dynamic and aggressive policy," he had changed his view. By now he believed that while such a policy "might result in the disintegration of the Soviet bloc," it would "almost certainly cause the disintegration of the free world bloc," while it would leave untouched "the terrible problem and threat of an unimpaired nuclear capability in the USSR itself." So these repeated suggestions had no operational effect. They serve only to remind us that James Byrnes was not the last American to jump to the conclusion that nuclear advantage is a ready instrument of political pressure.[55]

The Missile-Gap Myth Is Exploded

The definitive demonstration that there never was a missile gap did not come until 1960–61, when U.S. satellite reconnaissance persuasively demonstrated the absence of any large Soviet deployment. As it turned out in the end, only four of the intercontinental missiles of the first Soviet generation were ever deployed. By the end of his term Eisenhower had learned enough from the first satellite to be able to say with confidence in his last State of the Union Message that the "missile gap" showed every sign of being a fiction. The demonstration became conclusive in the summer of 1961, when new satellite photographs persuaded not only the new president and his secretary of defense, but also to the intelligence estimators of all three services. The "missile gap" as a public threat began with *Sputnik* and ended with American satellite reconnaissance. Intelligence obtained from satellites has continued, ever since, to play a decisive role in permitting reliable assessment of Soviet strategic strength.[56]

Probably the fact that the Soviets were the first to fly satellites, and also the first to use them for photography, helped to establish for this method of reconnaissance a level of international acceptance that was never achieved, to put it mildly, by the U-2 airplane. In a circuitous way, the "missile gap" itself contributed marginally to this happy result. The need for better information on the likeliest site for Soviet ICBMs, in April 1960, was the largest single cause of the CIA request for one more U-2 flight before the forthcoming Paris summit. Eisenhower reluctantly granted this request.[57]

When the plane was shot down, there followed a series of American public statements which Khrushchev delighted in proving false—he had the wreckage of the plane, the captured pilot, and the film to make his case. Eisenhower then found it necessary, belatedly, to announce his own responsibility, and for reasons of his own, probably related to the internal politics of the Soviet leadership, Khrushchev decided to break up the Paris summit of 1960 on this issue.[58] But before that happened de Gaulle engaged him on the general question of reconnaissance, and drew a most interesting response. Observing that the U-2 incident "arose from the state of international tension and the sharp differences which exist between the two camps," de Gaulle remarked that "overflights, whether by aircraft, missile or satellite, are of course a serious matter and they increase tensions." He then pointed out that "there is now a Soviet satellite which is going through the skies around the world and it crosses through French skies 18 times a day, of course higher than a plane." He noted that "In reality these satellites can take photographs and tomorrow they may be in a position to launch terrible destruction."[59]

Khrushchev flatly rejected this effort to establish a similarity between satellites and aircraft, and in his eagerness to separate the two he asserted that the Soviet Union had no objection to satellite photography. The Americans, he noted, had put up a satellite that photographed the Soviet Union, and he dismissed the matter as unimportant: "Let them take as many pictures as they want."[60]

In the tumult of the broken summit, and in his angry frustration over the messy American handling of the U-2 affair, Eisenhower was in no mood to rejoice over this important exchange, which he mentions only briefly in his memoirs.[61] But what Khrushchev did here, in real terms, was to accept the very Open Skies that Eisenhower had pressed upon him with no success at all only five years earlier. If part of this acceptance came from his pride in *Sputnik,* and part also from the fact that in 1960 no one anywhere knew how to shoot down a satellite, part of it also must have come from his desire to focus on the unpleasant character of aircraft intrusion. In the three years that followed, the Soviet government frequently denounced space reconnaissance, but by 1963 its own space reconnaissance was an important asset, and it returned to Khrushchev's initial position of tolerance. Insofar as the missile gap's possible existence led to the offending flight that produced these first reactions, it may have had at least one good result. The strategic peace of the following decades owes a great deal to the satellites whose legitimacy began to be accepted in Paris in the spring of 1960.

The Kennedy-McNamara Choices

John Kennedy came to the White House convinced that there was urgent need for a strengthened defense effort. He and those he appointed, both in the Defense Department and at the National Security Council, were opponents of the New Look. I was one of this group, as his special assistant for national security affairs—a title that originated in the Eisenhower administration. We believed that conventional military strength had been badly neglected in the Eisenhower years. Kennedy himself had been strongly influenced by army leaders like Maxwell Taylor and James Gavin, and he also shared the general view of veterans of the Truman administration that conventional strength was crucial to the effective defense of Europe in a way that Eisenhower and Dulles had not recognized. Improved conventional readiness was a first clear objective, and nothing that Kennedy and Secretary of Defense Robert McNamara learned in office ever changed that purpose.

It was different on the nuclear front. McNamara discovered within weeks that there was no discernible missile gap, but Kennedy was reluctant to admit so quickly that his campaign attack had been mistaken, and the administration waited until later in the year, when new satellite intelligence became compelling to every service, before it buried the missile gap in public. Kennedy and McNamara accelerated the production of the new weapons that they judged best—Polaris and Minuteman—while holding back others, most importantly the B-70 bomber, a high-altitude aircraft whose vulnerability to modern antiaircraft missiles made it a bad buy. By 1962 the combined decisions of Eisenhower and Kennedy had shaped the three-legged force that became famous as the triad, and as Herbert York has pointed out, the eventual force of 1,000 Minutemen, 656 Polaris missiles on submarines, and some 500 bombers was about the same as what Eisenhower had planned.[62]

The choices that Kennedy and McNamara concerted produced a force that met the political requirement of congressional approval when Congress as a whole would have liked more than the president asked for. The hardest political choice was not the acceleration of missile deployment but the refusal to build the B-70 bomber, to which both the air force and its congressional friends were deeply committed. They made a last-ditch effort to keep the plane alive in a reconnaissance model, and Kennedy was able to hold the line on that front only because Carl Vinson of Georgia, chairman of the House Armed Services Committee, accepted a compromise that promised further study in place of a proposed congressional order to proceed.[63]

This compromise, which emerged from a famous stroll that the two men took in the Rose Garden of the White House, rested on Kennedy's declaration that if necessary he would simply refuse to spend any money appropriated for this plan. In effect the most powerful man in the House decided that a direct challenge to the president on this narrow issue would be both unseemly and unsuccessful. In the main the B-70 was killed by timely recognition of its own flawed design, but the politically decisive recognition of this weakness came from an alert and active executive branch. A similar fate befell the still less persuasive plan for nuclear-powered aircraft in these years.

These notable cases deserve attention primarily not because they were bad designs whose weaknesses were understood before deployment, but rather because they underline the reality that strategic procurement in the age of technological revolution is not usually a question of more or less, or new and old—it is a question of good or not so good, where quality must be measured by many different tests. By the decisive criterion of the time—cost-effective, second-strike capacity for effective reply to any large-scale aggression—the strategic weapons developed under Eisenhower and preferred under Kennedy were excellent. The buildup that Eisenhower had begun and the relatively easy choices that McNamara recommended and Kennedy approved in 1961 and 1962 allowed the Kennedy administration to confront important crises with confidence that whatever difficulties they might present, there was no prospect whatever that the United States would be seen as an underdog in its strategic nuclear strength.

One big change was secret at the time and much misrepresented later. Kennedy's first year saw a sharp reduction in the total megatonnage of the U.S. stockpile, and that reduction has often been cited by officials of the Reagan administration as a demonstration of moderation in the management of the American deterrent. What actually happened is that the air force correctly decided that the strategic effectiveness of its large bombers would be increased by loading each aircraft not with a single bomb of some fifteen or twenty megatons, but with four bombs of about one megaton each. Each plane could then strike four times as many targets, and the militarily wasteful overkill of a single enormous explosion—much too big for any target but Moscow—would be avoided. Total megatonnage was reduced by some 9,400 megatons, almost 50 percent, and total capacity for destruction was multiplied. I do not remember knowing of this change at the time, and I think it is important primarily because it illustrates the general proposition that strategic striking power depends much more on numbers of weapons than on total megatonnage. The later misuse of this shift is also a remarkably clear example of the way the Weinberger Pentagon engaged in strategic flimflam; the reduction in megatonnage it so proudly cited was the incidental consequence of a military decision to multiply the real destructive power of the bomber force.[64]

Kennedy's clarity of choice among new systems was not matched, in 1961, by clarity in the assessment of strategic doctrine. The new administration was aware of the problem presented by the rigidity of the Single Integrated Operational Plan (SIOP), a matter on which I reported to Kennedy very early, and it was generally agreed that it needed attention. However it soon became clear to McNamara that it would be much easier to control strategic procurement if he did not at the same time challenge SAC's targeting doctrines. Nor was there any enthusiasm among us for approaching the matter through a revision of the document on basic national security policy that we inherited—a document with a modified but persistent emphasis on the use of nuclear weapons. Neither Kennedy nor his principal cabinet advisers, Rusk and McNamara, believed in general policy papers as a way of producing specific results, and although valiant efforts were made by planners under the leadership of Walt Rostow, the eventual decision was not to have any such paper. McNamara presently achieved some alterations in the guidance governing the SIOP, but the options prepared by strategic planners remained very large, and the basic policy of air commanders remained one of seeking both capabilities and plans sufficient for strategic victory. Kennedy's own attention remained focused on the simple basic imperative of avoiding nuclear war. In the summer of 1961 he went through a formal briefing on the net assessment of a general nuclear war between the two superpowers, and he expressed his own reaction to Dean Rusk as they walked from the Cabinet Room to the Oval Office for a private meeting on other subjects: "And we call ourselves the human race."[65]

In 1961 the most immediate hope for the reduction of nuclear danger lay in a nuclear test ban. Kennedy had believed in stopping tests from the time of Stevenson's proposal of 1956, and he believed that an effort more energetic than Eisenhower's was needed. Thus the negotiations on a comprehensive test ban were renewed in Geneva in March, but they made no progress. The Americans got some credit in world opinion for their new energy, and by contrast the Russians were seen to be dragging their feet. Unfortunately this foot-dragging turned out to have an explanation deeper than any specific bargaining point; in September the Soviets began a series of tests which included one monstrous explosion of fifty-seven megatons. Technically Moscow had not unilaterally broken the moratorium, because the French had already been testing and because the Eisenhower administration had also asserted American freedom to test. But the Soviet tests were a large and unpleasant surprise. Kennedy looked carefully at his own options and decided that the Americans must test in turn; the reasons were as much political as they were technical. The prospect of an early test ban faded.[66]

Even less successful was another early Kennedy initiative, an effort to launch a national program of civil defense. There were political considerations here too. The case of civil defense was championed by the Republican Nelson Rockefeller, who seemed then to be Kennedy's most likely challenger in the election of 1964. But more deeply Kennedy simply believed that nuclear danger was real and that if there should be nuclear war, a national shelter program could save tens of millions of Americans. It seemed to him a prudent form of insurance.

The civil defense proposal was put forward with inadequate preparation, and Kennedy's most important statement about it was unwisely placed in a speech about decisions on the Berlin crisis, with the result that it was wrongly perceived as a means of response to imminent danger. There were panicky and uninformed reactions, both from those who wanted immediate shelter and those to whom all civil defense was repugnant. A sensible program was eventually developed— aimed not at safety for every home, but at the encouragement of community shelters—but the program never won public support, and American civil defense has been rudimentary ever since.

His failure with civil defense remained troubling to Kennedy. He had clearly been wrong about the politics, but that was unimportant. Neither his support for the program nor Rockefeller's had any political effect. Nor was he much troubled by the initial imperfection of our supporting staff work; better work produced a better program. What bothered him, as indeed it still bothers me, is that in a world of real nuclear danger civil defense is indeed a prudent form of insurance, perceived as such in peaceable countries like Switzerland and Sweden, where truly national programs are accepted as a matter of course. As a political man Kennedy could recognize and respect public indifference, and while he did not back off from civil defense, he did stop pressing for it. But I agree with Theodore Sorensen that his enduring opinion was just as he stated it in a press conference on July 5, 1962: "These matters have some rhythm. When the skies are clear, no one is interested. Suddenly then, when the clouds come . . . then everyone wants to find out why more hasn't been done about it. . . . I think the time to do it is now."[67]

That is what I thought too and I still think so. Civil defense is not a reinforcement of deterrence; it is not a tool of crisis management; it certainly does not demonstrate will or confer superiority. But neither is it belligerent or provocative. It is what Kennedy called it—insurance, imperfect but relatively cheap—a way of mitigating a possible disaster, not a way of avoiding it or making it acceptable. The subject may be too dreadful for rational discussion. Perhaps the argument that you will want this if nuclear war ever happens may suggest that you want to be able to run larger risks of just such war. It is not really like life insurance because every individual already knows that he will die one day, so that life insurance is not an assertion about the long-run probability of death. The meaning of civil defense may not be the same for us as for the Swiss and the Swedes, because their governments are guarding against what their people know can never be the product of a Swiss or Swedish choice. But when our leaders talk of shelters, are they telling us that we are going to need them? What do they have up their sleeves, then? Why should we *plan* for what we *must* avoid?. Yet to talk with John Kennedy on this danger was to know that the reduction of nuclear danger was his highest single hope. Was he really wrong to recognize that the hope might fail and that then it would be good to have some shelter? My own conclusion is that he was right, but that the risk of public misunderstanding was grossly neglected by all of us.

These beginnings tell us much about John Kennedy, but not enough. Before he could reopen the quest for arms control or move toward reduction of superpower tension, he had to deal with two great crises: one over Berlin, which he shared with Eisenhower, and one over Cuba, which fell to him alone. What we do know from this early record is that this young president was not in doubt about his view of nuclear war. Twice, and from quite different political angles, he was asked about it in 1962. In July a Brazilian student asked him if Americans were not really "being prepared for war," through propaganda of all sorts. The answer was firm:

> . . . We have made it very clear that there is not going to be any winner of the next war. No one who is a rational man can possibly desire to see hostilities break out particularly between the major powers which are equipped with nuclear weapons. So your view of the United States in this regard is really inaccurate.[68]

Back in February he had been asked to comment on the charge of right-wing critics that his foreign policy was "based on a no-win policy in the Cold War." Here is the answer:

> Well, of course, every American whoever they may be, wants the United States to be secure and at peace and they want the cause of freedom around the world to prevail. Quite obviously that is our national objective. And what we are anxious to do, of course, is protect our national security, protect the freedom of the countries, permit what Thomas Jefferson called the disease of liberty to be

caught in areas which are now held by Communists, and some areas where people are imprisoned. We want to do that, of course, without having a nuclear war. Now, if someone thinks we should have a nuclear war in order to win, I can inform them that there will not be winners in the next nuclear war, if there is one, and this country and other countries will suffer very heavy blows. So that we have to proceed with responsibility and with care in an age where the human race can obliterate itself.[69]

VIII

Khrushchev, Berlin, and the West

FROM 1958 TO 1963, under the guiding hand of Nikita Khrushchev, there were more than four years of political tension over the future of Berlin. This long and intermittently acute crisis was closely related to the way in which the interested governments understood and misunderstood the politics of nuclear danger. It began in the time of Eisenhower and ended in that of Kennedy. While the courses followed by the two presidents were different, and while there was variety also in the flow and ebb of Soviet pressure, I believe this Berlin affair is best examined as a single phenomenon centrally defined by the purposes and choices of Khrushchev.

No one has made a larger contribution than Khrushchev to our understanding of what can and cannot be done with nuclear weapons. He played his largest and most dangerous role in 1962 on the improbable stage of Cuba, but there is a great deal to be learned from his less intense but longer attempt to rearrange the politics of Berlin and Germany by the interacting force of Soviet nuclear strength and what he hoped would be debilitating nuclear fear in the West. His four-year effort constitutes the most powerful demonstration yet recorded of the limited value of attempts at nuclear blackmail undertaken in the face of opponents with weapons, commitments, and will of their own. The Berlin crisis of 1958–63 does not display unbroken wisdom and foresight among Western statesmen, and their choices also offer lessons. But the greatest teacher—and fortunately also one of the best learners—in the crisis he began and ended was Khrushchev himself.

For more than a decade before 1958 Berlin was a place of constant political contest between East and West, and in the twenty-five years since 1963 this contest has continued, changing its shape in a most illuminating way as the 1970s began, and persisting to this day. The absence of any sharp crisis for a quarter of a century is striking, and it is certainly not what would have been predicted in 1963. We can learn a lot about nuclear reality by observing what happened in Berlin before and after Khrushchev's crisis. Yet his was the crisis in which there were real threats of war, and it is the best place to begin.

Khrushchev's Berlin crisis gives us what is otherwise missing in the nuclear age: a genuine nuclear confrontation in Europe. Governments were forced to ask themselves repeatedly what might make it necessary to fight, and in what measure and on what terms they must be prepared to use nuclear weapons. These questions are hardy perennials of theoretical analysis, political debate, and military planning. But there is a vast difference between a real crisis and an abstract analysis. We shall be able to look more clearly at European reality when we have first looked hard at the one major postwar European crisis that has had nuclear danger at its center. We will know something of what has in fact occurred when governments were required to think about these things in terms of real situations. What we shall see clearly is that they found the possibilities grim.

Outline of the History

Khrushchev's Berlin crisis began in the autumn of 1958, with his decision to assert that there must be a peace treaty between the wartime allies and Germany that would redefine the condition of West Berlin. If such a treaty were not accepted by the West within six months, the Soviet Union would make separate arrangements with East Germany and be free to see these new arrangements imposed on West Berlin, where the existing rights of the British, the French, and the Americans would have expired. The West would face in Berlin a surrounding adversary overwhelmingly superior in local strength, and could be forced to choose between the acceptance of East German authority and a resort to force.

Khrushchev hoped that the nuclear strength achieved by the Soviet Union in the 1950s would persuade the West that it must come to terms. In a sense he was trying to get concessions that would split the Atlantic alliance, and he was exploiting the new prestige of the apparent Soviet lead in missiles announced by *Sputnik*. In this way, the Berlin crisis of 1958–63 was a Soviet exercise in atomic diplomacy—an effort to use a new appearance of Soviet nuclear strength to force changes in the center of Europe. Both the atomic threat and the aim were made explicit in the first formal Soviet note of November 27, 1958. Characteristically, the threat was delivered only after a denunciation of the asserted threats of others:

> Methods of blackmail and reckless threats of force will be least of all appropriate in solving such a problem as the Berlin question. Such methods will not help solve a single question, but can only bring the situation to the danger point. But only madmen can go to the length of unleashing another world war over the preservation of privileges of occupiers in West Berlin. If such madmen should really appear, there is no doubt that strait jackets could be found for them.[1]

The political situation of Berlin, in 1958, remained in principle as it had been established by the agreements reached in World War II and the disagreements that almost immediately followed. Under the agreements, Berlin was a single city, occupied and administered by the victorious allies together, with troops of each—Russian, American, British, and French—occupying an assigned sector of the city, which lay far inside East Germany, 110 miles from West Germany. Because of the disagreements that were both a consequence and a partial cause of the cold war, Berlin had become operationally two cities. East Berlin, under Soviet control, had become essentially a part of Communist East Germany, while West Berlin remained part of the West, accustomed to democratic elections, holding itself to be part of the Federal Republic of Germany—West Germany—but protected, and ultimately ruled, by the governments of France, Great Britain, and the United States, each of which kept a few thousand troops in its sector of the city. Formally Berlin remained a single city, and access from one part to another remained largely open, both for Germans and for representatives of the occupying powers. But in political and military reality East Berlin was a part of the Soviet bloc, and West Berlin was an encircled outpost of the anti-Communist democratic world—an outpost whose importance to the West had been reinforced for all parties when the successful airlift of 1948–49 dramatically frustrated Stalin's land blockade.

The Western governments read Khrushchev's announcement of November 27 as a demand that there must be a new arrangement, either agreed or imposed. On the very day that the note was delivered the American response was firm: ". . . the United States will not acquiesce in a unilateral repudiation by the Soviet Union of its obligations and responsibilities formally agreed upon with Britain, France, and the United States in relation to Berlin. Neither will it enter into any agreement with the Soviet Union which, whatever the form, would have the end result of abandoning the people of West Berlin to hostile domination."[2]

There followed four years of intermittent tension, which did not end until after the successful resolution of the Cuban missile crisis of 1962, when it became plain that the Soviet Union would not press the question of Berlin to a final test of will. There were a few aftershocks even in 1963, notably in tests of allied determination by Soviet harassment of access on the Autobahn. The crisis had several phases, and each phase was begun and ended—like the crisis as a whole—primarily by decisions in Moscow.

Khrushchev's course was marked by alternate pressure and relaxation. The sense of urgency created by the six-month deadline of November 27 was eased in the spring of 1959 when the initial deadline was lifted and the two sides agreed to negotiate, first at the level of foreign ministers and later, at least prospectively, in a summit meeting. The foreign ministers' negotiations occupied nine weeks of the spring and summer, and were followed in September by Khrushchev's visit to the United States and his celebrated meeting with Eisenhower at Camp David. From that meeting emerged a carefully agreed but separately stated abandonment of any Soviet deadline, with an expectation of continued negotiations and a four-power summit meeting in Paris. But the friendly "spirit of Camp David" was soon replaced that winter by a renewal of Khrushchev's demands in increasingly vigorous speeches which stimulated increasingly firm reassertions of the wholly different American view of Berlin and indeed of Germany.

By the spring of 1960 the crisis had acquired a new sharpness, and preparations for the summit on both sides began to look like preparations for a disagreeable showdown. Matters were made worse for both sides after the American U-2 photographic intelligence airplane was shot down far inside the Soviet Union. When Eisenhower finally announced his personal responsibility for such overflights, Khrushchev reacted with demands that forced the quick adjournment of the Paris summit. There followed a period in which immediate tension was reduced by Khrushchev's announcement that he would await a new American administration; the climax of his crisis was accordingly deferred to 1961. That year began quietly, and Khrushchev delayed any heavy pressure for change in Berlin until his meeting with Kennedy in June at Vienna. Then he made up for lost time.

Khrushchev's long Vienna memorandum of June 4 reinstated an urgent demand for a satisfactory solution of the crisis. While it was couched in careful and superficially cooperative language, it once again insisted on an end to the three-power status of West Berlin. There followed a large-scale public campaign of Soviet pressure, including on June 15 a statement flatly imposing a new deadline for resolution of the problem: A peace treaty must be signed in 1961. Khrushchev had made the same demand privately in the Vienna talks. The Western response, especially from Washington, was energetic.

After six weeks of internal planning and debate, Kennedy made a major address announcing new defense measures and a reaffirmed commitment to the maintenance of American rights and obligations in West Berlin, "even in the face of force."[3]

Khrushchev's renewal of active pressure soon forced his own hand. The outward flow of refugees from East Germany through West Berlin, already much enlarged in earlier months, reached a new high level of fifty thousand a month in the first twelve days of August, propelled by a rising fear that the gates to freedom would soon be closed, a fear called *Torschlusspanik* (gate-closing panic). At a much lower level this hemorrhage of life and talent had been an original cause of Khrushchev's campaign; now his intensification of the crisis had made it unendurably large. The Communist powers could wait no longer. On August 13, shortly after midnight, they set up barriers between East and West Berlin which in a few days became the Berlin Wall. West Berlin remained free, but escape from the East was cut off. In the retrospective words of Willy Brandt, who was mayor of West Berlin at the time, "The Russians and the GDR [German Democratic Republic] accepted the political and psychological debacle of the wall's construction because they attached greater importance to an ability to consolidate the GDR behind it. Nobody can now deny that this opportunity has been exploited."[4]

The wall still marks the line of settlement of Khrushchev's Berlin crisis. There was tension after August 13. The renewed Soviet deadline for a peaceful settlement was not lifted until October, and continuing Soviet pressure both on routes of access and on remaining allied rights of entry into East Berlin led to a brief but dramatic confrontation of Soviet and American tanks on October 27. But there was no shooting, no attempt at any time to prevent effective Western support for the survival of West Berlin, and no separate peace treaty. In 1962 negotiations continued, and Berlin became quiet. In October 1962, the resolution of the Cuban missile crisis produced a cooling also of the crisis in Berlin. In a speech in East Berlin in January 1963, Khrushchev put his own end to the crisis, claiming, as he would in his memoirs, that the wall itself—the "border closing," in Moscow language—had produced a satisfactory result.

This bare-bones account of Khrushchev's Berlin crisis may make it look easy. It was not. The belief that it was intrinsically dangerous was never universal and seldom continuous, but it was strong and recurrent. Western leaders and their advisers differed on what the danger was and how to meet it, but I know of none who said there was no problem here. The danger may have been exaggerated, and I think in retrospect that it was, but it seemed great enough at the time.

What I remember of the Berlin crisis, with which I was directly engaged for two years in the Kennedy White House, is its persistence.

There was never a particular day on which it seemed likely that direct conflict would break out, but there was hardly a week in which there were not nagging questions about what would happen if . . . or what one or another of our allies would or would not support, or whether morale in West Berlin itself was holding up. Both the nature of the confrontation, centrally between Moscow and Washington, and the problem of defending an encircled city presented the question of resorting to nuclear weapons and Khrushchev himself was not hesitant in his reminders on this point. I remember the fall of 1961, in particular, as a time of sustained and draining anxiety, and I think Robert Lowell had it right when he wrote of that season,

> *All autumn, the chafe and jar*
> *of nuclear war;*
> *we have talked our extinction to death.* [5]

Khrushchev's Nuclear Threat

Judgment must come back to Khrushchev, to what he said and did and thought. We know all of what he said publicly, most of what he did, but not much, with any great certainty, of what he thought. But what I remember of 1961 and 1962 is that we thought it wise to take him seriously, as our predecessors had, and nothing has changed my mind.

We do not need to linger on the fascinating and difficult question of the reasons for Khrushchev's decision to try for change in Berlin. Many explanations have been offered: an ambition to break the Western alliance by humiliating the Americans, a desire to frustrate the military and political ambitions of the anti-Communist West Germans, a need to shore up his East German friends, a desire to be a better Communist than his Chinese critics, and so on and on. [6] For us it does not matter much just how these varied purposes were mixed in Khrushchev's mind. We need only to know that he wanted major change, and that in pursuit of such change he set loose a crisis that came to have a life and consequences of its own.

What is more interesting than these particular motives is the means that Khrushchev chose: nuclear threat. While many other pressures and incentives were deployed during this long crisis, the underlying threat was that the only escape from unendurable nuclear risk was for the West to accept change in West Berlin. Khrushchev had new and important nuclear strength in 1958, primarily in his rapidly growing force of missiles that could reach all of NATO Europe. He also had a seeming advantage in the race for intercontinental missiles. He made use of both, and it is probable that the existence of those changes in the strategic balance was itself a powerful element in his decision. A good Communist is expected to take advantage of changes in the correlation of forces, and there is no reason to doubt that when he began his Berlin crisis Khrushchev strongly believed that the nuclear position of the Soviet Union could somehow be translated into political gains. Whether he had carefully examined the problem of ways and means is much less certain.[7]

He started a crisis, but as the final result made clear, it was built on a bluff. As we look back we find all sorts of threats, along with intermittent expressions of goodwill, but we do not find a decisive challenge. For students of the technique called salami slicing—a process of little encroachments not easily resisted by democratic governments because each one in itself seems trivial—the Berlin crisis remains a treasure house of varied examples. But the action that requires either strong response or damaging acceptance does not exist here—with the signal exception of the wall. Except for the wall Khrushchev never took the actions he so often threatened and never came close to a forcible separation of the free people of West Berlin from their Western friends. What is decisive is that Khrushchev himself had no intention, at any point, of running a nuclear risk. He hoped that an asserted danger of nuclear disaster would make other governments responsive, but at the same time he was determined that no act of his should result in any risk of nuclear warfare that he could not himself control.

Without Soviet documents, this broad conclusion cannot be proved. Indeed not even documents would give proof in a matter so open to role playing. But what we do know is what did *not* happen. We know that at no point in the four years did anyone attempt to intrude on the life of West Berlin, or on the presence and authority of the Western allies, in such a way as to require either surrender or battle. There was salami slicing, but it was always far more slender than that, and it always stopped short of combat.

The most striking single thing that did not happen, indeed, was itself well short of open conflict: Khrushchev never signed his separate peace treaty with East Germany. Repeatedly and flatly, although not continuously, he insisted that this would happen. At the height of the crisis, in the summer of 1961, he was particularly blunt: A peace settlement in Europe must be attained before the end of the year; if others would not join, the Soviet and East German governments would sign a treaty alone, and control over Western access to Berlin would belong to the East Germans. The insistence on a separate peace treaty was a recurrent threat that its author never chose to execute.

Here we approach the central paradox of Khrushchev's effort. Western statesmen found the prospect of East German control over access routes highly unattractive, because they had no confidence in the good will or even the good sense of the East German government. Their best hope, in the event of such a shift of control, was that in fact final authority would remain in Soviet hands. But during his periods of heavy pressure, Khrushchev did not hesitate to attack this hope by pledges of his future support for the East Germans in any test of strength. "We shall sign the peace treaty and order our armed forces to administer a worthy rebuff to any aggressor if he dares to raise a hand against the Soviet Union or against our friends."[8] Any such encounter, as he never tired of pointing out, could only too easily lead to the nuclear war that no one wanted. But he himself was held back, at every moment of decisive choice, by this same danger. There was never anything about the possibility of igniting a Great Powers conflict that made Nikita Khrushchev ready to hand a lighted match to East Germany's Walter Ulbricht. Throughout his Berlin crisis Khrushchev was bedeviled by the intrinsic difficulty that the nuclear danger on which he relied for success was a danger that he knew he must himself stay clear of.

There is evidence of his understanding of this point in the curious manner of his threat making. Thus on August 11, 1961, in what may have been his most belligerent single appearance, a speech at a Soviet-Rumanian friendship meeting in Moscow, he began with threats and ended with reassurance: "We, of course, will sign a peace treaty with the German Democratic Republic." If in reply the imperialists should unleash a war, hundreds of millions might be killed. "They will force us, in self-defense, to deal crushing blows not only against the territories of the principal countries" but also against relative innocents; " . . . not only the orange groves of Italy but also the people who created them and who have exalted Italy's culture and arts" might perish, and also "cities, peoples, and historical monuments" of Greece. The speaker professed his sympathy for Italians and Greeks, and his threats against them were almost regretful in tone, but he was less sentimental about the West Germans, with their talk about reunification: "If such a war starts, there will very likely be no one and nothing in Germany to unite." But having made this sweeping set of threats, Khrushchev then circulated in the reception and talked cordially with Western diplomats, telling them there would be no war.[9]

This combination of threat and reassurance may well have seemed useful to Khrushchev barely twenty-four hours before the wall was to be started. Nothing could be a better psychological preparation of Western leaders for the acceptance of that next Soviet move than a firm reminder of general danger accompanied by a specific assurance that there need be no war. In the case of the wall, there was good reason for the Soviet government to expect no violent reply and good reason too for reinforcing that expectation by a combination of threat and reassurance. Yet wherever a strong Western reaction was more likely, the problem before Khrushchev remained precisely the same as the one he was trying to present to the West. In his own cooler way, Kennedy made the point at the end of August in a press conference.

> Q. Do you think, generally speaking, sir, that the crisis in Berlin has a better chance of being settled through negotiation, as you have suggested, rather than by force, as the Soviets have threatened upon occasion?
>
> THE PRESIDENT. Well, I don't see that there could be any solution—which would serve the world—to Berlin by force, and therefore I'm hopeful that all people involved will realize that in these days of massive forces available on every side that—for the future of the countries involved and for the human race—that we should attempt to work out a peaceful solution and that neither side should attempt to impose its will by brute force because in that case it would be unsuccessful and disaster would be the common result."[10]

Khrushchev understood the point, and indeed had understood it for years, as we know from a conversation between him and Averell Harriman in 1959. At the time, in a report published in *Life* magazine, Harriman chose to emphasize the firmness of Khrushchev's position.

> "Your generals," he said, "talk of maintaining your position in Berlin with force. That is bluff." Khrushchev spoke with angry emphasis. "If you send in tanks, they will burn and make no mistake about it. If you want war, you can have it, but remember it will be your war. Our rockets will fly automatically," he added, and his colleagues around the table chorused the word "automatically."[11]

What Harriman left out of this account, perhaps out of deference to a head of government, was what happened next. As he told it twenty years later to Glenn Seaborg:

> I laughed. He asked, "What are you laughing about?" I said, "What you're talking about would lead to war, and I know you're too sensible a man to want to have war." He stopped a minute and looked at me and he said, "You're right."[12]

Kennedy and the Wall

The wall that went up in Berlin in August 1961 has been an abomination ever since. In most countries most of the time, and especially in West Berlin itself, there has been a clear understanding that final responsibility for this offense against a great city and its citizens rests on the Kremlin. Yet from the first day onward there has also been a question for the West, especially for the American government, and in particular for John F. Kennedy: Could you and should you have prevented this?

The question was put to Kennedy at the time, and his answer was candid as far as it went, but incomplete. "Eastern Berlin and East Germany," he said, "have been under the control of the Soviet Union, really, since 1947 and '48."[13] What he did not add, although it was clear in his mind both before and after the wall went up, was that he should not use American military strength, conventional or nuclear, to challenge that Soviet control. He understood that legally Berlin was a single occupied city, and also that the circulation of citizens throughout Berlin had been accepted throughout the postwar years. But these realities, important as they must be to Berliners, were not matters for which he could ask Americans or their allies to fight. And he also noted, sometimes with a touch of irritation he tried not to show in public, that the questions came well after the fact, and that in the first days of the wall no ally, and no responsible American, had asked him to take action against it.

In reality no one in power in any major government believed in using force against the wall. Franz Josef Strauss, then the bitterly anti-Soviet minister of defense in the Federal Republic, told his sympathizers at the time that any immediate action against the wall "would risk World War III," and that "it was a risk neither he nor any responsible Western official would run for such a gain." Konrad Adenauer's memoirs report a still more searching comment from General de Gaulle, in December 1961, "that Berlin would already be under Soviet control if the West had used force on 13 August." We do not know what led General de Gaulle to this formidable conclusion, but it is not hard to understand how such a result could have come about. If we suppose, I think correctly, that there would have been no British or French support for an attempt to remove the wall by force, then the Americans would have had to act alone. It would then have been open to Khrushchev to move strongly against both the American garrison and the whole Western position in West Berlin, his local military superiority powerfully reinforced by the political claim that the American act of military provocation was simply a proof of the danger to peace presented by the outdated military occupation of West Berlin. It does not seem likely that in this situation of allied division and local defeat anyone would have been able to mobilize the West for further military action.[14]

A more subtle criticism, frequent in later studies, is that Kennedy himself had invited the wall by his insistent emphasis that what was vital was the defense of *West* Berlin.[15] The three essential requirements worked out in his first six months all related to that part of the city: its viability, free access to it, and the undisturbed presence of Western troops. Thus in his decisive public exposition, a television address of July 25, he spoke repeatedly of rights in West Berlin, and of Berlin as a whole only as the general location of the Soviet threat. Still more striking was this comment: "Today, the endangered frontier of freedom runs through divided Berlin. . . . The Soviet government alone can convert Berlin's frontier of peace into a pretext for war."[16] So had he not in effect told Khrushchev in advance that a wall "through divided Berlin" would not be forcibly challenged by the West? And was this not intentional, in that he knew the growing flood of refugees from East Germany would soon force Soviet action? Both Schlesinger and Rostow have reported that he knew and accepted, before August 13, that Khrushchev would have to do something— "perhaps a wall."[17]

I have no independent recollection that Kennedy foresaw a wall, and I am certain that he did not specifically expect a barrier through the middle of the city. I remember vividly his irritation after August 13 that there had been no warning from our intelligence services and our officials in Berlin. The irritation may well have been excessive, in that it is usually too much to expect that any particular secretly prepared move should be accurately predicted. That his own words may have given advance encouragement to Khrushchev, however, seems likely. What he did, deliberately and after prolonged consideration, was to base his Berlin policy on what mattered most—on what was worth a risk of war to the American government and people and to their principal allies, including in particular the government in Bonn. In so doing he did indeed define the interest to be defended as the continued freedom of *West* Berlin, and while he was well aware that Khrushchev was one of his most important readers, he paid much more attention to the need for Khrushchev to know what he *would* defend than for Khrushchev *not* to know what he *would not.* It must be accepted, I think, that by this process of definition and clarification he did make it somewhat easier for Khrushchev to choose the wall.

To judge this result we must consider the alternatives. Could Kennedy have regarded the whole of Berlin, in 1961, as a vital interest for which he could ask his countrymen to fight? He never thought so, and I do not remember that any such proposal came forward from any quarter in 1961. And if no one pressed such a conviction on the president—no true believer in the German connection, no disbeliever in negotiations—could anyone in fact expect that the American people as a whole would have understood and supported such a position? Was not Kennedy right when he pointed out who had controlled East Berlin for sixteen years?

It can be argued that it might have been wise at least to be less clear about it—to leave Khrushchev with greater uncertainty—to leave room in his mind for the possibility that a wall might mean a war. Certainly Kennedy could have spoken more vaguely, more of Berlin and less of West Berlin. I have played this game with the speech of July 25 and I find half a dozen places where a man with this purpose in mind could have put "Berlin" for "West Berlin." But the game shows the problem. The speech thus revised might have been more broadly deterrent to Khrushchev, but it would have been distinctly less persuasive to Americans, and persuasiveness to Americans was the first requirement for a speech announcing not only firmness, but a doubling and tripling of draft calls, a call-up of reserves, and new appropriations of over $3 billion. "Studies or careers will be interrupted; husbands and sons will be called away; incomes in some cases will be reduced." These painful requirements followed from Kennedy's conviction that such measures were required to persuade Khrushchev that the Western interest in *West* Berlin would be defended.

To the Kennedy administration West Berlin was indeed a vital interest of the West. As senior adviser on Berlin Kennedy had chosen Dean Acheson, who, in 1959, had been one of the first and most articulate expositors of the view that the stakes in West Berlin were real and great:

> For if Khrushchev could split the western alliance over Berlin and force the Allies ignominiously to withdraw, abandoning the 2,500,-000 citizens of West Berlin whom we had sworn to defend, Germany and all Europe would know that Khrushchev was master of Europe. And we Americans would have shown that we, too, knew that Khrushchev was master.[18]

Acheson further believed, in 1961 as in 1959, that strong and visible preparations were required, and in the main Kennedy agreed. But no such measures could be taken without setting before the American people a cause to which they would rally. The freedom of more than two million people reliant on American determination was such a cause. Freedom of circulation in an already divided city was not.

A different president might have played the hand differently. Eisenhower, as a believer in the value of uncertainty, might well have avoided the sharp definition of interests that Kennedy announced, and he would not have had to explain and justify new and costly defense measures, because he saw no need for such measures. In his memoirs Eisenhower called it a tragedy that the wall "evoked no quick or effective response" from anyone, but he did not say what he would have done or with what allied support.[19] I doubt that his different approach to Berlin would in the end have deterred the wall—that approach would not have reversed either the flow of refugees that made Khrushchev and Ulbricht need a wall or the balance of power and commitment in East Berlin that made it safe for them to build it.

None of this reaches the larger question of keeping open a path to freedom for all East Germans. Neither in 1961 nor later has it been argued that the Western allies could or should have tried to ensure that result. It was always within the power of Khrushchev and Ulbricht to put their barrier instead on the border between East Berlin and East Germany, an alternative seen beforehand as more likely by most but not all of the many American officials who speculated on the matter.[20] Obviously Khrushchev was under heavy pressure to act, and in a general way the prospect of his action was accepted. That he should do so by a wall through the middle of Berlin was odious—but not preventable, and not generally expected. On August 13 and thereafter it became necessary to come to terms with this further demonstration that wherever Soviet rulers have been determined to keep their hold, they have in the end brought down a barrier to keep unhappy people in.

There remains a smaller and more justified complaint against the American government—that it was slow to understand how deeply the wall affected the very people whose freedom and self-confidence were the touchstone of American policy and purpose. The wall required strong American reassurance to the citizens of West Berlin, and that reassurance could and should have been given more quickly. West Berlin could not be defended if the determination and self-confidence of its people were to fail, and the wall was a serious shock to both. Only the Americans could give the necessary first aid to morale. We did not at once understand this need. It took us almost a week to send Vice President Johnson, and another day to send in a battle group of fifteen hundred men over the Autobahn. It was not until August 30 that Kennedy announced the return to West Berlin of General Lucius Clay, who had been, for Germans, the hero of the airlift against the blockade of 1948–49. All this could have been done more rapidly, and it would also have been better if Kennedy himself had publicly denounced the wall more quickly than he did. To read his public statements for the remainder of 1961 is to see that his main purpose still was to focus attention on reducing the persistent danger to *West* Berlin. It was entirely understandable that these slow reactions to the wall should be criticized, and indeed a similar slowness in the reaction from Bonn was penalized in West Germany's September elections. But in fact the free people of West Berlin stood firm; encouragement from Washington did not come too late, and they formed no lasting grudge against the Americans.

The wall, from its first day to the present, has been protected by nuclear danger. West Berlin's Mayor Willy Brandt, whose hate for the wall was immediate, deep, and lasting, saw at once that an unpleasant part of his task was to "curb rash reactions;" he knew that there must be no explosion of activity that might run out of control.[21] Ever since August 1961 it has been clear at the wall, as everywhere else along the iron curtain, that the West will not make a military challenge to Soviet power in place. We will not ourselves be the initiators of open conflict in Europe. This position has been sustained in fact, though not always in verbiage, by every leader of every Western government since 1945. What Brandt probably had first in his own mind was the danger that angry reactions might be used to justify a Soviet grab for West Berlin. But beyond that, the final and fundamental protection of the Soviet iron curtain, at least since the 1950s, has been the risk that military action against it might bring on nuclear war. Many ardent and honorable anticommunists find it extremely hard to acknowledge the reality that nuclear danger forbids this direct military challenge to Soviet power. It is easier to denounce the wall and to imply or assert that braver men would have knocked it down. But nuclear danger, really and truly and unpleasantly, does prevent *military* challenge to the Soviet power in place in Europe.

Differing American Approaches

Let us turn back to the defense of West Berlin and examine the differing approaches of Eisenhower and Kennedy. There was no difference between them on the crucial importance of maintaining the Western position there and none on the importance of making it clear to Khrushchev that any interference with basic Western rights would be energetically resisted. Nor did either one ever doubt that Khrushchev must be kept aware that interference with Western rights would carry an unacceptable risk of nuclear war. On the ways and means of achieving this result, they had deep differences.

For Eisenhower it was essential that Khrushchev should clearly understand the determination of the Americans. As he explained it to his cabinet, the United States had to stand firm even should the situation come down to the last and ultimate decision, although neither he nor the State Department believed it would ever be allowed to go to that terrible climax.[22] Eisenhower matched this determination with a cautious readiness for negotiation and for meetings with Khrushchev which the Soviet leader clearly valued for their recognition of his stature. Occasionally Ike went further than hard-line critics liked, as in his public recognition that the situation in Berlin was indeed "abnormal."[23]

In private he could arouse concern even in a careful moderate like Llewellyn Thompson of the State Department by his readiness to reconsider the formal, and ineffective, Western insistence on the reunification of Germany. On this point, he told Thompson, he thought "there was much in what Khrushchev had said." He was prepared to be reasonable in looking for better answers in Berlin, but he was also determined to stand firm, and he believed that this determination rested on a plainly adequate capacity for response to any challenge. His country had the necessary strength, and he expected full public support as he himself supplied the firmness.[24]

Kennedy's view was at once similar and different. In the campaign his firmness had been plain, as Eisenhower recognized, and in his first mention of Berlin as president, he said simply that the new administration's view was "the same as the view expressed by the previous administration." But a week later he announced the appointment of Dean Acheson to direct a senior advisory group on the future of NATO, and by that act he invited new and different counsel on Berlin.[25]

Acheson, in the spring of 1961, was a man with a mission. In 1953 he had left office convinced that the American conventional military position required major reinforcement, and he had been alarmed from the first by Eisenhower's New Look, believing that it placed excessive reliance on nuclear weapons. In 1959, in the early months of Khrushchev's Berlin crisis, he had written a formidable essay, "Wishing Won't Hold Berlin," in which he attacked what he saw as an excessive reliance on nuclear threat and an insufficient conventional effort. He believed that Khrushchev's intentions in Berlin were serious, that the stakes were extremely high, that Khrushchev's central aim was to humiliate the United States and so disrupt the Atlantic alliance, and that he could not be effectively deterred by American nuclear strength alone. The critical hazard was the probability of a renewed and comprehensive blockade of Western traffic into Berlin. In his view, "to respond to a blockade of Berlin with nuclear strategic attack would be fatally unwise. To threaten this attack would be even more unwise."[26]

Acheson believed, in 1961 as in 1959, that the crucial ingredient of effective deterrence must be a large and plainly visible increase in the Western capacity to respond to Soviet provocation by other than nuclear means. His specific recommendations were less sweeping in 1961 than in 1959, but they were substantial: American ground forces in Germany should be increased by two or three divisions, and still larger increases should be made in the reserve forces held in the United States. The United States should be prepared to respond to any serious interruption of access by airlift and if necessary by a ground probe of two divisions.[27] Above all, the president should declare a national emergency. Such strong preparations for conventional ground fighting were in Acheson's view indispensable for any policy that aimed to forestall a Soviet decision to interrupt allied access.

In making his decisions of July 1961, Kennedy accepted most of

Acheson's recommendations but not the declaration of a national emergency. Acheson himself was not satisfied. He told State Department officials that in facing the Berlin crisis "this nation is without leadership."[28] But in substance, and in particular on the basic question of the military posture required for deterrence, Kennedy's emphasis on increased conventional military capability was Achesonian. It reflected a conviction among critics of the New Look that in a pinch the threat of "general war" would be dangerously unreliable unless there were substantial and believable means of conventional military action at lower levels. On this question the turn away from Eisenhower was sharp.

The difference here was long-standing. When Acheson criticized Eisenhower's Berlin policy in 1959, Eisenhower's rebuff was firm, and his answers to questions from the press were revealing. First, on March 4, he was asked about suggestions from people like Acheson that there ought to be "an immediate mobilization of NATO defense forces." He replied that general mobilization would produce a garrison state, and that "this would be the most disastrous thing we could do." A week later another questioner asked him whether it was Soviet strategy to get the United States "to spend itself into bankruptcy," and he replied, "I have said this time and time again." And anyway more troops would be useless. "We are certainly not going to fight a ground war in Europe. What good would it do to send a few more thousand or indeed even a few divisions of troops to Europe?"[29]

The next question went to the heart of the matter, and Eisenhower's answer was plainly heartfelt, if not totally clear:

> Q. . . . So, the question is: is the United States prepared to use nuclear war if necessary to defend free Berlin?
> THE PRESIDENT. Well, I don't know how you could free anything with nuclear weapons.
> I can say this: the United States and its allies have announced their firm intention of preserving their rights and responsibilities with respect to Berlin. If any threat, or any push in the direction of real hostilities is going to occur, it's going to occur from the side of the Soviets.
> Now, if that would become reality, and I don't believe that anyone would be senseless enough to push that to the point of reality, then there will be the time to decide exactly what the allies would, in turn, expect to do.[30]

The press was in a searching mood on that March 11, and the last question of the conference took Eisenhower a step further:

> Q. Mr. President, in answer to earlier questions, you seemed to have ruled out the possibility of a general war in central Europe. You

also said, I believe, that nuclear war doesn't free anyone. Is there, therefore, an in-between response that we could make in the event that the Russians really started trouble over Berlin?

THE PRESIDENT. I think we might as well understand this— might as well all of us understand this: I didn't say that nuclear war is a complete impossibility. I said it couldn't as I see it free anything. Destruction is not a good police force. You don't throw hand grenades around streets to police the streets so that people won't be molested by thugs.

This is exactly the way that you have to look at nuclear war, or any other. Indeed, even in the bombing of the, you might say, relatively moderate type that we had in World War II, we destroyed cities, but not to compel anything except the enemy to allow our ground forces to move forward.

And, I must say, to use that kind of a nuclear war as a general thing looks to me a self-defeating thing for all of us. After all, with that kind of release of nuclear explosions around this world, of the numbers of hundreds, I don't know what it would do to the world and particularly the Northern Hemisphere; and I don't think anybody else does.

But I know it would be quite serious.

Therefore, we have got to stand right ready and say, 'We will do what is necessary to protect ourselves, but we are never going to back up on our rights and our responsibilities.[31]

Eisenhower in this passage is almost surely engaged once again in "confusing them," but his underlying meaning is double. He is saying that nuclear war makes no sense, but that nonetheless we must stand firm, and the connecting proposition is one that he repeated over and over again in different ways through these last years: If Khrushchev knew that we would stand firm, he would not take any risk that might lead to nuclear war. Eisenhower never departed from a conviction that he expressed years later with graphic clarity to his trusted biographer, Stephen Ambrose. "There is nothing in the world that the Communists want badly enough to risk losing the Kremlin."[32] Nothing that happened in the crisis over Berlin suggests that he was wrong.

Kennedy's belief was the same, although perhaps not as confident: If Khrushchev properly assessed the danger, he should in fact be deterred. The difference between the two was over what was needed to make the danger clear. Eisenhower believed that it was enough "to stand right ready," and Kennedy believed that there must be military choices more credible and less suicidal than a rapid resort to general nuclear war. I cannot improve on Sorensen's summary of his view:

"If Mr. Khrushchev believes that all we have is the atomic bomb," he said, "he is going to feel that we are . . . somewhat unlikely to use it."

The President sought therefore to fill that gap with a rapid build-up of combat troops in Central Europe—with a contingent large enough to convince Khrushchev that our vital interests were so deeply involved that we would use any means to prevent the defeat or capture of those forces. This required a force large enough to prevent any cheap and easy seizure of the city by East German guards alone, which would weaken our bargaining power—and large enough to permit a true "pause," a month instead of an hour before choosing nuclear war or retreat, time to bring up reserves, to demonstrate our determination, to make a deliberate decision and to communicate at the highest levels before the "ultimate" weapons were used.

Only in this way, Kennedy was convinced, could Khrushchev be dissuaded from slowly shutting off West Berlin.[33]

This description tells us how Kennedy saw the problem of dissuading Khrushchev, but it does not tell us, and I believe nobody ever knew, just what Kennedy himself believed about the decision he would make if conventional battle were ever joined over access to Berlin in such a way that he was required to choose between defeat and the release of nuclear weapons. I remember vividly a short exchange between Acheson and Kennedy on the question. It came at the end of a meeting in the Cabinet Room on contingency plans for Berlin, I think in the summer of 1961, when only the three of us were left. The president asked Acheson just when he thought we would have to use nuclear weapons. Acheson's answer was more measured and quiet than usual. He said that he believed the president should himself give that question the most careful and private consideration, well before the time when the choice might present itself, that he should reach his own clear conclusion in advance as to what he would do, and that he should tell no one at all what that conclusion was. The president thanked him for the advice, and the exchange ended.

Acheson's statement came with an order and clarity that showed that it was itself the product of careful advance consideration. As I thought about its meaning at the time, I believed that a veteran was simply advising the president to be thoughtful, well ahead of time, about his personal responsibility for this most awesome choice. I now believe that Acheson had a further meaning, or at least that he had a view of what his own answer to the president's question would be. Unless he had changed his mind since 1959, what he believed was that the right final choice might be to accept defeat, and the loss of West Berlin, if the only remaining alternative were to start a nuclear war. The crucial evidence of this belief is in the essay he published in 1959 in *The Saturday Evening Post,* in a passage at the end of an extensive argument that Soviet restraint might well be induced by evident Western readiness for a sustained conventional battle to keep access to Berlin:

> One further contingency must be examined. It is the possibility that a military effort to keep the routes to Berlin open—prepared as well as possible and executed as well as possible—may fail without a nuclear strike by either side. Such a situation would show wisdom and restraint by both sides, but one should not rely on its probability.

Acheson went on to explain why in his view it would be better to have fought and lost than never to have fought at all, arguing that such an honorable but searing defeat could lead to a new and urgent effort for political, military, and economic strengthening of the West—a response to "disaster and hazard" as dramatic as those of 1947 and 1949—the years of the Marshall Plan and NATO, when he himself had been "present at the creation."[34]

This vision of revival after a local disaster has its own interest, but what is central for us is that the most ardent and eloquent advocate of energetic action to make nuclear risk credible to Khrushchev, a true believer in fighting hard with strong conventional forces for the freedom of West Berlin, nevertheless believed, at least in 1959, that at the moment of final choice, the course of "wisdom and restraint" might be to accept local defeat without the use of nuclear weapons. In 1961 Acheson was urging his own government to take measures that would believably increase the Soviet estimate of the nuclear risk in any interference with access to Berlin, so it is understandable that there is no reference to this earlier assessment in any account of his work in that year. One may even surmise that if he remembered what he had written for all the world to read two years before, he may have consoled himself with the thought that nothing is more secret than a sentence buried in a two-year-old weekly.

Whatever we may conclude about Acheson, we have no certain knowledge of what Kennedy himself believed he would do. Secretary of Defense McNamara has recently written that at some point he "recommended, without qualification," to President Kennedy and later to President Johnson "that they never initiate, under any circumstances, the use of nuclear weapons." McNamara believes they accepted his recommendation. But McNamara's own belief is that his conversation with Kennedy came well after the most intense months of the Berlin crisis, and I think he is right, simply because a conversation of this sort fits better with the later relationship of the two men, and also with their thoughts as affected by their continuing experience of exposure to the consideration of nuclear danger.[35]

We also know that for Kennedy in 1961, as for Eisenhower earlier, it was a political imperative in our relations with West Germany that we should have a clear and announced public position of readiness to go all the way to nuclear war if necessary, a requirement made even stronger by the new administration's fresh emphasis on conventional reinforcement. German opinion, especially at the higher political levels of Bonn, was understandably sensitive to any sign of weakening in the nuclear determination of the American government. It was an article of faith in the Adenauer government that the prevention of Soviet aggression of all sorts depended directly on Soviet fear of the American bomb. Moreover, precisely because of their understanding that the American nuclear commitment to their defense was an extraordinary guarantee for one country to give another, the Germans were in constant need of reassurance. Recently declassified papers remind me that as Sorensen was collecting suggestions for what became the Kennedy speech of July 25, the importance of this point was emphasized by Henry Kissinger, in advice telephoned from Cambridge. I passed the message on to Sorensen, reporting that "because our buildup is mainly conventional, it seems to him [Kissinger] important to make clear that our resolution on Berlin is not limited to such forces." I said that any language that did this job would be helpful, and in due course Sorensen took account of the point (which may well have come in from others too, or have been already in his mind). In the speech as delivered, the president said simply that our actions were designed "to make clear our determination and our ability to defend our rights at all costs—and to meet all levels of aggressor pressure with whatever levels of force are required." At the same time, and in the next sentence, Kennedy quite properly emphasized our own concern with intermediate levels of force: "We intend to have a wider choice than humiliation or all-out nuclear action." He thus succeeded in meeting the need for reassurance in Germany while maintaining the new American emphasis. For American opinion it was already important not to beat the drum of immediate nuclear danger.[36]

It was his awareness of this same difficulty that had made Eisenhower careful in his public comments. He never said to the world what he said in private, that the United States must be willing to "push its whole stack of chips into the pot." If Eisenhower had any doubts about what he would actually do at the moment of truth, it appears that he kept them to himself.[37]

Beyond this point there is a gap in what Berlin can teach us, and it is the same gap for Eisenhower and Kennedy. The distance between what Eisenhower said about the destructiveness of nuclear war and what he said about "standing right and ready" is wide, and with Kennedy the same gap is unfilled. Both Presidents believed they must persuade Khrushchev of their determination to stand firm. Each in his own way did what he thought best to ensure a credible posture of readiness to face nuclear danger. Both men knew what nuclear weapons could do. We do not know what either one would have done at a moment of final choice. It is interesting to know what Acheson wrote in 1959 when out of office, but what he himself chose to tell Kennedy two years later was to make up his mind and tell nobody. We do not know what, or how much, either Eisenhower or Kennedy had finally decided, nor what Khrushchev believed about them. We do know that the Soviet leader took no step that might have made it necessary for him to learn an American president's choice.

The Role of the Nuclear Balance

Khrushchev never chose to take any step that would have created a risk of nuclear war that he could not himself control. But was this caution a consequence of his awareness of American nuclear superiority, or was it rather that he understood the probable consequences of nuclear war for the Soviet Union no matter who had the stronger force? No decisive answer to this question is possible. Certainly there is no compelling evidence that American superiority was decisive for Khrushchev. We know that he understood what nuclear weapons could do, and in particular what they could do to the Soviet Union. He took special pleasure in frequent comments on what a few bombs could do to his West European neighbors, but in these same years he repeatedly noted that nuclear war could cause deaths in hundreds of millions and on both sides. It was what the Americans could always do, not American superiority as such, that created this risk to his own people.

American superiority might have had a different kind of influence. If the Americans should think that their relative position allowed them to press harder, then the danger to the Soviets in any particular challenge might be greater than if the Americans were more cautious. Thus Khrushchev was almost bound to ask himself whether the Americans displayed any sense of nuclear pushiness over Berlin. It is not easy for me to see how he could have found anything of this kind in either of the two presidents he faced there. Neither one ever asserted that any American nuclear advantage made him confident about contemplating a nuclear war. Neither one, as far as I can tell, ever thought that way, and even if their own convictions had not stopped them from any such public posture, they would have been held back by their shared respect for the American people's evident dislike of nuclear threat making. I do not think Khrushchev believed that American nuclear superiority inclined either of these two presidents toward nuclear risk taking.

But there is a third way of thinking about the matter. It is true that many Americans throughout this crisis considered that the United States had superior nuclear forces, and that this superiority would help to make Khrushchev cautious. This belief may well have helped them to support positions about the American commitment to West Berlin that Khrushchev then found it imprudent to challenge. Thus American superiority may in some degree have stiffened American determination. I believe that it did. Without supposing that our superiority would make a nuclear war anything but a shared catastrophe, many of us did tend to believe that the superiority of our force would increase both Khrushchev's caution and his respect for our determination to act. Yet the fact that in some measure we then believed these things does not in itself make them true. As I look back now, and reconsider what Khrushchev himself probably believed about nuclear war, I do not find it at all self-evident that American nuclear superiority was the decisive cause of his caution, or that it was an indispensable element in our own decision to stand fast. We have seen that Eisenhower and Kennedy—and Acheson himself—all believed that their basic objective must be to persuade Khrushchev not to run nuclear risks, and I am convinced that in these years, as now, the decisive nuclear reality for both sides was a risk of such enormous shared catastrophe that by comparison no numerical advantage or disadvantage in the nuclear balance could in the end count for much.[38]

We must not press this conclusion too far. If either side had felt itself to be in a position of decisive nuclear *inferiority* during the Berlin crisis, its behavior might indeed have been powerfully affected. We may define "decisive" here as meaning a level of inferiority such that the superior side might plausibly be expected to regard a general nuclear exchange as an acceptable result. If the "missile gap" had been real, for example, and so large that the Soviet Union could have contemplated a genuinely decisive first strike, then the American position on Berlin would have been hard to sustain. Joseph Alsop remembers asking Kennedy how he would have felt in such a case: "He answered by asking me not to pursue the subject; whenever he began to think about it, he said, he had too much trouble sleeping."[39] But there was never a missile gap. In all the years of the Berlin crisis neither side came close to having that kind of decisive advantage. Certainly the American superiority of these years never came near to creating in the American government any belief that a nuclear war could be less than catastrophic to the United States. The clarity and force of what both presidents believed on this matter are beyond question. We know less about Khrushchev; his prudence is apparent primarily from what he did not do. It may be that in estimating the dangers of nuclear war the Kremlin has always had a measure of acceptable damage higher than that of Eisenhower or Kennedy, but there is certainly nothing in Soviet behavior during the Berlin crisis—or indeed at any other time—to suggest that the possibility of receiving large numbers of nuclear warheads was seen in Moscow as a good thing to take chances on.

I belabor this argument because it became an unexamined assumption about the Berlin crisis, both at the time and later, that in the successful defense of West Berlin American strategic nuclear superiority was decisive. Both officials and outside analysts were drawn to the intuitively attractive argument that as in the general European balance so in Berlin the Soviet advantage in conventional strength could be counterbalanced only by American nuclear superiority. In 1966, in one of the most thoughtful and illuminating of all early studies of the period, Arnold Horelick and Myron Rush—senior research associates at the Rand Corporation, a leading center of strategic study in Santa Monica—referred to the decisive role of American strategic superiority in Berlin at least eight times; they took that role so much for granted that they nowhere undertook to explain how it had worked, or why a simple awareness of nuclear risk would not explain Soviet behavior just as well.[40]

The assumption that superiority has an influence that needs no demonstration has been frequent in the nuclear age. One reason for the casual omission of supporting argument lies in a failure to recognize how the prospect of a thermonuclear war really looks to a statesman who is making a choice to raise or lower the risk that it will actually happen. It is not what one can do to the enemy that is decisive when a political leader considers this risk. It is what such a war might do to his own country, his own power, and his place in history. Thus Harold Macmillan, in support of his campaign for a summit meeting, once reminded Eisenhower that in a nuclear war eight bombs "would mean twenty or thirty million Englishmen dead," and Eisenhower responded that "in the event of war, the United States would probably have losses many times those of Britain."[41] I find no reason to suppose that Khrushchev had a different primary concern.

Given the destructive power of thermonuclear weapons, war planners may think of one warhead, or perhaps ten—but I think not one hundred—as an acceptable level of damage to receive in one's own country, but the choice of an acceptable number is most unlikely to be governed by some marginally larger or smaller count of what one's own forces might do to another country. Nuclear war between the superpowers is not likely to have a winner and a loser as in encounters between battle fleets or ground armies or even contestants for air supremacy. Large-scale nuclear war between the Soviet Union and the United States in the years of the Berlin crisis would have produced an exchange of death and destruction in which both nations would have been ghastly losers, not only as against their own condition before the war but also in their postwar relation to the rest of the world. This reality was deeply understood by the men at the top on both sides, and what the crisis demonstrated in the end was that neither government, at any time, was disposed to make a choice that would let the danger of such a war pass out of its own control. Khrushchev's atomic threat was empty simply because the Americans had much more than enough to make nuclear war a terrible prospect for him too. Nor was this prospect in any way changed by his correct perception that his opponents were themselves reluctant to take avoidable nuclear risks.

The Berlin crisis is not a demonstration of the deterrent value of nuclear *superiority,* as so many have assumed, but rather a most powerful demonstration of the deterrent power, on both sides, of nuclear *danger.* It is also a demonstration that when such shared danger is recognized, the persuasiveness of any active nuclear threat, without more, is sharply limited. Khrushchev, Eisenhower, and Kennedy all placed high reliance on the adversary's lack of enthusiasm for nuclear war, and at the test all three were themselves constrained by their own parallel sentiments.

Certainly the Soviet leader attempted a large-scale deception as to the level and quality of his own nuclear strength. He made no precise numerical claims, but in his rhetoric he played strongly to the Western readiness to believe that his head start with *Sputnik* implied a massive advantage in nuclear missiles. In reality, as we have seen, there never was a missile gap, and by the fall of 1961 the new American administration had full confidence in its strategic strength. The decisive American exposure of Khrushchev's fraudulent pretension to superiority came on October 21, 1961, in a speech delivered to the Business Council by Deputy Secretary of Defense Roswell Gilpatric. Gilpatric's speech was his own, in the sense that he himself put the argument together, with staff help inside the Pentagon. But it was also an administration statement, encouraged by the president, and Gilpatric reviewed his text in advance in separate face-to-face meetings with Rusk, with McNamara, and with me. This speech included exposition of the measures taken "to improve the Western tactical position in Berlin," but its central theme was a sober affirmation of American nuclear strength, indeed superiority. Three sentences show the conclusions that Gilpatric supported with an extensive account of American strategic forces, though not with any comparable account of specific Soviet capabilities.

> The fact is that this nation has a nuclear retaliatory force of such lethal power that an enemy move which brought it into play would be an act of self-destruction on his part. . . . The destructive power which the United States could bring to bear even after a Soviet surprise attack upon our forces would be as great as—perhaps greater than—the total undamaged force which the enemy can threaten to launch against the United States in a first strike. In short, we have a second strike capability which is at least as extensive as what the Soviets can

deliver by striking first. Therefore, we are confident that the Soviets will not provoke a major nuclear conflict.[42]

The unanimous backers of this important speech had more than one audience in their minds. What Dean Rusk emphasized in a television interview the next day was the importance of not letting Khrushchev suppose we were weak. "Mr. Khrushchev must know that we are strong, and he does know that we are strong." But what both Gilpatric and I remember in particular is the importance of reassuring our allies. To them, even more than to us, there was political comfort in the existence of American nuclear superiority, and October 1961 was a good time for offering that comfort, not only because tension continued over Berlin, but because the affirmation of American nuclear strength would be helpful in our continuing effort to get European help on other military issues. Gilpatric remembers that the speech was reinforcing, later that fall, as he sought German support on offset payments for American troops in Europe.[43]

If Gilpatric's persuasive demonstration of American nuclear superiority was especially valuable in Bonn, and if the confidence and determination of that government were important to the unity of the alliance and its firmness over rights in Berlin, then we certainly have further evidence that in the Khrushchev crisis American nuclear superiority was politically helpful. To the degree that German officials believed in the value of superiority, Gilpatric's assurance was bound to be important, and of course the same thing was true among many in the United States. To Kennedy, as earlier to Eisenhower, what was decisive was that Khrushchev was deterred, and what deterred Khrushchev, I have been arguing, was nuclear *danger* and not the nuclear *balance.* But nuclear superiority comforted many in the West, and the Gilpatric speech, in that sense, was a reinforcement to the Western position. It was a part of the *political* defense of West Berlin, just as Khrushchev's threats were a part of a *political* assault on the Western presence there.

The Kremlin found Gilpatric's speech disturbing, coming as it did in the middle of the Twenty-second Party Congress, and a prompt but less than compelling answer was offered by the minister of defense, Marshal Rodion Malinovsky, whose primary quantitative boast was of the unmatched yields—twenty to thirty to one hundred megatons, he said—of Soviet warheads. Khrushchev himself, by contrast, fell back on a position he had already taken after Vienna, that Kennedy himself had there acknowledged the strategic equality of the two sides. In terms of a mutual deterrence made effective by the existence in both governments of an entirely adequate sense of nuclear danger, this estimate of general equality was right and reflected the ultimate reality of the strategic balance as indeed both Kennedy and Khrushchev understood it. When Rusk was asked about the Vienna discussion, in the same television interview, he made the point with eminent clarity: "When we use this world *equal* what is meant there is that in this confrontation of two great power blocs each side has a capacity to inflict very great damage upon the other. Therefore in terms of handling the relationships between the two power blocs, all responsible governments need to take that into account and not act irresponsibly or frivolously or not suppose that they can press in upon the vital interests of the other side without incurring very great risks." The power of this basic point is not undone by the irony that Rusk made it while arguing that there was some reality to American nuclear superiority.[44]

It cannot have been agreeable for Khrushchev to have his pretense of nuclear advantage persuasively exposed. Insofar as they related to the political resolution of the West, his attempted deceit and its exposure are a significant part of his Berlin failure. But Rusk's comment goes to the heart of what finally controlled the behavior of both sides over Berlin. The central governor of the crisis was a shared and continuous determination to avoid these "very great risks."

A Second Deterrent

There is a second deterrent, not specifically nuclear, that seems likely to have been operating in Khrushchev's Berlin crisis, a deterrent created in the Soviet mind by the backlash of Stalin's blockade ten years earlier. That blockade failed to force concessions on the German problem when it proved possible to keep West Berlin alive by an airlift—an enterprise conducted with his usual operational skill and energy by General Curtis LeMay. The Berlin blockade was a major cause of the establishment of NATO and the rearmament of the West, including West Germany. These consequences were not often publicly discussed by Soviet writers, but Khrushchev in his memoirs plainly recognized them, remarking in one place that "the West had managed to exploit the tension generated by the blockade," and in another, quite bluntly, that on West Berlin Stalin "suffered a defeat." I find it likely that the Soviet government believed with good reason that any new blockade could have parallel consequences in the further stimulation of Western unity and rearmament. If so, then a new blockade of Berlin, in this respect like a resort to nuclear weapons itself, was more useful as a threat than as a choice. This possible Soviet view deserves attention that it did not always get at the time. As Western leaders and their generals looked back at 1948–49, what they could see plainly was that airlift alone might no longer meet the needs of the rebuilt and prosperous Berlin of a later decade. But the earlier episode may well have had a quite different meaning in the Kremlin. There is a good deal in the details of what Khrushchev's people did and did not do in their salami slicing which suggests that in the end the Soviet leader preferred threat to action even at levels well short of nuclear danger. He was slicing not so much for the results per slice as to suggest that he could do much more if he chose. It seems reasonable to include among the probable causes of his caution a recognition that there could be other than nuclear costs in any increased pressure.[45]

In its nuclear aspect, Stalin's Berlin crisis was entirely different from Khrushchev's. Occurring as it did at a time of American nuclear monopoly, the blockade necessarily required Stalin to take his own account of nuclear danger, and in that straightforward sense the bomb was undoubtedly a constraining force. The Truman administration attempted to underline the risk by sending B-29 aircraft to Great Britain; a few B-29s, though not those that were sent, were capable of carrying atomic bombs. There was also inconclusive discussion within the administration on the role of nuclear weapons in the event of war, but President Truman firmly refused to shift control of the small stockpile of weapons—perhaps fifty in all—from the Atomic Energy Commission to the Pentagon; he also refused to delegate to anyone his own control over any decision to use the bomb. In effect he discouraged his secretary of defense, James Forrestal, from pressing his argument for a more clear-cut strategy of nuclear war. At the same time Truman decided firmly that it would be the policy of the United States to hold its position in Berlin, and that in pursuit of this policy "this Government is prepared to use any means that may be necessary." But the success of the airlift, plainly not expected by the Kremlin, was in the end decisive by itself, and as Stalin saw the surrounding costs in Western rearmament and in reinforced Western anticommunism, he let the blockade end, in the spring of 1949.[46]

That Khrushchev did not wish his own Berlin crisis to be a further cause of Western rearmament is strongly suggested by his sharp reaction to the measures that Kennedy announced on July 25, 1961. Neither Kennedy's military buildup nor his insistence that danger be recognized and faced was what Khrushchev wanted from Washington, and he may not have understood how his threats and deadlines by themselves constituted a formidable incentive to the very responses he found offensive. Although his bark remained worse than his bite, he became, like Stalin before him, a powerful stimulus to Western unity and resolution.

This stimulus was provided not only by threats and deadlines, but also by the rigidity of his performance as a negotiator. He made no effort to exploit the important interallied differences which existed throughout the crisis—especially between Washington and Bonn, the first urged onward in its taste for negotiation by London, and the second supported in every stiffness by Paris. We do not need to review the complex arguments that engaged the Western capitals, other than to note that there could have been divisive Soviet offers of compromise, which never came, on such issues as the real prospect of reunification, the nature of allied rights, the acceptance of borders, and the legitimacy of the existing regimes in Germany. In the White House at the height of the crisis there was a greater interest in such compromise than Kennedy ever chose to show publicly. On August 28 I reported to him the growing belief among those at work on our negotiating position "that we can and should shift substantially toward acceptance of the GDR, the Oder-Neisse line, a non-aggression pact, and even the idea of two peace treaties."[47] Clearly if we had heard proposals of this sort from Moscow, coupled with a prospect of reassurances on West Berlin, we would have had powerful reasons to press Bonn for concessions that did not come for another decade. But Khrushchev held back. He steadily refused to offer any renewed acceptance of the continuing validity of the three-power presence in West Berlin. Given the record of Soviet military power in the enforcement of political control over Eastern Europe, there was never any chance of Western acceptance of the change in West Berlin on which he insisted. His inflexibility simply ensured allied unity. When his nuclear bluff was called, he had no alternative means of achieving his desired result—always excepting the limited consolation of the wall to hold East Germans in.

The Agreement of 1971

There is one further episode relating to Berlin which throws light on the importance and lack of importance of the nuclear balance: the set of negotiations that produced a new agreement on that city in 1971. Since then the status of Berlin has been defined primarily by this Quadripartite Agreement, and it has proven a solid protector of the basic Western interest in that city. There has been nothing approaching a Berlin crisis of the sort we have been examining, and the sense of security in West Berlin has never been higher than in this period.

The primary architect of the Berlin agreement of 1971 was Chancellor Willy Brandt, whose courage and insight led him to propose and then to execute the changes in the West German position that led to agreement. Brandt was the prime mover in Bonn's decision to grant what Adenauer had always refused—a formal acceptance, in a treaty with the Soviet Union, of the boundaries set by World War II in Central Europe. In the treaty's language: "They regard today and shall in future regard the frontiers of all States in Europe as inviolable such as they are on the date of signature of the present Treaty, including the Oder-Neisse line which forms the western frontier of the People's Republic of Poland and the frontier between the Federal Republic of Germany and the German Democratic Republic." In return for this concession—or recognition of reality—the Soviet government in its turn joined in the Quadripartite Agreement under which it accepted for the first time a categorical obligation to ensure Western access to West Berlin: "The government of the Union of Soviet Socialist Republics declares that transit traffic by road, rail and waterways through the territory of the German Democratic Republic of civilian persons and goods between the Western sectors of Berlin and the Federal Republic of Germany will be unimpeded; that such traffic will be facilitated so as to take place in the most simple and expeditious manner; and that it will receive preferential treatment."[48]

This exchange of promises is one of the most important events in East-West relationships since 1945. While it is the product primarily of Brandt's initiative and Moscow's response, it is also a part of the complex process of Soviet-American negotiation in the early years of Nixon and Kissinger, and there were important contributions from London and Paris as well. Particular credit, by the common testimony of such different participants as Kissinger and Brandt, belongs to Kenneth Rush, then the American ambassador in Bonn. Fundamentally what we are dealing with here, with respect to Berlin itself, is a basic exchange of assurances of exactly the sort that neither side was willing to offer in the years of the Khrushchev crisis. Brandt's *Ostpolitik*—a fresh approach to Eastern Europe that was based firmly on continuing commitment to the Western alliance—produced not only Soviet guarantees on access but additional support for the new situation of Berlin in the form of changed relations between West and East Germany and also new Soviet guarantees of freedom of movement to and from West Berlin. New agreements between the two German governments registered and reinforced the existing balance between the very different political and economic positions of the two parts of Germany. In effect the whole set of agreements, explicitly entered into in a common commitment to "détente," placed the freedom and prosperity of West Berlin in a context in which the ultimate protection by the victorious Western allies was effectively supplemented by East German dependence on economic relations with Bonn, general European satisfaction with the relaxation of tension, and Soviet understanding that any major threat to West Berlin would be a death blow to the whole new political framework that would give powerful stimulus to precisely those attitudes and forces in Western Europe, and above all in West Germany, that were most feared in Moscow.

These constructive agreements took years to negotiate, and every party had deep concerns on which no agreement was possible. The West Germans were determined to keep alive their commitment to eventual all-German self-determination. The East Germans and their Soviet backers were determined to protect their own continuing purpose of limiting the connection between West Berlin and West Germany. Precisely because of the pain inflicted by the wall, the West Germans insisted that the Quadripartite Agreement must be on the subject of Berlin, not West Berlin. The negotiators had to find their way around these unsettled differences, and some of the results are untidy. The relations between West Berlin and West Germany are called "ties" in the English version, but the two Germanies use different words to translate that into German—the West Germans say *Bindungen* and the East Germans *Verbindungen*—"ties," perhaps, against "connections." More astonishing still, the Quadripartite Agreement is just that, in its agreed two-word title. It is not officially an agreement about any particular place, because the West Germans wanted it to be about "Berlin," while the Communists would have limited it to "West Berlin." The agreement is about accepted realities, but its shape also reflects conflicting hopes.

Since 1971 these conflicting hopes have been far less important than the human benefit of agreements whose central pledges have been kept. Millions of Germans have enjoyed a new freedom of movement across the accepted borders, and the condition and prospect of the free people of Berlin have been steadily sustained, mainly by themselves but also by their friends.[49] There have been recurrent petty squabbles over the exact relationship of West Berlin to West Germany, but it has regularly been practicable for the West German government to handle those squabbles for itself, sustained by its upper hand in economic affairs.

We must not be drawn into the enormous complexities of inter-German relations. What we have to observe is something much simpler and more fundamental. This great improvement in the basic situation of West Berlin, and in effect its disappearance as a cause of major crisis between the superpowers, was brought about in a season in which the nuclear balance between Moscow and Washington had changed dramatically in favor of the Russians. The years before the Berlin agreement were years of massive Soviet deployment of large-scale intercontinental missile systems, and that agreement itself was diplomatically interconnected with decisive progress toward the SALT treaty of 1972, which codified strategic parity—critics of SALT in the United States would say strategic Soviet advantage. Thus if we were to suggest that the direct determinant of the fate of Berlin was the strategic nuclear balance, we would have to reach the paradoxical conclusion that the situation in Berlin improved as the relative strategic strength of the Soviet Union rose. And there may be some limited reality to this connection, in that the Soviet concessions on Berlin may have been affected not only by Soviet eagerness for the reciprocal undertakings given by Brandt and his government, but also by a new self-confidence that did indeed have some relation to Soviet nuclear strength.

Soviet leaders themselves have asserted that their achievement of nuclear parity was what made the Americans and the West Germans more willing to accept the "postwar reality" of East Europe and East Germany, but this assertion does not fit well either with the political state of mind that led Brandt to his great initiative, or with the thinking that led Nixon and Kissinger to support the work of Rush.[50] What is more interesting is that Brezhnev, with the comfort of real strategic parity, was able to give guarantees to West Berlin that Khrushchev never even hinted at.

But the still deeper lesson is that we have here a classic instance of a problem resolved far short of nuclear threat by either side. The nuclear reality, in 1970 as in 1960, was that neither side had any appetite for nuclear danger. The border of vital interest for each side was defined by the line dividing Germany, glaringly completed by the wall itself. From direct and painful experience, Brandt understood the reality of the wall and its permanence within the time open for political action. His statesmanship, together with the sensible Soviet response and eventual enlightened support from his Western allies, reset the freedom of West Berlin in the context of a common commitment to détente in Europe. It was an achievement well worthy of the Nobel Prize that he won in 1971.

When we think of what it is that now defends the freedom of West Berlin we should be wary of any automatic translation of earlier beliefs into the present. In the end Khrushchev was deterred in 1958–63 by nuclear danger, and the same deterrent helped to prevent a Western reply in the case of the wall. We have seen how there was also a second line of deterrence in the prospective responses of the West to any intensified confrontation in Europe. Today nuclear danger still has a role, but it does not seem obvious that a sudden Soviet coup de main against West Berlin would set loose immediate war. That risk still exists, of course, and has its own effect in warding off any new pressure. Yet it seems likely that any sudden coup would be met not by war but by a strong and sustained reaction of anger, hostility, and rearmament all through the Western alliance. The first line of defense for West Berlin today is the Soviet interest in the survival of détente in Europe.

THE CRISIS over Berlin closely engaged the courage and good sense of political leaders in the West. In different ways, both Eisenhower and

Kennedy were tested and not found wanting. Nor did their country-men let them down, maintaining throughout the crisis a steady and strong approval of their government's refusal to abandon the people of West Berlin. Eisenhower spoke for himself, for his successor, and for his countrymen when he said to a group of congressional leaders, early in 1959, that "we have at stake 2.2 million free Germans who trust us and upon whom we may not turn our back."[51] Nuclear danger was made real because that basic sentiment was embodied and engaged by the Americans in West Berlin. With or without the conventional reinforcement that Eisenhower rejected and Kennedy accepted, the Berlin garrison in itself was always a trip wire to ultimate danger. Thomas Schelling was right when he wrote not long after the crisis that "while trip wire is a belittling term to describe an army, the role is not a demeaning one. . . . They represent the pride, the honor, and the reputation of the United States government and its armed forces; and they can apparently hold the entire Red Army at bay."[52] There is enough honor here for all concerned.

Yet in this great test the final honor belongs with the people of West Berlin. It was not just their freedom, but their indomitable spirit that engaged the American people and their government. The ordeal of Khrushchev's intermittent threats, the immediate and enduring pain of the wall, the sustained test of will imposed by geography and politics in combination, were met with a resilience that never failed. The Americans were good friends, and Brandt was a splendid mayor, but the final greatness of spirit was in the citizens of West Berlin, and without that the rest would have counted for little. Brandt remembers how Khrushchev expected the Berliners to give up under his pressure; he "had informed me through visitors that the problem of West Berlin would 'resolve itself,' that its inhabitants would clear out and economic life collapse. . . . He proved wrong."[53]

Khrushchev was in the wrong over West Berlin, and the proof was in the determination and defiance of the free citizens of that place. What held the Western allies together was not their concern for the balance of power, and certainly not any comfortable readiness for open conflict. Contingency plans were as troubling when first responses were to be conventional, under Kennedy, as when they were to become nuclear very fast, under Eisenhower. What held the allies together in spite of these unpleasant prospects was the shared convic-tion that it would be a betrayal to abandon the people of West Berlin. And what held Khrushchev back, in addition to the reality of nuclear danger, was his recognition that if war should come over West Berlin, he would be seen by the world as the one who started it.

It is not without sentiment that I recall the meeting between John F. Kennedy and the people of West Berlin, on June 26, 1963. No one who was there had ever seen anything like the outpouring of people of all ages to greet the young, but now tested, American leader. I remember the meeting not so much for the impression that Kennedy made on Berlin, though it was great, as for the impression the people of Berlin made on Kennedy. His understanding of the need to tell them of his admiration in some immediate and simple way had led him, in the airplane on the way to the city, to ask for some phrase that would have the meaning for these people of the old Latin words *civis Romanus sum.* The absence of any better student of German made me the one to suggest the phrase he used, and he used it both in his opening and again in his peroration, not as an American pledge and still less as a claim of American virtue, but as a way of saying "on behalf of my countrymen . . . that they take the greatest pride that they have been able to share with you, even from a distance, the story of the last eighteen years." The wall was "an offense against humanity," and one German out of four was still not free, but in the end all must be free, and the city and the country one day united "in a peaceful and hopeful globe." Meanwhile, "all free men, wherever they may live, are citizens of Berlin, and therefore, as a free man, I take pride in the words *'Ich bin ein Berliner.'* "[54]

The response was overwhelming, and it stayed with Kennedy, as a source of confidence, for the rest of his life. To have won, and at least in some measure to have earned, the extraordinary acclaim of this extraordinary citizenry was the reward that made him say to Sorensen, as he sat down in *Air Force One* to leave, "We'll never have another day like this one as long as we live."[55]

If the freedom of West Berlin was sustained against Khrushchev by nuclear danger, if nuclear danger was created by Western presence and firmness, and if that Western presence and firmness found both justification and reinforcement in the determination of the men and women of West Berlin, then in some final sense the ultimate defenders of free Berlin were the free Berliners themselves. That is true also in the age of détente.

IX

Cuban
Missile Crisis

O N SUNDAY, OCTOBER 14, 1962, two American U-2
aircraft, one of them piloted by Major Rudolf Anderson, Jr.,
took pictures over Cuba. A day later photoanalysts in Washington concluded firmly that the Soviet Union was installing in Cuba nuclear missiles that could reach the United States. After five days of analysis and argument in a small circle of his own selection, President Kennedy decided on October 20 to impose a naval quarantine on the further delivery of offensive weapons to Cuba and to insist on the prompt withdrawal of Soviet missiles already delivered. On the evening of Monday, October 22, he announced his decision to the country and the world. There followed a six-day international crisis of unprecedented severity in which the risk of nuclear war was almost universally believed to be greater than at any time before or since. After negotiations as complex and serious as they were brief, and military moves and countermoves in which astonishingly only one life was lost by hostile action—that of Major Anderson, on October 27—the acute phase of the crisis was ended on Sunday, October 28, by a public statement from Nikita Khrushchev undertaking to remove the missiles.

This crisis has been the object of study ever since. Forests have been felled to print the reflections and conclusions of participants, observers, and scholars. A further review might seem superfluous, if the episode were not central to our subject. There may also be advantage in combining in one account what I know as a participant and what I have since learned from the work of others and from my own study. My purpose is to attempt a clear assessment of the way in which those making decisions thought about these weapons and their meaning. What did Khrushchev and Kennedy think they were doing? How did these thoughts bring them into confrontation? What ended the crisis? What alternatives did the two men have, and why did they make the choices they did at each stage? In what ways was this truly a thermonuclear crisis and in what ways not? How close to catastrophe did we come? What did we learn?

Our Secret Choice of Naval Quarantine

While the crisis was brought on by Khrushchev, it is easier for Americans, and especially for me, to begin with the American side. Within the limits of records and memory—fallible but extensive—we know what we Americans thought and did. As usual we have no comparable evidence on the Soviet side. Moreover, what we thought then and what it seems sensible to think now about Soviet behavior are different, and it would be a mistake to confuse the two angles of judgment. So let us begin where the crisis began for President Kennedy: with the unwelcome news that against his warnings and expectations the Soviet government was clearly installing in Cuba nuclear weapons that could reach the United States. When I told the president the bad news, a little before nine o'clock on Tuesday morning, October 16, his first reaction, from which he never wavered, was that more than words would be needed to respond to this Soviet challenge. He had given explicit public warning that any such deployment would create "the gravest issues." In response to alarms raised by critics, most notably Republican Senator Kenneth Keating of New York, he had repeatedly denied that there was any evidence of the installation of such weapons, and he had repeatedly made it clear that he would know what to do, and would do it, if against his expectation Keating should turn out to be right. Beyond that, he had received repeated Soviet assurances, public and private, that no offensive weapons would be installed in Cuba. Some of these assurances were not without their ambiguities, but Kennedy was correct in his immediate and enduring judgment that there had been a concerted Soviet effort to mislead the United States government and its president on a matter of the highest importance, so that they could be presented with a fait accompli at some moment of Khrushchev's choice. Kennedy's instant conclusion that there must be an active response was tested repeatedly in the days that followed, among others by Robert McNamara on Tuesday morning and by me on Thursday evening. It was also tested by the president himself. Were his warnings to the Soviets, and his undertakings to his countrymen, so clear that inaction would be read as craven retreat at home and abroad? He reviewed them that first morning and concluded that they were.

Kennedy's warnings and promises of action are often slighted by those who believe that he overreacted, so it is important to understand how strong they were. They were given in the context of a heated domestic debate over the shape and meaning of Soviet shipments to Cuba. Kennedy was resisting proposals for military action against Cuba on the ground that nothing that we had observed required such drastic action. Thus his first statement on September 4 was more an assurance to his countrymen than a direct warning to Khrushchev:

> There is no evidence of any organized combat force in Cuba from any Soviet bloc country; of military bases provided to Russia; of a violation of the 1934 treaty relating to Guantanamo; of the presence of offensive ground-to-ground missiles; or of other significant offensive capability either in Cuban hands or under Soviet direction and guidance. Were it to be otherwise, the gravest issues would arise.[1]

On September 13, in a news conference, Kennedy went further and spoke words whose meaning was entirely clear, both at the time and as he read them again on October 16.

> If at any time the Communist buildup in Cuba were to endanger or interfere with our security in any way, including our base at Guantanamo, our passage to the Panama Canal, our missile and space activities at Cape Canaveral, or the lives of American citizens in this country, or if Cuba should ever attempt to export its aggressive purposes by force or the threat of force against any nation in this hemisphere, or become an offensive military base of significant capacity for the Soviet Union, then this country will do whatever must be done to protect its own security and that of its allies.
>
> We shall be alert, too, and fully capable of dealing swiftly with any such development. As President and Commander in Chief I have full authority now to take such action . . .

In response to a follow-up question he summed the matter up succinctly: ". . . *if Cuba should possess a capacity to carry out offensive actions against the United States . . . the United States would act* [emphasis added]."[2] In the light of these public commitments it was clear to the president throughout the crisis that every course of action must be measured by its effectiveness in removing the missiles.

Could anyone propose a course of diplomatic action that gave reasonable promise that the missiles would be removed? Or would a diplomatic course simply allow the Russians to complete their installation of the missiles and stand pat, showing the world that the United States either could not or would not take action to prevent or reverse a move against which the American president had given solemn and explicit warning? None of us who proposed a diplomatic beginning was ever able to offer a comforting answer to these further questions, except in terms of a visible readiness to go further than diplomacy if need be. No critic or commentator at the time or since has done better. If you start where John Kennedy started on October 16, you are forced to the conclusion that no direct diplomatic demarche, no appeal to the United Nations, no complaint of double dealing, would *by itself* have been effective. If diplomacy were to be successful, it must be diplomacy based on a persuasive readiness to use force if necessary. With or without diplomatic process, there must be a visible determination to act.

An overwhelming majority of Americans and their representatives in Congress would expect and demand the action that Kennedy had promised. If he were to begin by public diplomacy, he could expect an immediate clamor for deeds, not words, and a tumultuous babel of conflicting public advice as to what actions he should take, and how quickly, all in the context of continuing Soviet construction at the missile sites. He would be under enormous pressure to decide on early action, but in a situation far less favorable than the one in which he found himself for a few days, starting October 16. His judgment of the country's attitude is plainly reflected in an exchange with his brother a week later, when Russian ships were still sailing toward the newly established blockade line: "It looks really mean, doesn't it," said the president. "But then, really there was no other choice." The attorney general agreed, and added, "If you hadn't acted, you would have been impeached." The president said that was what he thought too.[3] One must discount here for the exaggeration of conversational shorthand and for the way brave men in a tight spot comfort one another: This is tough, but we had no alternative. The underlying point remains. The moment Americans knew what Khrushchev was doing, the overriding question would be what their own government was going to do about it. The question would be political, of course, but in every sense of that encompassing word. Reinforcing the natural instinct of Republicans to capitalize on warnings come true would be the anger and fear of a people whose government had been challenged in a way it had not expected on an issue of the highest possible emotional force. The shock of recognition that Kennedy himself had experienced on the morning of October 16 would be shared and sharpened as the news hit the nation, adding all the passions of public outcry to the same insistent question that had come to his lips at that first moment: What are we going to do about it? Khrushchev had acted, and now we knew it. It was our move.

The country would obviously have to know the bad news, and soon. It was equally obvious that the president should, if he could, announce that news himself, and at a time when he could also say what he was going to do about it.

A parallel and equally urgent need for a short period of secrecy was evident in the context of the contest with Khrushchev. It was obvious that he was attempting to complete a stolen march under the cover of assurances intended to deceive. He did not know that we had found him out, and he did not know that we were considering our response. It is possible that he thought we knew already, but if so he had no reason to believe that we planned to take any action; our public position was that everything we knew about was tolerable. I had made the point myself on national television only two days earlier, stating that so far "everything that has been delivered in Cuba falls within the categories of aid which the Soviet Union has provided, for example, to neutral states like Egypt, or Indonesia." The precise point of this way of stating the matter was that no nuclear weapons had ever been shipped to these states, and the distinction I was making could hardly have escaped Soviet attention. I also said, "I know there is no present evidence, and I think there is no present likelihood, that the Cubans and the Cuban government and the Soviet government would in combination attempt to install a major offensive capability." I do not think the Soviet government could have supposed that a senior member of the White House staff would make such a statement if he knew about nuclear missile sites.[4]

From our standpoint it was clearly best that Khrushchev should not know of our totally changed attitude until we were ready. Otherwise he might take further steps of his own that would complicate our choice. The fact that we were planning a response was a fact that he should not know, if we could help it, until we told him.

This double need for secrecy was quite different from the normal desire of all intelligence collectors, especially those privy to the work of the U-2, to protect their product. That natural institutional secretiveness might help us to keep the secret, but it was not the reason for keeping it. Indeed it was clear from the start that this decisive discovery must be revealed in due course, and when that time came the need for public persuasiveness rapidly overrode the ordinary rules of the U-2 community.

Thus on October 16 President Kennedy was determined to protect the secret revealed by the U-2 pictures until he had decided what to do. In my own way, I had recognized the importance of temporary protection of the secret from the moment I learned it over the telephone from Ray Cline of CIA, at about eight-thirty Monday evening, and decided not to call the president with the bad news that night. Cline and the photoanalysts would not be ready to show the pictures in a way that laymen could understand until the following morning, and what was even more important was that there was nothing the president could do that night without risk of a leak. If I had called him one of two results would have followed: Either he would have had a terrible night alone with the news, or he would have stirred up his administration by telephone calls and meetings that could easily have led to leaks. It seemed better to wait twelve hours and protect both his sleep and the secret.[5]

The president felt even more strongly about secrecy than I did. In his bedroom on Tuesday morning he recognized the need at once, and he drove the point home later that morning at his first meeting with those he had chosen to share his problem. Extraordinary precautions must be taken to prevent leaks. Moreover the immediate danger, as almost all of us knew almost instinctively, was not from Russian spies but from American newsmen who, fortunately for us, did not know the race was on. We could not know, that first morning, how much time we had, and we did not set a deadline for decisions and public announcements, but we guessed correctly that we had a few days to a week.[6]

We had some accidental good luck in our race with the press. The midterm political campaign that so often took the president away from our deliberations was an even worse distraction for normally attentive reporters. Here is a retrospective account from Hugh Sidey of *Time:*

> There were some breaks going for Kennedy. For one thing, the White House press corps was in total disarray because of the political campaign. They were dispatched on Fridays with duffel bags packed, and then through Saturday and Sunday there ensued a dusty race across America. . . . It was a job which drained all physical and mental energy. They struggled back to Washington on Monday and collapsed for two days at home, returned to the White House in time to get their new marching orders. What few hours they had between planes were spent in talking to politicians about the candidates and the districts that they would encounter during the coming week end. . . . Politics, the natural love of journalists and statesmen, was the consuming interest. The men simply could not cover the world and the campaign together. . . . Thus, the men deeply involved in the Cuban crisis had a rare freedom from the prying press.[7]

Sidey may protest a little too much, and the hardships endured in these highly coveted assignments require only moderate sympathy, but certainly the campaign in its own way helped to give us a few days of privacy we might otherwise have lost. This is, in my judgment, its only significant connection with the crisis, and it does not constitute a compelling reason for choosing a campaign season for such decisions. Whatever else it was, the missile crisis was not just what we wanted at the time.

We must act, and we must decide on our actions in secret; within those boundaries the discussion began. Unusually, for President Kennedy, most of the more intense arguments of the first week took place in his absence. He was absent mainly because his calendar could not be disturbed without danger to the secret, but partly it was also the wisdom of experience. In twenty-one months he had learned what we have seen repeatedly in this history, that in structured meetings counsel to presidents is often constrained. Yet as I remember him I doubt that he would have stayed away as much as he did if announced engagements had not required him to do so. Did the campaign do him another incidental kindness here?

Within forty-eight hours a single objective for our policy had been identified: the removal of the missiles. Moreover, we had reduced our options to two: a conventional air strike on the missile sites, and a naval quarantine on the delivery of offensive weapons.

The missiles must be removed. This was the president's immediate and firm determination, and it was the test against which other options fell away, either because they offered too little hope, or because in a situation which already appeared dangerous beyond the experience of any of us, they demanded too much. No diplomatic demarche, in and of itself, could offer a real prospect that the missiles would be removed. The most that was proposed by the senior diplomat in our early meetings, Charles Bohlen, was that we should test Khrushchev by a diplomatic exchange before choosing a course of action. But the president did not want to open communication until he knew what action he would take, and as discussion focused on this problem the question of a diplomatic demarche became secondary. We should decide what to say to the Russians, and when to say it, only after we knew what we were planning to do. Bohlen's recommendation was not ignored, and at different times more than one of us drafted messages that might be sent to Khrushchev without an accompanying announcement of a course of action, but these efforts only served to show the opportunities any such demarche would offer the Soviet leader: a rush to the United Nations, a public announcement of what he had done combined with a full defense of it and perhaps the issuance of blood-chilling threats.[8]

To get the missiles out—it was more than unaided diplomacy could be asked to do, but it was much less than some would have preferred. In particular it was less than the overthrow of the Castro regime. As far as I know, no one urged this objective strongly on the president to his face, and indeed I know of no member of our working group for whom this was the right primary target. For some in the Pentagon and the CIA, the removal of Castro was not only an end of great value in itself—a view which the president strongly shared—but one whose achievement could now be justified by his complicity in creating this clear and present danger. Kennedy and those he consulted directly disagreed. If the central objective was to get the missiles removed, one's attitude toward Castro, like one's view of diplomacy, must be assessed in the light of that purpose. It needed little thought to recognize that the decision to remove the missiles would not be likely to come easily from Castro; it was Khrushchev who must be persuaded. Castro was a hostile pawn, to be captured, threatened, or spared as the central purpose might dictate. It was not Castro's existence that had created the crisis; it was Khrushchev's missiles.

The missiles were the problem, and their removal was the solution. This reality gave early strength to the proposal for their elimination by an air attack with conventional weapons. This option was the president's first thought in the minutes after he heard the news, and the same first reaction occurred repeatedly as the circle of those informed was widened. The president chaired two meetings on Tuesday, and early in the first he made the flat statement that there would definitely be an air strike, at least against the missile sites, and perhaps against wider targets. Yet even on that first day he heard reservations on the political consequences of such action from Dean Rusk, and listening to the discussion of a surprise air attack, his brother wrote a note saying, "I now know how Tojo felt when he was planning Pearl Harbor."[9] In the second meeting, early in the evening, Robert McNamara became the first to suggest the existence of a course of action between the merely political, which had already been rejected, and the air strike: a "course of action that would involve declaration of open surveillance" and an immediate "blockade against *offensive* weapons entering Cuba in the future."[10] By Wednesday Robert Kennedy and Robert McNamara had become settled advocates of a naval blockade (not yet refined into a quarantine), and they had the strong support of Sorensen. In the beginning this proposal was not much more than an alternative form of action with the crucial advantage that it did not require instant killing, and from the beginning the primary objection to it was that it seemed to give no assurance of the early removal of the missiles. As argument continued the basic advantage endured while the basic objection was weakened. The blockade would not remove the missiles; it would not prevent the Russians from completing their installations if they had all the necessary materials at hand, and while the evidence was incomplete, no one could assume they did not. A blockade might produce a deeply embarrassing counterblockade, most obviously in Berlin, and it might require deadly force in its application. But it did not begin with sudden death, and it was a first step, not a last. If Khrushchev would not remove his missiles merely to lift the blockade—and not many argued that he surely would—further steps could be taken. It was this last argument, first put forward by Douglas Dillon, that in the end persuaded many of those who initially supported an air strike to join the gathering consensus for a blockade.

A particularly impressive and influential advocate of the blockade was Robert Lovett, whose role is often neglected because his advice was given in a very small group. The president and Lovett liked and respected each other. They were much alike; both had charm and wit; both knew that "life is unfair," and each understood and enjoyed the unusual grace of the other. If Lovett had been in good health in 1961, he could have had any job he would take in the administration. When he came to Washington at the president's request on Thursday, he talked first with me and then with briefing officers while the president was upstairs receiving deceptive assurances from Gromyko. It was Lovett's first encounter with the problem, and his quick conclusion was that a good strong blockade was the right first step. He would have included everything but food and medicine, but he recognized that a more limited beginning was also practicable, although he feared that we might be unwilling to strengthen it later. He thought an air strike might cause great bloodshed and would be an excessive first step in reply to an act which could not clearly be called aggression. He thought that "we would look ridiculous as the most powerful nation in the world if we grabbed a sledgehammer in order to kill a fly." Lovett's conclusion that it was best to begin with a less violent step was impressive both to the president and to Robert Kennedy, who joined the discussion in the president's office that followed Gromyko's departure. The attorney general and Lovett were delighted to find themselves in agreement with each other, and Lovett was called back to Washington more than once as the crisis continued. A man of great experience in war and peace, George Marshall's chosen undersecretary of state and later his successor as secretary of defense, well known as a disbeliever in the goodwill of the Kremlin, Lovett was a match in record and reputation to any advocate of a more drastic course.[11]

The advocates of an air strike were oddly assorted, and they never managed to concert their varied approaches into anything Kennedy found acceptable after Tuesday. The most formidable of them was Dean Acheson, whose argument was characteristically brisk. The emplacement of Soviet missiles in Cuba was wholly unacceptable; the president had already given fair warning. A military action to destroy those missiles was an entirely legitimate act of self-defense, and the action should be taken immediately, before the missiles became operational. To Acheson this action was both required and legitimized by the prospect that without it the United States would be subjected to a wholly intolerable level of nuclear threat from within its natural and historic area of predominance.

This view had strong supporters within the administration, but unfortunately for Acheson's argument the most energetic advocates of air strikes were the Joint Chiefs of Staff, whose version of this option was not Acheson's, and not calculated to be persuasive to the president. The Joint Chiefs, as a group, believed in adopting a military solution and executing it in a military manner. They preferred a conventional air strike to any other opening move. But where Acheson intended the air attack as a sharply limited blow against the missile sites alone, the Joint Chiefs, quite naturally from their own standpoint, saw it as a blow that should be struck with all the additional military measures appropriate to traditional air warfare: suppression of antiaircraft batteries, attacks on fighter bases, achievement and maintenance of air superiority, and the like. Between the air strike of Acheson and the air war of the Joint Chiefs there were differences that no one adequately explored.[12]

I know how inadequate this exploration was because for about twenty-four hours I was its straw boss. I was wary of the blockade—I thought it would not remove the missiles quickly and would invite a reply in Berlin. I also thought that the single most important lesson of our experience with crises, whether over Laos or Cuba or Berlin or the Congo or the resumption of nuclear testing, was that the president was ill-served if all reasonable options were not carefully explored. After only three days of study I thought it was too soon to settle on the blockade. On Thursday evening, spurred on by the quiet advice of my wife, Mary—"I hope you all will choose the least violent course you can"—I had reopened the question of a diplomatic course, but with no success whatever. On Friday morning, still uneasy with the blockade, I turned in the other direction and told the president that I thought the preference he had expressed for the blockade at the end of the discussion Thursday should not become final without further review. He also heard renewed argument that morning from the Joint Chiefs of Staff. If he was annoyed by these arguments, as Sorensen has reported, he did not show it to me, and my own belief is that in part of his mind he welcomed the prospect of a further test of options.[13] Since he was to be absent campaigning for the next twenty-four hours, there was time for one more look in his absence. So the two surviving alternatives—the air strike and the blockade—were debated once again in the working group that Friday morning. The upshot was a decision that each option should be developed further by a small subgroup through the rest of the day. I became the manager of the air-strike group.

Our group worked hard on Friday, but we worked only with the men and materials at hand. Our air strike remained the kind the military had in stock, not the kind that Acheson had in mind. Acheson had had his turn alone with the president on Thursday and had decided that Kennedy was not about to take his advice. On Friday morning he told me that he thought there was no point in pressing an argument that was already so strongly settled in the minds of the Kennedy brothers and McNamara, and he did not join our working group.

Our plan did continue to have the one clear advantage that it would remove the missiles quickly, and we were Achesonian in our argument that the provocation justified a direct response. But our air strike was neither limited nor surgical, and in its magnitude it did indeed present the dilemma that others had spotted almost from the beginning: Either it would be a ruthless surprise attack—in Sorensen's words "a U.S. initiated Pearl Harbor on a small nation"—or, if either public or private warning were given, it would have to take place in an environment in which Khrushchev could only too easily present himself to the world as the prospective victim of bloody aggression, justified in making terrible threats of his own.[14]

But if Friday's work on the air strike was unproductive, the day of challenge and further analysis was far more profitable for the blockaders. They were able to refine their proposal in many ways. This was the day it began to be a quarantine, and the change was no minor improvement.[15] It was also the day that the raw choice of naval action began to acquire the additions of diplomatic planning, legal justification, political exposition, and connection—the Dillon point—to further action if necessary. All this was fused in the crucible of a draft speech, and I do not recall a more remarkable demonstration of intellectual force in rapid written composition than the one Ted Sorensen gave in framing the necessary questions, eliciting answers from other members of the group, and then making a full draft of the resulting argument by working until three o'clock Saturday morning. His work was refined and improved in succeeding drafts. The most substantial and extensive changes were made by the president himself, but the draft Sorensen wrote that long Friday night marks in my own mind the point at which the president's advisers found a basic policy that he could be confidently expected to adopt. No such speech could be written for the air strike. It was not a solution for which any of us could write words that John Kennedy would speak.

We must return to the president's speech as it was delivered on Monday evening, but the intervening Saturday and Sunday offer other moments of instruction. The president cut short his campaign trip early Saturday—the white lie to the press was that he had a cold—and returned to the White House to hear argument and make his decision that afternoon. McNamara's presentation for the quarantine was masterful and Max Taylor's and mine for the air strike were not, but I think we all understood from the start that the president had come to know his own mind. In addition we had all read Sorensen's draft, and so had Kennedy. He quickly decided for the quarantine, subject only to a final discussion of the air strike with the responsible air commander. He also heard from Adlai Stevenson an eloquent argument for coupling the quarantine with immediate diplomatic moves such as an offer to see all of Cuba neutralized, an offer that would have required U.S. withdrawal from Guantanamo. He thought Stevenson's argument courageous but mistaken and rejected it.

Sunday was a day of intense preparation for the execution of the decision, and also the day when the president himself reviewed the requirements and prospects of the air strike for one last time with Pentagon leaders. The attack he heard described was massive, and the officer whose forces would carry it out, Major General Walter C. Sweeney, could not promise to destroy more than 90 percent of the Soviet missiles in his first attack. More important, neither he nor anyone else could guarantee beyond doubt that no Soviet missile would be fired in reply by a local commander. Discussion was quickly over, and the president's decision became final. The speech was reviewed; detailed diplomatic and military moves were planned and begun. The secret began to leak to the press. The president successfully appealed to *The New York Times* and *The Washington Post* not to tip his hand to the Russians, giving his word to James Reston of the *Times* that no military action would be taken before his public announcement of the crisis.

These arrangements with the two newspapers that covered the government most closely deserve a short review because times have changed on this front. We do not know just what was said to *The Washington Post,* but it is a safe bet that Kennedy talked directly to the publisher Philip Graham, who was his good friend and a frequent private counselor. I am confident that Graham found it easy to agree that the secret should be kept for one more day. What he did was to insist to reporter Murray Marder that his story of imminent decisions and official silence should not point specifically at Cuba, and Marder revised his story in a way that took Cuba out of the lead without taking it out of the story.[16]

Kennedy's conversations with the *Times* were more complex. They are vividly remembered by two notable *Times* reporters, James Reston and Max Frankel. By Sunday, October 21, the *Times* had learned that the Soviet missiles in Cuba had been found and that a major American response was imminent. Earlier in the week, before the *Times* had the story, Kennedy had learned of searching questioning by Reston (of me among others) and had obtained Reston's agreement to call him back before printing any story of an emerging crisis. So now Reston told the president what he knew. The president asked if he had found out what the American action would be, and Reston said he had not. Kennedy then asked Reston not to print the story on Monday morning. He said he would be announcing and explaining his decision on Monday evening and that it could be dangerous if his intent to act became known to the Russians before that speech—he is remembered as having said that Khrushchev might confront him with an "ultimatum," which suggests that in this conversation persuasion may have been more important to Kennedy than precision. We did fear some preemptive Soviet statement if there was a leak, but the word *ultimatum* is too strong. Reston told Kennedy that the decision would be up to the publisher. He then talked with Frankel and others who had been working on the story. They were wary of Kennedy's request, fearing that there might be open conflict on Monday if the *Times* held back the story. They remembered that they had come to regret holding back the story of the landing at the Bay of Pigs. Reston called Kennedy again and described the fear that there would be bloodshed before the president reported to the country. The president assured him that there would be no move against Cuba before the speech. Reston then recommended to the publisher, Orville Dryfoos, that the story should be held up, and it was.[17]

Looking at this episode twenty-five years later, one may be astonished, as Frankel now is, at the presumption of those young reporters, or impressed by Reston's instant readiness to take Kennedy at his word, or instructed by this reminder that the right way to "manage" the press in those days was to deal with it directly and honorably. Kennedy had asked for the calls he got, and he surely did not think that taking such calls was a distraction from his work on the crisis. It was part of that work, and not a small part. No one but the president himself could have stopped the *Post* and the *Times* that Sunday.

From the Announcement to the Settlement

On Monday, October 22, early in the evening, the country and the world were told. Only a few allied leaders had advance notice— Harold Macmillan on Sunday, when the president talked to Ambassador David Ormsby-Gore; de Gaulle early on Monday (Washington time) from Dean Acheson, the impeccable expositor of a decision he had opposed; and Adenauer and a few others from officials they had learned to trust. Congressional leaders were briefed two hours before the speech at five o'clock in the afternoon, and Ambassador Dobrynin was called in by Secretary Rusk at six o'clock. At seven o'clock the president began to speak.

Beginning with a bald announcement that the missile sites had been discovered, he went on to describe this "secret, swift, and extraordinary buildup" as "a deliberately provocative and unjustified change in the status quo which cannot be accepted by this country." Heavily emphasizing deliberate Soviet deception by false assurances,

public and private, denouncing the action as a flagrant defiance of
international agreements and charters, and also of his own repeated
public warnings, and noting that the missiles would be able to strike
most of the cities of the Western Hemisphere, the President went on
to list what he called, with emphasis, *"initial* steps":

> 1. strict naval quarantine on offensive weapons;
> 2. increased surveillance and readiness for the further action that
> would be justified if offensive Soviet preparations continued;
> 3. announcement that any nuclear missile launched from Cuba
> against any part of the hemisphere would be treated "as an attack by
> the Soviet Union on the United States, requiring a full retaliatory
> response upon the Soviet Union";
> 4. reinforcement of the base at Guantanamo and evacuation of
> dependents of military personnel;
> 5. an appeal for support to the Organization of American States;
> 6. the calling of an emergency meeting of the United Nations
> Security Council, and
> 7. a call on Khrushchev "to halt and eliminate this clandestine,
> reckless, and provocative threat to world peace."

There was much more: an appeal to the captive people of Cuba,
an explicit warning against any hostile moves against friends elsewhere, "including in particular the brave people of West Berlin," and
a general but strongly worded expression of readiness for new efforts
to remove tensions on both sides. But the heart of the speech was the
unacceptability of the missiles, the clear culpability of Moscow's secret
and deceptive act, the announcement of the American quarantine, the
demand for outright removal, and the threat of further action. Warning his fellow citizens that "this is a difficult and dangerous effort on
which we have set out," the president insisted, as he had all through
the week of debate, that "the greatest danger of all would be to do
nothing." We shall have to come back to a few questions of rhetoric,
but I know of no public document in the nuclear age that more faithfully reports a major course of action adopted by a president, and the
reasons for his choice.[18]

THE EVENTS that followed promptly proved the advantages of the
quarantine. The president's speech was more effective than we had
dared to hope beforehand. An overwhelming majority of Americans
accepted the danger and supported the president's course. By Tuesday
night the Organization of American States had exceeded the cautious
estimates of our Latin American experts and voted 19–0 to endorse the
quarantine. The leaders of the major NATO allies were staunch,
though there were tremors in leading British newspapers. Most of all

there was no sign of Soviet counteraction in Berlin or anywhere else. The quarantine proclamation was signed, but work on the missiles continued and seemed to have been speeded up.

On Wednesday morning the quarantine went into effect, and by the end of the afternoon a number of Soviet cargo ships had changed course or stopped, to avoid challenging it. It was at this point that Dean Rusk remarked, "We are eyeball to eyeball, and I think the other fellow just blinked." The remark had a larger meaning than those who heard it understood at the time. Rusk's metaphor was drawn from a game he had played as a child in Georgia: Two boys would put their heads face to face and stare into each other's open eyes until one or the other blinked; the blinker lost the game. I believed that day, and I believe still, that the Soviet decision not to challenge the blockade with any ship carrying military cargo was a clear signal that Khrushchev was not ready to press his gamble to open conflict. But work on the missile sites continued.[19]

Thursday the quarantine continued, challenged only by a tanker, which the president wisely left unboarded. The Soviet government, which seemed taken by surprise and uncertain of its own course, still refused to admit the existence of the missile sites, and Stevenson at the United Nations scored powerfully by challenging Soviet Representative Valerian Zorin to say plainly whether or not there were missiles in Cuba. When Zorin, evidently under instruction, refused to answer, Stevenson had the photographic evidence wheeled in on easels. Tension increased as work on the missile sites continued.

Friday the Soviets made a multiple demarche for settlement. The first approach came from Alexander Fomin, a senior KGB officer in Washington, and the second in a long private letter to Kennedy. Fomin's suggestion, made through John Scali, a respected reporter with the American Broadcasting Company, was as brief as Khrushchev's letter was long, but the possibility put forward in both was the same: What if the Soviets should agree to remove their missiles, while the Americans promised not to invade Cuba? Fomin was told that his approach was promising and that time was short, and a similar response to Khrushchev's letter was put in train. Although work at the missile sites continued, the events of Friday were encouraging.

Saturday was a dark day, requiring of John Kennedy the hardest decisions he had made since choosing the quarantine. A new and public Soviet message demanded the removal of American missiles from Turkey in exchange for the Soviet missiles in Cuba. As we tried to understand this shift, we also learned that a U-2 plane over Cuba—it turned out to be Rudolf Anderson's—was missing and presumably shot down. We were forced to confront the possibility that the Kremlin, or some part of it, was prepared to charge a price we could not pay, or to force a military test, or even conceivably both. Our spirits were not lifted by further news that another U-2, on routine reconnaissance in the Pacific, had strayed over Soviet territory, alerting Soviet fighters.

To give his diplomacy another chance the president held back from the bombing reprisal against antiaircraft missile sites that had earlier been agreed on as the right reply to any attack on our Cuban reconnaissance. After intense discussion he sent Khrushchev a public message accepting his proposal of Friday. Here he was helped by many, but most of all by his brother and by his adviser on Soviet behavior, Llewellyn Thompson (Thompson had taken over this role ten days earlier when Bohlen, to protect the secret, held to a scheduled sailing as the new ambassador to Paris). Later in the day, accepting a proposal from Dean Rusk, Kennedy instructed his brother to tell Ambassador Dobrynin that while there could be no bargain over the missiles that had been supplied to Turkey, the president himself was determined to have them removed and would attend to the matter once the present crisis was resolved—as long as no one in Moscow called that action part of a bargain.

Finally, the president instructed his brother to underline to Dobrynin the shortness of the time remaining before further American action would be necessary. Either the Russians would agree to remove their missiles, or we would take further action, and we must know the Russian choice by the next day, Sunday. Meanwhile, highly visible American preparations for both massive air assault and invasion were approaching completion.

On Sunday, at nine o'clock on a brightly sunlit morning, the Soviet answer was broadcast from Moscow. With its fifth sentence the severe phase of the crisis ended: "The Soviet Government . . . has given a new order to dismantle the arms which you described as offensive, and to crate and return them to the Soviet Union." The letter accepted "with respect and trust" Kennedy's offer to give assurances against an invasion of Cuba. There was no mention of the missiles in Turkey. It was my happy task to give this news to the president over the telephone. He was pleased.[20]

We need not linger over the weeks that followed. The missiles were removed. The inspection by the United Nations, which both leaders had approved, proved to be impossible because of Castro's opposition, but with Soviet cooperation aerial surveillance of the departing vessels provided conclusive evidence of the removal. Aerial surveillance also continued over Cuban air space, and no one interfered. After three weeks of bargaining in New York, the Russians agreed also to remove their IL-28 bombers. These out-of-date light bombers were not the cause of the crisis. Before October 16 we had been ready to tolerate them, but their removal had become politically important, at least in part because their ability to carry nuclear weapons had been mentioned in the president's speech of October 22. Llewel-lyn Thompson proved to be right in his belief that the Soviet government, having agreed to remove the missiles, would not in the end refuse to remove the elderly light bombers as well. In return for this further concession, President Kennedy ended the naval quarantine on November 20. The first meeting of the American officials assigned to the removal of the Turkish missiles took place on Monday, October 29, and those missiles were duly withdrawn the following April.[21]

Such is the outline of the events of a testing fortnight. We know from their direct testimony that it was a trying time for those with final responsibility. President Kennedy had been right when he remarked to Dean Acheson that this was the time when he must earn his salary, and in his memoirs Khrushchev describes his own anxiety as "intense." It was not an easy time either for members of the supporting cast, at least in the United States. I know of no member of our working group, rebaptized and slightly enlarged on October 22 as the Executive Committee of the National Security Council (ExCom), for whom this was not the most intense official experience of his life.[22]

Was There a Better Course?

There is some tendency for participants to tell war stories of these great events, but it remains a reasonable judgment that the conduct of both sides at the height of the crisis, and especially of the two leaders, was marked by prudence and skill. Both governments had made serious mistakes before the crisis broke on them, but in the days of immediate alarm—thirteen for Kennedy and six for Khrushchev—the two governments and their leaders did well, and it is not easy even now to construct for either side a clearly better result than the one that was reached on October 28.

In the immediate aftermath the principal criticism from Americans was that the crisis had not been used to achieve a broader result than the removal of the missiles. The fact that Fidel Castro was furious at the outcome and did his best to upset it was of little comfort to those for whom his survival was intolerable. Especially among leading Republicans there was resentment at Kennedy's readiness to offer assurances against invasion. Formally those assurances never took effect, because they were conditional on "United Nations observation and supervision," which Castro never allowed. But Kennedy never wavered from his own conviction that the United States should have invaded Cuba only as a last resort, if all else had failed to remove the offending missiles. In September 1963, with a new political strength that owed much to the successful outcome of the crisis, he explicitly challenged those critics who insisted that Castro must be overthrown. Did they accept and advocate the one plainly effective means to that end—"military invasion of Cuba?" For himself he was against it, as a "most dangerous" and "incendiary" action.[23] This challenge was not picked up, and from that day to this the most passionate of Castro's enemies in the United States have preferred words to action, perhaps even to thought. On the question of pressing matters to the overthrow of Castro, the lesson of hindsight is that Kennedy's forbearance was wise. The violent and massive ground and air campaign necessary to achieve such a result, and the inevitable guerrilla campaign thereafter, would have had costs and consequences far beyond any advantages, not only in Europe and Latin America, but also at home—let alone for Cuba itself. I am not aware of any serious analysis in all the years since 1962 in which anyone has attempted to demonstrate in detail that the rewards of a full-scale attack on Castro in that year would have outweighed its costs.

As for lesser forms of pressure on Castro, such as insistence on some pledge of good behavior in the Caribbean, or a requirement that the entire Soviet military presence in Cuba be removed, I believe that while we could have turned the screw a little further, we would soon have faced a rapid erosion of support at home and abroad. We would have been deeply embarrassed if we had tried to use the naval quarantine, which we had established with a single clear and publicly announced purpose, to press for other concessions much beyond those originally required. I do not find it surprising in retrospect that we gave no thought to such a course. Kennedy had consciously foreclosed that option by his original decision to make offensive weapons the issue. It would have been completely out of character for him to engage in tactics so clearly open to the charge of a double-cross.

The assertion that we should have sought such extra concessions is really a recommendation that we should have sought them from the start. But to do so would have weakened our opening position in a wholly unacceptable way, exposing us to the charge that we were indeed using a sledgehammer to swat a fly, and materially increasing the risk that a peaceful resolution would become impossible. The more I reflect on it, the plainer it seems that it would have been an act of folly to ask for anything beyond the removal of what was truly unacceptable. Indeed I believe that we went right to the edge of what was prudent when we insisted on the removal of the IL-28 bombers.

Criticism from the other flank, meager in the beginning, has become larger in volume and more serious in substance through the years, but it is still not persuasive. The most frequent complaint is that Kennedy announced and enforced his quarantine before attempting to settle the crisis by means of diplomatic communication and negotiation. This objection was registered early by Walter Lippmann, on

Thursday, October 25, and has been echoed by many others since, perhaps most eloquently by Lippmann's admirer and biographer Ronald Steel. Critics seldom argue directly that Kennedy should have allowed the missiles to remain in Cuba. Steel, for example, appears to believe that the right course would have been for Khrushchev to "quietly be told to take the missiles out." But neither Steel nor anyone else has told us why Khrushchev would have agreed to such a "quiet" request, or why he would not have been able to defend himself diplomatically forever as long as he did not have to expect some explicit resort to force by the Americans. Lippmann's own criticism, as Steel recognizes, did not extend to opposition to the quarantine. He simply thought that the president should have put Khrushchev on notice of his plan and of his forthcoming speech when he met with Gromyko on October 18. But this suggestion, which assumes and approves the quarantine, reduces to an assertion that Khrushchev might have responded more cooperatively with advance warning. Conceivably he might have, but much more probably not. As I have argued already, to tell him in advance was to offer him a chance to break the story in his own way with his own spin. It is not easy, on this hypothesis, to replay events in a way that improves on the actual result.[24]

After the crisis, Lippmann himself took a more sympathetic view. Explaining the American decision to act without consulting major allies, he offered the following defense:

> As I understand what went on, our allies were not consulted in the Cuban crisis because of the belief that the risk of war would have been much increased. The American intention was to react sharply, but to react for a limited aim and with limited means. Had this intention become known before it was announced—and in a consultation it would almost surely have become known—there was a probability that the Soviet government would take the initiative either by proclaiming defiantly the presence of the missiles or by denouncing the proposed quarantine as an act of piracy.
>
> Had that denunciation been made before the quarantine was proclaimed and enforced, both Moscow and Washington would have been committed to a collision course. Mr. Kennedy could not have gone backward. Mr. Khrushchev could not have done what in fact he did do, which was to accept the quarantine in what was, it seems to me, a rather elegant and nonchalant way.[25]

Lippmann's point about the danger of alerting allies was almost surely drawn from discussion with the president or with me. The transcripts now available show Kennedy making the point sharply himself in the very first meeting on October 16, where he replied to a suggestion of allied consultation by remarking, "Warning them, it seems to me, is warning everybody."[26]

If quiet diplomacy alone would not have removed the missiles, then perhaps some offer of a trade would have done the job. Here the classic example, and the one that Lippmann proposed on October 25, was the American missiles in Turkey. This argument may well seem to be reinforced by the fact, so deeply secret at the time, that an assurance from Kennedy on these missiles did indeed figure in the result of October 28. Could not Kennedy have offered at the beginning the same assurance he offered at the end, and so obtained the removal of the Soviet missiles without the tension and dangers of the quarantine?

But it is one thing to sweeten incentives a bit in a situation in which both sides have great common need for an early end to an increasingly dangerous confrontation, and quite another to try to trade off fifteen obsolete warheads you really do not want in exchange for a wholly new level of apparent strategic capability that your adversary is under no compelling need to give up. In the second volume of his memoirs, Khrushchev referred to Kennedy's assurance and described it as merely "symbolic" because the Jupiters "were already obsolete." Symbolic measures were helpful, he said, in "creating the impression of mutual concessions," and it seems entirely credible that this "impression" was useful to Khrushchev in carrying his colleagues with him in the decision to withdraw; that was our hope at the time. But without the quarantine, reinforced at the end by the threat of further action, it seems unlikely that Khrushchev would have found any Cuba-Turkey trade attractive. I know of no analysis or argument that makes even a passable case that diplomacy without more would have got the Soviet missiles out of Cuba at any such modest price. Those missiles had been put there to stay, not to be bargained away, as Khrushchev quite plainly tells us in his memoirs, and as nearly all students now agree.[27]

So the advocates of quiet diplomacy, unless they are talking of a warning just ahead of action, are forced back to the claim that the better course would have been to accept the Soviet deployment. While critics seldom embrace this view directly, they often observe correctly that more than one of us (McNamara is the favorite example) argued at one time or another during the crisis that these missiles made no decisive difference in the real strategic balance. The point is serious and requires further consideration, but it neglects a reality that could not possibly be neglected by the American administration in the five days after October 15—that the United States government had publicly pledged itself, in a manner wholly unambiguous to itself and its countrymen, not to accept any such deployment. It does no good to hunt for ambiguities and loopholes in the language. Kennedy knew what he had been warning against on September 4 and September 13, and so did the whole American body politic. Moreover, warning had come from others beside the president. The United States Congress, on September 26, less than three weeks before the missiles were discovered, formally adopted a joint resolution stating that "the United States is determined . . . to prevent in Cuba the creation or use of an externally supported military capability endangering the security of the United States."[28] The vote in the House was 386–7, and in the Senate 86–1, and the one senator in opposition argued that the resolution was not strong enough. The meaning is again unmistakable. It would thereafter have been impossible for any American president to deny that it was firmly declared national policy to keep nuclear missiles that could reach the United States out of Cuba.

Critics of Kennedy's choices rarely note the congressional resolution and often claim that his decision to choose and announce a course of action before beginning the negotiations was excessively affected by his feeling that his personal determination and courage were being tested. That he had such a feeling is certain—there was no way in the world for the challenge he faced on the morning of October 16 not to be a test of these qualities and many more. But he met those tests as much by restraint as by action. What forced his hand in the first place was what the United States government, both through him and through the Congress, had promised the American people.

It is his understanding of the consequences of a failure to honor this commitment to his countrymen that explains the firmness of Kennedy's rejection of all courses that did not give promise of getting the missiles out. It may have been a bit melodramatic for the two brothers to speak to each other of impeachment, and certainly they both could take opposition as a personal affront—in this respect the president had more tolerance than his fiercely protective brother—but the political consequences of accepting the missiles would not have been merely personal. Consider the triple indictment that critics like Keating—and, much more seriously, Eisenhower and Nixon—could and would have brought against the administration:

1. You said it wouldn't happen, and you were wrong
2. You said you would know how to stop it if it did happen, and you don't, and now
3. You say it doesn't matter, and it does.

Then the changes would have been rung on the dramatic and avoidable shift in the balance of power that had been achieved while the administration faltered, with demands for redoubled rearmament and renewed confrontation somewhere, somehow, soon, and under new leadership. At the same time, Khrushchev's successful gamble might well have tempted him toward further adventures. If so, 1963 and

1964 would hardly have been years of progress for the peacemakers and could only too easily have produced risks of war and nuclear dangers much higher than those of October 1962.

It is natural and understandable that, when people look back across twenty-five years of relatively tranquil if distempered coexistence both with Cuba and with hundreds of Soviet-based missiles that can reach the United States, some should find it hard to understand all this fuss about missiles in Cuba. But I do not think I exaggerate the consequences of inaction or ineffective protest in 1962. It is true that they are, in one sense, domestic political consequences, and it is not an accident that the two of us—McNamara and I—who argued briefly, at different times, for a solely diplomatic approach, were politically the least experienced of the civilians in our working group. It is sometimes assumed that Adlai Stevenson held this position for a time, but all of his suggestions for compromise were made within the context of explicit support for military action if necessary. It is a cardinal error to suppose that respect for the real political consequences of a foreign policy decision is unworthy. It is true that short-run popularity is often a poor guide to action, but a decent respect for the convictions of one's own people is different. Kennedy accepted, from October 16 onward, the probability that the crisis would damage the Democrats in the November election (after all, Keating had turned out to be right), and nothing he did or refused to do in the following two weeks had any connection with the prospect for November 6. His actions were governed by political considerations of a wholly different order. He was never prepared to accept the destructive and enduring consequences for his country of ineffective diplomatic palaver when effective action had been so plainly promised. If the missiles did not come out, no one would be able to conduct a sensible American foreign policy for years to come. As a matter of basic political diagnosis in October 1962 I find this assessment unanswerable.[29]

This argument would be quite different if the declared position of the administration and Congress had been different at the time. It thus becomes important to go back to the sources of the public warnings that both the president and Congress had given. Just what was it that made it so clear to Kennedy and to Congress in September and October that they should take a firm and flat stand against Soviet nuclear weapons in Cuba? It was not a calculation of the strategic balance. Such calculations came later and were never decisive in the president's choices. It was not that these weapons would make Castro more secure; Castro was an abomination, but not one that must be destroyed. It was not the fear of nuclear weapons landing on American soil, because that fear had been present for years. It was not even all of these points together. It was something different: a visceral feeling that it was intolerable for the United States to accept on nearby land of the

Western Hemisphere Soviet weapons that could wreak instant havoc on the American homeland. In ways which Americans did not bother to explain to themselves, the prospect of Soviet thermonuclear warheads on a next-door island was simply insupportable. It was possible to maintain, as Kennedy did, that Castro himself was not an intolerable threat to our security. It was even possible to accept the delivery of Soviet conventional weapons to assist in the defense of Cuba. But it was not possible in September 1962 to say that Soviet thermonuclear missiles in Cuba were acceptable. Once that question was raised to a level requiring a decision, only one position was possible. The fact that the president was prepared to accept lesser deployments made it all the more necessary for him to take a flat stand against this one. When the matter became a public question at the end of the summer, the answer was self-evident and quickly given.

Thus the compulsion to act that Kennedy felt so strongly from October 16 onward reflected not simply his own convictions, but those of the public. Nor could he have avoided the crisis if he had avoided the warnings. Kennedy himself looked briefly at that possibility on the afternoon of October 16, remarking that "last month I should have said that we don't care." But that is just what he could not have said, either as a matter of politics or as a matter of his own judgment.[30] In 1987 Sorensen noted that in his September warnings President Kennedy "drew the line precisely where he thought the Soviets were not and would not be" and suggested that if we had then known that they were putting in forty missiles we might have drawn the line at one hundred. I think it highly unlikely that any such choice would have been acceptable to the public, just as I think that scholarly criticism of Kennedy's September warnings and his October determination to act has not taken adequate account of the strong national conviction which both his warnings and his determination reflected.[31]

Our Failure to Give Timely Warning

These warnings of September and early October were indeed warnings against an event that the administration as a whole did not expect. They were issued in the context of broad assurances to the country that any cries of alarm over nuclear weapons in Cuba were unsupported by the government's evidence. But these warnings were not a bluff. All of us in the White House took it for granted, as did the American public, that Soviet nuclear weapons in Cuba were unacceptable. But no one, as far as I can remember, thought it necessary in September to consider what we would do if our warnings were disregarded. This was a failure of foresight, and one of the reasons for respecting the quality of the basic decision President Kennedy reached on October 20 is that he had to begin on the sixteenth almost from a standing start.

We must distinguish this mistaken expectation from the outrage which was our strong but temporary reaction to the news that Khrushchev was ignoring our warnings. Some accounts have it that when I told the president the bad news on October 15, his reaction was "he can't do this to me."[32] I don't think these words are quite right, but there is nothing wrong with the music. This initial reaction did not take account of the reality, which we recognized in the course of the day, that Khrushchev's adventure must have been put in train months before Kennedy's public warning. Khrushchev had not designed his challenge in spite of our warnings; rather he had not taken them sufficiently seriously to reverse a major decision of several months' standing which to him seemed on the brink of success. His challenge certainly required us to respond, but we soon understood that it must not be treated as something undertaken in the face of prior warning.[33] During Tuesday's second discussion, the president himself noted that it might have been hard for the Russians in September to turn back on an enterprise well under way, and said that "maybe our mistake was in not saying sometime *before* this summer" that if they did such a thing we would have to act. That failure was real and deserves separate attention.[34]

Khrushchev's belated and eventually self-defeating exercises in deception were also incompletely understood at the time. We were certainly correct in assessing them as a deliberate effort to deceive. In our anger on this point, which lasted through the crisis and beyond, we missed a somewhat different point. In retrospect it seems likely that Khrushchev was also trying, although clumsily, to take account of our warnings by offering assurances that all his deployments, of whatever sort, were *defensive.* Since we found it impossible to accept this reading, we assumed too easily that his assurances reflected *only* a vicious deception. His words were certainly intended to keep us complacent if indeed we still did not think the missiles were going in, but they were also intended to help us live with our own warnings once we found out. The clumsiness of Khrushchev's effort is nowhere more evident than in the probability that he deceived Ambassador Dobrynin too. I can find no other explanation for the fact that this careful and highly intelligent diplomat openly and directly told an untruth in a way that neither Khrushchev nor Gromyko did. The latter two always phrased their statements in terms of an avoidance of offensive weapons, but Dobrynin directly and explicitly assured Robert Kennedy that no nuclear missiles capable of reaching the United States were being placed in Cuba. I doubt that he had instructions to say exactly that, and I agree with both Kennedys that he too misunderstood.[35]

Let us return to our underlying error. We did not expect Khrushchev to put missiles in Cuba, which accounts for the relatively untroubled way in which we wrote our warnings in September. It also accounts for our failure to issue these warnings six months earlier, when their deterrent effect would have been greater. If we go by his memoirs, Khrushchev began to make his decision in a visit to Bulgaria in May 1962. There was probably also some collective discussion earlier and a collective decision later, but it is certainly plausible that the necessary formalities of such an official visit to a well-behaved satellite provided nourishment insufficient for Khrushchev's hyperactive mind and left him time for dangerous thoughts. If Kennedy and Congress had said in March or April what they said in September, would Khrushchev in May have come to believe in going ahead? It seems improbable.

One obvious but insufficient reason for our silence in the spring is our unexamined assumption that Khrushchev needed no warning. If it was self-evident to us that Soviet nuclear weapons in Cuba would be intolerable, should not that be obvious also to the Kremlin? Until the question was raised by Republican critics, it did not seem to call for comment. As it turned out, Khrushchev made a dangerously wrongheaded judgment, and we certainly failed to assess with care the forces driving him to take the gamble. When we thought of Cuba during 1962, at least until September, most of us thought first of our own frustrations, second about Castro's ambitions, and only after that about how Cuba might look to the Russians. But of course it was the view from the Kremlin that produced the fateful decision, so let us look at things from Khrushchev's side.

Khrushchev's Reasons and Why We Missed Them

With the advantages of hindsight, of memoirs, and perhaps most important of scholarly analysis, it is not hard now to find two motives for Khrushchev's action that we were not well placed to understand in 1962. The one that Khrushchev himself put first in all his later explanations was the Soviet desire to prevent the loss of Cuba. Here is Khrushchev on his Bulgarian reflections:

> One thought kept hammering away at my brain: what will happen if we lose Cuba? I knew it would have been a terrible blow to Marxism-Leninism. It would gravely diminish our stature throughout the world, but especially in Latin America. If Cuba fell, other Latin American countries would reject us, claiming that for all our might the Soviet Union hadn't been able to do anything for Cuba except

to make empty protests to the United Nations. We had to think up some way of confronting America with more than words. We had to establish a tangible and effective deterrent to American interference in the Caribbean. But what exactly? The logical answer was missiles.[36]

This argument was almost surely not enough in itself. There were other and less adventurous ways for Khrushchev to shore up his Cuban ally. But what is most interesting about this motive is that it simply did not occur to us in Washington before October 15. We knew that we were not about to invade Cuba and we saw no reason for the Russians to take a clearly risky step because of a fear that we ourselves understood to be baseless. We did not understand that Khrushchev might take our hostile words about Cuba, and the very attitudes of our own people that we understood so well on October 16, as meaning that all we had learned from the Bay of Pigs was that we should do it right the next time. Khrushchev certainly knew of our program of covert action against Cuba, and he could hardly be expected to understand that to us this program was not a prelude to stronger action but a substitute for it.

We were also inattentive to Khrushchev's second motive. Most American scholars now think that what moved him most was his belief that missiles in Cuba offered him a means of transforming, in one stroke, what he considered a highly unfavorable strategic nuclear balance of power.[37] Although some Soviet observers say that the defense of Cuba was the primary motive, they agree that he was moved also by strategic considerations.

From Suez onward Khrushchev had been practicing his own verbal atomic diplomacy, attempting to use direct and indirect nuclear threats to increase Soviet power and prestige, and believing through most of this period that this course was to his advantage. His most ambitious initiative, in Berlin, was based on a conviction that the Western allies, in the end, would prefer concessions to nuclear danger. He quite correctly understood that his middle-range rockets gave him an overwhelming nuclear superiority over the West Europeans, and he had translated this advantage into frequent reminders that in the event of general war it would take only a very few large weapons to make a desert of small countries like Macmillan's or Adenauer's. At the intercontinental level, he relied on pretense. The missile gap was mainly the product of American worst-case fears, but the Soviets did their clever best to look stronger in this field than they were, allowing the Americans, not for the last time, to advertise a level of Soviet intercontinental strength, both present and prospective, well beyond reality.[38]

By early 1962 this policy of verbal nuclear menace was in ruins. We have seen how in Berlin the Western allies correctly, if nervously, understood that Khrushchev at the pinch was unwilling to run the very risks he thought would shake the West. In London, Paris, and Bonn his blackmail failed. But the truly heavy blow, for Khrushchev, was the public collapse of the myth of the intercontinental missile gap and its replacement by an entirely credible official American announcement of substantial United States superiority in long-range nuclear strength. When Roswell Gilpatric made the real balance plain in October 1961, the Soviet leadership was forced to abandon its hope that nuclear bluff and pretense could bring political rewards. Worse yet, it was forced to consider that any political power stemming from intercontinental superiority could thenceforth be used against it.

Soviet leaders were prompt and resourceful in responding to the new challenge, reverting to the argument that the two large thermonuclear forces really created a kind of equality that both sides should recognize, as indeed Kennedy had in Vienna. In one part of his mind Khrushchev was too well aware of nuclear realities not to understand that equality in this sense was an unchangeable fact of life. But he had also been trained for decades to believe in the correlation of forces as the determinant of international issues, and he was now forced to consider the prospect that the Americans would try to play their newly strengthened hand. It is not an accident that the Soviets reacted to the Gilpatric speech, and others like it, as if these statements of American strategic strength were "a clearly organized campaign" designed "to intimidate the Soviet Union."[39]

For Khrushchev the newly proclaimed American intercontinental preponderance was a large and unpleasant force, and the more so because unlike most of his countrymen, even apparatchiks, he knew that the American claims were not overstated. They were indeed understated. Even in 1961 and 1962 U.S. intelligence continued to overestimate existing Soviet ICBMs by about 50 percent—seventy-five in October 1962, as against a later assessment of fifty. It is thus not surprising that he felt an urgent need to redress this balance, and the deployment to Cuba would have been most helpful to him from this standpoint. By the retrospective estimate of Raymond Garthoff, reconsidering an estimate he made at the height of the crisis, the deployments if completed would have increased the Soviet first-strike missile salvo by about eighty percent. As Garthoff and others noted at the time, deployment of forty launchers with eighty warheads could, if unimpeded, be followed by further deployments sufficient "to threaten the entire strategic balance of power."[40] That thoughts of this same sort were in Khrushchev's head is probable because of his belief that advantage and disadvantage in the strategic balance were of great political importance.

This assessment is reinforced not only by the match between this belief and the large deployments that he undertook, but also by two of his own comments, one contemporaneous and the other retrospective. In Bulgaria in May, at the very time when his memoirs tell us persuasively that he was hatching his scheme, he made pungent comments on what he called a nuclear threat by President Kennedy—an incautious interview with Stewart Alsop for *The Saturday Evening Post* that could be read to suggest that the Americans would go first if necessary. "We cannot but reckon with the statement made by Mr. Kennedy, since it introduces a new factor in the relations between our countries. . . . The President of the United States made an unwise statement. Is it wise to threaten someone who is at least your equal in strength?"[41] Khrushchev knew as he spoke that American strategic superiority was large. In the light of his own behavior as a practitioner of nuclear bluster, this attack on Kennedy's statement, at least in retrospect, conveys not confidence but deep concern, and his memoirs confirm this reading. He tells us plainly and believably that his purposes were not limited to the defense of Cuba.

> In addition to protecting Cuba, our missiles would have equalized what the West likes to call "the balance of power." The Americans had surrounded our country with military bases and threatened us with nuclear weapons, and now they would learn just what it feels like to have enemy missiles pointing at you; we'd be doing nothing more than giving them a little of their own medicine. And it was high time America learned what it feels like to have her own land and her own people threatened.

Khrushchev's feelings on this matter were not new. On his tour in the United States in 1959 he had told Walter Reuther that the Soviet Union was surrounded by U.S. bases and asked, "How would you feel if there were Soviet military bases in Mexico and Canada?"[42]

The strength of these feelings is unmistakable, but it would have come as a great surprise to most of us in the Kennedy administration if anyone had told us that thoughts of this sort were "churning" in Khrushchev's head as he "paced back and forth" in "solitary mental agony," in Bulgaria. We thought it self-evident that our country had already been exposed to exactly this kind of danger for years. Kennedy was the second president to have acknowledged mutual mortal danger as the inescapable relationship between the United States and the Soviet Union. We also believed that in the overall contest with the Soviet Union we were still on the defensive. It was not we who threatened destabilizing changes in Berlin or in Southeast Asia, or indeed, in reality, in Cuba. Kennedy's remark to Alsop, however incautious, was limited to the context of what might become necessary in response to major Soviet aggression.

Finally, we did not suppose that nuclear superiority conferred on us the opportunity for political coercion that Khrushchev took for granted. Certainly we did not think it wrong for Khrushchev to know that we were undeceived about the real situation, but our main object in the Gilpatric speech had not been to terrify the Kremlin, but to give encouragement to our own people and to our allies.[43]

It would be wrong to press this difference in outlook too far. Obviously Americans too in these years were uncomfortable about the prospect of standing at a great disadvantage in strategic delivery systems. This anxiety was what had made the "missile gap" a major issue. Obviously also there were plenty of powerful groups which took seriously the complex calculation of capability and survivability and targeting that made it natural for senior commanders of strategic forces always to want more. And there were already active schools of thought according to which strategic superiority was the indispensable requirement for the maintenance of what was called escalation dominance. My point is not that these forces were feeble, but rather that their state of mind was certainly not that of the senior members of the Kennedy administration, not in the White House, not in the State or Defense departments and not among the senior professional analysts in the Central Intelligence Agency. We simply did not think about the nuclear balance this way, and we gave wholly insufficient attention to the possibility that Khrushchev might think differently. Our cast of mind made his second motive invisible to us, and so we only too readily assumed that he was much too sensible to challenge us in the way that nuclear weapons in Cuba so obviously would. As a result we never came near to giving the warnings of September when they almost surely would have worked to deter—in April. In the words of Raymond Garthoff, "The United States failed to anticipate the Soviet action in Cuba because it failed to recognize how desperate the Soviet plight seemed in Moscow."[44]

John McCone, the director of the CIA, did have early suspicions of Soviet missiles in Cuba. His concern did not become serious until August, too late for a warning before the Soviet decision, but it developed soon enough to mark him as exceptional. His anxiety did not arise from bureaucratic wariness in his agency; his professionals did not agree with him, and I never knew McCone to try to bend their assessments to match his own opinions. He pressed his case as an individual, not as a representative of the agency, but he pressed it energetically. His hunch was strong enough to lead him to invite me for a morning walk in September, when we were both in Paris, to press his argument. He believed that the volume of material we had seen going into Cuba was too large and expensive—especially the air defense missiles—to be explained by anything less ambitious than the introduction of nuclear weapons. He had no more evidence than I did, and he fully recognized that hard evidence would be required for any final judgment. He was pressing for increased surveillance, and obviously he was right. Fortunately the decision to look harder was made in time, but it would have been made sooner if we had listened more attentively to McCone.[45]

McCone's advantage in this case was that he was himself a believer in nuclear superiority and in the high cost of losing it. He had been secretary of the air force and chairman of the Atomic Energy Commission under Eisenhower, and in these roles he had pressed for the expansion of strategic forces and the increased production of nuclear weapons. He did not believe in stopping the nuclear arms race but in winning it, and he worried continuously about losing it. There are all sorts of differences between McCone and Khrushchev, but on nuclear matters they were well placed to understand each other. So McCone got it right. Here is what Dean Rusk told the president about McCone's views on October 16: "About why the Soviets are doing this, Mr. McCone suggested some weeks ago that one thing Mr. Khrushchev may have in mind is that he knows that we have a substantial nuclear superiority, but he also knows that we don't really live under fear of his nuclear weapons to the extent that he has to live under fear of ours." The parallel with Khrushchev's own explanation is astonishing.[46]

The distinctive quality of McCone's warning is accentuated for me by the fact that his insight was not shared that summer by other members of the administration who held a correctly wary view of what the Soviets might be up to. Walt Rostow, for example, warned his colleagues in August that Khrushchev was faced with "frustrations" he might "seek to break out of," and he listed three: the arms race, Berlin, and Cuba, almost precisely the problems that later analysts have described as moving Khrushchev to his great gamble. But Rostow did not warn that missiles might be put in Cuba. Unlike McCone and Khrushchev, he did not believe in the overriding political importance of the thermonuclear balance.[47]

The Strength of the Quarantine

If hindsight suggests that the American warnings were late, it offers a quite different verdict on Kennedy's choice of the quarantine. That instrument proved effective beyond the president's expectations, and there was never any sign of the reply in Berlin that so many of us had feared. Moreover, it now seems reasonable to argue that the quarantine alone, properly reinforced and extended, would have forced the withdrawal of the missiles if we had been willing to wait.

No Soviet ship with a suspicious cargo ever challenged the quarantine line. In that sense the crucial issue was resolved on the afternoon that the other fellow blinked. But why did these ships stop? Partly of course for fear of confrontation, though a day or so later the Soviets did order a tanker to go through. Kennedy allowed that vessel to pass without boarding, but no Russian could have predicted that result with confidence. Thus it seems hard to conclude that it was fear of a challenge as such which governed the earlier decision, and as we thought about it, a stronger motive suggested itself: The Russians did not want us to seize those dry cargo ships and inspect what they were carrying. No one in the Kremlin wanted to give Soviet missile secrets to the imperialists. This unwillingness was certainly reinforced, on Wednesday, by the fact that the Soviet government had not yet admitted what it was doing. A vessel exposed as carrying missiles or missile equipment would have been an embarrassment. But we came to believe that secrecy was an even higher Soviet imperative. As the president summarized the matter on December 17 in a television conversation, the quarantine "had much more power than we first thought it did, because I think the Soviet Union was very reluctant to have us stop ships which carried with them a good deal of their highly secret and sensitive material."[48]

We might have understood this advantage beforehand (as indeed Llewellyn Thompson did), and we may have been misled once again by letting our own opinion get in the way of our understanding of the Soviet view of the matter, for we had relatively little interest in these same Soviet secrets. On the first day of our discussions, McNamara was asked whether it would do us any good "if we ever captured one of these things and could examine it and take it apart." His answer was "not very much," and no one disagreed. Nuclear intelligence professionals and weapons designers would probably have held very different views, but there were none at the table. The fact that these Soviet secrets did not deeply interest us probably made it harder for us to understand how much they were valued by their owners.[49]

As for Berlin, the Soviets went to great pains at the height of the crisis to ensure that nothing relating to that embattled city was allowed to intensify the crisis. There were no threats; instead there were assurances that the Soviet government would do nothing in Europe to contribute to the danger that the Americans had created in the Caribbean.[50] That Khrushchev hoped for eventual reinforcement of his pressure on Berlin from the deployment of missiles to Cuba still seems entirely likely. But such Soviet hope of reinforcement from a successfully completed installation was quite different from any desire to compound the dangers of the crisis in Cuba by a reciprocal resort to force in Berlin. What had defended Berlin before the Cuban crisis was Khrushchev's unwillingness to risk open war. Nothing in our quarantine altered this calculation, except to reinforce the prudence that had always governed his actions if not his words on Berlin. Those of us who feared reprisal in Berlin were taking too much counsel of our own long anxieties and too little note of demonstrated Soviet prudence. The more "expert" men were in attending to the Berlin crisis, the stronger their disposition to read the Soviet deployment to Cuba as a move in the Berlin game. The most striking illustration may be in the British Foreign Office. Shortly after the crisis a senior officer of that ministry told the American analyst Bernard Brodie that when they heard the Kennedy speech of October 22, he and his colleagues "expected, to a man, that the Russians would be in West Berlin the following day." As Brodie noted, "the very reverse is what came to pass."[51]

Having shared this mistaken fear, I am not disposed to make fun of it. I clearly should have listened harder to Llewellyn Thompson, and pressed him to develop further a judgment he put forward in our first week's discussions, that the Soviet government would not react to the surprise of our blockade by a blockade of its own in Berlin. He had correctly anticipated the position that is strongly suggested by what Gromyko said to the Supreme Soviet in December: "This [Cuban] crisis . . . made many people think how the whole matter might have developed if yet another crisis in Central Europe had been added to the critical events around Cuba."[52] Gromyko, true to his character, combined threat with self-righteousness, but the underlying reality is the same as the one that Thompson understood: the Soviet government in its pressure on Berlin might use nuclear threats, but it did not take nuclear risks.

In addition to the strength of its threat to Soviet missile secrets, and its absence of a dangerous connection with Berlin, the quarantine demonstrated a third advantage, one which had been predicted: It was far more responsive to command and control than an air attack could have been. No ship was stopped or boarded without direct authorization from the president, and the naval forces on both sides respected the decision of the two governments that mortal conflict should be avoided. There were imperfections in communication, and President Kennedy was startled to find on October 24 that the navy's surveillance of Soviet submarines led to their being required to surface in the presence of the United States Navy, usually by the exhaustion of their batteries, but possibly once or twice by the use of small practice depth charges.[53] There were also harsh words at moments of high tension between Robert McNamara and naval commanders; there was here a tension between political and operational concerns that was accentuated by a lack of reciprocal personal respect. While these edges of uneven management are not trivial, the naval quarantine, executed by decisively superior naval forces, proved vastly more controllable than the high-performance aircraft of 1962 could have been.

The quarantine had every virtue but speed in effect. It stopped the

Soviet deliveries; it did not provoke a counterblockade; its application could be sufficiently controlled on both sides to prevent unwanted hostilities. Moreover it had reserves of strength not yet called on. Validated by support from the Organization of American States, and respected by the Soviet government in its turnaround of weapons-bearing ships, the quarantine could have been expanded to cover deliveries of oil, and more. It seems unlikely that Khrushchev would have chosen to challenge a wider blockade, and if he had, the danger of uncontrolled escalation would have been much lower than with any other use of force. As Harold Macmillan told the House of Commons in November, by Friday October 26 "the President had won the battle of the ships."[54] But as the week wore on, with no resolution of the crisis, all these advantages paled in the shadow of the rising belief among us that time was running out. Whatever else it could and could not do, the quarantine gave no promise, by itself, of quick removal of the missiles already in Cuba, and that was what we thought we needed.

Robert Kennedy's account of what he said to Dobrynin on Saturday night is vivid: "We had to have a commitment by tomorrow that those bases would be removed. I was not giving them an ultimatum but a statement of fact. He should understand that if they did not remove those bases, we would remove them." I share McNamara's retrospective view that this account may be a shade more vivid than the truth, because tapes of Cabinet Room discussion on that Saturday show the president unready to "remove" the missile bases immediately. But I do believe that Robert Kennedy was instructed to convey a great sense of urgency and ask for a clear answer in one day.[55]

But why did an immediate resolution seem so urgent to us, especially on Friday and Saturday, and how far were we right in this judgment? That we held this conviction is clear—Robert Kennedy was speaking for a president whose instructions on this point had the unanimous support of his senior advisers. We believed that we were running out of time. But why?

The immediate sense of crisis on Saturday, I believe, owed much to the death of Major Anderson. That event was alarming in part because it might be the result of a top-level Soviet decision to fight in Cuba, but also because we thought it might force us into an early and heavy reply.[56] Hostile action of this sort, we had agreed earlier in the week, would require a prompt and punishing response, and when the president on Saturday held back from that response, he knew that pressure for action was bound to grow. The tradition of arms demanded not only that Anderson's death be avenged, but also that the men who would follow him be protected. Nor did anyone among us doubt that aerial reconnaissance must continue and in all probability be intensified. So unless we were to give up that reconnaissance or restrain it sharply against the advice of our senior military command-ers, we faced the early prospect of a contest for air supremacy over Cuba.

We did not require air supremacy over Cuba for its own sake, however, but only because we thought it vital to take pictures day by day over the missile sites. Was that because we needed to know exactly how many missiles there were? Not really. What we needed was that all the missiles should be removed under proper "observation and supervision," as the president said in his public reply to Khrushchev on October 27. But this requirement did not itself mean that we must look at every site every day, and it did not matter to us whether there were thirty or forty or eighty missiles to be taken out.

What we had been concerned with all along was the rapid and accelerating Soviet effort to make the missiles *operational.* From the beginning we had assumed that our problem would worsen when these missiles could actually be fired. To Dean Acheson, in a review of Robert Kennedy's posthumous book, *Thirteen Days,* it seemed clear from the start that the blockade "would give the Russians time for their technicians to make some or all of the missiles operational," and "once this occurred, Cuba would become a combination of porcupine and cobra."[57] Acheson's conviction that this must be prevented governed his unrepentant preference for an air attack. Sorensen, while rejecting the air attack, held a parallel view. A few months after the crisis he wrote: "All of us knew that, once the missile sites under construction became operational, and capable of responding to any apparent threat or command with a nuclear volley, the President's options would be drastically changed."[58] Sorensen is commenting here primarily on what had been thought in the first days of our deliberations, and he is correct. But our fear increased as continuing reconnaissance after the president's speech showed accelerated efforts at the missile sites. In the last days of the crisis we were still watching these efforts as if they were a capital point.

But were they? Grant that we had it right the first week. If the installations had been completed in secret and then revealed by Khrushchev in his own time and in his own way, the situation facing us would have been worse. Grant further that this prospect made it urgent for us to proclaim our own course before the installation was complete. Does it follow that the rate of construction should still have had the great influence that it plainly did on October 26, when the president told Rusk to tell Scali to tell Fomin that time was very short, and on October 27 when he told his brother to tell Dobrynin that we must have an answer the next day? As I look back on it, I do not think that any such position was required simply by the continuing Soviet efforts at the missile sites. I now believe that by that time the advantage had shifted in our direction in ways that we could have understood better than we did—and would have come to recognize if the warnings given by John Scali and Robert Kennedy had been rejected.

First and most important, by October 27 the missiles in Cuba were at best a paper cobra. We were never to know for certain whether they had warheads. In the fall of 1984 I had separate opportunities for reminiscences with two of the professional intelligence officers who worked on this problem in 1962. Both agreed that we never knew whether warheads arrived in Cuba or not; one now believes that they did and the other that they did not. In the face of this uncertainty the only prudent course was to assume that warheads might be in place.[59] But even if they were fully armed the missiles could not be used deliberately, because the Russians could not possibly ignore the plain warning in the president's speech of October 22 that any missile fired from Cuba would require "a full retaliatory response" on the Soviet Union. Khrushchev's letter of October 26 made it plain that he understood this warning. He was in control, he said, and he had never had any intention whatever of attacking the United States with these defensive weapons.[60]

Thus our successful exposure of Khrushchev's secret, together with our firm declaration of readiness to retaliate if necessary, had made his missiles unusable even for threats; far from brandishing them, he was already bargaining over their removal.

Porcupines the missiles might still be, because no one could be absolutely sure that if they were attacked directly, one or more might not be fired in angry reply. In some measure this risk had existed almost from the beginning. Even on October 16 General Taylor had pointed out that one of the missiles *might* be operational, and McNamara had remarked, "If we're talking about an air attack, we should consider it *only* on the assumption that we can carry it off before these become operational."[61] During that first week the prevailing belief was that in fact the missiles were not yet operational, and indeed one of the strongest arguments of the advocates of the air strike was precisely that it was important to remove the missiles while it was still safe to do so. Nor did the opponents of the air strike focus initially on the risk that some might already be operable. Their argument, especially as marshaled by Robert Kennedy, rested on broad moral grounds. But on October 21, when the president took one hard last look at the air-strike option, he learned that it was too late to assume that no missiles were ready, and by October 27 the prevailing estimate was that a number of the sites were operational. I find it hard to believe that in this situation we would ever have found a direct air attack on the missile sites an acceptable option. Any such attack *might* produce thermonuclear explosions on American cities, a risk we must not run as long as we had alternatives. I am confident, looking back, that this would have been the president's firm judgment.

Thus by October 27, and probably for some days before that, the question of levels of operability had become much less urgent than all of us had been supposing. The missiles could not be used deliberately, but the porcupine must not be provoked. There was no good case for rapid attack, and no great cost in delay.[62]

If we had been required to address this question on Sunday the twenty-eighth, I believe we would have found another path to a successful outcome, one less dangerous than the early direct attack on Cuba that was in the air on Saturday evening. We could have intensified our successful blockade, carefully limiting both our reconnaissance and any reprisals necessary to keep it in place, and waited for Khrushchev to give in. The blockade might not be decisive soon, but it was a certain winner over time. There was no way for either Soviet or Cuban forces to break it except by meeting our condition—the removal of the offensive weapons—and this condition had won the support of our own country and of our allies in the Americas and in Europe. A closer look would have shown us that the Soviet government *dared* not escalate in Europe, *must* not deliberately use its missiles in Cuba, and *could* not break the blockade. We could also have recognized that it would hardly have served Soviet purposes or helped Soviet prestige to endure an unbreakable and tightening blockade for long. Each week would have endangered the position of Khrushchev and his supporters much more than it endangered us. If we could be patient and careful, we had a winner in the blockade alone. I believe that just these kinds of thoughts would have forced themselves upon us on October 28 if Khrushchev had not delighted us with his Sunday-morning message. The president's mind was already moving in that direction. On Saturday evening, in an ExCom meeting that began at nine P.M., after his brother's talk with Dobrynin, he said that on the next day we could consider adding oil to the quarantine list, and on Sunday morning the indomitable McNamara got up early to work on that line of action.[63] The president was also considering diplomatic options.

Perhaps the largest obstacle to a more patient course was the feeling on Saturday that the situation was becoming so tense, so full of unpredictable encounters, so near to spinning out of control, that only an immediate conclusion could protect us from unacceptable risk of escalation even to a nuclear exchange. Yet there is an obvious contradiction between this reasonable motive for our Saturday messages and any actual attack on the missiles, with its own intrinsic risk of escalation. That difficulty would have been squarely before us on Sunday and Monday. While no one will ever know for sure how the argument would have come out, I think in retrospect that there was more to be learned from the events of the five days after October 22 than those of us on the American side had fully understood by Saturday night, and that further reflection on Sunday would have reinforced the president's already expressed preference for less dangerous moves.

A review of the choices Kennedy had already made by the evening of October 27 reinforces this opinion. It is true that he chose to begin by a public military action, because he found no hope in unaided diplomacy and no net gain in a diplomatic first round. In every choice after that opening decision he took the most moderate course he could find: naval action and not the air strike; a selective quarantine instead of a full John Paul Jones blockade; individual presidential selection of ships to be challenged; moderation and not anger in every message to Khrushchev; a refusal to react at once after Anderson was lost; a private assurance instead of a public rebuke on the Turkish missiles. Would Kennedy have ordered an air strike or an invasion on Monday or Tuesday when other moves were still open? I doubt it.[64]

Indeed as I look back, it appears to me that one essential and wholly characteristic part of the president's management of this crisis was his insistence on making his decisions one at a time and on relating each one to his current appraisal of the position of Khrushchev. As in a chess match, it was necessary in each new move to consider the last move of the opponent. The analogy to chess oversimplifies, because the process had more than two dimensions, and the possible moves were far more varied than in chess. The element of chance was high, and so was the possibility of intervention by third parties like Castro. The two sides were engaged in a set of actions and communications vastly more complex than any game conducted by two players making alternating single moves. Still, as in chess, each new action must respect the latest actions of the opponent. Moreover, the overall impact of moves and countermoves from Monday through Saturday had been to improve our position. The blockade had been respected; satisfactory proposals had come from Khrushchev; the unity of the West was strong, and Khrushchev had displayed great prudence. The events of Saturday, disquieting as they were, did not in fact outweigh the evidence of the preceding days, and they did not impose any requirement for rapid and violent American reaction. I think the president's restraint throughout the week was an augury of very careful play to come if Saturday's messages were unsuccessful.

Our Choices on October 27

Anxiety about continuing work on the missiles and the prospect of early air engagement were not the only causes of our intense desire for speed on Friday and Saturday. We were also driven by hope. On Friday we had received serious indications of a Soviet desire to settle the matter on a basis we found attractive: They would withdraw the missiles; we would promise not to invade Cuba, and the quarantine would end. Those indications were not conclusive. Fomin had simply asked Scali what our government would think of such a bargain, and Khrushchev's letter was both complex and imprecise. But taken together, these communications gave us high hope as Friday ended and made us eager to settle the matter on essentially these terms. We thought we could see daylight.

It was the disappointment of this hope that gave us so much pain on Saturday, with the killing of Major Anderson, the second U-2 off course in the Pacific, and above all Khrushchev's overnight shift to an explicit and public proposal that the Soviet missiles in Cuba should be exchanged for the American missiles in Turkey. Our distress reflected not only the liveliness of our earlier hopes but also, especially for the president himself, an intense dissatisfaction with the notion that the single remaining obstacle in the path to success should be the unwanted missiles in Turkey. To understand the strength of his feelings we must look back.

The deployment of Jupiters to Turkey was arranged in 1959, in spite of President Eisenhower's misgivings, as part of the NATO response to the emerging threat of Soviet missiles. The fifteen missiles in Turkey were there for Khrushchev to discuss on October 27 not because Kennedy, any more than Eisenhower, had wanted them there, but because, like Eisenhower, he had not acted on his own belief that it would be better if they were not. He had held this view since very early in his administration, before they were deployed, and at his repeated request the possibility of their cancellation or withdrawal had been repeatedly explored and regularly dropped. By the autumn of 1962 no senior official except General LeMay of the air force still believed that the Jupiters were good military weapons. The argument for inaction was simply that pressure for their removal would have political costs in Turkey that could be avoided by waiting until the vulnerable, cumbersome, obsolete, liquid-fuel Jupiters could be replaced by invulnerable, mobile, modern, solid-fuel Polaris missiles in submarines.

In August 1962, in the context of rising concern about Soviet shipments to Cuba, the president raised the subject again. The memorandum I sent out on August 23 asked his question: "What action can be taken to get the Jupiter missiles out of Turkey?" The question had received no formal answer when the crisis broke, and neither the president nor I as his agent had been pressing for action. The president was angry when they were still there on October 27, and in his anger he once or twice expressed himself as if he had given orders that had not been obeyed. But it was not so. He had known for a year and a half that the Turkish missiles could be removed only over the resistance of both the Turks and Washington's custodians of NATO solidarity (of whom, in one mood, he was the foremost). He had not pressed the matter home. Earlier in the crisis he had asked for further attention to the Turkish missiles, and for work on the ways of getting them off the diplomatic board. This request had useful consequences on Saturday, but it had produced no clear recommendation for action, and again the president had not pressed the matter. Many students of the crisis have been misled on this point, probably by Robert Kennedy and Kenneth O'Donnell, who undoubtedly heard incomplete and irritated versions from the president himself. But the record is clear. I agree with George Ball and Barton Bernstein that no decision to remove the missiles had ever been taken. Moreover, the president understood very well why the missiles were still in Turkey on October 27, and who had not ordered them removed, and why. There is something that makes one smile in Robert Kennedy's language: "The President believed he was President and that, his wishes having been made clear, they would be followed and the missiles removed." President Kennedy believed nothing of the sort, and neither did Robert Kennedy when he was himself the action officer. No one knew better than the Kennedy brothers the difference between wish and command, preference and decision, hope and action, in the executive branch of the United States government. It was one of Robert Kennedy's great qualities that he understood these differences so well, but in judging the behavior of departments not his own he sometimes forgot them.[65]

Now, at the height of the crisis, in a broadcast public letter, Khrushchev had presented the question of the Turkish missiles in a peculiarly galling fashion. On the one hand, the crisis could now be resolved if we would only do something we had been wanting to do, for our own reasons, for a year and a half. What could be more reasonable? But there was poison in the proposal too. If we would not press the Turks to a decision when there was no crisis, how could we explain ourselves if we were to force them to give up the Jupiters to save our own skins? And yet how could we deny the apparent fairness of the proposal? Our own most famous publicist, Walter Lippmann, had put it forward only two days before (and Llewellyn Thompson thought that the Soviets might see Lippmann's suggestion as our trial balloon). To us indeed there were differences; the missiles in Turkey had not been installed secretly, or lied about, and they were there as part of the collective defense of the West. But it would not be easy to make these points persuasively to the world—or to ourselves—if a refusal to withdraw those missiles should lead to war.

The discussion all day Saturday was intense. No one believed we could or should accept Khrushchev's new offer as it stood, but the president did not want to reject it either and sought other alternatives. Could NATO leaders recognize the danger themselves and propose a withdrawal as their contribution to the resolution of the crisis? He telephoned General Lauris Norstad, the NATO commander, and received no encouragement. Could the Turks contribute to peace by asking us to agree to the withdrawal? No one thought they could come to this view with the privacy and speed that would be needed to make such action effective. But the president's questions were not fruitless. By his persistent unwillingness to agree that he must flatly refuse to do what he had wanted to do all along, and by his insistent reminders that no one could really think the unwanted Jupiters were worth a war, he was forcing others to think harder about the choices he faced.[66]

The first decision that he reached was that we should try to get Khrushchev to settle on the basis of the proposal in his first letter—no American invasion of Cuba and no Soviet missiles there. That was the repeated advice of such varied members of our group as Sorensen, Nitze, Ball, Thompson, Robert Kennedy, and myself. It was also the preference of Rusk, McNamara, and Stevenson. The president never rejected this course, but he did not at first accept it. It was as clear to him as to the rest of us that Khrushchev's first proposal was better than his second, but he did not think the Soviet leader would go back to it. Khrushchev, he thought, was now in a strong position to press forward to complete the Cuban bases under the protective cover of a new proposal which he thought would "look like a very fair trade" to "any man at the United Nations or any other rational man."[67]

Kennedy also recognized more quickly than anyone else that if we should reject the missile trade and then go ahead with air strikes or an invasion, we would find our choice "very difficult to explain." He made the point repeatedly, perhaps most powerfully at the end of the afternoon: "We can't very well invade Cuba with all its toil, and long as it's going to be, when we could have gotten them out by making a deal on the same missiles in Turkey. If that's part of the record, I don't see how we'll have a very good war." That was why he thought, "We're better off to get those missiles out of Turkey and out of Cuba." The great obstacle to any such trade was that it would be seen in Europe as a sellout. Kennedy recognized this difficulty, but he was even more concerned with the prospect that European opinion would change sharply if bloody battles should begin in Cuba and spread to Turkey or Berlin. NATO might be firm now, but "we all know how quickly everybody's courage goes when the blood starts to flow."[68]

So Kennedy's understanding of the political power of Khrushchev's second letter made him pessimistic about the prospect of success in returning to the first. Yet in the end he not only chose that course but recognized the importance of giving it clear priority over any effort to persuade the Turks of the advantage of getting the missiles in their country off the board. Although he himself believed that it was urgent to address the Turks directly, he accepted the argument, advanced by his brother and me, that we should not say things to NATO or to the Turks that might get leaked to Khrushchev and lead him to stick to his second letter. He did not think the effort to go back to the first letter would be successful, but he respected the different opinion of Llewellyn Thompson, who said that for Khrushchev the important thing was "to be able to say, 'I saved Cuba, I stopped an invasion.' "[69]

In shaping the response to Khrushchev, the president got particular help from his brother and Dean Rusk. Robert Kennedy argued that it was important not only to go back to the proposals in Khrushchev's first letter but (1) to accept those proposals plainly, (2) to state our own view of their substance, and (3) to avoid unnecessary debate about missiles in Turkey. To see the real importance of this contribution we must begin by remarking that many writers (Robert Kennedy among them) have misunderstood it. He was not here proposing a next step that no one had mentioned before. Indeed the draft from the State Department that he was criticizing explicitly referred to "your letter of October 26" (the first letter) and urged "a rapid settlement," which that letter "suggests is possible."[70]

What Robert Kennedy did was to insist successfully on the value of a clear *acceptance* of Khrushchev's first proposal. If he had an adversary on this point it was not Adlai Stevenson and not the State Department, but his brother. The president initially resisted a direct assurance against invasion, for he knew that influential forces favored such an invasion. The editors of *Time* among others had been pressing for it even before the crisis. But now he accepted his brother's advice— "Send this letter and say you're accepting his offer." This argument was powerfully backed up by Sorensen. "Bobby's formula is a good one. Does it sound like an ultimatum if we say, we are accepting your offer[?]" I joined in, saying, "You've got to give him something to get him back on this track." But precisely because the resistance to this proposal came from the president himself, it was his brother's voice that counted most.[71]

The president had a second objection to his brother's suggestion. He saw no "policy difference" in the suggestion, and he did not think it was worth fighting over details of language with Ambassador Stevenson, the author of the new draft that his brother was criticizing. But when Sorensen proposed that there could be a new draft that would incorporate both Bobby's ideas and some of Stevenson's language, the President agreed, helped by some fraternal teasing.

> RFK: Why do we bother you with it? Why don't you guys work it
>   out and . . .
>   (Mixed voices)

> JFK: I think we ought to move. I don't—there's no question bother-
> ing me, I just think we're going to have to decide which letter
> we send . . .
>
> RFK: Why don't we try to work it out without you being able to
> pick . . .
> (Prolonged laughter)
>
> JFK: The one you're going to have to worry about is Adlai, so you
> might as well work it out with him.
> (Laughter—louder)[72]

So Sorensen and Robert Kennedy went off to do a new draft, which
Sorensen easily cleared on the telephone with Stevenson, whose real
interest was in avoiding a harsh tone and not in the sentences that
Robert Kennedy had found troublesome. The new draft proposed a
solution "along the lines" of Khrushchev's first letter; it stated "the
key elements of your proposal" as removal of offensive systems from
Cuba, an end of the U.S. quarantine, and American assurances against
an invasion of Cuba—all on the condition of "appropriate United
Nations observation and supervision." It stayed away from argumentation over Turkey. After review by the president, the message went
out.[73]

The afternoon meeting of ExCom adjourned after the approval of
this letter, and a smaller group moved from the Cabinet Room to the
Oval Office to talk over the second means of communication—an oral
message to be conveyed to Ambassador Dobrynin. As I remember it,
those present in the discussion that followed with the president were
Dean Rusk, Robert McNamara, Robert Kennedy, George Ball, Roswell Gilpatric, Llewellyn Thompson, Theodore Sorensen, and I. One
part of the oral message we discussed was simple, stern, and quickly
decided—that the time had come to agree on the basis set out in the
president's new letter: no Soviet missiles in Cuba, and no U.S. invasion. Otherwise further American action was unavoidable. This stern
part of the message was implicit in what we had been discussing all day,
and I do not recall that we had difficulty in agreeing on it. The president in particular was clear and insistent on this part of the message.

The other part of the oral message was proposed by Dean Rusk:
that we should tell Khrushchev that while there could be no deal over
the Turkish missiles, the president was determined to get them out and
would do so once the Cuban crisis was resolved. The proposal was
quickly supported by the rest of us and approved by the president. It
was also agreed that knowledge of this assurance would be held among
those present and no one else. Concerned as we all were by the cost
of a public bargain struck under pressure at the apparent expense of
the Turks, and aware as we were from the day's discussion that for
some, even in our own closest councils, even this unilateral private

assurance might appear to betray an ally, we agreed without hesitation that no one not in the room was to be informed of this additional message. Robert Kennedy was instructed to make it plain to Dobrynin that the same secrecy must be observed on the other side, and that any Soviet reference to our assurance would simply make it null and void.

Nothing about this decision is more remarkable than the way it was made. The meeting in the Oval Office lasted perhaps twenty minutes. The moment Dean Rusk made his suggestion it became apparent to all of us that we should agree. It would allow us to respond to Khrushchev's second proposal in a way that he might well regard as helpful, while at the same time it did not require us to engage NATO or the Turks in a public trade of "their" interests for "ours." No one could be sure it would work, but all of us believed it was worth a try.

That it was Rusk who made the proposal made it easier for the rest of us to support it. None of us could suppose that he was insensitive to the interests of allies, and none could think of him as eager to make unwise concessions to Soviet pressure. Of the nine of us, he was probably least inclined to help the Soviets at any real cost to anyone else. If he thought this assurance could properly be offered, it became relatively easy for the rest of us to agree. Rusk himself does not find his position remarkable. When I asked him in 1984 why he had been the one to make the proposal, he replied simply that the Turkish missiles were always "a phony issue." To him it was never a concession to tell Khrushchev that we were going to do what we had wanted to do for so long. He had a lively memory of his own private effort to get the Turks to give up the missiles as early as April 1961. At an Ankara meeting of the Central Treaty Organization he had walked in a garden in the evening with his Turkish opposite number, Selim Sarper, and had talked about the Jupiters on instructions from the president. Sarper had not disagreed with Rusk's low opinion of the military value of the Jupiters, but he had raised two objections. First, the Turkish government had only recently obtained parliamentary approval of its own contribution to the cost of the Jupiters (the missiles though not the warheads were to be Turkish owned), and it would be embarrassing to give them up so quickly. Second, it would be better for the self-confidence of the region to wait until there were enough Polaris submarines so that one or more could be stationed in the Mediterranean.[74]

Rusk did not come to his proposal unprepared. He had participated on the first Saturday and Sunday in discussions before the president of the possible need for a trade of some sort. Unlike some others, he had not objected to Stevenson's suggestion that a trade should be offered, and while he supported the president's decision that we should not *begin* by offering trades, there was a further discussion of the possibilities in the State Department on Sunday, and one participant in that discussion, Abram Chayes, remembers him as having "encouraged" further exploration of various trading options, not excluding Turkish missiles. Later in the week, on Thursday or Friday, Rusk saw the response that Ambassador Ray Hare sent back from Ankara to a cable drafted by George Ball, asking how the Turks would react to a trade of the missiles in their country. They would react badly, Hare answered, and if it had to be done it should be done secretly.[75] Finally, and I think most important of all, Rusk was deeply, indeed passionately, committed to the proposition that the central task of the secretary of state was to try to help the president—the *president*—not his staff or his relatives. He had been listening all day to the president's unwillingness to let an intransigent position on these unwanted weapons stand between his country and the safe removal of the Soviet missiles from Cuba. Rusk shared this sentiment, but even if he had not his mind would have turned to ways of meeting the president's concern. Characteristically, he had kept his counsel during the larger meeting. Now in the Oval Office, though he might have preferred a still smaller group, he spoke out.

To Dean Rusk it was and is clear that measured against the dangers we faced on October 27, this assurance was worth many times any possible cost. One cost we did avoid, with Soviet help. There was no leak. As far as I know, none of the nine of us told anyone else what had happened. We denied in every forum that there was any deal, and in the narrowest sense what we said was usually true, as far as it went. When the orders were passed that the Jupiters must come out, we gave the plausible and accurate—if incomplete—explanation that the missile crisis had convinced the president once and for all that he did not want those missiles there. Gossip about a possible deal did not vanish, but neither did it affect allied confidence in the United States. That the substitution of Polaris missiles for Jupiters improved the deterrent posture of the alliance was so obvious that the action essentially justified itself, and secrecy protected us from having to explain the ironic truth that it was a letter from Khrushchev that had brought us to take this obviously sensible and constructive step.

Secrecy of this sort has its costs. By keeping to ourselves the assurance on the Jupiters, we misled our colleagues, our countrymen, our successors, and our allies. We allowed them all to believe that nothing responsive had been offered in reply to Khrushchev's second message. We thus encouraged the conclusion that it had been enough to stand firm on that Saturday. Until the posthumous appearance of Robert Kennedy's *Thirteen Days* in 1969, both admirers and critics assumed that President Kennedy had been wholly unresponsive on the Turkish missiles. I remember intemperate but inconclusive conversations with people in both camps who had drawn natural but erroneous conclusions about Kennedy's "unwavering firmness" or his "unforgivable risk taking" on that Saturday. I suspect that part of the irritation on my side of such encounters lay precisely in the possession of knowledge I had promised not to share.

It remains the unanimous judgment of the surviving participants in the framing of this secret assurance that both the assurance itself and the secrecy with which we surrounded it were justified. The warheads for Jupiters in Turkey were worse than useless, and the president had full and single-handed authority to remove them. He was free to make this decision alone, and it was justified on the merits. With all its costs, secrecy prevented a serious political division both within the United States and in the Atlantic alliance. It would have been better if we had long since expressed in public the opinion Kennedy and Eisenhower both held in private, that such missiles were undesirable, but we had not done so. All day long most of us had been arguing that a public trade under Soviet pressure would have destructive effects in NATO, but no one had been able to dispute the president's insistent argument that we would be better off in reality if the Jupiters were out of Turkey. The president had every right to decide for himself that Jupiter warheads should come out, so that if a private assurance of such a decision could help to tip the balance between intensified crisis and an otherwise highly satisfactory resolution of it, it would be an act of great irresponsibility to hold that assurance back. So we thought that Saturday evening, and so we think today.

In 1987 the rest of us learned from Dean Rusk that on Saturday evening he had another discussion with the president, which produced a decision to prepare for further diplomatic action on the Turkish missiles if, as Kennedy expected, Khrushchev should insist on an open trade. The president believed such a trade might then be the best way out, and he decided that the way to do it might be in response to an appeal from U Thant, the secretary general of the United Nations. At Rusk's suggestion it was agreed that Rusk should call Andrew Cordier of Columbia University and ask him to be ready to propose such a step to U Thant. Cordier was selected because he had been a deputy to U Thant and had remained a trusted friend and also because Rusk was sure of his discretion. Rusk called Cordier, and Cordier agreed to be ready to move on a further signal, but neither he nor Kennedy had ever mentioned the matter to anyone still alive in 1987, and now both Kennedy and Cordier were dead.[76]

The fact that Kennedy and Rusk put this diplomatic contingency plan in place does not tell us what the president would have done if Sunday had produced a dusty answer from Moscow. It does tell us that a public trade was something that he wanted to be able to accept if he chose, and this alternative thus has the same standing as the preparation for tightening the naval blockade, which he encouraged McNamara to address that same evening. The privacy of the arrangement is parallel to that of the earlier decision to give Khrushchev a secret assurance on the Turkish missiles; only those present when each proposal was first mentioned were to know about it. Obviously if the public trade were to be put forward by U Thant and accepted by Kennedy, the whole world would know, but equally obviously what Kennedy intended was that if the "Cordier ploy" was executed, his own role in originating it should remain hidden. What we have here is a further demonstration of his awareness of the conflict between the *real* best interest of all—that the Turkish missiles should come out— and the inescapable *appearance* that a public Turkish trade would sacrifice the interest of a small ally in response to Soviet pressure. I cannot resist repeating what I said to him that Saturday morning: "In their own terms it would already be clear that we were trying to sell our allies for our interests. That would be the view in all of NATO. It's irrational, and it's crazy, but it's a *terribly* powerful fact."[77]

TWENTY-FIVE YEARS have passed, and I find myself less impressed by my own insistence on the reality of NATO sentiment than I am by the president's unwavering recognition that the basic interest of all concerned was to find a peaceful end to the crisis, and that the Turkish missiles, whatever the opinions of allies, did not justify bloodshed in Cuba. I also now believe that if he had decided to use the "Cordier ploy," he would have been able to marshal a formidable set of arguments in support of his acceptance of a public trade. He could have found much help within the ExCom itself. He could have asked McCone and Dillon, veterans of the Eisenhower administration, to join in making it clear that Turkish missiles had been a bad idea since before Kennedy was president; McCone on Saturday was particularly insistent that the missiles should come out of Turkey.[78] He could have asked Robert McNamara and General Taylor to spell out the gain in stable strength that would come from replacing the Jupiters with submarine-based Polaris missiles. He could have appealed—I think successfully—to both General Eisenhower in retirement and General Norstad on the job at NATO, to join in the defense of his decision as right in reality, however troubling in appearance. Norstad, unlike Eisenhower, was a believer in the Jupiters, and his messages to Kennedy on Saturday made it clear that he wanted no trade. Nonetheless I believe he would have understood that no good could come from a failure to support the president.

Among the NATO countries there would have been a mixed reaction. The temptation for de Gaulle to be critical would have been high; even without a visible Turkish trade he found the crisis a useful demonstration that the Americans were willing to put Europe in danger when their own immediate interests were at stake. On the other hand

Harold Macmillan, who supported Kennedy in his public rejection of the Turkish trade, would have backed him at least as strongly in accepting it; Macmillan wanted peace more than appearances. Other allies would probably have come out between these two. The most important politically would have been Turkey itself, and here the right special emissary (Rusk, or Robert Kennedy, or both) might well have been successful, and such a mission might even have been carried out before any full acceptance of U Thant's proposal. The Turks could have been promised a prompt Polaris deployment. They also might have asked for this or that new help from the American cupboard of conventional weapons, but why not?

Kennedy could have turned, as he did in the following year, to the yearning for peace among his own people. The eloquence that he and Sorensen successfully employed in 1963, from American University in the spring to Salt Lake City in the fall, could have been used in this case too. It is not at all clear that the public response to such a defense of an honorable end of danger would have been weak. We must bear in mind that the decisive concern of American public opinion was with Cuba, not Turkey, and the result in Cuba is exactly the same with a public trade as without it.

There would certainly have been criticism from hard-liners in the United States, but I do not believe that the administration itself would have been split. The White House staff would have been wholly and energetically loyal, and so would Rusk and McNamara and their senior colleagues, all of them believers in loyalty to the president and disbelievers in the utility of the Jupiters. In the military services there would have been dissent, but a strictly military argument in favor of keeping the Jupiters would not have been easy to make. If I guess right about help from Eisenhower and Norstad, I think it is safe to suggest that opposition in the Pentagon would have been muffled and endurable. Opposition from Senator Barry Goldwater could probably have been enjoyed.[79]

None of this tells us that the next step on Sunday or Monday would actually have been the "Cordier ploy." The president could also have tightened the blockade, and he could have held back for a time from an air strike or invasion. It is true that on Saturday afternoon there was a sense that such direct action might soon be unavoidable, but what Kennedy actually did in the rest of that day was to defer all decisions until Khrushchev had time to answer the messages sent through Dobrynin. There was talk of the need to attack the SAM site from which Anderson had been shot down, but the decision was to wait. There was talk of the need to defuse the missiles in Turkey so that we could take these possible targets off the board before bombs were dropped on Cuba, but no such order was given, and Kennedy himself argued that the Turkish attachment to the Jupiters might be one more reason for preferring "total blockade" to any stronger action against Cuba. There was indeed a recommendation from the Joint Chiefs of Staff that we should go ahead with a large air strike on Monday and an invasion a few days later. But I myself do not remember that this recommendation impressed anyone, and the Cabinet Room tapes now show that when General Taylor reported this recommendation, there was first a pause, and then a dry comment by Robert Kennedy, "That was a surprise," which produced a burst of general laughter.[80]

I cite this episode not to criticize the Joint Chiefs, but to underline the distance between their recommendation and the tenor of the Cabinet Room discussions led by the president. It was the president's choice, not that of the chiefs, that had kept all of them but Max Taylor at a distance from ExCom, and there was no way that they could be fully aware of the president's daylong preoccupation with finding a path to settlement through the tangle of Khrushchev's two messages. Still less could they know that their recommendation would be reported just after the president had agreed to let his brother and Sorensen redraft the reply to Khrushchev as a clear and definite acceptance of his first letter. They had been thinking in military terms about a military problem, guided in part by attacks on our reconnaissance aircraft and in part by their feeling that it had been understood all along that if the blockade did not do the job, we would go on to an air attack and invasion. It was also an element of their thinking that every service should be included in every enterprise. Finally, all the Joint Chiefs but Maxwell Taylor must have been concerned that a bunch of civilians were considering the next step *without consulting them.* Their recommendation showed that they were out of touch with their commander in chief, but the fault was not primarily theirs.

THE ASSURANCE on Turkish missiles remains far less important than the stick that Robert Kennedy carried to Dobrynin: a threat of further action within days, a statement that to avoid it there must be a quick Soviet agreement to withdraw the missiles, and a demand for an answer the following day. It is all very well to argue in retrospect that events were not that far in the saddle. What we told Khrushchev is clearly of great importance in the speed of his decision. Correctly or incorrectly, he concluded that time had indeed run out, or more precisely that he did not want to run the risk that it had. In reaching this conclusion he had more than Robert Kennedy's message to go by. The vast preparations for both air attacks and invasion were highly visible. In Havana the expectation of attack was at new heights. The smell of burning was indeed in the air.

I think it likely that a Saturday afternoon meeting between Scali and Fomin may have been particularly persuasive to Khrushchev. Scali was shocked by the Saturday proposal for a Turkish swap. He thought he had been made the go-between for a false lead. Rusk sent for him, asked him quietly what had happened, and sent him back to Fomin to see what he could find out. Scali was furious, and he did much more than ask for an explanation. "I denounced him for 'a stinking double-cross.'" Scali told Fomin that a missile swap was and would remain totally unacceptable. "'If you think the United States is bluffing,' I went on, 'you are part of the most colossal misjudgment of American intentions in history. We are absolutely determined to get those missiles out of there. An invasion of Cuba is only a matter of hours away.'"

Fomin repeatedly insisted that the suggestions he had put forward on Friday "were still valid," and put the blame for any mix-up on cable delays. But Scali was unappeased (although he later came to believe that Fomin's protestations were genuine), and the two men "parted on a frosty note." Sunday morning, after Khrushchev's message announcing his decision to withdraw the missiles, Fomin and Scali met again, and the Russian's first comment was: "I have been instructed to thank you and to tell you that the information you supplied was very valuable to Khrushchev in helping make up his mind quickly. And," he added with a smile, "that includes your 'explosion' of Saturday."

I believe that Scali's personal, uninstructed, and entirely genuine anger probably contributed to Khrushchev's Sunday decision. It is hard to doubt that Fomin's reports are among those he had in mind when he told the Supreme Soviet on December 12 that the cables received on October 27 had been read "as an extremely alarming warning signal."[81]

I have explained my belief that the president's next steps would have been less violent, simply because there were additional moves at sea that would carry growing costs to Khrushchev at much lower risk of unwanted escalation. But this judgment does not make the warnings of Saturday unjustified. In the situation as it had then developed there were indeed growing risks of more violent action on both sides, both by choice and by accident, and it was entirely reasonable that Khrushchev should be made aware of them. If I could replay the history and instruct John Scali not to show anger or warn that invasion was near, I would not do it.

Why Khrushchev Settled

The warnings of October 27 affected the speed of Khrushchev's response more than its substance. He had already decided by Friday morning, the twenty-sixth, that he would offer to remove his missiles, and once he took this position, he never abandoned it; the Turkish-swap proposal was a haggle, not a reversal. Even in our gloomiest moments on Saturday we knew that both his letters accepted our basic requirement that the missiles in Cuba must be withdrawn. We wanted only to hold him to the form of withdrawal he had already proposed. In understanding Khrushchev's course, it is important to go behind the American threats and assurances of Saturday night to his own decision of Friday, the most important single act in the second week of crisis. What led to this decision? The Soviet leader had certainly not made his enormous secret gamble for the purpose of pulling back so quickly, with or without an undertaking by Kennedy not to invade Cuba, with or without the dismantling of fifteen obsolete missiles in Turkey. Both of Khrushchev's letters were attempts to put a decent face on failure. Both of them offered to meet the one condition that Kennedy had made implacably clear, that the missiles must be withdrawn. What caused this reversal?

I think that Khrushchev recognized that he was in a situation in which he had no better choice. There was no prospect of gain and much to lose in any other course. He knew by Friday that the quarantine was effective, that it could be tightened, and that he could not evade it. He knew that the Americans were ready and able to attack Cuba both from the air and from the sea, and that there was no way for him to win those battles either. He had no promising move to make elsewhere. In particular there was nothing in this crisis that could encourage him to take the steps against West Berlin that he had been carefully avoiding for four years. Everywhere the political contest had gone against him—in the Organization of American States, in the United Nations, in Western Europe, and even in Africa, where non-aligned leaders canceled landing rights for Soviet planes that might have delivered warheads. Nor did he have anything to gain, in either the political or the military arena, by delay. It is true that a first reaction, by him or by someone high up on his side, had been to speed up work at the missile sites, but what good did that really do? His letters to Kennedy show that he understood perfectly well these missiles must not be fired if he could prevent it. To all this we must add, for Khrushchev as for Kennedy, the danger of unintended escalation. This possibility was a most important reason for avoiding unnecessary delay.

But the decisive consideration, on Friday and again on Sunday morning, was that in the Caribbean Khrushchev was in a position of such inferiority at every level of conventional strength that unlike the president he must fear not only the unpredictable consequences of accident, but the certainty of defeat at every level up to common catastrophe. If he had been the reckless risk taker whose possible existence we were required to consider on Saturday, he might have tried one more roll. But he was prudent; he remained in charge, and he chose to end the crisis. In retrospect it seems an easy and almost inevitable choice, hastened perhaps by Scali's outburst to Fomin, and also by Robert Kennedy's insistence on a rapid answer. But it was the situation, not the ultimatum, that was fundamental in the decision.

Khrushchev's Sunday announcement was both right and timely, and he had saved much from the shipwreck of his bold venture. Indeed, if you start from the position in which he had found himself early on Tuesday morning Moscow time, it is impossible not to have respect for the skill and energy of his reaction, as well as its prudence. Here is a man sixty-eight years old, probably awakened in the middle of the night to learn of the position just taken by his forty-five-year-old adversary in a speech to the world. He knows that his hope of a successful secret emplacement has been interrupted. He has been exposed as a deceiver, and Kennedy has announced a naval blockade that he is fully able to enforce. It must have been a bad moment.

In this situation it is not surprising that Khrushchev and his colleagues stalled for time. In terms of international reaction, that stalling was costly. Ambassador Zorin in the UN was exposed without defense to Stevenson's devastating attack. Tuesday and Wednesday for the Russians were days of standard-brand propaganda, and, one must suppose, indecision. Yet one absolutely crucial and correct decision was taken in time: the decision not to test the blockade with arms-bearing ships. The motive for this decision was not simply a desire to avoid a losing confrontation but a determination not to let nuclear secrets fall into the hands of the enemy. It was a hard decision and an easy one—hard in that it required a recognition of effective American power in place, but easy in that the alternative was so plainly undesirable. It is interesting that no Soviet commentator has yet publicly acknowledged this turnaround. Khrushchev himself flatly asserted in his memoirs that all his ships had sailed straight on through the hostile armada.[82]

Thus by Thursday Khrushchev had taken the first step to avoid direct humiliation. His next step was more affirmative and highly imaginative: a proposal to trade his missiles in Cuba for a promise from Kennedy not to invade that island. Members of the Kennedy administration have regularly claimed credit for wisdom and restraint in accepting this proposal, but it was Khrushchev's idea, not ours. Its value for him and his comrades is surely the one Thompson saw on October 27—it would save Cuba from the imperialists, as he boasted in his December speech. He was less successful with Castro, but in this crucial week Castro's good opinion meant little to both sides.

Khrushchev's letter of October 26 deserves a high place in the annals of crisis communication. The full text was released by the Department of State only in 1973, and many accounts, before and since, have been based on incomplete and loosely paraphrased quotations.[83] To read this full text in retrospect is to have renewed respect for the man who wrote it. First one is reminded that the letter was an answer to one from Kennedy written Wednesday night and delivered very early Thursday morning. In that response to an earlier and unhelpful message from Khrushchev, the president showed a moderation that Khrushchev did not miss. Kennedy explained again how he had publicly announced that the United States was bound to regard "any shipment of offensive weapons as presenting the gravest issues," and how in reliance on Soviet assurances he had

> urged restraint upon those in this country who were urging action in this matter. . . . And then I learned beyond doubt what you have not denied—namely, that all these public assurances were false and that your military people had set out recently to establish a set of missile bases in Cuba. I ask you to recognize clearly, Mr. Chairman, that it was not I who issued the first challenge in this case, and that in the light of this record these activities in Cuba required the response I have announced.
>
> I repeat my regret that these events should cause a deterioration in our relations. I hope that your Government will take the necessary action to permit a restoration of the earlier situation.[84]

Khrushchev's reply begins with the remark that "from your letter I got the feeling that you have some understanding of the situation which has developed and a sense of responsibility. I appreciate this." The change in temper is marked, and it lasts until the end of the crisis. The letter continues with an eloquent argument on the calamitous nature of war, and then an unrepentant effort to argue that whatever arms might be in Cuba, they could not be offensive because they were intended only to defend. Yet Khrushchev knows by now that Kennedy will not be moved by this semantic juggling: "Evidently, I shall not be able to convince you." He moves on to make two much more serious points. First, he is not about to fire the weapons in Cuba, whether they are called offensive or defensive. "You may regard us with distrust, but you can at any rate rest assured that we are of sound mind and understand perfectly well that if we launch an offensive against you, you will respond in kind." Second, he is not going to test the blockade with vessels carrying armaments. "I assure you that the vessels which are now headed for Cuba are carrying the most innocuous peaceful cargoes. . . . I assure you that the ships bound for Cuba are carrying no armaments at all. The armaments needed for the defense of Cuba are already there." In this oblique fashion Khrushchev asserts that all his undelivered weapons—no intermediate-range missiles were ever landed in Cuba—have suddenly become unnecessary. Since no weapons are now being sent through, the president can readily withhold "piratical actions," and he is strongly urged to do so.[85]

The letter goes on to explain the whole enterprise in terms of fear for the fate of Cuba. Khrushchev reminds Kennedy of the Bay of Pigs and of his acknowledgment in Vienna that it was a mistake. He also notes continuing help to "Cuban counterrevolutionary emigrants," and asserts that "the constant threat of armed attack and aggression has hung and continues to hang over Cuba." All this leads to the proposition that it is only this danger that has led to the Soviet deployment, and so it lays the basis for a cautious but clear proposal to remove "the armaments you call offensive" in return for American assurances against an attack on Cuba.

The letter concludes with the justly celebrated appeal against pulling on the rope of danger:

> If you have not lost command of yourself and realize clearly what this could lead to, then, Mr. President, you and I should not now pull on the ends of the rope in which you have tied a knot of war, because the harder you and I pull, the tighter this knot will become. And a time may come when this knot is tied so tight that the person who tied it is no longer capable of untying it, and then the knot will have to be cut. What that would mean I need not explain to you, because you yourself understand perfectly what dread forces our two countries possess.[86]

This three-thousand-word letter was delivered to the American Embassy in Moscow on Friday afternoon at 4:43 P.M. Moscow time. Unless we attribute to Khrushchev and his stenographers a superhuman speed in composition and transcription, we must assume that this fully developed argument, combining warnings, assurances, explanations, and proposals, was composed not later than Friday morning Moscow time, and possibly sooner. That in earlier messages Khrushchev blustered and stalled for time is much less remarkable than that he was able to assess the situation in this comprehensive way and make a constructive proposal only three days after the president's speech.

Khrushchev's letter was delayed en route. From the time of its arrival at the embassy in Moscow to the time of its complete arrival in Washington, almost twelve hours passed, the daytime and early evening hours of Washington's Friday. The message was translated by the Embassy before its transmission at seven P.M. Moscow time, and it was received in the Department of State in four sections, which arrived in irregular order at irregular intervals between six and nine P.M. Washington time. Given the seven-hour difference between the Moscow and Washington time zones, we have a transmission time of six to nine hours. The consequence was that this message did not get the same-day answer for which it cried out. We found it hopeful but complex, and after working for hours through Friday evening, we put off the reply until Saturday morning, at which point we found ourselves confronted with the Turkish-trade message as well. If Khrushchev's first letter had reached us even a few hours earlier, we would have been able to reply on Friday. Such a reply, delivered to Dobrynin by seven or eight P.M. Washington time, would surely have been in Khrushchev's hands on his Saturday morning. In that situation it seems reasonable to hope that the daytime activity in Moscow that produced the public broadcast of Khrushchev's Turkish-trade proposal at five P.M. Moscow time on Saturday would have been different. We were ill served by the delays in translation and transmission, and it was an entirely prudent and sensible change—one initiated by the Russians in the Turkish-trade letter—that every subsequent message was broadcast immediately.

After the crisis Kennedy ordered a review of its lessons for communications, and the delay in the receipt of this message of October 26 was inconclusively examined; no compellingly clear explanation was found. One titillating speculation attributed the delay to Kremlin intrigue. In those days outgoing cables from the American Embassy in Moscow, once encrypted, were entrusted to Soviet channels for initial onward transmission. A part of the long delay occurred at this stage, and there are some American officials who believe that the holdup was deliberate, caused by one or another Soviet leader who did not approve of the cable's contents. The Americans who hold this view assert that the length of the encrypted cable would have made it instantly recognizable to anyone who already knew of its existence. The matter is not subject to proof, and the relevant report remains classified, but this explanation is not inconsistent with either the technical or the political possibilities. In Khrushchev's memoirs there is a sentence that suggests that he may indeed have been criticized for sending the Friday letter on his own: "I take complete responsibility for the fact that the President and I entered into direct contact at the most crucial and dangerous stage of the crisis." Only a few months after the crisis Khrushchev talked with the American editor Norman Cousins in a way that suggested what some of that criticism might have been like: "When I asked the military advisers if they could assure me that holding fast would not result in the death of five hundred million human beings, they looked at me as though I was out of my mind or, what was worse, a traitor. . . . So I said to myself: To hell with these maniacs. If I can get the United States to assure me that it will not attempt to overthrow the Cuban government, I will remove the missiles."[87]

Speculation on the causes of this delay, with its damaging effect on the possibility of a more rapid resolution of the crisis, should not blind us to the fact that both the private and public letters, from Thursday onward, show on both sides a steady determination to resolve the matter without war. The Turkish-trade proposal was deeply disquieting to us, as we have seen, but not because it carried an immediate new threat. Moreover, the president's answer was not a rejection, but a rephrased acceptance, courteous if delayed, of a better offer only one day old. Even without the private assurance on the Turkish missiles that reply could hardly have been read by Khrushchev as intransigent. Both in tone and content every letter from Wednesday onward leaves the way open for a reply. The correspondence is one which in and of itself helped to create common ground, and even if Khrushchev had chosen a different next step on October 28, the rereading of these messages persuades me that if the crisis had continued, the messages too would have continued, and with the purpose on both sides of avoiding war.[88]

It is not pleasant to turn from Khrushchev's act of imaginative statesmanship to the much less impressive business of his proposal on the missiles in Turkey. My own assessment is that it was the ordinary Soviet effort to sweeten any agreement by one last haggle. I doubt that the Turkish question would ever have become a sticking point on the Soviet side, and in that sense the American response designed by Rusk and approved by Kennedy may have been more than Khrushchev deserved or needed. But just as it was wrong for Khrushchev to push on this essentially minor matter, so it was right for Kennedy to make the most forthcoming response he could in the light of his own situation, and no one can say for certain that this additional concession, so small in one sense, did not have its own importance in the speed and clarity of Khrushchev's final and best decision—the one he announced on October 28.

The Role of Nuclear and Conventional Balances

An enduring question for Americans is how much this satisfactory result is to be credited to the local military balance and how much to American nuclear superiority. Those who believe in the political weight of nuclear superiority have steadily maintained that it was decisive here. Henry Kissinger set an early example: "The crisis could not have ended so quickly and decisively but for the fact that the United States can win a general war if it strikes first and can inflict intolerable damage on the Soviet Union even if it is a victim of a surprise attack. . . . The credibility of our deterrent was greater than theirs."[89] Over the years American conservatives have come to take this view for granted, holding that Khrushchev's nuclear inferiority not only stimulated his adventure but caused his failure. Conversely, believers in the value of conventional strength on the spot have found encouragement in the evident effectiveness of the quarantine. Since indeed "success has a hundred fathers," it has been entirely natural for each of the armed services to praise its contribution, for each played an essential part.

The largest individual contribution may have been that of Rudolf Anderson, a reconnaissance pilot, not only on October 14, but still more on October 27. In traditional terms he remained unavenged, but when we consider the role of his death in the decisions and communications that brought a rapid and decisive turn away from danger in less than one day's time, it becomes hard to think of any single sacrifice in the service of the United States that ever had larger consequences for good. On the American side, the death of Anderson was a major force in producing the messages that Robert Kennedy carried to Khrushchev, and it now seems probable that the attack on his plane had a still larger impact on Khrushchev. In 1988 we have learned from responsible Soviet observers that the order to shoot at Anderson's plane was given by a senior Soviet commander on the spot, in violation of standing orders from Moscow not to shoot at American aircraft. If that is what happened—and I find it entirely credible—the news of the shoot-down must have been a severe shock to Khrushchev. Only one day earlier he had been telling Kennedy that neither of them must pull on the rope to the knot of war, and now one of his own commanders had given his end of the rope a fierce and forbidden tug. It seems likely that the shoot-down of Anderson was a powerful influence in persuading Khrushchev to step back from danger. To recognize and honor Anderson's role in this result is a better repayment to his memory than any act of vengeance could have been.[90]

Returning to the underlying question of the roles of nuclear and nonnuclear power, I have found the attribution of our success mainly to strategic superiority increasingly unpersuasive as time has passed. At first, and indeed for several years, it seemed to me sufficient to recognize and accept the importance of both kinds of strength, but in later years I have come to believe that such evenhandedness obscures a crucial difference. In conventional strength, effective and indeed substantial superiority was at once a necessity for the American president and a most compelling force on the Soviet chairman, but at the nuclear level it was not superiority but the fact of reciprocal mortal peril that was decisive. To put it another way, our purpose was to face Khrushchev with a situation in which his least unattractive choice was to withdraw the missiles. To achieve that result we must be able to show him, at the conventional level, the prospect of defeat, and that required effective and visible superiority. But at the nuclear level all that we needed was the strength to ensure that a nuclear war would never be attractive to him. In the formulation of Eisenhower, we needed enough. As six of us put it twenty years later:

> The decisive military element in the resolution of the crisis was our clearly available and applicable superiority in conventional weapons within the area of the crisis. U.S. naval forces, quickly deployable for the blockade of offensive weapons that was sensibly termed a quarantine, and the availability of U.S. ground and air forces sufficient to execute an invasion if necessary, made the difference. American nuclear superiority was not in our view a critical factor, for the fundamental and controlling reason that nuclear war, already in 1962, would have been an unexampled catastrophe for both sides; the balance of terror so eloquently described by Winston Churchill seven years earlier was in full operation. No one of us ever reviewed the nuclear balance for comfort in those hard weeks.[91]

Diligent students of the missile crisis have more than once asked me to compare this conclusion with a comment that McNamara made to Congress early in 1963: "We faced that night the possibility of launching nuclear weapons, and Khrushchev knew it, and that is the reason and the only reason why he withdrew those weapons." Questioners have suggested that this passage constitutes a recognition of the value of our nuclear superiority. The passage is an unfortunate one, but not for that reason. What McNamara was invoking was not nuclear superiority but the recognition of nuclear danger on both sides, and he was doing it with a vehemence that reflected not only the intensity of his own recognition of that danger at the time, but also his desire to head off a question suggesting that Khrushchev's decision could only be explained by some secret deal. We have here, in other words, not a declaration of the value of nuclear superiority, but an illustration of the difficulties created by our secret assurance. The full exchange shows how it happened, and it underlines the collateral costs of even the most justified deception:

> MR. WHITTEN: . . . Are you aware of any agreement, any assurance, by yourself or anyone else in high government office, to Khrushchev that if he would withdraw at the time under the conditions that you showed us, the United States would thereby commit itself to any particular course of action?
> SECRETARY MCNAMARA: I am not only unaware of any agreement, it is inconceivable to me that our President would enter into a discussion of any such agreement. Moreover, there were absolutely no undisclosed agreements associated with the withdrawal of the Soviet missiles from Cuba.

MR. WHITTEN: May I repeat again that by asking the question I am by no means making the charge. Only by asking the question can I get your answer.

I think the American people are seeking an answer in that area and are greatly disturbed. It is sort of unrealistic with Khrushchev's buildup that he suddenly would take this turn unless there was something which he expected.

SECRETARY MCNAMARA: If that is so, Mr. Whitten, the American people completely failed to understand what happened during that very important period of October. They failed to understand that we had a force of several hundred thousand men ready to invade Cuba. They failed to understand that had we invaded Cuba, we would have been confronted with the Soviets; that had we been confronted with the Soviets we would have killed thousands of them; that had we killed thousands of them, the Soviets would probably have had to respond; that they might have had nuclear delivery weapons there [that] might have been operational, and they might have been launched; and that in any event Khrushchev knew without any question whatsoever that he faced the full military power of the United States, including its nuclear weapons. That may be difficult to understand for some, but it is not difficult for me to understand, because we faced that night the possibility of launching nuclear weapons and Khrushchev knew it, and that is the reason, and the only reason, why he withdrew those weapons.[92]

This passage as a whole is not a declaration of the decisiveness of nuclear *superiority,* but a description of the military action in prospect, and the nuclear *danger* that both sides would then have faced. Certainly Khrushchev had to fear that result, but so did we.

What we knew about Soviet nuclear forces at the time was simply that they were large enough to make any nuclear exchange an obvious catastrophe for Americans too. Without counting the missiles in Cuba, the Soviets had a deployed strength of 50 on land (at the time we estimated 75) and 100 on submarines. They also had about 150 strategic bombers. We had to assume that in any nuclear exchange, no matter who started it, some of these missiles and bombers would get through with multimegaton bombs. Even one would be a disaster. We had no interest in any nuclear exchange other than to avoid it. The fact that our own strategic forces were very much larger gave us no comfort.

The nuclear balance may have had more meaning to Khrushchev and his colleagues. We have already observed that they had been watching the relative numbers closely and giving them political weight. The whole Cuban missile adventure resulted largely from Khrushchev's desire to narrow his newly exposed missile gap. He must have been well aware of the American missiles and the 1,300 SAC bombers that were arrayed against him. It is hard to doubt that he would have found the situation somehow more comforting if the balance had been different. But would that comfort have changed his behavior? The single most interesting element in the exchanges between Kennedy and Khrushchev at the height of the crisis is that both men take it for granted that neither one wants a nuclear war and that it would be a common disaster. I do not believe that this shared assumption would have been altered for either man by a more nearly equal nuclear balance.

One contention often made by those who believe in the role of the nuclear balance in the missile crisis is that if it were not for American nuclear superiority, Khrushchev would have reacted to our blockade by a blockade of his own against West Berlin. But as we have seen in our examination of the Berlin crisis, there is no evidence that it was American nuclear superiority that saved Berlin. Khrushchev's cautious behavior over Berlin is explained by the existence of real nuclear danger created by Western commitment, not by American superiority as such. It is true that during the missile crisis many of us wrongly feared a Soviet reaction against Berlin. It is also entirely possible that until the president's speech of October 22, Khrushchev himself had hoped to renew his pressure on Berlin after the missiles in Cuba had been secretly deployed and then publicly proclaimed by him. At that point he would indeed have had additional visible nuclear strength and also the political advantage of having demonstrated his own boldness and American weakness. But after Kennedy's speech it was quite another matter to force an enlargement of the crisis by blockading Berlin. That would simply have added to the risks in Cuba the very risks that Khrushchev himself had already found daunting in Berlin, and which he had chosen not to run in all the four years before his Cuban adventure. There was nothing in Kennedy's blockade that could encourage him to change his mind. Throughout the missile crisis the perceived connection between Cuba and Berlin was much more important in Washington than in the Kremlin. Our fear was not his hope.[93]

The point must not be pressed too far. One way to test the role of nuclear superiority is to ask ourselves how the two leaders might have behaved if the strategic balance at the time had been *reversed*— if the deliverable warheads of the Soviets had been numbered in thousands and those of the Americans in hundreds. In spite of the logic of mutual vulnerability when there is a significant level of survivable force on both sides, it seems unwise to take it for granted that a balance so reversed would have had no consequences for the behavior of either side. Would the Americans have been quite so ready to impose the quarantine? Would the Soviets have been so unwilling to run the risk of a counterblockade of their own in Berlin? The question is hypothetical, and in more than one way. If there had been this opposite imbalance, the Berlin question might have been pressed to some resolution earlier. In such a case the American rush to arms would already have been headlong, and American sensitivity about Cuba might already have reached explosive levels. In such a case too the problem bemusing Khrushchev in Bulgaria in May would have been altogether different. Nonetheless the contemplation of American behavior in the face of a ten-to-one inferiority in strategic weapons imposes wariness about the conclusion that once there is a reciprocal risk of catastrophe all differences in numbers become trivial. It does not strengthen a good argument to press it too far.[94]

The United States has never experienced dramatic overall inferiority, and the massive and variegated systems now deployed on both sides make any such imbalance a most improbable prospect for the future. "Parity," "overall equivalence," "compensating imbalances," "approximate equality," and the like have been the strategic reality at least since 1970, and it is relevant to ask whether the Cuban crisis would have been greatly different if that sort of strategic balance had existed in 1962. In such a case—say in the 1980s—it is possible that a few missiles in Cuba would not have had the political impact they had in 1962. The deployment might not have been attractive to Khrushchev or unacceptable to Americans. We should note that in 1984 the capabilities of Soviet submarines in the western Atlantic—essentially parallel to those of the missiles of 1962 in Cuba—were sensibly pronounced untroubling by Ronald Reagan: "If I thought there was some reason to be concerned about them, I wouldn't be sleeping in this house tonight. [*Laughter*] . . . No, I don't think they pose any particular threat at all."[95]

I think the result of the confrontation in 1962 would have been the same with strategic parity as it was with American superiority. The critical decisions might have been a little harder to make, because the risk of Soviet escalation might have seemed somewhat greater to Kennedy, and the temptation to seek some alternative to rapid withdrawal might have been larger for Khrushchev. One can imagine such differences slightly shifting the balance of anxieties, and so affecting the details of the result, but I do not believe that if Khrushchev had made the same opening move—a secret deployment to Cuba—the responses would have been different: a quarantine by Kennedy, withdrawal by Khrushchev, quiet in Berlin, and visible and concentrated efforts on both sides to keep well away from nuclear war. The *operating* forces would be the same in both cases. For Kennedy, the missiles must come out; conventional forces and political strength could be used to persuade Khrushchev to take them out, and both sides must stay well clear of any act that might produce nuclear war. For Khrushchev, any substantial risk of nuclear war would still be wholly unacceptable, and all other choices would remain unsatisfactory. In particular a counter-blockade at Berlin would still be too risky.

These relatively robust conclusions on the relative importance of the strategic balance force us to ask again why Khrushchev's gamble set off such a grave crisis. If such changes in nuclear capability would probably not change the basic outcome of this great encounter, why should we have run these great dangers to undo something that was not in itself all that important? And why should Khrushchev, for his part, have accepted risks that he must have known to exist even if he underestimated them?

Oddly, it is easier to explain Khrushchev's challenge, in these terms, than our own response. He did believe in atomic diplomacy, and he did think this move and only this move could quickly redress the balance of strategic power. If he underrated the risk of an American response, it was probably because in his attempt to act rapidly and secretly, he failed to consult with those who might have given him a better estimate of American attitudes. According to the Soviet officials who came to discuss the crisis at the Kennedy School of Government at Harvard in October 1987, he did make this error. They reported that the only diplomat with advance knowledge of the secret adventure was Andrey Gromyko, and sensitivity to American attitudes was never one of Gromyko's many professional assets.

But what was the reason for our response? To some nuclear strategists the answer is simply that the Soviet missiles in Cuba did indeed have major strategic significance. Thus Albert and Roberta Wohlstetter, in an influential early analysis, argued that it was wrong to dismiss Khrushchev's deployments as lacking military significance. The Wohlstetters noted that the first missiles, if tolerated, could have been followed by more: "The effect of such a rapid increase in power on the actual military balance could not be lightly dismissed." A parallel and even stronger analysis was made at the height of the crisis inside the government. On October 27, Raymond Garthoff, then a military-political analyst in the Department of State, estimated that the initial deployment, when completed, would increase Soviet first-strike strength by 40 percent. He noted that the missiles being installed would not be covered by U.S. warning systems, that they were highly reliable, accurate, and powerful, and above all, that in the absence of the quarantine there was no reason why the Soviets could not "literally multiply the number of launchers to a force large enough to threaten the entire strategic balance of power." The strongest opinions of all may have been those of air force commanders, who were bound to have a special wariness about these missiles. In the later words of General Thomas Power, who was then at the head of the Strategic Air Command, these missiles "could have hit us with virtually no warning" and were therefore a threat "to the preservation of our deterrent." For him that was "the main reason why we had to get these missiles taken out."[96]

Garthoff's analysis of October 27 obviously did not influence the choice that Kennedy had made the week before, but what is still more striking is that the calculation so compelling to Power was not impressive to Kennedy or indeed to most of his senior advisers, except for Douglas Dillon, John McCone, Paul Nitze, and the Joint Chiefs of Staff. Most of us agreed with McNamara's summary judgment at the outset, that the Cuban missiles did not change the strategic balance— "not at all,"[97] and I do not recall any serious discussion of the question in the ExCom. As we have seen already, what was decisive for the president was not the number of missiles in prospect, or their strategic value, but the political damage that the United States and its government would suffer if any nuclear missiles *at all* that could reach the United States from Cuba were tolerated.

We have here the most striking case on record of the degree to which the deployment of nuclear weapons can have consequences far beyond their direct military value. Kennedy tried to drive this point home at the end of the year when he remarked that if the missiles remained, "it would have politically changed the balance of power. It would have appeared to, and appearances contribute to reality." The explanation was generally accepted at the time, and in a broad way it still seems valid. But this effect is not one that can be assessed merely by assessing changes in the thermonuclear balance. Indeed if it is right to conclude that the missiles in Cuba would have had this effect, it becomes clear that any change in the balance of power here would have been a change determined more by our own perceptions than by those of Khrushchev. And what we perceived was more an intolerable affront than an unacceptable attempt to change the nuclear balance of power. Certainly calculations like those of the Wohlstetters, Garthoff, and Power would have been offered by critics if the missiles had remained, and those calculations would have contributed formidably to the embarrassment of the American government and the disillusionment of its friends. Just after the crisis Stewart Alsop wrote an article in which he gave McNamara credit for having "instantly recognized" that Khrushchev's deployment was "a trap, which had to be unmasked at any cost." Alsop's argument, which certainly did not come to him from McNamara, was the same as Power's: The missiles in Cuba would have bypassed our warning systems, and "the whole SAC bomber complex would have been nakedly exposed to surprise attack." Alsop concluded that "The World Balance of Power would have been shifted drastically in Russia's favor." This argument would have been pressed by many if the missiles had remained in Cuba.[98]

Yet I insist that in real terms Khrushchev's deployment would not have changed the balance of *applicable* power. We can quarantine Cuba just as well after the deployment as before, if we are truly determined to do so, and we can also stand fast in Berlin with just as much determination. The missiles in Cuba are in the end not a cobra, even when operable, if we do not accept them as such. Certainly we must respect them, but Khrushchev dares not use them. They would not allow Khrushchev any confidence that he could make a winning surprise attack; too many of our warheads would survive. If they must come out, as Kennedy so firmly insisted from the very beginning of the crisis, it is because we found them politically intolerable, and not because we must somehow remove a usable Soviet asset.

We are forced to these strange but compelling conclusions: Nuclear ambition caused the crisis; a sense of nuclear affront forced the response; an awareness of nuclear danger drove both governments toward rapidity of resolution; but it was conventional superiority on the scene that determined the eventual outcome.

How Great Was the Danger?

That this was the most dangerous crisis of the nuclear age does not tell us how dangerous it was. That the principals took it seriously we have already seen. Khrushchev found the smell of burning in the air, and Kennedy told Sorensen afterward that the odds on war seemed to him "somewhere between one out of three and even." Sorensen did not take this to mean that the president thought the risk of *nuclear* war was so large. The danger he saw was that Khrushchev might force a test of strength at some lower level, and that such challenge and response might lead to sustained combat of some sort. Even at the climax of the crisis Kennedy was worried not about an immediate resort to nuclear weapons, or even about the direct impact of a first or second step, but rather about the risks that might arise as one step followed another. These risks, as Arthur Schlesinger among others has noted, were probably overestimated on the crucial Saturday. In reality, great wariness was shown by both leaders. Whatever their worries, both about each other and about the possibility of unintended conflict, each of them was determined not to let matters spin out of control through any decision of his own. Each was at great pains to show to the other his understanding of the irrationality of any nuclear exchange. The largest single factor that might have led to nuclear war— the readiness of one leader or the other to regard that outcome as remotely acceptable—simply did not exist in October 1962.[99]

Nor does there appear to have been any prospect that less prudent men on either side might have forced riskier decisions on one government or the other. Concern that such pressure might arise in the

Kremlin was present in American thoughts on Saturday, and Khrushchev claims in his memoirs that Robert Kennedy expressed fear of the dangers from Washington hotheads in his talk with Dobrynin that evening. But President Kennedy in fact remained in wholly unchallenged command. If Robert Kennedy made some use of the men in uniform who were eager to fight, he was engaged in legitimate argumentation, and I think it unlikely that he went further. It is not easy for me to imagine Robert Kennedy telling anyone that his brother was not in full command.[100] It was always possible that if the crisis remained unresolved while episodes like the attack on Anderson were repeated or enlarged, there could have been increased pressure for action from military leaders, and they could have been joined by important politicians on Capitol Hill or elsewhere. There was clearly some concern in the White House about such pressure from "hawks" on October twenty-seventh, and it is entirely possible that Robert Kennedy shared some of this concern with Dobrynin. Yet my own clear recollection is that any risks of this sort were wholly outweighed, for most of us—and perhaps especially for Rusk and McNamara, who had senior operational responsibilities—by our confidence that the president's constitutional authority had now been reinforced throughout the country, both by his own performance and by the evident need of reliance on the commander in chief at such a time of trial.

As for Khrushchev, there is no evidence that he ever lost his personal control of Soviet choices. At the most he may have been persuaded by his colleagues on Saturday that he should test the prospect for a Turkish missile trade. The personal authority he demonstrated both in ending the crisis and in presenting the result as a success is strong evidence that he faced no immediate challenge from eager risk takers. Certainly there must have been those who thought the adventure a failure chargeable to their leader, and such opinions may have had a role in his forced retirement two years later, but there is no evidence that anyone sought to compound his folly at the height of the crisis. It was understandable that each side should have had worries of this sort about the other, but the retrospective judgment— one that I think both sides came to share quite quickly after the crisis ended—must be that the two leaders were prudent and that both remained in final control. This reality in and of itself means that the risk of general nuclear war was never high.

It remains possible that their interacting choices could have forced the hands of these two men. That was what each of them feared most as the crisis sharpened, and that fear was intensified on both sides by the fact that the very existence of the crisis was the consequence of just such actions by both men. Khrushchev's deployment had forced Kennedy to react, and Kennedy's reaction had forced Khrushchev to a disagreeable choice between withdrawal and local defeat. The possibilities the two men were forced to contemplate on Saturday were daunting, and neither of them could know what was next. In this situation, one's belief in the prudence of the adversary was bound to be incompletely comforting.

Yet it would be a mistake to conclude that the slide to unlimited escalation was only one move away on Saturday night. Let us look again at the prospects as they stood then. The worst that we could expect from Khrushchev that night was that he would reject our message and somehow try to extend the dickering he had begun on Friday, but he was in no position to take violent action. He had already shown his respect for our superiority at sea, and his choices inside Cuba were not impressive. He certainly did not stand to gain by maintaining or increasing the challenge created by the killing of Major Anderson the day before, and he had been warned of the dangers in that course. It was plain that we could win control of the air space over Cuba, and international acceptance of the need for surveillance was already clear. It was unlikely then that Khrushchev would risk a dangerous next step. Control of any escalation still rested with Kennedy, and I believe this decisive point would have been clear to us if we had found ourselves dealing with a different message from Khrushchev on Sunday.

Our own choices, as we have seen, were more attractive than those open to Khrushchev, and they did not enlarge the nuclear risk. Among military options the president had already indicated his preference for an expansion of the quarantine, which would permit a substantial period of increased pressure before a further hard decision was needed. We could also have kept it clear that it was not our U-2 surveillance but the resort to force against it that was dangerously wrong.

On balance, the prudence of both Kennedy and Khrushchev after the issue was publicly joined on October 22 is more impressive than the danger of unpredicted or uncontrolled episodes. The real lesson to be drawn from both Anderson's death and the accidental intrusion of a U-2 over the Soviet Union is that neither episode was likely to cause uncontrolled escalation. Such episodes, which have also occurred at less critical moments, are in fact *less* likely to have an escalatory effect when the sense of nuclear danger is strong and clear in both capitals.

Kennedy, in short, has more than one move left before he needs to run any risk of a nuclear reply. Even if he does not decide to settle by the "Cordier ploy," he has a number of wholly conventional options, and I believe that he would have tried more such moves on Sunday or later, so as to intensify his message to Khrushchev: The missiles in Cuba must come out, and they should be removed before danger became still greater, or the terms of settlement changed, or both. Actions and messages of this sort would have left both leaders in control of their forces and well short of nuclear choices. The existence of these options is one more demonstration of the conventional superiority the Americans enjoyed.[101]

The clear aversion of both sides to nuclear exchange suggests that Robert Kennedy was probably wrong to suggest later that an initial air strike would have risked blowing up the world. For Acheson and others a decisive requirement for an air attack was that it be delivered before the Soviet missiles were operational. We have seen how that opportunity passed sooner than we initially expected, and in that sense time ran out on the air strike. But an Achesonian president, for example Harry Truman, might have made a faster decision. I do not think that such an air strike would have had a *nuclear* risk greater than that in the quarantine.[102]

Such an attack on Soviet units would certainly have produced from the Russians a strong desire to punish us in return. But a nuclear exchange would still have been a wholly unacceptable option for Khrushchev, and indeed there would have been great Soviet wariness about any action that might detonate a nuclear reply—for example, a retaliatory conventional attack on missiles in Turkey. The search for retaliatory actions with acceptable risk would have been no more productive for the Kremlin than the search that must have been conducted on October 23 and 24. It is a mistake to conclude that an Achesonian air strike, executed by an Achesonian president while the missiles in Cuba were plainly not operational, would have had immediately catastrophic results.

This does not mean that such an air strike was as good a choice as the quarantine. To say that it would not have increased the risk of nuclear war is not to say that it would have had no other disadvantages. Its impact on Soviet-American relations would have been severe. It is not easy to imagine how Khrushchev could have portrayed an air attack as a Soviet success, as he so skillfully did in explaining the exchange of missiles for assurances against invasion. Instead of reduced tension in Berlin and elsewhere, there would surely have been open bitterness and a lasting sense of crisis, nor is it likely that the United States would have had the support from friends and allies that followed Kennedy's disclosure of the missiles, his quarantine, and his demand that the missiles be withdrawn. Certainly Stevenson at the UN could not have had the personal triumph he so fairly won on October 25. The burden of having caused a clear and present danger that Kennedy's course successfully imposed on Moscow would have been shifted in large measure to Washington.

On the first Saturday, as he made his nearly final choice of the quarantine, the president, asking for united support of his decision, remarked that those who preferred another course might well take comfort in the thought that whatever the decision the "losers" would probably look right in retrospect. The comment was kind, funny, and wrong. It also suggests the excessively gloomy view that Kennedy shared with most of the rest of us in that first week. We did not fully understand the strength of our own hand. Partly, as we have seen, this was a consequence of our exaggerated fear of the operability of the Cuban missiles. But our more serious failure was not to recognize the strength of our position—in both conventional military strength and political persuasiveness. Fear that the blockade would be ineffective was shared by its strongest advocates, and it was what made the president himself less than optimistic at the start.

What remains particularly impressive to me about Kennedy's choice is that he made it in spite of his belief that it was unlikely to work. He rejected the air strike option, in part because no one could promise him that such a strike would not provoke an immediate reply, but mainly because he found it an unacceptable initial action on wider grounds. While his brother's comparison of the air strike to Pearl Harbor was overdone, the argument for a combination of restraint and firmness, for keeping the responsibility both for the crisis and for subsequent bloodshed on Khrushchev, was compelling. I think it greatly to Kennedy's credit that he took the more moderate course even as he underestimated its effectiveness. He was a man of the generation that learned from Reinhold Niebuhr that in the end one must accept the obligation to choose the lesser evil, but it takes a special kind of courage to make that choice with grace when there is a smell of burning in the air.

This courageous acceptance of the lesser evil may be partly responsible for an error in our handling of the crisis: a certain excess in rhetoric, primarily in the speech of October 22. We were not wrong to make our case as strongly as we could, or to establish as wide a legitimacy as possible for the American conviction that these missiles must be removed. But I believe we would have done better to avoid some overblown phrases. As examples, I offer three passages that would have been just as persuasive, and somewhat less pretentious or nerve-racking or both, if the words I have put in italics had been deleted or sharply revised.

> . . . this sudden, clandestine decision to station strategic weapons for the first time outside of Soviet soil is a deliberately provocative and unjustified change in the status quo which cannot be accepted by this country *if our courage and our commitments are ever to be trusted again by either friend or foe.* [The claim is excessive and unnecessary.]

> Our policy has been one of patience and restraint, as befits a peaceful and powerful nation, which leads a worldwide alliance. We have been determined not to be diverted from our central concerns by mere irritants and fanatics. But now further action is required—and

it is under way; *and these actions may only be the beginning. We will not prematurely or unnecessarily risk the costs of worldwide nuclear war in which even the fruits of victory would be ashes in our mouth—but neither will we shrink from that risk at any time it must be faced.* [The assertion here is gravely overstated, and it has no useful operational meaning.]

I call upon Chairman Khrushchev to halt and eliminate this clandestine, reckless, and provocative threat to world peace and to stable relations between our two nations. I call upon him further *to abandon this course of world domination, and* to join in an historic effort to end the perilous arms race *and to transform the history of man.* He has an opportunity now to move the world back from *the abyss of destruction* [substitute "danger"] by returning to his government's own words that it had no need to station missiles outside its own territory, and withdrawing these weapons from Cuba—by refraining from any action which will widen or deepen the present crisis—and then by participating in a search for peaceful and permanent solutions.[103]

These alterations do not change the president's policy, and it seems to me certain that they would not have changed the course of the crisis, but they might have reduced the anxiety experienced by Americans of all ages in the week that followed October 22. At the very least they would have reduced the tendency of later observers to suppose that it was only Kennedy's egoism, his personal response to a personal challenge, that governed our decisions. It seems to me that when one's purpose is to lower nuclear danger, it is better not to inflate that danger in public rhetoric.[104]

Some Consequences of the Crisis

Within the administration the missile crisis reinforced the already commanding position of the president himself and reinforced his confidence in some of those who had been helpful in the hard choices of the crisis. Unfortunately there was an opposite effect on his relations with military leaders (always excepting Maxwell Taylor) and with Adlai Stevenson. As we have seen he had kept the military men at a distance, and their advice at the height of the crisis was not well connected with his own real concerns. The result was an increased skepticism in his view of military advice which only increased the difficulty of exercising his powers as commander in chief.

The immediate cause of the misunderstanding with Stevenson was a press report that Stevenson had advocated a "Munich" in the missile crisis. He had done nothing of the kind, and whoever had made these disparaging assertions to the reporting team of Stewart Alsop and Charles Bartlett plainly did not know that Kennedy himself had preferred compromise to conflict. It was the sort of gratuitous and anonymous sniping that has become common in later years, but it was rare under Kennedy, and it was made more damaging by the fact that Bartlett was known to be the president's close friend. Stevenson unwisely chose to take the matter seriously, and Kennedy unwisely failed to clear it up by a ringing denial of the false charge. Each man concentrated on the error of the other, and lasting damage was done.[105]

The failure with Stevenson and the failure with the Chiefs of Staff remain exceptional. What I remember clearly about this crisis is the courage and good humor of the president, who understood his own final responsibility while making intense and open use of information and advice from others. This recollection has been reinforced by the experience of listening repeatedly to the tapes of the discussion of October 27 in the Cabinet Room. The man at the dramatic center of these tapes is a man expecting and encouraging the open and honest advice of others, secure in his understanding that no one in the room has any doubt of his final responsibility and capacity for decision. Both Kennedy and his administration came out of the crisis with a new strength which was only reinforced by his insistent instruction that there should be neither bragging nor gloating.

Not all of us followed his instructions as well as he did himself. In particular I think we could have done more than we did to discourage the conclusion that this was a case of wonderfully coordinated and error-free "crisis management." Part of this failure is natural to the political world; winners seldom resist the temptation to accept the credit for victory. There was also a tendency for both participants and observers to be unduly impressed by the compact and relatively orderly movement of events through challenge and response to resolution; much of this movement was the result of unusual circumstances, not unusual management.

It is also true that we did not ourselves understand at the time how many loose ends there were. Only in recent years, for example, have I learned that air force generals seem to have taken it on themselves to give their alert orders in unencrypted language so that their message would more certainly reach Moscow, or that the naval campaign of surveillance over Soviet submarines may have been prosecuted well beyond the immediate requirements of the quarantine, or that the army's plan for invasion probably included the movement of tactical nuclear weapons to Cuba. I am not criticizing any of the services for such actions and plans, because even now I do not know enough to pass judgment (although I am confident that if invasion had ever been ordered, Kennedy or McNamara or Max Taylor or all three would have made sure that tactical nuclear weapons were left behind). The public record on all these examples remains incomplete, and I am only remarking that my own failure of understanding on such points, at a time when I was the president's staff officer for national security, in itself suggests imperfect crisis management. I entirely agree with Robert McNamara, rightly respected as the most attentive manager among us, who never loses an opportunity to make the point that the only really good way to "manage" such a crisis is to avoid it.

As we have seen in the last chapter, the outcome of the crisis led to the end of pressure against West Berlin. It was also the probable cause of new moves on both sides that led unexpectedly to the Limited Test Ban Treaty of 1963. The story of that treaty has been well told by Glenn Seaborg, chairman of the Atomic Energy Commission under Kennedy and Johnson.[106] I agree with Seaborg that what produced the treaty was steadily growing worldwide concern over the radioactive fallout from testing, and also that after the missile crisis Kennedy had strength that allowed moderation, and Khrushchev a new interest in agreements that seemed to put the Soviet Union and the United States on the same level.

Kennedy's new strength allowed him to plan for a "peace speech," in the spring of 1963 and to decide that he would not answer a new series of Soviet nuclear tests with a series of his own. The Soviets had broken the Eisenhower-Khrushchev moratorium in the fall of 1961 with a series of large tests. The Americans had tested in response, and now there had been a second Soviet series. Kennedy's decision not to reply was the result of his own assessment of the limited value of additional testing, and it allowed him to include in the "peace speech," delivered at American University on June 10, an announcement that the United States would not conduct nuclear tests in the atmosphere as long as other states did not do so. He went on to say that he hoped his declaration might help to get a treaty, and it did. On July 2 Khrushchev proposed a treaty limited to tests in the atmosphere, in outer space, and underwater. On July 25 in Moscow, after two weeks of careful bargaining, Averell Harriman initialed the treaty for the United States.[107]

The Limited Test Ban Treaty (LTBT) was indeed limited. At Kennedy's instruction Harriman tried for more in two ways. He tried to reconcile persistent differences over inspection so that the treaty could be made comprehensive, covering underground tests that could not be detected in those days without such inspection. He also tried to engage Khrushchev on the question of the danger that Kennedy saw in the emerging Chinese nuclear program. Khrushchev was unresponsive on both points. Harriman reported to Kennedy that the Limited Test Ban was as much as could be achieved and Kennedy agreed. In the process of ratification the administration gave assurances on continued underground testing that were honored in later years. The LTBT cleaned up the atmosphere, and it also prevented testing in space and underwater, but it did not stop continuing technological advance in the design of nuclear warheads. It also did not slow down the Chinese, and I share Seaborg's view that it was never clear just why Kennedy thought it might.

The Limited Test Ban was well worth having, a good first step. It was achieved primarily by world opinion, but there is honor enough also for the two American presidents who proposed it, for Harold Macmillan, who cheered them on, and for Nikita Khrushchev, whose acceptance of 1963 was as decisive as his rejections in preceding years.

THE RISK of nuclear war in the thirteen days was real, and the most important single consequence of the missile crisis may be that neither side wants to run such risk again. I have argued that the risk was small, given the prudence and the unchallenged final control of the two leaders, and I think that is the right retrospective judgment. But it is one thing to observe after a crisis is over that both sides are careful, and quite another to feel free to take such prudence for granted while the crisis lasts. Even if one judges, as I do, that a correct reading of the unfolding of events from October 22 onward should have given us steadily growing confidence in our ability to get the missiles out without war, we still could never forget the nuclear risk inherent in the confrontation. It might indeed be small, but in this apocalyptic matter the risk can be very small indeed and still much too large for comfort. I think even the most cheerful student of these events would agree that the objective risk of escalation to the nuclear level may have been as large as 1 in 100, and I think even the most determined believer in recovery from nuclear war would agree that, given a choice, one would not wish to accept even 1 chance in 1,000 of such escalation. If these guesses are close the nuclear danger during the crisis was at least ten times greater than either Kennedy or Khrushchev can have wished, and as I read the record, this danger drove them both toward a quick resolution. It greatly encouraged the negotiations from Thursday night to Sunday morning, and played as important a part in ending the crisis as American warnings of imminent conventional action.

To quantify this shared sense of nuclear danger, even in the most cautious manner, may be to trivialize it. Let me therefore put the point another way: The confrontation required both leaders to examine the possibility of nuclear war, but it did not lead them to double-check the detailed consequences of an exchange, or to review how such a war might be fought. Both of them had a healthy disrespect for such exercises, and both knew that the avoidance of such a war was imperative. What they understood was that nuclear war would be a disaster, and that they had come so near the precipice that there was a real chance of slipping over it. Their choices were much affected by that understanding.

Recognition that the level of nuclear danger reached in October 1962 was unacceptably high for all mankind may be the most important single legacy of the Cuban missile crisis. It is an episode full of instruction, and it has been read in many ways. All sorts of judgments have been offered on the performances of the leaders in governments principally involved, and I have here offered some of my own. In the aftermath many took the crisis as a reinforcement of conclusions reached beforehand, and in later years many others, especially in the United States, have read it as a reinforcement of political attitudes developed later. No one is immune from this temptation, and while the reading I have offered is as honest as I can make it, I too have present beliefs, and I am old enough to have had some views on nuclear matters before October 15, 1962. One of these views is that nuclear war would be good for no one. But I do not believe that I am merely peddling prejudice when I say that the preeminent meaning of the Cuban missile crisis, for participants and observers alike, and for the quarter century of history that has followed, is that having come so close to the edge, the leaders of the two governments have since taken care to keep away from the cliff.

In particular the missile crisis stands as a durable warning that we must not again be so far from understanding each other's commitments and fears. I cannot here improve on what Kennedy said in December:

> I think, looking back on Cuba, what is of concern is the fact that both governments were so far out of contact, really. I don't think that we expected that he would put the missiles in Cuba, because it would have seemed such an imprudent action for him to take, as it was later proved. Now, he obviously must have thought that he could do it in secret and that the United States would accept it. So that he did not judge our intentions accurately.

A few minutes later Kennedy indulged his taste for understatement by remarking that "nobody wants to go through what we went through in Cuba very often." In that final sense the teaching of these great events, as the participants learned it and also as it has been learned by others, was not how to "manage" a grave crisis, but how important it is not to have one. We must make it our business not to pass this way again.[108]

X

Beyond
the Big Two

NUCLEAR WEAPONS, especially to Americans, often seem to matter only to the United States and the Soviet Union. Our weapons protect—and Soviet weapons threaten—us and our friends; arms and arms control are a Soviet-American problem. This opinion is grossly incomplete. There are today nuclear weapons and nuclear capabilities in other countries, all of them now more friendly to us than to the Russians. This chapter begins with the choice to build weapons that has been made by three countries that are good friends of the United States—Britain, France, and Israel. It also takes note of the most important of our allies which has chosen not to have these weapons—West Germany—and it concludes with a brief discussion of the more general question of nuclear proliferation—the spread of these weapons to other countries. I here omit one remaining country with a visible weapon capability, the People's Republic of China. The Chinese case deserves separate treatment in the following chapter.

Great Britain[1]

The British government determined in 1941 that its long-run policy must be to have a bomb of its own, but the only way for the British to pursue that policy in wartime was to take as large a role as possible in a mainly American effort, and we have seen with what singleness of purpose Winston Churchill, after a slow start, sought that role, and how he also obtained from Franklin Roosevelt sweeping but personal assurances of continued postwar cooperation for military as well as civilian purposes. All this was done to advance the cause of a British bomb.

At the end of the war the new Labour prime minister, Clement Attlee, pressed on with this cause. While the formal decision was not taken until January 1947, from the end of the war onward Britain's aim was to have a bomb. Attlee's determination is clear from his acceptance of the recommendation, from his senior permanent official, that Sir John Anderson should be his chief adviser on this subject even though Anderson was a Tory and sat on the opposition's front bench. Attlee would not have made this unusual arrangement if he had intended to reverse Churchill's policy. What led to the formal decision in 1947 was not earlier hesitation, but the need for choices in the management of research on weapons. In an atomic energy program a decision on design and construction of nuclear warheads becomes necessary only after there is substantial progress toward obtaining enriched uranium or plutonium or both.[2]

In 1947, as in 1945 and 1941, British leaders were convinced that they must be present in this new field, that it was unacceptable for Great Britain not to have bombs. Attlee had hoped in his first year for some means of international control, and he had understood the importance of making no public statement that would undermine that hope. But nothing in the discussion of international control stood in the way of the quiet British research that went forward in 1945 and 1946. By the time it was necessary to decide about work on weapons, the prospect for international systems was so dim that the basic British position was swiftly reaffirmed: In a world with national atomic weapons, Britain must have her own.

The opinions of the two prime ministers were firmly supported by cabinet colleagues, military commanders, senior civilian officials, and scientific advisers. Only the physicist P.M.S. Blackett expressed reservations, and he made no converts. In another country with another inheritance it might have been possible for soldiers, scientists, politicians, or officials to look with sympathy on Blackett's central argument: that Great Britain could set an international example of holding back from nuclear weapons and standing independent between the dangerous Americans and the understandably fearful Russians. To those who supported Churchill and Attlee, Blackett was wrong about the Americans and wrong about the Russians, but most of all he was wrong about Great Britain herself. As Margaret Gowing, the official British historian, wrote:

> The British decision to make an atomic bomb had "emerged" from a body of general assumptions. It had not been a response to an

immediate military threat but rather something fundamentalist and almost instinctive—a feeling that Britain must possess so climacteric a weapon in order to deter an atomically armed enemy, a feeling that Britain as a great power must acquire all major new weapons, a feeling that atomic weapons were a manifestation of the scientific and technological superiority on which Britain's strength, so deficient if measured in sheer numbers of men, must depend. A bomb would not be ready in any case for five years, so that the decision was of the variety that was impossible *not* to take rather than of the type that must be taken for urgent and immediate purposes.[3]

This attitude dominated every decision in the ten years that followed, years in which the British developed their own nuclear and thermonuclear weapons, successfully testing the former in 1952 and the latter in 1957. Untroubled by either wartime urgency or the scientific uncertainties of the earlier American effort, unembarrassed by public debate, sustained by four prime ministers, and skillfully led by scientists and managers whose confidence in their own abilities was justified by their performance, the British nuclear program produced the result that the British government had decided to get. Britain became the third country to have nuclear weapons.

The years from 1945 to 1957 were full of great changes both in the general international scene and in the special world of nuclear energy, and these changes had important effects on the way British leaders thought about their program, but the underlying and controlling purpose never changed. There must be British nuclear weapons, and the steady application of British brains and British energy could be relied on to produce them. Most writers have focused on the more murky and irregular course of nuclear relations in this same period between Britain and the United States. These troubles deserve our attention, but they are marginal compared to the solidity, strength, and operational success of the British effort to make nuclear weapons.

This program was conducted with almost no public debate. In the 1980s, when we are familiar with the later history of ardent public concern in Great Britain—when Aldermaston marchers and unilateral disarmers have filled the headlines intermittently for three decades, and when only the Conservatives remain unequivocally committed to the British deterrent—the unchallenged secrecy of British policy in these early years is doubly astonishing. The formal decision of 1947 was known to only a few ministers, and nothing at all was said in Parliament. That Great Britain had a program in atomic energy was indeed well known, but this did not necessarily mean atomic weapons. Clement Attlee never referred in public to the weapons program while he was prime minister, and Churchill, returning to 10 Downing Street in 1951, was astonished at the progress that had been made.[4]

Attlee had reason for secrecy—it allowed him to avoid debate and suspicion at home and abroad as well as arguments that the undertaking was in conflict with the effort for international control. A public program would increase American doubts about cooperation in the development of a non-American weapon, and conversely the more secret the British effort the greater the prospect that sympathetic Americans would feel comfortable about assisting it. It was also believed—probably wrongly—by Foreign Secretary Ernest Bevin that an open program would somehow help or stimulate Soviet efforts. Finally, there was habit. The continuation of wartime secrecy was agreeable to those in charge.[5]

What is remarkable here, and not fully explained in any study I have seen, is that the decision to do all this in secret, with no public debate and almost no discussion in the House of Commons, seems to have aroused little British concern or comment at the time. Press speculation was limited in some degree by government warnings (so-called D-notices) of a sort that are foreign to American experience; these regulations constrained the discussion of specific projects and personnel, but not of policy. The avoidance of a policy debate was the product of a quite different process of choice, by politicians, publicists, and other citizens. Attlee's silence was challenged only rarely and ineffectively in the House of Commons. The British as a whole were apparently content to leave these matters to the prime minister and those he chose to help him.[6]

In May 1948, responding to an internal recommendation that the existence of the program should be made public in order to permit both internal communication and press acceptance of regulation, the government prearranged a question and answer in the House of Commons. The minister of defense was asked whether he was "satisfied that adequate progress is being made in the development of the most modern types of weapon." The answer was a masterpiece of misleading accuracy. The minister answered, "Yes, Sir," and continued, "As was made clear [in an earlier Ministry of Defense statement], research and development continue to receive the highest priority in the defence field, and all types of weapons, including atomic weapons, are being developed." The key here is that the minister began with a reference to a previously published statement. Neither politicians nor journalists much care about what has already been announced, and it would have taken a close student to note that grammatically the clause which mentioned atomic weapons was not necessarily covered by the reference to previous publication. The announcement passed unremarked and undebated.[7]

Yet if the words "atomic weapons" had been truly startling, the response would surely have been different. The British government's interest in such weapons was no longer a secret, and the British public and the House of Commons were content to leave the program unexamined. Only an occasional parliamentary questioner was annoyed by the Prime Minister's unresponsiveness: "When an Hon. Member asks the Prime Minister about the atomic bomb he looks at him as if he had asked about something indecent." If Labour had been in opposition, there might well have been more questioning and more debate, for then skeptics on the left would gladly have attacked their natural enemies the Conservatives. As it was, the prime minister's silence was not seriously challenged, and the Conservatives followed the lead of Churchill, who remarked in November 1945, without response from any member of the government, "This I take it is already agreed, we should make atomic bombs."[8]

As far as they could, the British would make their bombs with the help of the Americans. Here again the policy of the Attlee government was shaped by its inheritance. British participation in the American wartime effort had been productive for both sides, and those now responsible for the British project hoped that cooperation would continue and indeed grow stronger. While British scientists were confident of their own abilities, they knew how much they had learned in the wartime enterprise and how much American colleagues could now tell them if the American government would agree. British scientists also knew, rather better than their political superiors, the depth and quality of their own wartime contribution, and they also had a better sense than political leaders in either country of the critical role that the Frisch-Peierls memorandum and the Maud report had played in Roosevelt's decision. The British political leaders wanted American help, and they accepted the view of their scientists that they deserved it. This had been Churchill's position from the beginning. He had done what he could to achieve full partnership at Quebec in 1943 and had carried the matter further in the Hyde Park memorandum of 1944 whose second paragraph said that "full collaboration . . . should continue" after the war, "for military and commercial purposes."

But there were difficulties with the Hyde Park memorandum. It was a purely personal action by a president who never shared it with anyone in his administration, and the memorandum itself was self-contradictory. Full collaboration should continue, it said, but *full* collaboration had never existed, as men like Anderson and Chadwick knew. There had, in reality, been a wartime trade of limited but important British access for limited but important British help. British access to specific kinds of information had always required specific American consent, and Chadwick had been careful not to press for access where he did not think it would be granted. The cooperation that the Americans accepted was mainly what would advance the wartime enterprise of making a bomb in time to use it for victory. The partnership had been real, but the motives of the two sides had been different. The inheritance from the war included this difference, which was strengthened on the American side by the fact that among the Americans who continued to be advisers, like Groves and Bush, a relatively narrow view was strong. Roosevelt and Stimson were gone.

In November 1945, when Attlee came to Washington for a meeting on atomic energy, the leading item on the agenda was the effort for international control, and the best that Attlee could get on the less urgent matter of joint activity was one more hastily agreed paper asserting a common interest in "full and effective cooperation." When this paper was tested in practice it appeared that the two governments had different views of its meaning. For Truman the sharing of the American secret was governed by what he had said publicly back in October when he had distinguished sharply between the scientific knowledge that was available to everyone and the know-how that was an American secret, and he had specifically told the press that the secret know-how would not be shared even with allies. Nothing in his brief discussion of this subject with Attlee had changed his mind, and Robert Patterson, the secretary of war who reviewed the joint statement before Truman agreed to it, took the politically innocent view that the adjective *full*, for which John Anderson pressed, was acceptable because it had no important legal content. The agreement, therefore, did not truly resolve the difference of underlying purpose that had existed during the war, and when Attlee used it six months later to appeal repeatedly for the kind of cooperation that would help the British in factory-scale production, Truman was unresponsive. By then the mystique of the American secret, which Truman had done his share to enlarge, was entirely dominant in American politics, and Truman knew that legal limits on this kind of sharing would soon be imposed by Congress.[9]

On August 1, 1946, with the passage of the Atomic Energy Act (the McMahon Act), the argument between the two governments was overtaken by a flat prohibition on the delivery to any foreign nation of information on the production of fissionable materials or nuclear weapons. We do not know what exception might have been written into the law if the public, the Congress, and the Truman administration itself had fully understood the importance of the British connection in the speed of the American wartime effort. The Americans who knew that story best had little to do with the congressional decisions of 1946, and the British government made no separate effort of public explanation. There were a number of reasons for this British choice, but the most important was probably the habit of believing that cooperation, like everything else in the field of nuclear weapons, worked best when it worked in secret.

In later years Senator Brien McMahon told English leaders, including Churchill, that if he had properly understood the wartime partnership in 1946, the prohibition in the McMahon Act might well have been relaxed for Britain—not a sure guide to what would have happened if the British role had been made clear to Congress, but a reminder that no one in authority explained these connections at the time. Leo Szilard did speak about the importance of the Frisch-Peierls report, but he was hardly a spokesman for either government. If members of Congress had understood that without British help the bomb would probably not have been available in 1945 (a conclusion that I have found reasonable in Chapter III), it is not hard to suppose that the language of the McMahon Act would have been different. But no one made that point.[10]

The cutoff imposed by the McMahon Act did not change the British determination to restore and improve nuclear cooperation with the Americans. As the cold war developed in 1947, the two governments shared a sense of danger and even crisis. Moreover, as the American atomic energy program expanded and relied increasingly upon congressional understanding and support, the Truman administration found itself with two specific requirements for British help: additional supplies of uranium from the Belgian Congo, which would require the willingness of Britain to reduce its own agreed share of that supply, and a British abandonment of the clause of the Quebec agreement that required British consent to any American use of the bomb. Recognizing that the language of the Quebec agreement would be politically explosive if members of Congress ever learned about it on their own, President Truman decided on a full but private disclosure to leading senators, an unpleasant task that fell to Dean Acheson. Leading Republican senators were outraged that the American atomic monopoly should be so shackled, and it became clear that the Quebec agreement must be canceled. Fortunately the British wanted cancellation too, because they could not permanently accept Churchill's wartime concession that British work on the peaceful or commercial use of atomic energy would require the president's approval. The Quebec agreement had served its wartime purpose, but it did not fit the postwar imperatives of either side.[11]

Spurred by these needs for change, the Americans proposed and the British accepted a renewal of negotiation at the end of 1947, and in less than a month the two sides worked out what became known as the *modus vivendi.* The Americans were assured the supplies of uranium that they needed; the Quebec agreement was canceled and the Hyde Park memorandum too; in return it was agreed that there would be technical cooperation under terms to be settled jointly. The legal barriers of the McMahon Act remained in place, but the way was open for such cooperation as the Atomic Energy Commission and the Joint Committee on Atomic Energy might find unobjectionable.[12]

The *modus vivendi* was more satisfactory to the Americans than to the British, and it soon became clear what the underlying difficulty was. The British wished to use the new framework to get information that would help them make weapons, and growing recognition of this purpose on the American side brought with it a considerable sense of shock. Few American officials were fully aware of the historical record, and such interested parties as the Joint Chiefs of Staff and Lewis Strauss of the AEC felt strongly that there should be no American help for nuclear weapons production in the United Kingdom. In consequence the level of cooperation stayed low while the level of mutual misunderstanding went up. Yet as the cold war continued to grow more intense, military cooperation outside the field of bomb making continued to grow. Conspicuously, in 1948, the British allowed the United States to have B-29 bombers in England, and these were eventually provided with American nuclear weapons. In effect the United Kingdom agreed to become the principal forward base of American strategic forces.[13]

To an increasing number of people on both sides of the Atlantic it was apparent that there was a sharp contrast between the limits of the *modus vivendi* and the growing Anglo-American military and political cooperation on every other front. Beginning in 1948 and running through 1949 there was a further effort to find a new basis of agreement. But now the difficulty was in framing the American position, because of the differences among the State Department, the Pentagon, the Atomic Energy Commission, and the Congress, differences that were overcome only after careful negotiation within the government in Washington. The upshot was an American proposal for an integrated program in which the role of the British would be determined by overall strategic considerations. What this meant for Americans like Lewis Strauss was that it was not safe to produce nuclear weapons in Great Britain, a judgment hardly likely to be accepted by the British government. The negotiations were unfinished and their outcome unpredictable when on February 2, 1950 the British announced the arrest of Klaus Fuchs, a refugee physicist who had been at Los Alamos during the war as a member of the British team. The discovery that he was a longtime Soviet spy was a profound shock to Americans, and the whole negotiation on cooperation was stopped in its tracks.[14]

The British went on to make a bomb on their own. On October 3, 1952 they conducted their first successful test, in Australia, with no Americans present. This British achievement was more important in opening the road to cooperation than any other single event, and probably the second in importance was the earlier and surprising Soviet test in 1949. Each test, in its own way, undermined the mystique of secrecy. The Soviet bomb stimulated the American interest in further progress, and the British bomb was impressive evidence that the British might have something to contribute to such an effort.

With Churchill's return to power in 1951 and Eisenhower's election in 1952, the stage was set for renewed communication at the highest level between two believers in Anglo-American cooperation. Both disliked the impasse in the nuclear relationship. Nonetheless it was necessary to proceed slowly, and the prime minister was forced to respect the enormous postwar change in the processes of American decision making. But gradually American opposition to a closer relationship faded, and in 1954 the semisacred McMahon Act was amended to permit sharing information on what nuclear weapons were able to do and what size and shape they were.

Much larger steps were taken in 1957 and 1958. Again the initiative came primarily from the British prime minister, this time Harold Macmillan, but again Eisenhower responded quickly. The rapid British achievement of a successful H-bomb had made it plain that the British could make major technical contributions to a shared effort. The Americans were also eager to place some of their new ballistic missiles in the United Kingdom. Perhaps most important of all, in the aftermath of the bitter British-American split over Suez in 1956, the president and the prime minister were at one in their desire to renew their partnership. The president recommended, and Congress readily accepted, a further amendment to the McMahon Act permitting exchange of information on the design and production of warheads and the transfer of fissionable materials. Such exchanges and transfers were allowed only with countries that had made "substantial progress" on their own, and Britain was the only country that qualified. Thus it was the success of the British in their first purpose—obtaining the weapon—that produced success in the second—achieving a partnership with the Americans.[15]

The Anglo-American exchange of nuclear knowledge and nuclear materials that began in 1958 has continued ever since, to the technical advantage of both countries. Even more important is the further arrangement under which the Americans undertook to make available to the British modern methods of delivering their warheads. In this agreement the British were assured of access to an American air-to-ground ballistic missile system called Skybolt. From that time onward British nuclear warheads have depended for long-range delivery on American missile systems.

One of the great turning points in the competition over nuclear weapons is the shift of emphasis between 1955 and 1965 from the simple possession of warheads to the development of delivery systems. At the beginning all that was really needed for delivery was a large long-range airplane, preferably fast and high flying. In this field the British needed no help. But in the 1950s, as the age of ballistic missiles approached and as it became clear that aircraft armed only with bombs would have growing difficulty, both in surviving on their airfields and in penetrating modern defenses, British military planners, like their

American and Soviet colleagues, became convinced that an effective strategic deterrent must include ballistic missiles. Accordingly the British went ahead, as the two superpowers were already doing, with a mid-range, liquid-fueled, ground-based missile called Blue Streak, but when the British Chiefs of Staff concluded that this missile would be unacceptably vulnerable (a charge that could have been leveled also at its American cousins Jupiter and Thor), Macmillan used his American connection once again. In March 1960 he and Eisenhower, in a meeting in Washington devoted mainly to nuclear test ban negotiations, reached two understandings, "more or less" tied together in Macmillan's view: that the Americans should be allowed to establish a Polaris submarine base in Scotland and that the British should be allowed to obtain the American airborne Skybolt missile, which would prolong the effective lifetime of the British bomber force. Thereupon Blue Streak was canceled, and the future of the British strategic deterrent was tied to the right of access to an American missile. In 1960 this new arrangement went largely undebated in both countries, but two years later that omission was noisily filled in.[16]

France[17]

In February 1960 France became the fourth nation to set off a nuclear explosion, and by 1969, when General de Gaulle finally withdrew from power, the French nuclear forces were comparable to those of the United Kingdom. The French achievement is remarkable, and it encountered opposition within France that had no counterpart in any of the countries we have so far considered.

Before the war the French had been in the vanguard of nuclear studies, but the fall of France ended this effort until General de Gaulle established the French Atomic Energy Commission in October 1945 with Frédéric Joliot-Curie as its first high commissioner. In spite of the enormous demands of postwar recovery, Joliot and his colleagues pursued a basic research program of high quality. The new French team had the advantage that some of its members had worked in Canada in the wartime North American effort, and indeed three of them had given de Gaulle an account of the imminent American bomb when he visited Ottawa in July 1944, a step as natural for them as it would have been startling to the American keepers of the secret. But the new program was essentially French. By law and preference the Americans were committed to secrecy, and while there were some in Britain who would have preferred a more cooperative relation to France, their American connection was inhibiting and so was the natural inwardness of the British national effort. The French went their way alone, and it is not surprising that, in the words of one of de Gaulle's most ardent followers, Geoffrey de Courcel, the general's purpose from the start was "to give his country the means of catching up in the nuclear field, and so of breaking the atomic isolation in which the Anglo-Saxon powers enclosed themselves."[18]

Irritation with the Anglo-Saxons was a persistent element in the French pursuit of nuclear weapons, and English-speaking insensitivity kept this feeling strong. In his biography of de Gaulle, Jean Lacouture describes an astonishing encounter which shows how easily Americans could give offense. In September 1958, three months after his return to power, de Gaulle asked General Lauris Norstad, the NATO commander, for an account of NATO deployments in France:

> Norstad agreed, and made an extremely brilliant exposition, with his interallied staff in attendance. After congratulating him, the head of the French government asked the American general for a precise account of the deployment of nuclear weapons in France and of the targets assigned to them. Norstad: "Sir, I can answer only if we are alone." "So be it," said de Gaulle. The two staffs withdraw. "So then?" "Then, sir, I cannot reply to your questions, to my very great regret . . ." And de Gaulle in conclusion: "General, that is the last time, and make yourself understand it, that a responsible French leader will allow such an answer to be made."[19]

Lacouture's account comes from General Alain de Boissieu, de Gaulle's trusted son-in-law, and gives de Gaulle's view of the meeting, not Norstad's, but it is likely that Norstad really did feel that he could not give a full account of deployments and targeting. Yet it is implausible that Norstad, if he had bothered to ask, could not have obtained permission from Eisenhower to tell General de Gaulle whatever he wanted to know. This account does not suggest that either Norstad or de Gaulle proposed such an appeal. Lacouture cites the episode as reinforcing de Gaulle's determination that the defense of France must be under French control. But that determination was already ample, and I conclude that a very good American general must have done a very bad job of responding to a question that the head of the government of France had every right to ask.

But it was not because Anglo-Saxons are irritating that the French effort was made. It was because France must be France: "France," wrote de Gaulle in the opening paragraph of his memoirs of World War II, "is not really herself except in the front rank. . . . France cannot be France without greatness." It was never acceptable that France should be without nuclear weapons.[20]

Joliot himself disagreed. He always believed more in the industrial promise of atomic energy than in its military application. He was also a member of the French Communist party, and as the cold war intensified he came to assert first that French workers should refuse to make nuclear weapons and then that he himself would never give the smallest assistance to "any preparation of war against the Soviet Union." The government of the day removed him. What is remarkable, looking back, is that his leadership lasted until 1950. The opposition of the French Communist party to a French bomb persisted, but as it turned out this opposition helped other parties to muffle their considerable differences with one another. What emerged was a firm and widely supported position that France must not be held back by Stalinists.[21]

The partisans of a French weapon also saw to it that the road to a French bomb was not blocked by the effort for European unity led by the great French European Jean Monnet. Monnet's proposal for a European Defense Community was defeated by the French Parliament in 1954 after the other prospective partners rejected a French amendment protecting the French right to a French bomb. Similarly the friends of the French nuclear effort were able to ensure in 1957 that when Monnet and his friends effectively promoted the European Atomic Energy Community (Euratom), the language of the treaty which set it up left France free to pursue military uses of nuclear materials.[22]

After Joliot's departure, the French were free to make a bomb, not by any clear instruction from the premier of the day, but under the leadership of professional administrators who were supported by the ministers directly concerned. In the two dozen coalition governments of the Fourth Republic it was usually to the advantage of each new premier that the relevant ministers should be in favor of the nuclear program.

The work was slow compared to that in the three countries that were ahead of France, but it was steady and skillful, and the French were more concerned with direction than speed. By 1956 it was clear that a bomb would be ready for testing within five years.

Over this period the basic objective of those who believed in a French bomb was unchanging, and events provided almost continuous reinforcement to their convictions. The French faced repeated humiliations in the process of losing their former colonies. As the Germans moved toward rearmament, with American encouragement, the French felt acutely the need to reestablish a clear military distinction between themselves and their former enemies. When Britain acquired nuclear weapons, there was a need to match this ancient rival. Perhaps above all, the domination of the Western alliance by the United States, and a sense that American nuclear preponderance was decisive in that domination, reinforced French determination to have a bomb.

A particularly powerful stimulant to the French government was its extremely unhappy experience at the hands of all three of the existing nuclear powers in the Suez affair of 1956. In reality that crisis was neither caused nor resolved by nuclear weapons, but it did not look that way in Paris.

The Kremlin did rattle its rockets in the last days of the Anglo-French adventure, but this was merely propaganda designed largely to turn attention away from the much greater outrage of Soviet repression in Hungary. It was not the cause of the British decision to halt the operation. The Americans did play a crucial role in the British decision, but it was their financial strength, not their nuclear advantage, that was decisive. Eisenhower did refer to the danger of Soviet gains in the Middle East as he argued with Eden, but neither he nor Eden was impressed by Bulganin's references to Soviet rockets. Nor was there ever any thought in London or in Paris that the Suez operation itself would have been faster or easier with a few bombs. Nonetheless the best American students of the French nuclear program report that in the aftermath of Suez a large number of French political leaders, including Prime Minister Guy Mollet, drew the conclusion that if France were to stand up for herself in such cases in the future, she must have the bomb.[23]

Bertrand Goldschmidt, the best French historian on the subject, takes an even stronger view; he himself (I think wrongly) believes that the Soviet threat was a cause of the decisive American pressure on Anthony Eden, and he reports that in Paris "the Mollet government, which with the Israelis had prepared the Suez operation in the utmost secrecy, felt the affront it had just suffered. Its previous hostility toward atomic weapons . . . was transformed overnight into a determined and positive interest in national nuclear armament."[24]

With more psychological than logical power, French leaders put together their resentment of the American pressure on London and their dislike of the American nuclear advantage and concluded that if they could offset the advantage they could in future resist the pressure. How French possession of the bomb would have changed the course of events at Suez they did not say.

The role of the American bomb in the choices of France had begun long before Suez. As early as 1945 Joliot had put it to Sir John Anderson in London that "France and Britain together could 'hold the position vis-à-vis America better than either one alone,' " thus foreshadowing de Gaulle's own later argument that for Britain to choose partnership with the United States was to make a choice against Europe. And even earlier, in 1944, the scientist Bertrand Goldschmidt had thought it urgent to alert de Gaulle partly because of the need for the General to understand the "considerable advantage" that the new weapon would give the United States. For de Gaulle himself the escape from American leadership was a necessary part of his own view of the real destiny of France. In the debate of 1960 a French Catholic daily, *La Croix,* concluded that "France has constructed the atomic bomb and is preparing to construct an H-bomb not in order to use it against those who could become her adversaries, but to be able to be respected in the camp to which she belongs."[25]

If the Fourth French Republic had lasted beyond the spring of 1958, we might have a full case history of a country that acquired nuclear weapons mainly because its government never decided not to. As it happened, the decision of Prime Minister Félix Gaillard, in April 1958, that there should be a French test in 1960, occurred only two months before the return of Charles de Gaulle and the start of the Fifth Republic.

General de Gaulle had never had a merely permissive view of the French atomic adventure. He and his supporters had been its constant friends, and leading Gaullists had repeatedly defended and advanced the undertaking from positions of bureaucratic and even ministerial power. For de Gaulle prospective nuclear success was a trump card. Elsewhere he faced hard tasks—the most serious was the conflict in Algeria, and the most immediate was a new French constitution. But the bomb was his passport to international grandeur. It would place France back where she belonged, among the Great Powers, and France would be the only great Western power on the continent of Europe. His government gave its rapid development "absolute priority."[26]

De Gaulle's first hope was to build a new triangular relationship with the United States and Great Britain. He opened this campaign with a memorandum to Eisenhower and Macmillan in September 1958—the same month as his confrontation with Norstad—proposing a three-power organization "at the global, political, and strategic level" with two basic responsibilities: first, "to take common decisions on political questions affecting global security," and second, "to establish and if necessary to put in operation plans for strategic action, notably with respect to the use of nuclear weapons."[27]

Many students have concluded that this famous memorandum was intended from the first to be rejected, that de Gaulle must have known how unwilling the Americans would be to share their leading role, and that his conduct of the diplomatic exchanges which followed was designed to produce rejection. I disagree. After all, what de Gaulle proposed was exactly what he thought right: that France should be included in these great matters precisely because France was France. De Gaulle believed excessively in what great powers could do in concert, largely because he had only an outsider's view of the Anglo-American grand alliance of World War II—an enterprise whose continued existence in 1958 is assumed in his own account of his memorandum: "I therefore proposed that the alliance should henceforth be placed under a triple rather than a dual direction."[28]

Finally, and perhaps most important for our present purpose, General de Gaulle fully understood that nuclear danger was the decisive hazard of his time, so that the first responsibility of any nuclear power must be to play its full part against that danger. Neither Churchill nor any other master of rhetoric spoke of nuclear danger with more clarity and power than de Gaulle. Already in 1945 he had recognized that the bomb had "immense" consequences and also that it could cause "a worldwide cataclysm." In a 1960 television address after the breakdown of the Paris summit, he explained to his countrymen that the reality of nuclear danger was now understood by both East and West. Both sides knew that nuclear war would be "a disaster for everyone," bringing the risk, for both sides, that after the conflict they would have "neither powers, nor laws, nor cities, nor cultures, nor cradles, nor tombs."[29]

I do not find it odd that in 1958 de Gaulle should have proposed for his country, and for himself as its leader, the role of a full nuclear partner. The French bomb might be the ticket of admission to the *Club des Grands,* but the main work of that club must be to ensure the general nuclear peace.

The years since 1945 had not filled de Gaulle with confidence in the wisdom of the Anglo-Saxons. He believed that at Yalta they had failed to defend the interests of Europeans—and France had been absent. Thereafter, as he saw it, great events like the emergence of Red China had been met not with understanding but with mindless hostility. Now in 1958, the Americans were overreacting, once again, to troubles in Lebanon and in the Formosa Strait. It is not surprising that a man with these views should have believed that the safety of the world as well as the interest of France required her moderating presence at the high table of the free world's affairs.

The strongest evidence of de Gaulle's concern on this point is not in his initial memorandum but in a later letter to Eisenhower of May 25, 1959, which was not fully published until 1985. That letter covered particular points like the establishment of a new French command independent of NATO in the Mediterranean. General de Gaulle also noted the American unwillingness to share with the French the secrets of atomic armament, thus forcing the French "to discover them for ourselves and at great expense." To him this was a relatively minor matter compared to a larger concern:

> On this point, however, we can only express our regrets. But it is not like that with respect to the fact that America reserves entirely to itself the decision to use or not to use the nuclear forces at her disposal. For the consequences that could follow, for us, from any

unilateral action you might undertake in such a field could lead us to formulate explicit demands, and to adopt, as far as possible, measures of our own for our safety.

If there were no alliance between us, I would agree that your monopoly of the possible unleashing of nuclear conflict was justified. But you and we are bound together to a point where the opening of this sort of war, whether by you or against you, would automatically expose France to total and immediate destruction. She obviously cannot leave her life and death entirely in the hands of any other state whatever, even the most friendly. That is why France insists that it is essential for her to participate, if the case should arise, in any decision that might be taken by her allies to use atomic weapons and to launch them against given places at given times.[30]

I find no pretense in this *cri de coeur.* Nor is it surprising that de Gaulle went on to insist that as long as there was no agreement meeting this French demand, there could be no nuclear warheads based on her territory except under her complete and permanent control. This position was seen in Washington as a proof of French unwillingness to cooperate in NATO defense planning, and certainly de Gaulle did not regret that his decision was so understood. But his real argument went further: that it was unsafe for France to allow on her territory targets as dangerously attractive to Soviet planners as American-controlled nuclear weapons, in a situation where France had no role in the decisions about nuclear war that might be made by the Americans. When Eisenhower presented a further argument on this question of storing American nuclear weapons in France, de Gaulle's reply combined patience with firmness: "I think the future will allow us to arrive at an arrangement on this subject, whenever we have been able to agree that the opening of atomic war by the West anywhere in the world would require the joint decision of the United States, Great Britain, and France. In this matter it seems to me possible to consider that the beginning, quite soon now, of the deployment by France of French atomic weaponry will make things easier for us."[31]

The argument made secretly in this letter to Eisenhower was repeated more bluntly in a public speech at Grenoble in February 1960: "France considers that if, unfortunately, atomic bombs were launched in the world, none would be launched from the free world without her having accepted it, and that no atomic bomb be launched from her soil unless she herself makes the decision."[32]

The records known to me do not show any explicit American response to the demand so clearly set forth in the letter of May 1959. Eisenhower had dealt with the more general formulation in de Gaulle's first memorandum by an equally general objection. There could be no three-power concert, he wrote, because it was necessary to respect the interests and feelings of other friends. "We cannot afford to adopt any system which would give to our other Allies, or other Free World countries, the impression that basic decisions affecting their own vital interests are being made without their participation."[33] Eisenhower did not list the allies and friends he had in mind, but it is not hard to guess. In Europe he had to be concerned primarily with Adenauer's Germany, but also with a dozen other members of NATO, all of whom showed over the next few years that they were not ready to accept France as their leader in Europe. Eisenhower also knew how unfavorable the reception would be, in other parts of the world, to any appearance of a three-power concert. Anticolonial sentiment alone would make that certain.

But we do not know that Eisenhower ever went further, to explain to General de Gaulle that neither Congress nor the American people would accept any French authority over American strategic decisions and that it was quite wrong to suppose that Anglo-American cooperation in nuclear matters included any British power over American strategic decision making. Eisenhower could have explained that the real situation among the Anglo-Saxons was in fact just the opposite, that the abandonment of any British claim to a role in American decisions, by the cancellation of the Quebec Agreement, had been a necessary precondition to the limited Anglo-American cooperation allowed under the *modus vivendi* of 1948. There was no prospect whatever that any American president, however sympathetic to France, could grant a French veto over the American strategic deterrent.

To say that de Gaulle's demand was unacceptable is not at all to say that it was without justification. His argument has great strength. Who can wish his country's survival to be dependent on the good sense of others? Who can wish to increase his country's danger by accepting dangerous weapons on his territory without any control over the decisions that might bring them under attack? And how could this be the role of France for a man whose life had been dedicated to a quite different vision of his country's destiny? We have here no trivial misunderstanding on either side. The American president's determination to keep to himself the final responsibility for decisions on the use of nuclear weapons was at least as strong as de Gaulle's desire to share it. There could be no affirmative response to his central demand. I think that de Gaulle probably understood the American position even while he was trying to change it. He is not likely to have neglected altogether the question of what he would have thought and done if the positions of the two countries had been reversed.

When he was speaking to Frenchmen, and thinking about the requirements of France, de Gaulle could make it entirely clear that in his view the French requirement for nuclear weapons was of such a nature that France herself could never give up the right of independent decision about their possession and possible use. For him this was a matter of the very nature of France, as he explained in a speech at l'École Militaire on November 3, 1959:

> The defense of France must be French. This is a necessity which has not always been familiar in these recent years [a reference to French troops assigned to NATO]. I know that. It is indispensable that it become familiar again. If a country like France must make war, it must be her war. Her effort must be her effort. If it were otherwise, our country would be in contradiction with everything which it has been from its beginnings, with its role, with its esteem for itself, with its soul. Naturally, the defense of France, in the event, would be joined with that of other countries. That is in the nature of things. But it is indispensable that it be ours—that France defend herself by herself, for herself and in her way.

De Gaulle went on to insist that the need for national defense had been the very "raison d'être," in every epoch, of the government of France. And when he turned to nuclear matters, he drew the necessary conclusion:

> In consequence, it is evidently necessary that we be able to provide ourselves in the coming years with a force that can act on our account, with what is customarily called a "force de frappe," able to be deployed anywhere at any time. It goes without saying that the basis for this force will be a nuclear armament—whether we make it or buy it—which must belong to us. And, since eventually France can be destroyed from any point in the world, our force must be designed to act anywhere on earth.[34]

No one hearing this speech could suppose that the general was speaking of a force over which the president of the United States would have a veto.

Compared to the great issue of the final responsibility for making nuclear war, the question of catching up with the Anglo-Saxons is trivial, but it was never a small matter to de Gaulle, and it is not clear from the record that the Americans did all they could to deal with it. Eisenhower could have pointed out that except for the admittedly important field of nuclear technology there really was no Anglo-Saxon club to join in 1958, even leaving aside the special question of a role in the command of SAC. That London had close relations with Washington, and some influence, was obvious, but neither the relations nor the influence rested on formal arrangements. The vast wartime machinery of English-speaking staffs that de Gaulle had once observed as a proud outsider was long gone. What survived was a habit of close communication, more prized in London than in Washington, and frequently marked by disagreements that London found it prudent not to celebrate in public. On relations with China and crises in the Formosa Strait, for example, the British government was much closer to de Gaulle than to Dulles.

So de Gaulle was claiming membership in a club that no longer existed, and the privilege he sought could not be granted to anyone by the Americans. There was a third difficulty. The ticket of admission he was presenting—his bomb—was one the Americans were determined not to accept.

The role of the bomb as ticket of admission, in de Gaulle's mind, is clear. In 1945 he had moved swiftly to break the "atomic isolationism" of the Anglo-Saxons. Now in 1958 the work he had launched was about to bear its grimly gratifying fruit. As Geoffrey de Courcel remembered it, the meaning for the general was clear: "For him what mattered was to be able to say that France was politically a nuclear power, and to talk as equal to equal with the Anglo-Saxon powers." And it would have seemed to him entirely natural that the Americans and the British should understand this view of the bomb.[35]

But de Gaulle was presenting his ticket just as opinion in Washington was moving against any action that would increase the temptation among other nations to seek weapons of their own. By the end of the 1950s there was no significant element in the administration or in Congress which saw any advantage in making the possession of the bomb, even by a good friend, a passport to political or strategic influence. Eisenhower himself was quite untroubled by the prospect of a French bomb, which he was quite willing to see developed and indeed to assist if Congress would consent. But not even Eisenhower believed the possession of the bomb should confer special political influence in Washington. No one could deny that any American decision to use nuclear weapons might have grave consequences for France, but this proposition had equal force for many other countries. To make the possession of nuclear weapons the passport to special influence would be disruptive to good and confident relations with everyone but de Gaulle. The price was too high.

The very wide distance between what de Gaulle was asking and what Eisenhower could give does not justify the conclusion that de Gaulle made his proposal only for the purpose of recording Washington's refusal to accept it. When he finally gave it up, he did indeed go on to make trouble for the Anglo-Saxons, and in that process his supporters were led to rewrite the record, often denying that he had ever sought a role in the control of American strategic forces and often asserting that Eisenhower never even replied to the original memorandum. These misrepresentations are as unfair to de Gaulle as to Eisenhower. The effort we have been reviewing may show some French lack of respect for the interests of other allies and a certain contempt for

NATO as it then was. It may also show that de Gaulle was not interested in accepting or even exploring minor concessions. But it does not show at all that his basic demand was not serious.

What de Gaulle wanted was a place at the table where decisions that could mean life or death for France would be made. I do not assert that the demand was realistic, or even that de Gaulle was optimistic about its chance of success. I do conclude that he thought it right to try, that by his proud standards he tried hard, and that while he always knew he could make other choices if he was rebuffed, his own view was that the right and wise solution was for Eisenhower and Macmillan and de Gaulle to make themselves a triumvirate for the management of great affairs. As long as he had this hope, he saw no contradiction between such an arrangement and the independence of France. In May 1960, after the Paris summit, with (or against) Khrushchev, where indeed the three had been united, he made the point publicly. France must have nuclear arms, to keep her destiny in her own hands, but "it goes without saying [*il va de soi*] that such autonomy must have as a corollary a closer concert of the Western world powers, both in their policy and in their strategy."[36]

As late as August 9, 1960, in an appeal to Eisenhower for a three-man summit, de Gaulle made his point with passion: "My dear President, my dear friend, I have the feeling that we do have, you, Macmillan, and I, the possibility, at once certain and transitory, of organizing a real cooperation, political and strategic, of our West." He proposed that the three-man summit should undertake this work *corps à corps*—"body to body" is the literal translation; "face to face" is better English, but it does not do justice to the French. It would take a very cynical view of General de Gaulle to suppose that this appeal was merely a ploy.[37]

But in August 1960 Eisenhower was weary of summitry. The summit wrecked by Khrushchev was a recent and painful memory, and he may well have been weary too of de Gaulle's insistence on the unacceptable three-man top table for the West. Moreover, de Gaulle's letter contained a long list of issues on which Washington and Paris had disagreements most unlikely to be resolved in such a meeting. It was also election time at home. Eisenhower excused himself from the proposed meeting. De Gaulle's two-year effort had failed.

IN THESE SAME TWO YEARS the French nuclear weapons program went forward to its first great success, the explosion of a test device on February 13, 1960, at the Reggane test site in the Sahara. De Gaulle's first comment was a public telegram of thanks, which began HURRAH FOR FRANCE! SINCE THIS MORNING SHE IS STRONGER AND PROUDER. The general in charge of the program,

Albert Buchalet, had always believed that de Gaulle thought a successful French test would be "a political instrument that would permit him to sit at the table of the great powers," and the enthusiasm of this telegram strengthened that belief. That the success was deeply reinforcing to de Gaulle himself and to all those who had been engaged in the long and lonely French effort is amply attested by their own accounts.[38]

Yet the immediate political consequence of the Reggane test was divisive argument both at home and abroad. It led almost at once to a government proposal for a new two-billion-dollar-defense program to support a full-scale nuclear weapons system. There followed a debate which demonstrated that opinion in France was far from unanimous. Questions were raised about the vulnerability of the aircraft that would constitute the first delivery system, about the danger of putting a national program ahead of some form of allied effort, and about cost. While the program had its stout defenders in more than one party, majorities of those voting repeatedly rejected it, both in the Senate and in the Assembly. But the proposal had the full pledged endorsement of de Gaulle's government, and under the constitution of the Fifth Republic a bill with such endorsement could be defeated only by an absolute majority of all members of the Assembly. No such majority was attained by those opposed. De Gaulle's constitution, reinforced by his prestige, protected his decision. This result plainly owed much to the dramatic reality of successful testing.[39]

The first French test also stirred comment and criticism beyond the borders of France. It came at a time when the Americans, the Russians and the British had put in effect a moratorium on nuclear tests in the atmosphere, and there was widespread criticism of the French action from those in all countries who were trying to end such testing. To General de Gaulle this criticism was of little importance, since he understandably believed that the needs of France were not the same as those of countries which had already conducted extensive tests. He had expected such criticism and had assured the makers of the French bomb that he would protect them against all such pressures.[40]

A much larger matter was the absence of a sympathetic reaction in the United States. Eisenhower himself, as he had explained publicly only ten days before the French test, believed that it was time for a new cooperation between Washington and Paris. "I have always been of the belief that we should not deny to our allies what your potential enemy already has. We do want allies to be treated as partners and allies, and not as junior members of a firm who are to be seen but not heard." Eisenhower declared himself in favor of changes "to make our law more liberal." But his view was not shared in Congress. The leaders of the Joint Committee promptly made it clear that they were not ready to revise the McMahon Act in favor of France, and Eisenhower, keeping his irritation to himself, did not press the matter.[41]

The reasons for congressional resistance were many. Neither French scientists nor French generals had the same connections and influence in Washington that their British counterparts had built. Officers with influence on the Hill, like Admiral Hyman Rickover, were strongly opposed to the sharing of their secrets with a France which they thought open to easy Communist penetration, and the mythology of secrecy remained strong in the Joint Committee. Congressional opposition not only prevented a formal amendment to the law, but operated to chip away at specific offers of cooperation, as in submarine technology. Eisenhower himself always believed that if it had not been for congressional constraint, he "could have reached a satisfactory agreement with de Gaulle on the atom thing." But the contrast between his verbal expressions of friendliness and his government's failure to act had only negative effects in Paris, where doubts about American goodwill on the nuclear question were strong.[42]

In the Kennedy administration the balance shifted further against nuclear cooperation with France. The most important element in this new attitude was the growing belief that nothing good could come from additional national nuclear capabilities, and that only the two superpowers could now hope to have persuasive deterrent forces.

The classic analysis was presented early in 1961 by Albert Wohlstetter in *Foreign Affairs*. Wohlstetter found it foolish to encourage nuclear "sharing," and was particularly harsh in his criticism of the national deterrents being sought by countries like Britain and France. He found such undertakings not only "arduous" but "unlikely to pay off." The initial entrance fee was "merely a down payment," and effective second-strike deterrence, in his view, would prove beyond the capability of such smaller powers. He had only ridicule for the justifications offered by French theorists. To him it was not an accident that the first French deterrent vehicles were called Mirage, a wisecrack borrowed from the French writer François Mauriac. Both for Europeans and for Americans, Wohlstetter concluded, the best and safest form of nuclear umbrella was a closely controlled, centrally managed American set of forces.[43]

A year later, in the spring of 1962, this argument became the official position of the American government. After a secret speech at a NATO meeting in Athens McNamara described the new nuclear policy publicly at the University of Michigan in Ann Arbor. American forces would be kept large, varied, and capably deterrent. They would be closely controlled, and they would be capable of attack on clearly military targets. They would maintain "sufficient reserve striking power to destroy an enemy society if driven to it," but in the event of a nuclear war stemming from major Soviet aggression the objective would be "the destruction of the enemy's military forces, not of his civilian population." This strategy would give "a possible opponent the strongest imaginable incentive to refrain from striking our own cities." McNamara never abandoned this view of targeting, which is far different from a strategy of miscellaneous civilian destruction.[44]

McNamara noted that this kind of force did not come cheap; the United States program was running at fifteen billion dollars per year. He went on to disparage lesser nuclear capabilities:

> In particular, relatively weak national nuclear forces with enemy cities as their targets are not likely to be sufficient to perform even the function of deterrence. If they are small, and perhaps vulnerable on the ground or in the air, or inaccurate, a major antagonist can take a variety of measures to counter them. Indeed, if a major antagonist came to believe there was a substantial likelihood of its being used independently, this force would be inviting a preemptive first strike against it. In the event of war, the use of such a force against the cities of a major nuclear power would be tantamount to suicide, whereas its employment against significant military targets would have a negligible effect on the outcome of the conflict. Meanwhile the creation of a single additional national nuclear force encourages the proliferation of nuclear power with all of its attendant dangers.
>
> In short, then, limited nuclear capabilities, operating independently, are dangerous, expensive, prone to obsolescence, and lacking in credibility as a deterrent.[45]

Kennedy approved these two paragraphs. He had doubts about public debate with de Gaulle, but his high regard for McNamara overcame his reservations, though he did delete a sentence in which McNamara asserted that "in a world of threats, crises, and possibly even accidents" a small force "appears more likely to deter its owner from standing firm under pressure than to inhibit a potential aggressor."[46]

This incomplete amendment is characteristic of Kennedy's ambivalence on nuclear relations with General de Gaulle, whom he respected. He hoped that the two of them could come to a reasonable understanding, but he recognized that strategic deterrence was no simple task, and he strongly believed in close control over nuclear weapons. He also thought about the problem of relations with France in the context of his fear of rapid nuclear proliferation. He understood that the French were determined, but on balance, in the spring of 1962, he thought it wrong for the United States to help them. He explained his view repeatedly in response to reporters' questions, and the difference of tone between McNamara and Kennedy is plain:

> We do not believe in a series of national deterrents. We believe that the NATO deterrent, to which the United States has committed itself

so heavily, provides very adequate protection. Once you begin, nation after nation, beginning to develop its own deterrent, or rather feeling it's necessary as an element of its independence to develop its own deterrent, it seems to me that you are moving into an increasingly dangerous situation.

First France, and then another country and then another, until a very solid and, I think, effective defense alliance may be somewhat weakened. That, however, is a decision for the French. If they choose to go ahead, of course they will go ahead, and General de Gaulle has announced they are going ahead. We do not agree, but he cannot blame us if we do not agree anymore than we blame him if he does not agree with us.[47]

In a later press conference Kennedy was asked if the United States had now accepted "France's determination to build its own nuclear power," and his answer led to angry misunderstanding. "We have always accepted its determination to do so. What we have not agreed to is to participate in the development of a national deterrent. We believe that is inimical to the community interest of the Atlantic Alliance, that it encourages other countries to do the same."[48]

What Kennedy thought "inimical" was not the French effort, but that Americans should participate in it. But the language was imprecise; the words can be misunderstood to mean that the French action, not American help for it, was "inimical," and that is how it was read in France. French memories on the matter are long, and even twenty-five years later a distinguished French friend of the United States, François de Rose, remarked that Kennedy had called the French nuclear program an "unfriendly act."[49]

Kennedy should certainly have made his comment in a way that excluded this kind of misunderstanding, but even so his view would not have been popular in France. The American offense was the refusal to give the French the kind of help they were giving the British. It was too much to expect that the French should understand the different historical relationships we have been describing, or the evolution of American attitudes toward national nuclear efforts in the years after cooperation with the British had been renewed. One of the sharpest reminders was issued shortly after Kennedy's press conference by Raymond Aron, himself a sympathetic friend of the United States and a critic of the more overblown French notions of nuclear prestige and power:

. . . the Kennedy Administration, like the preceding Eisenhower Administration, has refused to face up to a major truth: that neither General de Gaulle nor any other French leader can admit the official Washington thesis according to which the dissemination of atomic weapons becomes dangerous when these weapons cross the Channel, but not when they cross the Atlantic.[50]

By the summer of 1962 there was an unpleasant split between the Kennedy administration and de Gaulle.

West Germany[51]

The Federal Republic of Germany does not make or own nuclear weapons, and no government in Bonn has ever come close to decisions like those we have just considered in London and Paris. But the German role in the nuclear defense of West Europe has been a major element in the politics of Europe and the Atlantic alliance for thirty years. West Germany relies heavily on nuclear weapons, not only for the deterrence of war, but for the arming of many hundreds of guns, aircraft, and missiles in her own armed forces. But the warheads are under the control of the American president. West Germany does not "have the bomb." For the Federal Republic and the United States, this remarkable result has been judged the best available for thirty years now, a judgment that would have occurred to no one in 1945.

What became West Germany was at first three zones of British, French, and American occupation, and at first all German armament was forbidden. Unlike their colleagues in Britain and France, the scientists in West Germany stayed out of postwar nuclear exploration.

From 1950 onward, rising cold war fears—stimulated by the Soviet bomb of 1949 and the North Korean attack of June 1950—convinced Truman and Acheson among others that the Atlantic alliance now required German rearmament. France and Britain objected, and while Adenauer was ready to do his part, he felt that his government must be treated as an equal by its western friends. Germany would not rearm as a second-class member of the team, and it took five years to reach an agreed plan. The Germans finally joined NATO in May 1955 and set out to raise a conventional force of 500,000 troops. Part of this 1955 agreement was a declaration by Chancellor Adenauer renouncing the production of nuclear weapons; it was a German choice, at least in form, and not an imposed inferiority. The absence of such a declaration would certainly have created difficulty, especially in Paris, but at the time the operational focus in all countries was on the need for conventional forces. NATO's Lisbon agreements of 1952 had looked to the establishment of an allied force of ninety conventionally armed divisions, and nuclear responsibility was still seen as resting with American strategic forces. Catherine Kelleher, the best American student of the German case, finds that in this period "there was hardly any expectation of a nuclear-armed Germany in the foreseeable future," and "all Germans looked upon atomic weapons production and possession as present subjects for great power aspirations, not for German demands."[52]

In the later 1950s, Eisenhower's New Look shifted attention toward nuclear strength, and the development of shorter-range tactical weapons created new possibilities for nuclear defense in Europe. Meanwhile it became clear that the Lisbon ground-force goals were politically unrealistic. By 1956 there was a clear prospect of American ballistic missiles of intermediate range. From 1957 onward the impact of *Sputnik* was felt in Europe as in the United States. In 1958 the urgency of all these questions was increased by the beginning of Khrushchev's Berlin crisis.

The first American response to this challenge came from General Norstad, the NATO commander in Paris. Beginning in 1956 Norstad developed and promoted two important nuclear proposals. The first was for the establishment of an American nuclear weapons stockpile in Europe, which could supply warheads that would make "an atomic delivery capacity available to more types of commands and to the forces of more countries." In the case of tactical weapons—for artillery, for air defense, and for short-range missiles—it was established policy by 1960 that the Germans would have the same delivery systems as the Americans, with control of the warheads and full authority over their use remaining in American hands.[53]

Norstad's second proposal was for the development of a NATO ballistic missile force to match the emerging threat of Soviet missiles that could hit Europe. At the end of 1957, the NATO Council of Heads of Government agreed that in view of Soviet weapons policies, "intermediate range ballistic missiles will have to be put at the disposal of the Supreme Allied Commander, in Europe." The proposal thus approved in principle did not quickly become real, but it marks the beginning of an effort to address the question of the kind of missile forces required for specifically European defense. In Britain and France the results were shaped by the preferences we have already observed. In addition to their own program, the British accepted American Thor missiles under joint control. The French agreed to accept such a force only if some of the missiles and warheads were put under their full control. Washington rejected this demand. The Germans held back; they believed in NATO missiles, but they did not want them in West Germany, the "foremost trench."[54]

In 1960 the State Department developed a competitor to Norstad's second initiative. Wary of encouraging national nuclear forces, fearful of German nuclear ambitions, and committed to European unification, Gerard Smith commissioned, and Robert Bowie produced, a report proposing what later became known as the multilateral force (MLF).

In its 1960 form it was to be a Polaris submarine force, initially established by the assignment of American vessels to NATO; later, if the Europeans wanted it, the proposed force could be manned by crews drawn always from at least three nations. The idea of such a collective force was outlined by Secretary of State Christian Herter at the NATO Council in December 1960, but by then it was clear that any decision must await the incoming president, John Kennedy.

The Kennedy administration took some months to develop its own initial view. Its attention was fixed first on the problem of Berlin, and then on what it saw as a primary need for conventional reinforcement. On nuclear weapons Kennedy concluded quickly that the missile gap was not urgent, and more slowly that it had never existed. He came to office opposed to the spread of national nuclear forces, and sympathetic to the goal of· European unification, but he also agreed with those in the State Department, and with Jean Monnet of Europe, that it was important to acknowledge Bonn's equality among European powers. Thus he came to believe in broad but conditional support for the policy that had been developed in the Herter State Department. At Ottawa in May, he announced that "the United States will commit to the NATO command five—and subsequently still more—Polaris atomic-missile submarines, which are defensive weapons, subject to any agreed NATO guidelines on their control and use." In the next sentence he encouraged the supporters of the multilateral force: "Beyond this, we look to the possibility of eventually establishing a NATO sea-borne force, which would be truly multilateral in ownership and control." Supporters of the MLF then began a concerted campaign, paying much more attention to these words of encouragement than to the conditions that Kennedy attached at the end of the sentence, "if this should be desired and found feasible by our Allies, once NATO's nonnuclear goals have been achieved."[55]

For the next year and a half, the effort to give substance to the MLF went forward under the leadership of the American State Department, though it soon became clear that Admiral Rickover would not approve multilaterally manned submarines. Without Rickover's approval no such proposal could have congressional acceptance, and attention shifted to the possibility of a force of surface ships. Naval officers with surface-ship experience and enthusiasm were assigned to the development of specific plans. By the fall of 1962, American officials were briefing European officials on an "Ottawa force" of twenty-five surface ships with two hundred Polaris missiles. The proposal still carried the Ottawa conditions of priority for conventional forces and genuine enthusiasm in Europe, but its supporters remained strongly convinced that with effective presidential support the conditions would be met or moderated because of the intrinsic merits of the enterprise. Then in

December 1962 the whole question of American policy on nuclear weapons in Europe was tested by a sudden need for new choices.

Nassau and After[56]

In December 1962 Kennedy and Macmillan met in Nassau, a meeting scheduled as a friendly wintertime parley, with no urgent agenda, on a warm and sunny British island. The crisis that transformed this meeting into one of unusual intensity and complexity had been wholly unpredicted.

The crisis was precipitated by a presidentially approved decision that the United States would not develop for itself the Skybolt air-to-ground missile on which the future of the British national nuclear deterrent then depended. Repeated and increasingly clear-cut assessments had demonstrated to McNamara's satisfaction that Skybolt was not good enough to be worth continued expensive development at a time when the success and cost-effectiveness of other weapons like Minuteman and Polaris were increasingly evident. McNamara was concerned that the matter be handled with minimal political difficulty in the United States, where Skybolt had strong friends among manufacturers and in the air force. That meant a proper hearing for the Joint Chiefs before the president could be asked for a final decision. The president was consulted; he agreed—as did Rusk and I—that McNamara was right about Skybolt and that the British should be warned. McNamara gave warning, but London understandably failed to recognize that the decision was inevitable. McNamara had promised to come to London for consultation on next steps before anything was said in public, but his trip was delayed, mainly by the aftermath of the Cuban missile crisis.

So it happened that the plan to drop Skybolt broke in the press before McNamara got to London for the promised discussions, thus creating a large problem for Macmillan. If Skybolt was not good enough for the Americans, how could it serve as the basic means of delivery for British nuclear weapons? Nor could the Americans solve the British problem by inviting them to pursue and purchase Skybolt for themselves. McNamara's decision, accompanied by his usual forceful public description of the shortcomings of the rejected weapon, damaged Skybolt's reputation, and when Kennedy supported him in a press conference, the case became hopeless, or so Macmillan concluded. When Kennedy began at Nassau with a sweetened offer to share half the cost, the prime minister observed "that although the proposed British marriage with Skybolt was not exactly a shotgun wedding, the virginity of the lady must now be regarded as doubtful."[57]

If Skybolt had lost its reputation, the obvious alternative was Polaris. That option had existed in 1960, when Skybolt had been preferred for British reasons of service preference—the Royal Air Force wanted to go on in the business of strategic deterrence, and the Royal Navy was not yet interested. Macmillan believed, I think correctly, that if he had pressed then for Polaris, Eisenhower would have granted it. He also believed that in 1960 the willingness of the Americans to supply modern missiles for British warheads had been fully compensated, in reality if not in form, by the British decision to accept an American Polaris base in Scotland. Now that Skybolt was an also-ran, he had a right to ask for a new American decision to provide Polaris. This belief was reinforced for Macmillan by an understandable but erroneous view of the early history of the wartime relationship. Here is the description in his memoirs:

> The project then known as "Tube Alloys" had been developed originally by British scientists. It was on grounds of safety as well as convenience that Churchill had agreed with Roosevelt that further development should be joint and carried out in the United States. But European countries knew perfectly well that Britain had been first in the field and might be said, up to the end of the War, to have had an equal share in the equity with America.

As we have seen earlier, the basic production decisions were entirely American, and the important contribution made by British science to Roosevelt's earlier decision to go ahead was not the product of a British decision for joint effort. But Macmillan's exaggeration was not contested at Nassau. He noted that both Kennedy and McNamara "seemed sometimes strangely ignorant of the immediate past," and he could have included others among us.[58]

But what mattered at Nassau was politics, not history. Macmillan had an absolutely vital political interest in obtaining Polaris. In his own party in Parliament a commanding majority were deeply committed to the British independent deterrent, and the future of that deterrent had been tied by Macmillan himself to American assistance in the means of delivery by modern missiles. In reliance on this American help, offered after the failure of their own Blue Streak missile, the British had made no further effort in missile development. Macmillan had been the primary architect of this Anglo-American partnership, and if Kennedy should now refuse the one missile that would meet British needs, the Macmillan government would be fatally undermined among its own supporters in the House of Commons.

As this reality became clear to Kennedy in the early days of the Nassau meeting, he quickly recognized it would be a mistake to give this kind of blow to the friendly head of a major allied government. The Americans had accepted and supported the British independent deterrent by word and deed since 1957. To refuse Polaris, as matters stood in Nassau, would damage Anglo-American relations in a quite fundamental way. Macmillan was marvelously eloquent in his evocation of British traditions and imperatives and Kennedy greatly liked both Macmillan and David Ormsby-Gore, his ambassador in Washington. But Macmillan could have been dull, and Ormsby-Gore just another diplomat, and the underlying imperative would still have been clear: Nothing could justify this kind of American damage to Anglo-American relations. Kennedy had hoped that Skybolt might still be adequate, but he understood the political problem presented by its damaged reputation. The British must have Polaris.

But nuclear relations between London and Washington could no longer be considered only from the standpoint of those two capitals. Anything the Americans did with the British was bound to have impact throughout the Atlantic alliance, especially in Bonn. By 1962, a decision to provide the latest American missiles to a single country required the American president to address the question of what he had to say about these matters to others. The most important, by now, was West Germany, and the proudest the France of General de Gaulle.

The French problem was daunting, given the distance between the preferences of Washington and Paris that had been clear for more than a year. But for Kennedy the right next choice was clear. He must make it plain to de Gaulle that he was now prepared to consider a program of assistance to France comparable to what he was ready to provide for Great Britain. Such an offer he would make, and if it were rejected by de Gaulle then at least it would be clear that the decision to go it alone was French.

The problem of policy toward other allies was more difficult. To provide Polaris to the British and to offer it to the French would raise the question whether and how far the Americans still believed in the multilateral force. The least that Kennedy must do was to reaffirm the American interest in that force. The most that he could hope for at Nassau would be a serious British commitment to participate in such a force, though the Americans and British already differed on the point.

The representative of the State Department at Nassau was George Ball, who believed the "first priority" of American policy "should be to bring about a politically united Europe." Given this conviction, and the belief that American leadership was the key to this unity, Ball opposed assistance to national nuclear forces. Kennedy backed his effort to gain British support for the multilateral force. In the end

Kennedy and Macmillan agreed in their final statement that "the purpose of their two governments with respect to the provision of the Polaris missiles must be the development of a multilateral NATO nuclear force in the closest consultation with other NATO allies." Other paragraphs of the agreement left it open for the British to claim that their own Polaris submarine force would be their contribution, but the meeting nonetheless became the launching pad for a new and sustained effort by Americans to make the MLF a reality. The Nassau meeting thus produced not only an agreement to provide Polaris to Great Britain, but also an offer to Paris, and what appeared to be a joint endorsement of the multilateral force.[59]

The Kennedy administration did its divided best to say to General de Gaulle that the president's offer of help was serious, but less than a month later, the general announced a double decision: He could not accept the kind of nuclear arrangement that he understood the Americans to be proposing, and he could not accept the United Kingdom as a member of the Common Market. He had taken the latter decision well before the Nassau meeting, but the British acceptance of American nuclear assistance, on what de Gaulle chose to see as unacceptably entangling American terms, allowed him to set his rejection of Britain in the context of his belief in unbridgeable differences between Europeans and Anglo-Saxons.[60]

De Gaulle's rejection of Kennedy's offer was equally flat. Because there were no suitable French submarines to put them in, there was no present French interest in Polaris missiles. Moreover, the Nassau agreement demonstrated the American conviction that there could be assistance only to nuclear forces that were "integrated" under an American commander. Since the essence of the French purpose was to have its own nuclear deterrent, integration would contravene French defense policy. De Gaulle recognized that the Nassau agreement left the British free to decide about the Polaris force in any case where Britain felt "that supreme national interests are at stake," but in his view the French requirement of an independent force could not be met by any such special right of withdrawal. He pronounced unacceptable all the entanglements and constraints which he attributed to integrated defense.[61]

I think de Gaulle's decision was rooted in conviction and not governed by the hasty and imperfect manner of Kennedy's offer. Certainly any offer emerging from an Anglo-Saxon summit was suspect. It is also likely that as an early expositor of the American position in Paris, Ball emphasized the importance of multilateral integration rather than the new readiness of Kennedy himself to assist the French deterrent. What de Gaulle wanted, from first to last, was a nuclear weapons force of his own. He had good reason to doubt that the offer from Nassau represented a durable change in the earlier American position, and he had no desire to get into a negotiation in which the Americans would try to trade their help for limits on French independence. So he would reject the offer and go his own way, asserting that the level of integration accepted by the United Kingdom was simply wrong for France. And then, going well beyond what his own basic policy required, he would assert that the Americans themselves, with all their nuclear strength, could not be relied on to provide the kind of nuclear protection that France, and Europe, required. "Deterrence is now a reality for the Russians as for the Americans, which means that in case of general atomic war, there would inevitably be terrible and perhaps mortal destruction for both countries. In such conditions no one in the world, and in particular no one in America, can say whether or where or when or how or to what extent American nuclear weapons would be used to defend Europe." This thrust was the more painful because it was plausible, and in less public comments French officials suggested that an independent French force could be used in some circumstances to trigger the American nuclear deterrent; it could be the "detonator," a highly offensive notion to Americans who wanted to keep that decision firmly in American hands. So Kennedy's offer produced French responses that put an end to any early prospect of major American nuclear help to France.[62]

Yet the United States did contribute importantly to the French nuclear deterrent, although not in the immediate area of nuclear weapons technology and not in the provision of any system as impressive as the Polaris missile. Before Nassau the Americans had agreed to the sale of tanker planes to refuel French nuclear forces. To the degree that this early French force was able to fire in all directions, it owed that capability to those tankers. Later, after much delay and debate, there were some sales of advanced computer equipment helpful to the French thermonuclear program. In a world in which large sales have many friends, a policy of total nonsupport is as hard to manage as one of general partnership.[63]

With Polaris assured to Macmillan, and French rejection clear, the effort for the MLF went forward. It became and remained a major element in American foreign policy for three years, until it expired from lack of political support at the end of 1965.

The rise and fall of the MLF has attracted much study. In terms of Washington politics it is a remarkable story, in that it was kept going mainly by the skill and energy of its backers in the State Department. It is also a remarkable story of interallied diplomacy, in which the political leaders of Britain, France, and Germany steadily behaved in ways that frustrated these Americans. Finally it is a case in which two presidents, Kennedy and Johnson, went through essentially the same cycle—a phase of encouragement and occasional advocacy and then a phase of insistence on a level of European support that they themselves came to believe would not be found.[64]

The MLF failed because it turned out that the underlying convictions of the decisive European governments—Britain, France, and West Germany—with respect to their relations to nuclear weapons, their relations to one another, and their relations with the United States, were all decisively different from those assumed or desired by the American supporters of the MLF.

The French view may be the clearest, and it may have been decisive. The French disliked the MLF from the beginning, and when it seemed near success, in 1964, they declared their opposition sufficiently to affect West Germany. For the French a German share in the MLF would blur the distinction, then so important in French eyes, that France was a nuclear power and West Germany was not. German acceptance of a large and complex American proposal would confirm precisely the American hegemony against which de Gaulle had set himself. To believers in European unity and an integrated NATO, the French attitude was quite simply perverse, but the operative reality was its strength. No move available to Washington could change this French position, and it could not be in the American interest to force the Germans to an unwanted choice between Paris and Washington.

Whatever they may have said at Nassau, the British never believed in the MLF. Macmillan and his two successors, the Conservative Sir Alec Douglas-Home and the Labourite Harold Wilson, resisted all proposals for direct British participation in the mixed manned-surface fleet. All three were also unsympathetic to the American view that a larger German role in nuclear matters was necessary to prevent a German effort to seek a German bomb. Like the French, the British believed the Germans could easily be held to Adenauer's pledge, and in any case they saw no gain in encouraging German participation through the MLF. Harold Wilson's comment was inelegant but sharp: "If you have a boy and wish to sublimate his sex appetite it is unwise to take him to a striptease show."[65]

The Germans initially supported the MLF, but only until they learned the strength of French opposition, and more because it was an American proposal than because of any strong German conviction. The German military were not enthusiastic about missiles based on surface ships. Although Adenauer himself was a backer (until he turned strongly Gaullist in retirement), his underlying motive was not German nuclear ambition, but the reinforcement of American engagement in Europe. The leading defense expert of the Social Democrats, Fritz Erler, was also in favor of joining the MLF discussions, but his purposes were to demonstrate a lack of interest in any national effort and to show dedication to "the closest possible integration of the American potential." As the MLF proposal stayed on the table, strongly supported by no third country, and increasingly opposed in different ways by France and Britain, it became steadily less attractive to the government in Bonn. In retrospect it is clear that while American advocates believed this force necessary to meet German concerns, its German supporters were moved primarily by their belief that this was the best way to hold on to the Americans. Both were wrong. It is a misunderstanding familiar in family life: I thought it was what *you* wanted.[66]

One important common element in this misunderstanding was that as the years passed, between 1957 and 1965, the perceived need for additional nuclear missiles in NATO steadily declined on both sides of the Atlantic. The missile gap disappeared; the Kennedy-McNamara strategic buildup went rapidly forward; five Polaris submarines were assigned to NATO; the sense of a rising Soviet threat was dramatically reduced after the Cuban missile crisis, and by 1963 West Berlin was plainly safe. By the mid-sixties there was no significant military claim of need for the numerical reinforcement that the multilateral force could give. It is not easy to win effective support for the costs and difficulties of a force for which no military need is felt.

Yet the objectives of the MLF, in the minds of those who had designed it, were always more political than military. At the beginning, a new military missile force was generally held to be needed, and this was the kind of force its backers found best on political grounds. The multilateral force may have been at least as good for military deterrence as the British Polaris, or any French system, but what really moved the British and French governments was a conviction of national need for national forces. This conviction was in itself a political force of decisive strength, and no parallel political force existed in the case of the MLF.

When tested from 1963 onward, in the pressure of proposal and counterproposal, the two political purposes that had inspired the MLF proved wholly insufficient to bring it into being. The first was a hope to turn nuclear weapons into an instrument for advancing the unity of Europe, and the second a fear that without membership in this shared force, the Germans would be dangerously drawn to the French and British course of national nuclear capability. The hope proved unattainable, and the fear groundless.

The unification of Europe was indeed a goal that attracted many members of the Kennedy administration, from the president on down. Enough was said and written to encourage the conclusion that Kennedy had a "grand design" for the construction of this kind of Europe as a full partner of the United States. He chose Independence

Hall in Philadelphia as the place, and July 4, 1962, as the date, for his most eloquent endorsement of "this vast new enterprise." A strong and united Europe, for Americans, would be not a rival but a partner, and while "the first order of business is for our European friends to go forward in forming the more perfect union" the president promised that when that job was done, the United States would be ready for "a concrete Atlantic partnership" with the new Europe. "I will say here and now, on this Day of Independence, that the United States will be ready for a Declaration of Interdependence."[67]

In such a united Europe there would certainly be need for a policy on nuclear weapons, and when Kennedy was asked about that the next day, he said that the United States would be ready to discuss any truly European proposal, but he noted that "so far no such proposal has come forward." In September in Copenhagen, with Kennedy's approval, I took the argument a small step further, making it explicit that if the new Europe should decide that "a genuinely multilateral European deterrent, integrated with ours in NATO, is what is needed and wanted," there would be no veto from the Kennedy administration.[68]

But in spite of rhetorical flourishes, Kennedy was not electing himself as the architect of the new Europe. He was simply making it clear, as the leaders of the European movement had asked, that there was no truth in claims that the Americans would fear a strong Europe as a rival. My own remarks were still more plainly defensive in purpose, designed to show that our opposition to small national forces should not be read as proof of a general American determination to exclude even a new and united Europe from nuclear weapons. Our position in the summer and fall of 1962 was that our foreign policy in general, and our nuclear policy in particular, were consistent with our sympathetic support for what we still saw as the growing unity of Europe.

It was one thing to give wanted encouragement to the European movement, but it was something else again to suppose that American proposals for the handling of nuclear weapons could themselves be a strong instrument for advancing the European idea, and this second way of thinking was strong among those pushing the MLF. The truth was, as events demonstrated, that for two of the three most important countries in Western Europe, the nuclear weapon was perceived mainly as an instrument for the protection of basic national strength and status. The British wanted a bomb of their own; so did the French. The unification of Europe was indeed the purpose of many distinguished Europeans, including Jean Monnet, but in the early 1960s there was nothing that Monnet or his friends in the American government could do to reverse the nuclear policy of France and Great

Britain. The attempt to use nuclear weapons policy as an instrument for transcending the nation-state in Western Europe was doomed to failure.

Yet I remember very few, in the Washington of the MLF years, who fully understood the commitment to national nuclear weapons that governed the policy of Britain and France. The determination of each of these two governments reinforced that of the other, in a manner which seemed foolish to good Europeans, but which can hardly be surprising as one looks back on the history of these two countries. To try to make nuclear weapons an instrument of European unification was to ignore the basic reason for their existence in both Britain and France.

The error about Germany is more understandable and more instructive. From the beginning, a leading purpose of the designers of the MLF was to do right by the West Germans. The theme of equal treatment for the new free society of the Federal Republic was central not only to the movement for European unity, but also to the broad policies of European cooperation and Atlantic alliance. The insistence on equality was also a hallmark of the Adenauer government. It did not seem safe to assume that Adenauer's unilateral renunciation of German nuclear weapons would last forever in the face of major national efforts in Britain and France. As Robert Bowie put it in 1963, that renunciation "over the long pull . . . can hardly keep Germany from demanding equal nuclear status with the United Kingdom and France." Neither Bowie nor anyone else believed that the Germans would deliberately decide to build a bomb. What they believed was that without equal treatment there would be frustration and bitterness in West Germany which could only lead to tension and cleavage that would gravely endanger the Atlantic alliance and even the political stability of the Federal Republic itself.[69]

After all, the American nuclear program had begun for fear of what Germany might do, and by the end of the 1950s the German economic miracle had made it plain that the Federal Republic would be the strongest economic and technological unit in Western Europe. Yet it was equally clear that a German nuclear effort would endanger the political stability of Europe because of the fears it would raise in every other European state. It was natural therefore to seek a way to satisfy Bonn that would remove the temptation for a German nuclear effort. As it turned out, however, neither the failure of the MLF nor any other event since 1963 has ever produced even the smallest sign of German interest in having a German bomb. A major reason for Germany's lack of interest in nuclear weapons of its own is what it learned from the results of the British and French efforts.

Britain and France as Nuclear Powers

As we look back at the role in world affairs of Britain and France in the generation since each of them became a nuclear power, what can we say that their nuclear status has done for them? First we may ask whether the nuclear weapon has proved, for either country, a ticket of admission to any top political table, the answer must be no, with the single exception of nuclear arms control.

In the case of Britain, which has had the bomb for almost thirty years, it was apparent even by the early 1960s that there was no correlation between British nuclear weapons and British international effectiveness, as Raymond Aron said after Nassau in criticizing over-blown French estimates of the importance of nuclear weapons. Noting that the Gaullist Michel Debré had asserted that nuclear weapons were indispensable for a wide variety of national objectives, including "all influence in international life," Aron remarked that "this might lead his readers to believe that Great Britain had derived enormous benefits from her national deterrent over the last ten years, when in actual fact the course of her diplomatic efforts during that period was a series of unmitigated failures."[70]

The years since Aron wrote do not show quite such a gloomy record, but leaving arms control aside for the moment, they also do not show evidence that Britain's nuclear status has had a positive influence on her relations with any other country. Nuclear weapons have not retarded the continuing British retreat from power in the Middle East and Africa. They did not help at the Falkland Islands, either in deterrence or in battle. They have not strengthened the Commonwealth or answered the Irish problem. They have not created or inspired a technological or scientific revolution to reverse persistent economic trouble. In fairness, very few leaders in Great Britain have ever supposed that nuclear weapons would or should do any of these things, but in France large claims were indeed put forward.

What makes the absence of nuclear weapons from the international role of France so striking is precisely that so many in that country agreed with de Gaulle's sweeping estimate of 1966, that "our country, becoming for its part and by its own means a nuclear power, is led to assume for itself the very extensive political and strategic responsibilities that this capability brings with it, responsibilities whose nature and dimensions evidently make them inalienable."[71]

It is not easy to find evidence of the exercise or even the existence of these extensive responsibilities. Where has the international role of France been larger because of the French bomb? Has that bomb had a role in Africa or in the Middle East? Have the nonnuclear neighbors of France been willing to accept French leadership because France has bombs and they do not? Has French influence been visibly greater in Moscow or London or Washington? Surely if the possession of the bomb had the political meaning that de Gaulle so confidently asserted, one would expect to find traces of that meaning in the historical record of the decades since he spoke. Ardent defenders of the Gaullist view often assert that the French bomb has reinforced French diplomacy, but I am aware of no concrete demonstration of these assertions.[72]

What this empty page of history suggests instead is that the nuclear weapons of middle powers like Britain and France simply do not give usable influence in daily international affairs. They are not replacements for the great fleets and armies that these countries had in earlier times. You cannot send a landing party, or garrison a colony, or capture a terrorist with atomic bombs, and everyone knows it. The bomb does not give you the means to undo the impact of Suez, or to reverse the verdict in Algeria, or to reappear in Asia.

If de Gaulle understood these limits on the bomb, he kept that understanding to himself. When he spoke as a strategist, he was at pains to assert that nuclear weapons were for the future of France what her defense and her war-making abilities had been in the past. Here is the argument he made on January 27, 1968, in explaining the strategy called *tous azimuts* [all directions] to a military audience:

> This is not the first time in our history that it has been this way! Vauban in his own time fortified all the frontiers of France, the Pyrenees, the Alps, our ports, and even Belgium. We have gone everywhere, we have made war everywhere, we have entered Madrid, Berlin, Moscow. We have made war in Europe, in the East, in America, in Asia. . . . There is no reason why this strategy, which in all ages has protected us against all, should not be perpetuated. By definition, indeed, our atomic armament must be for all directions.

The immediate impact of this doctrine was to annoy Americans in much the same way that Wohlstetter and McNamara had earlier annoyed the French. But what is more significant is the distance between this picture of worldwide strategy and the reality of the decades that followed. It is true that de Gaulle conceived of this nuclear strategy as a very long-term affair, "for generations. . . . In twenty years who will govern the United States and with what system? Who will govern the USSR? Germany? Japan . . . China?" While the last twenty years have produced no enormous change in these countries, except perhaps China, certainly no one can safely predict permanent stability anywhere. Still the absence of the French bomb from the international history of the last twenty years does suggest that when he asserted its political importance, General de Gaulle failed to recognize the degree to which the immensity of the bomb would limit its relevance in anything but a crisis of the very first magnitude.[73]

Even with respect to Europe, the French and British bombs have not conferred any usable advantage. No neighbor is awed by them, and no ally made more respectful. The Germans especially have concluded that the French and British forces are not badges of rank that need impress friends. Franco-German friendship certainly remains important. The German refusal to choose sides against France is plain in the adventure of the multilateral force. But it is not the French bomb that has this effect. It is rather the importance of overcoming a terrible historic hostility. The underlying requirement that France and Germany must be friends weighs as heavily on Paris as on Bonn. As de Gaulle himself said to his friend and follower Maurice Schumann four days before he left office, there was no longer any conceivable French foreign policy that was not "founded on the irreversibility of Franco-German reconciliation." This is not the product of the French bomb.[74]

Have their nuclear weapons made a difference, for France and Britain, in their relations with the Soviet Union? The answer here is less clear-cut. There have been no major crises engaging either one with Moscow since 1962, so that we have no case in which there has been a test of British or French confidence in the protective strength of their national deterrents. In episodes with lower levels of tension there has been no clear demonstration that the French and British are either stronger or weaker than their nonnuclear allies in responding to Soviet challenges and indeed no evidence that their nuclear capabilities have affected their political choices.

In at least one case, the relation of France to détente and cold war, we have a vivid contradiction between de Gaulle's own assertions and the historical record. In a press conference of October 1966, he said that "French nuclear forces provided a new and liberating element of a nature to reduce the tension provoked by the opposition of the two camps formed around the two giants." He went on to claim that "as France broke this stifling rigidity, one sees already the breakdown of the constant and gravely dangerous game which was called the cold war." But this is diplomacy by assertion, and what in fact happened was that the détente so proudly proclaimed from Paris was not confirmed by real political change in Europe. When de Gaulle's hopes were shattered by the Soviet invasion of Czechoslovakia early in 1968, the irrelevance of the French bomb was obvious. It could not bring détente; it could not change the bipolarity of divided Europe.[75]

There is indeed a strong connection to the Soviet Union in both British and French assessments of the adequacy of their nuclear forces. The two governments have accepted it as a necessary test of their national deterrents that they should be strong enough to make the

Soviet government reluctant to run the risk of nuclear attack on France or Britain. In the earlier decades of the nuclear age simply to have a bomb often seemed enough, so that a single successful test could be the moment to cry hurrah. But it soon became clear that a bomb alone is not enough. You have to have a force that can survive and respond. In the end, I believe, this criterion has been more of a measuring stick, in both countries, than an independently governing objective. A deterrent that does not deter one's only possible nuclear enemy is not a deterrent at all, though the need to deter the Russians is not necessarily the reason for having the force in the first place.

I am persuaded that the basic objective, historically, for both the British and French governments, has been to have a kind of power without which these two ancient sovereign powers could not truly be themselves. This requirement has been clear for each government at every moment of choice from 1945 onward, and it is not a matter of deterrent strategy as such. It is rather a matter of what Britain and France must have, as long as others have it, in order to meet their own standards of their own rank among nations.

There is a wonderful story that Wilfred Kohl reports of a French strategic analyst who sent a book of his to President de Gaulle. Presently the general wrote to thank him for his thoughts and then went on to stress that in his own mind the central question was clear: "Will France remain France?" De Gaulle certainly exaggerated the international political influence that a French bomb would confer, but I do not think it follows that he was wrong in this simpler view. It is not easy for a foreign observer to be confident that France would still be France, or Britain still be Britain, without their bombs. What is historically clear is that so far their governments have not thought so.[76]

The measuring stick of credible deterrent strength has played its own growing role through these decades. It is indeed a long way from a first successful test to a credibly survivable deterrent force, and the Skybolt affair itself is a reminder that there can be dramatic changes in what is needed for such a force. There was importance in the calculations of Wohlstetter and McNamara, although they overstated their case because they failed to acknowledge that for effective nuclear deterrence uncertain but real possibility may be enough. But what was wholly omitted from their calculations was the strength of the underlying conviction in the governments of Britain and France that nuclear weapons were indispensable to national self-respect.

To say that British and French nuclear forces seem to have satisfied their owners in this respect during the last generation is not at all to say that they will always have this effect. Both technological and political conditions can change, and so can national choices. It is also true that the task of deterring Moscow can have a growing or declining importance to each country, quite apart from its role of serving as a yardstick of nuclear status. The conclusion reached here rests on history, not on logical necessity. The record we have reviewed seems to me to show decisively that the nuclear weapons of Britain and France came into being because each nation felt that it could not be true to itself if it were to stand aside from this new weaponry.

When a nation makes such a decision—a decision that rests on its own sense of what its own role in the world requires—it is illusory to suppose that it will be easily discouraged by even the best of friends. The choice made by Britain and France in this generation could not be determined by the United States.

That too is a lesson of Nassau, but while Kennedy may have learned it, others believed that American leadership could indeed change basic British or French convictions and sometimes also that the cause of European unity, if the American government pressed it strongly enough, could govern British or French policy. As it turned out, the most that American policy could do was accommodate itself to the basic preferences of these two governments in their nuclear relationship to Washington. The British wanted and finally got and kept a junior partnership, fully integrated in NATO for planning purposes but under their own ultimate control—usable only by the decision of the prime minister. The French wanted and got independence, which for de Gaulle meant saying and doing things the American government disapproved. As Arthur Schlesinger reports, Kennedy came to think that de Gaulle believed he *needed* some sort of friction with the United States. Kennedy, and Johnson even more strongly, came to understand further that the right reply to Gaullist provocation was to ignore it.[77]

To LOOK at the record of West Germany, after reaching these judgments about Britain and France, is to see at once that the national imperative for nuclear status is simply missing in the German case. The West Germans are more directly exposed to both nuclear danger and nuclear blackmail than Britain and France. They have all the economic strength and technological sophistication they would need, and over the years their efforts in the field of nuclear power plants have given them the kind of head start from which it is no great distance to the basic materials for a bomb. But the development of these technological possibilities has been accompanied by a steadily declining belief, inside and outside West Germany, that there is any reason to expect change in the German renunciation of national nuclear weapons.

That was the lesson of the MLF case. What moved the Germans in that affair was their interest in engaging the Americans more closely, and in gaining such influence as they could over the American decisions. The easiest way to wreck the German-American connection would be a German desire to have a bomb. American sensitivity on this point was acute. Moreover the failure of the MLF did not arouse a German interest in a bomb, but if anything the opposite. As the German editor Theo Sommer explained to an American audience in 1966: "It made them aware of the severe limitations under which they operate in the nuclear field." He went on to quote Helmut Schmidt with evident approval—"Bonn has invested too much prestige in nuclear participation"—and he concluded, prophetically: "Indications are plentiful, then, that Germany might henceforth seek, for good political reasons, a low nuclear posture rather than a high one . . . there is no rational reason to fear or suspect the most dangerous reassertion of German nationalism: the combination of patriotism and atomic weapons."[78]

The German commitment to the American connection was broadly matched by the American commitment to the defense of West Germany, and it was fortunate that both commitments were strong, because there were many tensions in the relationship. The changes we have seen in American strategic policy were not always happily received in Bonn. Both the New Look and flexible response, when translated into the realities of the West German position, could sound like very bad news—the first seemed to bring nuclear war too close, and the second seemed to give an easy early run to the Soviet conventional forces. It is a tribute to the steady good sense of German leaders that they regularly worked their way through these fearful reactions to understanding with the Americans. Conversely, no American administration ever allowed the claims of its nuclear doctrine to outweigh the requirement of reassurance to Bonn. Eisenhower believed that only two American divisions were really needed in Europe, but there were more than six still in place in the Federal Republic when he left office. Kennedy and McNamara believed in conventional reinforcement, but they also delivered tactical warheads by the thousands to carry out understandings first reached in the Eisenhower years. On both sides, so naturally and easily that neither may have paid great attention, there was understanding that the unequal nuclear relationship must not be allowed to imply political inequality. Thus the Americans did not give to the French or to the British advantages they withheld from the Germans, and they did not use their nuclear protection to put political pressure on Bonn. Though nuclear disagreements and tensions were numerous, and indeed inescapable, there was no interallied nuclear blackmail.

What remains most remarkable in the German case is that national nuclear ambition never developed. We can be sure that the Germans were aware of the fierce disapproval that any attempt to get a national weapon would have produced among friends and adversaries alike, but what is more important is that the Germans themselves did not want the bomb. The British and French forces did not impress or tempt them; Sommer in 1966 found the French and British bombs "objects of mild derision in Germany, considered inefficient, costly and of doubtful value even in terms of prestige." Unlike their old rivals and neighbors, the Germans had turned away from their historic concern for greatness. In Sommer's words again: "The whole value system of nationalism has collapsed in Germany. So has the belief in a German mission." Greatness did not need to be restored. Sommer noted that in 1963 Germans were polled on the question "When did, in your eyes, Germany have it best during this century?" A dazzling 62 percent answered, "At present." No such answer would have been given in Britain or France. It was their happy present which the West Germans wanted to keep secure, internally by their own efforts, externally with American protection. These were not the building blocks of national nuclear ambition.[79]

The Israelis

The sixth state to choose a full-scale nuclear weapons program—skipping China for the moment—is Israel. In this case the historian's task is complicated by the fact that the government of Israel has maintained a policy of intense secrecy with respect to its nuclear program, has never conducted any detected nuclear test, and does not admit that it has nuclear weapons. For twenty-five years the formal position of the Israeli government has been the one announced in 1962: "There are no nuclear weapons in the Middle East and Israel will never be the first to introduce them."[80] The overwhelming weight of the evidence, from Israeli actions and statements, from assessments of other governments and international agencies, and finally from consideration of the purposes and concerns of succeeding governments of Israel, forces the judgment that this official Israeli position cannot be taken at its surface meaning.

The first and most important evidence of Israeli nuclear ambition is the history of the nuclear reactor at Dimona, which Israeli Prime Minister David Ben-Gurion tried to explain away in 1960 by saying that it was a textile factory. Here is an excellent short account by a professor at Hebrew University:

> The Israeli effort to acquire nuclear weapons began in the mid-1950s, when construction began on a French-designed reactor near Dimona in the Negev desert. This reactor, like many others, can be considered dual purpose, in that it can provide power as well as be used to make nuclear weapons. Compared to other such dual-use reactors, however, its design is particularly useful for the manufacture of weapons and generally ill-suited for power production.

Despite the great secrecy that surrounded the construction effort, it soon became clear that the highly secret and heavily guarded "textile" plant in the desert was really a nuclear reactor. By the late 1960s, it was generally acknowledged that Israel had the technical capability to produce fissile material (plutonium).[81]

The Dimona reactor uses uranium and heavy water and produces plutonium. To have what is needed for weapons, the plutonium thus produced must go through a reprocessing facility, and such a facility is now known to exist at Dimona. The International Atomic Energy Agency was the first to announce an Israeli reprocessing facility, in 1977, and in 1980 its existence and its French origin were confirmed by Francis Perrin. Perrin is the former head of the French Atomic Energy Commission, and his statement is persuasive.[82]

The basic nuclear capability thus revealed has also been confirmed by at least two eminent Israeli officials. In 1974 the president of Israel, Efraim Katzir, told Western journalists that his country would be able to use nuclear weapons if it had to: "Should we have need of such weapons, we could have them." One newspaper account reported Katzir as having added that if the need arose, Israel could convert capability into fact "in a short time—even in a few days." In 1984 the same point was made again by Professor Yuval Ne'eman, a senior nuclear physicist, a former member of the Israeli Atomic Energy Commission, and Minister of Science at the time he spoke. "Israel, fifteen or twenty years ago, saw to it that she would not be helpless. We have created a nuclear potential, we have skilled personnel, we have the infrastructure." Professor Ne'eman went on to keep his statement in verbal conformity with the policy of Israel: "but we have not crossed the nuclear threshold. We have no bombs." Yet his denials do not undermine his admissions. The Israelis, by the public statements of men who must be assumed to know, have had the means, for many years, to have nuclear weapons when they want them. It is verbal haggling whether they have "crossed the nuclear threshold." They may "have no bombs" that are complete, armed, and ready for instant delivery. But they may have dozens or even hundreds that need minutes or hours of work before use, and if that is their position, then Professor Ne'eman is telling the truth, but not the whole truth, and Israel in reality is a nuclear weapons state. I agree with Bertrand Goldschmidt, who reads the statement of President Katzir as "officially admitting that his country had the capacity to produce nuclear bombs, which no one doubted."[83]

I have begun with what we know from Israeli authorities because our central interest is in the decisions of political leaders. In that process we have regularly paid close attention to what responsible leaders themselves have said. Israeli leaders have said enough to make it clear that there is a major nuclear weapons program in Israel. Beyond that they have been silent, and not surprisingly the worlds of intelligence, journalism, scholarship, and speculation have tried to take up the slack. By 1974 the American Central Intelligence Agency was reporting its own assessment this way:

> We believe that Israel has already produced nuclear weapons. Our judgment is based on Israeli acquisition of large quantities of uranium, partly by clandestine means; the ambiguous nature of Israeli efforts in the field of uranium enrichment, and Israel's large investment in a costly missile system designed to accommodate nuclear warheads. We do not expect the Israelis to provide confirmation of widespread suspicions of their capability, either by nuclear testing or by threats of use, short of a grave threat to the nation's existence.[84]

This report did not become public until 1978, but in its report for 1975 the International Institute for Strategic Studies in London (IISS) stated: "In the Middle East the probable existence of a serious Israeli nuclear capability became more generally accepted." In April 1976, *Time* magazine published an extended account of the Israeli nuclear program. In the ten years that followed there was increasingly wide understanding that the Israeli program existed, although the Israeli government steadily refused to go beyond the position so often proclaimed.[85]

In 1986 *The Sunday Times* of London convincingly described an Israeli program much larger and more sophisticated than most outside observers had supposed. *The Sunday Times* conducted extended interviews with a thirty-one-year-old technician named Mordechai Vanunu, who had worked for almost ten years at Dimona, and who had left Israel, taking with him two reels of photographs and an extraordinary memory of what he had learned. Cross-checking Vanunu's account with first-class nuclear physicists in Great Britain and the United States, *The Times* was able to report Israeli production of plutonium several times greater than earlier estimates and also the means to produce components for thermonuclear weapons. Vanunu further reported the means to produce highly enriched uranium and neutron bombs, and his testimony showed that the Israeli program fully justified the designation of Israel as the sixth nuclear power. The production at Dimona was such that the Israelis could have "at least 100 and as many as 200 nuclear weapons of varying destructive power." In the words of the nuclear physicist Theodore Taylor: "There should no longer be any doubt that Israel is, and for at least a decade has been, a fully fledged nuclear weapons state. The Israeli nuclear weapons programme is considerably more advanced than indicated by any previous report or conjectures of which I am aware."[86]

The size and quality of the Israeli program, as thus revealed, help us to understand not only the program but its purpose. For thirty years, despite its own limited resources, and in a world in which not one other government has been steadily sympathetic to its purpose, Israel has worked to present its unfriendly neighbors with the reality that Israel cannot be defeated without the most compelling risk of nuclear and even thermonuclear devastation that would leave any "victor" in chaos. This is the capability the Israelis have achieved, and there are excellent reasons for believing that the achievement of exactly this capability has been the determined purpose of the men behind the program from the beginning.

Israel is a creation—if you prefer a re-creation—of a nation-state younger than the atomic age itself: independent only since 1948 and in continuous danger ever since. From the beginning its neighbors have denied its right to exist. To most Arabs, most of the time, Israel has been only "the Zionist entity." In their first twenty years the Israelis fought three wars. If they had lost any one of them, their national existence would have ended. Each of the three drove home its own lesson of danger. The first, in 1948, taught the passionate hostility of the neighbors. The second, the Suez adventure of 1956, taught the unreliability of such friends as Britain, France, and the United States. The third, the Six-Day War of June 1967, taught a triple lesson of self-reliance: in its origins, when no friend was ready to help stop the relentless Nasser; in its battles, where Israeli arms won a famous victory; and in its aftermath, when the hatred of the beaten Arabs reached new heights. Do not count on your friends; rely on yourself; know that you are alone in a sea of enemies.

Not to every Israeli leader, but to a decisive number of determined men, the reality thus revealed made it vital to achieve a nuclear capability. This was the steady purpose of David Ben-Gurion, and among his most important and steadfast supporters in this course were such notable Israelis as the soldier Moshe Dayan, the politician Shimon Peres, and the scientific administrator Ernst Bergmann. All of them believed that Israelis would have the necessary talents. Right at the beginning Ben-Gurion had made a boast of the same reality that had led Hitler to jeer at "Jewish" physics: "It is not impossible for scientists in Israel to do for their own people what Einstein, Oppenheimer, and Teller— all three Jews—have done for the United States."[87] There were excellent scientists in Israel before 1948. Young Israelis were also sent to learn the relevant sciences and technologies in the West. Scientists excluded from American nuclear laboratories because of associations like those of the youthful Oppenheimer found welcome and work in Israel.

By ingenious and multiple efforts the Israeli government also provided itself with uranium and heavy water, with enriched uranium, and with technical support in the construction of the necessary facilities.

The most important supplier was France—a certain indifference to the danger of sharing nuclear skills has marked French scientists and manufacturers through most of the nuclear age. The French connection appears to have been important at least until de Gaulle himself acted to limit it, in 1960, and to end it when the Israelis disregarded his advice and fought a preemptive war in 1967. Israel also appears to have had help from within the United States, finding Americans who were willing, for love or money, to help in providing needed equipment and perhaps also enriched uranium. Skills and connections developed over the decades of secret work that helped to build and supply Israeli conventional forces were plied with determination and success in nuclear matters too.

Because they "have no bombs" the Israelis do not have to say what they have them for. The complex doctrinal debates that have accompanied nuclear armament in other nuclear powers are missing in Israel. What is evident from Israeli attention to conventional forces is that no one in Israel has been tempted by the thought that nuclear weapons can be a happy remedy for an otherwise decisive conventional inferiority.

The Israeli bomb is thus not intended to be used lightly, or for direct deterrence of anything but an otherwise irresistible attack on the very life of Israel. How it would be used in such a case the Israelis do not say, but the evident existence of the Israeli bomb is a part of the political and military calculation in every capital concerned with the Middle East.

Judged by what she has done and can do, then, Israel is a nuclear weapons state; judged by what her leaders have been saying for more than twenty years, she is not. This ambiguity is well understood by Israelis. Public debate in Israel has not been extensive, but what there is turns mainly on the question whether a deliberate policy of ambiguity is better than the straightforward adoption of a public policy of nuclear capability and nuclear deterrence. Discussion of the existing Israeli program is off limits for those without the necessary clearances, and those who are cleared are bound to stay within the official position. What is instructive about this debate is that while debaters are usually at pains to say that they do not know what the Israeli nuclear capability may be, those who favor a public policy of nuclear deterrence seem to be quite untroubled by any question of difficulty or cost in having the capability which they recommend announcing, while critics of such a public policy often appear to take it for granted that an unannounced weapons program not only exists but is desirable.

Remarkably, the position of the Israeli government is accepted by the government of the United States, which has never been friendly to the development of nuclear weapons by Israel. In Eisenhower's time there was no military assistance of any kind for Israel, and as that policy

began to change in the Kennedy years, assistance was not only confined to conventional weapons, but accompanied by a deep concern
about the Dimona reactor, whose existence had become public in
1960. The intersection of these developments came in 1962, when
Kennedy's assistant Myer Feldman negotiated a simultaneous agreement that the United States would sell Hawk surface-to-air missiles,
and that in return Israel would permit regular visits by Americans to
Dimona, where they could judge for themselves whether or not the
installation was part of a weapons program. These bilateral visits continued until 1968, but they were not as seriously and rigorously conducted as they would have had to be to get the real story. My
recollection is that close concern with this issue ended with the death
of Kennedy.

I do not recall discussing the matter with Lyndon Johnson. There
are reports that in 1968 he learned of rising concern about Israeli
progress among the estimators in the CIA, but my successor, Walt
Rostow, remembers no presidential concern on this question. Certainly there were no nuclear overtones for Washington in the war of
1967, when I found myself temporarily back in the White House as
the responsible staff officer.

There was a similar absence of any visible Israeli weapons in the
Yom Kippur war of 1973, although there were rumors in later years
of emergency deployments of warheads at the order of Golda Meir.
The only action with a clearly nuclear component which was visible at
the time was the American alert of October 24–25, in which a midnight order from the White House increased the state of alert of all
U.S. armed forces. That action (discussed in Chapter XI) was designed
to give a message of political determination, not one of nuclear threat,
and the move that the Soviets had threatened and that the Americans
were trying to deter—a possible unilateral movement of Soviet airborne forces to Egypt—was in fact amply prevented by Sadat's unwillingness to accept it. In retrospect, the nuclear danger in this episode
seems small, in spite of the somewhat theatrical character of both the
Soviet threat and the American response. Not for the first or last time,
the statesman here was Anwar Sadat, who had no nuclear weapons and
no desire to test anyone to the point of nuclear danger. The war he
was fighting was a war for the pride of Egypt, not for the extinction
of Israel.

One way or another, nonetheless, it does appear that the 1973 war,
with its tumultuous aftermath, drew American attention to the Israeli
nuclear program. It was only a year later that the CIA reached its firm
conclusion that Israeli weapons existed, and it is reasonable to assume
that this assessment responded to renewed interest among senior members of the administration. What is most remarkable about the CIA's

conclusion, however, is that the United States does not appear to have acted on it. It obviously raised grave questions about the meaning of Israeli denials and revealed the deliberate clandestine entry into the world of nuclear weapons by a friendly country now deeply dependent on American military, political, and economic support.

The American government appears to have decided not to comment. The Nixon, Ford, Carter, and Reagan administrations have all followed this course, and none of the many writers of memoirs from all of these administrations has devoted even a sentence to the question of the Israeli bomb. The official American position became and remains as it was stated in the Carter administration, after the CIA reports became public.

> The Israeli government has declared that Israel is not a nuclear power and will not be the first to introduce nuclear weapons into the area. We accept this as the official position of the government of Israel.[88]

It is striking that this announcement was made by the White House press secretary, and not by the President or any senior political official.

This American choice, like the Israeli position itself, has never been publicly discussed by the American government, and it has had extraordinarily little attention in the United States. In countries where basic sympathy for Israel is lower, and suspicion of American motives higher, more has been said. It is easy for analysts not automatically friendly to Israel or the United States to conclude that the United States has been a willing silent partner in the whole Israeli effort.[89] So the American decision to accept and indeed to support the Israeli position has had costs, both to American reputation and to the general effort to limit the spread of nuclear weapons. American administrations, some with more energy than others, have been public backers of this cause ever since the days of Atoms for Peace, and many countries have come under direct American pressure because of programs much less impressive than that of Israel.

The simplest explanation for the absence of such pressure on Israel is that any American president must consider the domestic political cost of any choice that American friends of Israel will oppose. Contests over shipments of conventional arms to the Middle East are the most familiar example—the backers of Israel will always want more arms for Israel and less for Saudi Arabia. But I think it is too easy to assume that this particular pattern governs in the case of nuclear weapons policy, which is a question at once enormously large over the long run, and relatively small in its present-day immediacy. Whatever the Israeli nuclear program may be, it is not the product of an American decision, and if it conflicts with American preferences on nuclear proliferation, it is not at all clear that the situation would be improved by public American complaint. Does anyone suppose that the Israelis will give up a bomb for which they have worked with such determination because of the nonproliferation preferences of Americans? Their own scorn for international safeguards is deep-seated, and they have never been interested in signing the 1968 Treaty on the Non-Proliferation of Nuclear Weapons. If it is merely a matter of appearances, they can play the game of public virtue in this field as well as anyone in Washington. They are on record, for example, as supporters of a nuclear-weapons-free zone in the Middle East. There are elements in their proposal that make it most unlikely to complicate their own program for a long time—notably a requirement for political relations between Israel and her neighbors that has no present prospect of happening. Nonetheless their public position has as much surface respectability as do many American proposals in the field of strategic arms control. It is not easy to predict any useful consequence from American protest.

The serious question is not one of words but of action. If the United States should decide that it was indispensable to persuade Israel to give up its nuclear weapons, how would it do so? Would the United States go so far as to stop its programs of military and economic assistance? It is most unlikely that any administration would find such a course acceptable, either in terms of the national interest or in terms of American opinion. Nor is it likely that such a policy would bring the desired Israeli response.

A still deeper question is whether the United States would wish to accept the moral and political responsibility of forcing the abandonment of the Israeli nuclear weapons program, even assuming that it could. If that abandonment should take place, and if at some time in the future only a nuclear threat or even a nuclear response could prevent Israel from being overrun, would the United States do for the Israelis what it had made them unable to do for themselves? These lines of argument and speculation do not by any means exhaust the question, but they may be enough to suggest why it has seemed sensible in Washington to take the Israelis at their word. If there is nothing the American government is prepared to do that can end or even limit the Israeli nuclear program, then what purpose is served by verbal attacks on it? The United States has long since abandoned its public hostility to the programs of other friends like Britain and France. It may have had unfriendly thoughts about the Chinese program long ago, but it does not now complain of China's bomb. The Israeli case may be one more demonstration of the preposition that what you oppose before it happens is something which it is wise to accept when it becomes real.

The Problem of Nonproliferation

One of the most important and complex problems in nuclear policy is to find ways to limit the spread of nuclear weapons to other countries, and even to nongovernmental groups—revolutionaries, terrorists, or blackmailers. This problem has been given the name of nonproliferation. Americans and their government have believed in limiting the spread of such weapons ever since 1945, but finding an effective policy has not been easy. The difficulty can be quickly understood if we look at the forces that have led the present possessors of nuclear weapons to decide that they must have them. In every case the choice has been governed by a firm conviction that the weapon was required to protect the nation. The one partial exception here may be the United States itself. While Roosevelt's initial decision of 1941 was certainly governed by just such a need—not to let Hitler be first—the effort after 1944 was governed by momentum and the prospect of shortening a terrible war. The Soviet, British, French, Chinese, and Israeli decisions are all decisions about what each government believed its country simply must have. The considerations that led to the decision are not identical from country to country. Stalin saw that the equilibrium achieved at enormous cost in World War II had been suddenly upset by the American bomb. Britain and France in different ways decided that their countries could not be themselves without this weapon. China decided to have it, as we shall see, because Mao became convinced that China must have protection against American and then Soviet nuclear weapons. Israel must have the weapon because her existence was threatened by vastly greater Arab numbers, so that if she could provide herself with this ultimate deterrent, she must.

All of these are internal decisions, and any outside government trying to reverse any one of them would have had an extraordinarily hard job. The Americans tried not to help anyone except intermittently the British, yet in one degree or another, as it turned out, they helped everyone—by the example they set, the reports they published, the spies they did not screen out, the exports they did not prevent, and the people who went back and forth. Yet the Americans were not decisive in any case but their own. The spread of nuclear weapons has been the product of determined decisions in the states that have produced them.

We have not reviewed case by case the very much larger number of decisions *not* to have the nuclear weapon, which begin with Canada in 1945, but the same proposition can be asserted in almost all such cases: The decision not to have the bomb is a decision that most countries make for themselves. The most important partial exceptions are West Germany and Japan, where the decisions have been national but also required by the victors of World War II. There is a similar constraint upon the Communist states in Eastern Europe, clearly enforced by Soviet power. These exceptions underline the more general rule. When a sovereign state has the necessary resources, economic and human, and is unconstrained by defeat or domination, it becomes a matter of national choice whether to have the bomb or not. There is no case so far in which pressure from outside has been clearly decisive in preventing such a choice.

To state the matter only in this black-and-white form, however, is to miss the real importance of the influence that can be brought to bear in cases where the internal imperative is not immediately compelling. There are a number of such cases. The existing nuclear-weapon states—the five permanent members of the United Nations Security Council and Israel (in everything but her own public posture)—have been exceptional in the clarity and intensity of their decision. Today there is room for external influence in all the states that are now thought to be within reach of nuclear-weapon capability—usually listed as Argentina, Brazil, India, Pakistan, and South Africa. In each of these cases every outside country hopes that the government will hold back. There is still more room for influence in countries without the technical and economic strength that all these nearly nuclear nations possess. The man whose nuclear ambition may be the most disquieting of all is Colonel Muammar el-Qaddafi of Libya, but so far it has proved possible for other nations not to give him the help he would need to fulfill his ambition.

Nonetheless it is one thing to hope and quite another to be able to affect the choice, as we can see plainly by considering the one large international agreement that is aimed directly at the problem, the Treaty on the Non-Proliferation of Nuclear Weapons, also known as the Non-Proliferation Treaty of 1968 (NPT). This treaty was first proposed by Ireland in 1958, but it became possible only in the midsixties, when its nonnuclear supporters were joined by the Soviet Union and the United States, which had been held back in earlier years both by their mutual mistrust and by the complexities of such questions as the role of West Germany in NATO. The West Germans, as we have seen, did not want bombs of their own, but the possibility of such an arrangement as the MLF led the Soviets to press for language in any NPT that the Americans were bound to oppose. When the MLF faded away and there was a turn toward East-West détente, both in Germany and between the superpowers, the Non-Proliferation Treaty became possible and was energetically pushed by the United States after Lyndon Johnson made its conclusion a matter of high priority.

The treaty is simple in its principles, though not in its operations. It says that "nuclear-weapon states" will not help others to get such weapons, that "non-nuclear-weapon states" will not seek or receive such weapons or assistance in making them, and that they will accept safeguards to prevent diversion of nuclear energy from peaceful uses to nuclear weapons. In return all parties undertake to facilitate and have the right to take part in the peaceful uses of atomic energy. The states without weapons promise that there will be no proliferation among members, that the states without weapons will accept safeguards, and in return they are assured that they will have full access at moderate prices to what they need for peaceful uses. Among its members, the treaty has worked reasonably well, because the parties include only those nonnuclear-weapon states that have no serious interest in having nuclear weapons. Nations that already own such weapons and nations that do not want to own them have an obvious common interest in opposing proliferation, and complaints between nonnuclear and nuclear parties have been limited, in the main, to the places where international safeguards or national laws against proliferation are thought to conflict with reasonable access to what is needed for peaceful purposes. There are also recurrent complaints at the evident failure of the nuclear weapons states to make the progress in ending the arms race "at an early date" that they undertook to seek "in good faith" in Article VI of the treaty.

But the weakness of the treaty is that not one of the states that may be close to having nuclear weapons has signed it. Standing apart, along with China, France, and Israel, are Argentina, Brazil, India, Pakistan, and South Africa. Their absence does not mean that their interest in nuclear weapons is as strong as what we have found in the existing nuclear-weapon states, but it does mean that they are keeping their options open and that they commit no international offense by the steps they take to bring the possession of weapons closer.

What leaves room for external influence here is that the path from a real interest to a real capability is not short—longer indeed than it was in the early years when a first successful test automatically conferred full standing as a nuclear power, especially in the testing government's own eyes. India had a successful test in 1974, but India in 1988 still has the option not to "have the bomb." There is no Indian program comparable to the one that has become evident in Israel, and indeed no Indian leader has yet found it imperative to move from a test to a clear commitment to weaponry. The Indian position is clearly affected by what other countries do and refrain from doing, and in turn the actions of India greatly affect what is thought and done in Pakistan. In such a situation the choices of the United States and the Soviet Union are also highly relevant, and both will usually be well advised to give a higher rank to nonproliferation than officials with immediate political concerns may prefer.

Yet the connection between cause and effect is not simple in cases of this sort, and the nuclear question itself is not the only one that counts in the way that the government of Pakistan and India will move.

The relatively mechanical application of an antinuclear policy cannot be counted on to produce good results in a situation in which no one supplier, and indeed no one supply, is indispensable. Friendly support on one problem may help to induce moderation on another, and if the immediate danger is an irrevocable choice by one of these two countries, the single best hope of avoiding it may be in some conciliatory move by the other. Sometimes, but not always, superpowers can make such moves easier by their own behavior. Conversely an outside power that engages in active maneuvers against either of these countries can easily fan the flame of nuclear ambition. The Nixon administration, in its ill-advised "tilt" toward Pakistan in 1971, may well have helped to stimulate the Indian test of 1974.

In situations so complex and volatile sound policy cannot be set by formula. What makes sense in the subcontinent is not what will make sense in dealing with Brazil, and South Africa will remain unique. Some of these countries should remain our friends, no matter what they choose, but South Africa cannot be a friend while apartheid endures.

One further set of comments is suggested by what history itself has shown so far. In the long run possessing nuclear weapons is hard work, and in the absence of a threat, these weapons have little or no day-to-day value. The story we have been telling is mostly about the limited value of these weapons. It is hard to believe that there can be nuclear systems in any one country of the great Asian subcontinent or of South America without at least one competing nuclear system, sooner or later, in a neighboring state. It will not be easy then for either country in such a pair to have delivery systems clearly safe from surprise attack. And who will be more comfortable then, one side or both or neither? A related question about the eventual action of others can also be asked in South Africa. In the long run the countries that are close to having a bomb of their own will hold back only if that choice seems the lesser evil to them, but it may help them to consider whether it is truly in their interest to stimulate a mortal threat to themselves by presenting it to their neighbors.

XI

Called Bluffs

T HE FIRST THING to notice about the twenty-five years since the Cuban missile crisis is that nothing like it has happened again. There have been terrible events in these years, occasional moments of high tension, and a continuing competition in nuclear technology and deployment. There has been searing "conventional" warfare, as in Vietnam, and brutally repressive invasion, as in Afghanistan. Through most of this period there has also been debate in the West over nuclear deployment, whose most notable feature was the idea that Soviet nuclear deployments were creating a window of American vulnerability that would have the gravest consequences in the 1980s. This concern with "present danger" deserves attention, but it will help to begin with the remarkable fact that nothing of the sort has happened. The two superpowers have not become friends, but since 1962 they have continuously kept a decent distance from the nuclear danger that any confrontation between them must always present, and neither side has had any success with nuclear pressure on the other. There are episodes in this period that have been said to have such a color to them, but closely examined they show much more prudence than menace, and on both sides. Let us consider three cases in which this reality appears: one in the Middle East in 1973, one on the Sino-Soviet border in 1969, and one in Southeast Asia over the decade 1965–75.

Alert in the Middle East, 1973

The most conspicuous moment of superpower tension after Cuba was in the last moments of the Yom Kippur War. For about twelve hours, on the night of October 24 and the morning of October 25, 1973, senior officers of the United States government believed that there was imminent danger of a unilateral military intervention by the Soviet Union in Egypt.

The war against Israel that was begun on October 6 by Egypt and Syria led first to major Egyptian gains, then to a brilliant Israeli counterattack, and onward to a cease-fire produced mostly by Soviet-American diplomacy. The Americans were surprised by the outbreak of war, believing that neither Egypt nor Syria would dare to challenge the Israelis, but American diplomatic performance in the first two weeks was energetic and skillful. Slowly, but still in time, the Americans recognized that Israel faced a severe challenge. They ensured the resupply of armaments to Israeli forces while at the same time rejecting Israeli efforts to obtain American support for an internationally imposed restoration of the lines before October 6. Instead Kissinger proposed, and worked out in Moscow with Brezhnev, an agreement for a cease-fire that would leave unchanged, for the time being, the largely offsetting gains of Egyptians and Israelis. This proposal was voted by the United Nations Security Council in the early morning of October 22 (UN Resolution 338). It seemed a great achievement, but it left an Egyptian army almost encircled by Israeli forces east of the Suez Canal. The Israelis did not resist temptation. Within forty-eight hours the cease-fire was broken, and in the renewed fighting the Israeli encirclement of the Egyptian army was completed.[1]

After a day of diplomatic pressure, from Moscow to Washington to Jerusalem, the Soviet government raised the stakes, unappeased by Kissinger's relay of Israeli assurances that the cease-fire had been restored. Just after seven P.M. on October 24 (two A.M. October 25, Moscow time), Kissinger learned from Soviet Ambassador Dobrynin that the Soviets had decided to encourage a United Nations resolution that would call for the dispatch of Soviet and American troops to enforce the cease-fire. Two and one-half hours later, in an urgent and abrupt message from Brezhnev to Nixon, again telephoned by Dobrynin to Kissinger, the stakes were raised again. Brezhnev's message said, "If you find it impossible to act jointly with us in this matter, we should be faced with the necessity urgently to consider the question of taking appropriate steps unilaterally." It was apparent that the leadership in Moscow was working late.[2]

Kissinger says in his memoirs that he took this message to mean that he was facing "one of the most serious challenges to an American president by a Soviet leader." It would be "unthinkable" to join with Soviet troops in Egypt. That would put the Soviet Union back in Egypt "with our blessing"; our "friends among Arab moderates would be profoundly unnerved," and "Egypt would be drawn back into the Soviet orbit." Probably in the end the joint effort would collapse and create a U.S.-Soviet crisis in which "we would be alone." These forebodings could of course be dealt with, as Kissinger acknowledges, simply by rejecting the proposal for a joint military operation and reinforcing that rejection with a veto at the United Nations. The only hard point was that the Russians must also be discouraged from any *unilateral* landing. Kissinger swiftly concluded that this would have to be done "in a manner that shocked the Soviets." His account continues with a summary of Soviet air movements, airborne divisions on alert, and "other ominous reports." With these thoughts in his head as he read the message back to be sure he had it right, he warned Dobrynin against a unilateral move, and Dobrynin said he would report the warning to Moscow.[3]

Kissinger's next step was to call a meeting of senior officials—the secretary of defense, the chairman of the Joint Chiefs, the director of Central Intelligence, and three senior White House assistants. He himself chaired the meeting after learning from Alexander Haig, the White House chief of staff, that Nixon should not be waked up. When Haig curtly said no, Kissinger says he knew that "Haig thought the President too distraught to participate in the preliminary discussion." Earlier in the evening Kissinger himself, in a phone call, had found Nixon "as agitated and emotional as I had ever heard him," upset not by the crisis in the Middle East but by the tumultuous outburst that had followed his decision of October 20 to fire the Watergate prosecutor Archibald Cox, which had brought the resignation of Attorney General Elliot Richardson and two senior colleagues in what came to be called the Saturday night massacre. Nor was there any vice president who might take Nixon's place at the meeting, because Spiro Agnew had resigned and Gerald Ford was not yet confirmed. Kissinger, who was now both secretary of state and assistant to the president for national security, was bound to take the chair. He is right to describe it as "a daunting responsibility." Although Nixon was to claim from October 26 onward that the decisions which came out of this meeting were his own, the compelling evidence of all other accounts is that the men in this meeting acted in his name. The decisive figures were Kissinger and Secretary of Defense James Schlesinger, to whom Kissinger refers as his "partner" on this occasion.[4]

The meeting assembled in the White House basement at 10:40 P.M. One hour later the chairman of the Joint Chiefs, Admiral Thomas H. Moorer, executing a decision of the meeting, ordered an all-forces military alert called Defense Condition III. Because this general alert might not be observed quickly enough, the 82nd Airborne Division was also put on alert for movement, and additional movements of aircraft carriers were ordered, both within and toward the Mediterranean. Sixty B-52 bombers were ordered back from Guam to the U.S. mainland. The intent of these actions was to provide for the Soviets what Kissinger calls "noticeable action that conveyed our determination to resist unilateral moves." It was desired that the alerts should be noticed before the Soviets received the American reply to Brezhnev's message, and accordingly that reply, which was completed by two A.M., was not delivered to Ambassador Dobrynin for another three and one-half hours. Kissinger tells us that the reply was designed to be "conciliatory in tone but strong in substance." It plainly stated that "we could in no event accept unilateral action," which "would produce incalculable consequences which would be in the interest of neither of our countries and which would end all we have striven so hard to achieve."[5]

The Soviets made no unilateral move that night. By early morning the situation as seen from Washington had changed dramatically, as a result of decisions in Cairo and New York that had little to do with the American alert. Two messages from Egypt, answering American messages of the previous day, made it clear that Sadat fully understood and accepted the American rejection of a joint Soviet-American force and would now seek instead an "international force" that did not include Soviet or American troops. In Kissinger's words, "Egypt was withdrawing the request that had produced the crisis." Another early-morning message, from Ambassador John Scali at the United Nations, reported that the Security Council would respect the American rejection of a joint force and would instead proceed to consider a resolution that would not include the superpowers in any emergency force. Kissinger's judgment is correct: "We were on the verge of winning the diplomatic game." It was not a bit likely that the Soviet government would move troops to Egypt "without the sanction of either the host country or the UN."[6]

These two pieces of good news were well earned. The Egyptians were responding to timely messages of friendly warning, which Kissinger had sent on October 24. He had also instructed Scali to make clear at the United Nations the American opposition to any joint Soviet-American operation. In addition—and this third line of action may be still more important—Kissinger had conducted an energetic and successful effort to stop Israel's violation of the cease-fire. Since this Israeli violation was certainly the cause of the disquieting message the Soviets sent on the night of October 24, the renewed cease-fire was probably the most helpful single influence on their next decisions. When the Soviets did not act in the night they almost surely knew the Israeli guns were silent. Certainly they had received the firm assurances that Kissinger had sent out before Brezhnev's alarming message to Nixon arrived. It is also probable, though Kissinger and Nixon do not choose to say so in their memoirs, that there were additional assurances in the slow reply to the Brezhnev message. The full text of that message has not been made public, but if it was indeed "conciliatory in tone" as Kissinger says, it would naturally have included further assurance on the American view of Israeli obligations under the cease-fire. The Americans fully understood the legitimacy of Soviet concern on this point.[7]

These developments, all unrelated to the American alert, were more than enough to prevent any Soviet landing in Egypt. Nothing would have been less helpful to long-run Soviet interests than an uninvited and unsanctioned military intrusion when fighting had once more ended and the Security Council was proceeding with its supervision of a resolution unanimously approved only three days before. To suppose that the American alert is the main cause of the return of calm in the Washington morning of October 25 is to undervalue grossly the responses that had come from Egypt, the UN, and probably Israel, responses that ended the threat of Soviet unilateral intervention. Whether and how far the American alert also influenced Moscow is unclear, but we will come back to that.

As it turned out, the midnight alert played a bigger part in American public debate than in the resolution of the international crisis. Its existence became public within a few hours, much more rapidly than the participants in the basement meeting had expected. Coming as it did when both the press and the president were preoccupied with Watergate and its Saturday night massacre, the alert produced immediate speculation, as reporter Marvin Kalb put it to Kissinger in a press conference the next morning, "that the American alert might have been prompted as much perhaps by American domestic requirements as by the real requirements of diplomacy in the Middle East." Kissinger indignantly rejected the suggestion and went on to describe the alert as "precautionary." He also distinguished the situation sharply from one of confrontation. "We are not talking of threats that have been made against one another. We are not talking of a missile-crisis-type situation." In a comment as incisively clear as it was grammatically innovative, he underlined the crucial difference between October 1962 and October 1973: In the second case "there is no reason for any country to back off anything that it has not yet done."[8]

Kissinger's use of the moderate word *precautionary* was in part the result of a sensible desire to say nothing that might anger Moscow, and it certainly contrasts in temper with the expectation of imminent Soviet action that he describes in the night meeting: "During the night, the consensus emerged that the Kremlin was on the verge of a major decision. We expected the airlift to start at dawn in eastern Europe, about two hours away." This account may overstate the matter, for if Kissinger had really expected the Russians to take off so soon, it is hard to believe that he would have delayed the answer to Brezhnev until after noon, Soviet time. Nonetheless it was natural that there should be much more concern during the night than after the good news of the early morning, when diplomatic reports were encouraging and the threatened Soviet airlift had not happened.[9]

But the word *precautionary* was a diplomatic substitute for the truth. Kissinger's memoirs make it plain that the alert was not intended to foreshadow an American military reply, at least not as far as Kissinger himself was concerned. The alert was a message. "The readiness measures were our signal to Moscow," and it was to let that signal penetrate that the diplomatic message to Brezhnev was held up. So much did Kissinger value this unadorned military signal that he held back from informing any ally except Great Britain "because we wanted the Soviets to pick up our readiness measures themselves and not through allied leaks, which would inevitably include any reassurances we might have given and thus lessen the sense of determination we thought it essential to convey." Retrospectively he thought this procedure wrong, but the choice he made and his reasons for it make his purpose wholly clear: He wanted to send a signal of determination and danger that would deter.[10]

As we have seen, that signal was almost surely unnecessary because other obstacles to Soviet action were sought and found, and because the Israeli provocation was ended, just when and why we do not know. But it does not follow that no such signal should have been sent. In particular no one could be sure of Sadat's position ahead of time. For him the survival of his encircled army was a compelling necessity, and he might well be coming to think that only the Soviet Union could save it. It was therefore entirely possible, for those in the basement meeting at the White House, that Sadat had already agreed to support unilateral Soviet action if the Americans would not join. Given that possibility, there was every reason to send a signal that would encourage caution in Moscow. No one can be sure that the signal had the desired effect on the Politburo, but no one can be sure that it did not.

What is beyond argument is that the Soviet government itself had already taken steps of military readiness which themselves were intended, at least in part, as a serious political signal. We do not know how near the Soviet government came to action. Probably it had a good sense of the political difficulties in any unilateral action. The Soviet government surely knew, as the Americans could not, that Sadat had made no commitment to support any such intervention, and they could estimate ahead of time their own lack of enthusiasm for an action that would never win approval in the Security Council because of one or more Western vetoes. Yet insofar as their purpose was to send a signal that might encourage the Americans to put further pressure on Israel, they were making a point the Americans were sure to understand. Kissinger in particular recognized that one consequence of the cease-fire he had worked out in Moscow on October 2 1 and defended in Jerusalem on October 2 2 was that both the Soviet Union and the Arab world, and above all Sadat himself, would look to the United States to ensure Israeli compliance. Explaining his own concern at the first breakdown in the cease-fire, on October 2 3, he writes, "If the United States held still while the Egyptian army was being destroyed after an American-sponsored cease-fire and a Secretary of State's visit to Israel, not even the most moderate Arab could cooperate with us any longer."[11] Kissinger had been doing his best to stop the Israelis ever since, and one reason for his great concern over Brezhnev's threat of unilateral action was his fear that the Soviets now planned to use the broken cease-fire for their own ends. Unless his long account is incomplete, he does not seem to have recognized the strong possibility that when Brezhnev sent his alarming message he genuinely did not believe, as Kissinger genuinely did, that the cease-fire was again in force.

Sending diplomatic messages by military movements is an expensive form of communication and sometimes a dangerous one. In this case the danger never became great. Secretary of Defense Schlesinger's judgment in a press conference of October 2 6 seems sound: "We were very far away from a confrontation."[12] Both sides were sending military signals, but probably the signals were unnecessary, in that each side already respected and accepted what was most important in the message of the other: "Stop your Israeli friends," from Moscow to Washington; "Let's not have a direct confrontation in the Middle East," from Washington to Moscow. Kissinger finally concluded that insofar as it was a threat Brezhnev's signal was in fact a bluff, and it is to be doubted that Brezhnev gave any higher rank to a flight of B-5 2 aircraft from Guam to the United States. The use of such aircraft to convey a message of political warning should not be confused with the real nuclear danger that is inescapable in real superpower confrontation. Yet the power of such military signals may not be high if their weight is reduced by a lack of serious military intent. Thus Kissinger correctly remarks of later Soviet bluster that it was weakened by the absence of substance in Brezhnev's nighttime warning: "Once Brezhnev's big bluff had failed, Soviet threats had lost much of their credibility." But if it was only a bluff—if it was in reality only a signal, not a threat that Brezhnev truly intended to execute—then Kissinger exaggerates in a later chapter on the decline of détente. There he claims first that in the alert the Soviets "took us on frontally" and then that "the Soviets subsided as soon as we showed our teeth." That is a bit silly, especially as the Soviets plainly got what they most wanted that night, an Israeli cease-fire.[13]

The historic record was also rearranged by Nixon, who tried hard to enlarge both the gravity of the crisis and the importance of his own role. Beginning in a press conference two days afterward, on October 26, he painted a picture of imminent danger and lonely and decisive presidential fortitude that had almost nothing to do with reality. According to Nixon, he personally had ordered the alert, and it had been a real moment of test, "the most difficult crisis we have had since the Cuban confrontation of 1962." The messages on both sides had "left very little to the imagination," but fortunately Nixon had a quality he thought he must have inherited: "The tougher it gets, the cooler I get." Brezhnev had understood that he was dealing with the man who was strong enough to do "what he thought was right" in bombing Cambodia in May 1970 and North Vietnam in December 1972. "Mr. Brezhnev knew that regardless of the pressures at home" Nixon "would do what was right," and "that is what made Mr. Brezhnev act as he did."[14]

Kissinger saved his own posturing for his memoirs, but in his news conference the day before, he too had given the affair a deeper color of nuclear danger than it deserved. In the middle of a masterful review of events since October 6, he introduced an eloquent passage on the nuclear responsibilities of the superpowers.

> The United States and the Soviet Union are, of course, ideological and, to some extent, political adversaries. But the United States and the Soviet Union also have a very special responsibility. We possess—each of us—nuclear arsenals capable of annihilating humanity. We—both of us—have a special duty to see to it that confrontations are kept within bounds that do not threaten civilized life. Both of us, sooner or later, will have to come to realize that the issues that divide the world today, and foreseeable issues, do not justify the unparalleled catastrophe that a nuclear war would represent.[15]

These are honorable and important sentiments, but the speaker's choice of tense and mood, after a night of great tension, is troubling. Taken at their face value, these words suggest that one side or the other or both had recently been ignoring the danger of nuclear catastrophe. Otherwise why did Kissinger say that *"both of us . . . will have to come to realize"* that divisive issues do not justify nuclear war. No doubt Kissinger was stimulated by his experience of the responsibility for choice in a night of serious challenge and response, but insofar as he suggested that there had been any neglect of nuclear danger by anyone that night, he was going beyond the evidence.

Even below the nuclear level some of the prospects with which Kissinger embroidered his memoirs are unreal. There was, for example, no prospect that the United States would put its own troops into

Egypt in reply to a unilateral Soviet move. Kissinger reports on one page that on October 24 "we were determined to resist by force if necessary the introduction of Soviet troops into the Middle East," but by the morning of the twenty-fifth, he tells us, he and Nixon were talking only about their determination "to match any Soviet troop buildup in the area." The real possibility—greatly limited by congressional reluctance—was that some form of matching contingent might be put in territory held by Israel or in a friendly Arab state. Such a pair of superpower presences would have increased tension in the Middle East, but it would not by itself have led to conflict.[16]

In sum, the crisis of October 24–25, 1973, was not a moment of nuclear danger. The suggestion of unilateral Soviet military movement was dealt with primarily by timely and skillful diplomatic actions that had constructive effects on the positions of Egypt and Israel. The secretaries of state and defense worked well together in a situation of high pressure in which the president was temporarily unfit for duty. Their use of a military alert as a signal of serious concern may have been useful and may also have been unnecessary, but in the light of earlier and larger Soviet military movements it can hardly be called provocative. The rhetorical excess that followed was unfortunate, but it does not rub out a good night's work. In their behavior, if not in all their later words or those of their absent president, the men on watch took full account of the reality that this was a crisis that must be resolved very far short of nuclear risk.

The Chinese Bomb and the Sino-Soviet Border

In 1969, on the long border between the Soviet Union and China, there occurred a confrontation between nuclear powers that lasted longer than any other except Khrushchev's Berlin crisis of 1958–63. This one included ground force combat and real nuclear threats, along with striking demonstrations of determination and caution by both sides. But before we can consider the crisis we must introduce the world's fifth nuclear power—the People's Republic of China, last seen in these pages as a state without nuclear weapons that dared to challenge the Americans twice over Quemoy and Matsu.[17]

China is the first nuclear-weapon state whose decision to enter the field came after World War II. Because the country moved from Japanese surrender straight into intensified civil war, no such choice was open until the 1950s, and the initial position of Mao Zedong in 1946 was that the atomic bomb was "a paper tiger which the U.S. reactionaries use to scare people."[18] With respect to his own objective at that time, he turned out to be right. Nobody's bomb interfered in any way with the revolutionary war through which the Chinese Communists came to power on the Chinese mainland at the end of 1949.

We do not know exactly when Mao began to think that China must have a bomb of its own. He may have had that thought from the beginning. There are reports of great debates among his followers in Yenan after Hiroshima and Nagasaki, and it is at least possible that Mao's talk of paper tigers arose more from the need to shore up the courage of his own people than from an underestimation of the role that nuclear weapons could play in warfare or political conflict when one side had them and the other did not.[19]

In the years after he came to power, Mao certainly had to think about the American weapon. We have seen that there were threads of nuclear danger in the Korean war though we have found no solid evidence that Eisenhower's atomic diplomacy was decisive in producing the armistice of 1953. Still there is no doubt that Mao found the one-sided nuclear danger disagreeable, not only in Korea but still more in the first crisis over Quemoy and Matsu in 1954–55. The formal Chinese decision to start a nuclear weapons program was made in the middle of that crisis, on January 15, 1955. In an address to party leaders the next year Mao gave the illuminating explanation that "if we are not to be bullied in the present-day world, we cannot do without the bomb." The timing of this statement, just a year after Eisenhower's public warning over Quemoy, suggests which bully Mao then had in mind. He went on to argue that the need for the bomb and also for planes and artillery justified a cut in current "military and administrative expenditures" and greater spending on economic construction. That was what you must do, he said, if "your desire for the atom bomb" was "genuine and very keen." Otherwise, he said, "you will stay in the old rut." He left no doubt of his own choice.[20]

From the American standpoint it seems paradoxical that the first confrontation over Quemoy and Matsu should have been the precipitant of Mao's decision to go ahead. As we have seen, the real sentiment of Eisenhower was that he must do everything he could *not* to have to use nuclear weapons over those small islands, and his one public warning, which actually came in March, two months after Mao's decision, was intended only to encourage Chinese caution while conventional defenses on the two islands were strengthened. We have also seen that what was decisive for Eisenhower and Dulles, thoughout this crisis, and still more in the second one three years later, was their deep fear of a fall of dominos throughout the western Pacific; they felt themselves to be playing an entirely defensive hand.

But what becomes apparent when we consider the matter from the Chinese side is that the American government did not look or sound merely defensive. The Chinese knew about the doctrine of massive retaliation, and they read news stories about a new American readiness to use nuclear weapons in any conflict with China. They also knew that Chiang Kai-shek, on Taiwan, was still intent on a return to the mainland, and they paid more attention to noisy American sympathy with Chiang than to the less noisy but more important recognition in the White House that such an adventure was out of the question. Americans who remember what Maoists sounded like in the 1950s can remind themselves that Chinese rhetoric had a similar impact on opinion in the United States. When a statesman as sober as Zhou Enlai insisted that the liberation of Taiwan (Formosa) was "imperative" and promised "defeat after defeat" for American aggressors, Americans found it easy to conclude that the threat to peace came from the mainland. Yet American intelligence assessments continued to be generally cautious; even after the first attacks on Quemoy and Matsu in September 1954, the assessment was that China would not in fact make war over Taiwan.[21]

What was happening on both sides, we may now conclude, was that threatening words were used not so much to warn of action truly intended as to give an appearance of determination. The strong words on both sides were not so much a warning of action as a substitute for it. But if each side's rhetoric had a large role in stimulating the rhetoric of the other, there was an important difference in the eventual consequences. When one party has nuclear weapons and the other does not, exchanges of menace do not have equal weight. It is hard to avoid the conclusion that the precipitant of Mao's decision to have a bomb was a genuine perception of the Americans as nuclear bullies.

Yet the underlying cause of the Chinese choice lies deeper. I share the judgment of the scholars who have given the best account in English of the Chinese bomb, that the Chinese decision "rested on fundamental national interests as much as on the immediate security threat." Mao's commitment to revolution always included a fierce determination that China must escape forever from generations of humiliation at the hands of stronger states. The intense sensitivity displayed by Beijing at every Chinese border over the last four decades has reflected not so much an eagerness to expand as a passionate determination that the humiliations must not be repeated. If there had been no evident bone of contention like Taiwan, the new China might have waited in 1955 before undertaking a most difficult and demanding national nuclear effort, but it seems certain that there would have been precipitating reasons to make this fundamental choice at later dates. It is not easy in 1988 to imagine a China still standing back from the decision to have the bomb.[22]

In the opening years of their nuclear effort the Chinese sought and received extensive Soviet help. Between 1955 and 1958 the two countries signed no less than six agreements on nuclear cooperation. Arrangements were made for large-scale Soviet assistance, including not only technical support in the construction of a facility for the enrichment of uranium but also an undertaking to deliver "a sample of an atomic bomb." But on June 20, 1959, by the Chinese account, the Soviets "tore up the agreement" and refused to provide the sample bomb. This Chinese statement was issued in August 1963, after the open split between the two countries and during a bitter and sustained exchange of polemical messages. In its answer the Soviet government denounced the Chinese for betraying defense secrets of the socialist community, but it did not deny the existence of the agreement or even the plan to deliver a sample bomb. Indeed Khrushchev in his *Last Testament* confirmed the existence of such a plan and explained his own decision not to deliver the sample in pungent language: "We didn't want them to get the idea that we were their obedient slaves who would give them whatever they wanted, no matter how much they insulted us."[23]

The process by which the Soviet Union and China came to their great split is fascinating, complex, and far from clear. It is surrounded by clouds of doctrinal debate and punctuated by excessive expectations of help from the other party, especially on the part of Mao. In all this the nuclear threads are themselves tangled and often obscure, and we must be wary in judging cause and effect between political and nuclear elements in the split. The nuclear disagreement between Moscow and Peking was real, but so was the underlying political conflict. Perhaps the simplest judgment is also the most important: These differences repeatedly reinforced each other until in the end the Chinese bomb, first undertaken in conscious partnership with Moscow, became important primarily as a safeguard for China against the massive nuclear armament of a deeply antagonistic Soviet Union.[24]

The agreement to provide a sample bomb was reached in October, 1957, just after *Sputnik,* when both Mao and Khrushchev were optimistic about prospects for the continued rise of socialism and a parallel decay of imperialism. Mao was particularly hopeful, believing that the Soviet Union was moving toward a nuclear superiority that would effectively neutralize any nuclear threat from the United States and so allow new and rapid socialist victories. In Moscow in November he made his famous assertion that "the East wind is prevailing over the West wind . . . the forces of socialism are overwhelmingly superior to the forces of imperialism."[25] But in his eagerness for the exploitation of this new situation, Mao unwisely assumed that the newly impressive strategic might of Soviet Russia was available to support him in contests of his own selection. In 1958 he chose to renew his pressure on Quemoy and Matsu and made the distressing discovery that the Nationalists and the Americans could outmatch his artillery blockade with conventional air and sea power. Worse yet, the Americans were clearly the only superpower that was ready for escalation if necessary. Moscow offered no public word of deterrent protection until after it was clear that Mao's attempt had failed and the crisis was ending. Possibly Mao himself never intended that this island adventure should be colored by nuclear threats in either direction, but he surely did not want a nuclear threat from Washington that Moscow would not match. I think he expected more of his ally and less of his opponent than he found.

Mao's error here may have been the assumption that socialist solidarity would lead Moscow to run a nuclear risk in support of a Chinese initiative. He does appear to have supposed that it was reasonable to expect Khrushchev to stand beside him, matching any American threat with a Soviet counterthreat, even though Khrushchev had never approved the Chinese challenge over the offshore islands. This may be the high-water mark of third-party arrogance in the nuclear age—who else has tried to play his partner's nuclear trumps in his own adventure? In the circumstances what is remarkable is that the danger in this miscalculation was kept under control, first by the care and skill of Eisenhower, second by the evasiveness of Khrushchev, and third by Mao's own prompt and prudent acceptance of local frustration.

What remains unexplained on the Soviet side is the reason for the initial decision to help China get the bomb. That the Chinese wanted such help was entirely natural, and it is also clear that in the latter part of 1957 Khrushchev still hoped to maintain strong socialist solidarity between Moscow and Beijing. There were difficulties already, if only because from the death of Stalin onward Mao saw himself as the world's top communist. Soviet leaders could hardly be expected to share this view, but their decision to help the Chinese in the nuclear field demonstrates the strength of their belief in the need to respond to serious Chinese concerns. The Chinese may well have made the obvious argument that the United States and Great Britain had publicly renewed their nuclear cooperation earlier in the same year. We do not know how far the Soviet leaders considered the possibility that they might come to regret their help.

We do not even know just how much help the Soviet leaders initially intended to give. Khrushchev's discussion of the later decision not to deliver a sample bomb gives the impression that the idea of such a transfer came initially from "specialists" and that he learned of it only after the sample was packed up and ready to go, when the minister in charge, knowing that relations with China were no longer good, asked for instructions. It is an odd story, but not necessarily false. Specialists often perceive technical cooperation among allies as its own justification. In any case Khrushchev's account reinforces the impression that in this matter the Soviet government was less cautious than its overall record on nuclear questions would lead us to expect.[26]

Soviet prudence on the subject of nuclear danger was a major element in the growing political disagreement between Moscow and

Beijing during the later years of Soviet technical support for the Chinese bomb project. Proud of *Sputnik* as they were, the Soviets saw it more as a demonstration of their ability to ensure peace than as a stimulus for new adventures. In 1958 they began, with Eisenhower, the long negotiations that eventually led to the Limited Test Ban Treaty in 1963. The impact of such negotiations on China was inescapably negative—a power not yet ready to test naturally sees support for a test ban as an unfriendly act. Here as in some other respects the nuclear relation between Beijing and Moscow is reminiscent of the one between Paris and Washington.

A larger difference had to do with attitudes toward nuclear war itself. By the late 1950s, both Mao and Khrushchev were well aware of what general thermonuclear conflict would be like, and in real crises neither one was ever incautious. But Mao regularly insisted that nuclear war would bring the end of imperialism and the final victory of socialism, while Khrushchev argued that the right way to victory was by the peaceful proof that socialism was better. Soviet leaders were shocked, as early as 1957, when Mao expressed his harsh convictions in Moscow. During the bitter public debate of 1963, the Soviets quoted Mao's words back at him:

> "Can one guess," he said, "how great the toll of human casualties in a future war will be? Possibly it would be a third of the 2,700 million inhabitants of the entire world, i.e., only 900 million people. I consider this to be even low, if atomic bombs should actually fall. Of course it is most terrible. But even half would not be so bad. Why? Because it was not we that wanted it but they. It is they who are imposing war on us. If we fight, atomic and hydrogen weapons will be used. Personally I think that in the whole world there will be such suffering that half of humanity and perhaps more than a half will perish.
>
> "I had an argument about this with Nehru. In this respect he is more pessimistic than I am. I told him that if half of humanity is destroyed, the other half will still remain but imperialism will be destroyed entirely and there will be only socialism in all the world, and within half a century, or a whole century, the population will again increase by even more than half."

The Soviet polemicist found in this statement "exactly an orientation towards an armed conflict, towards a military solution of the contradictions between socialism and capitalism."[27]

When this attack was published, the Sino-Soviet contest was five years old and had been pressed by Mao with the intensity of a man accustomed to victory against heavy odds. Primarily by his choice there was open dispute about the long Sino-Soviet border, which in Chinese eyes was an unfair result of nineteenth-century Russian imperialism.

There was also competition for support in every communist party in the world and intrigue by each government aimed at producing internal division in the other. The words and the tactical processes of this conflict were those of communists, but the underlying differences were those of great national governments in angry competition. Nationalism had been present even at the very beginning as the two leaders seemed to agree that China should have the bomb. The Kremlin had seen this as an offer of junior partnership in return for which there would be acceptance of Soviet presence and privilege in China. Mao had seen it as a proper cooperation between socialist equals, in which the resulting weapons would be entirely Chinese, and he would not repay Soviet help with concession of any rights whatever inside China itself. Neither side seems to have explored these differences ahead of time, and if the two sides had understood each other better, there might well have been no large-scale Soviet assistance. In that event the Chinese bomb would have come later than it did. As it was, the Chinese enriched their uranium in the plant the Russians had made possible and moved on alone. They proved quick and able, and the first Chinese test took place on October 16, 1964, just two days after the forced retirement of Nikita Khrushchev.

In its very first statement after this test, the Chinese government declared that it would never be the first to use nuclear weapons in any conflict. This declaration was surrounded by much verbiage about the nuclear misbehavior of the United States and by further violent attacks on the Limited Test Ban Treaty. In the atmosphere of the time, the fact of the test and the shrillness of the propaganda far overshadowed the declaration of no first use, but in retrospect that declaration is significant. It is consistent with Mao's earlier declaration that the reason for having the bomb was not to be bullied, and also with actual Chinese behavior in the following years. No Chinese nuclear threat has ever been made except in terms of a readiness to reply to a nuclear attack, and Chinese deployments have been restrained. On all the evidence, it is the possession of usable weapons of retaliation, and not much more, that has been desired. It is also interesting that Chinese development of weapons that can reach American targets has been particularly slow. The weapon was first sought when Mao felt bullied by Washington, but it has been deployed to discourage bullying by Moscow.

There is Chinese pride in the Chinese bomb, but it is not the same kind of pride that we have found in other countries. The Chinese do not appear to believe that the possession of the atomic bomb is in itself a badge of status as a great power. They have regularly resisted the notion that nuclear-weapon states should have a special role even on nuclear matters, opposing the nonproliferation treaty precisely on the ground that it is based on distinctions between nuclear and nonnuclear states. The Chinese, like others before them, have occasionally represented their own nuclear strength as a shield for other peace-loving peoples, but their real interest has been to guard against nuclear threats to themselves.

It is of course not accidental that China should have been the first government to announce a policy of no first use. Chinese leaders have understood that the sheer size of China, both in area and in population, confers enormous advantages for her military defense. Her need for nuclear weapons was not a need for protection against the outmatching conventional strength of others. It was a need for a specifically nuclear deterrent to what were seen as specifically nuclear dangers. Eisenhower's mention of nuclear weapons in 1955 was in his eyes a temporary discouragement of Chinese aggression against Quemoy and Matsu. It was understandably read by Mao as American nuclear blackmail on a matter in which the real act of aggression was the American support of Chiang Kai-shek.

Nuclear danger from the Americans was probably overestimated again in Beijing a decade later. A notable American student of Chinese nuclear policy, Jonathan Pollack, reports a high level of anxiety in Beijing "in the middle of 1965 during a critical period of American escalation in Vietnam."[28] The evidence he cites is not wholly conclusive to a nonspecialist, but I find his judgment important because of his evident sensitivity to the complexities of Chinese political commentary. Having been in the White House at the time, I know that all through this period of crucial decision-making on Vietnam it was an overriding interest of Lyndon Johnson and all his senior advisers that the United States should take no action that might lead the Chinese to repeat in Vietnam their intervention in Korea. To say that Chinese fears were misplaced, however, is not at all to say that they did not exist, or even that there was no reason for them. In 1965 the Chinese nuclear capability was almost surely small, probably smaller in the view of Mao, who knew, than in the estimates of Washington, which were bound to be uncertain. Moreover there had been talk in Washington about the possibility of preemptive action against the Chinese bomb—talk, not serious planning or real intent—and late in 1963, after probing interviews, one of which was with me, Stewart Alsop had written an article that included a flat and inaccurate assertion that there was already an American policy decision for preemption.[29] This may be one more illustration of the ease with which unreal threats can create real fears, especially when direct lines of communication do not exist.

THE SECOND and larger case of Chinese nuclear fear came in the Sino-Soviet crisis of 1969. The episodic border fighting both reflected and enlarged a confrontation that had existed for years, but China was rather more to blame than the Soviet Union. According to one American analyst the Chinese were determined, after the Soviet invasion of Czechoslovakia in 1968, to show Moscow that China was not to be treated as a satellite and would not accept a Soviet presumption that disputes over borders or anything else must regularly be settled on Soviet terms. The long-standing disagreement on the precise location of the border left plenty of places, like islands in the Ussuri River, where each side could find reason to consider the presence of the other an affront. No one can say "who started it" in any particular encounter, but what is clear is that the Chinese were intent on demonstrating their determination not to be pushed around.[30]

The border fighting was sporadic and never large in scale, but it is the only case on record in which nuclear-weapon states have engaged in ground fighting with each other. Both sides were extremely careful, and no single encounter lasted more than a matter of hours, but neither side could be certain of the prudence of the other, and each was certainly aware of latent nuclear danger. The Soviets indeed engaged in atomic diplomacy by spreading semiofficial rumors of plans to use nuclear weapons—enough to stir alarm in the Nixon-Kissinger White House, and enough to produce a typically Maoist retort that any act of atomic aggression would be met by "revolutionary war." But in fact this public exchange was accompanied on both sides by quiet moves to defuse the crisis, at least as much from Moscow as from Beijing. In early October the Chinese announced that agreement had been reached to begin negotiations on the border conflict. The negotiations led nowhere, but the skirmishing and the crisis ended.[31]

It is extremely unlikely that the Soviet government had any intention of initiating a nuclear war over this border dispute, and indeed it seems probable that its warnings of nuclear danger were intended more to create pressure on China from other countries than to produce direct concessions from Beijing. I agree with the most careful American analyst of the Soviet side of this crisis, Thomas W. Robinson, in his conclusion that the actual use of the Soviet weapons would have been "scarcely imaginable." The Chinese bomb was bound to give the Soviets reason to avoid an exchange of nuclear warheads, and the whole affair must have confirmed the Chinese in a judgment that their investment in nuclear deterrence had been wise. When both sides play closed hands, we cannot be sure what either side was thinking, but we do know that the border crisis cooled off in stalemate. Nuclear threats were uttered, but the most that can be claimed for them is that they persuaded Zhou Enlai to meet Kosygin for a talk at the Beijing airport. They did not make him say very much, and in the end it was the Soviets who took the lead in easing the crisis.[32]

We certainly cannot assume that the Chinese bomb led to this result, because there would have been large and important reasons for the Soviet Union not to resort to nuclear weapons even if they had faced only conventional Chinese forces. In any event the Chinese did demonstrate both their own capacity to sustain a firm resistance along their own border and the unwillingness of the Soviet Union to apply against China the remedy of invasion that it had used in Czechoslovakia one year before.

There is an American myth connected with this episode, and—as in the case of the alert at the end of the Yom Kippur War—the principal myth maker is Richard Nixon. In 1985 he told Roger Rosenblatt of *Time* that he "considered using nuclear weapons" in this crisis. He said that he and Kissinger discussed the danger that the Soviets would "jump the Chinese" by an attack on their nuclear capability, and he went on "we had to let the Soviets know we would not tolerate that." An innocent reader would suppose that some communication of this sort went from Nixon to Brezhnev, but Kissinger's memoirs tell a very different story. The only official statements that he reports are two: a background briefing by the director of the CIA, reporting that the Soviets seemed to be exploring the possibility of a preemptive attack on China with "European Communist brethren," and a comment by Undersecretary of State Elliot Richardson, in a speech to a convention of political scientists, that the United States "could not fail to be deeply concerned" if the conflict should escalate into "a massive breach of international peace and security." These are not the messages that are suggested in what Nixon said to Rosenblatt. Kissinger tells us further that at the end of September he recommended a more serious response to continuing Soviet "probes," but that before Nixon could "act on this recommendation," the crisis ended. So whatever Nixon and Kissinger said to each other in this case, it seems clear that they did *not* give any nuclear warning to Moscow.[33]

China has faced no nuclear threat since 1969. There have been great changes in both foreign and domestic affairs, but none of these changes has engaged the Chinese bomb. It remains a finite deterrent against the risk of nuclear blackmail from the superpowers, and since no such blackmail has been attempted in those years, the Chinese bomb has been off stage. Nor has China sought to use its bomb for political advantage over nonnuclear neighbors. The Chinese military campaign of 1979 against Vietnam brought unpleasant lessons to both sides, but no audible nuclear threat.

Between China and the Soviet Union there has been no new crisis like that of 1969, but Chinese opposition to Soviet "hegemonic" behavior has continued. Meanwhile Chinese relations with the United States have improved dramatically, if unevenly. Because of the persistent difference over Taiwan, there are limits on this process, but it seems doubtful that the Chinese regret their decision to let the question of Taiwan face the test of time. The once-contested offshore islands remain in the hands of the Taiwan government, and they have not been threatened by anyone for nearly thirty years. That there will never be a change in the status of Quemoy and Matsu seems unlikely, but what seems more unlikely still is that those small islands will ever again be seen by anyone as a prize deserving defense by nuclear threat.

Both the rapidity and the moderation of the Chinese effort are remarkable. The test of 1964 was followed in less than three years by a three-megaton thermonuclear explosion. The Chinese appear to have hundreds of warheads of varied yields, and they have also built aircraft and missiles in moderate numbers and various ranges. Their missiles are based both on land and in submarines. They have had some thirty tests of nuclear devices. They are a nuclear-weapon state of roughly the same strength and standing as Britain and France. But they do not talk about it nearly as much as the others in their class, and indeed that very reticence is a demonstration of the Chinese under-standing—based on experience—of the abrasive and unfriendly effect of anything that looks or feels like atomic diplomacy.

The careful and moderate reality of Chinese nuclear policy was obscured at the beginning by absurdity in language. The bomb is not a paper tiger, and general nuclear war will not achieve victory for socialism. But the bomb as a prudent defense against any nuclear bully is quite different, and if that defense has not been needed, at least since 1969, it is not hard to conclude that in the view of the Chinese govern-ment the Chinese deterrent is untested precisely because it exists.

Vietnam

The largest event in American exposure to the world between 1965 and 1975 was the war in Vietnam. That disaster carries lessons that Americans are still struggling to understand. It is obvious that what the United States government tried to do did not work. South Vietnam was not saved from brutal subjection to a totalitarian re-gime, capable of many kinds of effective violence but incompetent in most other matters. The American effort in Vietnam had great costs for Americans and still more for the people on both sides in Viet-nam. Was there a better way to go about it, in military strategy, in level of engagement, in politics and diplomacy? Or should it have been recognized at the start, if not earlier then at least in 1965, that this effort could not succeed in the time or at the price the American people would accept? Such questions continue to attract retrospective analysis, as they should. The war was polarizing to American opinion in ways that were certainly not foreseen by Lyndon Johnson and those like me who supported him in the basic decision he made in 1965.

But for our present purpose the greatest single fact about Vietnam is one that is evident beyond argument: In seven years of warfare, from 1965 to 1972, and again in the final assault from Hanoi in 1975, not one of three American presidents ever came close to using a nuclear weapon. Between the one war that Americans lost and the tens of thousands of thermonuclear weapons in the massive American arsenal able to fire at almost any range, in any desired numbers, from land, sea, and air, there is no operational connection whatever. While that war was being lost, the nuclear forces always at the president's command were kept out of it.

The assumption of the time that Vietnam was no place for nuclear warfare was so strongly held, indeed, both in the government and in the country, that no memoir writer of the Washington of the day has bothered to explain it. Only Nixon even mentions the matter. Such fragmentary records as the Pentagon Papers are no better, and my own belief is that when the documentary record is fully available, not much more will be found on this subject. The record of public attention and discussion is equally thin. Once, when American forces at Khe Sanh were thought by some to be in danger of suffering the fate that overtook the French at Dien Bien Phu, General Westmoreland did want contingency planning for a nuclear strike to save them, but Johnson made it plain that he wanted no such proposal, and when Westmoreland "established a small secret group to study the subject," he was "told to desist."[34] Like Eisenhower over Quemoy and Matsu, though in a very different way—the way of forceful political insistence, not knowledgeable military management—Johnson saw to it that the American forces at Khe Sanh were effectively supported by other means. The moment of seeming emergency at Khe Sanh is the exception. The irrelevance of nuclear weapons is the rule.

But why? Surely it was not a shortage of warheads (as it had been to some degree in Korea). Very little, if at all, was it for fear that friends of Vietnam with warheads of their own, Russians or Chinese, would use some of them in reply. Nor could it be argued that there was a shortage of suitable targets. Ports, landing places, supply lines, bridges, and airfields could all have been hit decisively with relatively low-yield weapons and quite possibly with human losses lower than those of the war as it was actually fought. But no one close to any of these presidents ever proposed any such course. Why not?

We may begin to get an answer when we think of the effect of any such use of nuclear weapons on the Vietnamese. What kind of reaction would there have been, on both sides in divided Vietnam, to such attacks? Would what was decisive in a military sense have had terrible consequences not only in human terms but in the minds of the survivors? Could you, in that reaction, lose the war by winning it? And what would have been the reputation of the United States elsewhere—in the nearby countries whose future was so large a part of what had led the American government to persist, or in the rest of the newly independent world, or in Latin America, or in the Atlantic alliance? Careful answers to all these questions, I believe, would have been gravely deterrent in themselves. Yet I doubt that prudential calculations of this sort were at the root of the matter for these three presidents.

The decisive considerations were closer to home, in two connected but different judgments that I believe all three presidents shared: first, that it must be an absolutely primary concern of each successive president that he conduct himself so as not to be the one to bring nuclear war upon mankind, and second, that in the particular case of Vietnam no president could hope for understanding and support from his own countrymen if he used the bomb.

I think that these two considerations had different weights for the two men, Johnson and Nixon, who bore the main burden of the war. I doubt if Lyndon Johnson ever asked himself seriously how far the American people would support a decision to use the bomb in Vietnam, although he would certainly have known the answer. As far as I know, he never raised the question with senior advisers, and he would have known before asking that any decision to use the bomb would have brought the resignations of the two men he trusted most—his secretaries of state and defense. But here it was not other men's judgment that mattered; it was what he himself thought. I believe that on this matter Lyndon Johnson knew what he thought long before he was drawn into the Vietnamese commitments of 1965. Vietnam was a torment, but it was not a matter, in Lyndon Johnson's mind, that came anywhere near the level of importance that would require turning to the bomb. The bomb to Johnson was never a merely conventional weapon. He had said so with passion during the campaign of 1964.

After his opponent Barry Goldwater had made suggestions about delegating nuclear responsibility to military men, Johnson dealt firmly with these suggestions in press conferences, but he returned to the subject on Labor Day, in Cadillac Square, Detroit. After describing the catastrophe of general nuclear war—hundreds of millions dead, cities in ashes, fields gone barren, industry destroyed, and dreams vanished—he went on:

> Make no mistake. There is no such thing as a conventional nuclear weapon.
>
> For 19 peril-filled years no nation has loosed the atom against another. To do so now is a political decision of the highest order. And it would lead us down an uncertain path of blows and counterblows whose outcome none may know. No President of the United States of America can divest himself of the responsibility for such a decision.

There was certainly politics in this response to Goldwater's attitudes toward the bomb, but there was passionate conviction too.[35]

Johnson certainly believed that the American deterrent must be strong. He had feared the missile gap. He had supported what I have called the Eisenhower-Kennedy buildup, but to him this was a matter of what was needed to keep the nuclear peace. By 1964 he was entirely clear in his own mind that he would have no interest whatever in ordering the use of even one bomb, ever, except in the context of some overwhelmingly dangerous and direct confrontation with open Soviet aggression. If Johnson could have carried his country with him, I believe he would have made the Vietnam War larger in the hope of making it shorter. But the bomb was something else again—a danger so much greater that one must think of any use of it not in the terms of a battle or campaign, or even a war won or lost, but rather in terms of the long-term effect of any such use on the survival of man. It is not wrong, I believe, to conclude that for Johnson the use of the bomb in Vietnam was quite literally unthinkable.

Richard Nixon, before he became president, believed strongly in the value of nuclear threats. As vice president he had watched Eisenhower's handling of the Korean War in 1953, and he fully shared Eisenhower's view that it was the threat of nuclear weapons that had produced the armistice there. As he remembered it in 1985, Eisenhower had told Dulles to talk to Krishna Menon, the Indian ambassador to the United Nations, and Dulles had told Menon that unless the logjam was broken, it would lead to the use of nuclear weapons. In Nixon's view "it worked . . . it was the Bomb that did it."[36] The fact that there is no record of such a conversation anywhere else does not prove that it never occurred, and as we have seen Eisenhower himself believed that he had conveyed the same message on other channels. Nixon's evident belief in the connection between an American nuclear threat and the end of the Korean War is more important here than any possible imprecision in his recollection of the way the threat was conveyed.

What is much less clear from the record so far available is how far Nixon believed that he could end the war in Vietnam by a parallel process of threat. He does not refer to any specifically nuclear threat in the memoirs published in 1978, and in 1985 he told Rosenblatt that he had found the nuclear option unattractive, claiming that he "didn't see any targets in North Vietnam that could not have been as well handled by conventional weapons." There are reports from others that as he thought about Vietnam he had nuclear threats on his mind. H. R. Haldeman says that Nixon told him he wanted the North Vietnamese to believe that "I might do *anything* to stop the war," and Haldeman specifically refers to nuclear threats. At the Republican convention in August 1968, in a meeting with southern delegates,

Nixon answered a question about ending the war in Vietnam by saying, "I'll tell you how Korea was ended," and he then explained how
Eisenhower "let the word go out diplomatically . . . that we would not
tolerate this continued ground war of attrition." In the campaign of
1968 he also spoke of a secret plan to end the war; what was it?[37]

Kissinger, in his memoirs, is silent about nuclear options. He discusses the contingency planning in terms of a possible effort to force
"a rapid negotiated compromise," by mining ports and perhaps bombing rail links to China. He reports that the planning was desultory, and
that he eventually recommended that consideration of such options be
deferred; he thought they offered no prospect of "quick and 'decisive'
military action," and his retrospective assessment is that "I never examined it more than halfheartedly, largely because I and all members of
the Administration not only wanted to end the war but yearned to do
so in the least convulsive way."[38]

Whatever he hoped that Hanoi might believe, Nixon in office came
to recognize that he could not use nuclear weapons. Nonetheless he
still believed that Eisenhower had given successful warnings, and in
the summer of 1969 he launched a campaign of deliberate and repeated threat. In communications both direct and indirect he and
Kissinger made it clear that if there was not major progress toward
peace by November 1, the Americans would be forced "to take measures of the greatest consequences." In Nixon's own mind this was an
"ultimatum," and it seems likely that his initial hope was that it might
have the effect he attributed to the Eisenhower warnings of 1953. Yet
it is not likely that he ever really intended any large-scale action in that
year. Neither in his memoirs nor in a later short book on Vietnam does
he mention the contingency plans of 1969, and we do not know how
much he cared about that planning. His memoirs strongly suggest that
he wanted his threats to produce a political response although he never
intended to act on them. His real fear, he writes, was that Hanoi would
not believe him because of American public opinion. He could generate diplomatic pressure, "but the only chance for my ultimatum to
succeed was to convince the Communists that I could depend on solid
support at home if they decided to call my bluff."[39] When the maker
of a threat himself calls it a bluff, there is little reason to doubt his
verdict, and indeed the combined impression left by both Nixon and
Kissinger is that the word is precise.

The threats produced no remotely satisfactory response, and
Nixon, both understandably and characteristically, blamed this failure
on his domestic opposition. As the summer ended and the academic
year began, protest against the war was renewed, and on October 15
a quarter of a million people came to Washington for a moratorium
on the war. In Nixon's view it was this massive "protest for peace" that
"destroyed whatever small possibility may still have existed of ending

the war in 1969." His bluff had failed, and in his view the failure was the result of Hanoi's correct understanding that American opinion would prevent Nixon from acting.[40]

We do not know that Nixon would ever have made a decision to use the bomb in Vietnam even if American public sentiment had been very different, just as we do not know that Eisenhower would ever have used it in Korea. What we know of both men is that they thought nuclear threats worked in Korea, and what we know of Nixon is that he hoped he could do the same thing in Vietnam. We cannot know—he may not have known himself—what he would actually have done if he had been free to make the choice, because what stopped him before he reached that point was his conclusion that any use of the bomb in Vietnam would have totally unacceptable results inside the United States, enraging the opponents of the war and setting general opinion against the new administration with such force as to make it doubtful that the government could keep up the American end of the war.

Richard Nixon's belief in atomic diplomacy outlived his finding it unavailable in Vietnam, although that case is much the largest of his time in the White House. We have seen that he thought American warnings were useful in 1969 when China was threatened, and in 1973 when Brezhnev suggested that he might put troops in Egypt. He also told *Time* in 1985 that he considered the use of nuclear weapons in the Indo-Pakistan confrontation of 1973, but in that case the absence of any real nuclear message or intent is so plain that we need not review the matter. Nixon and Kissinger moved an aircraft carrier group into the Bay of Bengal, as part of an intense effort to protect West Pakistan from an attack that Mrs. Gandhi never intended to make. They angered the Indians, and their move may have stimulated the interest of Indians in obtaining the bomb for themselves. But no one, certainly not Nixon and Kissinger themselves, believed that this carrier force would ever have been used to make nuclear war on anyone.

Nixon's retrospective exaggeration of his role as a nuclear-threat maker only underlines the striking fact that in the case of Vietnam his own assessment, both in 1969 and thereafter, was that the bomb could have no place. What the American people would not accept, the nuclear-minded president could not plausibly threaten.

The choice in Vietnam was much less intense for Gerald Ford in 1975. By at least one measure the provocation was greater: The direct boundary crossing attack by large regular North Vietnamese forces was as flagrant as the North Korean aggression of 1950. But American response was forbidden not only by statute but by the settled determination of the American people that the very last place in which to have "another Vietnam" was Vietnam itself. So President Ford surely wasted no time thinking about the nuclear option in those last convulsive weeks in early 1975. The absence of such consideration nonetheless underlines the distance by then established between the anguish of Vietnam and the use, by threat or action, of the nuclear "master card." It also underlines a reality that Gerald Ford has frequently discussed in the years since he left the White House: his understanding that the central interest of any American president, with respect to nuclear weapons, is to see to it that he never does anything to make their use by anyone more likely. It is a state of mind that does not easily coexist with enthusiasm for nuclear diplomacy.[41]

Between Nixon's acceptance in 1969 of a constraint imposed by public opinion, and Ford's lack of interest in any kind of nuclear connection at the moment of sudden disaster in 1975, there stands one might-have-been. In his memoirs Henry Kissinger repeatedly insists that if it had not been for Watergate, Nixon's "executive authority" would not have been undermined, and Hanoi would never have dared to undertake its 1975 campaign. As I have argued elsewhere, there are many reasons to doubt this claim, but there is at least a possibility that for Kissinger himself, as for Nixon, there was lingering sentiment for the notion that the man whose resort to heavy bombing had brought temporary agreement in 1972 was just the kind of man whose determination to do *whatever* he had to do would be respected by Hanoi. Probably what Kissinger had in mind here was bombing, but probably only conventional bombing. We shall never know for sure, because by removing Nixon Watergate certainly removed any prospect of a lonely test of his will.[42]

What is apparent from the perspective of the present, with the Vietnam War now well behind us but not at all forgotten, is that among all the questions about that war which still stir debate and disagreement, the choice that is conspicuous by its absence from the discussion—the one that has no advocates—is the use of the bomb. I know of no serious retrospective argument that it was a mistake not to use it. There may be many who have had that thought, moved either by the anguish of personal loss or by the persistent if decreasingly popular belief that men like General LeMay and Admiral Radford were right in their conviction that this weapon should be as usable as any other. It is true that Barry Goldwater in 1964 spoke of the possibility of using low-yield atomic weapons there, but Goldwater was a genuinely special case among politicians, and his view of the bomb was one part of the reason for his overwhelming defeat in that year. Even Curtis LeMay never believed that nuclear weapons would be needed in Vietnam. He thought conventional air power, properly used, would bring victory. It is true that when LeMay ran for vice president, in 1968, as the running mate of George Wallace of Alabama, he refused to exclude the possibility of such a use of nuclear weapons, because of his conviction that it was unwise to tell the enemy what you would not do. By that refusal he gravely embarrassed Wallace. But this episode shows only how the ordinary politicians of 1968, learning from Goldwater's defeat, wanted to make no connection between Vietnam and nuclear weapons. LeMay's unwillingness to go against his own conviction was characteristic, and it does not change the reality that Vietnam and the bomb were wisely kept apart by all the presidents concerned, and that their shared judgment has not been seriously questioned since.[43]

TAKEN TOGETHER, these three cases—the American alert of October 1973, the Sino-Soviet border conflict of 1969, and the American acceptance of failure as against nuclear warfare in Vietnam— demonstrate the weakness of atomic diplomacy and the essentially secondary role of nuclear weapons in the regional conflicts of the decades that followed the Cuban missile crisis. These confrontations show great caution on the part of all states possessing nuclear weapons, caution not only with respect to their use, but also with respect to any step that might lead to a level of conflict in which someone else might be tempted to use them. The most nearly nuclear message in these cases is certainly the American alert of October 24, 1973, but even that was no more than a signal of what could be the eventual consequence of a whole series of interlocking steps that neither side took; it was not at all a threat of direct reply to a particular Soviet action.

XII

Debating
the Danger

THE THREE THIN CASES we have just examined are all
there is in the historical record of nuclear crisis after Cuba.
Instead of real danger the years since the Yom Kippur War have
brought us only *debates* about nuclear danger amid continuing strategic
stalemate. We have had prolonged and gradually expanding political
arguments over what nuclear weapons were good for and how to
decide on the size and shape of strategic forces. These debates had
substantial impact on such matters as the procurement of strategic
systems, the fate of arms control agreements, and the rise and fall of
particular political leaders. They also became entangled with technical
certainty and uncertainty in new and different ways. In the United
States the nuclear debates became so heated that for many their American opponents—not the bomb or the Russians or both together—
became the real enemy. These debates are unfinished as I write, and
there are elements in their history that are relevant to our inquiry.

Deterrence or Victory—McNamara and LeMay

We have seen how McNamara whittled the strategic forces of the
United States from what he found under development in 1961 and
how the resulting force allowed him and his president to reaffirm the
American claim to strategic superiority. The combination of strategic
bombers, submarine missiles, and land-based Minutemen—later

dubbed the Triad—is still our primary reliance more than twenty-five years later, and the most important change in that force since 1963 is one that also took shape while McNamara was at the Pentagon: the multiple-warhead missile called MIRV (multiple independently target-able reentry vehicle). We should also remember that McNamara had his hardest battles on nuclear systems over the ones that he rejected, like the B-70 bomber and the Skybolt missile.

But how much was enough? It was in wrestling with this question that McNamara produced the measuring stick that came to dominate the debate that followed: the criterion of "assured destruction." It took him about three years to get it clear in his own mind that this criterion was central, and along the way he advocated other capabilities too, but as he left office in early 1968 he stated his final position with clarity:

> One must begin with precise definitions. The cornerstone of our strategic policy continues to be to deter deliberate nuclear attack upon the United States or its allies. We do this by maintaining a highly reliable ability to inflict unacceptable damage upon any single aggressor or combination of aggressors at any time during the course of a strategic nuclear exchange, even after absorbing a surprise first strike. This can be defined as our *assured-destruction capability.*
>   . . . Assured destruction is the very essence of the whole deterrence concept. We must possess an actual assured-destruction capability, and that capability also must be credible. . . . If the United States is to deter a nuclear attack on itself or its allies, it must possess an actual and a credible assured-destruction capability.
>   When calculating the force required, we must be conservative in all our estimates of both a potential aggressor's capabilities and his intentions. Security depends upon assuming a worst plausible case, and having the ability to cope with it. In that eventuality we must be able to absorb the total weight of nuclear attack on our country—on our retaliatory forces, on our command and control apparatus, on our industrial capacity, on our cities, and on our population—and still be capable of damaging the aggressor to the point that his society would be simply no longer viable in twentieth-century terms. That is what deterrence of nuclear aggression means. It means the certainty of suicide to the aggressor, not merely to his military forces, but to his society as a whole.[1]

The capability so severely described was one that McNamara believed to have been clearly achieved in 1968, not only by the United States but by the Soviet Union too. One may object to the flatness of his assertion that effective deterrence required "the certainty of suicide." I believe myself that a quite moderate *risk* of suicide is itself an effective deterrent; sane leaders do not play Russian roulette. In terms of what each great nation *could* do to the other, even after the most sweeping and successful surprise attack, the situation of 1968 is the situation of every year since; it is where we are today. Moreover, understanding of this "balance of terror" goes clear back to Churchill and Eisenhower in the 1950s. What McNamara did was to argue that this "assured-destruction capability" should be the purpose of strategic deployment. In the beginning it was precisely his refusal to seek more that stirred complaint.

Curtis LeMay did not believe in mere second-strike retaliation. It was not what he wanted for the United States, and he believed in denying it to the Soviet Union. He believed in being able to win a decisive victory in strategic warfare, and his own name for what he preferred was "the strategy of pre-emptive counterforce." He had been guided by that strategy in his planning as commander of SAC for nine years between 1948 and 1957. If ever the Soviet adversary decided on war against the United States, LeMay believed, the United States could know it before the blow came. "I was prepared to beat him to the draw and attack all of his bomber and missile bases. In accordance with the Joint Chiefs of Staff my purpose was to destroy his war-making capability, particularly in the strategic nuclear area."[2] LeMay fully recognized that such a preemptive strike could be undertaken only at the orders of the president, but this was the strategy he believed in. As David Rosenberg has shown, he was quite right in saying that his purpose was the one assigned to SAC by the Joint Chiefs of Staff, although the Joint Chiefs made no serious effort to monitor his choice of targets.[3] LeMay's plan for victory was what he had been taught to look for as a young devotee of air power and what he believed he had put into effect as a field commander in World War II. As chief of staff of the air force in the early McNamara years he continued to believe that the United States would be able to fight and win a strategic nuclear war as long as his government would provide the necessary weapons. Exactly on this point McNamara's criterion of assured destruction stood in his way, as both men understood. The kinds of weapons required for assured destruction by a second strike were far from sufficient for LeMay's mission.

In 1962 McNamara briefly adopted as his own a nuclear strategy of city-sparing counterforce. In the event of major Soviet aggression, he said, the purpose of any American nuclear attack should be "the destruction of the enemy's military forces, not of his civilian population," and he expressed the hope that the adoption of such a strategy, with ample forces always held in reserve, would protect the cities on both sides because it would give the opponent "the strongest imaginable incentive to refrain from striking our own cities."[4] He soon found that he had set a standard he could not meet. There was no attainable level of force that would permit a satisfactory degree of "destruction of the enemy's military forces." The Soviets could always build additional survivable strategic nuclear forces sufficient to destroy the United States in reply, and their determination to have such forces was predictable. McNamara gradually but firmly concluded that because of the nature of nuclear weapons and the priorities of both superpowers, the right course was for each to attend to its own means of assured second-strike destruction and to accept a parallel means on the other side.

McNamara did not find immediate public support as he began to explain these sentiments in public appearances. In February 1963 he remarked in a House hearing that he saw a time coming when neither side could hope "to preclude a devastating retaliatory blow." He drew sharp complaints, and there is almost a plaintive tone in his comment to the Advertising Council the following month:

> I have spoken on a number of occasions of the declining relative value of our nuclear superiority. I am continually surprised at the complaints which such statements arouse, as though the problem would go away if we stopped talking about it. Yet of course we are not talking about a policy . . . it is not a policy which we can choose to follow or not to follow, but a fact of life and a fact which we can ignore only at great peril to our national security. The increasing numbers of survivable missiles in the hands of both the United States and the Soviet Union are a fact of life. Neither side today possesses a force which can save its country from severe damage in a nuclear exchange. Neither side can realistically expect to achieve such a force in the foreseeable future. And these, too, are facts of life.[5]

In these years the annual analyses of his experts showed that no matter who attacked first, and no matter what targets were chosen, the opponent could always make a devastating reply. The consequences of Soviet attacks on cities were routinely examined because such attacks were always possible and because high levels of urban destruction were so obviously unacceptable for Americans. These analyses routinely produced the tens of millions of casualties that had daunted Eisenhower in earlier years.

A further advantage of this kind of analysis was that it provided a means of testing the effectiveness of U.S. forces against a second criterion which came forward from his staff in those years: the criterion of "damage limitation." If nuclear war ever came, it would obviously be in the American interest to limit damage to its own society, and for several years after 1963 McNamara used this criterion as a supplementary means of assessing the new systems advocated by one service or another.[6]

The trouble with damage limitation, however, was that each side was determined to be able to inflict overwhelming damage on the other, even after absorbing a first strike. In 1964 McNamara concluded that there was a clear conflict between one side's purpose of limiting damage and the other side's purpose of maintaining a capacity for assured destruction. If one side could always achieve assured destruction, the other could not achieve satisfactory damage limitation. As he put it to President Johnson in a long secret paper of December 3, 1964, "our damage limiting problem is their assured destruction problem and our assured destruction problem is their damage limiting problem." He went on to argue that there was no combination of damage limiting measures that could not be overcome by the Soviet Union.[7]

So McNamara came to believe that the criterion of "damage limitation" could not be met, and assured destruction became his single decisive standard for the measurement of what was needed. He applied that standard in a highly conservative way, using worst-case assumptions about future Soviet capabilities. Moreover in his recommendations for procurement he regularly went above the levels required by strict analysis. When he chose to have 1,000 Minuteman missiles, he was choosing a number that Congress would find acceptably large, not a number that he himself could demonstrate as strategically necessary. There were critics who argued then and later that a smaller number would have been enough, but the politically important alternatives before McNamara at the time were those desired in the air force—anywhere from 2,400 missiles to 10,000.[8]

Much of the debate over McNamara's performance, both at the time and later, turned on questions of style and methods of management. "Civilian whiz kids" were thought to be interfering in military matters. There was some justification for some of this concern. The way you must think about combat command is genuinely different from the way you can think about paper capabilities, and not all strategic analysts know how to think about the real world of war. There was also McNamara's highly developed ability to apply the results of analysis to the quite different process of advocacy. He was a formidable antagonist, and senior military men dislike losing.

But the fundamental obstacle that McNamara and his band presented to LeMay was not a matter of style. As LeMay saw it, McNamara was turning his country's back on the capacity for victory through air power in nuclear war. But LeMay did not see that it was not McNamara, but the realities of thermonuclear warheads, that made victory a mirage. LeMay understood that he faced an additional difficulty here: "A strategy which rested on our initiating a war ran against the American philosophy."[9] But the underlying problem was the unavoidable and growing Soviet capacity for a devastating reply to even the strongest preemptive strike. LeMay's successor as commander of SAC, General Thomas Power, recognized this problem candidly after his retirement. Power noted that no matter how successful an initial American attack might be, "some of their bombers and missiles would escape destruction and succeed in mounting a counterattack, exacting a high price with their nuclear payloads." Power decided that preemptive war was an unlikely choice, because "so long as there is the slightest hope that we can prevent a Soviet attack through diplomatic means or a strong posture of deterrence, our government, backed by the majority of the American people, would in my opinion be opposed to more drastic measures." This is a judgment that became more and more widely shared by military men and civilians alike as LeMay's strategy was overtaken in the years 1965 to 1975 by the belated but massive Soviet deployment of strategic missiles. By the end of the 1970s it was entirely clear to senior commanders that an all-out nuclear exchange would have no victor in any normal sense. In the Senate hearings on SALT II in 1979 Senator James Exon of Nebraska asked, "What would be left" of the two superpowers "after an all-out nuclear exchange?" General Richard Ellis, a successor to LeMay and Power as commander of SAC, gave an authoritative answer: "It would be a catastrophic event of such magnitude that I don't think the human mind could understand it . . . it would be difficult to distinguish . . . which would be the victor or the vanquished." Air force leaders continued to believe in war-fighting capabilities, but for deterrence, not for victory. By the end of the 1970s the dream of preemptive victory was dead.[10]

The inevitability of mutual destruction in general nuclear war was not at all the same as a policy or doctrine of planning only for "the mass destruction of enemy civilians," as the Nixon administration repeatedly and falsely suggested. The strategic targeting of SAC, from Eisenhower's time through Johnson's, was governed by the standards inherited by strategic air commanders from World War II. First came the destruction of enemy offensive strength, now primarily nuclear, and then the destruction of urban-industrial targets as well to ensure defeat. Most targets were always in the first category. In 1962, for example, on the official list of 1,860 Soviet-bloc targets projected for 1969 (as one guide to force planning), 1,650 were military and only 210 urban-industrial. There was also, from McNamara's time onward, a fully planned option not to attack targets in cities. But no one could guarantee that cities would be spared by the other side, and in any case any large attack on military targets would itself be catastrophic in human terms. When McNamara talked of assured destruction he was talking of what nuclear war could do in the same way as General Eisenhower earlier and General Ellis later. He was not talking about deterrence by a merely city-busting force.[11]

Strategic Defense and SALT I

The second great battlefield over assured destruction has been on the question of strategic defense, first fought out during McNamara's last years and Nixon's first term. The issue appeared to be settled by the Anti-Ballistic Missile Treaty of 1972 (part of SALT I), under which the United States and the Soviet Union agreed to severe limitations on defense against ballistic missiles. The path to this agreement was long and tortuous. It involved changes of positions by both governments and also extended debate among experts and politicians. I vividly remember one of these debates—an effort by McNamara, at the Glassboro summit of 1967, to persuade Soviet leader Alexey Kosygin that ballistic missile defenses would be bad for both sides because they would merely intensify offensive deployments. Kosygin, obviously protecting a firm Kremlin position, had himself a good time making the argument so persuasive on the surface—that such defenses were a natural and proper way of protecting one's own country and people. But as Raymond Garthoff has demonstrated, the argument that McNamara was making was already well understood, if not generally accepted, in Moscow, and over the two years that followed it gained in strength. Soviet readiness for sharp limits on ballistic missile defense became wholly clear as soon as the SALT talks began at the end of 1969.[12]

The Soviet readiness for limits is less remarkable than the eventual American acceptance of them. When the issue first required presidential choice, in the later years of the Johnson administration, American decision makers had both new incentives for strategic defense and higher technical capabilities than the Soviets. The incentives were provided by the unwelcome demonstration in the late 1960s that the large Soviet missile deployments prematurely predicted after *Sputnik* were now at last becoming a reality. Soviet intercontinental missiles increased from 250 to 1,000 between 1966 and 1969 alone, with a parallel if smaller deployment of submarine-based missiles. Moreover the Soviet land-based missiles were much larger than the American Minuteman, though less sophisticated. Over time their sophistication was sure to increase—they would carry many warheads in each missile, and the accuracy of the systems would improve. They would present a threat that Americans would expect their Department of Defense to try to ward off, as it had tried to ward off Soviet bombers a decade earlier in large programs of air defense.

What made the United States turn away from strategic defense in the years between 1967 and 1972 was not the preference of presidents but the interacting force of other American opinions and the preference of the Kremlin. Johnson had ordered a reluctant McNamara to put forward a limited missile defense program in 1967. Nixon in 1969 strenuously supported a somewhat different program, but against his expectations he encountered strong resistance in Congress. This opposition was the product of many forces. There was widespread skepticism—notably among scientists—as to the effectiveness of defenses against missiles and there was opposition to large new military programs in these later Vietnam years. Proposals for defensive deployments also generated local fear and opposition: If this defensive battery is proposed for our neighborhood, someone must think it's a prime target. Finally, there was the view which McNamara had put to Kosygin: Defensive deployments were bound to stimulate ever larger and more sophisticated offensive systems on both sides. There is no way to know the relative strength of these varied considerations, but in combination they almost killed the ABM appropriation in August 1969, when an amendment removing all funds for the Nixon program failed in a tie vote broken in favor of the administration by Vice President Spiro Agnew.[13]

Nixon then decided that the right course was to use the ABM program as a bargaining chip while he could, and after negotiations of great complexity the SALT I agreements were signed in Moscow in the summer of 1972. The most important agreement was a treaty of unlimited duration banning defense against strategic missiles except at two sites in each country. The exception was further limited to a single site by a 1974 amendment (ratified in 1976). Today the Soviet Union attempts to defend Moscow as its single site, and the single American site for defending missiles in North Dakota has been closed down. The effort to constrain offensive weapons in SALT I was much less successful, because neither side would give up important forces or plans for modernization, but a five-year interim agreement was reached that did put temporary, high, and incompletely agreed limits on the offense.

MIRV

What SALT I did not address was an offensive capability, MIRV, that both sides were pursuing in these years, with the Americans in the van but with no doubt in either government that both sides would have it unless it could somehow be banned by agreement. When a missile is MIRVed, it is able to carry many warheads—3 to 14 in existing American missiles—and deliver them on separate targets. Land-based MIRVs in silos, when both sides have them, have a powerfully destabilizing effect because they tend to put a premium on striking first. Let us assume, for illustration, that each side has 100 missiles, with 5 warheads each, and let us assume further that each side has a 95 percent chance of destroying an opponent's missile in its silo by firing 2 warheads at it. Then the side that goes first can reduce the hostile force from 100 missiles to about 5 by firing 40 missiles with 200 warheads, and keeping 60 missiles in reserve. The attacker attains a decisively superior position. The example oversimplifies, but it makes the essential point. The fixed MIRVed ICBM is a good killer but not a good survivor, especially as accuracy improves on both sides. That is what is wrong with most Soviet ICBMs and more than half of American ICBMs in 1988. If it were not for other survivable forces on both sides—submarines, alert bombers, and mobile ICBMs, these MIRVed ICBMs in silos would be a constant source of tension for both sides. They compare most unfavorably with the systems that went before.

The first strategic missiles had only one warhead, and both accuracy and reliability were much less good than they are today. If we go back to our two forces each with a hundred missiles and give them the single warheads and the lower accuracy of the 1960s, we can see that neither one could profitably attack the other. You could fire first with all your missiles, or with fifty, or with ten, and you would then be worse off than when you started, because your enemy would have more warheads left than you. The first ICBMs were good second-strike weapons, but MIRV has made their successors bad ones.

The destabilizing character of MIRV is not so hard to understand that it was not noticed before it was deployed. What happened was that other considerations were always found more important at moments of choice. As usual we can see that process most clearly on the American side. MIRV was always technically easy, especially when compared with the much more conspicuous possibility of these same years—ABM, the defense against ballistic missiles. MIRV was always appealing to military commanders who measured their preferences more by what they could deliver than by what the Soviets might later possess, and it was a particularly attractive prospect in years in which McNamara had set a firm upper limit on the deployment of missiles, leaving MIRVs as the only way to get more missile-carried warheads. As Herbert York has reminded me, the notion that an expensive carrier could properly have more than one warhead was entirely natural to commanders whose basic attitudes had been shaped by aircraft carrying bombs. Moreover, McNamara himself was not opposed to MIRV. He had to consider not only its political value in his defense of limits on missile deployment, but also the prospect that multiple warheads would be a powerful means of penetrating any Soviet ABM system—the more incoming warheads such a system had to find and kill, the less it would be able to nullify the American strategic deterrent.

This argument was weakened when it was decided in the Nixon years that the United States would seek to deal with the problem of

ABM by a treaty. But by then the MIRVs were scheduled for early deployment, both in silos and in submarines, and they were much wanted by the Joint Chiefs of Staff, whose support would be needed for any strategic treaty. The Joint Chiefs were joined by McNamara's successor, Clark Clifford, and still more strongly by Nixon's secretary of defense, Melvin Laird. Nixon and Kissinger decided not to overrule the Pentagon, and the only American proposal on MIRV that was put forward in SALT I was for a test ban with on-site inspection, in those days an excellent way of ensuring Soviet rejection. The Soviets for their part were content with an equally nonnegotiable proposal: an uninspected ban on deployment, with testing unconstrained. There were able officials and a small group in Congress who tried to stop MIRV, but they were always far behind the curve of Defense Department decision making, and in any case the cause of stopping MIRV never had top priority for more than a few.[14]

The Reaction Against SALT I

The Anti-Ballistic Missile Treaty of 1972, all but barring defensive systems, left the Soviet Union and the United States open to attack from each other's strategic missiles. In that sense it reinforced the reciprocal vulnerability that had been recognized by both governments since the middle of the 1950s. These arms control arrangements were by far the largest achieved in the nuclear age, and they were surrounded by agreements on other subjects, by basic "Principles of Relations," and by a bilateral rhetoric of détente that had worldwide appeal. It was a major achievement, but the victory for restraint was less solid than it seemed. In the months after the signature of the treaty there were two sharp warning signals, one from Donald Brennan, a noted defense analyst, and the other from Senator Henry Jackson.

Less than a month after the signing, Brennan published in *National Review* a remarkable article in which he attacked both the offensive limitations and those on strategic defense. His central target was what he called the "concept of mutual assured destruction." That concept, he asserted, had become dominant, and he went on to give it a name:

> The concept of mutual assured destruction provides one of the few instances in which the obvious acronym for something yields at once the appropriate description; for it, that is, a Mutual Assured Destruction posture as a goal is, almost literally, mad. MAD.

Brennan's complaint was not grounded in a demonstration that a particular defensive system would be effective. His argument was broader: "A major nuclear war could happen;" the government was supposed to "provide for the common defense," and "we should not deliberately create a system in which millions of innocent civilians would be exterminated should the system fail." The argument ignores the realities of thermonuclear missiles. Brennan conceded that "if technology and international politics provided absolutely no alternative, one might reluctantly accept a MAD posture," thus admitting that if the friends of the ABM Treaty were right about the technological realities they might be right about the treaty, at least for the time being; Brennan never quarreled with the political judgment that the Soviets would always want effective offensive systems. But that was not the thrust of his paper, which avoided technical assessment in a manner that was to become characteristic of the critics of MAD. Brennan had been one of the first serious students of nuclear arms control, and he had himself for some years opposed defense against ballistic missiles, but now he was rejecting a judgment on the real balance between the offense and the defense which analysts on the other side of the argument thought to be *imposed* by the technological realities. In 1972 Brennan, as he expected, proved to be in a small minority. Nonetheless he had invented a powerful acronym and he had sounded an alarm against MAD and "MAD-vocates" that would be heard more loudly in later years.[15]

The second warning signal, from Senator Jackson, related not to strategic defense but to the offensive balance. In Jackson's view the limits accepted in the interim agreement were unbalanced in favor of the Soviets. The underlying difficulty was in the continuing expansion of the Soviet strategic arsenal. The American negotiators had made determined efforts to produce lower limits on Soviet forces than were achieved, but their bargaining position was not strong because there were no large new American programs that could be cut back in return for parallel Soviet concessions. Both sides in the end accepted arrangements in which both their existing forces and their new programs were essentially unconstrained, except for a few older Soviet missiles. The Soviet land-based missiles thus accepted were both more numerous and much larger than American ICBMs, and many were not comforted by the counterbalancing American advantage in bombers and submarines or even by the fact that the Americans would be first in the field with multiple-warhead missiles. For defenders of the treaty like Kissinger, the decisive point was the considerable American lead in number of warheads because after all it was warheads that were the killers. But critics pointed out that the large Soviet missiles, with their ability to carry heavier loads, would presently be able to carry their own multiple warheads.

The critics of the agreement did not have the votes to defeat it, but under the leadership of Senator Jackson they were able to introduce a sentence in the joint resolution accepting the interim agreement; it became known as the Jackson amendment. In that sentence the Congress "urges and requests the President to seek a future treaty that, inter alia, would not limit the United States to levels of intercontinental strategic forces inferior to the limits provided for the Soviet Union."[16] In its formal language the amendment was not binding on the president, but it was a powerful warning that a treaty governing offensive weapons would be severely questioned in the Senate if it were thought to permit Soviet strategic superiority.

In one sense the Jackson amendment was moderate. It implicitly recognized that the Russians would accept no treaty confirming American strategic superiority. Given the strength of earlier American attachment to just such superiority, this congressional acceptance of equality with the Soviet Union was important. It was a match to the significant change that Nixon himself had made in 1969. After an election campaign in which he had repeatedly called for the reestablishment of strategic superiority he announced, one week after his inauguration, that he preferred the word *sufficiency,* since talk about superiority could simply stimulate "the other side" by "putting it in an inferior position" and "giving great impetus to its own arms race."[17]

In this quick change Nixon took a constructive step that his predecessors had resisted. Kennedy in particular had held up the flag for strategic superiority. In 1960 he had made it part of his campaign that America must be number one again, and in office he regularly pointed with pride to the improvement in strategic posture that he was making. The nonexistence of the missile gap was a matter that he preferred not to discuss because the next question would be why he had made it an issue in his campaign, and he never got a good answer to that question from me, although he kept asking. Instead he regularly claimed credit for timely and effective improvements. The very last of his public papers is a speech he would have given to Texas Democrats in Austin on the afternoon of November 22. He would have said that he had kept a pledge of 1960 in Fort Worth "to build a national defense which was second to none—a position I said, which is not 'first, but,' not 'first, if,' not 'first, when,' but first—period." The speech goes on to cite the Polaris and Minuteman programs, the doubling of alert forces and number of strategic warheads, as well as conventional improvements. Kennedy was well aware that in the larger sense the two superpowers were headed toward strategic stalemate, but that is not what he chose to emphasize in public in what was already the beginning of an election year.[18]

Lyndon Johnson also claimed superiority. He was moderate in new procurement, careful about nuclear danger, earnest in his attempt to limit the spread of nuclear weapons, and energetic in distinguishing himself from Barry Goldwater on just this subject, but in his few references to strategic balance he spoke of American advantage. As to rockets, he said once, "We have more than anyone—twice as many." And on bombers, "We have more than twice as many as anyone."[19] It is characteristic of Johnson that these casual boasts were part of a general argument against rattling the rockets or boasting about the bombers, but he never took the next step of giving up the notion of superiority. Nixon's shift to "sufficiency" was a major step toward recognition of the reality that superiority was out of reach.

Politically, on the evidence of the decade after 1972, there was a great difference between the national acceptance of "sufficiency," which came quite easily, and any acceptance of apparent Soviet advantage. Sufficiency was in fact the right standard, the same one that Eisenhower had implicitly accepted when he said, back in 1956, "enough is certainly a plenty," and warned against judging military strength "by the numbers racket" of counting this or that particular class of weapons to see who had more.[20]

But when Jackson insisted that future agreements should not impose "inferior" limits on the United States, he was setting a standard that proved to have great political appeal. The interim agreement embodied a highly visible Soviet superiority in the size of land-based missiles. In 1972, as the Nixon administration successfully argued, that superiority was counterbalanced by a number of American capabilities, most notably by the American advantage in missiles with multiple warheads. But in the years that followed the numbers of large Soviet missiles increased, and they came to have multiple warheads of their own. The Jackson amendment became an ever more formidable hurdle for any new agreement.

An unfortunate episode in the negotiation and ratification of the interim agreement strongly reinforced the zeal with which Senator Jackson and his able assistant Richard Perle watched out for shortcomings in later strategic agreements. The Americans tried hard to get clear limits on large Soviet missiles. The Soviets agreed that they would not expand the numbers of their "heavy" missiles, meaning the large SS-9, but they were unwilling to accept an American proposal that all new missiles over a certain smaller size should be classed as "heavy" and forbidden. The Soviet government was already committed, as American negotiators knew, to the production of a new missile that would exceed the limits the Americans were proposing. In this situation Kissinger resorted to a unilateral declaration of what the Americans would consider forbidden as "heavy," and he then assured Senator Jackson that this declaration, with other clauses, gave full protection against such new missiles, saying that "no missile larger than the heaviest light missile that now exists can be substituted." The Soviets went ahead with just such a missile, smaller than SS-9 but larger than any previous "light" missile, and no effective complaint was

possible because no one could claim that a unilateral American statement was binding on the Soviets. The congressional leaders had been
misled.[21]

For men like Perle, this new missile, the SS-19, modern, MIRV,
and eventually numerous (360, with 2,160 warheads) became a scary
illustration of the failings of the SALT process. Perle and others talked
as if better negotiators would have succeeded in blocking the SS-19
and as if the arms control process was responsible for a massive new
addition to Soviet throwweight. Their talk was not persuasive because
Brezhnev would hardly have agreed to cancel a fully developed missile
of this quality in 1972, especially as no balancing American concession
was offered. There were other avoidable shortcomings in SALT I—the
consequence, as Kissinger later admitted, of the mistrustful secretiveness with which Nixon and Kissinger treated their own negotiators—
but SALT I did not produce the SS-19, and the SS-19 did not change
the basic strategic balance. What we shall never know is what would
have happened if the Nixon administration had resisted the temptation
to mislead Congress and had said simply that the Soviet refusal to
accept tighter limits was part of the reality of this first major agreement.
Given the national popularity of SALT and the strong position of the
administration that summer, it is hard to believe that such a straightforward approach would have prevented ratification, and it certainly
would have reduced the force of the backlash that came when the
misleading assurance was exposed.

The Window of Vulnerability

Beginning in 1976 and continuing for a decade, many apparently
qualified Americans argued that the Soviet Union was achieving a clear
strategic superiority that was bound to create a "window of vulnerability," which Moscow would use to produce dramatic Soviet gains and
American losses on the international political scene. Their argument
does not seem to have had great impact on public opinion or political
behavior, except as a modest contribution to the perception that President Jimmy Carter was weak on national defense. But the shape of the
argument is striking, and so are the predictions made by its advocates.
Still more striking is the distance between these predictions and what
happened.

The best place to study this window of vulnerability is in the
publications of an organization called the Committee on the Present
Danger, organized in 1976 under the leadership of Eugene Rostow
and Paul H. Nitze. Its purpose was to arouse Americans against the
delusion of détente and to stimulate support for defense against Soviet

pressures of all sorts around the world. Our particular concern is with its analysis of the strategic nuclear balance between the Soviet Union and the United States, and its view of the connection between that balance and Soviet expansion.

The committee believed that in 1976 Soviet military strength was growing, while the American defense effort was far too small. Observing that American defense spending as a percentage of gross national product had reached the lowest level in twenty-five years, and observing also the steady and even dramatic expansion in Soviet military strength over the preceding decade, it foresaw a dangerous future: "If we continue to drift, we shall become second best to the Soviet Union in overall military strength; our alliances will weaken; our promising rapprochement with China could be reversed. Then we could find ourselves isolated in a hostile world, facing the unremitting pressures of Soviet policy backed by an overwhelming preponderance of power. Our national survival itself would be in peril, and we should face, one after another, bitter choices between war and acquiescence under pressure."[22]

Beginning from this gloomy forecast, the committee found particular danger in the prospect of Soviet superiority in strategic nuclear forces. In early 1977 it reported, "we are convinced, and there is widespread agreement among knowledgeable experts, that *if past trends continue, the USSR will within several years achieve strategic superiority over the United States* [original emphasis]."[23] The principal instrument of this superiority, as the committee understood it, would be the very large Soviet deployment of land-based missiles with vastly greater throwweight than anything in the American arsenal. As Nitze wrote:

> It is a copybook principle in strategy that, in actual war, advantage tends to go to the side in a better position to raise the stakes by expanding the scope, duration or destructive intensity of the conflict. By the same token, at junctures of high contention short of war, the side better able to cope with the potential consequences of raising the stakes has the advantage. The other side is the one under greater pressure to scramble for a peaceful way out. To have the advantage at the utmost level of violence helps at every lesser level. In the Korean war, the Berlin blockades, and the Cuban missile crisis the United States had the ultimate edge because of our superiority at the strategic nuclear level. That edge has slipped away.[24]

In an earlier formulation Nitze's view of the Soviet view was stated still more sharply:

> The nuclear balance is, of course, only one element in the overall power balance. But in the Soviet view, it is the fulcrum upon which all other levers of influence—military, economic, or political—rest.[25]

Nitze argued further that if the Soviets achieved a strategic nuclear superiority, they would "consider themselves duty bound by Soviet doctrine to exploit fully that strategic advantage through political or limited military means."[26] In particular he believed that Soviet superiority in ICBM throwweight would make possible a Soviet first strike against U.S. ICBMs and other military targets that would create such a gross American inferiority that the American president could make no rational response. "It is a horrible prospect," he told the Senate Foreign Relations Committee in 1979.[27] Nitze did not assert that the Soviet government would actually make such an attack; what he insisted was that they could and would use this superior capability to support remorseless expansion by other means. In the words of his colleague Eugene Rostow, testifying on behalf of the Committee on the Present Danger one week later, "It is our contention that the political consequences of an adverse shift in the strategic nuclear balance would be catastrophic." Rostow asserted that such a shift was inevitable in the absence of prompt and drastic remedial measures which in fact were not taken.[28]

The window of vulnerability found many frightened believers who expressed their fears in 1979, during Senate hearings on the SALT II Treaty that Carter had signed. That treaty left intact the Soviet advantage in heavy missiles. The most eloquent prophet of peril may have been Henry Kissinger, who argued that long years of neglect—here he generously included his own time in office—intensified by cancellations and delays in the Carter administration, had produced a situation in which the Soviet Union was bound to have a general strategic superiority in the years just ahead. Like Nitze and Rostow he particularly emphasized the vulnerability of U.S. land-based missiles, and he believed that because of this vulnerability Soviet willingness to run risks "must exponentially increase." Like Nitze and Rostow he foresaw a "period of maximum danger" in the coming five years. Kissinger surprised many who had heard him make very different arguments while in office, and his explanations of his change of mind raised questions, but they need not detain us because what matters here is simply that when he predicted the same years of maximum danger as Nitze and Rostow, he joined them in getting it wrong. The Soviet numerical advantages that troubled all these men have continued to exist, but nothing has happened from 1979 to the present that can plausibly be explained in terms of any Soviet exploitation of strategic superiority.[29]

There is something abstract in the argument that an advantage of throwweight in a single weapons system will remorselessly translate into catastrophic political consequences, and it is important to understand that these opinions were reinforced—understandably but illogically—by a strong sense that Americans in office had dangerously soft-headed ideas that were having a damaging effect on American policy. The notion that Russian superiority in the size and numbers of ICBM missiles would set loose a campaign of coercive Soviet diplomacy was more than a deduction from "a copybook principle." It was a way of sounding the alarm against ideas and men that were thought dangerously soft, not so much about this question as about such separate elements of the problem as the Soviet view of nuclear war and the Soviet commitment to aggressive expansion. There developed in these years a substantial volume of argument that neither Soviet deployments nor Soviet military doctrines were consistent with the notion that the Soviet leadership shared the prevailing American opinion that a capacity for assured destruction—a large survivable second-strike force—was the right measuring stick for strategic nuclear forces. Up to a point, and in ways that are important for understanding why the Soviet government made the enormous strategic investments that it did, these analysts were right even though their conclusions were wrong.

Soviet Deployment and Soviet Doctrine

Soviet deployments of nuclear weapons systems were indeed vast and varied between 1965 and 1975. The Soviet Union built much larger missiles than the American Minuteman and many more of them; it deployed less effective but more numerous submarines; it attended continuously to civil defense and air defense, and its efforts in antimissile defense, before and after SALT, were larger than those of the Americans, though still of only marginal operational value. In SALT I Soviet negotiators sturdily protected their right to deploy new systems they then had under development, and by 1975 their systems were receiving MIRV warheads. It was plain that the Soviets had not decided simply to match the Americans and then stop, and while administrations in power continued to believe and declare that the strategic balance remained strong and stable—there was no disagreement on this point among men in office throughout the 1970s—there was room to ask what Soviet leaders really did believe about nuclear weapons.

The most excited analysis, not surprisingly, came from a member of the Committee on the Present Danger, Professor Richard Pipes, a specialist in Russian history. Where Nitze had found danger in the "copybook principle" of strategy by which anyone who had a lead in the most powerful weapons could inevitably impose his will all down the line, Pipes found danger in the particular beliefs and acts of the Soviet military leadership, and reported his findings in July 1977 in an article for the monthly *Commentary* whose extraordinary title encapsulated a most alarming view of Soviet nuclear doctrine: "Why the Soviet Union Thinks It Could Fight and Win a Nuclear War." The article was essentially a comparison of certain aspects of Soviet and American thought on these matters. Pipes chose to compare Soviet military doctrine on fighting a nuclear war with that of one small group of civilians in the United States. Crudely misunderstanding the nuclear policy of McNamara as one close to "minimum deterrence," Pipes wrongly assumed that American procurement and targeting had been governed by a policy based only on retaliatory strikes at Soviet cities. His essay compared this straw man to the Soviet military doctrine that the solution to the problem of nuclear war was to be able to win it. He concluded that "there is something innately destabilizing in the very fact that we consider nuclear war unfeasible and suicidal for both, and our chief adversary views it as feasible and winnable for himself."[30] Pipes believed that Soviet superiority would dampen American resolution and encourage Soviet adventures. Indeed by 1978 he was saying that the Russians "already begin to treat us as inferiors," a clear sign of danger.[31] The Pipes article attracted unusually wide attention, partly because of its frightening title and partly because the author had recently served on a panel that correctly criticized American intelligence estimates for underestimating Soviet plans for deployment.

Pipes was by no means alone in challenging the notion that Soviet strategic thought was benign. More careful analysts reached conclusions that were less sweeping, but still sufficient to show that the Soviet military view of strategic nuclear power did not include the proposition that the destructiveness of nuclear weapons required a new and different way of thinking about what they were good for. Soviet military leaders believed that there were two right ways to think about nuclear weapons: first, to have enough of them so that if the imperialists should force a war, the Soviets could crush the enemy; and second, to make the strongest possible arrangements for defense—active and passive, air defense and civil defense—so as to reduce nuclear damage to the Soviet Union. It was clear that Soviet military leaders of the 1970s had not reached McNamara's conclusion that one side's effort for damage limitation was bound to be frustrated by the other side's commitment to assured destruction. In place of second-strike assured destruction the Russians wanted the strongest and earliest strike against the aggressor—doctrinally they were much more like LeMay than like McNamara. But where LeMay's belief in strategic preemption was the product of air force victories sought and won, the Soviet conviction was more the consequence of all that their country had suffered in allowing Hitler an initially successful surprise in 1941. In principle the Soviets wanted the best possible offense for destroying the aggressors' ability to strike and the best possible defenses for damage limitation.

Yet when the arguments of these more expert analysts are carefully read, it appears that not one of them wrote anything that supported the assertion in the title of the Pipes essay, that the Soviet Union thought it could fight and win a nuclear war. No matter how firm the demonstration that Soviet doctrine called for both usable superiority and strong defense—two goals that McNamara had discarded—there would always be a sentence that made plain the analyst's recognition of Soviet awareness that however it might be in theory, a nuclear war would have its own reality.

Thus John Erickson, a senior British expert, in 1979 after reviewing the opinions of Khrushchev and his successors: "Clearly, Soviet strategy recognised (and still does recognise) the sensible need to avoid nuclear war as a possible contingency (if waged by the United States and her allies, for here is power enough to destroy the Soviet Union)," even though "the Soviet Union was unwilling (as it is now) to entertain any concept of deterrence which would *increase* Soviet vulnerability." And thus Fritz Ermarth, a senior analyst with experience at the CIA, the Rand Corporation, and the National Security Council, after describing the strong Soviet "tendency to preempt" if necessary and their interest in having "a going-in force balance in which they have an equal or better chance of winning" a general nuclear war: "This is not to argue that the Soviets do not foresee appalling destruction as the result of any strategic exchange under the best of conditions. In a crisis, Soviet leaders would probably take any tolerable and even costly exits from the risk of such a war."[32]

The best summary of all this that I know was written by a younger scholar, David Holloway. In a remarkable book of 1983, called *The Soviet Union and the Arms Race,* Holloway spelled out with care the behavior and the doctrines of the Soviet leadership, and concluded that:

> The Soviet Union has approached the problem of nuclear war in the way that states have traditionally approached the question of war. It has sought to ensure its own security by increasing its military strength.

But then he added:

> The Soviet leaders have been forced to recognize that their relationship with the United States is in reality one of mutual vulnerability to devastating nuclear strikes, and that there is no immediate prospect of escaping from this relationship. Within the constraints of this

mutual vulnerability they have tried to prepare for nuclear war, and
they would try to win such a war if it came to that. But there is little
evidence to suggest that they think victory in a global nuclear war
would be anything other than catastrophic.[33]

The doctrine preached victory, even in nuclear war. But the real
understanding was more sober. Moreover, the judgment is unanimous. Even Pipes, when his broadside is read with care, distinguishes
between doctrine and reality. After writing that "the Soviet leadership
could not accept the theory of mutual deterrence," he emphasized in
a footnote that he was talking only about theory, because "the Russians
certainly accept the *fact* of deterrence." Two years later in another
paper Pipes promoted his footnote to the main text and wrote that one
of the four underlying propositions of Soviet nuclear strategy was that
"the destructive potential of nuclear weapons is so enormous that
great-power conflict likely to lead to nuclear war ought to be
avoided."[34]

Warnings about nuclear blackmail thus reflected not Soviet or
American reality, but the state of mind of believers in present danger.
Nitze believed that Soviet nuclear superiority would lead as a matter
of doctrinal necessity to successful nuclear coercion, and Pipes believed that the existence of a Soviet theory of war fighting would have
a dangerous impact even though in fact Soviet leaders accepted the
reality of nuclear deterrence. The Committee on the Present Danger,
in its more general broadsides, reached still more sweeping conclusions: in 1978, "America is becoming Number 2." In 1982, "the
United States has become second best." In 1984, things are worse yet;
the question is "Can America catch up?" and the answer is "not at the
present and projected rate of increase in the overall defense effort."
And like its strategic mentor Paul Nitze, the committee saw the heart
of the danger in Soviet strategic superiority, which "guarantees that
the United States will face mounting Soviet pressures and the unacceptable choice between military defeat or political submission."[35]

The test for believers in the window of vulnerability has come
under Ronald Reagan. Throughout his time in the White House, the
strategic balance has been essentially unchanged by the measurements
of the believers in present danger. In the ICBM balance that they
found crucial, the Soviet "advantage" has in fact increased, as Soviet
MIRVing has gone forward and as the Soviet military has begun the
deployment of new systems with new megatons. The Carter administration's delay in the deployment of the MX, which troubled these
critics in 1979, has been followed by even longer delays in both terms
of the Reagan administration. Because of the retirement of the old and
inaccurate Titan II missiles (a sensible move long overdue), the throw-

weight of American ICBMs will be smaller when Mr. Reagan leaves the White House than it was when he got there.

Let us take time out here to examine the strange case of the MX missile. Neither administration should be faulted for the delay in its deployment.[36] MX is a large, ten-warhead ballistic missile designed to succeed the Minuteman and to counterbalance the heavy Soviet missiles. From the beginning it has faced political and technical obstacles that were not foreseen by its designers in the air force. It was originally designed to fit into Minuteman silos, but when it came under review by Secretary of Defense Harold Brown and his principal technical adviser, William Perry, in the Carter administration, they concluded that it would be foolish to put a ten-warhead missile in a fixed silo where it could be knocked out by a two-warhead attack. MX-in-Minuteman flagrantly violated the standard of second-strike survivability that had been established by Eisenhower and strongly enforced by Kennedy and McNamara; ten warheads in a single silo were a fat and easy target. Brown set his people to work to find a way of basing the missile that would meet the standard of survivability, and after a number of possibilities had been examined and debated he settled on a scheme that involved moving each missile around in a complex tracking system so that it could be hidden from the Soviets in any one of some twenty-three otherwise empty firing points. The system would be deployed over thousands of square miles in the West that looked empty to the planners but amply populated to the inhabitants. It was impossible to sit through a thorough briefing on this plan, complete with charts and acronyms, without nostalgic recollection of the first great master of zany design, Rube Goldberg. I used to listen to such briefings as a member of an advisory committee in the Carter years. It was a form of cruel and unusual punishment that always left me wondering whether the administration inflicted such briefings on itself as well as its committees. Yet I admit that I never encountered a better proposal for ensuring some useful survivability for this misbegotten missile; its basic design was incompatible with a sensible basing mode.

Although he had been an early and eloquent believer in the window of vulnerability and thought the MX missile the right remedy, Ronald Reagan had no difficulty in accepting the insistence of his friend Senator Paul Laxalt of Nevada that the multiple-shelter MX with its enormous racetrack would be unwelcome in Nevada and Utah. Patiently, and with inexhaustibly renewed enthusiasm for one bad design after another, Defense Secretary Caspar Weinberger continued the search for a sensible basing mode. In the end he came back to the Minuteman silos on the recommendation of a bipartisan committee of strategic notables—all preselected friends of MX—led by Lieutenant General Brent Scowcroft.

In a report as skillful politically as it was incomplete logically, the Scowcroft commission defended MX-in-Minuteman. It put to one side the criterion of second-strike survivability that had governed missile procurement for more than twenty years, insisting (without a supporting argument) that it was urgent to begin to match the capabilities of heavy Soviet missiles. In a spirit of compromise it cut the proposed number of missiles in half—from 200 to 100. To balance its report it acknowledged two facts of durable importance: first, that its unmatched survivability justified "the increasing importance of the ballistic missile submarine force," and second, that the vulnerability of Minuteman was not at all a window of vulnerability for the whole strategic deterrent. The commission's second point was a little complicated, but compelling: A surprise attack on Minuteman could be launched only by long-range strategic missiles, which would be detected "within moments after the launch," thus permitting American strategic bombers to be safely airborne in large numbers, ready to retaliate, well before any long-range attack arrived. But if the bombers were attacked first, as by submarine-based missiles on a shorter, quicker flight, the "massive nuclear detonations" on the airfields would clearly justify an immediate decision to launch from the Minuteman silos, so that only empty holes would be left for the long-range surprise attack to hit. Such quick decisions to retaliate would be fateful, but the reply to nuclear aggression can never be comfortable, only better than no reply at all. The Scowcroft commission, with the advantage of its standing as a body chosen by Reagan, thus closed the window of vulnerability by its acknowledgement of facts that had been clear to serious analysts all along.[37]

The Scowcroft commission saved the life of MX-in-Minuteman but not without further bargaining between Congress and the president. Senators and congressmen divided sharply over the wisdom of buying weapons that remained tempting targets protected only by the greater survivability of the other parts of the triad. In 1988 it appears that forty to fifty MX-in-Minuteman may eventually be deployed; the air force is still trying to get more MX elsewhere—perhaps on railroad cars. If there are other new ICBMs in the American future, they will probably be smaller missiles with only one or two warheads which will not be such rewarding targets. Nothing now on hand or on order will come close to balancing the Soviet advantage in ICBM throwweight that was so frightening to believers in present danger.

None of the dreadful Soviet pressure feared by these believers has in fact been exerted in the years for which they predicted it. The strategic "imbalance" that they described as politically compelling still exists, but there has been no attempt at Soviet coercion. Rostow's "catastrophic" political consequences have not followed. Kissinger's "period of maximum danger" passed, and Soviet risk taking did not "exponentially increase." Nitze's "copybook" logic proved to be irrelevant.

I press the point not because these men were so imprudently sure of themselves when they spoke, but because their error is so instructive. Beset by their fears, they neglected the question that would always come first for any Soviet leader contemplating nuclear war. They pushed aside the point that Eisenhower had explained to his countrymen in 1954—the Soviet leaders would think first of what nuclear weapons could do to their homeland and themselves. Nitze got past it in part by accepting fanciful estimates of the effectiveness of Soviet civil defense, and Pipes got past it in part by emphasizing theory over facts. Neither of them chose to look closely at the risks the Soviet government would have to accept if it started a nuclear war.

Consider the uncertainties and risks attending the attack on Minuteman, the favorite scenario of believers in present danger. No Soviet planner could assure his government that a planned surprise would be a real surprise. Especially during a crisis—much the most likely time for attack or threat of attack—Americans would be highly alert to Soviet behavior. Even without an early warning to Washington, no Soviet planner could promise his masters that the Americans would not fire their own ICBMs when their satellites detected the launch of hundreds of Soviet missiles. No Soviet planner could prevent the escape of alert strategic bombers, and no Soviet air defense could prevent some of those bombers from getting some of their warheads to targets. No Soviet planner could prevent the survival of American submarines at sea, and none could foretell what targets their thousands of warheads might hit. No Soviet planner could give any assurance whatever that the Soviet Union, after the best possible surprise attack, would not find itself hours later a radioactive ruin.

The magnitude of what could happen was correctly suggested by Jimmy Carter, who defended the adequacy of the American deterrent in 1979 by noting that the warheads on a single Poseidon submarine could "destroy every large- and medium-sized city in the Soviet Union." This statement drew heavy fire from believers in Soviet superiority, who claimed that it showed Carter to be an adherent of the dangerous doctrine of "minimum deterrence," under which the ability to hit some number of cities was all you needed. It is true that Carter was no enthusiast for a strategic buildup; he made new systems pass a severe examination, and he rejected both the B-1 bomber and the neutron bomb. He also talked with longing about a world without nuclear weapons. But when he told what one submarine could do he was describing a danger that any Soviet leader must take into account.[38]

Nitze and his friends argued that the American president would be mad to reply to an attack on Minuteman with a massive attack on Soviet cities, since such an attack would surely bring a parallel reply. The argument has force, but it neglects the many choices between a counter-city spasm and no reply at all. Many kinds of retaliation would be open to a president, and a general counter-city attack could well be held in reserve. It is a good and complex question just what targets the Americans should try to hit in response to Soviet nuclear attacks, but what remains genuinely strange is Nitze's argument that the best available choice would be surrender. Stranger still is the notion that the Soviet Union could ever have confidence in advance that this would be the American choice.

Part of the trouble here goes back to the misunderstanding about the meaning of McNamara's criterion of assured destruction. McNamara believed and said that this criterion required a capacity to destroy the Soviet Union as a functioning society. The destruction he had in mind clearly included cities—urban-industrial targets, in the jargon. He never said, and he did not believe, that only cities should be targeted or that they should be the targets of first choice if nuclear war ever came. The target lists of SAC were comprehensive when he came to the Pentagon and still more comprehensive when he left. He had succeeded in requiring a limited number of attack options in addition to the single, massive, all-purpose attack that he found in the first SIOP when he arrived, but the number of warheads assigned to each option remained large. His real success had been to insist on a way for the president to withhold forces, and one of his persistent hopes was that in the event of war American avoidance of urban attack could be used to discourage Soviet forces from attacking American cities. There were—and still are—technical difficulties in withholding, but it is wrong to confuse McNamara's criterion of sufficiency with a doctrinal preference for city busting. It is true that the criterion lent itself to misunderstanding, but those who were most ardent in distorting it usually knew what they were doing. The development of varied options began under McNamara, and when Nitze began to worry about present danger, in the middle of the 1970s, there was no such narrow choice between city busting and surrender as he chose to assume.[39]

Yet no matter how "moderate" the first attacks of either side might be, there would always remain a risk, which no planner or decision maker could ignore, that the exchanges would become disastrously large. That was the real point of Carter's comment on what one Poseidon could do. Who could tell whether the war would stop after one strike by each side, or two, or ten, or how the choice of targets might change as the horror continued? To fling open the door to nuclear war by an attack on Minuteman—something like two thousand warheads aimed at one thousand targets—was to run an enormous risk of incalculable catastrophe. To use the threat of such an attack for blackmailing was so clearly implausible that the nightmare of the Present Dangerites could never have come to pass. In the end Eisenhower and Kennedy and McNamara too had it right. The thousands of survivable warheads in the forces they shaped were plenty, even in the face of Soviet forces with larger missiles and more powerful warheads. Enough was enough.

Deterrence in Europe Again

From 1977 to 1987 the Carter and Reagan administrations struggled with the most complex and confused of all the American efforts to ensure effective nuclear deterrence in Europe. We are much too close to this affair to write its history with confidence, but a few of its remarkable features deserve notice. The most remarkable of all may also be the hardest to explain. A matter that arose from an exaggerated fear of a particular new Soviet deployment ended ten years later with a superpower treaty that provided for the destruction of that Soviet system—the SS-20 missile—and also the countervailing but much less numerous missiles that the Atlantic alliance had, with great political effort, deployed in response. In effect, the long contest which arose from the Soviet decision to deploy eventually ended in a draw.

My own belief is that both the initial allied decision to organize a response and the eventual agreement owed much more to politics than to strategic reality. The SS-20, an intermediate range missile aimed at West European targets, did not confer on the Soviet Union any superiority that it could translate into coercive advantage unless the allies were so weak as to give in to bluff. In the event there were large numbers of unmatched SS-20s in place between the first deployment in 1976 and the arrival of the first new allied weapons in 1983. They produced no effective Soviet pressure of any sort. What they did instead was to provoke a strong political response, especially in West Germany.

Helmut Schmidt, the West German chancellor who took the lead in asserting the need for an effective allied response, was not himself easily frightened by Soviet missiles. His insistence on this requirement was much less a matter of strategic calculation than of the political need for new American action. I think that Schmidt was moved less by fear of the SS-20 than by mistrust of Jimmy Carter. Certainly there were technical arguments to the effect that the SS-20 was a dangerously better weapon than the SS-4 and SS-5 it had replaced—cumbersome and vulnerable weapons that had been aimed at Europe for twenty years (the same weapons that Khrushchev had unwisely tried to put in Cuba). But the technical argument was much less important for

Schmidt than his belief that the Carter administration must be persuaded to prove its solidarity with Western Europe.[40]

The political pressure in which Schmidt was the prime mover set loose the technical and analytic professionals who truly believed that the safety of Europe depended on particular responses to particular Soviet weapons systems; it also gave new encouragement to those who had believed in the 1950s that Europe-based missiles like the Jupiter were badly needed, and in the 1960s that they should not have been withdrawn. Midrange weapons in the theater are what is needed, said men who appeared not to remember that submarine missiles had long since been committed to NATO and would be modernized in their turn. So a "high-level group" of middle-level allied defense officials produced a plan for the deployment of new warheads, some on ground-launched cruise missiles (GLCMs) and some on a land-based ballistic missile called the Pershing II. The weapons they selected were the ones that interested manufacturers had at hand, and their choices had less to do with any clear strategic assessment than with the interests of particular services and countries—the army wanted the Pershing II because it was an army weapon; the British did not want new weapons at sea. The West Germans insisted that the new weapons be accepted on the territory of at least one other continental ally. That requirement alone might have wrecked the enterprise, because North European allies proved hesitant, but the requirement was met by the unexpected and welcome firmness of the Italians. The allied proposal for new deployments was approved in NATO at the end of 1979. The agreed numbers were 108 Pershing IIs and 464 GLCMs.

In order to be responsive to important antinuclear opinion in Western Europe, NATO adopted a double track—deployment if necessary, but arms control if possible. The door was thus left open for a Soviet effort to prevent the new allied deployment while offering the smallest concessions possible. There followed a Soviet political campaign in which propaganda and diplomacy were united, even including occasional nuclear bluster from Andrey Gromyko. This effort produced a determined response from NATO. Whether or not the new allied deployment was needed for deterrence, it was plainly undesirable that an allied decision should be reversed by Soviet pressure. The firmness of the governments that mattered most—London, Bonn, Rome, and Paris—was only reinforced by Soviet behavior. An interesting diplomatic effort at compromise was led by Paul Nitze. After a "walk in the woods" with a Soviet colleague he put forward a proposal for reduced deployments on both sides, but first Washington and then Moscow rejected it. In terms of alliance politics, the Nitze scheme was at least as good as what eventually happened, but doctrinaires in the Reagan Pentagon successfully opposed it.[41] The alliance persisted, and deployments began on schedule at the end of 1983.

At first most observers believed that the story would end there. A Soviet deployment perceived as threatening had led to a NATO response, and in spite of both Soviet pressure and the antinuclear sentiment of many in Europe, the alliance had held firm. But in the first year of the leadership of Mikhail Gorbachev the Soviet government made a new decision. If it could not defeat the new deployment by propaganda and pressure, it would seek to remove it by concession. After an amount of haggling that was unprecedentally small by traditional Soviet standards, Gorbachev negotiated an agreement that was signed at the Washington summit on December 8, 1987 and ratified in time for the Moscow summit six months later. In essence he accepted a proposal that Reagan had made five years earlier—the so-called zero option: no SS-20s and no allied midrange missiles. More than that, Gorbachev accepted procedures for verification that had no precedent. On the evidence of what was in the new treaty, the Politburo had decided that its interests would be best protected by the abandonment of both the challenging Soviet missiles and the frightening allied response.

There can be no certainty about the reasons for this dramatic shift in the Soviet position, but it has a number of possible causes. One part of the new allied deployment, the Pershing II missile, almost surely appeared to Soviet analysts to give the Americans a new and serious capability for a limited first strike. The Pershing II was highly accurate and could hit its target in some ten or twelve minutes. The Americans said it could not quite reach Moscow, but the Soviets found this assurance incompletely comforting, if only because the range of a missile is always open to technical improvement. Like their American counterparts, Soviet analysts have a professional addiction to worst-case analysis. By comparison the Soviet SS-20 had no such extraordinary capability, and its European targets could be covered by many other Soviet weapons. Finally, and perhaps most important, Gorbachev may well have a better understanding of nuclear weapons than his predecessors. It may be that he prefers stable stalemate to unstable competition.

There are important questions in this story. Was there miscalculation here? Did the Soviet government fail to foresee that its deployment of the SS-20—in its view probably a routine decision to provide prudent modernization of a class of weapons that had been deployed for nearly twenty years—would be read in Western Europe as a provocative act? Did the Americans for their part recognize the degree to which their deployment of Pershing II might cause distress in Moscow? Some of them have admitted that they did not. It seems clear that the zero option was initially proposed and promoted by the Reagan administration because it seemed both publicly appealing and predictably unacceptable in the Kremlin. A good question for both sides is whether it was necessary for them to spend many billions of dollars to install and then remove these competing systems. Could the results of 1987 have been reached at no cost if the two sides had been more sensible in the competitive 1970s?

There is also, in all this, a political contest that centers on the choices of European members of NATO. The double-track position adopted by NATO—build and negotiate at the same time—was necessary for domestic political reasons, but it invited Soviet efforts to split the alliance. The underlying difficulty here is the same one we have examined in earlier decades: the complexity of the process by which the nuclear weapons of the United States can be used to generate more reassurance than fear among allies who have no such weapons of their own. The INF debate showed determination in the necessary number of governments, but both the deployment plan and the eventual agreement aroused conflicting sentiments which give warning that before they begin the next serious negotiation on the balance of weaponry in Europe the political leaders of the alliance will do well to examine their options with more care than ever. It will be as unwise to leave military choices mainly to military men—Thor and Jupiter come to mind—as to attempt complex military solutions to essentially political problems—remember the case of the MLF. And high-level groups should be formed at a really high level—the "experts" are usually not expert on issues in which political reassurance is central.

Strategic Defense Again

On March 23, 1983, in what may be the loneliest presidential decision on nuclear matters since October 1941, Ronald Reagan announced "a program to counter the awesome Soviet missile threat with measures that are defensive." He called on the American scientific community "to give us the means of rendering these nuclear weapons impotent and obsolete." With these words he set in motion the undertaking that the world calls Star Wars and that he and his subordinates call the Strategic Defense Initiative—SDI. Probably no undertaking in his presidency has come to mean more to Ronald Reagan than this one, and from the beginning his aim has been high: "Tonight we're launching an effort which holds the promise of changing the course of human history." Reagan has insisted in later years that this initiative was his own, and there is every reason to accept his claim. Enthusiasts for strategic defense had his ear, notably Edward Teller, and he had been encouraged in some measure by the Joint Chiefs of Staff, but this initiative was not the product of careful analysis by anyone, and some of his most senior advisers were taken by surprise.[42]

What drove him to this initiative was his own passionate belief in two propositions. First, he was unwilling to accept the prospect of permanent vulnerability to total destruction. As he said two days later to reporters, "It is inconceivable to me that we can go on thinking down the future, not only for ourselves and our lifetime but for other generations, that the great nations of the world will sit here, like people facing themselves across a table, each with a cocked gun, and no one knowing whether someone might tighten their finger on the trigger." Second, he believed that the same men who had made the danger could unmake it. Reagan saw both the danger and the prospect in more than merely national terms—he was genuinely ready, for himself, to share any new solution with the Russians—but at the same time both his concern and his hope were intensely American. It was the danger to Americans that was especially intolerable, and it was American scientists and American "strengths in technology" that could put things right. On March 23 Reagan was indeed sharing with his countrymen his own strongly held and quite personal "vision of the future."[43]

To translate a vision into a program was not easy. The first step was to get expert and supportive advice. Two outside committees were formed, one on strategy (the Hoffman panel) and one on technology (the Fletcher panel), and presently both reported affirmatively—the strategists were preselected believers in strategic defense, and the technologists were preselected believers that technology should try to rise to any challenge.[44] Taking the reports as encouragement to proceed, the administration set up a Strategic Defense Initiative Office (SDIO) and proposed a five-year research program of twenty-six billion dollars. No program has had more ardent and continuous advocacy from Ronald Reagan ever since, but the results have been modest. Lack of congressional enthusiasm, together with the heavy pressure of continuing large federal deficits, has kept annual appropriations well below the administration's targets. It seems likely in 1988 that the first five-year research phase will be funded at about $16 billion, less than two-thirds of the level the administration has proposed. There were significant research programs on these subjects before the Star Wars speech, and the increase over what would have been spent in the relevant fields if there had been no Reagan speech is probably less than half of what the president has sought.

Compared to the size of the challenge, the research results through 1987 have been thin, but the debate about the program has been thick. At the center of that debate has been the question whether strategic defenses, assuming that they can be developed and deployed, are worth having. Those in favor of the program have argued mainly that there must be a better answer than continued exposure to thermonuclear devastation, while opponents say that no achievable defense can prevent that exposure. The central question in this debate is whether the ability to inflict mutual assured destruction is imposed by both technological reality and the strategic imperatives of the two super-powers, or is merely an unwise policy preference inherited from the 1960s. Initial preferences on this subject are often governed by political priorities; there is a high correlation between anti-Soviet feeling and enthusiasm for SDI, and also between disbelief in strategic defense and hope for better relations with the Soviet Union. Except at the extremes, there has been agreement in principle that the question is whether, and to what extent, defensive deployments can be effective. Reagan told high school students in Glassboro, New Jersey, in 1986, such a defense would "enable us to put in space a shield that missiles could not penetrate, a shield that could protect us from nuclear missiles just as a roof protects a family from rain."[45] It is hard to find anyone who would be against such a system, but unfortunately it is also hard to find anyone with technical qualifications who thinks that such a system can be had.

Even within the administration only one official regularly asserted that the president's leakproof shield was obtainable—his loyal and zealous defense secretary. Weinberger's enthusiasm was immediate, and it was the more remarkable because less than a year before the Star Wars speech he had expressed his own strong belief that there was no early prospect of any useful strategic defense; he had strongly asserted the adequacy of the research program of 1982 and had opposed a new level of effort because "we do not have any indication at this point that it is anything on which we could put our reliance. If we did, we would be dangerously misleading the President and the country." What converted Weinberger was not any change in the technical prospects, but Reagan's lonely decision, in which he had no role. He was out of the country at the time and learned of the Star Wars proposal only after it had been put into the text of a presidential speech on other defense needs.[46]

The president's program gave new hope to many different groups—to those who believed that defensive weapons were the best way to deal with the enduring problem of the vulnerability of American ICBMs, to advocates of many different and competing technologies, to those who wanted defenses for allies, and even to a few who renewed their long-time advocacy of large-scale civil defense—this last was the position of Edward Teller. All of these believers professed themselves supporters of the president's initiative, but almost none was a true believer in his dream. The case of Teller is interesting because of his own role in persuading Reagan to pursue the program. It is not clear why it would be necessary to have civil defense in a world with a leakproof shield. But Teller does not believe in a leakproof shield. In 1986 he said flatly, "A complete defense is completely impossible. To rely on such a defense would be even more completely absurd."[47]

Teller was writing in the London monthly *Encounter,* and his remarks were intended as encouragement to supporters of British and French nuclear forces, whose value might indeed be reduced if there were effective Soviet defenses. But his statement was unqualified, and I believe it reflects his conviction about American defenses too: They are desirable, but they will not make offensive warheads obsolete or fallout shelters unnecessary.

This division between Reagan and his advisers, visible but not publicly admitted, gravely affected both the debate and the development of the SDI program. The president remained committed to the leakproof defensive roof, but everyone else was working for a more modest purpose: the strengthening of nuclear deterrence. The president's vision, from the start, was directly tied to new technologies and the extensive use of space, because no one believed that an effective general defense could be created without a powerful attack on Soviet missiles in the first minutes of their flight, the boost phase. A multiphase, space-using, high-technology, directed-weapons model was the centerpiece of the technical briefing offered to guests at the White House on the occasion of the first speech, and in 1985 Reagan's own preferred name for what he wanted was "the strategic space shield." This objective was admittedly distant in time. The Fletcher panel placed "an effective defensive capability" in the twenty-first century. This time span did not grow shorter in the first years of the program, and in 1987 the American Physical Society published an authoritative report which estimated that "even in the best of circumstances, a decade or more of intensive research would be required" before there could be "an informed decision about the potential effectiveness and survivability of directed energy weapons systems." Thus a real decision to go ahead with the "space shield" that was advertised at the beginning—a decision like Franklin Roosevelt's in 1941 or Harry Truman's in 1950—will not be possible for Reagan or for his successor even if that successor serves two terms. If the physicists are right, the "strategic space shield" will be an object of research at least until 1997.[48]

Ignoring this reality, Reagan talked as if his program was already assured of eventual success. On the fourth anniversary of his initial speech he stated flatly that "it is possible for us to design and build a strategic defense," and he spoke as if the prospect of effective defense was clear: "All humanity can begin to look forward to a new era of security when the burden of nuclear terror is lifted from its shoulders." This was not true. By 1987 the balance of effort was shifting from long-range research on a complete system of strategic deterrence to developmental work on a partial system, from exotic directed-energy weapons to more conventional systems of kinetic energy weapons. The president still insisted that he wanted to defend people, not missiles, but his own program was shifting its direction. Even Caspar Weinberger, by 1987, was emphasizing the defense of "retaliatory forces" by "a less than one hundred percent defense."[49]

Changes of emphasis like this one, combined with annual shortfalls in appropriations, have produced a research program that is a long way from providing the best of circumstances. Shortly after his retirement from his position as the first chief scientist of the program, Gerald Yonas described the financial situation of the program as "funding chaos," caused by the gap between what the Pentagon planned and what Congress voted. "Programs have to stop and start up again, and people have to be shifted. There's an enormous amount of inefficiency and waste in this type of situation." It is interesting that in the same speech Yonas emphasized three limited defensive systems that would defend hardened military targets, or specific areas, or give protection against attack by terrorists. None of these three programs would come anywhere near Reagan's dream.[50]

THE RELATION between Star Wars and arms control was complex. For Reagan, whose commitment was not just to research but to success, there must be no new agreement blocking his dream. He accepted advice that a repudiation of the ABM Treaty of 1972 would not be necessary in the early years of the effort, but he clearly believed that in the long run the achievement of a space shield was vastly more important than the survival of the treaty. While he correctly claimed for SDI that it was a major force in the Soviet decision of 1985 to return to arms control negotiations, he repeatedly refused to allow his favorite program to become a "bargaining chip" in the renewed negotiations. At the Reykjavík summit in October 1986 he refused to consider any new agreement to limit the testing of defensive devices. The managers of SDI were already committed to demonstrations, as early and dramatic as possible, as a most important way of building support for the program, a bad habit learned from both weapons promoters and the space program. An attempt was made to clear a path for space testing by a new interpretation of the ABM Treaty, but the practical result of this bit of trickiness was to produce a congressional prohibition of such testing. The adversarial attitudes that marked the Reagan administration's approach to strategic policy at every stage became a formidable political barrier to Reagan's most cherished initiative.

Internationally Reagan's unbending refusal to accept limits on SDI blocked one tantalizing possibility for new strategic agreement—a bargain in which there might be concessions by each side that responded to the most urgent fears of the other. The prospect of a large-scale American effort on strategic defense was not attractive to the Kremlin. Only four days after Reagan's launching speech the Soviet leader Yuri Andropov roundly denounced it, insisting that since the United States was already developing and upgrading its offensive forces "at full tilt" with the aim "of acquiring a first nuclear strike capability," the attempt to build defenses as well was "a bid to disarm the Soviet Union in the face of the U.S. nuclear threat." Although no American could yet say how to build a space shield, there was great Soviet respect for what American technology might do and a strong Soviet desire to have limits on any such effort. Since the new American interest in strategic defense was itself largely the consequence of American concern about what the enormous Soviet missile force could do, James Schlesinger (first, I think) and then others of whom I was one suggested in 1984 and 1985 that there was a possibility of a grand compromise in which each side would accept new limits on what the other side feared most: The Soviet side would accept sharp limits on heavy missiles as part of a major reduction of offensive forces by both sides, and the Americans would accept reaffirmed and perhaps modernized constraints on strategic defense. At Reykjavík in the fall of 1986 it became clear that the new Soviet leader Mikhail Gorbachev intensely desired just this kind of new agreement, but Reagan refused to consider it.[51]

At Washington in December 1987 the two leaders again failed to agree. In the words of the American negotiator Max Kampelman, "They kicked the can down the road," by compromise language that left the Americans free to decide that the ABM Treaty permits some testing in space, while leaving the Soviets free to respond to any such testing by new moves of their own. Soviet acceptance of this indeterminate language was undoubtedly affected by the fact that a few weeks before the summit meeting the administration accepted a congressional prohibition on space testing for the coming fiscal year. There was no progress on this question at the Moscow summit in May 1988, and the probability, as I write, is that the final choices of the superpowers on any new strategic agreement will not be made while Reagan is president. Star Wars turned out to be a possible bargaining chip—a more important one than most of its critics had initially expected—but at least through the spring of 1988 Reagan preferred the "vision" to the bargain.

The most accomplished nuclear strategist in the Reagan administration was Fred Charles Iklé, an undersecretary of defense. In 1985 he presented a revealing argument for strategic defense in an essay with a characteristically apprehensive title: "Nuclear Strategy: Can There Be a Happy Ending?" His answer to his own question was clear; there would be no happy ending in a continued acceptance of mutual vulnerability, repugnant on moral grounds, demoralizing to democracies, and favorable to the Soviet Union because a Soviet ruler "schooled in the uses of terror for political ends could lay iron hands on the deepest emotions and fears of a great many people in the West." Iklé found his window of vulnerability not in any imbalance of weapons systems but in a durable psychological imbalance between totalitarian terrorists and fearful democrats, and his conclusion was categorical. "For the future, the 'balance of terror' cannot favor the defense of a democratic alliance. Sooner or later, it will favor those most at ease with, those most experienced in, the systematic use of terror."[52]

For Iklé the solution was so obvious that he left out altogether the question whether it would work. "The key now for the needed trans-formation is technological development to make effective defensive systems possible for the United States and our allies." He thought only dogma stood in the way, and his objective was not Reagan's space shield for citizens but something much more narrowly defined, "non-nuclear missile defenses capable of negating the military utility of a Soviet missile attack and of diminishing its destructiveness." If Iklé thought there was any serious prospect of a comprehensive defense of American cities and citizens he did not say so—nor did he say why fearful democrats would be able to resist the totalitarian terrorist if their lives still lay bare to his missiles. It turned out that what he really wanted from strategic defenses was not all that different from what Eisenhower and Kennedy and indeed McNamara had wanted: surviva-ble second-strike forces—it was the "militarily important targets" that he was most concerned to defend. If defenses could prevent a disarm-ing first strike, they would make any such attack irrational, and Iklé could relax. In the end it was the survivability of weapons, not people, that he found decisive. He protested in his rhetoric that the object was to eliminate the vulnerability of each side to "massive nuclear destruc-tion" but his *means* for doing that was to make such a strike irrational, not to make it impossible. His honesty did him credit, but it did not reinforce his president's dream.[53]

The decisive difference between Iklé and McNamara, then, was not a matter of dogma but one of technological estimates. McNamara had concluded in the 1960s that the deployment of strategic defenses would lead only to an intensified superpower competition in the de-ployment of all sorts of systems that would leave both sides worse off than before. That view had won the day. Iklé believed in the 1980s that a sufficiently sustained and determined effort at improved de-fense—one directed in particular at defending the American deter-rent—would be successful, and that such a defense could open the way to a new balance in which both superpowers would be more secure. Paul Nitze candidly recognized that there could be tricky problems in any such transition, and Iklé emphasized one of them: The Russians might not play. "Should the Soviet leaders choose to preserve their doomsday capability at any price, the prospects for arms control would be bleak indeed." Tricky as the question of Soviet choice might be, however, it was likely to be dominated in the end by the technological question. If strategic defense could be good enough, everyone would want it. How good could it be?[54]

The technological prospects for strategic defense were as complex and uncertain in 1983 as the vision of Ronald Reagan was clear and definite. He launched his program without the encouragement of such clear technical insights as the Maud conclusions that Bush had reported to Roosevelt in October 1941, and indeed without the specific problem in physics that Harry Truman decided to attack when he made his decision on the hydrogen bomb. All strategic defenses, and especially all strategic space shields, partial or complete in their attempted coverage, would be systems of response to attack with a complexity exponentially different from that of the most sophisticated warhead.

Another and equally significant difference for SDI was that it must cope with a predictably energetic Soviet attempt to frustrate any defensive system, as Nitze and Iklé feared. There had been a sense of competition in earlier decisions; for Roosevelt it was Hitler who must not get ahead, and for Truman it was Stalin. Yet the technological undertakings they launched did not have to face the question whether an adversary could make their new weapon ineffective. If they could be made, there would be a way to deliver them. But a strategic defense system must be effective in the face of a determined effort to overcome it. This difference was regularly neglected in Reagan's speeches, but regularly acknowledged by the managers of SDI, who asserted that one of their most important tasks was to make sure that all prospective systems were exposed to the strongest possible challenge by the best possible "Red Teams," experts assigned to think about Soviet responses to any given scheme.

In its first four years the SDI produced no proof whatever that it could ever meet Ronald Reagan's standard of effectiveness, or even Fred Iklé's. What did emerge, largely through the efforts of Paul Nitze—now the president's "senior adviser" on arms control—was the establishment of two criteria for judging any system of strategic defense. First, it must itself be survivable—there was no point in building a system that was easier to knock down than to put up. Second, it must be "cost-effective at the margin"—a phrase borrowed from economics, which meant simply that it must be cheaper for the United States to maintain a given level of defensive effectiveness than for the Soviet Union to degrade that level—for example, by enlarging the offensive threat, by making missiles and warheads harder to attack (especially in the boost phase), by threatening elements of the defensive system (especially in space), and by shifting emphasis (as the United States is already doing with its own offensive forces) from land-based to sea-based systems and from ballistic missiles flying through space to cruise missiles flying through the air. The Red Teams of SDI have many choices.

Although Nitze's standards of survivability and cost-effectiveness were challenged by such promoters of SDI as Weinberger, who preferred to say that a system must simply be "affordable," they were accepted by Ronald Reagan, notably in a statement praising the supporters of SDI on the fourth anniversary of his launching speech. He said "they understood that a system not only had to work but also had to be able to survive attacks itself and be more cost-effective than proliferating offenses." Reagan did not doubt that these standards would be met. In the same statement he spoke as if success were certain, and what he plainly had in mind was the space shield to protect people. Ronald Reagan already knew in his heart that his dream would pass the Nitze tests.[55]

But he did not know it in his head, because in 1987 no one could know it that way. No one knew how to make large space-based systems *survivable,* and no one could promise that any deployment would be *cost-effective* because no one knew how to estimate the costs of either defensive systems or counters to them, even to the right number of zeroes. Reagan's space shield simply could not be tested against the Nitze criteria while he was president, so his acceptance of those criteria was more of a marker for later administrations than for his own. It had no dampening effect on his own bright hopes.

Yet the Nitze standards helped considerably to prevent premature commitment to systems that could not claim to meet them. The standards, indeed, had a common sense that was helpful to those on both sides not committed by faith to support or to oppose strategic defense. Nitze's test, logically, was the same as the one that had long since been accepted, if not always honored, in judging new offensive systems. What made the original triad attractive was that each of its three legs could meet the basic test—the ability to survive and strike back—in a cost-effective way.

One of these systems, the manned bomber, had faced a persistent and sustained challenge from Soviet air defenses. Soviet investment in strategic air defense was often noted with fearful respect by advocates of SDI who believed that the Soviet preoccupation with strategic defense of all sorts was proof of some higher wisdom. But a closer look suggested a different answer. As he had done before in the disputed case of the H-bomb decision, Herbert York in 1986 reviewed the evidence in the case of American bombers against Soviet air defense and concluded that over a period of forty years Soviet air defense had cost about 500 billion dollars, and American bombers about 50 billion. Yet "never during all that time have they been capable of seriously blunting a U.S. air attack." By the Nitze criteria the Soviet air defense program was a hideously expensive failure.[56]

The debate over SDI began right after Reagan's speech of March 23, 1983, and continues as I write. Much remains unsettled, but much is also clear. What is unsettled is whether and how far any defense against ballistic missiles will be found acceptable by the Nitze criteria, or indeed by other tests, like that of the overall value of the ABM Treaty. What is clear is that any limited defense will leave essentially unchanged the strategic stalemate we now have—one that rests in the end on mutual vulnerability. The leakproof space shield that is Ronald Reagan's dream will not become real for decades, if ever. The strategic stalemate remains much stronger than SDI.

Debating Doctrine

The strategic stalemate has also proved stronger than the attempts to produce improvements in war-fighting doctrine that marked not only the Reagan administration but the earlier terms of Nixon, Ford, and Carter. All these administrations addressed the problem of strategic targeting doctrine, and each in its own way modified the formal guidance to strategic planners. After each change spokesmen alternated between boasting of their reforms and insisting on the essential continuity of U.S. strategic policy. What they seldom emphasized was that none of their doctrinal adjustments matched the existing capabilities or the projected deployments of American forces and that none of them had any effect on the underlying and decisive reality of shared vulnerability.

There were good reasons for this repeated attention to the problem of nuclear targeting. It made sense to insist that cities must not be the only targets in the plans, although it was not helpful to neglect the reality that cities had never been the only targets—always excepting the plan to attack Japan in 1945. It also made sense that any president who might find the use of nuclear weapons unavoidable should have more than one choice of targets and weapons. In particular it would probably be wise, in any first resort to nuclear warheads, to withhold any direct attack on centers of population. It was also important to be able to respond in a measured and presidentially chosen way to a Soviet attack. Certainly it would have been imprudent to suppose that the only possible Soviet attack was the massive preemptive effort to win that then appeared so prominent in Soviet military thought.

The difficulty with revisions of strategic targeting doctrine was not in the statement of sensible objectives, but in meeting them when the real work of targeting was done. Take the sparing of cities. Here the obvious problem is that many of the most important military targets are in or near cities; the seaport and naval base are examples for any one who lives in an American coastal metropolis such as New York. Moreover, if you made a visible decision to spare your opponent's cities, you might encourage him to put crucial targets in cities, where they would be sheltered by your pledge—and if this worry reminds you of rule making among clever children playing games, it may tell you what some strategic planners are like. A compromise on this question was announced by Elliot Richardson when he was Nixon's Secretary of Defense: the United States would not target "cities as such." Just how many warheads would hit how many cities in any given attack on targets not themselves "cities as such" is a question that policy makers seldom ask and that strategic planners do not eagerly discuss, but an illuminating public report does exist.

In the 1970s the Arms Control and Disarmament Agency (ACDA) reported to Congress a model retaliatory attack by U.S. forces, which it claimed was based on existing targeting doctrine; cities as such were not targeted, but military and industrial targets were not spared because they happened to be in cities. Casualties on each side were on the order of one hundred million, and were reported as "only a part of the total disaster." In that attack sixty warheads were aimed at targets in Moscow, and attacks just as severe in relation to population were made on 80 percent of all cities and towns with populations of twenty-five thousand or more. Arms Control officials do not speak for SAC, and their assessments are not always dispassionate, but I know of no official objection to the targeting in this report.[57]

Quite aside from the enormous hazards of any "general exchange," there is trouble for strategic planners in the complex interconnection between one use of strategic weapons and another. Leaders of SAC have historically been dedicated to what they have seen as their primary task—the ability to execute the strongest possible attack—or counterattack—on Soviet war-making capabilities, so that most of the weapons at their disposal have been designed and targeted for early large-scale use. To fire anything less than a full salvo from a missile submarine is to risk the loss of its remaining warheads to a prompt counterattack on the location that may be exposed by the firing of even one missile. But what sort of limited war would you have after firing a couple of hundred warheads from one submarine? The case of the MX missile may be even more striking. If you invest enough money in weapon-by-weapon command and control, you can fire a single missile, but how "small" would your action be? The ten warheads of one MX missile have a total destructive power one hundred times as great as the bomb that fell on Hiroshima. I recognize that these are extreme cases. You could use bombers or single-warhead Minuteman missiles in a more discriminating way, but those uses too would have risks and complexities. Planners working on limited options do not have an easy task. It is really not surprising that when Caspar Weinberger was asked in 1982 what he thought of the chances of controlling any sustained nuclear conflict he answered, "I just don't have any idea; I don't know that anybody has any idea."[58]

A still deeper difficulty in meeting the demands of new targeting doctrines is that when military planners set out to plan attacks that would do everything the new doctrines asked for, while maintaining in reserve the force required to meet the continuing (and even expanded) requirement for further reply to further attack, they regularly found themselves without enough warheads to do the job. There were many reasons for this shortage. Strategic planners with a hard eye on what can go wrong are conservative about what it takes to get through and kill a given set of targets. As intelligence improves and doctrinal requirements increase, the number of targets of all sorts expands. Some sets of targets, like the leadership class that was so interesting to thinkers in the Carter White House, are spread all over the place; they can be "collocated" in cities; they can be sent to deep shelters; they can also be hidden.

To be able to do such large-scale "limited" jobs and at the same time to be ready for a full role in full-scale war would require forces that the United States simply did not have, and there was no answer in adding warheads, not only because two could play at that game but because so many Soviet targets could be moved around, or hidden, or even fired first. American strategic planners knew that many among their own commanders, faced with the terrible choice, would rather fire their missiles than let them perish unused; they had to ask themselves how to cope with a parallel preference on the Soviet side. Above and beyond all these difficulties was the question that would surely come from any president in a situation so desperate that he must consider the use of nuclear weapons; if we do this to him, what will he do to us? *Any* answer would be a guess, but any *honest* answer would have to respect the reality that there was no American attack of any size or shape that could reliably protect the country from a terrible reply. Assured destruction of all sorts remained a capability of the other side, with or without the existence of carefully designed American options. Whatever other value any particular targeting doctrine might have, it could not change that reality.[59]

The Freeze

The nuclear stalemate that planners could not escape proved equally resistant in these years to the arguments of arms controllers and antinuclear activists. Arms controllers on the whole would have been content with relatively modest steps to strengthen strategic stability and get firm upper limits on offensive forces, but the best of them were well aware of the excessive magnitude of the forces permitted to both sides by the SALT II treaty that was signed in the spring of 1979, hotly debated at Senate hearings in that summer, and forced onto the shelf by the Soviet invasion of Afghanistan at the end of the year. The SALT II process in itself contributed to new American weapons as the need for Senate support led Carter to approve new programs for which he himself had little enthusiasm.

The ardent opponents of all nuclear weaponry had even less impact on the superpower stalemate. An awakened awareness of the nature of nuclear war did develop in the later 1970s, and it was intensified by the careless rhetoric and the large military buildup of the early Reagan years. Believers in nuclear moderation were numerous in Congress, and while most of the new programs were approved, there was effective and growing opposition to such ill-conceived systems as MX-in-Minuteman.

But the largest single effort to slow the arms race, the nuclear freeze movement, was also the least successful. It found friends in Congress, but only after its leaders agreed to widen its original purpose to include a freeze by the Soviet Union too. In 1984 it also won the support of the Democratic candidate, Walter Mondale, but a bilateral freeze never came close to happening. There was much that was right and strong about the movement for a freeze. No one could think for even a few minutes about what a hundred warheads might do and not conclude that when the two great rivals had tens of thousands between them, enough might be enough. There was also good sense in the notion that the two should simply stop where they were, as a first step. But the freeze in its official form called for a bilateral, verifiable, and sweeping agreement, and that was very much easier to demand than to get. Such a freeze would have been hard to negotiate because of special Soviet concerns with third countries like China, but it was also hard to sell to the American people as a whole because so many Americans remained persuaded that the best defense was to have an excellent offense (and maybe defense too). Americans wanted arms limitation, but they also wanted not to tie their hands at a time when men they trusted, in and out of uniform, in and out of the White House, said that we must build new systems or fall dangerously behind. In the end the underlying motivation of the leaders of the freeze came from their opposition to *American* weaponry, and that motive was never dominant in more than a minority of American minds.[60]

BEHIND the rhetoric, first of present danger and then of future safety, there was much less than met the ear. There was no Soviet coercion, and neither was there early prospect of escape from nuclear vulnerability under a space shield. The strategic balance in 1988 is essentially what it was ten years before. New warheads have been deployed by thousands on both sides, but older warheads have been withdrawn, and the overall numbers of weapons and of megatons have not changed much on either side. No new deployment has had any large effect on the enduring strategic stalemate. It is true that one important part of Ronald Reagan's rhetoric changed: An American strategic force that was depicted as dangerously inferior in 1980 became in his view a fully effective deterrent in time for the election of 1984, and his newly found confidence in the strategic balance continued to grow stronger in his second term. But in reality the changes made in these years by his own new departures was small. There was no MX on station before 1986, and only a handful of B-1 bombers. The most important improvements of the 1980s have come in the deployment of accurate cruise missiles both at sea and on strategic aircraft—Carter programs modestly enlarged by Reagan. One is forced to ask whether it would not have been better to go through this period with a lower dose of unnecessary fear.

The enduring strength of the stalemate lay in the survivable second-strike forces of both sides. Each could make replies of many kinds to any surprise attack; neither could hope to win, and the possibility of catastrophe in any open conflict between the two was obvious and large. McNamara was right. In the 1970s and the 1980s what he had come to understand in 1964 remained entirely true: When each side could certainly deliver many kinds of destruction, neither side could meet the standard of limiting damage to itself. The governing reality of the nuclear balance is the prospect of shared and sweeping catastrophe in any resort to nuclear warheads by either side. It is not surprising that this reality has been stronger than either the nightmares of believers in present danger or the hopeful vision of Ronald Reagan.

There is considerable comfort in this demonstration by history of the strength and stability of the strategic stalemate. It rests in 1988 on the same enormous phenomenon that has sustained it since the 1950s—on what each superpower can most assuredly do to the other, and on the caution that this enormous reality imposes on both sides. Just as persistent as this reality is the recognition it has had from statesmen. Soviet leaders have respected it, and so indeed has Ronald Reagan. I have not found all his opinions persuasive, but it is important to remember to his credit a short sentence that he has been repeating since the spring of 1982: "A nuclear war cannot be won and must never be fought."[61] There is no better basic guideline to the politics of the bomb.

▮ XIII ▮

Lessons
and Hopes

W E HAVE COME A LONG WAY. We have seen these weapons made and used in World War II and then not used again. We have seen men learning about them, deciding their countries must have them, feeling their cautionary weight in crisis, trying with very modest success to bring them under control, and debating the ways to deal with their danger. Of course the story does not stop. The record provides its own warning against prediction. Who would have picked Cuba ahead of time as the site of the gravest crisis of the time? Surprise has been the commonplace of the nuclear age. It may be imprudent to offer conclusions, but it would be worse to hold them back. On balance the major lessons of this history are more encouraging than not: lessons of attention to both danger and survival, lessons of prudence and rationality, and lessons on the pertinence of such ancient moral imperatives as truthfulness, courage, and hope.

The Abundant Arsenals

In the fiftieth year of the age of fission, the bombs abound. Together the two superpowers have more than fifty thousand warheads. Small parts of these two forces could bring ruin to both nations. Britain, France, and China may have a thousand or two among the three of them; comparatively, these forces are small, but the gross destructive power in British, French, and Chinese hands is hundreds of times greater than anything ever found in a peacetime arsenal before the atom was split. In terms of what each of these three forces could do to any enemy in all-out nuclear conflict, they are much more like the superpower arsenals than they are like the capabilities of merely conventional forces in any age. At least two more countries are as close to a bomb as they want to be. India has had an explosion but may not have made warheads. Israel has had no evident explosion, but it would be a most imprudent government which did not assume that if the Israelis should ever decide to use bombs, they would be right at hand.

The forces that have driven governments to have the bomb, and then to have it in large quantities, are not trivial. In each of the first five cases the national decision to have this weapon was essentially unchallenged. It would take a great revision of basic policy and purpose to change the decisions of Roosevelt, Stalin, and Attlee, to reverse the process of development that governed successive French prime ministers through the 1950s, or to change the judgment of Mao that for nuclear deterrence China must be dependent on no one but herself. The five sets of motives are entangled in specific historical situations, but they all rest on the deep conviction that it is intolerable to accept a future in which others have this weapon and not we, where "we" in every case means the responsible leaders and scientists of a nation that will not willingly accept second rank. Even for Stalin it was not "I" but "we." For the Indians and the Israelis it is different. The bomb for India remains a doubtful prize in that something about this apocalyptically destructive standard of greatness is not truly Indian. The bomb for the Israelis is something they have decided they must have at hand not merely to match or outmatch some nuclear competitor, and not for prestige, but as protection against a continuing and presently nonnuclear threat of national extinction.

To have the bomb was the initial imperative, but soon after having it came the need to have enough. That need has been greatest for the two superpowers, each concerned with what the other might have or come to have, and each drawn by fear and hope to the pursuit of technological and military "advances," some of them impressive in their raw capabilities and others disappointing. The hydrogen bomb certainly "worked," but effective air defense has been always out of reach for both sides. Bombers are followed by ballistic missiles; MIRVs are added; accuracy improves. Missile defenses are planned, then held back by agreement, and then dreamed of again. The complexity of the sets of systems has multiplied, and so have the numbers of warheads.

Both governments have found it a heavy task to have what they think is enough. Only intermittently has either side felt that its nuclear position and prospects were satisfactorily sufficient. The Americans felt that way in the first years after Hiroshima, until the rude shock of the first Soviet test. The two sides then competed all through the 1950s, to get H-bombs and then ballistic missiles. After 1962 the Americans had another few years, perhaps as many as ten, when the Eisenhower-Kennedy triad seemed safely in place, and enough was enough. But what was enough for the Americans was more than enough to stir a strong Soviet response. The decade between 1965 and 1975 was marked by a massive Soviet buildup, which eventually produced renewed American fear. Since the midseventies Moscow has been less uneasy about the strategic balance than Washington, but neither side has been truly comfortable. In the eighties the pace of technological competition and of new deployments has quickened in both countries. Meanwhile MIRVs on both sides have multiplied the numbers of warheads on strategic ballistic missiles. In the 1970s, a time when the prophets of present danger saw the United States as standing still or even sliding back, the numbers of such American warheads went from two thousand to seven thousand. Only in raw megatonnage has there been even modest restraint on either side. The two mammoth sets of offensive systems now have fewer warheads in the multimegaton class and less total explosive power than they once had. But these reductions tell us more about the irrational megatonnage of earlier years than about present arsenals, which remain excessive on both sides.

The decisions leading to massive and varied deployments have been dominated by the conviction in each government that it could not tolerate the nuclear superiority of the other. In their initial decision to have the bomb, the British and French certainly, and the Chinese perhaps, had a similar conviction that they must not be "behind." But soon all three were forced to understand that it would be hard enough to have a force that no hostile superpower could wholly destroy, so that its survivable reply must be respected. The nuclear powers of the second rank have been governed not by any search for parity, but by their sense of what will allow them self-confidence in their dealings with the superpowers. Their calculations have regularly included the question of the value of these weapons for their relations with friendly nations as well as with the not-so-friendly Russians.

The Tradition of Nonuse

The competition to develop and deploy nuclear weapons and fragmentary defenses against them is far less arresting, at the end of the first half century, than the fact that since the first two bombs were dropped in August 1945 no government has used a single warhead against an enemy. In my opinion no government has ever come close.

Plans for use and war-fighting doctrines have existed. Moments of danger have occurred, but such moments have been few, and the real risk has been more in what might have gone out of control than in the intentions or desires of responsible leaders. Open atomic threats have been generally ineffective, and their value—even their existence—often exaggerated in retrospect. We have found an instructive difference between doctrine and behavior, theory and practice, in the time of Dwight Eisenhower. The weapons were secretly asserted to be "as available for use" as any others, and both the president and his secretary of state, in many ways so different from each other, were agreed on the value of readiness to threaten use. But the real choices of this careful and experienced president tell a different story—one of respect for the opinions of Asian adversaries and European friends, of steady understanding that nuclear weapons are different, and of close control that was recognized and accepted by all subordinate commanders. In the age of Radford and LeMay, the doctrines in which they deeply believed—that nuclear weapons should be used whenever needed, even in small wars—these doctrines were disregarded at every moment of choice. A tradition of nonuse took root and grew strong, proving itself most conspicuously in the Vietnam War, where the use of nuclear weapons was the one solution that had no serious advocate. The best consequence of that war is that it reinforced the tradition of nonuse.

The Soviets have not used the bomb either, and while estimates of Soviet decision making must be made without access to Soviet archives, the public record makes clear the great distance between Soviet nuclear bluster and Soviet nuclear action. There is no evidence that the Soviet government has ever come close to using even one of its warheads, and no evidence that Soviet bomb rattling has had any large effect anywhere. The most dangerous moments may also be the most revealing—moments of confrontation with the United States over Berlin and Cuba, and at a much lower level with China over a long common border. In these moments what is most visible in retrospect is Soviet caution, as clear when the immediate opponent has only a small supply of nuclear warheads—China in 1969—as in facing an evidently superior United States in 1962. The Soviets have faced nothing as painfully unsuccessful as the American effort in Vietnam, but they have encountered reverses at least as large politically: the "loss" of Yugoslavia, the "loss" of Egypt, and largest of all, the "loss" of China. For Soviet leaders too the nonuse of nuclear weapons is now a strong tradition, and as far as anyone in the West can tell, that shared tradition is as welcome on one side of the iron curtain as on the other.

What Thomas Schelling in 1960 was the first to call the "tradition" of nonuse is the most important single legacy of the first half century of fission.[1] Its power is visible in the behavior of superpowers, lesser nuclear powers, and nonnuclear nations. No government that has nuclear weapons is now unaware of the enormous political cost of using them for any but the gravest and most obviously defensive reasons. No government without such weapons needs to be easily coerced by nuclear threats from others, because both history and logic make it clear that no government will resort to nuclear weapons over a less than mortal question. Having and not having nuclear weapons are not now a part of the ordinary daily currency of international politics.

The tradition of nonuse has strengthened with each decade. It is a long distance from the untroubled choice of Harry Truman in 1945 to the politically compelled decision of Richard Nixon in 1969 that he simply could not make the nuclear threat in Vietnam that he believed he had seen Eisenhower use successfully in Korea. The forces arrayed against breaking the tradition were overwhelming to Nixon in 1969, and they are stronger now.

The existence of the weapons and the absence of their use have their roots in the same enormous fact: that nuclear explosions are vastly more deadly than any ever known before. Fear of what these weapons can do in the hands of an enemy has been the driving force in the creation of nearly every nuclear arsenal, and the same fear has been decisive at moments of crisis in producing caution among decision makers.

The Future Survival of the Superpowers

The United States and the Soviet Union threaten not only each other's existence, but the whole human future. Only these two governments have had moments of direct confrontation in which nuclear danger became a present and visible reality to all the world. It has been and is still a matter of the greatest importance that these two arsenals should never be engaged against each other.

The double reality is that the arsenals cannot be abolished and that neither country can now build an effective defense of its homeland. For both governments, whatever their leaders may claim to hope, it is impossible to suppose that nuclear weaponry can be altogether abandoned. Absent the open world of Niels Bohr, these two adversarial systems of politics and power, beset by mutual mistrust and possessing such numbers of warheads that their abolition could never be verified for sure in either country, will not let go of the one protection they have found against the warheads of the other. Each arsenal may get larger or smaller, but there is no early prospect that either side will give up its ability to reply to a first strike by the other. Reagan's personal vision of a space shield that blocks the missiles as a roof keeps out the rain is a dream with no basis in technical possibility. Technology makes it possible and mutual fear makes it inescapable that the two great offensive deterrents will remain for a long time to come.

When political leaders in Moscow and Washington think about nuclear war, what they think about first is what such a war could mean for their own country, and they have understood for more than thirty years that this war must not happen. No one in either government can hope to know what the full effect of a nuclear attack on the homeland would be. The "literature" on the physical effects of nuclear explosions is enormous, and insofar as it is honest it recognizes that the subject is surrounded by enormous uncertainty. Only two primitive weapons have ever been used in war, and those two events do not begin to tell us what could happen to a whole society under large-scale assault. Uncertainties about targeting policy and levels of operational effectiveness are equally inescapable. Who knows what kind of attack or response would in fact be ordered at the terrible moment of choice, and who can tell in advance just how many of what weapons would work as their designers intended? The "fog of war" was familiar to Tolstoy in the nineteenth century and to generals and statesmen on all sides in the two great world wars of the twentieth century. But the fog that shrouds the unknown realities of a nuclear war between the two superpowers has wholly new dimensions.

Leaders cannot see through this fog, but they still know all they need to know: that they do not want to bring on their own country a nuclear strike. Given the warheads currently deployed, just one incoming strategic warhead on just one strictly military target—a missile silo perhaps, or a submarine base—would be the worst event for either government since World War II. Ten warheads on ten such targets would be much more than ten times worse, presenting not only immediate and hideous devastation, but questions of the utmost urgency and foreboding about the next decisions of both sides. A hundred warheads, on no-matter-what targets, would be an instant disaster still more terrible. A thousand warheads would be a catastrophe beyond all human experience. Any and all of these things could happen with an expenditure of only a fraction of the weapons at the ready in each country. As I put it almost twenty years ago, "There is no level of superiority which will make a strategic first strike between the two great states anything but an act of utter folly."[2]

There are only two situations in which the deterrent power of these appalling possibilities might be overcome. One is the prospect of some defeat or disaster so large and so unacceptable that the hazards of nuclear war would seem preferable. The other is the possibility of a disarming attack on the nuclear systems of the adversary. Let us call one the fear of conventional disaster, and the other the hope of nuclear victory, where both the disaster and the victory are very large indeed. We can dismiss the hope of nuclear victory, because as we have seen both sides have ceased to believe in such a prospect; both have been amply deterred *in fact.* There is no reason for either side to allow any such prospect to the other.

Nor has either superpower ever faced a prospect of any conventional disaster even remotely large enough to provoke use of nuclear weapons. Each side has carefully avoided that kind of challenge to the other. When we looked at Khrushchev's Berlin crisis of 1958–62 we found that the existence of this nuclear danger—this real possibility—was in itself fully deterrent to Khrushchev himself. We do not have to know just what Eisenhower and Kennedy would have done to know that their Soviet adversary had no desire to find out. A parallel caution on the American side has been so visible as not to require detailed study.

It has become common practice in the nuclear decades not to run such risks. Exceptional cases like the attempt to take West Berlin and the placement of missiles in Cuba are now assessed on both sides as unsuccessful and imprudently dangerous. Nothing could do more for the recognized reduction of nuclear danger than strengthening the conditions that will discourage such adventures. In this connection it is not trivial that Mikhail Gorbachev has made a sweeping and categorical denial of any Soviet desire to challenge the West by force, either in Europe or in the Middle East.[3] Words alone are not enough, but they are an important beginning. They can be used to encourage behavior that fits them and to challenge behavior that does not. I believe there would be a parallel benefit in a more general American acknowledgement that our opposition to communist oppression in Eastern Europe does not include the readiness to run a risk of war; the historical record on the matter is clear.

Depriving the other power of any rational hope of nuclear victory has so far proved relatively easy for both governments. We have seen this "second-strike capability" challenged by technological change, and we have seen its sturdiness debated hotly in the years in which many Americans perceived a window of vulnerability. But we have also found no moment since the 1950s when either government could see any prospect of nuclear victory at acceptable cost. From the Geneva summit of 1955 to the time of Reagan and Gorbachev in the late 1980s political leaders have agreed that a Soviet-American nuclear war would be a shared disaster.

We have seen that early in his presidency Eisenhower recognized the importance of second-strike survivability in deterring surprise attack. In his years the groundwork was laid for the survivable triad—bombers, submarines, and land-based missiles. In the Kennedy years attention shifted to the next question: "How much is enough?" We have seen how crudely that question was answered by the criterion of survivable second-strike forces sufficient to produce "assured destruction" even after absorbing the strongest possible Soviet first strike. Mathematical estimates of this kind of enoughness changed from time to time, and no one paid much attention to them. More important was a different assessment: that beyond a certain point, when thousands of the most important targets had been hit, the value of additional warheads would be affected by the law of diminishing returns. It was in this brutal sense that enough was considered enough in 1965. This crude criterion was reinforced by recognition that there was no way to get and keep a satisfactory capability for limiting damage to ourselves. There was survivable overkill on both sides.

We can make a simpler and still more brutal estimate now at the end of the 1980s, when the number of warheads that can survive for a second strike may be five times larger than twenty years ago, before the multiple-warhead submarine missile. American second-strike forces are—to put it mildly—ample. By any measure of Soviet appetite for self-destruction, the Kremlin is deterred from getting into a general nuclear war.

So is the United States. Even when the United States had a monopoly, no American political leader was tempted to start a nuclear war with the Soviet Union, and once the Soviet Union had survivable weapons of its own it was plain that "preventive war" was impossible. There has been an enduring belief that massive Soviet conventional aggression might require a nuclear response, and since 1949 our policy has been to use nuclear weapons if necessary in reply to Soviet aggression in Europe. There has been a similar appearance of readiness in relation to Korea since 1953, and in relation to the Middle East since 1979. None of these undertakings reflects a desire to pick a nuclear quarrel with the Soviet Union. From Eisenhower onward, American leaders have understood that any American choice that brought even a small number of nuclear warheads on targets in the United States would be a disaster. Eisenhower and Kennedy accepted the reality of two-way deterrence in years when others with less understanding and less responsibility thought they saw an American nuclear superiority with great strategic and political weight. What Eisenhower and Kennedy found conclusive was what could, and must not, happen to the United States.

It is sometimes argued that democracies are more readily deterred than dictatorships, and it is certainly true that under Stalin there was a Soviet ruthlessness about human life that has no American parallel. But if historically there has been an imbalance in ruthlessness, there is a second imbalance that runs the other way. The people of the Soviet Union—emphatically including their leaders—remember a "merely conventional" war, between 1941 and 1945, that has no match in the

American memory. Those who have known the worst of the conventional World War II are the most wary of any World War III. It is an error of the most insensitive sort (and one that is frequent among right-wing analysts) to suppose that this Soviet experience weighs on the side of belligerence and not caution.

The stalemate that keeps nuclear peace between the superpowers is so deep and strong that it is not affected by the relative ruthlessness of the two societies or their different experiences of twentieth-century war. What each can do to the other, whoever goes first, is more than enough to stay every hand that does not belong to a madman. Leaders on both sides have been sane, and they have also been watched by sane associates.

The imperative of avoiding nuclear war imposes great caution on both governments. In the words of Raymond Aron in 1966, there is a "solidarity of the Great Powers against the total war of which they would be the first victims." They remained determined, as he thought they were when he wrote, "not to interdestroy themselves."[4]

This mutual deterrence has been steady through more than three decades of dramatic variations in the relative numbers of warheads, in the explosive power of arsenals, in the accuracy and reliability of delivery systems, and in the degree of vulnerability of particular systems on each side. The record makes it clear that the sturdiness of the balance does not rest on having as much of this or that system as the other side. Such partial enumerations are not a good guide to the basic strategic assessments of the political decision makers on both sides. What each side has always seen in the other is a capability for strategic reply that makes it wholly unacceptable to run any avoidable risk of nuclear war. It is, to repeat, what can happen to your own side that counts most. We have found uninterrupted awareness of that danger on both sides, and what demonstrates it most clearly is what each side does *not* do at moments of real crisis—it does not make any move that could end its own control over nuclear danger. That is the caution we have seen in Berlin from 1958 to 1963, in Cuba in the autumn of 1962, and on the Soviet-Chinese border in 1969. There is no visible correlation between any numerical advantage and this caution.

There is a parallel lack of correlation, throughout this period, between merely numerical measures of strength and what the leaders of the two powers believe about nuclear war. On the American side the pattern is intrinsically unchanging from Eisenhower to Reagan: There will be only losers in any general nuclear war. On the Soviet side there is change, but it is not what believers in the importance of numerical superiority would expect. It is Khrushchev, with his forces outweighed and outnumbered, who tries nuclear blackmail, and his generals who write of socialist victory in any general war. In 1968, when hundreds of big Soviet missiles are coming on line, it is the military leader Marshal V. D. Sokolovsky who warns that the losses of a world nuclear war would be suffered by both sides. In the age of excessive Soviet throwweight that has followed, the Soviet government has continually strengthened its assertions on this point, until Gorbachev can say in 1987 that "a nuclear tornado will sweep away socialists and capitalists, the just and sinners alike."[5]

No Superpower War

The most important thing that the United States and the Soviet Union can do to stay clear of the "nuclear tornado" is to see to it that they have no war of any kind with each other. Here too we have a good historical record to build on. Each government has been extremely cautious about the use of military force against the other. Stalin's blockade of Berlin and Kennedy's blockade of Cuba were limited, and neither led to open battle. Nonetheless these examples ought not to be repeated; the real lesson of the crises over Berlin and Cuba is that neither side should take such risks again.

The avoidance of war means the avoidance of all steps that can bring Soviet and American forces into open conflict with one another. This leaves room for contests in which each of the superpowers supports some other combatant, and even for conflicts in which one side is directly engaged against forces supported by the other, as in Korea, Vietnam, and Afghanistan. But each side has an interest in avoiding direct military challenge to the other, and the reality of nuclear danger makes that interest very large indeed.

I do not argue that a single battle between regiments or cruisers or fighter aircraft will inevitably mean nuclear war. The interest in avoiding such a war would not end with the first exchange of shots, and we will come back to the war-ending problem. Nonetheless it is easier to avoid escalation before combat than after, and the prudence historically displayed by the leaders of both countries in the avoidance of open combat deserves attention and imitation from their successors.

In Europe this constraint holds both sides back behind the borders set at the end of World War II. Each side knows that the other will fight if those lines are crossed, and neither side can have any certainty that the resulting conflict would be contained below the nuclear level. The danger here is not primarily a matter of doctrine or of specific deployments, and there is a certain unreality in debates among "experts" about the precise weapons systems and doctrines that will deter. Deterrence is inherent in what any nuclear power can do if it chooses, and also in the possibility that open warfare may drive one side or both to permit in anger what it would never consider in peace. However much one may hope and pray, as I would, that such a war could be kept limited, the danger of unlimited escalation is inescapable.

Clearly the superpowers should avoid open conflict with each other in outer space. Space-based defensive systems will always be open to attack, and so far the evidence supports the view that such systems are easier to knock down than to put up. There are important existing assets in space whose vulnerability is also likely to be high, particularly the reconnaissance satellites that are essential to American confidence in strategic parity. The value of peaceful behavior in space will be high, and to sustain it will require agreements respected by both governments. Such understandings may require both sides to accept space reconnaissance that is troubling to particular interests—for example the ability of Soviet satellites to keep track of American surface ships. The matter is complex, and the achievement of international understanding will not be easy, but the peaceful use of space has had a broadly stabilizing effect for almost thirty years, and both sides have a strong interest in protecting it.

What has actually happened should not blind us to the significance of what has not. Even more instructive than crises over Berlin and Cuba are the military challenges that have not been made in the nuclear years. We have made no military response to repeated Soviet acts of repression in areas that matter more to Moscow than to Washington, and although Moscow has continually sought to separate the United States from its friends and allies, most conspicuously in Western Europe, there has been no Soviet resort to warfare in the area. Even in Berlin, where Khrushchev tried atomic diplomacy, the attempt was in the end exposed as a bluff.

The Acceptance of Coexistence

The avoidance of war implies the acceptance of coexistence. This proposition has been emotionally hard for many in both countries, but since it is only by war that either one can hope to bring an end to the power of the other, it follows that each must accept the other's existence. Internal change may come—has already come—to one or both, but change imposed by external force is excluded.

When I speak of coexistence, I am not going beyond the plain meaning of the word: that neither makes war on the other. The word is suspect to some Americans because it has sometimes been used to mask Soviet policies that are not benign. Nonetheless the word itself is straightforward, and we should remember that the first man to use it in the National Security Council was George Humphrey, no friend of communism. What led Humphrey to advocate "a policy of coexistence" in 1954 was the imperative that there should not be nuclear war with the Soviet Union.[6] Both sides have in fact been practicing coexistence in the nuclear decades, and the prospect that they will continue can be greatly improved by more explicit recognition of what they have gained from the avoidance of war.

What is not so clear is the behavior that each country should expect of the other and require of itself under the imperative of coexistence. We cannot here make general rules that will easily command general support, but we can read a few lessons from the historical record:

> First, it greatly serves the interests of both sides that they should not have open battle with each other.
>
> Second, neither should trespass by its own armed force of any kind against the clear and strong commitment of the other; that is the rule for peace in Europe and in the Caribbean.
>
> Third, all nuclear forces should be designed for survivable sufficiency, since nothing more can be achieved, and since the attempt to get more will only arouse political fear and disturbing reply; that is the lesson of American overarmament in the fifties and sixties (with thermonuclear weapons and MIRVs) and Soviet overarmament thereafter.
>
> Fourth, the stakes in other parts of the world should never be allowed to reach the nuclear level; understanding of this point has been plain in the cases of Vietnam and Afghanistan, and I believe it now applies also to Korea, Japan, and the Middle East.

The defense of the two Koreas from one another is best assured by the visible unwillingness of either superpower to support hostilities begun by its Korean ally. The Soviets made that mistake once, and their behavior over a thirty-five-year period argues that they have no intention of making it again. Nor will the United States support South Korea if it should begin a war. The situation is not comfortable, but it is stable, and an American nuclear threat is not now the indispensable stiffener that the Eisenhower administration believed it to be in 1953. There need be no hurry in any formal revision of a long-standing declaratory policy, but it will be right for every president after Ronald Reagan to examine with care his own view of what kind of weapon it would ever be wise to use first in Korea.

A similar inquiry is needed in the still more important case of Japan. In the strategic situation of Japan, so plainly defensive and so clearly defined by the surrounding seas, there is no reason to believe that there need ever be a situation in which only a first use of nuclear weapons could ward off defeat. Japanese self-confidence is sturdy, based as it is on recognition that there are no Soviet invaders in prospect. With good sense on both sides, the Americans and the Japanese together can keep nuclear danger out of the Japanese future.

The Middle East is a good place for a firm and early American decision that the United States will not be the first to use nuclear weapons. We have seen wars of many kinds in that region in the last forty years, but none in which there was any call for American warheads. The American alert of 1973, as its authors have acknowledged, was no more than a diplomatic signal in a situation in which there was no desire by either superpower for any direct encounter. In early 1980, after the Soviet invasion of Afghanistan, American fear of further Soviet advance led to the announcement of the so-called Carter Doctrine, which seemed to promise a first use if necessary, but no one has ever presented a persuasive argument that such a use could lead to a good result. The nation which is first to use nuclear weapons in the Middle East runs an overwhelming risk of becoming the long-term loser in the area simply because it will inevitably be held responsible for whatever happens next. The strategic defense of the Middle East requires less apocalyptic kinds of strength. Here as elsewhere in the developing world it is the political and social stability of the countries of each region that matters most, and American nuclear weapons can make no contribution to that.

This negative judgment obviously does not constitute a policy. It does not tell us how to discourage Soviet troublemaking of the sort that has helped to make Ethiopia a disaster area. Neither détente nor confrontation offers a sovereign remedy in such cases. My own belief is that over time it will turn out that neither superpower can hope to bring much of the third world under its durable control. All sorts of forces, demographic, economic, ideological, and nationalistic, are arrayed against any such result. Otherwise the study of nuclear danger can tell us very little about such hard areas for American policymakers as the Middle East or Central America or the Philippines, just as it cannot tell the Politburo how to handle its overextension in Afghanistan and in Africa.

The superpowers do share one great common interest in all countries without nuclear weapons: that such countries should steer clear of nuclear danger by not seeking warheads for themselves. It will take much careful work, and a new level of mutual trust, to find ways to advance this common interest more effectively, but the challenge is clear and the rewards would be great. The United States and the Soviet Union have cooperated to some degree in the effort to constrain nuclear weapons development in South Africa. There will be both need and opportunity for further cooperation in pursuing a clear common interest.

The Failure of Atomic Diplomacy

As the tradition of nonuse grows stronger, the role of atomic diplomacy necessarily shrinks. What you can do only at very great risk to yourself, you cannot plausibly threaten for any ordinary political purpose. When we add up the achievements of atomic diplomacy we find a thin record. Khrushchev's bluster won no rewards. Boasts of the power of nuclear warning, as by Truman in his old age to Senator Jackson about Iran, prove to be only imagined war stories, understandable but not credible. We have seen that there must be doubt about the effect of Eisenhower's signals in Korea, and still more doubt about the recollections of Richard Nixon. In the real record the Nixon threats never happened. Only in the cases of Quemoy and Matsu is there a significant likelihood that a nuclear threat was decisive, a small harvest. The legends of atomic diplomacy have been appealing to those who oppose all nuclear weapons and easily believe whatever is said against them, but they have also been too readily accepted by those who believe that whoever is "ahead" in nuclear strength will dominate whoever is "behind."

The ineffectiveness of atomic diplomacy was certainly not predicted at the beginning. In 1945, at the end of an enormous war, it was only too natural to suppose that a weapon vastly more powerful than any before it would confer a new level of influence. It would have been astonishing if some Americans had not had that expectation. But the expectation was quickly disappointed, and the same thing happened repeatedly in later years. Both in Killian's report of 1954 and in Gaither's of 1957 there were urgent recommendations for the conduct of a diplomatic campaign designed to bring about a durable settlement with Moscow while the United States still had a clear upper hand in nuclear strength, on the theory that this upper hand could be translated into a diplomatic success. Nothing came of these recommendations. Neither Eisenhower nor Dulles ever showed any practical interest in such diplomacy. On the Soviet side the evidence is not so clear, but in the 1970s there was enough Soviet talk about improvements in the correlation of forces to suggest that some Soviet leaders expected political rewards from nuclear strength. But the fact that atomic diplomacy has attracted advocates only makes the absence of its effective practice all the more impressive.

It is a long way from Khrushchev's nuclear threats to the calm and collected Soviet posture in years of undoubted Soviet strategic strength. Only Gromyko, in the 1980s, was still including nuclear threats in his diplomatic repertoire, trying to frighten Western Europe away from new deployments. In this respect as in others Gromyko was a voice from the past. He was also ineffective.

The Case of Europe

The successful coexistence of these extravagantly overequipped nuclear powers has been possible because there is literally nothing at all—no place, no ally, no "sphere of influence"—where dominance is a truly vital interest to both at once. The Soviet establishment of communist regimes in Eastern Europe was a basic cause of the *cold* war, because it was so sharply at odds with the expectation of the West that victory would mean freedom for all the peoples Hitler had overrun, but the resulting oppression has not been a cause of *real* war. Since 1945 there have been many grim happenings in Eastern Europe, and some have gravely affected relations between the superpowers, but there has been no moment of nuclear danger in this harsh history, because the interest of the United States in these countries is not and never has been a war-fighting interest. The tension between the sentiment of Americans with ties to Eastern Europe and our national unwillingness to make that part of the world a fighting interest has been a recurrent embarrassment to political leaders who have used words about American concern for "captive nations" that are much stronger than any actions the country has ever been ready to take.

I am not suggesting that it is nuclear danger as such that limits the American interest in Eastern Europe. I do not believe that the United States would have acted more strongly over Hungary or Czechoslovakia or Poland if there were no bomb. Quite aside from the nuclear stalemate, there is no American stake in those countries that compares to the interest of the Soviet Union in maintaining untroublesome regimes in the countries along her western border, across which invaders have been coming for centuries. This Soviet interest greatly outweighs the strong human feelings of individual Americans with and without ancestral ties to those countries. What happens in Eastern Europe can have great affect on Soviet-American relations, but it carries no danger of open conflict and therefore none of nuclear war.

There is a parallel absence of danger in Western Europe, as long as the countries of that region are self-confident and the tradition of mutual trust between them and the United States is maintained. While the Atlantic alliance holds together, the Russians are not coming. There is need for armed forces and need for nuclear deterrence, but these requirements do not have to pass the tests imposed by defense analysts professionally preoccupied by the possible outcomes of an extended war. The Soviet Union wants no war of any kind in Western Europe—easy pickings yes, but open warfare no. We need the Atlantic alliance to make it clear to them and to ourselves that there are no easy pickings. NATO has never been as strong in military terms as its professional commanders would like, but it has never come close to failure.

It has been hard in this European case to understand the role of nuclear weapons. The primary nuclear deterrent is American, while the primary exposure is not. It is the countries nearest to the Russians that most need protection, and none of them has its own nuclear weapons. There has also been a mistaken belief that the American nuclear umbrella could be protective only if the Americans continued to have strategic superiority. That notion is both a natural historical inheritance and a misleading export of politically naïve American strategic analysis. We have seen that for statesmen there has been a basic strategic standoff since the 1950s. It has been recognition of nuclear danger and not respect for American nuclear advantage that has ensured prudence in Moscow.

What establishes this deterrent danger is not American doctrine, and not American nuclear warheads in particular locations, but the American military presence there and the American political commitment which it represents and reinforces. The decision to use nuclear weapons will never be easier in Western Europe than anywhere else, and that theater offers no more promising outcome for any first use of these weapons than any other. But where there is a serious American engagement there is inescapable nuclear danger in any Soviet aggression—more than enough to deter. The American engagement that was enough to defend West Berlin in 1958–63 is enough to defend Western Europe today.

A defense based on nuclear weapons alone would not sustain the self-confidence of Western Europe; it would not persuade those nearest to the Soviet Union that no Kremlin leader would be tempted to try for easy pickings. Conventional forces are indispensable. There is a continuing need to keep them respectably modern and well trained, and in the future as in the past governments will do less than their military commanders would like. But these forces today are no mere trip wire. They are a guarantee that aggression against Western Europe would mean war between the superpowers, with all the risks that are inherent in that.

It is sufficient to recognize this nuclear danger as a reality, and better not to attempt judgment in advance as to where or how a president might ever give the nuclear command. As we have seen, different presidents have had different doctrinal preferences, and every president has been careful. There are vulnerabilities in every clear-cut doctrine. I myself joined with old friends in 1982 to argue that it would be much better if NATO would provide itself with conventional strength so great that it could formally and confidently adopt a policy of no first use of nuclear weapons.[7] In the years that have passed since we made that proposal it has become plain once again that our European allies will not make the balancing conventional investment because they do not think it necessary. They do not think that Soviet conventional strength is evidence of Soviet intent to make war against the West, and on the record they are right. In this situation it is well that awareness of nuclear danger should persist on both sides, as indeed it would even if there had been a full exchange of pledges on no first use.

An important less-than-nuclear deterrent in Europe is the enduring cost to the Soviet Union of any move to change a border by force, even if large-scale war should be avoided. Even such a limited grab would have the effect that Acheson foresaw in a successful Soviet coup at Berlin: It would galvanize the West and impose on the Soviet Union the increased danger to her own security that her policy in Europe is designed to fend off.

The most important purpose of the Western alliance is to underpin the political independence and self-confidence of its own members over the long run. The Soviets hope for gains in Europe, but the gains they seek are political. In the wonderful words of Sir Michael Howard, the American military presence was needed in the first place "not just in the negative role of a *deterrent* to Soviet aggression, but in the positive role of a *reassurance* to the West Europeans." Initially it was feared in Europe that there might be no general recovery of war-torn societies. But recovery came, and Western Europe has never had a better forty years. Yet the American role persists, and it is still double—to make deterrence credible and reassurance strong. In this situation it is both unseemly and destructive for American leaders to parade a fear of aggressive eight-foot Russians as so many have done in the last ten years. Michael Howard made his classic statement when this rhetoric was at its worst, and he made the point with painful clarity: American propaganda on the Soviet threat and the need for massive rearmament was spreading more fear than encouragement, until in 1982 it was "against the prospect of nuclear war itself" that the Europeans required reassurance. That reassurance today can come only from the president of the United States, and the basic message is as simple as this: "We are here, and the Russians are not coming."[8]

In 1988 I cannot say that this reassurance would be strengthened if the American government should press for a new NATO doctrine of no first use, but I do think that the next American president can very well say—in the absence of some major adverse change in Soviet behavior—that he confidently expects to sustain the tradition of nonuse during his time in office, and I think that such a statement would be reassuring. I think also that every president should examine with care the question that Kennedy put to Acheson over Berlin: At what point should he resort to nuclear weapons? I believe that both Americans and their allies prefer that the American president should have thought hard about that.

American leaders can also reassure Europe by reaffirming the reality and the value to the West of détente in Europe. We have seen that détente is now the first line of defense for West Berlin, and the American government has been uncharacteristically modest in not claiming credit for its own contribution to that result. Détente in Europe is not yet as strong as it should be, and what happened in 1980 to Solidarity in Poland had an inescapably chilling effect on East-West relations. But in Berlin and in the two Germanys détente endures, and even the wall begins to look out of date. The Soviet Union could destroy European détente in a day, but only at great cost to itself. In the hands of the self-confident détente is an important deterrent.

There is one further element of great potential importance in the security of Europe: the nuclear weapons of the British and the French. We have seen how these weapons were developed for reasons of national self-esteem, and we have seen also that their day-to-day political utility has been small. But it is wrong to suppose that they have no bearing on the possibility of a crisis caused by open Soviet aggression in Europe. There has been no such crisis since 1945, and indeed no hint of Soviet aggressive action since the pressure on West Berlin was relaxed in 1963. The relatively low importance of British and French weapons in the Berlin crisis does not tell us much about the future, because these forces—especially that of France—were then small, and also because that crisis was by its very nature a test of *American* political will. It would be another matter in the future if the Soviets should threaten open armed aggression against any part of NATO. The Soviet government would then have to ask itself what it would say about peace and war, not only to Washington, but also to London and Paris, and it is a heavy probability that it would wish to offer peace and immunity from attack to all three. Any such offer would be potentially divisive, but it would also be a demonstration of the deterrent value of all three Western nuclear forces. It would therefore constitute a reminder to the three governments that their weapons can be daunting to Moscow just as far as the will of each government can believably reach.

Like other possessors of nuclear weapons, the British and French decided to have them long before they considered the design of delivery systems or the choice of possible targets or even the question of the occasion that might justify the use of the weapon. Neither the promoters of these forces nor their critics have a notable record of analytic foresight as to what they would be good for. To men like Churchill and DeGaulle such analytic questions were trivial compared to the basic point that their great nations must not be absent from this rank of power. But the simplicities of the early years may not be good enough for the future, as indeed they are not for Americans either. The British and French nuclear forces are now facing a requirement for modernization with costs and complexities that require a new attention to questions about their value and especially their connection to deterrence in Europe. The balance of opinion is not the same in the two countries, and the channel remains politically wide. Western Europe has not developed the political coherence that great men sought in the first postwar decades. Moreover nuclear weapons can easily breed interallied mistrust. Ingenious nuclear "solutions" like the multilateral force have not always been helpful.

The growing community among former enemies suggests how much shared concern there is now among Britain and France and their West European allies. The choices ahead in the two nuclear-weapon countries are choices for leaders in London and Paris, and the historical record does not encourage unsolicited advice from Americans. The United States has sensibly learned to accept what it could not prevent. There is now a long-standing public partnership with Great Britain, and more recently the connections between the United States and France on these matters have been closer than either government has chosen to say. It would be better for all these countries and for their friends if they would tell the truth about their relationships. The general security of the West can be considerably reinforced if it turns out that there are affordable solutions to the open question of the future of British and French weapons. Such solutions could reinforce both national and European self-confidence. To put it modestly, the nuclear protection of Western Europe is no longer dependent only on the political will of the American president.

Yet the American connection remains essential today, and it is unlikely that European nuclear weapons alone will in the next twenty years make it sensible for the Americans to disengage. There is a particularly strong connection now between the American deterrent and the political stability of West Germany. There have been recurrent shocks in relations between Bonn and Washington, most of them caused by American insensitivity. I believe that an American government which puts reassurance and détente ahead of fear and confrontation will have no great trouble repairing such temporary damage. As long as Western Europe is politically self-confident, respectable in conventional strength, and properly reassured by British, French, and American presence—or even American presence alone—the Atlantic alliance is sure of peace.

The Future of Strategic Deterrence

What the second-strike triad has done for nearly thirty years the United States must go on doing: it must maintain nuclear capabilities such that no Soviet leader ever comes to think that a "nuclear tornado" is an acceptable choice. Because we live in an age in which we must expect the unexpected from science and technology, we must not let past success make us complacent about the future. In particular it would be wrong to let the ballyhoo that has marked recent advocacy of strategic defense give all forms of research and development a bad name. There should be sustained attention to the survivability of the strategic deterrent force, and it is predictable that there will be need for future contributions as notable as those made by the designers and operators of intercontinental bombers, hidden strategic submarines, and—in their own time—survivable Minutemen. A study of history is not the place for an assessment of specific future systems, but it is right to underline as a lesson of that study that the most important test of their quality will be their ability to survive a first strike and reply effectively.

The importance of survivability can also be underlined by remarking that reliable deterrence requires more than the ability to make a single terrible retaliation. Current strategic doctrine is correct in its insistence that in any reply to nuclear attack the United States must always hold in reserve forces whose continuing capabilities will block any hope that the enemy can impose surrender. My own view is even stronger: I believe that if one had to choose a single decisive measure of sufficiency for strategic forces over the next thirty years, it would be their capacity to survive sustained and repeated attack.

The most important and most often neglected element in this capability is the requirement of survivable command and control. There must be a capacity for responsible and effective choice by the president or his authorized delegate, and that capacity must survive the worst an enemy can do. This proposition has been clearly understood at the top of the Pentagon for at least a decade, but there is still much that is not as good as it should be in our systems of communication and our plans for keeping responsible centers of authority alive and effective. It is true that capacity for retaliation, for example from submarines, can exist in deterrent quantity even after central systems of command and control have been knocked out, but there are compelling reasons for doing much better than we have so far in making such a knockout difficult. Survival of central command and control on both sides could make an enormous difference in the level of catastrophe arising from nuclear war at any level.

The Imperative of War Ending

A closely related but neglected proposition is that if ever a nu-clear war begins, no matter how or by whose choice, the ending of that war will become an enormously important objective for both sides. One reason for this neglect is reluctance to confront the real-ity that since Ronald Reagan is entirely right when he says that "a nuclear war cannot be won," any nuclear war will have to end with-out victory for either side—by some joint decision of contestants both of whom are losers. That prospect is deeply unattractive to many Americans in and out of uniform (and probably to many Sovi-ets too). In the relatively marginal case of Vietnam, American ac-ceptance of failure came with the greatest reluctance and only after great national suffering. Bias against peace without victory is deep-seated—so deep-seated that many analysts are unaware of their own subjection to it and therefore unable to confront the fact that once a nuclear war has begun it would be disastrous for both sides to let the exchanges get worse. Nuclear escalation can lead only to a shared and expanding disaster. It follows that the least bad thing that the combatants can do is to stop. Their chances of achieving this result will be uncertain at best—which is of course why neither one will ever have got into this terrible situation on purpose—but those chances will be better if there continue to be leaders on both sides who can communicate with each other and with their own nu-clear forces.

Consider the case of ending a nuclear war begun by the Soviet Union. What response or lack of response has the best chance of bringing such a war to an end? I am not confident that I know the right answer to this question, but I do believe that the question itself is the right one. Once a nuclear war has begun, it is a literally vital interest for both combatants that it should end before it gets totally out of control.[9]

One way to think about the right answer is to try to see what answers would probably be wrong, and the most obvious answers of this sort turn out to be the ones routinely suggested by analysts of nuclear escalation. Given that each side has enormously redundant capabilities for destruction of all kinds, the one plainly suicidal course is to go on raising the stakes. The better choice then may be to reply at a level more moderate than that of the initial attack. It is even conceivable that there could be an attack that should receive no nu-clear reply at all. The president who chose not to reply with nuclear weapons to a single limited nuclear strike—a single warhead, perhaps, at a single strictly military target—might well be both wise and brave. It is well to remember that when Kennedy held back from instant reaction to the unauthorized Soviet attack on Rudolf Anderson's U-2, he turned out to be right.

But let me turn to the question of the shape of a second strike designed for war ending; that is the response that requires nuclear plans and capabilities prepared in advance. This subject has engaged the serious attention of many analysts, and complaints against plans for excessively destructive retaliation have come as often from believers in nuclear victory as from disbelievers in nuclear deterrence. A strong argument made by many is that there is a compelling difference between having a survivable capacity for assured destruction, a powerful deterrent to war of any kind between the superpowers, and a decision to inflict that destruction after deterrence has failed. The chance that a full retaliatory strike would be an act of national suicide is appallingly high. But it is hard to suppose that a large-scale nuclear attack on Americans or their allies could wisely be left with no reply at all.

For illustration let us assume an attack in which twenty or thirty warheads, aimed at military targets at home or abroad, have killed two hundred thousand people; the numbers are deliberately arbitrary. In nuclear terms, this is a small event, but in ordinary military and human terms it is enormous. What response has the best chance of ending the war?

I believe that the answer to this question may lie in recognition of the most important underlying political reality of any nuclear exchange—that each side must be vastly more distressed by the warheads it receives than pleased by the warheads it delivers. For this reason the nuclear strike in our example can be made a dreadful disaster for the enemy by a response that is clearly and visibly smaller than the initial attack. Let us suppose that we make a reply with half as many warheads—ten or fifteen, also aimed at military targets, preferably lower in yield, and designed to kill fewer people, indeed just as few as possible. I believe that such a reply would be entirely sufficient to demonstrate the urgency of an immediate cease-fire, and such an immediate cease-fire—no matter who had gained or lost what before the nuclear exchange began—is the best available next step for both sides. Further use of nuclear weapons by either side could only lead on to further replies in which both sides would have further terrible losses.

In any situation in which nuclear weapons were being used by the two superpowers, no matter how it started and no matter how small the first use, the notion of victory in the traditional sense would be an illusion. In a world with thousands of survivable weapons on both sides there can be no such victory. In this situation a strategy that is visibly *not* one of escalation presents a clear-cut invitation to stop. No one can guarantee that the invitation will be accepted; any nuclear war will have among its hazards the possibility that one side or the other or both, once the horror begins, may be unable to recognize the commanding shared interest in cease-fire. But I think one can say of the less-than-equal reply that it has a commandingly better chance of eliciting a rational response than any reply that enlarges the scale of destruction.

The less-than-equal reply has one further advantage: It fits the requirement that one's own arsenal must never be exhausted. In a war of full-scale retaliation there is a real danger of early exhaustion. Strategic planners are familiar with the traditional double requirement that a second strike must be as effective as possible against enemy strategic power and that ample reserves must be held back. They also know that no single strike, first or second, can disarm the enemy; effective damage limitation is beyond their reach. So they are led to plan very large attacks that will *not* bring victory. Planners can try to escape this difficulty by calling for more procurement, but the trouble is that even if their calls should be answered even more abundantly than in recent decades, both the number of targets and the unknown location of many of them will always outrun the planners' capabilities. In the world of strategic parity the planners have always had enough for deterrence, but never enough for victory. In that situation the attempt to win is the way to suicide.

The Wide Band of Strategic Parity

Strategic stability between the superpowers, as we have seen, does not depend on a closely calibrated equality of their nuclear forces. We have not bedeviled our discussion with extended statistics on weapons systems, but we have seen that ever since each side has had a substantial second-strike force, neither side has ever believed that it had a usable nuclear superiority, and neither has had any significant success with atomic diplomacy. It has been clear to both governments that in a general strategic exchange the result must be Aron's "interdestruction" of both countries. Given survivable overkill on both sides, there is a parity of mortal danger that is not sensitive to this or that specific difference in numbers of warheads or megatons. At the strategic level what McNamara has called "the band of parity" is wide.[10]

To understand this reality is also to understand that it is not sensible to allow decisions on strategic forces to be governed by the false perception that measures of marginal advantage have the kind of weight that we assume when we count the pawns in chess games or the tanks and battleships in conventional arms races. Only too often responsible men have allowed themselves to be persuaded that such perceptions are a good argument for new deployments not otherwise required. But the demands on our national budget are such that it is foolish to let false perceptions cost us tens of billions; it is cheaper and better to correct the false perceptions. It is obviously essential to maintain sufficient survivable strength, but beyond that level—no matter what the other side does—the right thing to do is to talk sense and save money.

Prudent Modernization

I am not suggesting here that there is no case for nuclear modernization. Strategic survivability itself can require change—as in the move away from MIRVs in silos that has been so intensely resisted by the friends of the vulnerable MX-in-Minuteman. There is also a need for capabilities much more discriminating than those designed primarily for large-scale use. The president in search of the right reply to a small nuclear strike—not a likely event, on the historical record, but entirely possible—will not wish to fire large salvos, whether or not he sees value in a less-than-equal strike. The nuclear forces of the United States should have a modest number of single-warhead weapons of low yield and high accuracy, precisely to encourage nuclear war ending. Quite possibly such forces can be designated from among the systems already on hand or on order. In modest numbers such weapons would not change the stable strategic balance of the superpowers, but they could well provide the right answer to any "small" first use by anyone. There is also great promise in highly accurate conventional weapons, and the importance of the tradition of nonuse gives them a special importance for use against all kinds of less-than-nuclear aggression.

The Indispensable Military Professionals

American understanding of the strange realities of nuclear strategy may be strongest today among military professionals. There are great difficulties in their way, and of course there are military strategists as wrongheaded as any civilian. The problems of analysis are forbidding, and so are the problems of tradition. The targeting priorities of the 1950s rested on convictions deeply rooted in air force experience and on a balance of forces very different from present reality; plans were designed for the knockout victory that is wholly out of reach today. But military professionals have not missed the new realities of the age of bilateral overkill. They are the ones who now know best the limitations of existing plans, and they have long recognized that communication, in the widest sense of the word, is more important even than

accuracy. They also understand that nothing in the continuing technological revolution lessens the vital deterrent role of strategic nuclear
forces. Even when earlier commanders thought they could win strategic victory, the political purpose of that ability was always deterrence—
that the war should never happen. The requirements for professional
dedication, skill, and integrity are if anything greater than ever. I
cannot improve on a comment that President Kennedy made to air
force cadets in 1963. He was dealing with the notion that air force
officers of the future would be "nothing more than 'silent silo sitters,' "
and he was assuring them that "nothing could be further from the
truth":

> The fact that the greatest value of all of the weapons of massive
> retaliation lies in their ability to deter war does not diminish their
> importance, nor will national security in the years ahead be achieved
> simply by piling up bigger bombs or burying our missiles under
> bigger loads of concrete. For in an imperfect world where human
> folly has been the rule and not the exception, the surest way to bring
> on the war that can never happen is to sit back and assure ourselves
> it will not happen. The existence of mutual nuclear deterrents [sic]
> cannot be shrugged off as stalemate, for our national security in a
> period of rapid change will depend on constant reappraisal of our
> present doctrines, on alertness to new developments, on imagination
> and resourcefulness, and new ideas. Stalemate is a static term and not
> one of you would be here today if you believed you were entering
> an outmoded service requiring only custodial duties in a period of
> nuclear stalemate.[11]

I have been using the word *stalemate* myself as shorthand for the
strategic parity that makes nuclear war something for both sides to
avoid, but Kennedy was surely right to insist that this situation is
neither static nor undemanding.

The President and Commander in Chief

Yet military men cannot have sole responsibility for nuclear weapons policy. From the very beginning this subject has been presidential.
Congress has also had a great role, but nuclear doctrine, assessment of
nuclear danger, and above all decisions on use or threat of use have
always been presidential. In this situation nothing is more important
than sustained understanding between the president and decision makers in the Pentagon, and nothing has been harder to get.

Let us look again at the hard question of the nature and purpose
of any American use of nuclear weapons if nuclear war does come—"if
deterrence fails," in the deceptively cool phrase of the experts. On this

hard matter there has been no clear understanding between presidents and planners. Such understanding is not easy to get when targets are given sharply different values or when officials disagree about when the United States itself should begin nuclear warfare. We have seen how Eisenhower and Radford, united in warm mutual respect, treated each other as allies within the government on this subject. Nonetheless they had different priorities when they were faced by choices in Indochina or on the offshore islands. We have seen that when Robert McNamara set up the criterion of "assured destruction" as a measure of what was enough, neither he nor the two presidents he served ever succeeded in tackling the next question: Just which strategic attack should be ordered in this or that situation? McNamara instead reached the conclusion that the United States must never go first and that the Soviet Union was amply deterred. He shared his second judgment with the world and his first only with the two presidents.

In later administrations there were new efforts to refine strategic nuclear doctrine, but a gap remained between presidents and planners. The doctrinal adjustments approved by later presidents were the result of serious analytic efforts, especially under defense secretaries James Schlesinger, in the administrations of Nixon and Ford, and Harold Brown, in the administration of Carter, but there is still much distance between all these conceptual adjustments and the world in which strategic planners try to translate doctrine into operational plans. There has been fault at both ends of this line of communications—too much possessiveness at SAC, and not enough sustained attention from commanders in chief. But fault is not the point.

What we must ask is how to do better. Here I think the starting point must be in a new effort to connect the political objective of avoiding nuclear war with the military ways and means of maintaining effective deterrence. The crude control that all our presidents have retained, both over broad levels of procurement and over final decision on use, is not in itself sufficient for long-term safety. Both strategic plans and crisis management, when technology imposes complexity and rapid choice may be imperative, require a better connection between political authority and military choice than there has been in any administration so far, and the necessary attention and effort must come from all concerned, especially the president himself.

There are three specific situations in which the role of the president is critical:

> First, only the president has the standing to make choices that affect the balance of responsibilities and resources among the military services, and such choices are necessary as technology affects what can survive. A strong secretary can make recommendations, but only the president can make them stick and have them respected.

Second, only the president can explain with authority what nuclear options he does and does not want in the event of a desperate need for choices. The distance between strategic plans and real presidential needs can be a convenience for both sides in ordinary times, but it could be catastrophic at a time of necessary choice.

Third, it is important that in any crisis there should be firm presidential control over all actions that could lead an adversary to fear imminent attack. Sometimes such measures are important to ensure survivability—one example is the aircraft on air alert—but no president in the future will want any command to make its own decisions, as the Strategic Air Command did in the missile crisis, about the signals it wants Moscow to get.

The President and the Truth

It has not been easy to get the truth told clearly in nuclear matters, and failure on this front has led to mistakes and danger. Advocates of this or that preferred policy have often been careless with the truth, but the best place for truth telling and the worst place for its absence is the White House.

Roosevelt made two central decisions: to make the weapon if possible, and not to consider what to do with it until later. I find the first decision better than the second. It is not easy to see what would have been gained by a public discussion of the Manhattan Project before the time of Roosevelt's death, but what is also missing here is any internal process by which there could be serious consideration of the choices that were so incompletely studied in the short time between Roosevelt's death and Truman's decision. That internal process was wholly blocked in Roosevelt's last months by the interaction of his established policy of secrecy, his insistence that policy decisions must be his alone, and the weariness that he and Stimson shared. What we know of his own state of mind is too little to tell us what would have happened if he and his advisers had addressed the nuclear question as they addressed other strategic choices, but we know enough to regret this empty page of history.

The presidents of the nuclear age have a mixed record in seeking and telling the truth about our nuclear predicament. They have all understood nuclear danger, and the attacks on Hiroshima and Nagasaki have remained exceptional. The tradition of nonuse owes much to American presidents, and it is striking that in all the nuclear debates of recent years there has been no serious interest in proposals to shift the final responsibility for the command and control of these weapons away from the president. Yet we must also note the mixed record of our presidents, both in public exposition and in assuring the careful analysis of choices within the government.

Roosevelt kept it all too much to himself. Truman was too quick in his judgments. Eisenhower's theory and practice were different in ways that confused both citizens and commanders, and later he failed to make it clear why he was right about the absence of a missile gap. Kennedy understood the danger better than he explained it, and he missed a chance to make it clear that no one could be "number one" in this field. Johnson recognized, as well as any political leader I ever met, what nuclear weapons were *not* good for, but both in choices and in explanation of them, he and his lieutenants were less effective. Nixon recognized that *sufficiency* was a much better term than *superiority,* but he was genuinely confused about atomic diplomacy, and neither he nor Kissinger was even remotely straightforward. Ford understood nuclear danger, but he had too little time, and he did not sieze his one big chance to lead in finishing SALT II and taking it to the country. Carter understood nuclear danger in both human and technical terms, and his secretary of defense was honest and intelligent, but the decisions of his administration were constrained both by excessive secrecy and by imperfections in such inherited undertakings as the SALT II treaty and the MX missile. Ronald Reagan has understood one big thing—that a nuclear war must never be fought—but he has failed to understand many other things that are not small, and he leaves to his successor a record of internal confusion and public misinformation which is the worst we have had so far.

This inheritance offers the next president an opportunity to reestablish a truly presidential capability for analysis and decision. This means, among other things, that he should seek the kind of technical counsel that Eisenhower and Kennedy got from the president's Science Advisory Committee, although he should certainly not replace one set of precommitted advocates by another, or imitate Reagan by appointing biased advisory committees to give surface respectability to positions already uncritically adopted. He can connect the presidency to military advisers in a way that no president has yet done in nuclear matters, and here the best model may be Franklin Roosevelt as a "conventional" commander in chief.[12] The president as commander in chief has been missing all too often in the planning, the procurement, and the doctrinal guidance of nuclear defense policy.

One wide-open opportunity is the chance to discard the process of selective truth telling that became a national disgrace under Reagan and Weinberger. The country and the world need good data on the complex realities of nuclear weapons, and it is a scandal that the fearful official propaganda of the 1980s has required regular and authoritative correction from analysts outside the administration. Nothing would do more for confidence and understanding than a determined official effort to tell the truth, for example with respect to SDI.

Truth alone is not a policy, of course. Avoiding war, maintaining coexistence, assuring strategic stability, and working for new agreements are all hard tasks for the next president, and for his successors. Nor can a new policy of "candor" be established by a single speech. Truth and understanding are not static, and the process by which a president achieves and shares them must be continuous. What I am emphasizing here is the extraordinary political opportunity that is presented by the extraordinary failure of recent years.

Truth telling will help in dealing with the Congress, with allies, and with the Kremlin. We have had repeated troubles on all three lines, and we have also seen moments of clarity and renewed understanding. We need not suppose that all difficulties can be resolved by improved communication, but neither should we forget the costs of failure.

There is obviously a parallel value in straightforward communication from the other end of the line. There has been folly as well as wisdom in the work of Congress. There has been weakness in communication from allies to us, as from us to them. Our communication with the Soviet Union has been gravely hampered by the Soviet belief that the less any adversary knows about Soviet capabilities the better for the Soviet Union, a dangerous illusion which has had a persistently negative effect on nuclear stability. Fortunately, there has been improvement, even before Gorbachev, and there is prospect of still greater change under his leadership. *Glasnost*—openness—is not the same as free speech, but it can make a great contribution to enduring nuclear peace. In particular it can make a great contribution to reliable arms agreements.

Even more important, as time goes on, may be Gorbachev's understanding that nuclear war between the superpowers would "spell suicide" for both. He also understands that efforts by either side to get ahead will "gain nothing." From a master politician, his way of stating the matter is compelling: "Any striving for military superiority means chasing one's own tail. It can't be used in real politics."[13]

Arms Control

The historical record does not show us that arms control can be expected to remove all nuclear danger, but it does show us that it can help. Acheson and Lilienthal and Oppenheimer were right in their conclusion of 1946 that the elimination of nuclear weapons would require an international authority with reliable monopoly of the ways and means of making them. Unfortunately their proposal was wholly incompatible with the political reality of the time. One great state had a temporary monopoly that it would not surrender except on conditions that a second great state was wholly determined not to accept. We have also seen that none of the states now having clear access to nuclear warheads has been held back by any outside influence. But these sweeping conclusions do not tell us that arms control is a failure, only that its success must be measured by less absolute standards. Has the effort for arms control helped the two superpowers toward stable coexistence? Has the effort to limit the spread of nuclear weapons helped in some countries to prevent a decision to have warheads? My own answers are cautiously affirmative. The superpowers have been helped by their agreements, and the world as a whole is less dangerous than it would be if there were not a serious and growing awareness, worldwide, that there is both danger and cost in seeking national nuclear arsenals.

Arms control agreements have been hard to get, politically vulnerable, and so far limited in scope. For both superpowers the acceptance of agreement has always required assurance that the basic deterrent balance would be preserved, and it is no accident that limits on atmospheric testing and on strategic defense have been easier to get than limits on offensive deterrent forces. There have also been grave issues of confidence—especially American fear of cheating by the Soviets and Soviet fear of technological breakout by the Americans.

It remains possible to establish a stronger and more sustained process for doing what we have done only episodically in the past—identifying and reaching agreements that are helpful to both sides in reducing danger. The greatest of these dangers at present is that changes in deployment may weaken the common confidence that neither side has any interest in resorting to nuclear war. The threat to this shared confidence presented first by the excessive deployment of large Soviet silo-based missiles and then by the possibility of American space-based strategic defense is precisely what gives attraction to the grand compromise that seems attainable but hard to get as I write.

Arms control of this sort can never be a substitute for the attention to nuclear danger and nuclear reality that is required of presidents and their subordinates, but as the imperative of coexistence becomes more clearly understood in both governments, the role of careful and substantial arms agreements can be enlarged.

Nor should the two sides limit themselves to the formal treaties that are familiar. Treaties are not the only way to get ahead, and the treaty process in the United States allows a minority of the Senate to block progress. Given the wide band of parity there is room on each side for unilateral moderation. It can save money and leave real parity intact. Each side can make choices of this sort that are at once advantageous to itself and encouraging to the other. This is what Kennedy did in 1963 when he decided not to match the second set of Soviet tests, and it is what Gorbachev may well do in the field of conventional arms. A process of this sort could go a long way to undo the damage their strategic competition has done to the political relations between the superpowers. Gorbachev has it right when he says that the arms race is the most important obstacle to good Soviet-American relations.[14]

We cannot take it for granted that the years of Gorbachev will be a time of major progress in arms control or indeed in Soviet-American relations. Nonetheless there is good reason for hope. At the very least it makes sense for the United States government to make progress of this sort a primary objective. Soviets and Americans can if they will make progress through the recognition of the underlying realities that make stable coexistence a shared objective. Neither country can have more than stable and self-confident deterrent strength, and neither can accept less. Our interest in stability is equal. No one on either side can want mutual assured destruction to happen. Both must prefer mutual assured deterrence. We could let MAD have that less confusing meaning, and we could also call it SANE—for survivably adequate nuclear effectiveness. Best of all, we could forget acronyms and simply recognize our overwhelming common interest in avoiding Aron's "interdestruction."

I return to the hope in *glasnost*. Nothing has been more dangerous to both countries than the practice of secrecy and deception. It creates a fearful mistrust that leads to excessive responses. Consider the case of the Krasnoyarsk radar—a Soviet early-warning installation that violates a provision of the ABM Treaty which requires that early-warning radars shall be placed only near national borders. Krasnoyarsk is deep in Siberia, far from the Soviet border. To put the radar there is a plain violation of the treaty, made worse by official Soviet claims that it is really not a radar for the detection of hostile missiles, but for observation of satellites. This silly claim allowed Reagan officials to make their own false accusation that the Krasnoyarsk radar was part of a secret Soviet ABM system. What has gradually become clear, with some recent Soviet help, is that the radar in Krasnoyarsk is not designed to help knock American missiles down, but only to detect them early enough for Soviet missiles to be launched on warning before being destroyed in their silos. The radar was probably put in Krasnoyarsk for economy. To cover the same angles of approach with systems at the Soviet border might have required two radar sites, not one, and the construction of at least one of them would have been made vastly more expensive by the need to build in East Siberian permafrost. It would have been better to explain all this openly—less dangerous in the end for both sides. This kind of openness will not be learned by either side overnight, but precisely because Soviet secrecy and deception have been more pervasive than our own, it is right to find special hope in Gorbachev's *glasnost.* [15]

Courage

Survival in the nuclear age requires many virtues—candor and caution and imagination and effort—but the one that has impressed me most over the years is courage: the courage to face the danger, to face and tell the truth, and not to accept the false protection of believing what is not true. It is not true that we can get rid of this danger by perfect defense; it will take courage to admit it. We cannot get rid of it by early abolition or by early international control—the political realities of sovereign states and of closed societies forbid that. We have to live with the nuclear reality as it is, working to improve it when we can, but looking it in the eye. In 1950, just after Truman's fateful and secretly concerted decision on the H-bomb, Robert Oppenheimer made my point better than I can. He was denouncing the fearfulness that led to excessive secrecy, but his prescription has a broader meaning; it tells us what was most important also about the people of West Berlin in 1958–63 and about John Kennedy in the Cuban missile crisis:

> Wisdom itself cannot flourish, nor even truth be determined, without the give and take of debate or criticism. The relevant facts could be of little help to an enemy; yet they are indispensable for an understanding of questions of policy. If we are wholly guided by fear, we shall fail in this time of crisis. The answer to fear cannot always lie in the dissipation of the causes of fear; sometimes it lies in courage.[16]

Hope

Courage is hard without hope, and it is easy to lose hope in the face of nuclear realities. Neither the weapons nor the two great adversarial governments can be wished away. There will be nuclear danger in the next decade and the one after that, and indeed as far ahead as we can see. In that situation it is only too easy to conclude that sooner or later the general catastrophe will come. That conclusion is wrong. It is true that if there is a given chance of disaster, however small, in any one time period, and if that chance remains the same or increases, the disaster will one day come. Thus if the risk of nuclear catastrophe in any one year was one in one hundred in 1962, as it may have been, and it had stayed that way year in and out, the chance of such a disaster by 1988 would be 23 percent, by 2100 75 percent, by 2200 91 percent.[17]

But the odds do not have to stay the same. History suggests that they can be reduced. Nuclear weapons have been with the world since 1945, and each ten-year period in that time has turned out to be less dangerous than the one before it. Even when we count in the special tensions over Berlin and Cuba in the second decade, the overall risk that there would be open nuclear warfare was lower then than in the earlier years in which so many believed that the new weapon would have a necessarily central role in any serious war. Still more plainly, the decades after Cuba have been less dangerous than before. The Reagan administration came in on a tide of fear, but it is going out in a season of hope, and the dangers its partisans predicted never came to pass.

Both great governments have learned to respect the nuclear danger and to practice, if not always to preach, coexistence. They have been slow about arms control and still have much to learn about it, but both are now doing better than they were. We are in danger still, but the risk of catastrophe at the end of the 1980s is much lower than in earlier decades.

Reduction of the risk, decade by decade, is our best hope for long-run survival. It is a mathematical law that if you do not reduce the risk from one time period to the next, you face inevitable catastrophe, but it is also a mathematical law that if you keep reducing the risk, your chance of durable safety can be very good. Thus if the overall chance of general nuclear disaster *per decade* was one in fifty in the decade of the sixties (when most of the danger was in one week of 1962), and if it is one in two hundred two decades later, if we can make it one in eight hundred for the first decade of the twenty-first century, and so on after that, the chance of permanent escape will be 99 percent.[18]

Obviously the mathematics of probability do not of themselves produce safety. Real reductions of risk come only from real choices. Moreover technological and political change, from one decade to another, will always require new choices. No one can tell today whether the risk of catastrophe will go up or down in the future, and still less can anyone predict the wisdom or folly of future decision makers.

If we judge by history, it is right to expect that our progress away from danger will be slow and not always steady. As we learn from the first effort at international control, it is wrong to hope for an immediate twenty-foot jump when ten is the best on record. Yet it is also true, as men like Bohr and Oppenheimer understood at the beginning, that the terrible power inside the nucleus offers hope as well as peril. If the two superpowers stay clear of war with one another, and if they go on reducing their common nuclear danger, it is not wrong to hope that a time will come in which they learn how to get beyond the age of survivable overkill. If and when they do that, I believe, the achievement will rest on a politics of trust that exists on neither side today. In the long run only mutual trust, not arms control as such, can end any military rivalry. But accepted coexistence and shared support for strategic stability can over time make important contributions to trust. No one who looks at the realities of political behavior in our time can suppose that Niels Bohr's open world is close, but his prescription remains persuasive, and it is not wrong to hope that over the long run the message that Roosevelt and Churchill failed to heed when they heard it from Bohr may yet be understood by all.

Meanwhile there is work enough in smaller steps toward safety. Good choices are not easy, but the record shows that they are not impossible. The choices of the first fifty years, however imperfect, have kept the two superpowers out of war with one another. The danger between them remains mortal, but their understanding of that danger and of each other is better than it was. Our survival in the first fifty years of danger offers encouragement to renewed pursuit of truth, resolute practice of courage, and persistence in lively hope.

Bibliography

ABBREVIATIONS

Cab   Files of the British War Cabinet Scientific Advisory Committee, Public Records Office, London, England.

DDE   Papers of Dwight D. Eisenhower, Dwight D. Eisenhower Library, Abilene, Kans.

FDR   Papers of Franklin D. Roosevelt, Franklin D. Roosevelt Library, Hyde Park, N.Y.

FRUS   Foreign Relations of the United States (Washington, D.C.: U.S. Government Printing Office, 1945–1952–54).

HST   Papers of Harry S. Truman, Harry S. Truman Library, Independence, Mo.

JFK   Papers of John Fitzgerald Kennedy, John Fitzgerald Kennedy Library, Boston, Mass.

MED   Records of the Manhattan Engineer District, 1942–48, Modern Military section, National Archives, Washington, D.C.

OSRD   Records of the Office of Scientific Research and Development, National Archives, Washington, D.C.

Prem   Premier files of Winston Churchill, Public Record Office, London, England.

ARTICLES AND PAPERS

"ABC's Issues and Answers," Transcript, October 14, 1962.

Acheson, Dean. "Dean Acheson's Version of Robert Kennedy's Version of the Cuban Missile Affair." *Esquire,* February 1969, pp. 76–77.

————. Oral history, JFK.

————. " 'Total Diplomacy' to Strengthen U.S. Leadership for Human Freedom." *Department of State Bulletin* 22 (March 20, 1950): 427–30.

————. "Wishing Won't Hold Berlin." *Saturday Evening Post,* March 7, 1959, pp. 32–33, 85–86.

Alsop, Joseph. "After Ike, the Deluge." *Washington Post,* October 7, 1959, p. A17.

————. "Comments." *Foreign Policy,* no. 16 (Fall 1974): 83–88.

————, and David Joravsky. "Was the Hiroshima Bomb Necessary? An Exchange." *New York Review of Books,* October 23, 1980, pp. 37–42.

————. "Affairs of State: The Real Meaning of the Test Ban," *Saturday Evening Post,* September 28, 1963, p. 20.

Alsop, Stewart. "Kennedy's Grand Strategy." *Saturday Evening Post,* March 31, 1962, pp. 11–17.

————. "Our New Strategy: The Alternatives to Total War." *Saturday Evening Post,* December 1, 1962, pp. 13–19.

————. "Our Gamble With Destiny." *Saturday Evening Post,* May 16, 1959, pp. 23, 114–18.

Arneson, R. Gordon. "The H-Bomb Decision." *Foreign Service Journal* 46 (May 1969): 27–29, (June 1969): 24–27, 43.

Aron, Raymond. "De Gaulle and Kennedy: The Nuclear Debate." *Atlantic Monthly,* August 1962, pp. 33–38.

Bernstein, Barton J. "The Atomic Bomb and American Foreign Policy, 1941–45: An Historiographical Controversy." *Peace and Change* 2 (Spring 1974): 1–16.

————. "The Cuban Missile Crisis: Trading the Jupiters in Turkey?" *Political Science Quarterly* 95 (Spring 1980): 97–125.

————. "The Perils and Politics of Surrender: Ending the War with Japan and Avoiding the Third Atomic Bomb." *Pacific Historical Review* 46 (February 1977): 1–28.

————. "A Postwar Myth: 500,000 U.S. Lives Saved." *Bulletin of the Atomic Scientists,* June/July 1986, pp. 38–40.

————. "Truman and the H-bomb." *Bulletin of the Atomic Scientists* 40 (March 1984): 12–18.

————. "The Week We Almost Went to War." *Bulletin of the Atomic Scientists* 32 (February 1976): 12–21.

Blechman, Barry M., and Douglas M. Hart. "Afghanistan and the 1946 Iran Analogy." *Survival* 22 (November/December 1980): 248–53.

————. "The Political Utility of Nuclear Weapons," *International Security* 7 (Summer 1982): 132–56.

————, and Robert Powell. "What in the Name of God Is Strategic Superiority?" *Political Science Quarterly* 97, no. 4 (Winter 1982–83): 589–602.

Blight, James G., Joseph S. Nye, Jr., and David A. Welch. "The Cuban Missile Crisis Revisited." *Foreign Affairs* 66 (Fall 1987): 170–88.

Bowie, Robert R. "Strategy and the Atlantic Alliance." *International Organization* 17 (Summer 1963): 709–32.

Bundy, McGeorge. "Building the Atlantic Partnership: Some Lessons from the Past," *Department of State Bulletin,* October 22, 1962, pp. 601–5.

————. "Early Thoughts on Controlling the Nuclear Arms Race: A Report to the Secretary of State, January 1953." *International Security* 7 (Fall 1982): 3–27.

————. "To Cap the Volcano." *Foreign Affairs* 48 (October 1969): 1–20.

————. "Vietnam, Watergate and Presidential Powers." *Foreign Affairs,* 58 (Winter 1979/80): 397–407.

————, George Kennan, Robert S. McNamara, and Gerard Smith. "Nuclear Weapons and the Atlantic Alliance." *Foreign Affairs* 60 (Spring 1982): 753–68.

Burke, Arleigh A. "The Threat Confronting Us." *Vital Speeches of the Day* 25 (March 15, 1959): 332–35.

Committee on the Present Danger. "Can America Catch Up? The U.S.-Soviet Military Balance." November 1984.

Compton, Karl T. "If the Atomic Bomb Had Not Been Used." *Atlantic Monthly.* December 1946, pp. 54–56.

Cousins, Norman. "The Cuban Missile Crisis: An Anniversary." *Saturday Review,* October 15, 1977, p. 4.

————. "Modern Man Is Obsolete: An Editorial." *Saturday Review of Literature,* August 18, 1945, pp. 5–9.

Cuban Missile Crisis Meetings, October 16, 1962, presidential recordings transcripts, President's Office files, JFK.

————. October 27, 1962, presidential recordings, President's Office files, JFK.

Davis, Elmer. "No World, If Necessary." *Saturday Review of Literature,* March 30, 1946, pp. 7–8, 50–55.

"De Gaulle's 1958 Tripartite Proposal and U.S. Response." *Atlantic Community Quarterly* 4 (Fall 1966): 455–58.

Department of State Bulletin, March 20, 1950; January 19, 1958; December 15, 1958; November 13, 1961; September 24, 1962; October 22, 1962; November 12, 1973; November 19, 1973.

Dower, John W. Review of *Japan's Secret War* by Robert K. Wilcox. *Bulletin of the Atomic Scientists* 43 (August–September 1986): 61–62.

Dulles, John Foster. "Policy for Security and Peace." *Foreign Affairs* 32 (April 1954): 353–64.

————. "The Threat of a Red Asia." *Department of State Bulletin,* April 12, 1954, pp. 539–42.

Finney, Nat S. "How F.D.R. Planned to Use the A-Bomb." *Look,* March 16, 1950, pp. 23–27.

Foot, Rosemary. "Nuclear Threats and the Ending of the Korean Conflict." Unpublished paper.

[Gaither report.] Deterrence and Survival in the Nuclear Age: Report to the President by the Security Resources Panel of the Science Advisory Committee, November 7, 1957, DDE.

Garthoff, Raymond L. "The Meaning of Missiles." *Washington Quarterly* 5 (Autumn 1982): 76–82.

————. "New Thinking in Soviet Military Doctrine." *The Washington Quarterly* 11 (Summer 1988): 131–58.

Gordon, Leonard H. D. "United States Opposition to Use of Force in the

Taiwan Strait, 1954–62." *Journal of American History* 72 (December 1985): 637–60.

Hahn, Otto. "The Discovery of Fission." *Scientific American,* February 1958, pp. 76–84.

Halperin, Morton H. "The Gaither Committee and the Policy Process." *World Politics* 13 (April 1961): 360–84.

Hampson, Fen Osler. "The Divided Decision-Maker: American Domestic Politics and the Cuban Crises." *International Security* 9 (Winter 1984/85): 130–65.

Harriman, Averell. "My Alarming Interview with Khrushchev." *Life,* July 13, 1959, pp. 33–36.

Heisenberg, Werner. "Research in Germany on the Technical Application of Atomic Energy." *Nature,* August 16, 1947, pp. 211–15.

Hersey, John. "Hiroshima." *New Yorker,* August 31, 1946.

Holloway, David. "Entering the Nuclear Arms Race: The Soviet Decision to Build the Atomic Bomb, 1939–45." *Social Studies of Science* 11 (1981): 159–97.

————. "Research Note: Soviet Thermonuclear Development." *International Security* 4 (Winter 1979/80): 192–97.

Howard, Michael. "Reassurance and Deterrence." *Foreign Affairs* 61 (Winter 1982/83): 309–24.

Iklé, Fred Charles. "Nuclear Strategy: Can There Be a Happy Ending?" *Foreign Affairs* 63 (Spring 1985): 810–26.

Kissinger, Henry A. "Reflections on Cuba." *Reporter,* November 22, 1962, pp. 21–24.

Knebel, Fletcher, and Charles W. Bailey. "The Fight Over the A-Bomb," *Look,* August 13, 1963, pp. 19–23.

Lawrence, E. O. "Historical Notes on Early Activities of Ernest O. Lawrence in Connection with the Tubealloy Project." E. O. Lawrence Papers. University of California, Berkeley.

Lear, John. "Ike and the Peaceful Atom." *Reporter,* January 12, 1956, pp. 11–21.

Lebow, Richard Ned. "The Cuban Missile Crisis: Reading the Lessons Correctly." *Political Science Quarterly* 98 (Fall 1983): 431–58.

Lippmann, Walter. "Cuba and the Nuclear Risk." *Atlantic Monthly,* February 1963, pp. 55–58.

Lovett, Robert. Oral history, JFK.

McKelway, St. Clair. "A Reporter with the B-29s." *New Yorker,* June 23, 1945, pp. 26–39.

McNamara, Robert S. "The Military Role of Nuclear Weapons: Perceptions and Misperceptions." *Foreign Affairs* 62, no. 1 (Fall 1983): 59–80.

Nathan, James A. "The Missile Crisis: His Finest Hour Now." *World Politics* 27 (January 1975): 256–81.

Nitze, Paul H. "Assuring Strategic Stability in an Era of Détente." *Foreign Affairs* 54 (January 1976): 207–32.

Oppenheimer, J. Robert. "Atomic Weapons and American Policy." *Foreign Affairs* 31 (July 1953): 525–35.

————. "International Control of Atomic Energy." *Foreign Affairs* 26 (January 1948): 239–52.

————. "Niels Bohr and Atomic Weapons." *New York Review of Books*, December 17, 1964, pp. 6–8.

Peierls, Rudolf. "Atomic Germans." *New York Review of Books*, July 1, 1971, pp. 23–24.

Pipes, Richard. "Why the Soviet Union Thinks It Could Fight and Win a Nuclear War." *Commentary* 64 (July 1977): 21–34.

Pollack, Jonathan D. "Chinese Attitudes Towards Nuclear Weapons, 1964–9." *The China Quarterly*, April-June, 1972, p. 244–71.

"Report of the President's Commission on Strategic Forces." April 6, 1983.

Roberts, Chalmers. "The Day We Didn't Go to War." *The Reporter*, September 14, 1954, pp. 31–35.

Rosenberg, David Alan. "American Atomic Strategy and the Hydrogen Bomb Decision." *Journal of American History* 66 (June 1979): 62–87.

————. "The Origins of Overkill: Nuclear Weapons and American Strategy, 1945–60." *International Security* 7 (Spring 1983): 3–71.

————. "Reality and Responsibility: Power and Process in the Making of United States Nuclear Strategy 1945–68." *The Journal of Strategic Studies* 9 (March 1986): 35–52.

————. "Toward Armageddon: The Foundations of United States Nuclear Strategy, 1945–61." Unpublished ms.

————. "U.S. Nuclear Stockpile, 1945 to 1950." *Bulletin of the Atomic Scientists*, May 1982, pp. 25–30.

Rusk, Dean; Robert McNamara; George W. Ball; Roswell L. Gilpatric; Theodore Sorensen; and McGeorge Bundy. "The Lessons of the Cuban Missile Crisis." *Time*, September 27, 1982, pp. 85–86.

Sachs, Alexander. "Early History Atomic Project in Relation to President Roosevelt, 1939–40." Typescript, MED.

Sagan, Scott D. "Nuclear Alerts and Crisis Management." *International Security* 9 (Spring 1985): 99–139.

Scali, John. "I Was the Secret Go-Between in the Cuban Crisis." *Family Weekly*, October 25, 1964, pp. 4–5, 12–14.

Schilling, Warner R. "The H-Bomb Decision: How to Decide Without Actually Choosing." *Political Science Quarterly* 76 (March 1961): 24–46.

Sclove, Richard E. "Atomic PreMunitions: Frederick Soddy and the Social Responsibility of Scientists." Cambridge, Mass.: Center for International Studies and Program in Science, Technology, and Society, M.I.T., 1980.

Seversky, Alexander de. "Atomic Bomb Hysteria." *Reader's Digest*. February 1946, pp. 121–26.

Shepley, James. "How Dulles Averted War." *Life*, January 16, 1956, pp. 70–80.

Sokolski, Henry. "Atoms for Peace: A Non-Proliferation Primer?" *Arms Control*, September 1980, pp. 199–231.

Steel, Ronald. "Endgame: *Thirteen Days* by Robert Kennedy." *New York Review of Books*, March 13, 1969, pp. 15–22.

Stimson, Henry L. "The Decision to Use the Atomic Bomb." *Harper's Magazine*, February, 1947, pp. 97–107.

————. Diary, June 1, 1945, Yale University Library, New Haven, Conn. Other citations.

"Talking Moonshine." Editorial, *Scientific American,* November 1933, p. 201.

Teller, Edward. "What Helps Superpower 'Star Wars' Stability?" *Encounter,* September-October 1986, pp. 68–69.

Thirring, Hans. "The Super Bomb." *Bulletin of the Atomic Scientists* 6 (March 1950): 69–70.

Time, March 19, 1945; November 12, 1945; November 19, 1945; July 31, 1950, p. 12; January 28, 1980.

Twining, Nathan, The John Foster Dulles Oral History Collection.

WNET. "MacNeil/Lehrer NewsHour," February 15, 1985, "Missile Crisis Recalled," interview with Fidel Castro; also unpublished transcript of the interview provided by the program.

Weinberger, Caspar W. "Why Offense Needs Defense." *Foreign Policy* 68 (Fall 1987): 3–18.

Welch, David A., and James G. Blight. "The Eleventh Hour of the Cuban Missile Crisis: An Introduction to the ExComm Transcripts." *International Security* 12 (Winter 1987/88): 5–29.

Wieseltier, Leon. "When Deterrence Fails." *Foreign Affairs* 63 (Spring 1985): 827–47.

Wohlstetter, Albert. "Nuclear Sharing: NATO and the N+1 Country." *Foreign Affairs* 39 (April 1961): 355–87.

———. "The Delicate Balance of Terror." *Foreign Affairs* 37 (January 1959): 211–34.

——— and Roberta Wohlstetter. "Controlling the Risks in Cuba." *Adelphi Papers,* no. 17 (April 1965).

BOOKS

Acheson, Dean. *Present at the Creation: My Years in the State Department.* New York: W. W. Norton & Company, 1969.

Adams, Sherman. *Firsthand Report: The Story of the Eisenhower Administration.* New York: Harper & Brothers, 1961.

Adenauer, Konrad. *Erinnerungen, 1959–1963.* Stuttgart: Deutsche Verlags-Anstalt, 1968.

Adomeit, Hannes. *Soviet Risk-Taking and Crisis Behavior: A Theoretical and Empirical Analysis.* London: George Allen & Unwin, 1982.

Aliano, Richard A. *American Defense Policy from Eisenhower to Kennedy: The Politics of Changing Military Requirements, 1957–1961.* Athens, Ohio: Ohio University Press, 1975.

Allison, Graham T. *Essence of Decision: Explaining the Cuban Missile Crisis.* Boston: Little, Brown & Company, 1971.

Alperovitz, Gar. *Atomic Diplomacy: Hiroshima and Potsdam: The Use of the Atomic Bomb and the American Confrontation with Soviet Power.* New York: Simon & Schuster, 1965.

Alsop, Joseph, and Stewart Alsop. *The Reporter's Trade.* New York: Reynal & Company, 1958.

———. *We Accuse! The Story of the Miscarriage of American Justice in the Case of J. Robert Oppenheimer.* New York: Simon & Schuster, 1954.

Ambrose, Stephen E. *Eisenhower.* 2 vols. New York: Simon & Schuster, 1983–84.

———. *Ike's Spies: Eisenhower and the Espionage Establishment.* Garden City, New York: Doubleday & Company, 1981.

The American Physical Society Study Group. *Science and Technology of Directed Energy Weapons,* April 1987.

Arnold, H. H., and Ira C. Eaker. *Winged Warfare.* New York: Harper & Brothers, 1941.

Aron, Raymond. *The Great Debate: Theories of Nuclear Strategy.* Garden City, New York: Doubleday & Company, 1965.

———. *Mémoires.* 2 vols. Paris: Julliard, 1983.

———. *Paix et guerre entre les nations.* 4th edition. Paris: Calmann-Levy, 1966.

Babyonyshev, Alexander, ed. *On Sakharov.* New York: Alfred A. Knopf, 1982.

Ball, Desmond. *Politics and Force Levels: The Strategic Missile Program of the Kennedy Administration.* Berkeley: University of California Press, 1980.

——— and Jeffrey Richelson, eds. *Strategic Nuclear Targeting.* Ithaca: Cornell University Press, 1986.

Ball, George W. *The Discipline of Power: Essentials of a Modern World Structure.* Boston: Little, Brown & Company, 1968.

———. *The Past Has Another Pattern: Memoirs.* New York: W. W. Norton & Company, 1982.

Batchelder, Robert C. *The Irreversible Decision, 1939–50.* Boston: Houghton Mifflin Company, 1962.

Baxter, James Phinney. *Scientists Against Time.* Boston: Little, Brown & Company, 1946.

Baylis, John. *Anglo-American Defense Relations, 1939–80: The Special Relationship.* New York: St. Martin's Press, 1981.

Beard, Edmund. *Developing the ICBM: A Study in Bureaucratic Politics.* New York: Columbia University Press, 1976.

Bell, Coral. *Survey of International Affairs: 1954.* Edited by F. C. Benham. London: Oxford University Press, 1957.

Beres, Louis Rene, ed. *Security or Armageddon: Israel's Nuclear Strategy.* Lexington, Mass.: D.C. Heath and Company, 1986.

Bernstein, Barton J., ed. *The Atomic Bomb: The Critical Issues.* Boston: Little, Brown & Company, 1976.

Bernstein, Jeremy. *Hans Bethe: Prophet of Energy.* New York: Basic Books, 1979.

Beschloss, Michael R. *Mayday: Eisenhower, Khrushchev and the U-2 Affair.* New York: Harper & Row, 1986.

Betts, Richard K. *Nuclear Blackmail and Nuclear Balance.* Washington, D.C.: The Brookings Institution, 1987.

Beyerchen, Alan D. *Scientists Under Hitler: Politics and the Physics Community in the Third Reich.* New Haven: Yale University Press, 1977.

Bidault, Georges. *D'Une Résistance à l'autre.* Paris: Les Presses du Siècle, 1965.

Blackett, P.M.S. *Fear, War, and the Bomb: Military and Political Consequences of Atomic Energy.* New York: Whittlesey House, McGraw-Hill Book Company, 1949.

Blight, James G., and David A. Welch. *On the Brink: Americans and Soviets Reexamine the Missile Crisis.* New York: Farrar, Straus & Giroux, 1989.

Blumberg, Stanley A., and Gwinn Owens. *Energy and Conflict: The Life and Times of Edward Teller.* New York: G.P. Putnam's Sons, 1976.

Bohr, Aage. "The War Years and the Prospects Raised by the Atomic Weapons." In *Niels Bohr: His Life and Work as Seen by His Friends and Colleagues,* pp. 191–214, edited by S. Rozental. New York: John Wiley & Sons, 1967.

Bottome, Edgar M. *The Missile Gap: A Study of the Formulation of Military and Political Policy.* Rutherford, N.J.: Fairleigh Dickinson University Press, 1971.

Boyer, Paul. *By the Bomb's Early Light: American Thought and Culture at the Dawn of the Atomic Age.* New York: Pantheon Books, 1985.

Branch, Christopher I. *Fighting a Long Nuclear War.* National Security Affairs Monograph Series 84–5. Washington, D.C.: National Defense University Press, 1984.

Brandt, Willy. *People and Politics: The Years 1960–75.* Boston: Little, Brown & Company, 1976.

Brians, Paul. *Nuclear Holocausts: Atomic War in Fiction, 1895–1984.* Kent, Ohio: The Kent State University Press, 1987.

Brodie, Bernard. *Strategy in the Missile Age.* Princeton: Princeton University Press, 1959.

Brodie, Bernard, ed. *The Absolute Weapon: Atomic Power and World Order.* New York: Harcourt, Brace & Company, 1946; reprint ed., Freeport, N.Y.: Books for Libraries Press, 1972.

Brodie, Bernard. *War and Politics.* New York: Macmillan Company, 1973.

Buchan, Alastair, ed. *A World of Nuclear Powers?* The American Assembly, Columbia University. Englewood Cliffs, N.J.: Prentice-Hall, 1966.

Bundy, McGeorge. *The Strength of Government.* Cambridge: Harvard University Press, 1968.

Burns, James MacGregor. *Roosevelt: The Soldier of Freedom.* New York: Harcourt Brace Jovanovich, 1970.

Bush, Vannevar. *Pieces of the Action.* New York: William Morrow and Company, 1970.

Butow, Robert J. C. *Japan's Decision to Surrender.* Stanford: Stanford University Press, 1954.

Byrnes, James F. *All in One Lifetime.* New York: Harper & Brothers, 1958.
———. *Speaking Frankly.* New York: Harper & Brothers, 1947.

Calvocoressi, Peter. *Survey of International Affairs: 1953.* Edited by Coral Bell. London: Oxford University Press, 1956.

Cantril, Hadley. *Public Opinion, 1935–1946.* Princeton: Princeton University Press, 1951.

Carnesale, Albert, and Richard N. Haass, eds. *Superpower Arms Control: Setting the Record Straight.* Cambridge: Ballinger Publishing Company, 1987.

Carter, Ashton B., and David N. Schwartz, eds. *Ballistic Missile Defense.* Washington, D.C.: The Brookings Institution, 1984.
———, John D. Steinbruner, and Charles A. Zraket, eds. *Managing Nuclear Operations.* Washington, D.C.: The Brookings Institution, 1987.

Carter, Jimmy. *Public Papers of the Presidents of the United States: Jimmy Carter, 1977–1980–81.* Washington, D.C.: United States Government Printing Office, 1977–82.

Catudal, Honoré M. *Kennedy and the Berlin Wall Crisis: A Case Study in U.S. Decision Making.* Berlin: Verlag, 1980.

Chayes, Abram. *The Cuban Missile Crisis: International Crises and the Role of Law.* New York: Oxford University Press, 1974.

Childs, Herbert. *An American Genius: The Life of Ernest Orlando Lawrence.* New York: E.P. Dutton & Co., 1968.

Churchill, Winston S. *Closing the Ring.* Boston: Houghton Mifflin Company, 1951.

———. *The Grand Alliance.* Boston: Houghton Mifflin Company, 1950.

———. *The Hinge of Fate.* Boston: Houghton Mifflin Company, 1950.

———. *Triumph and Tragedy.* Boston: Houghton Mifflin Company, 1953.

Clark, Dick, ed. *United States-Soviet Relations: Building a Congressional Cadre, Second Conference, July 14–18, 1987.* Wye Plantation: Aspen Institute for Humanistic Studies, 1987.

Clark, Ronald W. *The Birth of the Bomb: The Untold Story of Britain's Part in the Weapon that Changed the World.* London: Scientific Book Club, 1961.

———. *Tizard.* Cambridge: MIT Press, 1965.

———. *The Greatest Power on Earth: The Story of Nuclear Fission.* London: Sidgwick & Jackson, 1980; published in the United States as *The Greatest Power on Earth: The International Race for Nuclear Supremacy.* New York: Harper & Row, 1980.

Cochran, Thomas B., William M. Arkin, and Milton M. Hoenig. *Nuclear Weapons Databook.* Vol. 1: *U.S. Nuclear Forces and Capabilities.* Cambridge: Ballinger Publishing Company, 1984.

Coit, Margaret L. *Mr. Baruch.* Westport, Conn.: Greenwood Press, 1975; originally Boston: Houghton Mifflin Company, 1957.

Committee for the Compilation of Materials on Damage Caused by the Atomic Bombs in Hiroshima and Nagasaki. *Hiroshima and Nagasaki: The Physical, Medical, and Social Effects of the Atomic Bombings.* New York: Basic Books, 1981.

Compton, Arthur Holly. *Atomic Quest.* New York: Oxford University Press, 1956.

Conant, James B. *My Several Lives.* New York: Harper & Row, 1970.

———. *Anglo-American Relations in the Atomic Age.* London: Oxford University Press, 1952.

Cousins, Norman. *Modern Man Is Obsolete.* New York: The Viking Press, 1945.

Craven, Wesley Frank, and James Lea Cate, eds. *The Army Air Forces in World War II,* Vol. 5, *The Pacific: Matterhorn to Nagasaki, June 1944 to August 1945.* Chicago: University of Chicago Press, 1953.

Dallek, Robert. *Franklin D. Roosevelt and American Foreign Policy, 1932–1945.* New York: Oxford University Press, 1979.

de Ménil, Lois Pattison. *Who Speaks for Europe? The Vision of Charles de Gaulle.* New York: St. Martin's Press, 1977.

Detzer, David. *The Brink: Cuban Missile Crisis, 1962.* New York: Thomas Y. Crowell, 1979.

Diehl, Paul F., and Loch K. Johnson, eds. *Through the Straits of Armageddon: Arms Control Issues and Prospects.* Athens, Ga.: The University of Georgia Press, 1987.

Dinerstein, Herbert S. *The Making of a Missile Crisis: October 1962.* Baltimore: Johns Hopkins University Press, 1976.

Divine, Robert A. *Foreign Policy and U.S. Presidential Elections, 1952–1960.* New York: New Viewpoints, 1974.

Documents on American Foreign Relations, 1954, 1955, 1956, 1958, 1961, 1962. New York: Published for the Council on Foreign Relations by Harper & Brothers, 1955–63. *Documents on American Foreign Relations,* 1970. New York: Published for the Council on Foreign Relations by Simon and Schuster, 1975.

Documents on International Affairs, 1961, 1962. London: Issued under the auspices of the Royal Institute of International Affairs by Oxford University Press.

Donovan, Robert J. *Eisenhower: The Inside Story.* New York: Harper & Brothers, 1956.

Dower, John W. *War Without Mercy: Race and Power in the Pacific War.* New York: Pantheon Books, 1986.

Drell, Sidney D., Philip J. Farley, and David Holloway. *The Reagan Strategic Defense Initiative: A Technical, Political, and Arms Control Assessment.* A Special Report of the Center for International Security and Arms Control. Stanford: Stanford University, 1984.

Duffy, Gloria (Project Director). *Compliance and the Future of Arms Control.* Report of a project sponsored by the Center for International Security and Arms Control, Stanford University, and Global Outlook. Cambridge: Ballinger Books, 1988.

Dyson, Freeman. *Weapons and Hope.* New York: Harper & Row, 1984.

Eayrs, James. *In Defence of Canada: Peacemaking and Deterrence.* Toronto: University of Toronto Press, 1972.

Eden, Anthony. *Full Circle.* Boston: Houghton Mifflin Company, 1960.

Edwards, John. *Superweapon: The Making of MX.* New York: W.W. Norton & Company, 1982.

Eisenhower, Dwight D. *Crusade in Europe.* Garden City, N.Y.: Doubleday & Company, 1948.

———. *The Eisenhower Diaries.* Edited by Robert H. Ferrell. New York: W. W. Norton & Company, 1981.

———. *The Papers of Dwight David Eisenhower.* Edited by Alfred D. Chandler, Jr., and Louis Galambos. Baltimore: The Johns Hopkins University Press, 1970–1984.

———. *Public Papers of the Presidents of the United States, Dwight D. Eisenhower,* 1953–1960–61. Washington, D.C.: U.S. Government Printing Office, 1958–1961.

———. *The White House Years: Mandate for Change, 1953–56.* Garden City, N.Y.: Doubleday & Company, 1963.

———. *The White House Years: Waging Peace, 1956–61.* Garden City, N.Y.: Doubleday & Company, 1965.

Èly, Paul. *Mémoires: L'Indochine dans la Tourmente.* Paris: Librairie Plon, 1964.

Enthoven, Alain C., and K. Wayne Smith. *How Much Is Enough? Shaping the Defense Program, 1961–1969.* New York: Harper & Row, 1971.

Erickson, John, and E. J. Feuchtwanger, eds. *Soviet Military Power and Performance.* Hamden, Conn.: The Shoe String Press, 1979.

Evans, Medford. *The Secret War for the A-bomb.* Chicago: Henry Regnery Company, 1953.

Feis, Herbert. *The Atomic Bomb and the End of World War II.* Princeton: Princeton University Press, 1966.

Fermi, Laura. *Atoms for the World: United States Participation in the Conference on the Peaceful Uses of Atomic Energy.* Chicago, Ill.: University of Chicago Press, 1957.

Fleming, Donald, and Bernard Bailyn, eds. *The Intellectual Migration: Europe and America, 1930–1960.* Cambridge: Belknap Press of Harvard University Press, 1969.

Foot, Rosemary. *The Wrong War: American Policy and the Dimensions of the Korean Conflict, 1950–1953.* Ithaca: Cornell University Press, 1985.

Forrestal, James. *The Forrestal Diaries.* Edited by Walter Millis. New York: The Viking Press, 1951.

Freedman, Lawrence. *The Evolution of Nuclear Strategy.* New York: St. Martin's Press, 1981.

———. *U.S. Intelligence and the Soviet Strategic Threat.* Boulder, Colo.: Westview Press, 1977.

Frisch, Otto R. *What Little I Remember.* Cambridge: Cambridge University Press, 1979.

Furniss, Edgar S., Jr. *De Gaulle and the French Army: A Crisis in Civil-Military Relations.* New York: Twentieth Century Fund, 1964.

Gaddis, John Lewis. *The Long Peace: Inquiries Into the History of the Cold War.* New York: Oxford University Press, 1987.

Gallup, George H. *The Gallup Poll: Public Opinion, 1935–1971.* 3 vols. New York: Random House, 1972. Vol. 1: 1935–48.

Garthoff, Raymond L. *Détente and Confrontation: American-Soviet Relations From Nixon to Reagan.* Washington, D.C.: The Brookings Institution, 1985.

———. *Intelligence Assessment and Policymaking: A Decision Point in the Kennedy Administration.* Washington, D.C.: The Brookings Institution, 1984.

———. *Reflections on the Cuban Missile Crisis.* Washington, D.C.: The Brookings Institution, 1987.

———, ed. *Sino-Soviet Military Relations.* New York: Frederick A. Praeger, 1966.

Gaulle, Charles de. *Discours et messages.* 5 vols. Paris: Librairie Plon, 1970.

———. *Lettres, notes, et carnets, 1958–1960.* Paris: Librairie Plon, 1980–85.

———. *Mémoires de guerre.* 3 vols. Paris: Librairie Plon, 1954–59.

———. *Memoirs of Hope: Renewal and Endeavor.* Translated by Terence Kilmartin. New York: Simon & Schuster, 1971.

George, Alexander L., and Richard Smoke. *Deterrence in American Foreign Policy: Theory and Practice.* New York: Columbia University Press, 1974.

———, David K. Hall, and William E. Simons. *The Limits of Coercive Diplomacy: Laos, Cuba, Vietnam.* Boston: Little, Brown & Company, 1971.

Gilpin, Robert. *American Scientists and Nuclear Weapons Policy.* Princeton: Princeton University Press, 1962.

Giovannitti, Len, and Fred Freed. *The Decision to Drop the Bomb.* New York: Coward-McCann, Inc., 1965.

Goldschmidt, Bertrand. *Le Complexe Atomique.* Paris: Fayard, 1980. American Edition: *The Atomic Complex.* LaGrange Park, Ill.: American Nuclear Society, 1982.

———. *The Atomic Adventure: Its Political and Technical Aspects.* Oxford: Pergamon Press, 1964.

Golovin, I. N. *I. V. Kurchatov: A Socialist-Realist Biography of the Soviet Nuclear Scientist.* Bloomington, Ind.: Selbstverlag Press, 1968.

Gorbachev, Mikhail. *Perestroika: New Thinking for Our Country and the World.* New York: Harper & Row, 1987.

Goudsmit, Samuel A. *Alsos.* New York: Henry Schuman, 1947.

Gowing, Margaret. *Britain and Atomic Energy, 1939–45.* London: Macmillan & Co. Ltd., 1964.

———. *Independence and Deterrence: Britain and Atomic Energy, 1945–52.* 2 vols. London: Macmillan & Co., 1974. Vol. 1: Policy Making; Vol. 2: Policy Execution. Also New York: St. Martin's Press, 1974.

Gravel, Mike, ed. *The Pentagon Papers: The Defense Department History of United States Decisionmaking on Vietnam.* 4 vols. Boston: Beacon Press, 1971. Vol. 1.

Greenwood, Ted. *Making the MIRV: A Study of Defense Decision Making, 1904–1945.* Cambridge: Ballinger Publishing Company, 1975.

Grew, Joseph C. *Turbulent Era: A Diplomatic Record of Forty Years.* 2 vols. Boston: Houghton Mifflin Company, 1952.

Griffith, William E. *The Sino-Soviet Rift.* Cambridge: MIT Press, 1964.

Grosser, Alfred. *The Western Alliance: European-American Relations Since 1945.* New York: Continuum, 1980.

Groueff, Stephane. *Manhattan Project: The Untold Story of the Making of the Atomic Bomb.* Boston: Little, Brown & Company, 1967.

Groves, Leslie R. *Now It Can Be Told: The Story of the Manhattan Project.* New York: Harper & Row, 1962.

Hagerty, James C. *The Diary of James C. Hagerty: Eisenhower in Mid-Course, 1954–55.* Edited by Robert H. Ferrell. Bloomington: Indiana University Press, 1983.

Hahn, Otto. *Otto Hahn: A Scientific Autobiography.* Translated and edited by Willy Ley. New York: Charles Scribner's Sons, 1966.

———. *Otto Hahn: My Life.* Translated by Ernst Kaiser and Eithne Wilkins. New York: Herder & Herder, 1970.

Haldeman, H. R., and Joseph DiMona. *The Ends of Power.* New York: Times Books, 1978.

Halperin, Morton H. *China and the Bomb.* New York: Frederick A. Praeger, 1965.

———. *Nuclear Fallacy: Dispelling the Myth of Nuclear Strategy.* Cambridge: Ballinger Publishing Company, 1987.

Hansard's Parliamentary Debates (House of Commons), 5th series, vol. 537 (1954–55).

Harriman, W. Averell. *America and Russia in a Changing World.* Garden City, N.Y.: Doubleday & Company, Inc., 1971.

Harrison, Michael M. *The Reluctant Ally: France and Atlantic Security.* Baltimore: The Johns Hopkins University Press, 1981.

Hartcup, Guy, and T. E. Allibone. *Cockcroft and the Atom.* Bristol: Adam Hilger, 1984.

Heisenberg, Elisabeth. *Inner Exile.* Boston: Birkhäuser, 1984.

Heisenberg, Werner. *Physics and Beyond: Encounters and Conversations.* Translated from the German by Arnold J. Pomerans. New York: Harper Torchbooks, Harper & Row, 1971.

Herken, Gregg. *The Winning Weapon: The Atomic Bomb in the Cold War, 1945–50.* New York: Alfred A. Knopf, 1980.

Hersey, John. *Hiroshima.* New York: Alfred A. Knopf, 1946.

Hewlett, Richard G., and Oscar E. Anderson, Jr. *The New World, 1939/1946.* Vol. 1: A History of the United States Atomic Energy Commission. University Park, Pa.: Pennsylvania State University Press, 1962.

Hewlett, Richard G., and Francis Duncan. *Atomic Shield, 1947/1952.* Vol. 2: A History of the United States Atomic Energy Commission. University Park, Pa.: Pennsylvania State University Press, 1969.

———. *Nuclear Navy, 1946–62.* Chicago: University of Chicago Press, 1974.

Hillenbrand, Martin J., ed. *The Future of Berlin.* Montclair: Allanheld, Osmun Publishers, 1980.

Hilsman, Roger. *To Move a Nation: The Politics of Foreign Policy in the Administration of John F. Kennedy.* Garden City, N. Y.: Doubleday & Company, 1967.

Holland, Lauren H., and Robert A. Hoover. *The MX Decision.* Boulder, Colo.: Westview Press, 1985.

Holloway, David. *The Soviet Union and the Arms Race.* New Haven: Yale University Press, 1983.

Holton, Gerald. *The Advancement of Science, and Its Burdens.* Cambridge: Cambridge University Press, 1986.

Hoopes, Townsend. *The Devil and John Foster Dulles.* Boston: Little, Brown & Company, 1973.

Horelick, Arnold L., and Myron Rush. *Strategic Power and Soviet Foreign Policy.* Chicago: University of Chicago Press, 1966.

Hull, Cordell. *The Memoirs of Cordell Hull.* 2 vols. New York: Macmillan Company, 1948.

Hutchins, Robert M. *The Atomic Bomb Versus Civilization.* The Human Events pamphlets, no. 1. Washington, D.C.: Human Events, 1945.

Iklé, Fred Charles. *Every War Must End.* New York: Columbia University Press, 1971.

Irving, David. *The Destruction of Dresden.* London: William Kimber, 1963.

———. *The German Atomic Bomb: The History of Nuclear Research in Nazi Germany.* New York: Simon & Schuster, 1967.

Jervis, Robert. *The Illogic of American Nuclear Strategy.* Ithaca, N.Y.: Cornell University Press, 1984.

Johnson, Lyndon B. *Public Papers of the Presidents of the United States: Lyndon B. Johnson, 1963–1968–69.* Washington, D.C.: U.S. Government Printing Office, 1965–70.

Jones, R. V. "Winston Leonard Spencer Churchill." In *Biographical Memoirs of Fellows of the Royal Society,* 1966, vol. 12, pp. 35–105. London: Published by The Royal Society, 1966.

Jungk, Robert. *Brighter than a Thousand Suns: A Personal History of the Atomic Scientists.* Translated by James Cleugh. New York: Harcourt, Brace and Company, 1958.

Kahn, Herman. *On Escalation: Metaphors and Scenarios.* New York: Frederick A. Praeger, 1965.

Kalicki, J. H. *The Pattern of Sino-American Crises: Political-Military Interactions in the 1950s.* New York: Cambridge University Press, 1975.

Kaplan, Fred. *The Wizards of Armageddon.* New York: Simon & Schuster, 1983.

Kaplan, Morton A., ed. *Great Issues of International Politics.* 2nd edition. Chicago: Aldine Publishing Company, 1974.

Kaplan, Stephen S. *Diplomacy of Power: Soviet Armed Forces as a Political Instrument.* Washington, D.C.: The Brookings Institution, 1981.

Kase, Toshikazu. *Journey to the Missouri.* New Haven: Yale University Press, 1950.

Kelleher, Catherine McArdle. *Germany and the Politics of Nuclear Weapons.* New York: Columbia University Press, 1975.

Kennan, George. *Memoirs.* 2 vols. Boston: Little, Brown & Company, 1967–72. Vol. 1: 1925–50; Vol. 2: 1950–63.

Kennedy, John F. *Public Papers of the Presidents of the United States: John F. Kennedy, 1961–63.* Washington, D.C.: United States Government Printing Office, 1962–64.

———. *The Strategy of Peace.* Edited by Allan Nevins. New York: Harper & Brothers, 1960.

Kennedy, Robert F. *Thirteen Days: A Memoir of the Cuban Missile Crisis.* New York: W.W. Norton & Company, Inc., 1969. The 1971 edition includes an afterword by Richard E. Neustadt and Graham T. Allison.

Kevles, Daniel J. *The Physicists.* New York: Vintage Books, 1971.

Khrushchev, Nikita S. *Khrushchev in America.* New York: Crosscurrents Press, 1960.

———. *Khrushchev Remembers.* Translated and edited by Strobe Talbott. Boston: Little, Brown & Company, 1970.

———. *Khrushchev Remembers: The Last Testament.* Translated and edited by Strobe Talbott. Boston: Little, Brown & Company, 1974.

Killian, James R., Jr. *Sputnik, Scientists, and Eisenhower: A Memoir of the First Special Assistant to the President for Science and Technology.* Cambridge: MIT Press, 1977.

Kinnard, Douglas. *President Eisenhower and Strategy Management: A Study in Defense Politics.* Lexington: University of Kentucky Press, 1977.

Kissinger, Henry A. *The Necessity for Choice: Prospects of American Foreign Policy.* New York: Harper & Brothers, 1961.

———. *Nuclear Weapons and Foreign Policy.* New York: Published for the Council on Foreign Relations by Harper & Brothers, 1957.

———. *White House Years.* Boston: Little, Brown & Company, 1979.

———. *Years of Upheaval.* Boston: Little, Brown & Company, 1982.

Kistiakowsky, George B. *A Scientist at the White House: The Private Diary of President Eisenhower's Special Assistant for Science and Technology.* Cambridge: Harvard University Press, 1976.

Kohl, Wilfrid L. *French Nuclear Diplomacy.* Princeton: Princeton University Press, 1971.

Kraft, Joseph. *The Grand Design: From Common Market to Atlantic Partnership.* New York: Harper & Brothers, 1962.

Kramish, Arnold. *Atomic Energy in the Soviet Union.* Stanford: Stanford University Press, 1959; reprint ed., Ann Arbor: University Microfilms International, 1986.

Kull, Steven. *Minds at War: Nuclear Reality and the Inner Conflicts of Defense Policymakers.* New York: Basic Books, Inc., 1988.

Kuniholm, Bruce R. *The Origins of the Cold War in the Near East.* Princeton: Princeton University Press, 1980.

Labrie, Roger P., ed. *SALT Handbook: Key Documents and Issues 1972–1979.* Washington, D.C.: American Enterprise Institute for Public Policy Research, 1979.

Lacouture, Jean. *De Gaulle.* 3 vols. Paris: Editions du Seuil, 1984–86.

———. *Pierre Mendès France.* Paris: Editions du Seuil, 1981.

Lamont, Lansing. *Day of Trinity.* New York: Atheneum, 1985; original ed. 1965.

Lang, Daniel. *From Hiroshima to the Moon: Chronicles of Life in the Atomic Age.* New York: Simon and Schuster, 1959.

Larrabee, Eric. *Commander in Chief.* New York: Harper & Row, 1987.

Larson, David L., ed. *The "Cuban Crisis" of 1962.* Boston: Houghton Mifflin Company, 1963.

Leahy, William D. *I Was There: The Personal Story of the Chief of Staff to Presidents Roosevelt and Truman Based on His Notes and Diaries Made at the Time.* New York: Whittlesey House, McGraw-Hill Book Company, 1950.

Leebaert, Derek, ed. *Soviet Military Thinking.* London: George Allen & Unwin, 1981.

LeMay, Curtis E., with Dale O. Smith. *America Is in Danger.* New York: Funk & Wagnalls, 1968.

Lewis, John Wilson, and Xue Litai. *China Builds the Bomb.* Stanford: Stanford University Press, 1988.

Library of Congress, Congressional Research Service. *The U.S. Government and the Vietnam War: Executive and Legislative Roles and Relationships.* Washington, D.C.: U.S. Government Printing Office, 1984.

Lilienthal, David E. *The Journals of David E. Lilienthal.* Vol 2: *The Atomic Energy Years 1945–1950.* New York: Harper & Row, 1964.

Lowell, Robert. *For the Union Dead.* New York: Farrar, Straus & Giroux, 1964.

L'Université de Franche-Comté et l'Institut Charles-de-Gaulle. *L'Aventure de la Bombe: De Gaulle et la dissuasion nucléaire (1958–69).* Paris: Librairie Plon, 1985.

Macmillan, Harold. *At the End of the Day, 1961–63.* New York: Harper & Row, 1973.

———. *Pointing the Way, 1959–61.* New York: Harper & Row, 1972.

———. *Riding the Storm, 1956–59.* New York: Harper & Row, 1971.

Major, John. *The Oppenheimer Hearing.* New York: Stein & Day, 1971.

Malone, Peter. *The British Nuclear Deterrent.* New York: St. Martin's Press, 1984.

Martin, John Bartlow. *Adlai Stevenson and the World.* Garden City, N.Y.: Doubleday & Company, Inc., 1977.

Martin, Laurence, ed. *Strategic Thought in the Nuclear Age.* Baltimore: The Johns Hopkins University Press, 1979.

Marwah, Onkar, and Jonathan D. Pollack, eds. *Military Power and Policy in Asian States: China, India, Japan.* Boulder, Colo.: Westview Press, 1980.

Masters, Dexter, and Katharine Way, eds. *One World or None.* New York: Whittlesey House, McGraw-Hill Book Co., 1946; reprint ed., Freeport, N.Y.: Books for Libraries Press, 1972.

McCloy, John J. *The Challenge to American Foreign Policy.* Cambridge: Harvard University Press, 1953.

McLin, Jon B. *Canada's Changing Defense Policy, 1957–63: The Problems of a Middle Power in Alliance.* Baltimore: The Johns Hopkins University Press, 1967.

McNamara, Robert S. *Blundering into Disaster.* New York: Pantheon Books, 1986.

———. *The Essence of Security.* New York: Harper & Row, 1968.

Mickiewicz, Ellen Propper, and Roman Kolkowicz, eds. *International Security & Arms Control.* New York: Praeger Publishers, 1986.

Miller, Steven E., and Stephen Van Evera, eds. *The Star Wars Controversy.* Princeton: Princeton University Press, 1986.

Monnet, Jean. *Memoirs.* Garden City, N.Y.: Doubleday & Company, 1978.

Morison, Samuel Eliot. *History of United States Naval Operations in World War II.* Vol. 12: *Leyte, June 1944–January 1945.* Boston: Little, Brown & Company, 1958.

Moss, Norman. *Men Who Play God: The Story of the H-Bomb and How the World Came to Live with It.* New York: Harper & Row, 1968.

Neustadt, Richard E. *Alliance Politics.* New York: Columbia University Press, 1970.

New York Times, Hiroshima Plus 20. New York: Delacorte Press, 1965.

Newhouse, John. *Cold Dawn: The Story of SALT.* New York: Holt, Rinehart & Winston, 1973.

———. *De Gaulle and the Anglo-Saxons.* New York: The Viking Press, 1970.

Nicholas, H. G., ed. *Washington Despatches 1941–1945: Weekly Political Reports from the British Embassy.* Chicago: The University of Chicago Press, 1981.

Nichols, K. D. *The Road to Trinity: A Personal Account of How America's Nuclear Policies Were Made.* New York: William Morrow & Company, 1987.

Nixon, Richard. *Public Papers of the Presidents of the United States: Richard Nixon, 1969–1974.* Washington, D.C.: United States Government Printing Office, 1971–75.

———. *RN: The Memoirs of Richard Nixon.* New York: Grosset & Dunlap, 1978.

Nogee, Joseph L. *Soviet Policy Towards International Control of Atomic Energy.* Notre Dame, Ind.: University of Notre Dame Press, 1961.

O'Donnell, Kenneth P., and David F. Powers, with Joe McCarthy. *"Johnny, We Hardly Knew Ye."* Boston: Little, Brown & Company, 1972.

Oppenheimer, Robert. *Letters and Recollections.* Edited by Alice Kimball Smith and Charles Weiner. Cambridge: Harvard University Press, 1980.

Pearson, Lester B. *Mike: The Memoirs of the Right Honourable Lester B. Pearson.* 2 vols. New York: Quadrangle Books, 1972–73.

Peierls, Rudolf. *Bird of Passage: Recollections of a Physicist.* Princeton: Princeton University Press, 1985.

Pfau, Richard. *No Sacrifice Too Great: The Life of Lewis L. Strauss.* Charlottesville: University Press of Virginia, 1984.

Pierre, Andrew J. *Nuclear Politics: The British Experience with an Independent Strategic Force, 1939–70.* London: Oxford University Press, 1972.

Pocket Books editors. *The Atomic Age Opens.* New York: Pocket Books, 1945.

Pogue, Forrest C. *George C. Marshall: Statesman 1945–1959.* New York: Viking Penguin Inc., 1987.

Pope, Ronald R., ed. *Soviet Views on the Cuban Missile Crisis: Myth and Reality in Foreign Policy Analysis.* Washington, D.C.: University Press of America, 1982.

Power, General Thomas S., USAF (Retired), with Albert A. Arnhym. *Design for Survival.* New York: Coward-McCann, 1964.

Prados, John. *The Sky Would Fall, Operation Vulture: The U.S. Bombing Mission in Indochina, 1954.* New York: Dial Press, 1983.

———. *The Soviet Estimate: U.S. Intelligence Analysis & Russian Military Strength.* New York: Dial Press, 1982.

Prochnau, William W., and Richard W. Larsen. *A Certain Democrat: Senator Henry M. Jackson, A Political Biography.* Englewood Cliffs, N.J.: Prentice-Hall, Inc., 1972.

Proceedings of the American Philosophical Society, 90, No. 1.

Quandt, William B. *Decade of Decisions: American Policy Toward the Arab-Israeli Conflict, 1967–1976.* Berkeley: University of California Press, 1977.

Reagan, Ronald. *Public Papers of the President of the United States: Ronald Reagan, 1981–1984.* Washington, D.C.: United States Government Printing Office, 1982–86.

———. *Weekly Compilation of Presidential Documents.* October 21, 1985; June 23, 1986; March 30, 1987. Washington, D.C.: United States Government Printing Office.

Rees, David. *Korea: The Limited War.* New York: St. Martin's Press, 1964.

Reid, R. W. *Tongues of Conscience: Weapons Research and the Scientists' Dilemma.* New York: Walker & Company, 1969.

Reiss, Mitchell. *Without the Bomb: The Politics of Nuclear Nonproliferation.* New York: Columbia University Press, 1988.

Rhodes, Richard. *The Making of the Atomic Bomb.* New York: Simon & Schuster, 1986.

Roberts, Chalmers M. *First Rough Draft: A Journalist's Journal of Our Times.* New York: Praeger, 1973.

Robin, Gabriel. *La Crise de Cuba (Octobre 1962): Du Mythe à l'histoire.* Paris: Economica, 1984.

Roosevelt, Franklin D., and Felix Frankfurter. *Roosevelt and Frankfurter: Their Correspondence, 1928–1945.* Annotated by Max Freedman. Boston: Little, Brown & Company, 1967.

Roosevelt, Franklin D. *The Public Papers and Addresses of Franklin D. Roosevelt, 1928–45.* 13 vols. New York: Random House, Macmillan Company, and Harper & Brothers, 1938–50. 1939, 1944–45 vols.

Roosevelt, James, with Bill Libby. *My Parents: A Differing View.* Chicago: Playboy Press, 1976.

Rose, Francois de. *European Security and France.* Urbana: University of Illinois Press, 1985.

Rosecrance, R. N., ed. *The Dispersion of Nuclear Weapons: Strategy and Politics.* New York: Columbia University Press, 1964.

Rosenblatt, Roger. *Witness: The World Since Hiroshima.* Boston: Little, Brown & Company, 1985.

Rostow, W. W. *The Diffusion of Power: An Essay in Recent History.* New York: The Macmillan Company, 1972.

————. *Open Skies: Eisenhower's Proposal of July 21, 1955.* Austin: University of Texas Press, 1982.

Rovere, Richard H. *The Eisenhower Years.* New York: Farrar, Straus & Cudahy, 1956.

Rozental, S., ed. *Niels Bohr: His Life and Work as Seen by His Friends and Colleagues.* New York: John Wiley & Sons, 1967.

Samii, Kuross A. *Involvement by Invitation: American Strategies of Containment in Iran.* University Park, Pa.: The Pennsylvania State University Press, 1987.

Sapolsky, Harvey M. *The Polaris System Development: Bureaucratic and Programmatic Success in Government.* Cambridge: Harvard University Press, 1972.

Scheinman, Lawrence. *Atomic Energy Policy in France under the Fourth Republic.* Princeton, N.J.: Princeton University Press, 1965.

Schelling, Thomas C. *Arms and Influence.* New Haven: Yale University Press, 1966.

————. *The Strategy of Conflict.* Cambridge: Harvard University Press, 1980.

Schilling, Warner R., Paul Y. Hammond, and Glenn H. Snyder. *Strategy, Politics, and Defense Budgets.* New York: Columbia University Press, 1962.

Schlesinger, Arthur M., Jr. *A Thousand Days: John F. Kennedy in the White House.* Boston: Houghton Mifflin Company, 1965.

————. *Robert Kennedy and His Times.* Boston: Houghton Mifflin Company, 1978.

Schnabel, James F. *The History of the Joint Chiefs of Staff: The Joint Chiefs of Staff and National Policy, Volume I 1945–47.* Wilmington, Del.: Michael Glazier, 1979.

Schoenbrun, David. *The Three Lives of Charles de Gaulle.* New York: Atheneum, 1966.

Schwarz, Jordan A. *The Speculator: Bernard M. Baruch in Washington, 1917–1965.* Chapel Hill: The University of North Carolina Press, 1981.

Seaborg, Glenn T. *Kennedy, Khrushchev, and the Test Ban.* Berkeley: University of California Press, 1981.

Segrè, Emilio. *Enrico Fermi, Physicist.* Chicago: University of Chicago Press, 1970.

Shea, William R., ed. *Otto Hahn and the Rise of Nuclear Physics.* Boston: D. Reidel Publishing Company, 1983.

Sherry, Michael S. *The Rise of American Air Power: The Creation of Armageddon.* New Haven: Yale University Press, 1987.

Sherwin, Martin J. *A World Destroyed: The Atomic Bomb and the Grand Alliance.* New York: Alfred A. Knopf, 1975.

Sherwood, Robert E. *Roosevelt and Hopkins: An Intimate History.* New York: Harper & Brothers, 1948.

Sidey, Hugh. *John F. Kennedy, President.* New York: Atheneum, 1963.

Sigal, Leon V. *Fighting to a Finish: The Politics of War Termination in the United States and Japan, 1945.* Ithaca: Cornell University Press, 1988.

Slusser, Robert M. *The Berlin Crisis of 1961: Soviet-American Relations and the Struggle for Power in the Kremlin, June–November 1961.* Baltimore: The Johns Hopkins University Press, 1973.

Smith, Alice Kimball. *A Peril and a Hope: The Scientists' Movement in America: 1945–47.* Chicago: University of Chicago Press, 1965.

Smith, Gerard. *Doubletalk: The Story of SALT I.* Garden City, N.Y.: Doubleday & Company, 1980.

Smyth, Henry De Wolf. *Atomic Energy for Military Purposes: The Official Report on the Development of the Atomic Bomb under the Auspices of the United States Government, 1940–45.* Princeton: Princeton University Press, 1945.

Sokolovskiy, V. D. *Soviet Military Strategy.* Edited by Harriet Fast Scott. 3rd ed. New York: Crane, Russak & Company, Inc., 1975.

Sorensen Theodore C. *Decision-Making in the White House: The Olive Branch or the Arrows.* New York: Columbia University Press, 1963.

———. *Kennedy.* New York: Harper & Row, 1965.

Spector, Leonard S. *Nuclear Proliferation Today.* New York: Vintage Books, 1984.

Speer, Albert. *Inside the Third Reich: Memoirs by Albert Speer.* Translated by Richard and Clara Winston. New York: Macmillan Company, 1970.

Steinbruner, John D. *The Cybernetic Theory of Decision: New Dimensions of Political Analysis.* Princeton: Princeton University Press, 1974.

Stern, Philip M. *The Oppenheimer Case: Security on Trial.* New York: Harper & Row, 1969.

Stimson, Henry L. and McGeorge Bundy. *On Active Service in Peace and War.* New York: Harper & Brothers, 1948.

Strauss, Lewis L. *Men and Decisions.* Garden City, N.Y.: Doubleday & Company, 1962.

Stromseth, Jane E. *The Origins of Flexible Response.* New York: St. Martin's Press, 1988.

Subrahmanyam, K., ed. *Nuclear Myths and Realities: India's Dilemma.* New Delhi, India: ABC Publishing, 1981.

Sulzberger, C. L. *A Long Row of Candles: Memoirs and Diaries, 1934–54.* Toronto: Macmillan Company, 1969.

Szilard, Leo. *The Collected Works of Leo Szilard: Scientific Papers.* Edited by Bernard T. Feld and Gertrud Weiss Szilard. Cambridge: MIT Press, 1972.

———. *Leo Szilard: His Version of the Facts. Selected Recollections and Correspondence.* Edited by Spencer Weart and Gertrud Weiss Szilard. Cambridge: MIT Press, 1978.

Talbott, Strobe. *Deadly Gambits: The Reagan Administration and the Stalemate in Nuclear Arms Control.* New York: Alfred A. Knopf, 1984.

Tatu, Michel. *Power in the Kremlin: From Khrushchev to Kosygin.* New York: The Viking Press, 1969.

Thirring, Hans. *Die Geschichte der Atombombe.* Wien: "Neues Osterreich" Zeitungs und Verlagsgesellschaft, 1946.

Toland, John. *The Rising Sun: The Decline and Fall of the Japanese Empire, 1936–45.* New York: Random House, 1970.

Truman, Harry S. *Memoirs by Harry S. Truman.* 2 vols. Garden City, N.Y.: Doubleday & Company, 1955–56. Vol. 1: *Year of Decisions.* Vol. 2: *Years of Trial and Hope.*

———. *Off the Record: The Private Papers of Harry S. Truman.* Edited by Robert H. Ferrell. New York: Harper & Row, 1980.

———. *Public Papers of the Presidents of the United States: Harry S. Truman, 1945–1952–53.* Washington D.C.: United States Government Printing Office, 1961–66.

Tsou, Tang, ed. *China in Crisis.* Vol. 2: *China's Policies in Asia and America's Alternatives.* Chicago: The University of Chicago Press, 1968.

Tyroler, Charles II, ed. *Alerting America: The Papers of the Committee on the Present Danger.* Washington, D.C.: Pergamon-Brassey's International Defense Publishers, 1984.

Ulam, Adam B. *Stalin: The Man and His Era.* New York: The Viking Press, 1973.

U.S. Atomic Energy Commission. *In the Matter of J. Robert Oppenheimer: Transcript of Hearing before Personnel Security Board.* Washington, D.C.: United States Government Printing Office, 1954.

U.S. Department of State. *Foreign Relations of the United States, 1943–1955–1957.* Washington, D.C.: United States Government Printing Office, 1963–86.

U.S. Department of State. *The International Control of Atomic Energy: Growth of a Policy.* Washington, D.C.: United States Government Printing Office, 1946.

U.S. Department of State. Committee on Atomic Energy. *A Report on the International Control of Atomic Energy.* Washington, D.C.: U.S. Government Printing Office, 1946.

The United States in World Affairs, 1954, 1955, 1958. New York: Published for the Council on Foreign Relations by Harper & Brothers.

Vonnegut, Kurt, Jr. *Slaughterhouse-Five: Or the Children's Crusade, A Duty-Dance with Death.* New York: Delacorte Press, 1969.

Walker, Richard Lee. *Strategic Target Planning: Bridging the Gap between Theory and Practice.* National Security Affairs Monograph Series 83–9. Washington, D.C.: National Defense University Press, 1983.

Wallace, Henry A. *The Price of Vision: The Diary of Henry A. Wallace, 1942–1946.* Edited by John Morton Blum. Boston: Houghton Mifflin Company, 1973.

Waller, Douglas C. *Congress and the Nuclear Freeze.* Amherst: The University of Massachusetts Press, 1987.

Walzer, Michael. *Just and Unjust Wars: A Moral Argument with Historical Illustrations.* New York: Basic Books, 1977.

Weart, Spencer R. *Scientists in Power.* Cambridge: Harvard University Press, 1979.

Weiner, Charles. "A New Site for the Seminar: The Refugees and American Physics in the Thirties." In *The Intellectual Migration: Europe and America, 1930–1960*. Edited by Donald Fleming and Bernard Bailyn. Cambridge: Belknap Press of Harvard University Press, 1969.

Weissman, Steve, and Herbert Krosney. *The Islamic Bomb*. New York: Times Books, 1981.

Wells, H. G. *The World Set Free: A Story of Mankind*. New York: E.P. Dutton & Company, 1914.

Westmoreland, William C. *A Soldier Reports*. Garden City, N.Y.: Doubleday & Company, 1976.

Wheeler-Bennett, John W. *John Anderson, Viscount Waverley*. New York: St. Martin's Press, 1962.

Wich, Richard. *Sino-Soviet Crisis Politics: A Study of Political Change and Communication*. Cambridge: Council on East Asian Studies, Harvard University and distributed by Harvard University Press, 1980.

Wilcox, Robert K. *Japan's Secret War*. New York: William Morrow & Company, Inc., 1985.

Williams, Francis. *Twilight of Empire: Memoirs of Prime Minister Clement Attlee*. Westport, Conn.: Greenwood Press, Publishers, 1978; originally A. S. Barnes and Company, 1960–61.

Wilson, Jane, ed. *All in Our Time: The Reminiscences of Twelve Nuclear Pioneers*. Chicago: Reprinted from the Bulletin of the Atomic Scientists, 1975.

Wyden, Peter. *Day One: Before Hiroshima and After*. New York: Simon & Schuster, 1984.

York, Herbert F. *The Advisors: Oppenheimer, Teller, and the Superbomb*. San Francisco: W. H. Freeman and Company, 1976.

———. *Does Strategic Defense Breed Offense?* Lanham, Md.: University Press of America, 1987.

———. *Making Weapons, Talking Peace: A Physicist's Odyssey from Hiroshima to Geneva*. New York: Basic Books, 1987.

———. *Race to Oblivion: A Participant's View of the Arms Race*. New York: Simon & Schuster, 1970.

Zhukov, G. K. *The Memoirs of Marshal Zhukov*. New York: Delacorte Press, 1971.

Notes

CHAPTER I

1. There is argument as to exactly what Rutherford said; this version, nearly contemporaneous, comes from an approving editorial, "Talking Moonshine," in *Scientific American,* November 1933, p. 201. I owe the reference to Kevles, *The Physicists,* p. 271. For a different version, see Richard Rhodes, *The Making of the Atomic Bomb,* pp. 27–28. Here as elsewhere in this admirable volume we have Leo Szilard's "version of the facts."

2. Soddy, "Radium," *Professional Papers of the Corps of Royal Engineers* 29 (1903): 250–51. I owe this citation to Richard E. Sclove, and much of my understanding of Soddy to his excellent unpublished paper, "Atomic PreMunitions: Frederick Soddy and the Social Responsibility of Scientists."

3. Wells was not the very first, as Paul Brians notes in his excellent study of atomic war in fiction, *Nuclear Holocausts,* at pp. 4–5. Radium had inspired earlier works by lesser writers.

4. The importance of this work is described in many places, but notably in Smyth, *Atomic Energy for Military Purposes,* pp. 17–18; the hydrogen and lithium example is also Smyth's, p. 22. An excellent account is in Hartcup and Allibone, *Cockcroft and the Atom,* chap. 5.

5. Smyth, *Atomic Energy for Military Purposes,* p. 9.

6. The best account known to me is in Weart, *Scientists in Power,* pp. 44–47.

7. Fermi's work in this period and later is described with understanding admiration by his "friend, disciple, and fellow scientist," Emilio Segre, in *Enrico Fermi, Physicist;* at Appendix 2 is Fermi's own Nobel speech on his work, which was "semipopular" to Segre, just right for me. The speech is particularly enlightening because it was delivered, ironically, one month before Fermi's work was overtaken by the discovery of fission.

8. Hahn, "The Discovery of Fission," p. 78.

9. Ibid., p. 80.

10. Ibid., p. 82.

11. Weart, *Scientists in Power,* p. 59.

12. Frisch, *What Little I Remember,* pp. 116–17.

13. This account rests primarily on Weart, *Scientists in Power.* Chaps. 4–10 offer a thorough and systematic study of the French effort in 1939–40, along with penetrating comparisons with the progress of others in the same period.

14. Clark, *The Birth of the Bomb,* p. 21, quoted in Weart, *Scientists in Power,* p. 86.

15. Weart, *Scientists in Power,* chaps. 7–9.

16. Ibid., pp. 138–39.

17. Ibid., p. 103.

18. Ibid., p. 150; and Goldschmidt, *Le Complexe Atomique,* p. 38.

19. Irving, *The German Atomic Bomb,* pp. 35–36, 49–50. Originally published in London under the title *Virus House,* this volume is much the best single account of the German uranium effort in World War II. Controversy surrounding other historical works by Irving should not be allowed to shadow this one, which stands up well to critical reading and comparison with other evidence.

20. Hahn, *Otto Hahn: A Scientific Autobiography,* pp. 162–72, and *Otto Hahn: My Life,* p. 155; Heisenberg, *Physics and Beyond,* p. 195.

21. For Hahn's budget see Irving, *The German Atomic Bomb,* p. 230, and for Hahn's extraordinarily high priority, p. 155. For the way German scientists cheerfully corrupted the meaning of the designation "decisive for the war effort"—*kriegsentscheidend*—see Beyerchen, *Scientists Under Hitler,* pp. 190–91.

22. This summary account rests heavily on Irving, *The German Atomic Bomb.* I share Beyerchen's judgment that Irving's account is more accurate than the earlier and conflicting assessments of Goudsmit (dumb Germans) and Jungk (noble Germans). See Goudsmit, *Alsos,* and Jungk, *Brighter than a Thousand Suns.*

23. Peierls, "Atomic Germans," p. 23.

24. Heisenberg's account of these beliefs is in *Physics and Beyond,* pp. 170–75. The book is composed largely of reconstructed conversations consciously in the manner of Thucydides, but rather less compelling; still Heisenberg is a witness of stature. His somewhat complacent assumption of German leadership in 1945 is reported in Goudsmit, *Alsos,* p. 113.

25. The 1939 report is in Irving, *The German Atomic Bomb,* p. 53; the later estimate of the U-235 problem and the opinion on the German development program are in Heisenberg, *Physics and Beyond,* p. 180.

26. Holton, *The Advancement of Science, and Its Burdens,* p. 160.

27. There are accounts of the Germans' reaction to Hiroshima in Groves, *Now It Can Be Told,* pp. 333–37, and in Reid, *Tongues of Conscience,* pp. 118–122. Groves gloats; Reid tries to understand. Heisenberg's later conclusion is in *Physics and Beyond,* p. 180.

28. Varied versions of this encounter are given by Heisenberg, *Physics and Beyond,* pp. 181–82; by Reid, *Tongues of Conscience,* pp. 95–100; by Jungk, *Brighter than a Thousand Suns,* pp. 102–4; and very briefly in an essay by Aage Bohr, in *Niels Bohr,* ed. Rozental, p. 193.

29. Letter of Heisenberg to Jungk, quoted by Jungk, *Brighter than a Thousand Suns,* p. 103.

30. Bernstein, *Hans Bethe: Prophet of Energy,* p. 77; Bethe tells me, after reading an earlier draft, that he heard this explanation not from Heisenberg himself but from a third party; Rhodes, *The Making of the Atomic Bomb,* p. 389, quoting from Elizabeth Heisenberg, *Inner Exile,* pp. 77 ff.

31. Jungk, *Brighter than a Thousand Suns,* pp. 103–4.

32. Gowing, *Britain and Atomic Energy, 1939–45,* p. 248.

33. Irving, *The German Atomic Bomb,* pp. 102–3.

34. Speer, *Inside the Third Reich,* pp. 228, 336. For a fuller account of Hitler's view of German scientists, and theirs of him, see Beyerchen, *Scientists under Hitler,* especially chap. 10.

35. This elusive anecdote is told three different ways: by Irving, *The German Atomic Bomb,* pp. 77–78; by Goudsmit, *Alsos,* p. 165; and by Jungk, *Brighter than a Thousand Suns,* p. 95.

36. Speer, *Inside the Third Reich,* pp. 226–27.

37. The attitudes of Von Braun and Dornberger, and in particular their determined and skillful effort to win Hitler's support, are well treated in Reid, *Tongues of Conscience,* pp. 80–84, 104–8.

38. Speer, *Inside the Third Reich,* p. 227.

39. Heisenberg, "Research in Germany on the Technical Application of Atomic Energy," p. 213.

40. Speer, *Inside the Third Reich,* p. 226; confirmed in Irving, *The German Atomic Bomb,* p. 298.

41. Heisenberg, "Research in Germany on the Technical Application of Atomic Energy," p. 214.

42. This section depends heavily on the first volume of the British official history by Gowing, *Britain and Atomic Energy, 1939–45.* This distinguished work has made all earlier studies of only marginal interest; it is a model of clarity and accuracy.

43. Gowing, *Britain and Atomic Energy, 1939–45,* p. 37.

44. Ibid., p. 42. The Frisch-Peierls memorandum is a two-part document. One part is technical, and the other, written in layman's language, is broader and addresses such political questions as the "extreme importance" of secrecy, "since any rumor about the connection between uranium-separation and a super-bomb may set a German scientist thinking along the right lines." Professor Gowing's judgment fits both parts of the memorandum, although she herself had seen only the more technical paper when she wrote. The other part, shorter and in some respects still sharper, was discovered only later, by William Clark, who found a copy in the papers of Sir Henry Tizard, the first British official to receive the memorandum. It is printed in Clark's *Tizard,* at pp. 215–17.

45. The Maud report is printed in Gowing, *Britain and Atomic Energy, 1939–45,* pp. 394–436; the conclusions on the bomb are at p. 398. The Maud Committee in fact overstated what "any capable physicist" would be likely to perceive, but the conviction that others might see the possibilities was central to the urgency of its recommendation.

46. Gowing, *Britain and Atomic Energy, 1939–45,* pp. 96–7.

47. Ibid., p. 106.

48. Ibid., p. 95; Anderson's life has been told in a friendly and informal way by Wheeler-Bennett, *John Anderson, Viscount Waverley.*

49. Gowing, *Britain and Atomic Energy, 1939–45,* pp. 90–96.

50. Ibid., p. 105.

51. Ibid., pp. 95–103.

52. The basic book on the American effort is the official history, Hewlett and Anderson, *The New World;* it is extraordinarily reliable. An excellent large-scale treatment with emphases quite different from my own is Rhodes, *The Making of the Atomic Bomb.* It came to hand after this chapter was drafted, but I have found it a most helpful double-check on my relatively brief account.

53. Kevles, *The Physicists,* p. 219, and chap. 14. Kevles's conclusion is not accepted by some of my friends among physicists, but I find his argument persuasive.

54. Weiner, "A New Site for the Seminar: The Refugees and American Physics in the Thirties," in *Intellectual Migration,* p. 228.

55. Kevles, *The Physicists,* pp. 282–86. Alvarez on Lawrence is in *All in Our Time,* ed. Wilson, p. 15. This is a splendid collection of recollections by physicists of the years before Alamogordo.

56. Oppenheimer, *Letters and Recollections,* pp. 207–8. This meticulously edited and sensitively selected collection is the most valuable single volume we yet have on Oppenheimer's life up to 1945.

57. Much the best book about Szilard is *Leo Szilard: His Version of the Facts. Selected Recollections and Correspondence,* edited by Spencer Weart and Gertrude Weiss Szilard. It is indeed Szilard mainly as he saw himself and thus incomplete, but the integrity of the editing is such that one can also understand why others saw him differently. Except where otherwise noted this book is the basis of the following account of his role in the first approach to Franklin Roosevelt.

58. Szilard, *Leo Szilard: His Version of the Facts,* p. 54.

59. Ibid., p. 82.

60. Ibid., p. 84.

61. A straightforward account of the Sachs visit is in Hewlett and Anderson, *The New World,* p. 17. Sachs's own version is in his still unpublished "Early History Atomic Project in Relation to President Roosevelt, 1939–40," typescript, MED. The Einstein letter is in FDR and is printed in many places, conveniently in Szilard, *Leo Szilard: His Version of the Facts,* pp. 94–96.

62. Hewlett and Anderson, *The New World,* pp. 21–23; also Sachs, "Early History Atomic Project."

63. Sachs's "Early History Atomic Project" includes as Exhibit 1 the nine-page essay on what made Hitler possible that he claims to have read aloud to the president and commended as "concentrated sense that makes the proposal urgent." If Roosevelt really listened through this pompous account of the errors of interwar statesmanship, he deserves high marks for patience. And if he did, there may well be truth in the account given by Jungk, *Brighter than a Thousand Suns,* pp. 109–10; here Sachs is quoted as remembering that he had *two* conversations with Roosevelt, boring him in the first and persuading him only at breakfast the following day, by telling an apocryphal story of how England was saved from Napoleon by the French emperor's refusal to let Robert Fulton build him a fleet of weatherproof steamships. *Si Non è vero . . .*

64. Hewlett and Anderson, *The New World,* pp. 23–24.

65. Szilard, *Leo Szilard: His Version of the Facts,* p. 115.

66. Compton, *Atomic Quest,* p. 29.

67. Hewlett and Anderson, *The New World,* pp. 22–24.

68. Bush, *Pieces of the Action,* p. 36. A year later Roosevelt enlarged the enterprise by creating an Office of Scientific Research and Development (OSRD) with broader powers. He made Bush its director. NDRC continued with an advisory role within OSRD, and Conant became its chairman.

69. The achievement of Bush is attested in many places. The official history by Hewlett and Anderson, *The New World,* is important here, and there is the value of a contemporary eye in Baxter, *Scientists Against Time.* An excellent later account is in *The Physicists,* chaps. 19 and 20. Henry Stimson's judgment is in Stimson and Bundy, *On Active Service,* p. 465.

70. Carroll Wilson, conversation, May 16, 1980.

71. Kevles, *The Physicists,* p. 294.

72. Roosevelt's letter to Briggs of June 15, 1940, is in Atomic Bomb File, FDR. The main story is in Hewlett and Anderson, *The New World,* pp. 24–26. Bush's draftsmanship is confirmed in Bush, *Pieces of the Action,* p. 38.

73. This description of Breit comes from between the lines of orthodox accounts, which are not directly critical, and was confirmed in an interview of July 1, 1980, by I. I. Rabi, whose description of Breit's capacity to miss the point I quote.

74. Compton, *Atomic Quest,* pp. 5, 29–30.

75. E. O. Lawrence, "Historical Notes on Early Activities of Ernest O. Lawrence in Connection with the Tubealloy Project," E. O. Lawrence Papers.

76. I. I. Rabi, interview, July 1, 1980; Gowing, *Britain and Atomic Energy, 1939–45,* p. 84.

77. E. O. Lawrence, "Historical Notes on Early Activities of Ernest O. Lawrence in Connection with Tubealloy Project," E. O. Lawrence Papers; and Hewlett and Anderson, *The New World,* pp. 33–36.

78. Vannevar Bush to Frank B. Jewett, June 7, 1941, Bush-Conant correspondence, folder 4, OSRD.

79. The role of Bainbridge is sketched in Clark, *The Birth of the Bomb,* pp. 131–32, and in Lamont, *Day of Trinity,* pp. 28–29. The estimate of Bainbridge's quality as a witness is my own.

80. The National Academy of Sciences reports of May and July are amply summarized in Hewlett and Anderson, *The New World,* pp. 37–39, from which I quote. The full text of the May report has been declassified and, along with the July report, is available at the National Academy of Sciences. The November 1941 report is in the Bush-Conant correspondence, folder 18, OSRD.

81. Conant, *My Several Lives,* p. 278.

82. Hewlett and Anderson, *The New World,* pp. 42–43.

83. "Report of the National Defense Research Committee for the First Year of Operation, June 27, 1940, to June 28, 1941," PSF Collection, FDR. Sherwin, in *A World Destroyed,* pp. 36–37, suggests that Roosevelt read this passage, but that seems highly unlikely. Not only does Bush clearly assume in his last sentence that the president would *not* see it, but it stretches the imagination to suppose in that warlike season, with no interested staff to guide

him, no meeting with the author, and no warning in the covering letter, the president would have turned to pages 34 and 35 of a sixty-page report. The report tells us what Bush thought, not what Roosevelt knew.

84. Conant, *My Several Lives,* p. 279.

85. Vannevar Bush to James Conant, October 9, 1941, Bush-Conant correspondence, folder 5, OSRD.

86. Vannevar Bush to Franklin Roosevelt, March 9, 1942, Bush-Conant correspondence, folder 5, OSRD.

87. Rhodes, *The Making of the Atomic Bomb,* p. 378.

88. Roosevelt's view of Conant, and Conant's diplomacy over the tercentenary fuss, are reflected in the Conant and Harvard files at FDR Library. The exchanges between Roosevelt and Lowell—which Conant correctly found unworthy of both—are also in *Roosevelt and Frankfurter: Their Correspondence,* ed. Freedman, pp. 322–27.

89. Oliphant's visit is assessed in Hewlett and Anderson, *The New World,* p. 43, and in Gowing, *Britain and Atomic Energy, 1939–1945,* pp. 116–17, 121. Lawrence pays special tribute to Oliphant's persuasiveness, and records his understanding of the necessary American role, in "Historical Notes on Early Activities of Ernest O. Lawrence in Connection with the Tubealloy Project," E. O Lawrence Papers. In *Leo Szilard: His Version of the Facts,* at p. 146, Szilard's version is that the Americans owed Oliphant a medal.

90. I. I. Rabi, interview, July 1, 1980.

91. Hewlett and Anderson, *The New World,* p. 42.

92. Ibid., p. 45. The fact that this request was written after the conference with FDR is evident in that Bush explicitly reserved all policy questions as outside the sphere of the Academy committee, a reservation that reflects the president's instructions to him.

93. National Academy of Sciences Committee on Uranium, report to the president, November 6, 1941, Bush-Conant correspondence, folder 18, OSRD.

94. Different assessments are offered on this point in Hewlett and Anderson, *The New World;* Compton, *Atomic Quest;* and Szilard, *Leo Szilard: His Version of the Facts.*

95. Hewlett and Anderson, *The New World,* pp. 78–83.

96. The most recent (1985) speculative account of the Japanese effort is Robert K. Wilcox, *Japan's Secret War.* An authoritative and moderate review is by John W. Dower in *Bulletin of the Atomic Scientists,* August–September 1986, pp. 61–62.

CHAPTER II

1. Hewlett and Anderson, *The New World,* pp. 71–75, 119–20; Goudsmit, *Alsos,* pp. 65–71.

2. Hull, *The Memoirs of Cordell Hull,* 2:1111, and Burns, *Roosevelt: The Soldier of Freedom,* p. 490, both refer to Franklin Roosevelt's preference for the title "commander in chief."

3. James B. Conant, "A History of the Development of an Atomic Bomb," OSRD.

4. Hewlett and Anderson, *The New World*, p. 103.

5. U.S. Atomic Energy Commission, *In the Matter of J. Robert Oppenheimer*, pp. 12–14. This transcript of the hearing on Oppenheimer before the personnel security board in Washington in 1954 was originally printed by the Government Printing Office that year. The hearing transcript reprinted by MIT Press (Cambridge, 1971) has the advantage of an index.

6. Carroll Wilson, conversation on Bush and Conant, Cambridge, Mass., May 16, 1980; Groves, *Now It Can Be Told*, pp. 42–44, 46–52, 54–59; Groueff, *Manhattan Project*, pp. 54–62.

7. Morison, *Leyte*, p. 397.

8. Groves, *Now It Can Be Told*, p. 184; this probably refers to a meeting of December 30 described in Hewlett and Anderson, *The New World*, pp. 333–34.

9. Truman, *Public Papers*, 1945, pp. 1–6. Underlining is as in text.

10. Truman, *Year of Decisions*, p. 42; *New York Times*, April 17, 1945, p. 1.

11. Hewlett and Anderson, *The New World*, p. 343.

12. Truman, *Year of Decisions*, pp. 87, 419; Stimson, "The Decision to Use the Atomic Bomb," pp. 99–100; Stimson and Bundy, *On Active Service*, pp. 99–100, 629–36; Groves, *Now It Can Be Told*, pp. 265–66.

13. Groves, *Now It Can Be Told*, pp. 266–67.

14. Ibid., p. 265.

15. U.S. Atomic Energy Commission, *In the Matter of J. Robert Oppenheimer*, p. 32.

16. *FRUS, Conferences at Malta and Yalta*, 1945, p. 984.

17. Dower, *War Without Mercy*, pp. 51–57. Dower's book is a powerful account of racism on both sides of the Pacific war.

18. Truman, *Public Papers*, 1945, p. 3.

19. Stimson, "The Decision to Use the Atomic Bomb"; memorandum for director, Historical Division, WDSS, George A. Lincoln Papers, United States Military Academy, West Point, N.Y.; extract from minutes of meeting held at the White House, June 18, 1945, Records of the Joint Chiefs of Staff, National Archives.

This strong sense of what *must* be prepared for and *could* happen survived into the postwar debate, and defenders of the use of the bomb, Stimson among them, were not always careful about numbers of casualties expected. Revisionist scholars are on strong ground when they question flat assertions that the bomb saved a million lives. What the best of them do not question, however, is the reality of the conviction in the Pentagon that without the bomb there must be readiness for repeated invasions of the home islands against resistance that could be fierce and sustained. A strong but fair comment is Bernstein, "A postwar myth: 500,000 U.S. lives saved," *Bulletin of the Atomic Scientists*, June/July 1986, pp. 38–40.

20. Groves, *Now It Can Be Told*, p. 267.

21. This section was written before the appearance of Michael S. Sherry, *The Rise of American Air Power*, which covers the turn to urban area bombing

with massive authority. I have amended my account so that it does not conflict with Sherry's.

22. Roosevelt, *Public Papers,* 1939, pp. 454, 589. Arnold and Eaker, *Winged Warfare,* pp. 133–34.

23. Batchelder, *The Irreversible Decision,* p. 174.

24. *New York Times,* March 6, 1944, pp. 1, 22; March 7, 1944, p. 4; March 9, 1944, p. 16; Roosevelt, *Public Papers,* 1944–45, p. 392; Batchelder, *The Irreversible Decision,* p. 174.

25. *New York Times,* August 18, 1945, p. 3.

26. Craven and Cate, *The Army Air Forces in World War II,* 5:611.

27. Ibid., pp. 616–17.

28. Ibid., p. 617.

29. The best nonfiction account known to me is by David Irving, *The Destruction of Dresden.* This book had an American edition, but the nature of the Dresden holocaust was not widely understood in the United States until the publication in 1969 of Kurt Vonnegut's brilliant novella of fantasy and anger, *Slaughterhouse-Five: Or, The Children's Crusade, A Duty-Dance with Death.* Vonnegut knew what had happened at Dresden because he had been there as a prisoner of war.

30. See, for example, front-page accounts in the *New York Times,* March 10, 11, and 16, 1945, and the editorial, March 26, 1945, p. 18; *Time,* March 19, 1945, p. 32; *Newsweek,* March 19, 1945, p. 34.

31. McKelway, "A Reporter with the B-29s," Part III, *The New Yorker,* June 23, 1945, pp. 35, 36, 39.

32. Stimson, diary, June 1, 1945.

33. Groves, *Now It Can Be Told,* pp. 266–76; Hewlett and Anderson, *The New World,* p. 365.

34. The best single account of the full process of military planning for the bomb's first use is in Sigal, *Fighting to a Finish,* chap. 4. Sigal gives greater weight than I would to the need for justifying the money spent on the bomb, but I am sure he is right about the desire to contribute to victory that animated men as different as Groves and Stimson.

35. Hewlett and Anderson, *The New World,* pp. 344–46.

36. Ibid.

37. Ibid., p. 358; Compton, *Atomic Quest,* pp. 238–39.

38. Sherwin, *A World Destroyed,* Appendix L, p. 302.

39. "Not available" is the way most accounts have it; some say "out of the city," but Sherwin correctly notes that Stimson was in Washington that day (*A World Destroyed,* pp. 212–13). Stimson noted in his diary that he saw Felix Frankfurter in his office to listen to Frankfurter's report of the concerns of Niels Bohr; see chap. 3 (Stimson, diary, June 12, 1945). One assumes that the hard-pressed secretary was protected by his staff from a sudden and possibly unexplained request for a meeting on a subject that belonged to the Interim Committee; he had tried to get the decks cleared that day to work on another subject.

40. The report is published in Smith, *A Peril and a Hope,* Appendix B, pp. 560–72.

41. Compton, *Atomic Quest,* p. 239.

42. Sherwin, *A World Destroyed,* Appendix M, pp. 304–5.

43. Szilard, *Leo Szilard: His Version of the Facts,* p. 186.

44. A similar point is made by Feis, *The Atomic Bomb and the End of World War II,* p. 201.

45. *FRUS, Conference of Berlin (The Potsdam Conference),* 1945, 2:1361–68.

46. Sherwin, *A World Destroyed,* Appendix O, pp. 307–8; Smith, *A Peril and a Hope,* pp. 52–53.

47. McCloy's actions and opinions have come out over the years in McCloy, *The Challenge to American Foreign Policy,* pp. 40–42, in Giovannitti and Freed, *The Decision to Drop the Bomb,* pp. 135–39, and in Wyden, *Day One,* pp. 171–74. The present account rests primarily on my own conversations with McCloy. See also Stimson, diary, June 19–July 2, 1945.

48. Groves, *Now It Can Be Told,* p. 266.

49. Leahy, *I Was There,* pp. 440–42; Eisenhower, *Crusade in Europe,* pp. 455–56; also Knebel and Bailey, "The Fight Over the A-Bomb," on the views of Marshall and Groves.

50. Szilard, *Leo Szilard: His Version of the Facts,* p. 186.

51. McCloy always remembered the shock around the cabinet table as just like the reaction among his Yale friends to any reference to Skull and Bones. Stimson, Bundy, and Lovett were members, and McCloy, as an Amherst man, took a properly irreverent view of this solemnity.

52. Groves, *Now It Can Be Told,* pp. 273–75.

53. Compton, *Atomic Quest,* p. 237.

54. Truman, *Off the Record,* pp. 55–56.

55. Stimson, "The Decision to Use the Atomic Bomb," p. 107; Stimson and Bundy, *On Active Service,* p. 633.

56. Groves, *Now It Can Be Told,* p. 345.

57. Stimson, "The Decision to Use the Atomic Bomb," p. 102; Stimson and Bundy, *On Active Service,* p. 633.

58. There is debate on the casualty levels at Hiroshima and Nagasaki. The figures I use are for the number of prompt deaths estimated by the Committee for Compilation of Materials on Damage Caused by the Atomic Bombs, in *Hiroshima and Nagasaki,* p. 367. That committee seems to me to have reviewed the available evidence, with the advantage of time, in a way that makes its estimate far more credible than the earlier and lower figures of the American Strategic Bombing Survey. But all figures are estimates, and the committee repeatedly emphasizes the difficulties in the estimations.

59. The judgments of all those principal figures except Marshall are given in their respective memoirs. Marshall's views are comprehensively and judiciously assessed by Forrest C. Pogue in *George C. Marshall, Statesman,* pp. 16–25. There is also a particularly vivid report of his opinions in June 1947 by Lilienthal, in *The Journals of David E. Lilienthal,* 2:198; this account incidentally makes it entirely clear that Marshall always assumed the bomb would be used when ready, that he truly anticipated a need for invasion, and that he was surprised by the bomb's shock value in providing the Japanese with an immediate reason to "surrender without complete loss of face." Marshall's was the controlling military opinion, partly because of his commanding prestige, but also because of his senior operational responsibility for both the Manhattan Project and the bombing plans.

60. Grew, *Turbulent Era*, 2:1424–28; Stimson, diary, May 29 and June 19, 1945; Stimson, "The Decision to Use the Atomic Bomb," pp. 102–4; Stimson and Bundy, *On Active Service*, pp. 619–25.

61. *FRUS, Conference of Berlin (The Potsdam Conference)*, 1945, 1:889–92; Stimson, diary, July 2, 1945; Stimson, "The Decision to Use the Atomic Bomb," pp. 102–4; Stimson and Bundy, *On Active Service*, pp. 619–25.

62. *FRUS, Conference of Berlin (The Potsdam Conference)*, 1945, 1:885–87, 896.

63. Roosevelt, *Public Papers*, 1944–45, p. 359; Gallup, *The Gallup Poll*, 1:511–12.

64. When Stimson raised the question of timing at Potsdam on July 17, the day after Truman and Byrnes arrived, he found it already settled. *FRUS, Conference of Berlin (The Potsdam Conference)*, 1945, 2:1265–68.

65. Stimson, diary, July 24, 1945.

66. *FRUS*, 1945, 6:626, 631–32.

67. *New York Times*, August 11, 1945, pp. 1, 12; July 31, 1945, p. 18.

68. See Toland, *The Rising Sun*, pp. 810–77; Butow, *Japan's Decision to Surrender*, pp. 228–33; Kase, *Journey to the Missouri*, pp. 198–272; Alsop and Joravsky, "Was the Hiroshima Bomb Necessary? An Exchange."

69. Butow, *Japan's Decision to Surrender*, pp. 228–33; but contrast this with Bernstein, "The Perils and Politics of Surrender."

70. Grew, *Turbulent Era*, 2:1406–42; Stimson and Bundy, *On Active Service*, p. 829. McCloy's judgment was registered sharply to William L. Laurence in 1965, "I am absolutely convinced that had we said they could keep the emperor, together with the threat of the atomic bomb, they would have accepted, and we would never have had to drop the bomb." *New York Times, Hiroshima Plus 20*, p. 122.

71. This is my reading of the Stimson diary for the whole period, and also my recollection of Stimson's retrospective view in 1946.

72. Intercepts are in *FRUS, Conference of Berlin (The Potsdam Conference)*, 1945, 1:873–883, 2:1248–64.

73. *FRUS, Conference of Berlin (The Potsdam Conference)*, 1945, 1:883.

74. Truman, *Off the Record*, p. 53.

75. *FRUS, Conference of Berlin (The Potsdam Conference)*, 1945, 1:905. In speaking of new American actions Marshall referred explicitly to the U.S. landing in Japan, but he was undoubtedly thinking of the bomb as well.

76. Byrnes, *All in One Lifetime*, pp. 290–91; Stimson, diary, July 23–24, 1945; Bernstein, "The Atomic Bomb and American Foreign Policy: The Route to Hiroshima," in *The Atomic Bomb: The Critical Decisions*, pp. 94–120.

77. Truman, *Memoirs*, 1:416.

78. The principal propagators of this false conclusion were British physicist P.M.S. Blackett and American Gar Alperovitz. Blackett in *Fear, War, and the Bomb* used no direct evidence, but merely argued that because Japan was so obviously beaten already there *must* have been an ulterior motive; the argument was excellent polemics but bad history, showing complete ignorance of the way the men at the top of the American government in fact thought about the war. In *Atomic Diplomacy* Alperovitz at least tried to look at the record, but his performance was both sloppy and tendentious. He reached the conclusion he wanted, but his own evidence repeatedly failed to sustain it. In support of

his view that from April onward Truman built his policy toward the Soviet Union on toughness to be backed by the bomb, Alperovitz was driven to a fantastically Machiavellian view of Truman, who is pictured as having duped Harry Hopkins into a purely tactical mission of delay to Moscow—a distortion of the much simpler and better real relations of those two men, and a striking example of the way in which critics of the American government are often comforted by assuming conspiracy when the reality is only confusion. Truman in this period went this way and that in his view of Russia; in the course of 1945 most of his advisers—and indeed most Americans—were doing the same thing. In reaching the conclusion that at least from May onward Truman "saw it [the bomb] primarily as a way to end the war before Russia entered" (1985 edition, p. 164), Alperovitz not only offered no evidence but ignored the extensive documentary record (still thicker today) showing that Truman continued to be firmly in favor of Russian entry at least until he heard the results of Alamogordo in Potsdam, a time at which the decision to use the bomb as soon as possible was long since firmly set in his own mind. Alperovitz repeatedly refers to Truman's somewhat different view of late July as if it had existed earlier. It did not.

In a new edition published in 1985, Alperovitz allowed himself the firm conclusion that "military factors alone . . . simply cannot explain the choices made during the final two months of the war" (p. 53), thus neglecting the settled practice of using every promising weapon just as fast and just as destructively as possible, and the settled commitment of two successive commanders in chief to the pursuit of total victory at the earliest possible moment. These, as we have seen, were not necessarily the best military policies, but they were certainly clear and strong in the middle of 1945, and it takes a very selective historiography to deny their relation to Hiroshima.

79. The best general essay on various views of the bombing decision is by Bernstein, "The Atomic Bomb and American Foreign Policy, 1941–45: An Historiographical Controversy." Bernstein's summary of the complaints of serious revisionist historians against Alperovitz is more severe than my own.

80. Aide-memoir of conversation between the president and the prime minister at Hyde Park, September 18, 1944, in *FRUS, The Conference at Quebec, 1944,* pp. 492–93; memorandum of conference, September 22, 1944, and Vannevar Bush to James Conant, September 23, 1944, Bush-Conant correspondence, OSRD.

81. Roosevelt, *Public Papers, 1944–45,* p. 412; Burns, *Roosevelt: Soldier of Freedom,* p. 456; Roosevelt, *My Parents: A Differing View,* pp. 169–70. James Roosevelt says his father "planned to use the bomb," but his account leaves room for such uses as warning and threat; his father was simply assuring him, a marine officer serving in the South Pacific, that there would be no need for any invasion of Japan. (I am grateful to Susan Elter, archivist at the FDR Library, for this citation.)

82. Finney, "How FDR Planned to Use the A-Bomb"; Wallace, *The Price of Vision,* pp. 499–500.

83. Conversations with McCloy, 1984–85.

84. Toland, *The Rising Sun,* pp. 792, 828; Giovannitti and Freed, *The Decision to Drop the Bomb,* pp. 265–81; Butow, *Japan's Decision to Surrender,* pp. 231–33.

85. Stimson, "The Decision to Use the Atomic Bomb," pp. 105–6, and Stimson and Bundy, *On Active Service,* p. 630. Stimson's account quotes Compton, "If the Atomic Bomb Had Not Been Used."

86. Toland, *The Rising Sun,* pp. 806–7; Butow, *Japan's Decision to Surrender,* pp. 158–65.

87. Wallace, *The Price of Vision,* p. 474; Bernstein, "The Perils and Politics of Surrender," pp. 9–10.

88. Walzer, *Just and Unjust Wars,* pp. 263–68.

89. Szilard, *Leo Szilard: His Version of the Facts,* pp. 211—12.

90. Walzer, *Just and Unjust Wars,* p. 262.

91. I here paraphrase Walzer, *Just and Unjust Wars,* p. 267; he goes on to criticize the insistence on unconditional surrender in terms not unlike my own but considerably more harsh; here I think he may be insensitive to the strength of the case for severe defeat, extended occupation, and imposed constitutional change, as means to prevent renewed Japanese militarism.

CHAPTER III

1. Vannevar Bush to Conant, October 9, 1941, folder 5, OSRD.

2. The two official accounts are Hewlett and Anderson, *The New World,* chapter 8, and Gowing, *Britain and Atomic Energy, 1939–1945,* chaps. 4, 5, and 9. A thoughtful but overargued account is in Sherwin, *A World Destroyed,* chap. 3; Sherwin's contention—that British-American cooperation was a consequence mainly of British and American anticommunism—occasionally outruns his evidence.

3. Hewlett and Anderson, *The New World,* pp. 259, 261; Churchill, *The Hinge of Fate,* p. 380.

4. Churchill, *The Hinge of Fate,* pp. 380–81 and Hewlett and Anderson, *The New World,* pp. 73–75.

5. All quotations are from Churchill, *The Hinge of Fate,* pp. 379–83.

6. Vannevar Bush to John Anderson, September 1, and October 1, 1942, Bush-Conant correspondence, folder 1, OSRD. See also Hewlett and Anderson, *The New World,* pp. 262–65.

7. American opinions of Akers are reflected better in memoirs than in official papers. See particularly Groves, *Now It Can Be Told,* pp. 128–29, and Bush, *Pieces of the Action,* p. 283.

8. The two memoranda are J. B. Conant to Vannevar Bush, October 26, 1942; and James B. Conant memorandum, January 7, 1943, Bush-Conant correspondence, folder 12, OSRD. The second memorandum is also in Gowing, *Britain and Atomic Energy, 1939–1945,* p. 156.

9. Gowing, *Britain and Atomic Energy, 1939–1945,* pp. 157–60.

10. Sherwin, *A World Destroyed,* p. 283.

11. Vannevar Bush, memorandum of conference with Harry Hopkins and Lord Cherwell at the White House, May 25, 1943, and Vannevar Bush, memorandum of conference with the president, June 24, 1943, both in OSRD, Bush-Conant correspondence, folder 2. All quotations in these conversations are from these memoranda.

12. Harry Hopkins to the prime minister, June 17, 1943, FDR; Hewlett and Anderson, *The New World,* p. 264.

13. Churchill to Roosevelt, July 9, 1943, FDR; Hewlett and Anderson, *The New World,* p. 274.

14. These meetings are also well reported on both sides; the official histories are both excellent, and the supporting documents show clearly the way both sides came to understand each other better. See Gowing, *Britain and Atomic Energy, 1939–1945,* pp. 166–70; and Hewlett and Anderson, *The New World,* pp. 275–77.

15. Hewlett and Anderson, *The New World,* pp. 275–76.

16. This meeting is particularly well reported in Gowing, *Britain and Atomic Energy, 1939–45,* pp. 167–69, and also in a detailed contemporary American record by Harvey H. Bundy, conveniently available in *FRUS, Conferences at Washington and Quebec,* 1943, pp. 634–36.

17. Roosevelt to Churchill, July 20, 1943, FDR.

18. Gowing, *Britain and Atomic Energy, 1939–45,* p. 264; Oppenheimer, "Niels Bohr and Atomic Weapons."

19. Gowing, *Britain and Atomic Energy, 1939–45,* pp. 266, 267.

20. Ibid., p. 242.

21. Ibid., pp. 138; 165, note 1.

22. Ibid., p. 201.

23. Ibid., p. 234; Vannevar Bush to John Anderson, August 6, 1943, and John Anderson to Vannevar Bush, August 6, 1943, Bush-Conant correspondence, folder 2, OSRD.

24. The American record shows that the prime minister proposed all three of these clauses toward the end of a long discussion in which none of the three had been mentioned before. *FRUS, Conferences at Washington and Quebec,* 1943, p. 636.

25. See the discussion of the Hyde Park memorandum below.

26. Byrnes expressed this doubt on May 18, in an early meeting of the Interim Committee; Hewlett and Anderson, *The New World,* p. 354.

27. Bush to the president, August 7, 1943, Bush-Conant correspondence, folder 2, OSRD.

28. Conant, *Anglo-American Relations in the Atomic Age,* pp. 32–33.

29. The four best discussions of Bohr's whole effort are in Gowing, *Britain and Atomic Energy, 1939–1945,* pp. 346–66; Oppenheimer, "Niels Bohr and Atomic Weapons"; Alice Kimball Smith, *A Peril and a Hope,* pp. 5–13; and Aage Bohr, "The War Years and the Prospects Raised by the Atomic Weapons," in *Niels Bohr,* ed. Rozental, pp. 196–210. These complementary accounts, each unusually scrupulous and sensitive, are the sustaining pillars of what follows. Through the courtesy of Aage Bohr, I have also been able to consult his memoranda of July 21, 24, and 25, 1945, which are in the Niels Bohr archive at the Niels Bohr Institute in Copenhagen.

30. Aage Bohr, "The War Years and the Prospects Raised by the Atomic Weapons," Oppenheimer, "Niels Bohr and Atomic Weapons," p. 6.

31. Felix Frankfurter, copy of memorandum left with H. L. Stimson, May 3, 1945, Oppenheimer Papers, Library of Congress.

32. Gowing, *Britain and Atomic Energy, 1939–1945,* p. 349.

33. Ibid., pp. 352–56.

34. R. V. Jones, "Winston Leonard Spencer Churchill," in *Biographical Memoirs of Fellows of the Royal Society,* vol. 12, p. 88. Jones's account is especially interesting because he helped arrange the meeting and because he met Bohr right afterward in the street and got an early firsthand report. I owe this reference to Ronald Clark, *The Greatest Power on Earth,* pp. 175–76, 319–20.

35. Niels Bohr, memorandum, July 3, 1944, Oppenheimer Papers, box 34, Library of Congress.

36. Gowing, *Britain and Atomic Energy, 1939–1945,* pp. 351, 352.

37. Once again the only record is from Bohr's side; the most detailed and trustworthy reconstruction is in Gowing, *Britain and Atomic Energy, 1939–45,* pp. 356–57—almost surely based in part on contemporary reporting from Bohr to Halifax to Anderson—but see also Aage Bohr, "The War Years and the Prospects Raised by the Atomic Weapons," pp. 206–7.

38. *FRUS, The Conference at Quebec,* 1944, pp. 492–93.

39. Bush wrote two long memoranda on September 22 and September 23, 1944, Bush-Conant correspondence, folder 20A, OSRD. Cherwell also reported; his version is drawn on by Gowing, *Britain and Atomic Energy, 1939–45,* p. 341.

40. To Hull: Sherwin, *A World Destroyed,* pp. 285–86—this letter from FDR is a real find; to Stimson: Stimson and Bundy, *On Active Service,* pp. 580–81.

41. Gowing, *Britain and Atomic Energy, 1939–45,* p. 351.

42. Harriman to Hopkins, September 9, 1944, in *FRUS, The Conference at Quebec,* 1944, pp. 198–99.

43. See *FRUS, The Conference at Quebec,* 1944, pp. 327–28, where Roosevelt is reported—by Harry White, to be sure—as agreeing with Henry Morgenthau that the Soviets "were holding back" because of their suspicion of Anglo-American policy toward Germany.

44. This general background is well recounted in Robert Dallek, *Franklin D. Roosevelt and American Foreign Policy, 1932–1945* (New York: Oxford University Press, 1979), pp. 465–75. Professor Dallek goes wrong, I think, in suggesting at p. 471 that Roosevelt spoke to Bohr as he did because "it was his way of telling Moscow that he was ready to entertain a Soviet role in ultimate control of atomic power." This speculation is quite inconsistent with Roosevelt's general way of communicating to Stalin and also with his obvious desire for reassurance on Bohr's discretion in his later talk with Bush and Cherwell, but one odd guess does not undo a solid and careful work of synthesis.

45. *FRUS, The Conference at Quebec,* 1944, pp. 466–67.

46. Stimson and Bundy, *On Active Service,* p. 581; Dallek, *Franklin D. Roosevelt and American Foreign Policy,* pp. 477–78. See Sherwood, *Roosevelt and Hopkins,* pp. 813–19, 832.

47. Stimson, diary, December 31, 1944, and Sherwin, *A World Destroyed,* pp. 134–36, and Appendix H, pp. 290–91. Professor Sherwin's conclusions are different from mine, and I think stretched beyond the evidence. But his publication at appendix H of the unexpurgated first draft of Churchill's important memo to Eden of March 25, from which this account of Roosevelt's "casual" suggestion is quoted, is a fine example of his sweeping grasp of the sources.

48. Stimson and Bundy, *On Active Service,* p. 616.

49. Hewlett and Anderson, *The New World,* p. 344.

50. Byrnes, *Speaking Frankly,* p. 262; "Notes of the Interim Committee Meeting, May 31, 1945," in Sherwin, *A World Destroyed,* Appendix L, p. 301.

51. Science Panel, "Recommendations on the Immediate Use of Nuclear Weapons, June 16, 1945," in Sherwin, *A World Destroyed,* appendix M, pp. 304–5.

52. Hewlett and Anderson, *The New World,* p. 369.

53. Harrison to Stimson, June 26, 1945, in Sherwin, *A World Destroyed,* Appendix H, pp. 305–6.

54. Byrnes, *Speaking Frankly,* p. 263; Churchill, *Triumph and Tragedy,* p. 670.

55. Byrnes, *Speaking Frankly,* p. 263.

56. Churchill, *Triumph and Tragedy,* p. 640.

57. Ibid., p. 670; Anderson to Churchill, March 7, 1945, Prem 3/139.

58. Smuts to Churchill, June 15, 1944, Prem 3/139.

59. Churchill, *Closing the Ring,* p. 125.

60. Gowing, *Britain and Atomic Energy, 1939–45,* p. 163.

CHAPTER IV

1. The best accounts of the first public reactions are in the contemporary press. *The New York Times,* which had been alerted to the question by a special and secret assignment of its star reporter on science, William L. Laurence, as official reporter for the Manhattan Project, used ten of its thirty-eight pages on August 7 to report on different aspects of the story. That edition is still the simplest source for the statements of Truman, Churchill, and Stimson. Truman's statement is also in *Public Papers,* 1945, pp. 197–200; Churchill's is in Gowing, *Independence and Deterrence,* 1:17–18. The best general compilation of such reports and comments I have found is in *The Atomic Age Opens,* ed. Geddes for Pocket Books, printed that very August; this small volume makes it entirely clear that from the first there was a deep and general understanding of the sheer magnitude of what had happened, as well as the greatest difficulty in reaching a clear sense of what to do about it. Additional evidence on the first American reaction from perceptive British observers is in *Washington Dispatches,* ed. Nicholas, pp. 598–600. Since this chapter was drafted, we also have Boyer, *By the Bomb's Early Light,* chap. 1. The estimated yield announced by Truman was somewhat high. The Hiroshima bomb is now estimated at a yield of about 13 thousand tons—13 kilotons, and the Nagasaki bomb at 22 (Committee for the Compilation of Materials, *Hiroshima and Nagasaki,* p. 30).

2. There is no comprehensive study of all these reactions. For some but not all of them, see Boyer, *By the Bomb's Early Light,* chaps. 2–4. I attempt no survey of my own because what is most notable about the course of decision making in these months is that the advice and comment of publicists had little effect on it. Any careful study would have to consider such immediate works as Norman Cousins's, "Modern Man Is Obsolete: An Editorial," an extended

appeal for world government printed in the *Saturday Review of Literature,* August 18, 1945, pp. 5–9, and published in revised form as *Modern Man Is Obsolete* by The Viking Press in October. A closely parallel argument was repeatedly put forward by President Robert Hutchins of the University of Chicago, for example in *The Atomic Bomb Versus Civilization* in December 1945. In November there was a thoughtful symposium at a joint meeting of the American Philosophical Society and the National Academy of Sciences, printed in *Proceedings of the American Philosophical Society* 90, no. 1. The social scientists Jacob Viner and Joseph Willets showed particularly acute understanding of difficulties that escaped Cousins and Hutchins. In March 1946 a remarkable group of scientists published essays in support of the brilliantly appealing title of a collection called *One World or None,* ed. Dexter Masters and Katharine Way. The most notable political argument in this collection was an extended appeal by Walter Lippmann for a system of law enforceable against individuals; the argument is lucid and the solution extraordinarily irrelevant to the real world of nation-states—especially, if not uniquely, the real world of Soviet Russia. A pessimistic response to this volume was written by Elmer Davis under the harsh title "No World, If Necessary," *Saturday Review of Literature,* March 30, 1946, pp. 7–8, 50–55.

    3. Cantril, *Public Opinion,* p. 20; *Public Opinion Quarterly* 9 (1945): 385.

    4. Truman, *Memoirs,* 1:421–22, and *Public Papers,* 1945, pp. 212, 213.

    5. Truman, *Off the Record,* p. 56, *Public Papers,* 1945, p. 213.

    6. Truman, *Public Papers,* 1945, pp. 212–13.

    7. Henry D. Smyth, *A General Account of the Development of Methods of Using Atomic Energy for Military Purposes under the Auspices of the United States Government, 1940–45.* A more convenient and slightly revised version called *Atomic Energy for Military Purposes* came from Princeton University Press a month later. This edition also included the British official report with its brief but lively account of the Frisch-Peierls memorandum. Yet neither version gave a full account of the influence of British work on the basic American decision to go ahead.

    8. Goldschmidt, *The Atomic Complex,* p. 68.

    9. Groves, *Now It Can Be Told,* pp. 350, 351; Stimson, diary, August 9, 1945. See also Hewlett and Anderson, *The New World,* pp. 400–401, 406–7.

    10. Groves, "Foreword" to Smyth, *Atomic Energy for Military Purposes,* p. v.

    11. Thus *Time,* November 12, 1945, pp. 28–29: "In Northern Bohemia the Russians took over the Jachymov mine, famed for its uranium deposits." *Time*'s reporting of the early months of the public atom was excellent. On the same page of this issue the magazine reported "twelve key points" it had managed to abstract from the mass of reporting in the three months after Hiroshima. As a measure of what careful and intelligent observers could know by November it is helpful. Indeed it would be comforting if point 9 were better understood even today:

TWELVE POINTS

From the mass of fact and solid evidence about atomic fission, *Time* has abstracted twelve key points:

1. Atomic weapons will overshadow peacetime uses of atomic energy. . . .

2. No military or scientific defense can be expected.

3. Breaking up cities is the only practical defense idea so far advanced. . . .

4. Much larger atomic charges are in prospect. . . .

5. Atomic weapons might kill 20% of a nation's people in an hour. No nation lost 10% of its people by military action in all the years of World War II.

6. No big secret protects the atomic bomb. The U.S. alone knows some engineering quirks, which other nations may learn in a few years.

7. All major powers have access to the necessary raw materials. . . .

8. The cost of atomic weapons is not prohibitive. Any nation that can afford a large army or navy can afford them.

9. Out-producing the enemy is not much advantage in atomic warfare. Two hundred bombs may be better than 100, but 10,000 is no better than 5,000, because 5,000 would destroy all important targets in a country. . . .

10. Atomic weapons increase the incentive to aggression by multiplying the advantage of surprise.

11. International control will be extremely difficult. . . .

12. Publication of atomic research data will mitigate distrust, but complete national or international control of atomic research is impossible.

12. Smith, *A Peril and a Hope,* pp. 83–84.

13. Truman, *Public Papers,* 1945, p. 382.

14. Ibid., August 16, 1945, pp. 224–29; August 23, pp. 229–35; September 6, pp. 310–13; September 12, pp. 315–20.

15. The text of the Stimson memorandum, with his own later commentary, is in Stimson and Bundy, *On Active Service,* pp. 638–45.

16. Stimson and Bundy, *On Active Service,* p. 641.

17. This episode is recounted in a memorandum for the record by Harrison, August 18, 1945, in Harrison-Bundy files, MED. I owe the reference to Sherwin, who prints the memo in *A World Destroyed,* Appendix Q, pp. 314–15.

18. Stimson and Bundy, *On Active Service,* pp. 644–45.

19. Acheson, *Present at the Creation,* pp. 123–24; Stimson and Bundy, *On Active Service,* p. 668; Forrestal, *The Forrestal Diaries,* p. 95; Wallace, *The Price of Vision,* pp. 483–84.

20. *New York Times,* September 22, 1945, pp. 1, 3.

21. Wallace, *The Price of Vision,* p. 491; Truman, *Memoirs,* 1:527.

22. Patterson's memo is in *FRUS,* 1945, 2:54–55; Wallace's is in *The Price of Vision,* pp. 485–87; and Bush's memo of September 25 is in Bush-Conant correspondence, file 6, OSRD.

23. Acheson's memo of September 25 is in *FRUS,* 1945, 2:48–50.

24. Ibid.

25. *New York Times,* September 22, 1945, p. 3; Herken, *The Winning Weapon,* p. 32; Anderson to Truman, and Vinson to Truman, President's Secretary file, box 199, HST; Anderson to Truman, *FRUS,* 1945, 2:50.

26. Truman, *Public Papers,* 1945, pp. 362–66.

27. Acheson, *Present at the Creation,* p. 125. For the White House changes in the draft I am indebted to Gregg Herken's diligence. See Herken, *The Winning Weapon,* pp. 35, 347.

28. Truman, *Public Papers,* 1945, pp. 379–84.

29. Herken's discussion of Truman's mood in this period is in *The Winning Weapon,* pp. 35–40. His view of Truman is not altogether mine, but his accounts of Groves's influence and of Truman's candid talk with his old friend, Fyke Farmer, are important.

30. Truman, *Memoirs,* 1:527–28. This account is confirmed in Schnabel, *The History of the Joint Chiefs of Staff,* vol. 1, 1945–47, pp. 258–61, where Lovett's role is recounted. The full text of what the Chiefs eventually put in writing is in a memorandum, Leahy to President, October 23, 1945, JCS Records, National Archives.

31. Truman, *Public Papers,* 1945, p. 383.

32. From minutes of meetings of secretaries of state, war, and navy, October 10 and 16, 1945, in *FRUS,* 1945, 2:55–56, 60.

33. The Bush-Byrnes memorandum of November 5, 1945, is in *FRUS,* 1945, 2:69–73.

34. Bush, *Pieces of the Action,* p. 296; Truman, *Public Papers,* October 3 and 27, 1945, pp. 362–66, 428–30; *FRUS,* 1945, 2:69–73.

35. Acheson, *Present at the Creation,* p. 132.

36. *FRUS,* 1945, 2:69–73.

37. Smith, *A Peril and a Hope,* chap. 15; *New York Times,* November 11, 1947. Daniel Koshland, quoted in Smith, ibid., p. 213.

38. Pearson's account is in *Mike,* 1:258–63. A thorough secondary account is that of James Eayrs, *In Defense of Canada,* 3:276–81. In emphasizing that the Canadians found the United Nations a congenial forum, I do not at all mean to suggest that they were blind to the need to approach the Russians. One of Pearson's versions of what he said (quoted by Eayrs) refers specifically to the need to include the Russians soon. Moreover, both Pearson and Eayrs report that Mackenzie King insisted on revision in the communiqué to remove any impression that the three leaders were merely passing the buck to the UN. Still the Canadians, on balance, were a force in support of working through the UN, not directly with Moscow. As is usual in Canadian international affairs, the best studies on this general subject are Canadian. See especially McLin, *Canada's Changing Defense Policy,* chap. 6, and Eayrs, *In Defense of Canada,* chap. 5. I have also had helpful advice from my old friend George Ignatieff.

39. Williams, *Twilight of Empire,* p. 103.

40. I add the italics to draw attention to the parallel with the Stimson memorandum handed to Truman two weeks later. Attlee's memorandum and the officials' paper he received on August 25 are in the Public Record Office, in Prem 8/116.

41. Gowing, *Independence and Deterrence,* 1:65.

42. See, for example, *Time,* November 19, 1945, p. 29. Gowing, *Independence and Deterrence,* p. 65, gives a graphic account of Churchill's comment.

43. The draft Churchill saw and the full text of his comments are in Prem 8/116; the passage that was cut out is on p. 215.

44. The full text of the final message is in Gowing, *Independence and Deterrence,* 1:78–81.

45. Ibid.

46. Halifax's report to Attlee and Bevin is in Prem 8/116, p. 174.

47. Gowing, *Independence and Deterrence,* 1:70–71; *International Control of Atomic Energy,* report by officials, October 29, 1945, Gen 75/10, Prem 8/116.

48. *International Control of Atomic Energy,* report by officials, October 29, 1945, Gen 75/10, Prem 8/116, p. 6.

49. Ibid., p. 4.

50. Ibid., p. 6.

51. Ibid., pp. 6–7. Attlee's arguments are to be found in an unfinished and undated handwritten memo, Prem 8/116, pp. 43–44, in minutes of a cabinet meeting of November 2, 1945, Prem 8/116, pp. 40–42; and in a finished memorandum circulated to the cabinet on November 5; Gen 75/12, in Prem 8/116, pp. 37–38.

52. Gen 75/12, pp. 1–2; Gen 75/10, p. 3.

53. Gen 75/12, p. 3.

54. Prem 8/116, 75/1, memo of August 28, 1945, p. 2.

55. The recommendations of the officials are in Gen 75/10, p. 10; Attlee's comments are in Gen 75/12, p. 4.

56. There is in fact no firsthand contemporary record of the meeting. The three men met alone; Mackenzie King was an inveterate diarist but his diary for this period has vanished; Attlee's accounts are short; I have here quoted from Truman, writing almost ten years later in *Memoirs,* 1:539. Most writers have wrongly assumed that this discussion took place on Sunday during a Potomac cruise.

57. Truman, *Public Papers,* 1945, pp. 472–75.

58. Byrnes's statement of November 16 is reprinted in the U.S. Department of State, *The International Control of Atomic Energy: Growth of a Policy,* pp. 121–24. The messages to and from Molotov and the three-act play with Bevin are in *FRUS,* 1945, 2:576–600.

59. Molotov's frivolous suggestion and its withdrawal are told in Byrnes, *Speaking Frankly,* p. 267. Conant's more general observations, and a valuable contemporary memorandum, are in Conant, *My Several Lives,* pp. 484–87.

60. We do not know just what forces moved Byrnes to act as he did, but probably the trigger was a letter from Bush to Cohen on January 4 enclosing a memorandum by his assistant, Carroll Wilson. Wilson had been a member of a working group set up by Byrnes before Moscow, and he had reached strongly reasoned conclusions on the need for study of the ways and means of inspection and control and also on the question of "stages" and of the character and quality of the U.S. technical lead. Hewlett and Anderson, *The New World,* pp. 531–32, and papers of Carroll Wilson.

61. The best example of this problem of time may be Conant. He had the most important single full-time job in American higher education; he had

given it short shrift in the war years; he now felt a compelling need to give Harvard his full attention, and his trustees, the fellows of Harvard College, felt the same way and perhaps more so. See Conant, *My Several Lives,* pp. 475, 477.

62. The role of Marks in all this was generously acknowledged by Acheson both briefly in his memoirs, *Present at the Creation,* p. 152, and at greater length in testimony for Marks when the latter was nominated later in the year to be the first general counsel of the Atomic Energy Commission. *Confirmation of Atomic Energy Commission and General Manager,* hearings before the Senate section of the Joint Committee on Atomic Energy, pp. 280–82.

63. Acheson, *Present at the Creation,* p. 153; Lilienthal, *The Journals,* 2:14–15. The two best general accounts of the process which led to the Acheson-Lilienthal Report are Hewlett and Anderson, *The New World,* pp. 531–54, and Daniel Lang, "Seven Men on a Problem." I also had the advantage of discussion with Carroll Wilson, who was lent by Bush to be secretary of the board of consultants and became a full participant in its work—a task which led to his appointment at the end of the year as the first general manager of the Atomic Energy Commission.

64. The Acheson-Lilienthal report, formally cited as U.S. Department of State, Committee on Atomic Energy, *A Report on the International Control of Atomic Energy,* pp. 5, 21.

65. Hewlett and Anderson, *The New World,* p. 536.

66. Ibid., pp. 535–36.

67. Lilienthal, *The Journals,* 2:27.

68. U.S. Department of State, Committee on Atomic Energy, *A Report on the International Control of Atomic Energy,* pp. viii, 5–6, 39–43, 54–55.

69. So Acheson reported to Lilienthal, who put it in *The Journals,* 2:59. The best account is in Hewlett and Anderson, *The New World,* p. 555.

70. The best political life of Baruch by far is Schwarz, *The Speculator.* Schwarz has a careful account of Baruch's role in atomic energy control at pp. 490–507, but it is more useful for detail than for an understanding of Baruch's basic attitude.

71. On attitudes toward Baruch see Acheson, *Present at the Creation,* p. 154; Lilienthal, *The Journals,* 2:30; and Schwarz, *The Speculator,* pp. 490–94.

72. Truman, *Off the Record,* p. 87. The Baruch-Truman falling out, which interested Baruch far more than it did Truman, is best followed in Schwarz, *Speculator,* pp. 521–26.

73. The best account of this phase is in Hewlett and Anderson, *The New World,* pp. 556–66, but see also Herken, *The Winning Weapon,* pp. 159–63; and Schwarz, *The Speculator.*

74. Hewlett and Anderson, *The New World,* p. 566.

75. Lilienthal, *The Journals,* 2:58; see also p. 53. Most of the memoranda exchanged are printed in *FRUS,* 1946, 1:790, 851; see also the excellent and detailed account in Hewlett and Anderson, *The New World,* pp. 566–74. Herken, in *The Winning Weapon,* pp. 164–70, seriously overstates the degree to which Baruch pushed Truman and Byrnes away from the content of the Acheson-Lilienthal report; on the difference of spirit between a Baruch and a Lilienthal he is much more persuasive.

76. Acheson's views are in *Present at the Creation,* p. 155, and at great length in *FRUS,* 1946, 1:983–88.

77. *FRUS,* 1946, 1:847. The best account of the meeting of May 17 and the eventual acceptance of Baruch's view of the veto is in Hewlett and Anderson, *The New World,* pp. 562–74.

78. Truman, *Memoirs,* 2:6.

79. Baruch, "Mem/Con," June 7, 1946, Baruch Papers. Truman's comment to Attlee and King is in Truman, *Memoirs,* 1:539. The two memoranda Truman approved are in *FRUS,* 1946, 1:838–40, 846–51.

80. For Lilienthal's assertion, see Lilienthal, *The Journals,* 2:60; for Acheson, see Hewlett and Anderson, *The New World,* p. 565, and Acheson, *Present at the Creation,* p. 155.

81. Gromyko's speeches are well handled in Nogee, *Soviet Policy toward Control of Atomic Energy,* pp. 36–8 and 45–6; Truman to Baruch, July 10, 1946, Baruch Papers.

82. This conversation did not take place until October 21. It was led for the Americans by Eberstadt; the only Soviet participant was A. A. Sobolov, the assistant secretary general of the United Nations. See *FRUS,* 1946, 1:955–60; the thoughts of the Moscow embassy are at 1:1016–17.

83. Although some, like Oppenheimer, had moments in which they feared that Baruch and his group always expected Soviet rejection (cf. Lilienthal, *The Journals,* 2:40), it is wrong to confuse probabilities with certainties; Schwarz, *The Speculator,* p. 502; Baruch to Truman, June 6, 1946, *FRUS,* 1:839.

84. A particularly interesting example is the first report of the Scientific and Technical Committee of the Atomic Energy Commission (AEC, c. 3/3) of September 27, 1946. This report was approved unanimously, and while it made no recommendations on the specific ways and means of effective international control, it is impossible to read it through today without observing that it powerfully supports the basic thesis—the initial Oppenheimer thesis—that nothing less than an international authority with operating control of dangerous activities would be able to do the job. It is particularly explicit on the danger of clandestine diversion from a nominally peaceful reactor or separation plant, and the difficulty of preventing any such diversion by external inspection. History has grimly confirmed this analysis in Israel and India.

85. Memo of conference of members of U. S. and Canadian delegations, August 1, 1946, *FRUS,* 1946, 1:872.

86. Baruch to Truman, March 26, 1946, in *FRUS,* 1946, 1:767–68.

87. Schwarz, *The Speculator,* pp. 484–89.

88. A conveniently sympathetic and loyal account of these basic attitudes is in Coit, *Mr. Baruch,* particularly pp. 552–608.

89. This is the sense of the astonishing memorandum that Groves wrote to himself in January 1946 and shared with John Hancock in June, in *FRUS,* 1946, 1:1197–1203.

90. Lilienthal's address to the American Chemical Society is reprinted in *Bulletin of the Atomic Scientists,* October 1, 1946, p. 14. Oppenheimer's remark to Hancock on April 5, 1946, is in *FRUS,* 1946, 1:779.

91. This is how Oppenheimer, in a mood approaching despair, sounded to Lilienthal on the night of July 23, just before Gromyko's root-and-branch rejection of the Baruch plan. Lilienthal, *The Journals,* 2:69–70.

92. Committee for the Compilation of Materials on Damage Caused by the Atomic Bombs in Hiroshima and Nagasaki, *Hiroshima and Nagasaki: The Physical, Medical, and Social Effects of the Atomic Bombings.*

93. Hersey, *Hiroshima;* see also "Hiroshima," in *The New Yorker,* August 31, 1946, p. 32.

94. Lilienthal, *The Journals,* 2:12, on January 22, 1946; *FRUS,* 1946, 1:850.

95. Lilienthal, *The Journals,* 2:11, 16.

96. Acheson, *Present at the Creation,* p. 153.

97. Lippmann, "Today and Tomorrow" column, July 18, 1946, Walter Lippmann Papers.

98. Lippmann, "Today and Tomorrow" column, October 2, 1945, Walter Lippmann Papers.

99. Thus, among many others, on October 7, 1945, in the speech that led to the Reelfoot Lake press conference: "We have the greatest production machine that the world has ever seen. We conclusively proved that free government is the most efficient government in every emergency." And at Reelfoot Lake the next day: "I don't think it would do any good to let them in on the know-how, because I don't think they could do it anyway." Truman, *Public Papers,* 1945, pp. 380, 382.

100. *New York Times,* January 27, 1953.

101. This is part of Lilienthal's description of what Acheson told him on January 16 in their first meeting; Lilienthal, *The Journals,* 2:11. Corroborating evidence that his question was part of the original charge to Acheson is to be found in the Papers of Carroll Wilson, in Hewlett and Anderson, *The New World,* p. 533, and in Acheson, *Present at the Creation,* p. 152.

102. U.S. Department of State, Committee on Atomic Energy, *A Report on the International Control of Atomic Energy,* p. ix.

103. Herken, *The Winning Weapon,* p. 39, quoting a memorandum of the conversation by the old friend, Fyke Farmer.

104. There is some incidental evidence. A year later, writing an undelivered statement about Lilienthal, Truman confused the Acheson-Lilienthal report with the very different Smyth report. Truman, *Off the Record,* p. 127. The absence of direct discussion between the president and the framers of a "great state paper" has to be astonishing to anyone who worked for John F. Kennedy on these questions, but it does not seem to have surprised the ten men themselves; the point is not mentioned by either Acheson or Lilienthal.

105. Truman, *Off the Record,* p. 80.

106. Holloway, "Entering the Nuclear Arms Race," p. 183, quoting from a Soviet article reviewing an unpublished biography of Vannikov. Holloway's work is outstandingly careful and reliable; both his command of the evidence and his judgments on its implications have been most helpful to me.

107. Zhukov, *The Memoirs of Marshal Zhukov,* p. 675; Kramish, *Atomic Energy in the Soviet Union,* p. 78.

108. Holloway, "Entering the Nuclear Arms Race," pp. 182–83; Ulam, *Stalin,* p. 625; Truman, *Memoirs,* 1:416.

109. Holloway, "Entering the Nuclear Arms Race," pp. 178–83.

110. This parallel I draw from Holloway, "Entering the Nuclear Arms Race," pp. 183–84.

111. *FRUS,* 1945, 2:48–50.

112. Ibid., 1945, 5:885–86.

113. Report prepared by Thomas P. Whitney, *FRUS,* 1945, 5:935–36. Harriman's description of Whitney is at p. 933.

114. This record has been thoroughly examined and ably analyzed by Nogee, in *Soviet Policy towards International Control of Atomic Energy.* Nogee did not know then what we know now about Stalin's early and firm determination to have his own bomb, but the other points in my present argument owe much to his work.

115. Gromyko in the 321st meeting of the UN Security Council, June 16, 1948, quoted by Nogee, *Soviet Policy towards International Control of Atomic Energy,* p. 136. See also an earlier parallel statement of March 1947, p. 87.

116. Nogee, *Soviet Policy towards International Control of Atomic Energy,* p. 136.

117. Kramish, *Atomic Energy in the Soviet Union,* p. 94, and Nogee, *Soviet Policy towards International Control of Atomic Energy,* pp. 11–12, 14, 65, 234–35.

118. Nogee, *Soviet Policy towards International Control of Atomic Energy,* pp. 67, 122.

119. Bush to Byrnes, November 5, 1945, *FRUS,* 1945, 2:71.

120. The full text of this letter is in *New York Times,* September 18, 1946; a substantially complete version is in Wallace, *The Price of Vision,* pp. 589–601 (quoted passages at pp. 591, 593, and 594). This excellent volume, edited by John Norton Blum, shows in earlier entries how opinion in Washington was divided on the emerging cold war during the preceding months and contains a powerful essay on Wallace as a diarist in which Blum gives Wallace rather more credit for vision than I can. I believe that Wallace judged American and British behavior more critically than it deserved, and that of Russia less so; it has not been a useful formula for enlarging public understanding or winning political leadership in this country.

121. *FRUS,* 1946, 1:939–43.

122. Nogee, *Soviet Policy towards International Control of Atomic Energy,* p. 124 (citing AEC, C. 1/PV. 42).

123. *FRUS,* 1946, 1:861–65. This opinion was expressed in a memorandum Kennan wrote to himself during a time at the War College.

124. Zhukov, *The Memoirs of Marshal Zhukov,* pp. 674–75; and see also Holloway, "Entering the Nuclear Arms Race," pp. 182, 185.

125. There is no fully satisfactory account of this process, but the careful reader of Hewlett and Anderson, *The New World,* can follow much of it, pp. 471–72, 531–32. I have also learned from talking with Carroll Wilson and Joseph E. Johnson.

126. One picks Bush here because there is no other remotely likely source of Truman's early and firm conclusion on this point, but we should note that Truman himself once seemed to deny the indebtedness. Truman, *Public Papers,* 1945, p. 419.

127. Stimson and Bundy, *On Active Service,* p. 643.

128. The principal dissenting "expert" was Alexander P. de Seversky, an apostle of air power who was impressed by the fact that much remained standing at Hiroshima. His article, "Atomic Bomb Hysteria," published with fanfare in the *Reader's Digest* in February 1946, pp. 121–26, was remarkable

mainly for its total failure to take account of what these things could do if used in numbers much greater than two.

129. Hewlett and Anderson, *The New World*, p. 104.

130. Ibid., p. 417.

131. Holloway, "Research Notes: Soviet Thermonuclear Development," pp. 192–93.

132. "Nomination of David E. Lilienthal," speech of Robert A. Taft, April 2, 1947. I owe the reference to Evans, *The Secret War for the A-Bomb*, pp. 210, 288. This is a foolish book that contains many interesting facts.

133. Oppenheimer, "International Control of Atomic Energy," p. 250.

134. Herken, *The Winning Weapon*, p. 367, note 14; a particularly interesting but atypical argument to this effect was made by George Kennan to Dean Acheson, in *FRUS*, 1946, 1:860–65.

135. Arnold Wolfers, "The Atomic Bomb in Soviet-American Relations," in *The Absolute Weapon*, ed. Brodie, pp. 111–97, especially pp. 113–14.

136. Lippmann's column of October 10, 1946, contains his sharp assessment of Baruch's rigidity and Stalin's intentions, which he correctly inferred from the Soviet leader's statement of September 24, in answers to questions from Alexander Wirth of the *London Sunday Times*, that monopolistic possession of the atomic bomb cannot long continue. The text, crudely translated, is in *FRUS*, 1946, 1:786. Lippmann's column also contains reaffirmation of his basic support for the Acheson-Lilienthal report. His own belief in a still more sweeping project and design of world organization is restated in "Why We Are Disarming Ourselves."

CHAPTER V

1. The basic reference work for the events in this decision is Hewlett and Duncan, *Atomic Shield*, vol. 2: *A History of the United States Atomic Energy Commission*, chap. 12. The probable date of the Soviet test is discussed at p. 366. Truman's announcement is in Truman, *Public Papers*, 1949, p. 485, and the announcement of his decision to authorize work on the hydrogen bomb is in *Public Papers*, 1950, p. 138. The book that has most affected my own thinking is York, *The Advisors*.

2. Golovin, *I. V. Kurchatov*, p. 64; Sakharov, "An Autobiographical Note," in *On Sakharov*, ed. Babyonyshev, pp. xii–xiii.

3. Churchill's speech of March 1, 1955, is in Great Britain, Parliament, *Hansard's Parliamentary Debates* (House of Commons), 5th series, 537 (1954–55); see cols. 1895, 1897–98. His "first comprehensive review" is a speech delivered on February 17, 1954, by Representative W. Sterling Cole in U.S. Congress, House, Eighty-third Congress, Second Session, February 18, 1954, *Congressional Record*, Appendix, pp. A1349–51.

4. United States Atomic Energy Commission, *In the Matter of J. Robert Oppenheimer*, p. 467; *FRUS*, 1949, 1:491.

5. Truman, *Years of Trial and Hope*, pp. 295, 306.

6. Lilienthal, *The Journals of David E. Lilienthal*, 2:391. Truman had not seen the matter quite as clearly in 1945; see chap. 11.

7. Forrestal, ibid., p. 464; Forrestal, *The Forrestal Diaries,* p. 487.

8. Truman, *Years of Trial and Hope,* p. 305. See also Rosenberg, "American Atomic Strategy and the Hydrogen Bomb Decision," p. 76. The policy document, *NSC 30,* is in *FRUS,* 1948, 1:624–28.

9. Truman, *Public Papers,* 1949, p. 485.

10. Conversations with George Kennan, 1981–83, and McMahon to Johnson, *FRUS,* 1949, 1:483.

11. Thirring's discussion was in a book called *Die Geschichte der Atombombe* published in Vienna in 1946. The chapter was finally translated and reprinted in *Bulletin of the Atomic Scientists,* March 1950, pp. 69–71, but only after Truman's public announcement of the decision to develop an H-bomb. At p. 67 the *Bulletin's* editors explained their own participation in the conspiracy of silence: "We feared that any discussion of this subject in the *Bulletin* might foster the belief that America was actively engaged in developing thermonuclear weapons, and that this might stimulate the atomic arms race and further exacerbate international relations."

12. Hewlett and Duncan, *Atomic Shield,* p. 417; see chap. IV.

13. Lilienthal, *The Journals,* 2:210; U.S. Atomic Energy Commission, *In the Matter of J. Robert Oppenheimer,* p. 69.

14. Rosenberg, "U.S. Nuclear Stockpile, 1945 to 1950," *Bulletin of the Atomic Scientists,* May 1982, p. 26.

15. Lilienthal, *The Journals,* 2:552–53.

16. *FRUS,* 1949, 1:562.

17. Strauss, *Men and Decisions,* pp. 216–17. Strauss had a draft of this memorandum as early as September 30, according to Hewlett and Duncan, *Atomic Shield,* p. 373.

18. Golden to Strauss, September 25, 1949; the text was made available to me by its author.

19. Hewlett and Duncan, *Atomic Shield,* p. 374.

20. U.S. Atomic Energy Commission, *In the Matter of J. Robert Oppenheimer,* p. 777; Lawrence was accompanied to Washington by Luis Alvarez, an excellent physicist and Los Alamos veteran who had helped to arouse Lawrence to this Washington expedition. Alvarez kept a diary which allowed him to report all these Washington conversations, and an earlier visit with Teller, in his testimony at the Oppenheimer hearing. Hewlett and Duncan, *Atomic Shield,* p. 378; and conversation with Nichols, 1982.

21. U.S. Atomic Energy Commission, *In the Matter of J. Robert Oppenheimer,* pp. 714–15. The activities of advocates and opponents are dispassionately and extensively covered in Hewlett and Duncan, *Atomic Shield,* chap. 12.

22. McMahon's work is recorded not only in Hewlett and Duncan, *Atomic Shield,* but also in the Oppenheimer hearing, and in his own communication to Truman, noted below. Borden appears in most books about Oppenheimer; his cast of mind is best revealed in his letter about Oppenheimer to J. Edgar Hoover, in U.S. Atomic Energy Commission, *In the Matter of J. Robert Oppenheimer,* pp. 837–38.

23. Lawrence is followed with detailed sympathy in Herbert Childs, *An American Genius.* The flavor of the man is wonderfully conveyed in a memorandum recording his appearance before the officials working on what became *NSC 68,* on March 20, 1950, in *FRUS,* 1950, 1:200–201.

24. Strauss, *Men and Decisions,* pp. 157, 212.

25. Conversation with William Golden, 1982.

26. This account of the mid-October position of the Joint Chiefs rests on the contemporary personal notes of Kenneth Nichols, who has kindly shared them with me.

27. Oppenheimer was also probably preferred by Lilienthal. See Conant, *My Several Lives,* p. 500. Conant had been led to expect that the president planned to make him the chairman, but when he got a message suggesting that Lilienthal preferred Oppenheimer, he cheerfully made the nomination himself.

28. Between 1945 and 1947 Oppenheimer held chairs at Berkeley and at the California Institute of Technology. Professors in very great demand sometimes allow themselves to be drawn into such double appointments. The usual result is increased public prestige for both places and lowered effectiveness of performance. But in Oppenheimer's case it was the claims of public policy that reshaped his life away from teaching and research. The postwar role of Oppenheimer and of the General Advisory Committee is readily verified in Hewlett and Duncan, *Atomic Shield,* and more dramatically, if less precisely, in the testimony of the Oppenheimer hearing, U.S. Atomic Energy Commission, *In the Matter of J. Robert Oppenheimer.*

29. Years later, on a long flight to a thermonuclear test in the Pacific, Seaborg and I sat beside each other. While I was lost in a combination of fatigue and bemused anticipation, he passed the time by revising the proof sheets for the new edition of a scientific text.

30. Conant's reservations about Strauss and Truman's response were discovered by James G. Hershberg and are described in a thesis on Conant that Hershberg wrote as a Harvard senior in 1982. I am grateful for his permission to draw on his thesis and also to Theodore Conant for telling me of this contribution to knowledge about his father. James Conant's own account of Truman's offer and his decision not to accept it (Conant, *My Several Lives,* pp. 493–95) omits the decisive role of Truman's prior commitment to Strauss, but Hershberg's evidence, from Conant's contemporary correspondence, is compelling.

31. York, *The Advisors,* pp. 155–56.

32. Ibid., pp. 156–58.

33. Lilienthal, *The Journals,* 2:582–83.

34. Ibid., 2:583–584, 590.

35. *FRUS,* 1949, 1:573–76.

36. Lilienthal, *The Journals,* 2:594; "Views of David E. Lilienthal," italics in original; this and other documents submitted to the President by Lilienthal on November 9 are printed without some annexes in *FRUS,* 1949, 1:576–85.

37. Truman to Souers, *FRUS,* 1949, 1:587.

38. The best general account of the staff process is in Hewlett and Duncan, *Atomic Shield,* pp. 391–99, 403–9. The work in the Pentagon has been carefully traced by Rosenberg, "American Atomic Strategy and the Hydrogen Bomb Decision," and the processes in the State Department are covered by Acheson, *Present at the Creation,* especially p. 348. The best source of documents is *FRUS,* 1949, 1:585–617, and 1950, 1:1–44, 503–23.

39. Compton's letter of November 9 is in Strauss, *Men and Decisions,* p. 440, and its prompt delivery is described on p. 233.

40. McMahon's letter, with apparently minor deletions of still-classified material, is in *FRUS,* 1949, 1:588–95. His visit to Truman is reported in Moss, *Men Who Play God,* pp. 30–31.

41. Strauss to Truman, November 25, 1949, *FRUS,* 1:596–98; also in Strauss, *Men and Decisions,* pp. 219–22.

42. *FRUS,* 1949, 1:595–96. In his diary in June 1945 Truman had placed Bradley with Robert E. Lee, John J. Pershing, and—at that time—Dwight Eisenhower in a military pantheon whose members he contrasted with "Custers, Pattons, and MacArthurs." Truman, *Off the Record,* p. 47.

43. Rosenberg, "American Atomic Strategy and the Hydrogen Bomb Decision," pp. 81–82. I have considerable sympathy still for General Bradley's position. It corresponds to the information available to him—there is no evidence that he ever heard of the Fermi-Rabi alternative, which we have yet to examine, and without that alternative the choice before Truman did seem sharp: Do this or let the Russians get ahead. In 1968 I publicly expressed the view that the military advice to proceed with the H-bomb was correct (in Bundy, *The Strength of Government,* p. 22). The different view I shall be expressing in this chapter rests on arguments not presented to General Bradley in 1949 and not examined by me in 1968.

44. This story is in Lilienthal, *The Journals,* 2:595. Truman incorrectly identified the report he had seen as one which Lilienthal was handing him, and Lilienthal himself never knew what document Truman was in fact referring to. My own belief is that it was the General Advisory Committee report of October 30, the only relevant report in circulation at this stage.

45. Acheson, memorandum of telephone conversation, January 19, 1950, *FRUS,* 1950, 1:511–12.

46. Truman to McMahon, January 5, 1950, "Super Bomb" file, President's Secretary file, box 201, HST.

47. *FRUS,* 1950, 1:517.

48. Lilienthal, *The Journals,* 2:632–33; Arneson, "H-Bomb Decision," p. 27.

49. *FRUS,* 1950, vol. 1: the Joint Chiefs of Staff memo of January 13 is at pp. 503–11; the formal recommendation, at p. 517.

50. *New York Times,* February 1, 1950, p. 1.

51. For the March action, see *FRUS,* 1950, 1:541–42, and also Rosenberg, "American Atomic Strategy and the Hydrogen Bomb Decision," pp. 84–85.

52. York, *The Advisors,* pp. 158–59.

53. Ibid., p. 54.

54. Hewlett and Duncan, *Atomic Shield,* p. 383; Moss, *Men Who Play God,* p. 31.

55. Dennison's letter is in President's Secretary's file, box 21, HST, and the list of the staff that actually served is in *FRUS,* 1949, 1:587. Of Dennison's nominees only Lauris Norstad survived.

56. *FRUS,* 1949, 1:574–75, 592–93.

57. Acheson, *Present at the Creation,* p. 346.

58. Oppenheimer to Kennan, November 17, 1949, *FRUS,* 1949, 1:222–23.

59. York, *Advisors,* p. 156. Conant appears to have been the draftsman; his signature came first, out of alphabetical order.

60. *FRUS,* 1949, 1:575.

61. *FRUS,* 1950, 1:516.

62. Interview with Dean Acheson, February 16, 1955, memoirs file, HST.

63. From remarks made at a meeting of the Advertising Council at the White House of February 16, 1950, printed in the *Department of State Bulletin,* March 20, 1950, p. 429.

64. Truman, *Public Papers,* 1950, p. 116.

65. For a different view, see Schilling, "The H-Bomb Decision."

66. Oppenheimer to Conant, October 21, 1949, in U.S. Atomic Energy Commission, *In the Matter of J. Robert Oppenheimer,* pp. 242–43.

67. Ibid.; my view of what Los Alamos would have done rests in part on conversation with Stanislaw Ulam in 1982.

68. U.S. Atomic Energy Commission, *In the Matter of J. Robert Oppenheimer,* p. 81.

69. York, *Advisors,* p. 156. It is a mark of the haste with which the report was drafted that Oppenheimer here asserts that exploration would require "proof-firing." It did not, as events showed.

70. Bernstein, "Truman and the H-bomb." *Bulletin of the Atomic Scientists* 40 (March 1984): 12–18.

71. *FRUS,* 1949, 1:593. There are security deletions which leave McMahon's argument opaque.

72. York, *Advisors,* p. 156.

73. York, *Advisors,* pp. 96–103. I have presented York's conclusions rather than the details of his argument, which rest on the characteristics of the two programs as they in fact evolved. The first Soviet thermonuclear test was of a device that fell far short of being a full-scale fusion weapon, and it had a yield in the submegaton range, comparable to an American fission device tested in the same year. Moreover, York found both technical and political reasons for believing that the U.S. development after Soviet warning signals in 1953 would probably have been faster than the one that began in 1950: The computers of the later time were much more effective, and the sense of unity and urgency among scientists would have been greater. In assessing York's conclusions we must remember that he was himself an enthusiastic participant in the H-bomb enterprise from the beginning, so that his second thoughts are informed by direct knowledge of the way things actually happened at the time. I am not aware of any persuasive rebuttal—or indeed of any detailed criticism at all—of his analysis.

74. For a similar conclusion see Bernstein, "Truman and the H-Bomb."

75. See, for example, Lilienthal, *The Journals,* 2:626–30, the entry of January 31, 1950.

76. Kennan's argument is in *FRUS,* 1950, 1:22–44, and his retrospective comments are in his *Memoirs, 1925–1950,* pp. 471–76.

77. For a sample of these comments see *FRUS,* 1950, 1:293–324.

78. Lilienthal, *The Journals,* 2:552.

79. Truman's comment is in *FRUS,* 1949, 1:481, and it was made in a meeting attended by Louis Johnson.

80. *FRUS,* 1949, 1:559–63; Lilienthal, *Journals,* 2:510.

81. Rosenberg, "The Origins of Overkill," p. 23.

82. Truman, *Public Papers,* 1950, p. 727.

83. Jackson's account is in *Time,* January 28, 1980, p. 13. Basic diplomatic exchanges are in FRUS, 1946, vol. VII, pp. 340–43 (Kennan), and vol. VI, pp. 732–36 (Smith), together with an unusual editorial report that there is no evidence of any "ultimatum," at VII, p. 348. An excellent general account of the crisis is in Kuniholm, *Origins of the Cold War in the Near East,* pp. 304–342. A good essay on the absence of an ultimatum is Blechman and Hart, "Afghanistan and the 1946 Iran Analogy," *Survival,* November/December 1980. An interesting argument that Truman's messages did constitute a threat, if not an ultimatum, is in Samii, *Involvement by Invitation,* chap. 4.

84. Truman, *Public Papers,* 1952–53, pp. 1124–25.

85. Truman, *Public Papers,* 1952–53, p. 1201.

CHAPTER VI

1. Eisenhower, *Crusade in Europe,* p. 443.

2. Eisenhower, *The Papers of Dwight David Eisenhower,* vol. 7, nos. 946, 969; vol. 8, nos. 1198, 1296, 1634, 1668.

3. Eisenhower, *The White House Years,* 1:23, quoting his contemporary letter to Lucius Clay on the Dulles argument.

4. The best single monograph on American policy in the Korean war is Rosemary Foot, *The Wrong War,* and the best essay on nuclear threats in that war is Ms. Foot's paper, "Nuclear Threats and the Ending of the Korean Conflict." Ms. Foot finds the administration's readiness for nuclear war clearer than I do, but on the role of nuclear threats we are in substantial agreement. Another serious essay is Blechman and Powell, "What in the Name of God Is Strategic Superiority?"

5. Adams, *Firsthand Report,* pp. 48–49.

6. Eisenhower, *The White House Years,* 1:181.

7. *FRUS,* 1952–54, 5:1811; Robert J. Donovan, *Eisenhower: The Inside Story,* p. 116. Donovan was a favored recipient of authoritative information, but his own phrase, "atomic missiles," is not clear. There were no missiles, in the usual nuclear sense of the word, in 1953. Sherman Adams uses the same phrase in *Firsthand Report,* p. 48.

8. Rees, *Korea: The Limited War,* pp. 404–5; the quotation is in the text of Eisenhower's statement on his return from Korea, in the *New York Times,* December 15, 1952, p. 6.

9. Eisenhower, *The White House Years,* 1:181.

10. Donovan: *Eisenhower: The Inside Story,* p. 116. An excellent argument that most of the signals of warning and determination that came out of Washington in these months were not primarily nuclear is developed by Barry M. Blechman and Robert Powell in "What in the Name of God Is Strategic Superiority?" pp. 589–602.

11. *FRUS,* 1952–54, 15:769–70.

12. Ibid., 15:1062, 1065, 1067.

13. Ibid., 15:1139, 1140, 1143.

14. The Dulles report is at *FRUS*, 1952–54, 15:1068–69. The "basic instructions" are at pp. 923–25. Clark's recollection is reported in Blechman and Powell, "What in the Name of God Is Strategic Superiority?" pp. 594–95; Eisenhower, *The White House Years*, 1:180.

15. Eisenhower, *The White House Years*, 1:248; *FRUS*, 1952–54, 15:1654–55.

16. Hagerty, *The Diary of James C. Hagerty*, p. 3. DDE; *FRUS*, 1952–54, 15:1700, 1705, 1707.

17. Quotes are from *NSC 162/2*, October 30, 1953, paragraph 39.B, in *FRUS*, 1952–54, 2:593, conveniently reprinted in *the Pentagon Papers*, ed. Mike Gravel, 1:426. Eisenhower's direct part in these specific decisions is best described by Glenn H. Snyder, in Schilling, Hammond, and Snyder, *Strategy, Politics, and Defense Budgets*, pp. 427, 436–38. Snyder's essay, "The 'New Look' of 1953," although subject to some amendment on details, remains the best single analysis of Eisenhower's decisions of 1953 and their immediate consequences.

18. *FRUS*, 1952–54, 2:520; the "carefully prepared paper," *NSC 141*, January 19, 1953, DDE, does not contain precise numbers; its general conclusions are printed in *FRUS*, 1952–54, 2:209–22. Its principal architect was probably Paul Nitze, then the State Department's director of policy planning.

19. This story is persuasively told by Snyder, "The 'New Look' of 1953," pp. 437–38, evidently on the basis of interviews with participants in the deliberations. The phrase "the major deterrent" appears twice in *NSC 162/2*, in *FRUS*, 1952–54, 2:584, 585, and Gravel, ed., *The Pentagon Papers*, 1:418, 419.

20. Eisenhower, *The White House Years*, 1:453. See also *Public Papers*, 1954, p. 330.

21. Eisenhower, *The White House Years*, 1:454.

22. Snyder, "The 'New Look' of 1953," pp. 427–37; *FRUS*, 1952–54, 2:447, 521, 533.

23. *FRUS*, 1952–54, 2:532, 533.

24. Ibid., 2:447, 533, 546.

25. Ibid., 2:546, 547.

26. Ibid., 2:456, 574, 592.

27. Ibid., 2:786.

28. Ibid., 2:789.

29. Ibid., 2:461, 696, 786, 833, 836–37; *NSC 5501*, paragraph 35.

30. Eisenhower, *Public Papers*, 1954, p. 698.

31. Ibid., 1954, p. 701.

32. *FRUS*, 1952–54, 2:397, 457, 806; Eisenhower, *Public Papers*, 1953, p. 618, September 27.

33. *FRUS*, 1952–54, 2:640, 641; impromptu remarks of John Foster Dulles before the Republican Woman's Centennial Conference, Washington, D.C., April 7, 1954, John Foster Dulles Papers, Princeton University Library. I was led to this press release by Richard Rovere's report of the speech in *The Eisenhower Years*, p. 199.

34. Eisenhower, *Public Papers*, 1953, pp. 816–17, December 8; 1955, p. 358, March 23.

35. Ibid., 1954, pp. 261–62; and 1955, p. 332, March 16. See below in Quemoy-Matsu section.

36. Eisenhower, *Public Papers,* 1955, p. 332; *Time,* July 31, 1950, p. 12.

37. Speech of John Foster Dulles, secretary of state, before the Council on Foreign Relatons, January 12, 1954, in *Documents on American Foreign Relations, 1954,* pp. 7–15.

38. Ibid.

39. This discovery was made by Douglas Kinnard. See his *President Eisenhower and Strategy Management,* p. 140. That the relevant handwriting of this sentence is in fact that of Eisenhower has been confirmed for me by Alice Boyce. The exact words in Eisenhower's handwriting are: "The basic decision was to depend primarily upon a great capacity for retaliation—instantly."

40. See the discussion of surprise attack in Chapter VII.

41. Eisenhower, *Public Papers,* 1954, p. 11, January 7.

42. Careful and impartial summaries of these reactions are in *United States in World Affairs, 1954,* and in *Survey of International Affairs, 1954.*

43. Dulles, "Policy for Security and Peace," pp. 356, 358–60.

44. Eisenhower, *Public Papers,* 1954, p. 306, March 10; and p. 322, March 17.

45. Ibid., 1954, pp. 325–26.

46. Ibid., 1954, pp. 372–81.

47. Ibid., 1954, pp. 377–79.

48. Ibid., 1954, pp. 374–75.

49. Ibid., 1954, pp. 375–76.

50. Ibid., 1954, pp. 375–76.

51. *FRUS,* 1952–54, 2:799.

52. The best recent account of this affair is in John Prados, *The Sky Would Fall.* Prados finds Eisenhower somewhat less wary than I do, but his use of the historical evidence is sweeping and careful.

53. *FRUS,* 1952–54, 13:1038; Eisenhower, *Public Papers,* 1954, p. 253; *FRUS,* 1952–54, 13:949. This *FRUS* volume, published in 1982, makes most previous accounts of the American response to Dien Bien Phu out of date, but it has been admirably used by William Conrad Gibbons in Library of Congress, Congressional Research Service, *The U.S. Government and the Vietnam War,* pt. 1, chap. 4, against which I have checked my account.

54. *FRUS,* 1952–54, 13:952, 971; Eisenhower, *Public Papers,* 1954, pp. 383, 421, April 7, and April 24.

55. *FRUS,* 1952–54, 13:1014, 1038.

56. Ibid., 1952–54, 13:953, 1150, 1159.

57. Ibid., 1952–54, 13:1204. One may note in passing that in 1954 the president could describe a possible covert operation to a major publisher and his editor-in-chief with no apparent fear of disclosure.

58. Radford's belief in air action is attested most plainly by his own memorandum reporting the special meeting of the Joint Chiefs, in *FRUS,* 1952–54, 13:1198–99. When the proposal was criticized in later years he backed away from it; it is not mentioned in his memoirs and the question is fudged in his oral history, in the Dulles Papers at Princeton University Library. His conversation with Ély is best reported by the latter in his *Mémoires,* pp. 75–76. Ély says that Radford raised the question of air action

at Dien Bien Phu "with a certain insistence." See also *FRUS*, 1952–54, 13:1201–2, 1159.

59. Eisenhower, *Public Papers*, 1954, p. 306; *FRUS*, 1952–54, 13:1163–68, for the minutes of the NSC meeting of March 25, 1954.

60. Dulles, "The Threat of a Red Asia," p. 540.

61. *New York Times*, March 30, 1954, p. 1.

62. *FRUS*, 1952–54, 13:1210–11.

63. The only official account we have is a State Department memorandum approved by Dulles, in *FRUS*, 1952–54, 13:1224–25. The principal competing source is an extremely careful and specific account by Chalmers Roberts in *The Reporter*, September 14, 1954, pp. 31–35. This report is in many respects the more persuasive of the two; Roberts was one of the most careful and thorough reporters of his careful and thorough generation.

64. *FRUS*, 1952–54, 13:1224.

65. These conditions are stated in different ways in the phone conversation, in *FRUS*, 1952–54, 13:1230; in a report by Sherman Adams of the April 4 meeting, in *FRUS*, 1952–54, 13:1236, and Sherman Adams, *Firsthand Report*, p. 122; and in the minutes of the NSC meeting on April 6, in *FRUS*, 1952–54, 13:1254.

66. *FRUS*, 1952–54, 13:1236–38.

67. The Eisenhower-Dulles conversation is in *FRUS*, 1952–54, 13:1241–42, and the cable of rejection at p. 1242.

68. *FRUS*, 1952–54, 13:1361–62, 1386–96; *New York Times*, April 25, 1954, p. 1; and Sulzberger, *A Long Row of Candles*, pp. 1001–3.

69. Nathan Twining, John Foster Dulles Oral History Collection, pp. 29–30.

70. Richard Nixon, *RN: The Memoirs of Richard Nixon*, p. 154.

71. *FRUS*, 1952–54, 13:1270–72.

72. *FRUS*, 1952–54, 13:1351. Dulles was in the United States between trips to Europe only from April 17 through April 20, and this luncheon is his only recorded meeting with Radford in that interval.

73. *FRUS*, 1952–54, 13:1927.

74. Ibid., 13:1928, 1933.

75. Ibid., 13:1261, 1374, 1928.

76. Bidault, *D'Une Resistance à l'autre*, p. 198.

77. For an excellent but somewhat different account of this episode, see John Prados, *The Sky Would Fall*, chap. 10.

78. *FRUS*, 1952–54, 13:1447–48.

79. Ambrose, *Eisenhower*, 2:184.

80. *FRUS*, 1952–54, 13:1467.

81. Bell, *Survey of International Affairs*, 1954, p. 121, quoting from House of Commons Debate, fifth series, vol. 525, col. 1052, March 23, 1954.

82. *FRUS*, 1952–54, 13:1437.

83. Eden, *Full Circle*, p. 139.

84. Ibid.

85. Shepley, "How Dulles Averted War," p. 72.

86. Lacouture, *Pierre Mendès-France*, pp. 246–49.

87. The two crises over Quemoy and Matsu have been analyzed with particular power by George and Smoke, *Deterrence in American Foreign Policy*,

chaps. 9 and 12, and by Kalicki, *The Pattern of Sino-American Crises,* chaps. 6 and 8. The advantage of examining both is that George and Smoke found that these crises were unnecessary and damaging to the United States, while Kalicki found them to have left a "positive legacy" of stability. I also have a particular debt in this section to my friend Morton Halperin, a close student of these crises.

88. *United States in World Affairs,* 1958, p. 320; Hoopes, *The Devil and John Foster Dulles,* p. 450.

89. The document is printed in Eisenhower, *The White House Years,* 2:691–93. The paper was prepared by Dulles and presented with advance approval from the secretary of defense and Chairman Radford. Whitman file, DDE diary, box 22, DDE. Eisenhower tells us in *The White House Years,* 2:295, that the final version was one which Dulles and he "studied, edited, and agreed on."

90. Eisenhower, *The White House Years,* 1:473–74.

91. Ibid., 2:693.

92. Hoopes, *The Devil and John Foster Dulles,* p. 265.

93. Eisenhower, *The White House Years,* 1:466.

94. Ibid., 1:467.

95. Roberts, *First Rough Draft,* p. 123.

96. Eisenhower, *Public Papers,* 1955, p. 215.

97. U.S. Congress, Senate, Eighty-fourth Congress, First Session, January 27, 1955, *Congressional Record,* 101:819–20.

98. Eisenhower, *The White House Years,* 1:476.

99. Ibid., p. 477; Goodpaster's report is in *FRUS,* 1955-1957, 2:366–7.

100. *New York Times,* March 9, 1955, p. 4; Eisenhower, *Public Papers,* 1955, p. 332; Eisenhower, *The White House Years,* 1:477.

101. *FRUS,* 1955–57, 2:358–59.

102. Eisenhower, *The White House Years,* 1:478; Eisenhower, *Public Papers,* 1955, p. 358.

103. Eisenhower, *The White House Years,* 2:693.

104. Telephone call to General Twining, September 2, 1958, 8:48 A.M., John Foster Dulles papers, box 9, DDE.

105. *Documents on American Foreign Relations,* 1958, p. 439; *New York Times,* September 5, 1958, p. 1. In the press briefing Dulles allowed himself to be described only as "a high official," but the disguise was quickly torn off.

106. Eisenhower, *Public Papers,* 1958, p. 698.

107. The author of this particular phrase is Richard P. Stebbins, who wrote *United States in World Affairs,* 1958, p. 322. Many other contemporary writers made the same large but accurate assertion; it had a special resonance at a time when memories of the armadas of World War II were still fresh.

108. *Documents on American Foreign Relations,* 1958, pp. 446–47.

109. Khrushchev's letter of September 19 is in the *New York Times,* September 20, 1958, and the Chinese statement of September 1, 1963, is printed in Appendix C of *Sino-Soviet Military Relations,* ed. Garthoff. I have also found help in chap. 7 of this volume, a discussion by John R. Thomas of the Quemoy crisis of 1958.

110. Eisenhower, *The White House Years,* 2:299, 302.

111. For a different view, compare Hoopes, *The Devil and John Foster Dulles,* pp. 448–49, where Eisenhower is seen as "painted into a corner" by Dulles; Eisenhower, *The White House Years,* 2:299.

112. Memorandum from the president to the secretary of state, April 5, 1955, *FRUS,* 1955-1957, 2:445–50. For an excellent account of Eisenhower's general attitude toward Chiang's ambitions, see Leonard H. D. Gordon, "United States Opposition to Use of Force in the Taiwan Strait," pp. 637–60; Eisenhower, *Public Papers,* 1958, p. 716, press conference, October 1.

113. Sorensen, *Kennedy,* p. 205; Kennedy, *Public Papers,* 1962, pp. 509–10, 512.

114. Eisenhower, *Public Papers,* 1955, p. 332.

115. H. G. Hopwood to commander in chief, Pacific, December 20, 1958, Defense Department, Washington, D.C.

116. Ibid.

117. Eisenhower, *Public Papers,* 1953, p. 2.

118. Ibid., 1953, pp. 820, 822.

119. A sanitized version of this document is to be found in *FRUS,* 1952-54, 11:1056–91. I published an abbreviated version, "Early Thoughts on Controlling the Nuclear Arms Race," in *International Security* 7 (Fall 1982): 3–27. This version includes the nonrepetitive parts of the argument, less a dated discussion of air defense. In addition to Oppenheimer, Bush, and Dulles, the panel's membership included John S. Dickey and Joseph E. Johnson, both deeply committed believers in efforts for international cooperation. Their participation was of particular value in underscoring for official readers the grimness of the conclusions reached. I was the panel's secretary.

120. *FRUS,* 1952-54, 2:1065–68.

121. Ibid, 2:1059, 1062.

122. Ibid., 2:1078–79.

123. Ibid., 2:1079.

124. NSC 151, "Interim Report by the Ad Hoc Committee of the NSC Planning Board on Armaments and American Policy," *FRUS,* 1952-54, 2:1151–57; United States Atomic Energy Commission, *In the Matter of J. Robert Oppenheimer,* pp. 48, 95; and Oppenheimer, "Atomic Weapons and American Policy."

125. C. D. Jackson memorandum of September 30, 1954, *FRUS,* 1952-54, 2:1526–28; John Lear, "Ike and the Peaceful Atom," pp. 11, 12. This article is clearly based largely on interviews with Jackson and James Hagerty.

126. Dwight D. Eisenhower to Milton Eisenhower, December 11, 1953, Whitman file, DDE diary, box 4, DDE.

127. This is the way the question was stated by Cutler to Strauss as reported in Strauss to the president, September 17, 1953, *FRUS,* 1952-54, 2:1219. This passage is also quoted in Strauss, *Men and Decisions,* p. 357.

128. Strauss to the president, September 17, 1953, *FRUS,* 1952-54, 2:1219. With characteristic intellectual dishonesty Strauss omitted Eisenhower's second sentence from his own later account. In similar fashion he recreated his initial reaction after the proposal had been enthusiastically received by the public, allowing Robert Donovan to believe two years later that the temper of his skeptical memorandum was defined by the single

phrase "the idea is novel." See Robert Donovan, *Eisenhower: The Inside Story,* p. 186.

129. Dulles to Eisenhower, September 6, 1953, and Eisenhower to Dulles, September 8, 1953, *FRUS,* 1952–54, 2:457–63.

130. Memorandum to the president, September 21, 1953, Jackson Papers, box 41, DDE; memorandum to the president, C. D. Jackson, October 2, 1953, *FRUS,* 1952–54, 2:1225–26.

131. Memorandum to the president, C. D. Jackson, October 2, 1953, *FRUS,* 1952–54, 2:1225–26.

132. Memorandum to the president, October 23, 1953, *FRUS,* 1952–54, 2:1234–35.

133. Strauss, *Men and Decisions,* pp. 357–58.

134. Laura Fermi, *Atoms for the World: United States Participation in the Conference on the Peaceful Uses of Atomic Energy,* and conversations with I. I. Rabi, 1982–84.

135. Sokolski, "Atoms for Peace: A Non-Proliferation Primer?" pp. 199–231.

136. *United States in World Affairs, 1955,* p. 285.

137. Eisenhower, *Public Papers,* 1953, pp. 817, 822; *The Eisenhower Diaries,* p. 261.

138. Ibid., pp. 261–62; compare with Eisenhower's memoirs, *The White House Years,* 1:255.

139. *Survey of International Affairs, 1953,* p. 122.

140. Eisenhower, *The Eisenhower Diaries,* p. 262.

141. Eisenhower, *Public Papers,* 1955, pp. 713–16.

142. Eisenhower, *The White House Years,* 1:520–21.

143. Ibid., 1:521.

144. Much the best record of the origins and purposes of the Open Skies proposal is Rostow, *Open Skies.* W. W. Rostow had a major part in the genesis of the proposal, and in one of a series of retrospective studies of the interconnection between ideas and action, he has produced a carefully researched monograph in which many of the relevant documents are marshaled. His conclusions are not mine, but his work provides the best present guide to what happened.

145. Log–1955 folder, C. D. Jackson Papers, box 56, DDE, cited in Rostow, *Open Skies,* pp. 159–64. This is Jackson's contemporary memorandum of a private lament delivered to him alone after dinner on July 11. Even after a heavy discount in recognition of Jackson's taste for the dramatic, it remains a revealing paper.

146. Rostow, *Open Skies,* p. 26.

147. Ibid., p. 29.

148. Ibid., p. 47.

149. Ibid., pp. 46, 50–52, 135.

150. Ibid., pp. 52–53, 55.

151. Eisenhower, *The White House Years,* 1:519; Rostow, *Open Skies,* pp. 46, 106.

152. Memorandum on limitation of armament, June 29, 1955, John Foster Dulles Papers, Subject series, box 4, DDE.

153. Rostow, *Open Skies*, p. 63; Eisenhower, *The White House Years*, 1:521.

154. Henry Cabot Lodge to the UN General Assembly, December 5, 1955, in *Documents on American Foreign Relations, 1955*, p. 454.

155. This point is well argued by Rostow, *Open Skies*, pp. 78–84.

156. Khrushchev, *Khrushchev Remembers*, p. 392.

157. Khrushchev, *Khrushchev Remembers: The Last Testament*, p. 537; *New York Times*, July 22, 1955, p. 3.

158. Speech of Lewis Strauss to the Atomic Industrial Forum and the American Nuclear Society, September 28, 1955, in *Documents on American Foreign Relations, 1955*, p. 478.

159. Eisenhower, *Public Papers, 1955*, p. 728.

160. *Documents on American Foreign Relations, 1956*, p. 509.

161. On this episode the indispensable source is U.S. Atomic Energy Commission, *In the Matter of J. Robert Oppenheimer*, the text of the hearing and related documents, published first by the Atomic Energy Commission in 1954 and reprinted by the MIT Press in 1971 with an index and an excellent introduction by Philip Stern. The two best general accounts are Philip Stern, *The Oppenheimer Case* and Ralph Major, *The Oppenheimer Hearing*.

162. U.S. Atomic Energy Commission, *In the Matter of J. Robert Oppenheimer*, p. 837.

163. Eisenhower, *The Eisenhower Diaries*, pp. 260–61, entry for December 3, 1953.

164. Pfau, *No Sacrifice Too Great*, pp. 158–60, 162, 184.

165. Stern, *The Oppenheimer Case*, pp. 129–30.

166. Pfau, *No Sacrifice Too Great*, pp. 147, 159, 162.

167. U.S. Atomic Energy Commission, *In the Matter of J. Robert Oppenheimer*, pp. 14, 137.

168. U.S. Atomic Energy Commission, *In the Matter of J. Robert Oppenheimer;* in the "Texts of Principal Documents and Letters" pamphlet. Gordon Gray is quoted on p. 21, Lewis Strauss on p. 51 (pp. 1019 and 1049 of MIT ed.).

169. U.S. Atomic Energy Commission, *In the Matter of J. Robert Oppenheimer*, pp. 149, 167.

170. Stern, *The Oppenheimer Case*, p. 384; *New York Times*, June 7, 1954, p. 24.

171. U.S. Atomic Energy Commission, *In the Matter of J. Robert Oppenheimer*, pp. 892–96, and in the "Texts of Principal Documents and Letters" pamphlet, p. 18 (p. 1016 of MIT ed.).

172. U.S. Atomic Energy Commission, *In the Matter of J. Robert Oppenheimer*, pp. 710, 726–27.

173. U.S. Atomic Energy Commission, *In the Matter of J. Robert Oppenheimer*, "Texts of Principal Documents and Letters," p. 15ff (p. 1013ff of MIT ed.).

174. Ibid., pp. 13, 20–21 (pp. 1011, 1018–1019 of MIT ed.).

175. Ibid., pp. 20, 21 (pp. 1018, 1019 of MIT ed.).

176. Stern, *The Oppenheimer Case*, p. 267.

177. Hagerty, *The Diary of James C. Hagerty*, p. 61.

178. Stern, *The Oppenheimer Case*, pp. 225–26, 345–46.

179. U.S. Atomic Energy Commission, *In the Matter of J. Robert Oppenheimer*, "Texts of Principal Documents and Letters," pp. 43–48 (pp. 1041–46 of MIT ed.). (Nichols has now given a much more balanced account of the case in *The Road to Trinity*, pp. 304–9, 312–24.)

180. Ibid., p. 54 (p. 1052 of MIT ed.).

181. Ibid., p. 51 (p. 1049 of MIT ed.).

182. Ibid., pp. 51–54 (pp. 1049–52 of MIT ed.); Strauss, *Men and Decisions*, p. 295; "An Act for the Development and Control of Atomic Energy," approved August 1, 1946, in U.S., *Statutes at Large*, 1946, vol. 60, pt. 1, pp. 755–75; section 10 on the control of information is at pp. 766–68.

183. The charges are in U.S. Atomic Energy Commission, *In the Matter of J. Robert Oppenheimer*, "Texts of Principal Documents and Letters," pp. 52–53 (pp. 1050–51 of MIT ed.); the rebuttals are at p. 66 (p. 1064 of MIT ed.). The word "ugly" is in Strauss, *Men and Decisions*, p. 294.

184. U.S. Atomic Energy Commission, *In the Matter of J. Robert Oppenheimer*, "Texts of Principal Documents and Letters," pp. 51, 54 (pp. 1049, 1052 of MIT ed.).

185. Strauss, *Men and Decisions*, p. 294; U.S. Atomic Energy Commission, *In the Matter of J. Robert Oppenheimer*, pp. 295, 848, 875, 886.

186. Hagerty, *The Diary of James C. Hagerty*, p. 61.

187. Eisenhower, *The White House Years*, 1:312. The intensity of the argument over the H-bomb controversy in the hearing was even greater than what appears in the published record. Much of the most energetic argumentation was deleted by security officers on the ground that it contained classified information. The student who wants the full record that led Gray to find Oppenheimer insufficiently enthusiastic about offensive capabilities must turn to the record of classified deletions released by the Department of Energy in 1983. See U.S. Atomic Energy Commission, "In the Matter of J. Robert Oppenheimer: Record of Classified Deletions Noted in Unclassified Copy Printed by U.S. Government Printing Office, 1954," Department of Energy, Washington, D.C.

188. Stern, *The Oppenheimer Case*, pp. 422–23; *New York Times*, June 30, 1954, p. 9.

189. Eisenhower, *The White House Years*, 1:312–13; U.S. Atomic Energy Commission, *In the Matter of J. Robert Oppenheimer*, "Texts of Principal Documents and Letters," p. 51 (p. 1049 of MIT ed.).

190. Lloyd K. Garrison, in his written responses to Philip Stern, in Stern, *The Oppenheimer Case*, p. 523; U.S. Atomic Energy Commission, *In the Matter of J. Robert Oppenheimer*, pp. 972, 992; on Oppenheimer's distress over the Chevalier incident, see, for example, p. 888.

191. Conversation with I. I. Rabi, 1982.

192. Killian, *Sputnik, Scientists, and Eisenhower*, pp. 223–24.

193. Teller's suffering and his recognition of his "grave mistake" are described in Blumberg and Owens, *Energy and Conflict*, pp. 364–68. I learned of Borden's rejection in conversation with a former colleague in 1983; Stern pointed me in this direction by his guess that it might have been so in *The Oppenheimer Case*, pp. 448–49.

CHAPTER VII

1. These estimates and others that follow of total megatonnage in different years are those of Thomas B. Cochran in a letter to me, April 18, 1984. Cochran believes them accurate to within plus or minus 15 percent. As senior author of the *Nuclear Weapons Databook* of the Natural Resources Defense Council, Cochran is the best independent authority I have found on stockpile levels. More generally, I have relied in this section on Rosenberg, "The Origins of Overkill: Nuclear Weapons and American Strategy."

2. General LeMay's estimate is in Curtis E. LeMay, *America Is in Danger,* pp. 284–85.

3. The extraordinary standards set at SAC by LeMay are attested in any number of places, notably in Rosenberg, "The Origins of Overkill," p. 18ff, but I rely in particular on conversations with General David C. Jones, who was LeMay's aide in the early days of SAC. Having myself been an aide to a distinguished senior commander—Admiral Alan G. Kirk in World War II—I believe that an observant aide gets an unrivaled look at his boss, and General Jones is a highly observant man.

4. Eisenhower, *The White House Years,* 1:453.

5. LeMay, *America Is in Danger,* pp. 82–83.

6. Memorandum of conference with the president, August 13, 1960, Whitman file, DDE diary, box 51, DDE.

7. Rosenberg, "The Origins of Overkill," p. 64.

8. Ibid., p. 35.

9. Kistiakowsky, *A Scientist at the White House,* pp. 399–400, 413–14, 415–16, 421.

10. Memorandum of meeting with the president, February 18, 1959, White House Office, Office of the Special Assistant for National Security Affairs, Special Assistant series, box 4, DDE; memorandum of conference with the president, January 2, 1960, White House Office, Office of the Staff Secretary, Subject series, box 2, DDE; and memorandum of meeting with the president, August 25, 1960, Whitman file, DDE diary, boxes 33 and 51, DDE; Kistiakowsky, *A Scientist at the White House,* diary entry of October 6, 1960, p. 400.

11. Rosenberg, "The Origins of Overkill," pp. 47–48.

12. Memorandum of conference with the president, January 20, 1959, White House Office, Office of the Staff Secretary, Subject series, box 38, DDE.

13. Memorandum of meeting with the president, February 18, 1959, White House Office, Office of the Special Assistant for National Security Affairs, box 4, DDE.

14. The best account of the Technological Capabilities Panel (TCP) and its report is Killian's own, in *Sputnik, Scientists, and Eisenhower.* Killian's pride in the TCP and its work is both evident and entirely pardonable. The first and more general volume of the report was declassified, with only marginal deletions, in 1976: Technological Capabilities Panel, Science Advisory Committee, "Meeting the Threat of Surprise Attack," vol. 1, February 14, 1955,

White House Office, Office of the Staff Secretary, Subject series, box 16, DDE.

15. The most comprehensive and fair-minded account of the development of the ICBM is Beard, *Developing the ICBM,* pp. 145–202.

16. Killian, *Sputnik, Scientists, and Eisenhower,* p. 68; Technological Capabilities Panel, Science Advisory Committee, "Meeting the Threat of Surprise Attack," vol. 1, February 14, 1955, White House Office, Office of the Staff Secretary, Subject series, box 16, DDE; Rosenberg, "Toward Armageddon," unpublished ms., pp. 223–24.

17. Hewlett and Duncan, *Nuclear Navy 1946–62,* p. 308.

18. Rosenberg, "Toward Armageddon," unpublished ms., pp. 228, 230; Sapolsky, *The Polaris System Development,* pp. 29–32; Hewlett and Duncan, *Nuclear Navy,* p. 310.

19. Hewlett and Duncan, *Nuclear Navy,* pp. 370–71.

20. The interaction, not all kindly, is reported in Sapolsky, *The Polaris System Development,* chapter 2.

21. Killian, *Sputnik, Scientists, and Eisenhower,* p. 76.

22. This standard brand phrase is taken from the comprehensive exposition of government policy issued by Eisenhower in the course of the 1956 campaign, on October 24, Eisenhower, *Public Papers,* 1956, p. 999.

23. *New York Times,* October 16, 1956, p. 18.

24. Eisenhower, *Public Papers,* 1956, pp. 997–1002.

25. Memorandum of conference with the president, March 24, 1958, White House Office, Office of the Staff Secretary, Subject series, box 3, DDE.

26. Ibid.

27. Eisenhower, *The White House Years,* 2:478, 653.

28. Killian, *Sputnik, Scientists, and Eisenhower,* pp. 2–3.

29. Roberts, *First Rough Draft,* pp. 149–50.

30. Joseph Alsop and Stewart Alsop, *The Reporter's Trade,* pp. 361–64. Certainly Roberts and the Alsops were nearer to the temper of the Gaither group than *The New York Times.* As far as I can tell, the *Times* had the honor of publishing the first account of the panel's conclusions, on November 23, 1957, and its story was devoted exclusively to recommendations for a fallout shelter program. Civil defense was the assignment the panel had been given initially by the White House, but it was in no sense the main topic of the report. See the Gaither report, *Deterrence and Survival in the Nuclear Age: Report to the President by the Security Resources Panel of the Science Advisory Committee,* November 7, 1957, White House Office, Office of the Special Assistant for National Security Affairs, NSC series, box 22, DDE.

31. Eisenhower, *Public Papers,* 1957, p. 811; and 1958, p. 30.

32. A particularly good account of these battles is in York, *Race to Oblivion.*

33. Joseph Alsop, "After Ike, the Deluge," *Washington Post,* October 7, 1959, p. A17; Stewart Alsop, "Our Gamble With Destiny," *Saturday Evening Post,* May 16, 1959, pp. 23, 114–18; and Edgar M. Bottome, *The Missile Gap,* p. 97. Bottome, in Appendix A, has an excellent set of published estimates of present and future missile gaps in this period.

34. Freedman, *U.S. Intelligence and the Soviet Strategic Threat,* pp. 67, 71–72; Eisenhower, *The White House Years,* 2:547. For a much more sweeping view

of the value of the U-2 in disproving the "missile gap," see Ambrose, *Ike's Spies*, pp. 276–78.

35. Eisenhower, *The White House Years*, 2:225; Beschloss, *Mayday*, pp. 125, 157; Killian, *Sputnik, Scientists, and Eisenhower*, p. 83.

36. Eisenhower, *Public Papers*, 1960, p. 26. The questioner, Sarah McClendon of Texas, was a reporter the sharpness of whose enquiries enlivened many a press conference for a generation; I remember that Kennedy used to recognize her when he wanted to test his own ability to turn back a heavy question with a light reply.

37. Burke, "The Threat Confronting Us," pp. 332–33.

38. Kistiaskowsky, *A Scientist at the White House*, p. 243; Burke, "The Threat Confronting Us," p. 333.

39. Eisenhower, *Public Papers*, 1954, p. 375; Kistiakowsky, *A Scientist at the White House*, p. 149.

40. Freedman, *U.S. Intelligence and the Soviet Strategic Threat*, pp. 76, 77; Prados, *The Soviet Estimate*, p. 89, from declassified documents; Kistiakowsky, *A Scientist at the White House*, p. 219.

41. Prados, *The Soviet Estimate*, pp. 90–91.

42. Bottome, *The Missile Gap*, p. 119; Prados, *The Soviet Estimate*, pp. 91, 94.

43. Eisenhower, *Public Papers*, 1960, p. 145; Kistiakowsky, *A Scientist at the White House*, p. 239.

44. Kistiakowsky, *A Scientist at the White House*, p. 161.

45. Kennedy's most important speech on the gap was delivered in August 1958, in *Congressional Record*, Eighty-fifth Congress, Second Session, 104:-17569–73, and reprinted in 1960 in his *Strategy of Peace*, pp. 33–45.

46. Quoted in Divine, *Foreign Policy and U.S. Presidential Elections*, p. 255.

47. Aliano, *American Defense Policy from Eisenhower to Kennedy*, p. 50; Adams, *Firsthand Report*, p. 415; Halperin, "The Gaither Committee and the Policy Process," p. 364.

48. Kistiakowsky, *A Scientist at the White House*, pp. 262–67, 280–81.

49. Albert Wohlstetter, "The Delicate Balance of Terror," pp. 211–34.

50. Ibid., p. 217.

51. Kissinger, *Nuclear Weapons and Foreign Policy;* and Kissinger, *The Necessity for Choice*, pp. 26, 39.

52. Eisenhower, address to the Third Special Emergency Session of the General Assembly of the United Nations, August 13, 1958, *Public Papers*, 1958, p. 607.

53. Gaither report, White House Office, Office of the Special Assistant for National Security Affairs, NSC series, box 22, DDE, p. 15, italics as in the original. It is interesting that the word *decisive* is defined in a footnote as follows: "(1) ability to strike back is essentially eliminated; or (2) civil, political, or cultural life are reduced to a condition of chaos; or both (1) and (2)." The panel here seems to believe in counterforce victory or assured destruction or both.

54. Killian report, Technological Capabilities Panel, Science Advisory Committee, "Meeting the Threat of Surprise Attack," vol. 1, February 14, 1955, White House Office, Office of the Staff Secretary, Subject series, Box 16, DDE, p. 11.

55. *FRUS*, 1952–1954, 2:459, 834; the handwriting on the first document (memorandum by the secretary of state, September 6, 1953, located in Whitman file, International series, box 33, DDE) is that of Eisenhower, as verified by Alice Boyce.

56. Freedman, *U.S. Intelligence and the Soviet Strategic Threat*, p. 73; Eisenhower, *Public Papers*, 1960–61, p. 919.

57. Beschloss, *Mayday*, p. 242.

58. Tatu, *Power in the Kremlin*, pp. 41–68, also Beschloss, *Mayday*, p. 290.

59. Meeting of chiefs of state and heads of government, Paris, May 16, 1960, Whitman file, International series, box 40, DDE, pp. 9–10.

60. Ibid., p. 11; also Beschloss, *Mayday*, pp. 288–89.

61. Eisenhower, *The White House Years*, 2:556.

62. York, *Making Weapons, Talking Peace*, pp. 193–97. For a different view see Ball, *Politics and Force Levels*, passim.

63. Sorensen, *Kennedy*, pp. 347–48.

64. A brief account of this big change is in Cochran, Norris and Hoeing, *Nuclear Weapons Databook*, II, p. 17.

65. Diehl and Johnson, eds., *Through the Straits of Armageddon*, p. ix.

66. Glenn T. Seaborg, with Benjamin S. Loeb, *Kennedy, Khrushchev, and the Test Ban*, chaps. 5–12.

67. Kennedy, *Public Papers*, 1962, p. 543.

68. Ibid., p. 586.

69. Ibid., p. 141.

Chapter VIII

1. Soviet note of November 27, 1958, in *Department of State Bulletin*, January 19, 1959, pp. 81–89.

2. *Department of State Bulletin*, December 15, 1958, p. 948.

3. *Documents on American Foreign Relations*, 1961, pp. 137–41; "Text of Khrushchev's Fireside Chat on Vienna Issues," *Current Digest of the Soviet Press*, July 12, 1961, p. 7; Kennedy, *Public Papers*, 1961, p. 534.

4. Brandt, *People and Politics*, p. 25.

5. Robert Lowell, "Fall 1961," in *For the Union Dead*, pp. 11–12. I was struck by the poem when I first read it, and not only because of these lines. In that fall Lowell found a "point of rest" in the reliable movements of the pendulum of a grandfather clock; so did I.

6. For a careful review of the many Soviet purposes asserted by different writers, see Adomeit, *Soviet Risk-Taking and Crisis Behavior*, pp. 183–94.

7. Horelick and Rush, *Strategic Power and Soviet Foreign Policy*, pp. 108–16; George and Smoke, *Deterrence in American Foreign Policy*, pp. 401–3; and for a different view see Adomeit, *Soviet Risk-Taking and Crisis Behavior*, pp. 247–53.

8. Quoted in *Documents on International Affairs*, 1961, p. 315.

9. *Current Digest of the Soviet Press*, September 6, 1961, pp. 10–11; *New York Times*, August 12, 1961, pp. 1, 3.

10. Press conference, August 31, 1961, in Kennedy, *Public Papers,* 1961, p. 574.

11. Moscow Embassy to Department of State, conversation between N. S. Khrushchev and Governor Harriman, June 23, 1959, Department of State; Harriman, "My Alarming Interview with Khrushchev," p. 33.

12. Glenn T. Seaborg with Benjamin S. Loeb, *Kennedy, Khrushchev, and the Test Ban,* p. 252. Ambassador Thompson's official report of the Harriman-Khrushchev meeting, declassified in 1983, does not include this remembered exchange, but I do not believe that Harriman made it up.

13. Press Conference, October 11, 1961, in Kennedy, *Public Papers,* 1961, p. 662.

14. Strauss's views are given by Kelleher, *Germany and the Politics of Nuclear Weapons,* p. 166, and Adenauer's comment in his *Erinnerungen,* 1959–63, p. 123, is reported by Adomeit, *Soviet Risk-Taking and Crisis Behavior,* p. 298.

15. Catudal, *Kennedy and the Berlin Wall Crisis,* particularly pp. 200–203. Catudal goes too far in suggesting collusion between the White House and Senator Fulbright, who said publicly on July 30 that the Russians and East Germans had a right to close their borders; he misreads as a sign of agreement a sarcastic "helpful" in a memo from me to the president.

16. Kennedy, *Public Papers,* 1961, p. 539.

17. Schlesinger, *A Thousand Days,* p. 394; Rostow, The *Diffusion of Power,* p. 231.

18. Acheson, "Wishing Won't Hold Berlin," p. 33.

19. Eisenhower, *The White House Years,* 2:629.

20. Catudal, *Kennedy and the Berlin Wall Crisis,* pp. 216–19, 229–30, 243.

21. Brandt, *People and Politics,* p. 30.

22. Minutes of cabinet meeting, March 13, 1959, Whitman file, DDE diary, box 25, DDE.

23. Eisenhower, *Public Papers,* 1959, p. 698.

24. Memorandum of conference with the president, October 21, 1959, Whitman file, DDE diary, box 29, DDE; Eisenhower dictation, December 1960, Whitman file, DDE diary, DDE.

25. Kennedy, *Public Papers,* 1961, pp. 38, 67.

26. Acheson, "Wishing Won't Hold Berlin," p. 85.

27. Catudal, *Kennedy and the Berlin Wall Crisis,* p. 146.

28. Ibid., p. 182, citing John Ausland.

29. Eisenhower press conferences of March 4 and 11, 1959, in *Public Papers,* 1959, pp. 227, 243–44.

30. Eisenhower press conference, March 11, 1959, in *Public Papers,* 1959, p. 245.

31. Ibid., p. 252.

32. Ambrose, *Eisenhower,* 2:150.

33. Sorensen, *Kennedy,* p. 588.

34. Acheson, "Wishing Won't Hold Berlin," p. 86.

35. McNamara, "The Military Role of Nuclear Weapons," p. 79; and conversation with McNamara, November 1985.

36. McGeorge Bundy, memorandum to Theodore Sorensen, July 22, 1961, JFK; Kennedy, *Public Papers,* 1961, pp. 535.

37. Memorandum of conference with the president, March 6, 1959, 5:00 P.M., Whitman file, DDE diary, box 39, DDE.

38. For a quite different speculation on Khrushchev's interest in the nuclear balance, see Paul H. Nitze, "Assuring Strategic Stability in an Era of Détente," p. 216.

39. Alsop, "Comments," p. 87.

40. Horelick and Rush, *Strategic Power and Soviet Foreign Policy,* pp. 119, 121, 124, 126, 127, 140 (twice), and 180. The only effort in this book to demonstrate by analysis that it was superiority that mattered comes at pages 190–91, where the authors hypothesize a new Berlin crisis in a situation of strategic parity, and find it hard to handle; the argument is thin, and it explicitly acknowledges that increased Soviet pressure "would still be risky."

41. Eisenhower, *The White House Years,* 2:354–55.

42. Slusser, *The Berlin Crisis of 1961,* p. 373, quoted from *Documents on Disarmament,* 1961.

43. "Secretary Rusk Interviewed on 'Issues and Answers,'" *Department of State Bulletin,* November 13, 1961, p. 802; conversation with Gilpatric, 1986.

44. Slusser, *The Berlin Crisis of 1961,* pp. 375, 382–85; Horelick and Rush, *Strategic Power and Soviet Foreign Policy,* pp. 85–89.

45. Khrushchev, *Khrushchev Remembers,* p. 452, and *Khrushchev Remembers: The Last Testament,* p. 501.

46. Forrestal, *The Forrestal Diaries,* pp. 451–91; *FRUS,* 1948, 2:971.

47. Memorandum to the president, August 28, 1961, National Security files, Country series, box 82, JFK.

48. For the treaty between the Federal Republic of Germany and the Union of Soviet Socialist Republics, see *Documents on American Foreign Relations,* 1970, pp. 105–6, and for the Quadripartite Agreement, *Documents on American Foreign Relations,* 1971, pp. 166–70. Air access was not treated in the Quadripartite Agreement because it was already governed by adequate four-power documents.

49. At this writing the best recent account of the situation is *The Future of Berlin,* ed. Martin J. Hillenbrand. The measured optimism of this volume is impressive because of the stature of the editor and his contributors.

50. I was reminded of this Soviet assertion by Robert Legvold, "Soviet Union and the Issue of Military Power," in *United States-Soviet Relations,* ed. Clark, pp. 17–18.

51. Memorandum of conference with the president, March 6, 1959, 10:30 A.M., Whitman file, DDE diary, box 39, DDE.

52. Schelling, *Arms and Influence,* p. 47.

53. Brandt, *People and Politics,* p. 40.

54. Remarks in the Rudolph Wilde Platz, Berlin, June 26, 1963, *Public Papers,* pp. 524–25. If Kennedy had not been dependent on my feeble German, he would have said, *"Ich bin Berliner,"* because that is the right translation for "I am a Berliner," and also because *"ein Berliner,"* colloquially, can mean a doughnut. Fortunately the crowd in Berlin was untroubled by my mistake; no one in the square confused JFK with a doughnut.

55. Sorensen, *Kennedy,* p. 601.

CHAPTER IX

1. This statement, unaccountably, is not in Kennedy, *Public Papers,* and can be found conveniently in *New York Times,* September 5, 1962, in *Department of State Bulletin,* September 24, 1962, p. 450, and in *Documents on American Foreign Relations,* 1962, p. 376. Like most of the other public documents of the crisis it is also in Larson, *The "Cuban Crisis" of 1962,* second ed., an invaluable vade mecum for students of the crisis.

2. President's news conference of September 13, 1962, in Kennedy, *Public Papers,* 1962, pp. 674–75.

3. Robert Kennedy, *Thirteen Days,* p. 67.

4. "ABC's Issues and Answers," transcript, October 14, 1962. My statement may not have seemed remarkable to the people in the Soviet Embassy, because at the time they knew as little about the Cuban missile sites as I did.

5. Some months later a newsmagazine criticized this decision and the president, for the first time, asked me about it. After looking up the facts about his travels, I sent him the following explanation, now available in the President's Office files at the JFK Library:

MEMORANDUM FOR THE PRESIDENT   March 4, 1963

You asked me the other night why I didn't call you the evening of the 15th of October, when Ray Cline reported the hard evidence of MRBM's in Cuba to me (at about 8:30 P.M.). I'm not sure I gave you a full answer, and you really need it for your memoirs—and perhaps even sooner if some reporter asks you. As I remember it, my thinking was like this:

1. This was very big news, and its validity would need to be demonstrated clearly to you and others before action could be taken. The blow-ups and other elements of such a presentation would not be ready before morning. I was satisfied that the word was going out quietly to those with an immediate need to know. The one obvious operational need was for more photography, and that was in hand.

2. It was a hell of a secret, and it must remain one until you had a chance to deal with it. Thus everything should go on as nearly normally as possible; in particular there should be no hastily summoned meeting Monday night. Chip Bohlen and I, for example, should not leave a dinner at my house where there were knowledgeable guests, and others, I knew, were in the same spot.

3. On the other hand this was not something that could be dealt with on the phone except in the most limited and cryptic terms. What help would it be to you to give you this piece of news and then tell you nothing could be done about it till morning?

4. Finally, I had heard you were tired. You had had a strenuous campaign week end, returning from Niagara Falls and New York City at 1:40 Monday morning.

5. So I decided that a quiet evening and a night of sleep were the best preparation you could have in the light of what would face you

in the next days. I would, I think, decide the same again unless you tell me different.

McG. B.

The president never did "tell me different."

6. Cuban missile crisis meetings, October 16, 1962, pt. 1, p. 19, presidential recordings transcripts, President's Office files, JFK. So far there are transcripts of the presidential recordings for two days of the crisis, October 16 and October 27. Those tapes were made secretly by President Kennedy, and among those recorded I believe only the president and his brother knew of the taping. I doubt if most of us would have favored such taping if we had been consulted, but the tapes have obvious value for historians. The transcript of October 16 was made by the research staff at the Kennedy Library, and the transcript of October 27 was made by me after I was allowed to listen to it and discovered its historical value. Full transcripts are available at the Kennedy Library. Useful shorter versions have been edited by Marc Trachtenberg, for October 16, and James Blight, for October 27. They are printed in *International Security,* Summer, 1985, and Winter, 1987–8.

7. Sidey, *John F. Kennedy, President,* pp. 329–30.

8. Schlesinger, *Robert Kennedy and His Times,* p. 513; Sorensen, *Kennedy,* p. 685; Bernstein, "The Week We Almost Went to War," p. 17. Bernstein's judgment that Kennedy welcomed an opportunity for public confrontation is wrong; he simply saw no effective alternative.

9. Robert Kennedy, in *Thirteen Days,* at p. 31, writes that he passed the note to the President, but Arthur Schlesinger has found an earlier memorandum in which he said that he passed it to Sorensen (*Robert Kennedy and His Times,* p. 976, note 33). Sorensen cannot now remember who got it, but I am inclined to think he did simply because unless the seating was extraordinary, the Attorney General would have had to reach across the table to pass the President a note, and he seldom if ever did that.

10. Cuban Missile Crisis Meetings, October 16, 1962, pt. 1, p. 27, and pt. 2, p. 9, presidential recordings transcripts, President's Office files, JFK.

11. This account rests on my own recollection and on Lovett, oral history, JFK, pp. 44–52.

12. Acheson, oral history, JFK, pp. 22–25; and Allison, *Essence of Decision,* pp. 198–99, 202–6.

13. Sorensen, *Kennedy,* p. 692.

14. Sorensen memo to the president, October 20, 1962, Papers of Theodore C. Sorensen, Classified Subject file, box 48, JFK.

15. The best account of the emergence of the quarantine is in Chayes, *The Cuban Missile Crisis,* pp. 14–17, 25–40. Chayes omits the interesting detail that an earlier call for a "quarantine" of Cuba had come from Richard Nixon on September 18. See *New York Times,* September 19, 1962, pp. 1, 3.

16. Conversation with Murray Marder, 1987.

17. This account rests on conversations of 1987 with Reston and Frankel. Schlesinger, in *A Thousand Days,* p. 809, reports that there was also a direct call from Kennedy to Dryfoos.

18. Kennedy, *Public Papers,* 1962, pp. 806–9.

19. Conversation with Dean Rusk, 1984.

20. *Department of State Bulletin,* November 19, 1973, p. 652.

21. Chayes, *The Cuban Missile Crisis,* p. 98.

22. Acheson, oral history, JFK; Khrushchev, *Khrushchev Remembers,* p. 497.

23. Kennedy, *Public Papers,* 1963, p. 676, press conference, September 12, 1963.

24. Steel, "Endgame," pp. 15–22. Steel's belief about Khrushchev is on p. 21.

25. Walter Lippmann, "Cuba and the Nuclear Risk," p. 57.

26. Cuban missile crisis minutes, October 16, 1962, pt. 1, p. 17, presidential recordings transcripts, President's Office files, JFK.

27. A particularly careful and early assessment is that of Horelick, "The Cuban Missile Crisis: An Analysis of Soviet Calculations and Behavior," pp. 363–89, at 367–78. The argument is elaborated in Horelick and Rush, *Strategic Power and Soviet Foreign Policy,* pp. 126–40. Among others who reach similar conclusions persuasively are Allison, *Essence of Decision,* pp. 50–56, 240–41; Dinerstein, *The Making of a Missile Crisis,* pp. 155–56, 186–87; Lebow, "The Cuban Missile Crisis: Reading the Lessons Correctly," p. 453–54. For an eccentric but imaginative argument that the crisis came out just as Khrushchev planned it, see Robin, *La Crise de Cuba.* See also Khrushchev, *Khrushchev Remembers: The Last Testament,* pp. 511–12.

28. *The "Cuban Crisis" of 1962,* ed. Larson, p. 33

29. The best account of Stevenson's position is in John Bartlow Martin, *Adlai Stevenson and the World,* pp. 721–25. The otherwise excellent analysis of Alexander George contains an unreferenced story that when I broke the news to him on October 16, the President asked me if action could be deferred until after the election. The story has no foundation in fact. That the election would probably be affected in some way by the crisis was self-evident, but the relative importance of the election as against the crisis was less than 1 to 100 in our minds. Alexander George, "Cuban Missile Crisis, 1962," in George, Hall, and Simons, *The Limits of Coercive Diplomacy,* p. 89. For an argument like my own, but more complex and subtle, see Hampson, "The Divided Decision-Maker."

30. Cuban missile crisis minutes, October 16, 1962, pt. 2, p. 15, presidential recordings transcripts, President's Office files, JFK.

31. Sorensen's comment is reported in Blight, Nye, and Welch, "The Cuban Missile Crisis Revisited," p. 181.

32. This phrase first appeared in Neustadt and Allison, "Afterword," 1971 edition of Robert Kennedy, *Thirteen Days,* p. 122. It is almost certainly the result of conversation between Neustadt and me.

33. The best retrospective analysis of these questions that I know is in Allison, *Essence of Decision,* pp. 230–37, but Allison incorrectly assumed that Kennedy's first reaction was durable.

34. Cuban missile crisis minutes, October 16, 1962, pt. 2, p. 36, presidential recordings transcripts, President's Office files, JFK.

35. Robert Kennedy, *Thirteen Days,* p. 25. The view that Dobrynin misunderstood is reinforced by the assertions of Soviet authorities at Harvard, in October, 1987, that he was not among the few who knew of the secret

adventure before October 22. He was then a relatively junior officer. For more on the Harvard meeting see Blight and Welsh, *On the Brink.*

36. Pope, ed., *Soviet Views on the Cuban Missile Crisis,* p. 123, or Khrushchev, *Khrushchev Remembers,* p. 493.

37. Dinerstein, *The Making of a Missile Crisis,* pp. 150–83; Allison, *Essence of Decision,* pp. 237–44; Horelick and Rush, *Strategic Power and Soviet Foreign Policy,* pp. 126–40; Horelick, "The Cuban Missile Crisis: An Analysis of Soviet Calculations and Behavior," pp. 363–89; and Garthoff, *Reflections on the Cuban Missile Crisis,* pp. 8–11.

38. On this and the following paragraphs, see Horelick and Rush, *Strategic Power and Soviet Foreign Policy,* chaps. 3–5.

39. Ibid., p. 85, quoting Radio Moscow. See also chap. 8 above.

40. Garthoff, *Reflections on the Cuban Missile Crisis,* pp. 138–46.

41. *Pravda,* May 20, 1962, reported in *Current Digest of the Soviet Press,* June 13, 1962, p. 7. See Stewart Alsop, "Kennedy's Grand Strategy," pp. 11–17.

42. Khrushchev, *Khrushchev Remembers,* p. 494; *Soviet Views on the Cuban Missile Crisis,* ed. Pope, p. 125; Khrushchev, *Khrushchev in America,* p. 129.

43. My interpretation here diverges from that of Roger Hilsman, who believes the speech was principally an effort to impress Moscow. I do not remember it that way, but it would not be unusual if different officials had different motives for supporting the action. See Hilsman, *To Move a Nation,* p. 162.

44. Garthoff, *Intelligence Assessment and Policymaking,* p. 27. Garthoff's paper is a masterly analysis of an interdepartmental strategic review conducted at the president's request in the summer of 1962. The review, of which Garthoff was staff director, was unusual in its integrated analysis of U.S. strategic programs and intelligence estimates of Soviet capabilities and intentions. But as Garthoff demonstrates, the state of mind underlying the resulting report was that of policymakers and analysts whose principal concern was whether we were doing enough. The notion that we might be doing so much that we would stimulate an adventurous Soviet response was simply not considered. The report, with minor deletions for security, was declassified through Garthoff's efforts and is printed in an appendix to his paper.

45. The photographs of October 14 were taken in good time, but they had been delayed, first by our own caution in overflying Cuba, then by an unworthy bureaucratic squabble between the CIA and the Air Force over control of the mission, and finally by weather. If our primary interest here were in the intelligence process, these matters would deserve further attention. Hilsman, *To Move a Nation,* has a good participant's account and assessment, pp. 160–92, and Dinerstein, *The Making of a Missile Crisis,* notes interesting warning signals in Castro's speech of July 26, 1962, pp. 175–78. Our underweighting of such uncertain but suggestive evidence was important not because we could have taken action on it, but because it was one further cause of the delay in the indispensable photography.

46. McCone himself was out of town as the crisis broke, at his stepson's funeral. Dean Rusk's comment is in Cuban missile crisis meetings, October 16, 1962, pt. 1, p. 14, presidential recordings transcripts, President's Office files, JFK.

47. Rostow describes his concern in *The Diffusion of Power,* pp. 253–60. It is reflected plainly in papers he has sent me: highlights of discussion at the secretary of state's policy planning meeting, August 28, 1962, and Rostow's speech, "The Present State of the Cold War," at the Free University of Berlin, West Berlin, Germany, October 18, 1962.

48. Kennedy, *Public Papers,* 1962, December 17, p. 889. Harold Macmillan's account (too often neglected by American writers) shows that Kennedy recognized this element in the quarantine's effectiveness as soon as ships with suspected cargo began to turn back; Macmillan, *At the End of the Day,* pp. 198–99.

49. Cuban missile crisis meetings, October 16, 1962, pt. 2, p. 47, presidential recordings transcripts, President's Office files, JFK.

50. Zorin to African and Asian diplomats, quoted by Detzer, *The Brink,* pp. 202–3.

51. Brodie, *War and Politics,* p. 431.

52. *Pravda,* December 14, 1962, reported in Horelick and Rush, *Strategic Power and Soviet Foreign Policy,* p. 140.

53. Robert Kennedy, *Thirteen Days,* p. 69; Scott D. Sagan, "Nuclear Alerts and Crisis Management," pp. 112–18; and George, "The Cuban Missile Crisis, 1962," pp. 113–14. Sagan argues that the procedure was unduly risky, while George finds that it may well have been particularly impressive to Khrushchev.

54. *Documents on International Affairs,* 1962, p. 239.

55. Robert F. Kennedy, *Thirteen Days,* p. 108, and Cuban Missile Crisis Meetings, October 27, 1962, pp. 40–48, presidential recordings, President's Office files, JFK. McNamara's view of what Robert Kennedy probably said is in Blight and Welch, *On the Brink,* chap. 3.

56. We were never sure at the time whether the fatal attack on Anderson, by a newly operational surface-to-air missile unit, was the result of Soviet or Cuban orders.

57. Dean Acheson, "Dean Acheson's Version of Robert Kennedy's Version of the Cuban Missile Affair," in *Esquire,* p. 77.

58. Sorensen, *Decision-Making in the White House,* p. 31.

59. For a judicious assessment of this problem see Garthoff, *Reflections on the Cuban Missile Crisis,* pp. 20–22.

60. Some critics have complained that Kennedy overstated matters here by speaking of "a *full* retaliatory response," and they may be right in the sense that an all-out nuclear attack would probably have been an excessive and self-destructive response. But the object here was to warn of nuclear retaliation, not to define its precise character. It is doubtful that anyone on either side paid much attention to this adjective at the time.

61. Cuban missile crisis meetings, October 16, 1962, pt. 1, pp. 13, 18, 24, presidential recordings transcripts, President's Office files, JFK.

62. Barton Bernstein has written perceptively on the tendency among us to put too much weight on operability, in "The Week We Almost Went to War," p. 17. On the other hand, Arthur Schlesinger, in an otherwise brilliant chapter of *Robert Kennedy and His Times,* seems to me to err in assuming that in the later days short deadlines were justified as a way of preventing an operability not yet achieved. Schlesinger correctly notes that no one could

confirm the presence of warheads, but he neglects the point that no one could confirm their absence (p. 518).

63. Summary record of NSC Executive Committee meeting, October 27, 1962, 9:00 P.M., JFK.

64. For an excellent analysis that reaches a parallel conclusion, see George, "The Cuban Missile Crisis, 1962," in *The Limits of Coercive Diplomacy*, pp. 128–29, and for highly relevant reflections see Albert Wohlstetter and Roberta Wohlstetter, "Controlling the Risks in Cuba," pp. 17–20.

65. See George Ball, *The Past Has Another Pattern*, pp. 500–502, and Bernstein, "The Cuban Missile Crisis: Trading the Jupiters in Turkey?" pp. 103–4. For an account as sincere as it is mistaken, see O'Donnell and Powers, *"Johnny, We Hardly Knew Ye,"* p. 337. See also Robert Kennedy, *Thirteen Days*, p. 95.

66. Cuban missile crisis meetings, October 27, 1962, passim, presidential recordings transcripts, President's Office files, JFK.

67. Cuban missile crisis meetings, October 27, 1962, p. 3, presidential recordings transcripts, President's Office files, JFK.

68. Ibid., pp. 3, 67, 28, 27.

69. Ibid., p. 31.

70. Ibid., pp. 35–36.

71. Ibid., pp. 36, 38, 37.

72. Ibid., pp. 37, 38.

73. *The "Cuban Crisis" of 1962*, ed. Larson, pp. 187–88.

74. Conversation with Dean Rusk, 1984. A parallel account is in a letter from Rusk to James Blight, quoted in Welch and Blight, "An Introduction to the ExCom Transcripts," *International Security*, Winter 1987–88, footnote 36. There is no tape of the meeting in the Oval Office, and my account rests on my own memory.

75. Chayes, *The Cuban Missile Crisis*, p. 81; the Hare cable was recalled to my memory by Barton Bernstein's account of it in Bernstein, "The Cuban Missile Crisis: Trading the Jupiters in Turkey?" p. 108.

76. Rusk's letter is quoted in Blight, Nye, and Welch, "The Cuban Missile Crisis Revisited," *Foreign Affairs*, Fall 1987, at p. 179.

77. Cuban missile crisis meetings, October 27, 1962, pp. 4–5, presidential recordings transcripts, President's Office files, JFK.

78. Ibid., p. 57.

79. For an early argument that the cost of a public Turkish-Cuban swap would have been acceptable, see Bernstein, "The Cuban Missile Crisis: Trading the Jupiters in Turkey?" pp. 97–126. Bernstein's argument concedes, more readily than I now would, that a public swap would have caused serious political damage both to Kennedy personally and to the prospects for moderate U.S. policy, but he argues that if Khrushchev had insisted on a public pledge, Kennedy should have accepted, because otherwise the next step was bound to be an invasion, with excessive costs and dangers. Here he neglects the possibility of other less dangerous steps like a tightening of the quarantine.

80. Cuban missile crisis meetings, October 27, 1962, pp. 28, 39, 50–53, presidential recordings, President's Office files, JFK. The defusing of the

Turkish missiles was put forward by McNamara as a step he would recommend before any attack on the missile sites in Cuba, but there is no record of any decision to take that step. McNamara and I are confident that no such step would have been approved on a day when our final judgment was to try not to advertise our anxiety about the Turkish missiles. The widespread later belief that defusing was ordered seems to come from overreading and overstatement in *Thirteen Days,* at p. 98.

81. This account rests mainly on John Scali, "I Was the Secret Go-Between in the Cuban Crisis," *Family Weekly,* October 25, 1964, pp. 4–5, 12–14. A closely parallel account is in Hilsman, *To Move a Nation,* pp. 217–19, 222–24, and both are based on Scali's contemporaneous memoranda. That Scali's strong language on Saturday was his own idea is evident in his own account and also confirmed to me by Dean Rusk: "He used his own body English in that." Khrushchev dated his alarming cables at the morning of Saturday, October 27, which neatly fits a report on the first Fomin-Scali exchange, not the second. But this may be mere coincidence; Khrushchev was forced to fudge the timing of events in his speech because he chose not to discuss or even mention the Turkish swap letter of Saturday. The comment to the Supreme Soviet is in *Soviet Views on the Cuban Missile Crisis,* ed. Pope, p. 87, and in *Current Digest of the Soviet Press,* January 16, 1963, p. 5.

82. Khrushchev, *Khrushchev Remembers,* p. 496; *Soviet Views on the Cuban Missile Crisis,* ed. Pope, p. 129.

83. The full exchange of ten letters is printed in *Department of State Bulletin,* November 19, 1973, pp. 635–55. The letters also appear, with helpful comment, in *Soviet Views on the Cuban Missile Crisis,* ed. Pope, pp. 28–67.

84. *Department of State Bulletin,* November 19, 1973, p. 639.

85. Ibid., pp. 643–44.

86. Ibid., p. 645.

87. Khrushchev, *Khrushchev Remembers,* p. 497; *Soviet Views on the Cuban Missile Crisis,* ed. Pope, p. 132; Cousins, "The Cuban Missile Crisis: An Anniversary," p. 4.

88. The messages to Khrushchev were drafted by Sorensen, who had been draftsman for many earlier letters in what we called the penpal correspondence. The practice that both sides had in this correspondence was almost surely helpful in the Cuban crisis.

89. Kissinger, "Reflections on Cuba," pp. 21–24.

90. The best account of the new Soviet evidence is in Blight and Welsh, *On the Brink,* forthcoming.

91. Rusk, McNamara, Ball, Gilpatric, Sorensen, and Bundy, "The Lessons of the Cuban Missile Crisis," *Time,* September 27, 1982, p. 85.

92. U.S. House, Subcommittee of the Committee on Appropriations, *Department of Defense Appropriations for 1964,* hearings, Eighty-eighth Congress, First Session, pp. 30–31.

93. The best argument I have seen on the other side of this question is in Betts, *Nuclear Blackmail and Nuclear Balance,* pp. 109–123.

94. I owe this speculation, though not my own conclusions, to my friend George Quester in conversation.

95. Reagan, *Public Papers,* 1984, vol. I, pp. 730–31.

96. Albert Wohlstetter and Roberta Wohlstetter, "Controlling the Risks in Cuba," p. 12; Garthoff, *Intelligence Assessment and Policymaking*, pp. 32–33; Power, *Design for Survival*, p. 154.

97. Cuban missile crisis meetings, October 16, 1962, pt. 2, p. 12, presidential recordings transcripts, President's Office files, JFK.

98. Kennedy, *Public Papers*, 1962, p. 898. Alsop, "Our New Strategy," p. 15.

99. Sorensen, *Kennedy*, p. 705; Schlesinger, *Robert Kennedy and His Times*, pp. 528–29.

100. Schlesinger, *Robert Kennedy and His Times*, p. 521; Khrushchev, *Khrushchev Remembers*, pp. 497–98.

101. For a parallel argument see Albert Wohlstetter and Roberta Wohlstetter, "Controlling the Risks in Cuba," pp. 18–19.

102. The suggestion that "the world might have been blown up" was made by Robert Kennedy in an interview two days before his death. Ronald Steel, in "Endgame," p. 22, goes further: "Had Acheson and the other hawks had their way probably none of us would be here to conduct these postmortems." Arthur Schlesinger, *Robert Kennedy and His Times*, reports a similar comment by RFK on November 30, 1962, p. 525, and note 120, p. 979.

103. Kennedy, "Radio and Television Report to the American People on the Soviet Arms Buildup in Cuba," October 22, 1962, *Public Papers*, 1962, pp. 807–8.

104. But compare with Sorensen, *Decision-Making in the White House*, pp. 46, 47.

105. The best account of this unhappy affair is Schlesinger's, in *A Thousand Days*, at pp. 835–38.

106. Glenn T. Seaborg, with Benjamin Loeb, *Kennedy, Khrushchev, and the Test Ban*.

107. The decision not to be the first to test again in the atmosphere was entirely the president's; I know because I heard him making it as he reviewed some paper I was showing him. When I heard him I suggested that if he was sure of his position the decision could well be announced in the "peace speech." He agreed at once and I passed the word to Sorensen.

108. Kennedy, *Public Papers*, 1962, pp. 898, 901.

CHAPTER X

1. The basic record for the British story from 1945 to 1952 is in Margaret Gowing, *Independence and Deterrence*, vol. 1. Three excellent general studies are Andrew J. Pierre, *Nuclear Politics;* John Baylis, *Anglo-American Defense Relations, 1939–80*, and Peter Malone, *The British Nuclear Deterrent*.

2. Gowing, *Independence and Deterrence*, vol. 1, chap. 2.

3. Ibid., vol. 1, p. 184. Blackett's basic memorandum in opposition is at pp. 194–206.

4. Gowing, *Independence and Deterrence*, vol. 1, pp. 179–85; for Churchill's surprise, see p. 406.

5. Gowing, *Independence and Deterrence,* vol. 1, pp. 179–85, and for Bevin's view, p. 28.

6. Gowing, *Independence and Deterrence,* vol. 1, pp. 210–13.

7. Ibid., vol. 1, p. 212.

8. Ibid., vol. 1, pp. 52, 174.

9. Hewlett and Anderson, *The New World,* pp. 467–68, 479–80; Gowing, *Independence and Deterrence,* vol. 1, pp. 75–76, 95–107.

10. Gowing, ibid., pp. 107–8.

11. Hewlett and Duncan, *Atomic Shield,* pp. 273–75; Gowing, *Independence and Deterrence,* vol. 1, pp. 120–23; Acheson, *Present at the Creation,* chap. 18.

12. Gowing, *Independence and Deterrence,* vol. 1, chap. 8; Hewlett and Duncan, *Atomic Shield,* pp. 275–84; Pierre, *Nuclear Politics,* pp. 127–31; Baylis, *Anglo-American Defense Relations,* pp. 36–38. Gowing prints the agreement at pp. 266–72, and so does Baylis, at pp. 142–47.

13. Hewlett and Duncan, *Atomic Shield,* pp. 287–89.

14. Ibid., pp. 293–314; and Gowing, *Independence and Deterrence,* vol. 1, chap. 9.

15. Eisenhower, *The White House Years,* 2:122–25, 219; Macmillan, *Riding the Storm,* chap. 10; and Malone, *The British Nuclear Deterrent,* pp. 58–61.

16. Macmillan, *Pointing the Way,* pp. 252–54.

17. On the French bomb there are two excellent American studies, Scheinman, *Atomic Energy in France under the Fourth Republic,* and Kohl, *French Nuclear Diplomacy;* the latter is centered on de Gaulle. There is also an illuminating set of Gaullist papers and comments in L'Université de Franche-Comté, *L'Aventure de la bombe.* The most interesting French writer on nuclear history is Bertrand Goldschmidt, *The Atomic Adventure* and *The Atomic Complex,* and the most formidable French analyst was the late Raymond Aron.

18. The report to de Gaulle in Ottawa was reported by de Gaulle in 1954 in his *Memoires de Guerre,* vol. 2, p. 242. See also Bertrand Goldschmidt, in L'Université de Franche-Comté, *L'Aventure de la Bombe,* p. 25. De Courcel's comment is in *L'Aventure de la Bombe,* p. 16.

19. Lacouture, *De Gaulle,* 3:466; see also de Gaulle, *Memoirs of Hope,* pp. 257–58.

20. De Gaulle, *Mémoires de Guerre,* vol. 1, p. 1, quoted by Kohl, *French Nuclear Diplomacy,* p. 61.

21. Scheinman, *Atomic Energy in France under the Fourth Republic,* pp. 40–57, 78–85.

22. Ibid., chap. 5; Monnet, *Memoirs,* pp. 400–402, 417–26.

23. Scheinman, *Atomic Energy in France Under the Fourth Republic*, pp. 171–74; Kohl, *French Nuclear Diplomacy,* pp. 35–37.

24. Gildschmidt, *The Atomic Complex*, p.137.

25. Joliot to Anderson in Gowing, *Independence and Deterrence,* vol. 1, p. 9; Bertrand Goldschmidt, in L'Université de Franche-Comté, *L'Aventure de la bombe,* p. 25; *La Croix,* February 29, 1960, quoted in Kohl, *French Nuclear Diplomacy,* p. 105.

26. L'Université de Franche-Comté, *L'Aventure de la bombe,* passim; "absolute priority" is in Lacouture, *De Gaulle,* 3:461.

27. Full text in de Gaulle, *Lettres, notes et carnets,* 1958–60, pp. 83–84, and also in Grosser, *The Western Alliance,* p. 187.

28. De Gaulle's comment is in *Memoirs of Hope,* p. 202.

29. Press conference, October 12, 1945, de Gaulle, *Discours et messages,* 1:637–38; radio and television speech, May 31, 1960, 3:218.

30. De Gaulle, *Lettres, notes et carnets,* 1958–1960, pp. 225–28.

31. Ibid., p. 263.

32. Harrison, *The Reluctant Ally,* p. 97. Harrison also led me to de Gaulle's letter of May 25, 1959, which he obtained from the Eisenhower Library before its French publication and discusses at pp. 90–91, 96.

33. Eisenhower's letter was made public in 1966 in a submission by the Department of State to Senator Henry Jackson's Subcommittee on National Security and International Operations, of the Committee on Government Operations. It is printed in *The Atlantic Alliance: Hearings,* Eighty-ninth Congress, Second Session, 1966, and reprinted as "De Gaulle's 1958 Tripartite Proposal and U.S. Response," in *Atlantic Community Quarterly* 4 (Fall 1966): 455–58, and also in appendix 1 of Lois Pattison de Menil, *Who Speaks for Europe? The Vision of Charles de Gaulle,* pp. 193–94. I owe the latter two references to the distinguished French scholar Alfred Grosser, who cites them in firm but courteous refutation of the Gaullist legend that Eisenhower never answered de Gaulle's memorandum. Grosser, *The Western Alliance,* p. 352, note 10.

34. De Gaulle, *Discours et messages,* 3:126–27.

35. De Courcel's remark is in L'Université de Franche-Comté, *L'Aventure de la Bombe,* p. 16.

36. Radio and television speech, in de Gaulle, *Discours et messages,* 3:220.

37. De Gaulle, *Lettres, notes et carnets,* 1958–60, p. 389. For judgments of de Gaulle's purpose that are different from mine, see Newhouse, *De Gaulle and the Anglo-Saxons,* chap. 3; Kohl, *French Nuclear Diplomacy,* pp. 70–81; and Lacouture, *De Gaulle,* 2:638–92. Kohl notes that in his memoirs de Gaulle wrote that he expected the "evasive" replies he got, and that they set him free to go his own way. I think that like most statesmen de Gaulle habitually put a brave gloss on his accounts of efforts that did not succeed. An assessment nearer my own is in Harrison, *The Reluctant Ally,* pp. 100–101.

38. The telegram is in Kohl, *French Nuclear Diplomacy,* p. 103. For Albert Buchalet's opinion, see his "Les Premières Étapes," in L'Université de Franche-Comté, *L'Aventure de la bombe,* pp. 52–53; for de Gaulle's reaction see *Memoirs of Hope,* p. 215; and for the sentiment of the supporters of the French effort, see *L'Aventure de la bombe,* passim.

39. For the legislative process and the debate, see Kohl, *French Nuclear Diplomacy,* pp. 114–19, but see also Pierre Messmer's account in L'Université de Franche-Comté, *L'Aventure de la bombe,* pp. 93–98, and for a comprehensive review of arguments against the program, see Furniss, *De Gaulle and the French Army,* pp. 200–205.

40. L'Université de Franche-Comté, *L'Aventure de la Bombe,* p. 70.

41. Press conference, February 3, 1960, Eisenhower, *Public Papers,* 1960, p. 152.

42. Harrison, *The Reluctant Ally,* p. 78; Newhouse, *De Gaulle and the Anglo-Saxons,* pp. 21–24; Kohl, *French Nuclear Diplomacy,* pp. 107, 110. Kohl quotes Eisenhower's belief from an interview reported by David Schoenbrun, *The Three Lives of Charles de Gaulle.*

43. Wohlstetter, "Nuclear Sharing: NATO and the N + 1 Country," *Foreign Affairs* 39 (April 1961): 355–87, reprinted in Rosecrance, *The Dispersion of Nuclear Weapons,* pp. 186–221.

44. *Documents on American Foreign Relations,* 1962, p. 233.

45. Ibid.

46. Declassified documents remind me that I recommended deletion of this whole passage at the time as needlessly offensive to the French. McNamara disagreed, arguing that the argument was needed for better American understanding of the issue and also that the French would not be upset; they simply would not agree. Kennedy reviewed the speech alone on a weekend and made his decision by amending the draft. It is pertinent that all these thoughts had already been expressed by McNamara in Athens to an audience that included French leaders. McGeorge Bundy, Memorandum for the president, June 7, 1962, and remarks of Secretary of Defense Robert S. McNamara at the commencement exercises, University of Michigan, June 7, 1962, National Security Council files, Departments and Agencies, Department of Defense, box 274, JFK.

47. News conference of May 17, 1962, in Kennedy, *Public Papers,* 1962, p. 402.

48. News conference of June 27, 1962, in Kennedy, *Public Papers,* 1962, p. 513.

49. François de Rose's comment is in his *European Security and France,* p. 41. A more excessive recollection is that of the Gaullist Burin de Roziers in L'Université de Franche-Comté, *L'Aventure de la bombe,* p. 351, where Kennedy is misquoted as calling the French program "an inimical action toward the United States."

50. For the understandable resentments of Frenchmen who had helped in the allied wartime effort, see the works of Bertrand Goldschmidt. Aron's reminder is in his "De Gaulle and Kennedy: The Nuclear Debate," *Atlantic Monthly,* August 1962, p. 34.

51. The outstanding study of West Germany is Kelleher, *Germany and the Politics of Nuclear Weapons.*

52. Kelleher, *Germany and the Politics of Nuclear Weapons,* pp. 25, 28, 29.

53. Ibid., p. 125; and Steinbruner, *The Cybernetic Theory of Decision,* p. 175.

54. Steinbruner, *The Cybernetic Theory of Decision,* p. 178; Kelleher, *Germany and the Politics of Nuclear Weapons,* pp. 130–31.

55. Kennedy, Address before the Canadian Parliament in Ottawa, on May 17, 1961, *Public Papers,* 1961, p. 385.

56. The best account of Nassau as a product of interacting errors of perception by the American and British governments is in Neustadt, *Alliance Politics,* chap. 3.

57. Macmillan, *At the End of the Day,* p. 358.

58. The British Service preferences are described by Pierre, *Nuclear Politics,* pp. 200–201, and Malone, *The British Nuclear Deterrent,* pp. 66–67. See also Macmillan, *At the End of the Day,* pp. 356, 360. Macmillan's version of history was undoubtedly encouraged by the official account that Churchill prepared and Attlee released in 1945. See Gowing, *Independence and Deterrence,* vol. 1, p. 16. But even Churchill never claimed anything as expansive as "an equal share in the equity."

59. Ball stated his priority in *The Discipline of Power* at p. 95. The Nassau joint statement is in Kennedy, *Public Papers,* 1962, pp. 908–10.

60. Macmillan's memoirs show that de Gaulle's opposition to British entry into the Common Market had been made clear the week before in a de Gaulle–Macmillan meeting at the French Palace of Rambouillet. After a grand pheasant shoot in which Macmillan "was alleged to have shot seventy-seven," the two men talked at length for two days, and Macmillan found the discussions "about as bad as they could be from the European point of view." The visit "left me in no doubt that de Gaulle would, if he dared, use some means, overt or covert, to prevent the fruition of the Brussels negotiation." Macmillan, *At the End of the Day,* pp. 345, 354–55. This result was not disclosed to the Americans at Nassau.

61. De Gaulle, *Discours et messages,* 4:66–76.

62. Ibid., especially p. 73; On the detonators, see Harrison, *The Reluctant Ally,* pp. 126–27; Jean Klein in L'Université de Franche-Comte, *L'Aventure de la bombe,* pp. 182–83; and Aron, *The Great Debate,* pp. 142–43.

63. Kohl, *French Nuclear Diplomacy,* pp. 249–50.

64. The most detailed account of the MLF is Steinbruner, *The Cybernetic Theory of Decision,* whose focus is on American decision making, and whose excellent history is more important than its theoretical superstructure. The German element is in Kelleher, *Germany and the Politics of Nuclear Weapons,* and chaps. 9 and 10.

65. Quoted by C. L. Sulzberger in *The New York Times,* October 19, 1964, p. 32. I owe this reference to Catherine Kelleher.

66. Adenauer and Erler are discussed in Kelleher, *Germany and the Politics of Nuclear Weapons,* p. 238.

67. Kennedy, *Public Papers,* 1962, p. 538. For the argument that Kennedy had more than an eloquent hope here, see Joseph Kraft, *The Grand Design.*

68. Ibid., p. 546; McGeorge Bundy, "Building the Atlantic Partnership: Some Lessons from the Past," *Department of State Bulletin,* October 22, 1962, pp. 601–5.

69. Bowie, "Strategy and the Atlantic Alliance," p. 725, quoted by Steinbruner, *The Cybernetic Theory of Decision,* p. 260.

70. Aron, *The Great Debate,* p. 103.

71. De Gaulle, *Discours et messages,* 5:18.

72. Instructively sweeping and vapid comments of this sort are collected in L'Université de Franche-Comté, *L'Aventure de la bombe,* pp. 339–53. The Gaullist commentators appear to believe that to assert the international impact of the French bomb is to demonstrate it.

73. The best account I have seen of the strategy of *tous azimuts* is in Lacouture, *De Gaulle,* 3:477–83. Lacouture obtained a reconstruction by listeners of the speech of January 27, and my quotations come from the text he prints at p. 480. A similar version in *L'Aventure de la bombe,* at pp. 210–11, contains this striking sentence after the one on entering Madrid, Berlin, and Moscow, "Of course we have not entered London!"

74. Lacouture, *De Gaulle,* 3:312.

75. De Gaulle, *Discours et messages,* 5:105–6.

76. Kohl, *French Nuclear Diplomacy,* p. 150.

77. Schlesinger, *A Thousand Days,* p. 871.

78. Theo Sommer, "The Objectives of Germany," in ed. Buchan, *A World of Nuclear Powers?* pp. 53–54.

79. Ibid., pp. 52–54.

80. Spector, *Nuclear Proliferation Today,* p. 122.

81. Steinberg, "Deliberate Ambiguity," in *Security or Armageddon,* ed. Beres, p. 30.

82. Spector, *Nuclear Proliferation Today,* p. 132; Weissman and Krosney, *The Islamic Bomb,* p. 110, 113.

83. Goldschmidt, *The Atomic Complex,* p. 187; Spector, *Nuclear Proliferation Today,* p. 129; Zeev Eytan, "A Nuclear or Conventional Defense Posture?" in *Security or Armageddon,* ed. Beres, p. 88.

84. Spector, *Nuclear Proliferation Today,* pp. 128–29.

85. IISS Strategic Survey, 1975, p. 13; *Time,* April 12, 1976, p. 39.

86. *The Sunday Times* (London), October 5, 1986, p. 1, and conversation with Taylor, 1986.

87. Weissman and Krosney, *The Islamic Bomb,* p. 111.

88. Steinberg, "Deliberate Ambiguity," in *Security or Armageddon,* ed. Beres, p. 34.

89. See for example, Christopher Raj, "Israel and Nuclear Weapons," in *Nuclear Myths and Realities,* ed. Subrahmanyam, chap. 6.

CHAPTER XI

1. The most revealing single account of the Yom Kippur alert is in Kissinger, *Years of Upheaval,* pp. 545–613. Three important secondary analyses are Quandt, *Decade of Decisions,* pp. 165–206, Blechman and Hart, "The Political Utility of Nuclear Weapons," *International Security,* vol. 7, no. 1, pp. 132–56, and Garthoff, *Détente and Confrontation,* pp. 368–85.

2. Kissinger, *Years of Upheaval,* p. 583.

3. Ibid., pp. 583–85.

4. Ibid., pp. 585, 581, 597.

5. Ibid., pp. 587–91; Garthoff, *Détente and Confrontation,* p. 379.

6. Ibid., p. 592.

7. Ibid., p. 587. The version that Nixon prints is the most extensive we have. It contains a paragraph whose opening sentence asserts that there is no information indicating "that the ceasefire is being violated on any significant scale," but the rest of the paragraph is omitted (Nixon, *RN,* pp. 939–40).

8. *Department of State Bulletin,* Nov. 12, 1973, pp. 589–92.

9. Kissinger, *Years of Upheaval,* p. 587.

10. Ibid., pp. 589–90.

11. Ibid., p. 571.

12. *Department of State Bulletin,* Nov. 19, 1973, p. 622.

13. Kissinger, *Years of Upheaval,* pp. 612, 980.

14. Nixon, *Public Papers,* 1973, pp. 900, 902, 904–5.

15. *Department of State Bulletin,* Nov. 12, 1973, p. 585–86.

16. Kissinger, *Years of Upheaval,* pp. 580, 593, and Garthoff, *Détente and Confrontation,* p. 376.

17. The most important English language study of the origins of the Chinese bomb is John Lewis and Xue Litai, *China Builds the Bomb,* which gives a compelling account of the extraordinary achievement of determined and talented Chinese over the ten years between Mao's decision in early 1955 and the explosion at Lop Nur late in 1964. I have tried to take account of this pathbreaking work in this brief account and in chap. VI, but serious students of Mao's basic decision to go ahead will want to examine the first three chapters of *China Builds a Bomb;* the authors have an understanding of Chinese Communist thinking in the 1950s that I cannot claim to match.

18. Ibid., p. 6.

19. The best assessment that I have found on Mao's early view of the bomb is in Morton Halperin's essay, "Chinese Attitudes Toward Nuclear Weapons," in *China in Crisis,* ed. Tsou, vol. II, pp. 137–41.

20. Mao's 1956 statement is cited by Pollack in *Military Power and Policy in Asian States,* ed. Marwah and Pollack, at p. 97, quoting from *Peking Review,* no. 1, Jan. 1, 1977, p. 13.

21. Lewis and Xue Litai, *China Builds the Bomb,* chap. 2.

22. Ibid., p. 35

23. Chinese statement of August 15, 1963, in Griffith, *The Sino-Soviet Rift,* p. 351; Khrushchev's comment is in his *Last Testament,* p. 269.

24. See Lewis and Xue Litai, *China Builds the Bomb,* pp. 60–65.

25. Cited in Chinese statement of September 1, 1963, in *The Sino-Soviet Rift,* ed. Griffith, pp. 375–76.

26. Khrushchev, *The Last Testament,* pp. 268–69.

27. Soviet statement of Sept. 21, 1963, in *The Sino-Soviet Rift,* ed. Griffith, p. 445.

28. Pollack, "Chinese Attitudes Toward Nuclear Weapons," *China Quarterly,* April–June 1972, p. 245.

29. Alsop, "Affairs of State," *Saturday Evening Post,* September 28, 1963, cited in Halperin, *China and the Bomb,* p. 125.

30. Wich, *Sino-Soviet Crisis Politics,* pp. 41–64 and 207–17.

31. Ibid., pp. 198–206: Kissinger, *White House Years,* pp. 183–186.

32. Robinson, "The Sino-Soviet Border Conflict," in *Diplomacy of Power,* ed. Kaplan, p. 291; Wich, *Sino-Soviet Crisis Politics,* pp. 199–206.

33. Nixon's comments to Rosenblatt are in *Time,* July 23, 1985, p. 53; they are reprinted in Rosenblatt, *Witness,* pp. 78–9. Kissinger's account is in *White House Years,* pp. 184, 186.

34. Westmoreland, *A Soldier Reports,* p. 338. General Westmoreland thought it a mistake "to fail to consider this alternative," but he also recognized that any use of nuclear weapons would require a political decision, and his own earlier decision to fight at Khe Sanh was based on an assessment that Khe Sanh was defensible by strictly conventional means; the assessment turned out to be correct.

35. Johnson, *Public Papers,* 1964, p. 1051.

36. *Time,* July 23, 1985, p. 50; also in Rosenblatt, *Witness,* p. 69.

37. *Time* and Rosenblatt, as cited; Haldeman, *The Ends of Power,* pp. 82–83; Nixon's comment to southern delegates is reported in Halperin, *Nuclear Fallacy,* p. 40.

38. Kissinger, *White House Years,* pp. 284–88.

39. Nixon, *RN,* pp. 396–98.

40. Ibid., p. 403.

41. I have heard such comments from President Ford in more than one meeting.

42. Bundy, "Vietnam, Watergate, and Presidential Powers," *Foreign Affairs,* Winter, 1979–80.

43. Goldwater is quoted by Halperin, in *Nuclear Fallacy,* at p. 156; LeMay's judgment is in *America Is in Danger,* at p. 263.

CHAPTER XII

1. McNamara, *The Essence of Security,* pp. 52–53.

2. LeMay, *America Is in Danger,* p. 83.

3. Rosenberg, "The Origins of Overkill," pp. 34–38.

4. McNamara, address at Ann Arbor, June 16, 1962, in *Documents on American Foreign Relations,* 1962, p. 233.

5. These quotations come from McNamara's file copies of his public statements, which he has kindly shared with me.

6. Draft memoranda for the president, December 6, 1963, December 3, 1964, November 1, 1965, office of the secretary of defense.

7. Draft memorandum of December 3, 1964, pp. 18, 25–26.

8. Enthoven and Smith, *How Much Is Enough?* p. 195.

9. LeMay, *America Is in Danger,* p. 83.

10. Power, *Design for Survival,* pp. 80–81; The Ellis assessment is in Hearings, Senate Committee on Armed Services, Ninety-sixth Congress, First Session, SALT II Treaty, part II, pp. 779–80.

11. Desmond Ball, "The Development of the SIOP, 1960–83," in Ball and Richelson, *Strategic Nuclear Targeting,* p. 66. See also Rosenberg, "Reality and Responsibility," and Rowan, "The Evolution of Strategic Nuclear Doctrine" in *Strategic Thought in the Nuclear Age,* ed. Martin.

12. Garthoff, "BMD and East-West Relations," in Carter and Schwartz, *Ballistic Missile Defense,* pp. 297–303. I was at Glassboro as a temporary staff officer working on the problems arising from the Six-Day War.

13. Newhouse, *Cold Dawn,* pp. 150–57.

14. The rise of MIRV in the McNamara years is still told best in Greenwood, *Making the MIRV,* and the most powerful account of the failure of efforts to deal with MIRV in SALT I is in Smith, *Doubletalk,* chapter 4.

15. Brennan, "When the SALT Hit the Fan," *National Review,* June 23, 1972, conveniently reprinted in *Great Issues of International Politics,* ed. Kaplan, second edition.

16. Public Law 92-448, Sept. 30, 1972, conveniently reprinted in *SALT Handbook,* ed. Labrie, p. 142.

17. Nixon, *Public Papers,* 1969, p. 19.

18. Kennedy, *Public Papers,* 1963, pp. 897–98.

19. Johnson, *Public Papers,* 1963–64, vol. II, p. 1303.

20. Eisenhower, *Public Papers,* 1956, pp. 474–75.

21. This affair is detailed by Garthoff in *Détente and Confrontation* at pp. 171–74 and is conceded in substance by Kissinger in *White House Years,* p. 1239, where he refers to his statement to the leaders this way: "We overestimated the restraining effect of such a unilateral statement." The full exchange with Senator Jackson is printed in Hearings, Senate Committee on Foreign Relations, Ninety-second Congress, Second Session, Strategic Arms Limitation Agreement, p. 406.

22. *Alerting America,* ed. Tyroler, p. 5.

23. Ibid., p. 14.

24. Ibid., p. 160.

25. Ibid., p. 28.

26. Nitze, "Assuring Strategic Stability in an Era of Détente," *Foreign Affairs,* January 1976, p. 217.

27. Senate Foreign Relations Committee, Ninety-sixth Congress, First Session, SALT II Treaty, part I, p. 529.

28. Ibid., part II, p. 373.

29. Ibid., part III, pp. 224–25. Kissinger's discussion of the strategic balance while in office remains remarkably enlightening. A notable address in Texas, on March 22, 1976, is largely reprinted in the first issue of *International Security.* The speech includes a persuasive argument against the notion that specific numerical advantages of the sort that led to the notion of a window of vulnerability could in fact affect Soviet pressure in regional matters.

30. Pipes, "Why the Soviet Union Thinks It Could Fight and Win a Nuclear War," *Commentary,* July 1977, p. 34.

31. *Alerting America,* ed. Tyroler, p. 26.

32. Erickson, "The Soviet Military System," in Erickson and Feuchtwanger, *Soviet Military Power and Performance,* p. 27; Ermarth, "Contrasts in American and Soviet Strategic Thought," in *Soviet Military Thinking,* ed. Leebaert, p. 66.

33. Holloway, *The Soviet Union and the Arms Race,* p. 179.

34. Pipes, op. cit., p. 29; *Alerting America,* ed. Tyroler, p. 167.

35. Ibid., pp. 202, 235; Committee on the Present Danger, "Can America Catch Up?" 1984, p. 59.

36. Two serious studies of MX are Edwards, *Superweapon,* and Holland and Hoover, *The MX Decision.*

37. "Report of the President's Commission on Strategic Forces," April 6, 1983, pp. 11, 7–8.

38. Carter, *Public Papers,* 1979, p. 108. Carter's description was technically imprecise because no single submarine could target cities in all parts of the Soviet Union, but his central point was right—no Soviet leader wants his country to be hit by the warheads of even one Poseidon submarine.

39. See references in note 11 above.

40. The best general account of all this is in Talbott, *Deadly Gambits,* part one.

41. Ibid., chapter 6.

42. Reagan, *Public Papers,* 1983, pp. 437–43.

43. Ibid., pp. 442, 448.

44. The unclassified summaries of these two reports are in Miller and Van Evera, *The Star Wars Controversy,* pp. 273–322.

45. Reagan, *Presidential Documents*, June 23, 1986, p. 839. He continued to make statements just as absolute in 1987 and 1988.

46. Weinberger's opinion of 1982 is in Hearings, U.S. Senate, 97th Congress, Second Session, Foreign Relations Committee, "Nuclear Arms Reduction Prospects," April 29, 1982, p. 46; Weinberger's lack of connection to the Star Wars initiative was revealed by Richard Perle in a debate with me in New York, June 3, 1987.

47. Teller, "What Helps Superpower 'Star Wars' Stability," *Encounter*, Sept.-Oct. 1986, p. 68.

48. Reagan, speech in Milwaukee, Oct. 15, 1985, *Presidential Documents*, Oct. 21, 1985, p. 1255; Report of the American Physical Society Study Group, *Science and Technology of Directed Energy Weapons*, April 1987, p. 2.

49. Reagan, *Presidential Documents*, March 30, 1987, p. 290; Weinberger, "Why Offense Needs Defense," *Foreign Policy*, Fall 1987, p. 17.

50. *Aviation Week and Space Technology*, February 2, 1987, p. 20.

51. Andropov's comment was widely reported, and I rely on quotations given in Drell, Farley, and Holloway, *The Reagan Strategic Defense Initiative: Technical, Political and Arms Control Assessment*, p. 105. p. 107. Schlesinger's suggestion was first put forward in a symposium at the Mitre Corporation, on October 25, 1984. It is reprinted in the Proceedings of the Symposium and in *The Star Wars Controversy*, ed. Miller and Van Evera.

52. Iklé, "Nuclear Strategy: Can There Be a Happy Ending?" *Foreign Affairs*, Spring 1985, pp. 822, 823.

53. Ibid., pp. 824, 825.

54. Ibid., p. 825.

55. Reagan, *Presidential Documents*, March 30, 1987, p. 290.

56. York, *Does Strategic Defense Breed Offense?* pp. 20–21, 24.

57. U.S. Arms Control and Disarmament Agency, "An Analysis of Civil Defense in Nuclear War," December, 1978, printed as Appendix 2 to Hearings, Ninety-fifth Congress, Second Session, Senate Committee on Banking, Housing, and Urban Affairs, *Civil Defense*, January 8, 1979.

58. *New York Times*, August 10, 1982, p. 8.

59. There are many important lines of analysis that undergird this brief account of the tension between strategic doctrine and the reality of large-scale nuclear exchanges. The works I have found most helpful are Jervis, *The Illogic of American Nuclear Strategy*, *Strategic Nuclear Targeting*, ed. Ball and Richelson, and two pamphlets by military professionals, Walker, *Strategic Target Planning*, and Branch, *Fighting a Long Nuclear War*.

60. Waller, *Congress and the Nuclear Freeze*.

61. Reagan's first use of this comment came in one of his weekend radio broadcasts, on Saturday, April 17, 1982. He has used it since on many occasions around the world, and he and Gorbachev have used it in two summits. In his first use he was careful to point out that the idea was not new. "Those who've governed America throughout the nuclear age and we

who govern it today have had to recognize that a nuclear war cannot be won and must never be fought." Reagan, *Public Papers,* 1982, vol. I, p. 487.

CHAPTER XIII

1. Schelling, *The Strategy of Conflict,* p. 260.
2. I quote myself from "To Cap the Volcano," *Foreign Affairs,* October 1969. In that article I wrote of bombs on cities—on one or ten or a hundred. That kind of calculation was commonplace when warheads were large and inaccurate, but it can be misread to suggest a preference for such targets, so I make the same basic point here in a different way.
3. Gorbachev, *Perestroika,* pp. 178, 202–3.
4. Aron, *Paix et Guerre,* p. 7. The French phrase is *résolus . . . à ne pas s'entredétruire.*
5. Gorbachev to the International Forum, February 16, 1987, reported in Foreign Broadcast Information Service, February 17, 1987, p. AA18.
6. *FRUS,* 1952–54, vol. II, p. 837.
7. Bundy, Kennan, McNamara, and Smith, "Nuclear Weapons and the Atlantic Alliance," *Foreign Affairs,* Spring 1982. An excellent 1988 assessment of Soviet thinking is Garthoff, "New Thinking in Soviet Military Doctrine."
8. Howard, "Reassurance and Deterrence," *Foreign Affairs,* Winter 1982–83, pp. 310, 318.
9. The decisive political importance of keeping control is a point often forgotten by strategic analysts. Three exceptions are Albert Wohlstetter, Paul Bracken, and Fred Iklé. See Wohlstetter and Brody, chap. 5, and Bracken, chapter 6, in *Managing Nuclear Operations.* See also Iklé, *Every War Must End,* a book which states the right problem in its title, although it does not fully explore the answers. Two excellent recent essays are Quester, "War Termination and Targeting Strategy," in *Strategic Nuclear Targeting,* ed. Ball and Richelson, pp. 285–305, and Wieseltier, "When Deterrence Fails," *Foreign Affairs,* Spring 1985
10. McNamara, *Blundering into Disaster,* pp. 44–45.
11. Kennedy, *Public Papers,* 1963, p. 441.
12. See Larrabee, *Commander in Chief,* for a splendid account of this performance.
13. Gorbachev, *Perestroika,* p. 219.
14. Ibid., p. 218.
15. As I write, the best overall assessment of Krasnoyarsk is in Duffy, *Compliance and the Future of Arms Control.* The subject is indexed under Abalakovo (an alternative place-name for the site).
16. I owe this quotation to Robert Gilpin, *American Scientists and Nuclear Weapons Policy,* at p. 342. The statement was made on February 12, 1950 on Eleanor Roosevelt's radio program "Roundtable," and is reprinted in the *Bulletin of the Atomic Scientists,* vol. 6, no. 3, March 1950, at p. 75.

17. What produces these results, as a pocket calculator will show, is what happens when you raise .99, the chance of survival in any one year, to the 26th power, the 138th, and the 238th.

18. I owe an amateur's interest in probability to teachers at Groton and Yale, but in presenting this particular example I have been tutored by Steven Brams of NYU and Richard Garwin of IBM, each of whom has addressed this question in the nuclear context. The governing formula is that if you reduce a small risk regularly, by a given fraction in each time interval, the risk all the way to eternity is $R/(1 - N)$, where R is the risk in the current time period and N is the amount by which you reduce that risk over each time interval. R in my case is .005 (1 in 200) and N is .5, the reduction of 50 percent per decade that will produce the reduction over two decades which is here asserted for the past and assumed for a successful future. I am warned by my tutors to emphasize that such formulas are indicators of possibilities, not predictors.

Index

ABOUT THE AUTHOR

Born in Boston in 1919 and educated at Groton School, Yale College, and Harvard's Society of Fellows, MCGEORGE BUNDY has been a student of nuclear danger since 1945, when he went to work with Henry L. Stimson on their account of Stimson's public life, *On Active Service.* Since then he has been continuously concerned with this subject, as a teacher of American foreign policy at Harvard (1949–60), as special assistant for national security affairs at the White House in years that included nuclear crises in Berlin and in Cuba, and as president of the Ford Foundation in a time when the support of independent work on this subject became one of the foundation's major programs. Since 1979, as professor of history at New York University, he has been at work on this book.